BIBLICAL EPICS IN LATE ANTIQUITY
AND ANGLO-SAXON ENGLAND:
DIVINA IN LAUDE VOLUNTAS

Biblical Epics in Late Antiquity and Anglo-Saxon England

Divina in Laude Voluntas

PATRICK McBRINE

UNIVERSITY OF TORONTO PRESS
Toronto Buffalo London

ISBN 978-0-8020-9853-5

Toronto Anglo-Saxon Series

Library and Archives Canada Cataloguing in Publication

McBrine, Patrick, 1974–, author
Biblical epics in late antiquity and Anglo-Saxon England : divina in laude voluntas /
Patrick McBrine.

(Toronto Anglo-Saxon series)
Includes bibliographical references and index.
ISBN 978-0-8020-9853-5 (cloth)

1. Epic poetry, Latin – History and criticism.   2. Christian poetry, Latin – History and
criticism.   3. Christianity and literature – England – History – To 1500.   4. Bible – Criticism,
interpretation, etc. – History – Middle Ages, 600–1500.   5. Bible – In literature.   I. Title.
II. Series: Toronto Anglo-Saxon series

PA6053.M33 2017   873.009   C2017-900056-X

This book has been published with the help of a grant from the Federation for the
Humanities and Social Sciences, through the Awards to Scholarly Publications Program,
using funds provided by the Social Sciences and Humanities Research Council of Canada.

University of Toronto Press acknowledges the financial assistance to its publishing
program of the Canada Council for the Arts and the Ontario Arts Council, an agency
of the Government of Ontario.

For my wife, Caroline,
and for Kieran, Ellie, and William

Contents

Preface

The purpose of this book is to provide an accessible introduction to the Latin biblical epics of late Antiquity (c. 300–600) that were known in Anglo-Saxon England (c. 600–1100). The first five chapters introduce the poetry of Juvencus, Cyprianus, Sedulius, Avitus, and Arator, whose work was read and studied throughout the Anglo-Saxon period. These chapters form the core of the book and focus on the Latin approach to biblical versification and the evolution of the genre over the course of late Antiquity. Chapter 7 turns to the reception of this literature in Anglo-Saxon England, in the writings of Aldhelm, Bede, and Alcuin, whose poetry bears witness to the pervasive influence of Latin biblical epic on Anglo-Latin literature. The discussion concludes with analyses of episodes in Old English biblical verse, specifically in *Genesis A*, *B*, and *Exodus*, in order to consider how poets of the two traditions, Latin and English, approach the same scenes. Above all, the purpose of this book is to promote knowledge of a body of writing that was important to the Anglo-Saxons and played a vital role in the instruction of Latin verse and the dissemination of biblical lore.

In the course of finishing this book, I am grateful to a number of people. First, thank you to Suzanne Rancourt at the University of Toronto Press for her support in the publication of this book and to Michel Pharand for his careful attention to the manuscript. Thank you to George Clark at Queen's University for years of guidance and friendship. Thank you to George Rigg at the University of Toronto for weekly readings in late antique Latin verse over the course of a year. Those sessions led to many insights and a translation of the *Carmen paschale* of Sedulius. To David Townsend, I am grateful for support in the early stages of this project and for his friendship and guidance over the last decade. To Toni Healey and the *Dictionary of Old English*, I owe my knowledge of the corpus and its resources. Toni's attentive eye has saved me on more than one occasion, and her suggestions for Chapter 8 (Old English Biblical Verse) have been invaluable. Thank you to Gernot Wieland at the University of British Columbia for reading early drafts of this book in my dissertation and for serving as my external examiner, and thank you to Julia Warnes at the University of Toronto for proofreading early drafts of the chapters on late Antiquity. Thank you also to Yale University for access to Sterling, Beinecke, and Divinity during my years in New Haven, and to Southern Connecticut State University and the English Department for supporting this project. Thank you to Roy Liuzza, Damian Fleming, and Mark Sundaram for reading a draft of my chapter on Old English biblical verse and for their thoughtful suggestions. And thank you especially to Andy Orchard for suggesting this project initially and for years of teaching and friendship. Much of what is good about this book is owing to his influence, and (as Arator would say) "si quid ab ore placet, laus monitoris erit."

Finally, thank you to my family and above all to my wife, Caroline, for enduring these last ten years. I do not think that she will read Sedulius again, but to her and our children, Kieran, Ellie, and William, I dedicate this book.

Patrick McBrine (Toronto, 31 January 2017)

Abbreviations

AJP	American Journal of Philology
ALLG	Archiv für lateinische Lexikographie und Grammatik
ASE	Anglo-Saxon England
ASPR	Anglo-Saxon Poetic Records
CCSL	Corpus Christianorum Series Latina
CSASE	Cambridge Studies in Anglo-Saxon England
CdV	Carmen de uirginitate
CE	Carmina ecclesiastica
CM	Classica et Mediaevalia
Cp	Carmen paschale
ELN	English Language Notes
EC	Les Études Classiques
ES	English Studies
Ev	Euangeliorum libri quattuor
CMCS	Cambridge Medieval Celtic Studies
CSEL	Corpus Scriptorum Ecclesiasticorum Latinorum
JAC	Jahrbuch für Antike und Christentum
LSE	Leeds Studies in English
HE	Historia ecclesiastica gentis Anglorum
MÆ	Medium Ævum
MGH	Monumenta Germaniae Historica
MLN	Modern Language Notes
NM	Neuphilologische Mitteilungen
PIMS	Pontifical Institute of Mediaeval Studies
PL	Patrologia Latina
PRIA	*Proceedings of the Royal Irish Academy*
REA	Revue des Études Augustiniennes

RMAL	Revue du Moyen Age Latin
SP	Speculum
TAPS	Transactions of the American Philosophical Society
TAPA	Transactions of the American Philological Association
TMLT	Toronto Medieval Latin Text
VC	Vigiliae Christianae

BIBLICAL EPICS IN LATE ANTIQUITY
AND ANGLO-SAXON ENGLAND

Chapter One

Introduction

Sed non ut dignum tanti praeconia facti
Eloquium captent: diuina in laude uoluntas
Sufficit et famulo monstrari munere uotum.

[But I do not sing, that my praise of so great a story may capture the eloquence
it deserves. My will to praise the Divine is enough and that this humble offering
makes that wish clear.]

– Avitus, *Historia spiritalis* (5.6–8)

The subtitle of this book, *Biblical Epics in Late Antiquity and Anglo-
Saxon England: Divina in Laude Voluntas*, is based on the above quotation from Avitus of Vienne's sixth-century biblical epic (c. 500), *De
spiritalis historiae gestis* (hereafter *Historia spiritalis*).[1] The relevant lines
appear in the preface to his versification of Exodus, *De transitu maris rubri* (*On the Crossing of the Red Sea*), which emphasizes the baptismal
symbolism of the passage through the waters. The will of Avitus to praise
God through poetry is common to all of the writers in this study, and so it
affords a fitting theme for this book. Moreover, despite his words to the
contrary ("Sed non ut dignum tanti praeconia facti / Eloquium captent,"
5.6–7), Avitus, like every biblical versifier, Latin and English, does indeed
strive to capture the eloquence worthy of the renowned deeds of the Bible.
The general purpose of this book is to consider the manner in which this

---

1 For the text see Peiper, ed., *Alcimi Ecdicii Aviti Viennensis Episcopi Opera*, MGH Auct. A.

will is carried out in the biblical versifications of late Antiquity and the early Middle Ages.

Contribution of This Book

More precisely, the goal of this book is to provide an accessible introduction to the late classical Latin biblical epics known and studied in the Anglo-Saxon period, namely, Juvencus' *Euangeliorum libri* (c. 330), Cyprianus' *Heptateuch* (c. 400–25), Sedulius' *Carmen paschale* (c. 425–50), Avitus' *Historia spiritalis* (c. 500), and Arator's *Historia apostolica* (c. 544).[2] There is now ample evidence in the surviving manuscripts and booklists of the period, not to mention myriad echoes of this literature in Anglo-Latin writing, to confirm that these texts were part of a programmed study of Latin poetry meant to serve as devotional reading and introduce the Anglo-Saxons to the style of classical hexameter verse through biblical epic. There is at present, however, no book that treats these poems all together and with a view to assessing their reception in the later Anglo-Saxon period. That, then, is the primary objective of this book: to introduce each of these texts (chs. 2–6) and to consider how they are important for our reading of Anglo-Latin (ch. 7) and Old English poetry (ch. 8).

Defining Biblical Epic

The Latin genre of biblical epic evolved continually over the course of late Antiquity (c. 330–544 CE), changing with the tastes of its writers and audiences, so that no two poems in this tradition are quite the same.[3] In simple terms, a Latin biblical epic is a poem based on one or more books of the Bible that incorporates features of classical epic.[4] As Paul-Augustin

---

2 Huemer, ed., *Gai. Vetti Aquilini Iuuenci Euangeliorum Libri Quattuor*; *Sedulii Opera Omnia*; Peiper, ed., *Cypriani Galli Poetae Heptateuchos*; for the text of Avitus, see note 1 above; and Orbán, ed., *Aratoris Subdiaconi Historia Apostolica*, 2 vols.

3 The year 330 is the approximate date of the first Latin biblical epic, *Euangeliorum libri quattuor*, and 544 is the year in which Arator dedicated his versification of Acts, *De actibus apostolorum*, to Pope Vigilius in Italy, effectively marking the end of the Latin genre in late Antiquity.

4 See also the definition of Roberts, *Biblical Epic and Rhetorical Paraphrase*, p. 4, n. 12: "poems written in the dactylic hexameter which owe their narrative continuity to a biblical sequence of events."

Deproost defines them, "the poems normally placed within the category of biblical epic aspire to translate the stories of the Bible into the language, images, meter, in short the literary conventions of classical epic."[5] Moreover, though much space and time separate the two, the later genre of Old English biblical verse is defined in similar terms by Paul Remley as "compositions which maintain reasonable fidelity to biblical narratives while evincing their own distinctive poetical identities."[6] Those distinctive poetic identities refer to the English author's response to conventions in Germanic-heroic verse, but the general approach to biblical versification is comparable. In each case, the goal is transformation, to create the illusion that those biblical stories had always been a part of the older tradition even as they stood apart from it.[7] Latin- and English-speaking audiences knew the truth, of course, that this was all slight of hand, but they were willing to entertain the illusion, so long as the pleasures of pagan verse did not taint the more wholesome literature of the Bible. Balance was the key and only a few writers managed to devise a formula that won them any lasting fame; but their legacy endured for more than a millennium, inspiring generations of poets well into the Middle Ages.

Audiences of Biblical Epic

The initial audience for Latin biblical epic was the literary elite of late Antiquity, sophisticated readers who were familiar with both the Bible and classical literature. "After the Edict of Milan," as Michael Roberts puts it, "and the emperor's increasing patronage of Christianity, the poet could count on attracting cultivated readers for whom a recasting of the biblical narrative in the culturally prestigious idiom of Latin (primarily

---

5 Deproost, "L'épopée biblique en langue latine," 14: "les poèmes que l'on range habituellement sous cette étiquette 'épopée biblique' prétendent effectivement traduire des histoires bibliques dans le langage, les images, le mètre, bref les conventions littéraires de l'épopée antique ..."

6 Remley, "Biblical Translation: Poems," in *The Blackwell Encyclopedia of Anglo-Saxon England*, 66–7.

7 See further Morhmann, *La langue et le style de la poesie Latine chrétienne*, 155.

Vergilian) epic would have a special appeal."[8] That was certainly the case with Juvencus' *Euangeliorum libri* (c. 330), a versification of the Gospels dedicated to Emperor Constantine, whose formal endorsement of Christianity in 313 (The Edict of Milan) opened the way for Juvencus and many other Christian writers eager to establish a corpus of Christian literature. In fact, all of the biblical epics of late Antiquity appealed to highly educated readers who could appreciate the sophisticated interplay of sources in the genre; one need only look to scholarly editions of these texts to find lists of learned individuals who knew them very well. Huemer's edition of Juvencus, for one, contains endorsements by such famous writers as St Jerome, Isidore of Seville, Eugenius of Toledo, and many others who cited or echoed the poem in approbation of its merit.[9] These were all highly literate individuals, many of them highly placed in the Church.

The situation was somewhat different in Anglo-Saxon England, where Latin was not the native language of the English and where biblical epic arrived only after the conversion to Christianity around 600 CE. The Anglo-Saxons had to struggle with this literature more than their continental neighbours, but they became familiar enough with it to initiate their own tradition of Latin hexameter verse in the "classical" style, that is, poetry based on the Christian model of late antique writing. Thus Aldhelm's verse and prose *De uirginitate* (*On Virginity*), Bede's two lives of St Cuthbert (*Vita Cuthberti*) and Alcuin's lives of St Willibrord (*Vita Willibrordi*), all treated in chapter 7, follow in the footsteps of Sedulius, who wrote the original *opus geminatum* ("twinned work") with his *Carmen* and *Opus paschale*, a versification of the Gospels.

Vernacular audiences of Old English biblical poetry were probably not for the most part members of the literary elite, given the appeal of English writing to a more general audience. On the other hand, passages in *Genesis A* and *Exodus* (ch. 8) obviously appeal to sophisticated readers, and so we must be careful about generalizations. But given the fidelity of these poems to the basic events of the Bible over any symbolic messages, it is likely that this poetry was meant primarily to disseminate knowledge of the Scriptures

---

8   Roberts, "Vergil and the Gospel," 47. See also p. 59 of the same article: "The *Ev.* could expect an enthusiastic readership among cultivated Romans for whom its Vergilian idiom would only enhance the appeal of Juvencus." See also Deproost, "L'Épopée Biblique," 24 and 21, where Deproost imagines an extremely cultivated audience participating in the culture of its author. See also Evenepoel, "The Place of Poetry in Latin Christianity," 39; and McClure, "The Biblical Epic and Its Audience in Late Antiquity," 305–21.

9   See further Huemer's introduction, *Euangeliorum libri*, esp. i–xxiv.

in popular form. Again, however, because many of these poems can and do move unpredictably between passages of literal description and figurative allusions, it is safest to say that the audience of the English genre was a mixed but mainly general one.

Purposes of Biblical Epic

As the title of this book suggests, there is a sense that these biblical poems represent in large the author's will to praise God. So the progenitor of the Latin genre, Juvencus, concludes his preface to *Euangeliorum libri* with the hope "that [he] may speak things worthy of Christ" ("ut Christo digna loquamur," *Ev. Praef.* 27), and a century later the poet Sedulius proclaims a similar desire to "speak the truth and … praise the Lord-Thunderer with all [his] heart and soul" ("manifesta loqui, Dominumque tonantem / Sensibus et toto delectet corde fateri," *Cp.* 1.27–8). Avitus says much the same thing – "My will to praise the Divine is enough for me" ("diuina in laude uoluntas / Sufficit," *Hist. spirit.* 5.7–8) – and so does Arator, the sixth-century versifier of Acts, who declares, "there is a burning in my heart to celebrate the labours of the men by whose voice faith finds a path in the world" ("Sensibus ardor inest horum celebrare labores, / Quorum uoce fides obtinet orbis iter," *Epist. Vigil.*, 17–18), and "I will be guilty, if I ever stop giving thanks to Him" ("Esse reus potero, grates si reddere cessem," 15), that is, God.

Poets in the later English genre are less outspoken in every respect than their Latin predecessors, but the first work in the vernacular tradition, *Genesis A*, begins with the following words: "It is very right that we should praise the Guardian of heaven, the Glory-King of hosts, with words and love him in our hearts" ("Us is riht micel ðæt we rodera weard, / wereda wuldorcining, wordum herigen, / modum lufien"). Moreover, the only named biblical poet of the period, Caedmon, whose other works have not survived, begins his *Hymn* in the same way: "Now we should praise the Guardian of the Kingdom of Heaven …" ("Nu sculon herigean heofonrices weard …"). Other poems in the Junius collection of biblical poetry likewise emphasize the importance of giving praise to God. So in the context of the fall of Lucifer, the author of *Genesis B* writes, "He had to render praise to God … to thank his Lord" ("Lof sceolde he drihtnes wyrcean … and sceolde his drihtne þancian," 256b–7), although Lucifer's pride compels him to do "something worse" ("to wyrsan þinge," 259a). At the end of *Exodus*, the Israelites give due thanks and praise to God for delivering them out of Egypt (*drihten heredon*, 576b), and their faith, as Moses says, will earn them "great glory" (*Bið eower blaed micel*, 564b). It is like the glory God's angels enjoyed in heaven ("Wæs heora blaed micel," *GenA* 14b), when they still praised the Lord (*þeoden heredon*, 15b). Therefore, this theme of praise is an ongoing concern for the poets of the Junius Manuscript and for those of the Latin tradition as well.

There is also a strong didactic element to all of the Latin and Old English biblical poems. As Michael Roberts describes it, the wider justification for the genre, beyond its entertainment value, is attached to the "Christian purpose of spiritual instruction, moral edification or biblical exegesis."[10] The German scholar, Reinhart Herzog, uses the term *Erbauung* ("edification") in much the same way, and Klaus Thraede before him refers to "der überwiegend moralisch-didaktischen Auffassung der Poesie" ("the predominantly moral and didactic conception of [this] poetry").[11] So while delight, or *delectatio*, is a strong draw for audiences, an important function of this literature, as Siegmar Döpp puts it, is attached to its "didaktische Intention" ("didactic intention").[12]

Overview of Chapters

The purpose of this book, apart from sharing what these poems are about, is to consider how their authors promote the values of Christianity. A summary overview of the chapters will thus be useful at this point. Following the present chapter, chapter 2 introduces the work of the Spanish priest and poet, Juvencus, whose verse rendition of the Gospels, *Euangeliorum libri Quattuor* (c. 330), establishes many of the normative practices in the Latin genre. In his preface, Juvencus confronts conventional themes of epic, notably immortality (*Inmortale nihil mundi*, 1), but also the lofty deeds of men (*homines sublimia facta*, 6), fame, praise (*famam laudesque*, 8), and the glory of the poets themselves (*gloria uatum*, 11). These Juvencus must convert (as it were) for Christian audiences to serve the "glory of the Creator" (*genitoris gloria Christus*, 24), whose "life-giving deeds" (*uitalia gesta*, 19) eclipse the heroic exploits of old, "which bind lies to the deeds of ancient men" ("quae ueterum gestis hominum mendacia nectunt," 16). Unlike those, Christ's life is without falsehood

---

10   Roberts, *Biblical Epic*, 107.

11   The didactic function of biblical epic is expressed early on as *Erbaulichkeit* by Herzog in his fundamental study, *Die Bibelepik der lateinischen Spätantike*; see also Thraede, "Epos," 983–1042, 1006.

12   See also Döpp, *Eva und die Schlange*, 19–22, for the purpose of biblical epic.

(*falsi sine crimine*, 20) and it reveals the true path to immortality (*Inmortale decus*, 18). As such it is more than worthy of epic song.

In versifying the Bible, Juvencus moves systematically through the text of the Gospels, favouring Matthew, and authenticating his poetic rendition with verbal links to the Bible. Thus, for example, his versification of the Lord's Prayer begins, "Sidereo genitor residens in uertice caeli / Nominis, oramus, ueneratio sanctificetur" ("Father residing in the starry height of heaven, / may the veneration of your name, we pray, be hallowed," 1.590–1), and echoes of the original can be heard in the words, *caeli* ("heaven"), *nominis* ("name"), and *sanctificetur* ("be hallowed"), the last of which appears verbatim in the Bible: "Pater noster qui in caelis es sanctificetur nomen tuum" ("Our Father who art in heaven, hallowed be thy name"). Such fidelity is part of the reason why Jerome calls the poem a *paene ad uerbum* translation of the Bible, that is, "almost word for word."[13] That being said, the poetic diction Juvencus adds to the prose – and this can be seen even in the excerpt of the Lord's Prayer above – introduces shades of meaning into the original story, and a careful reading of many scenes in *Euangeliorum libri* reveals a subtle, renovating hand at work, showing that Juvencus adapts much of what he adopts. The purpose of this chapter, then, after a brief introduction to the author and some biblical and classical features of his poem, is to examine key scenes in the text, to show how the author blends biblical language with that of classical poetry. More often than not, Juvencus strikes a balance between the sacred and profane, which accounts in large part for the popularity of the work, but he also manages to introduce subtle commentary through his choice of diction. Such commentary may suggest a point of contrast with the values of classical epic, what German scholars call *Kontrastimitation*, while other additions develop themes that are important to the author, such as the "life-giving deeds of Christ" (*Christi uitalia gesta, praef.* 19), which he highlights in the preface and emphasizes throughout his translation of New Testament miracles. In many ways, therefore, this chapter is the most important one in the book, because it introduces the Latin genre, its normative features, and a general template for all subsequent discussions.

Chapter 3 introduces the *Heptateuchos* (hereafter the *Heptateuch*) of the poet Cyprianus Gallus, a versification of the Old Testament written at the beginning of the fifth century (c. 400–25). In style, the *Heptateuch* owes much to the foundational work of Juvencus and it is likewise a *paene*

---

13 See further Huemer, ed., *Euangeliorum libri*, vi.

ad uerbum translation of the Bible. That much is clear from the first words, "Principio dominus caelum terramque locauit" ("In the beginning the Lord established heaven and earth," 1), which nearly renders the language of the original ("In principio fecit deus caelum et terram," Gen. 1:1).

Little is known about the author himself (his name is a fabrication), but it is apparent from analyses of the metre and his choice of poetic diction that Cyprianus is a less gifted poet than Juvencus. He shares with him an exuberant love of classical verse, especially of the *Aeneid*, but this same (youthful?) exuberance leads him to some unfortunate choices, not the least of which is the decision to attempt to versify all of the historical books of the Old Testament. That is over-ambitious, and judging from the general obscurity of the author and his work throughout late Antiquity and the Middle Ages, it appears the poem never enjoyed the kind of success and status *Euangeliorum libri* did. Even so, flashes of virtuosity reward the persistent reader, including the author's rendition of the temptation and fall of Eve (*Gen.* 72–90), the description of the Flood (*Gen.* 287–321), and the destruction of Sodom and Gomorrah (*Gen.* 661–7). The story of Pharaoh's pursuit of the Israelites through the wilderness and into the waters of the Red Sea also captures some of that eloquence worthy of so great a story. Ultimately, the greatest virtues of the *Heptateuch* are its economy of style and close proximity to the biblical narrative, which make this poem an accessible and at times forceful rendition of the Old Testament.

Chapter 4 introduces the *Carmen paschale* of Sedulius (c. 425–50), a free and florid rendition of the Gospels and arguably the greatest achievement in the genre. Not only is Sedulius a skilled imitator of his epic predecessors, especially Vergil, but his translation of the Gospels is at once inventive and faithful to the original. His preface, written in elegiac distichs and not dactylic hexameter, which is itself notable, transforms the image of a Roman banquet into a metaphorical, Eucharistic feast for the consumption of spiritual food. No *paene ad uerbum* translation, this and all subsequent poems in the genre range farther afield to explore the deeper symbolism of the Bible and the connections between the Old and New Testaments. Thus Sedulius exhorts his reader, "Cognoscite cuncti, / Mystica quid doceant animos miracula nostros" ("Let us all recognize what these mystical miracles teach our souls," 4.263–4), and unlike Juvencus or Cyprianus, who remain detached from their narratives in observance of epic decorum, Sedulius and his successors intervene frequently in their poems, to guide the reader in the interpretation of the Bible. Consequently, the complexity of the genre, which was determined mainly by the juxtaposition of classical and Christian sources, now increases to include a symbolic dimension. Thus the description of the advent of the Magi in Book 2 (2.89–101) includes biblical language augmented by classical-poetic diction, but it also contains symbolic meaning with a doctrinal message. The three gifts of the Magi now stand for religion (*pro religione*, 2.93), for the threefold power of God, the Holy Trinity ("in triplici uirtute sui," 2.101). With such depth of interest and symbolism, it is easy to see why the *Carmen paschale* was among the most popular biblical epics of late Antiquity and the Middle Ages, because it offered not only an alternative to the pagan verses of the *Aeneid* but a rich source of devotional reading for the ruminating mind.

Chapter 5 introduces Avitus and his *De spiritalis historiae gestis* (hereafter *Historia spiritalis*), a very free rendition of the Old Testament with emphasis on the theme of salvation history. It was written around 500 CE. If the greatest virtues of the *Heptateuch* are its economy of style and general accessibility, the opposite is true of this work, which is expansive and magniloquent, at times to the point of obscurity. The poem contains five books, which cover the Creation, the Fall, God's Judgment of Adam and Eve, the Flood, and the Crossing of the Red Sea. Each book is linked loosely to the scriptural narrative and shows that Avitus is more concerned with developing dramatic action and characters that exhibit greater emotional and psychological depth than their biblical counterparts; and much of everything promotes the symbolic importance of the Old Testament over its literal meaning. So the drama of the Fall is raised to epic proportions; we see into the devil's mind, his hatred of God and man, and his determination to ruin both (2.90–116). We also see the internal struggle of Eve and the psychological turmoil that leads to her downfall (2.208–34), and we learn that Christ is to be the new Adam (*nouissimus Adam*, 3.21) who will atone for the sins of the first father (*prime pater*, 1.7). Equally, the stories of the Flood and Crossing of the Red Sea contain dramatic re-enactments of the Bible with symbolism related to Baptism. The whole narrative is intricately composed of recurrent images linking the events of each book to the larger framework of salvation history, and although the expansive nature of the text can be excessive, *Historia spiritalis* remains one of the most vivid and entertaining poems on the Old Testament.

Chapter 6 introduces the final biblical epic of late Antiquity, Arator's *De actibus apostolorum* (hereafter *Historia apostolica*), a free rendition of Acts alternating between passages of biblical translation and biblical commentary. It was written around 544 CE. As Arator himself says, "I shall in turn set out what the letter reveals and whatever mystical sense is given to my heart" ("Alternis reserabo modis quod littera pandit/Et res si qua mihi mystica corde datur," *Epist. Vigil.* 21–2). This can be seen, for example, in his treatment of the storm at sea in Acts 27:13–20, which begins with a fairly straightforward account of the incident (2.1067–81), followed by an explanation of its greater significance in terms of Christian salvation (2.1131–51). What is more, although Arator is far freer in his adaptation of the Bible than Juvencus, Cyprianus, or Sedulius (though not Avitus) and pursues the mystical sense of Acts with ardent fervour, he does not (as many argue) lose sight of the Bible.

Unlike Avitus, who favours lofty poetic diction almost for its own sake, Arator reacts more to the semantic depth of language and its potential to express literal and figurative meaning, simultaneously. Indeed, Arator's fondness for wordplay permeates *Historia apostolica*, so that the challenge for the reader at times is to follow the poet's mental path from scenes of literal description to more symbolic interpretations. A passing reference to Troas in Acts 20.6 leads Arator into a digression on Troy, epic, and the proper place of praise (2.757–71), followed immediately by an interpretation of sleep as spiritual blindness, and all of this comes before his actual commentary on the deeper, general significance of the episode. But there is great richness in *Historia apostolica*, which offers plenty of instruction with delight.

Following these first five chapters on Juvencus, Cyprianus, Sedulius, Avitus, and Arator, chapter 7 sets out to account in some measure for the reception of this literature in Anglo-Saxon England. The chapter begins with a discussion of the Anglo-Saxon school curriculum and the place of Latin biblical epic in it. Evidence is given for knowledge of these poems in the surviving manuscripts, references on booklists, and verbal echoes in Anglo-Latin writing. The list of echoes is not exhaustive, but it does provide a sense of which works were well known and which parts of them. Analysis of two anonymous versifications of the Lord's Prayer from this period also provides a case study of how deeply the influence of that literature can go. The discussion then shifts to the work of Aldhelm, Bede, and Alcuin, the most prominent Latin poets of the period, each of whom was very well acquainted with the late antique tradition of biblical epic. The extent of their debt to this literature, however, has yet to be gauged fully, and so this section aims to show how these writers incorporated their knowledge of the earlier genre into their idiosyncratic compositions in Anglo-Latin, in particular in Aldhelm's *Carmen de uirginitate*, Bede's versified *Vita Cuthberti*, and Alcuin's *Vita Willibrordi*, but also in their other poetry. In short, this chapter provides much new evidence to support the argument that Aldhelm, Bede, and

Alcuin were deeply indebted to the language and style of the late antique Latin biblical epics.

Chapter 8 turns to the Old English versifications of the Bible in the so-called Junius Manuscript and specifically to *Genesis A*, *Genesis B*, and *Exodus*, which have in common many scenes with the earlier Latin genre. The primary goal of this chapter is to provide an objective analysis of Old English biblical verse from the point of view of someone familiar with the Latin tradition and to consider what vernacular poets may have in common with their late antique predecessors. Simply put, there is much to suggest that the working *modus operandi* of the English versifier is more like that of the Latin poet than not, especially in their shared desire to validate the scriptural poetry with verbal links to the Bible and to adopt features of traditional poetic diction (now from the Germanic tradition), to augment the entertainment value of the biblical story. There is also good reason to believe that the impetus towards extra-literal meaning in poems like the Old English *Exodus* owes as much to the earlier work of Sedulius, Avitus, and Arator as it does the liturgy or biblical commentaries in prose.

Finally, chapter 9 provides a brief summary and conclusion of the discussion as well as a few suggestions for future work in the field. In simple terms, there is a need for more translations of these texts and treatments of their reception in Anglo-Latin and Old English literature. This book only scratches the surface.

Summary of Scholarship

Scholarly interest in the Latin and Old English versifications of the Bible has increased steadily over the last fifty years, gaining momentum in recent decades. A brief sketch here will be helpful. Important, early surveys include Max Manitius' *Geschichte der Christlich-lateinischen Poesie* (1891),[14] E.R. Curtius' *Europäische Literatur und lateinisches Mittelalter* (1948),[15] and F.J.E. Raby's *A History of Christian Latin Poetry* (1953).[16] Each says something about the tradition of biblical epic in the wider scope of early Christian literature. Klaus Thraede's 1962 article "Epos" treats

---

14 Manitius, *Geschichte der Christlich-lateinischen Poesie*; see also *Geschichte der lateinischen Literatur des Mittelalters*, 3 vols.

15 Curtius, *Europäische Literatur und lateinisches Mittelalter*; see also Trask, trans., *European Literature and the Latin Middle Ages*.

16 Raby, *History of Christian Latin Poetry from the Beginnings to the Close of the Middle Ages*.

the development of Greek and Latin epic, specifically, but includes a survey of the Latin biblical poems.[17] Thraede also introduces the term *Konstrastimitation*, which scholars now use regularly to define those moments in Christian poetry when a writer appears to adopt classical-poetic diction to suggest a point of contrast with the earlier tradition.[18] Thus Eve eats the apple, because she wants to be like God (*deo*), but Avitus uses the plural form, *dis* ("the gods"), because her ambition, like that of the pagan deities and Satan, is motivated by self-interest and a lust for power.[19] Christian poets would say, that is not what God is like.

Treatments of biblical epic, specifically, include Reinhart Herzog's fundamental study, *Die Bibelepik der lateinischen Spätantike* (1975), which emphasizes the devotional and edifying purpose of this literature in the fourth century.[20] Fontaine's *Naissance de la poésie dans l'occident chrétien* (1981) ranges more broadly, but includes many insightful discussions of the biblical epics.[21] Michael Roberts' *Biblical Epic and Rhetorical Paraphrase in Late Antiquity* (1985) is among the most influential surveys of the genre, which approaches biblical versification from the point of view of the procedures of rhetorical paraphrase.[22] "For Herzog, as for me," writes Roberts, "the biblical epic is an expression of the devotional needs of the Christian community. But my approach insists on the importance of rhetoric and the exercise of the paraphrase in the development of this new branch of Christian literature in the West."[23] Among other things, Roberts' work has helped to popularize the use of rhetorical language in the study of biblical epic, including such terms as "abbreviation," "omission," "amplification," "variation," etc.,

---

17   Thraede, "Epos," 983–1042; see also his article on Arator, "Nachträge zum Reallexikon für Antike und Christentum: Arator," 187–96. For a roughly contemporary survey in English, see also Hudson-Williams, "Virgil and the Christian Latin Poets," 11–21.

18   See further Thraede, "Epos," 1039; see also Sandnes, *The Gospel According to Homer and Vergil*, 58–9.

19   The passage appears in Book 1 (2.220–1): "she wants to be like God, and the poison creeps in, wounding her with ambition" ("Dis tamen esse cupit similis serpitque uenenum / Ambitione nocens").

20   Herzog, *Die Bibelepik der lateinischen Spätantike*; and his later article, "Exegese – Erbauung – Delectatio," 52–69; finally, "Juvencus," 331–6.

21   *Naissance de la poésie dans l'occident chrétien*; see also Fontaine and Pietri, eds., *Le monde latin antique et la Bible*.

22   Roberts, *Biblical Epic and Rhetorical Paraphrase*. Aside from his individual articles, see also "The Latin Literature of Late Antiquity." See also Kirsch, *Die lateinische Versepik des 4 Jahrhunderts*, which was published in the same year.

23   Roberts, *Biblical Epic*, 61.

which scholars now use to characterize the relationship of biblical poets to their sources. Finally, Roger Green's *Latin Epics of the New Testament: Juvencus, Sedulius, Arator* (2006) contains an excellent survey of these writers and their versifying *modus operandi*.[24] His article "Birth and Transfiguration: Some Gospel Episodes in Juvencus and Sedulius" (2007), moreover, provides a model exemplum of how to approach a passage of biblical verse, not just by isolating its classical and Christian sources, but by suggesting how particular allusions and rhetorical devices function in the context of the poetic narrative.[25] In other words, he does not lose sight of the individual achievement of the author.

The above works are supplemented by numerous studies of individual authors, which have helped to deepen our understanding of the genre. They include Jean-Michel Poinsotte's *Juvencus et Israël: la représentation des Juifs dans le premier poème latin chrétien* (1979), which explores anti-Semitism in *Euangeliorum libri*.[26] Carl Springer has written three books on Sedulius, including *The Gospel as Epic in Late Antiquity: The Paschale Carmen of Sedulius* (1988), *The Manuscripts of Sedulius* (1995), and a recent translation, *Sedulius: The Paschal Song and Hymns* (2013).[27] Two important monographs on Arator were published in 1990: *L'Apôtre Pierre dans une épopée du VIe siècle: L'Historia apostolica d'Arator* (1990) by Paul-Augustin Deproost,[28] and Schwind's *Arator-Studien* (1990).[29] Richard Hillier's 1993 book, *Arator on the Acts of the Apostles: A Baptismal Commentary*, makes it a trifecta.[30] In the same year, Daniel Nodes published a general study of *Doctrine and Exegesis in Biblical Latin Poetry* (1993) that provides valuable context for the extra-literal meaning of the biblical epics; eight years earlier he also published an edition of Avitus for *The Fall of Man: De Spiritalis Historiae Gestis, Libri I–III* (1985).[31] Knowledge of *Historia spiritalis* has

---

24 *Latin Epics of the New Testament.*

25 See further Green, "Birth and Transfiguration," 135–71; also, "The *Evangeliorum Libri* of Juvencus," 65–80; and "Approaching Christian Epic," 203–22.

26 Poinsotte, *Juvencus et Israël.*

27 Springer, *The Gospel as Epic in Late Antiquity*; *The Manuscripts of Sedulius: A Provisional Handlist*; *Sedulius: The Paschal Song and Hymns*; see also "The Biblical Epic in Late Antiquity and the Early Modern Period," 103–26.

28 Deproost, *L'Apôtre Pierre dans une épopée du VIe siecle.*

29 Schwind, *Arator-Studien.*

30 Hillier, *Arator on the Acts of the Apostles.*

31 Nodes, *Doctrine and Exegesis in Biblical Latin Poetry*; *The Fall of Man*; "Avitus of Vienne's Spiritual History," 185–95.

also been advanced by two books published in 1999: Alexander Arweiler's *Die Imitation antiker und spätantiker Literatur in der Dichtung "De spiritalis historiae gestis" des Alcimus Avitus*[32] and Nicole Hecquet-Noti's two-volume edition of Avitus, *Avit de Vienne: Histoire Spirituelle*.[33]

In addition to numerous other articles on the biblical epics, several commentaries have appeared over the last thirty years, most in German, and these have helped to temper generalizations about individual texts and the genre as a whole.[34] As Green says, "commentaries of this kind are extremely useful, not only in their analyses of particular sections – the closeness of the paraphrase, the possibilities of exegetical nuance, and the analysis of classical influence on Juvencus' language are favoured topics – but also because they form valuable testing grounds for some of the more generalizing studies of recent times."[35]

Anglo-Latin studies have advanced significantly in the last thirty years, due in large part to the influence of Michael Lapidge, and while he is among only a few to have addressed the reception of Latin biblical epic directly, awareness of the genre has been increasing steadily. Lapidge's two volumes on *Anglo-Latin Literature* (1993 and 1996) offer a wealth of context, but his chapters on Aldhelm, Bede, and the Anglo-Saxon school curriculum in particular are fundamental to chapter 7 of this book.[36] His translations in *Aldhelm: The Prose Works* (with Herren, 1979) and *Aldhelm: The Poetic Works* (with Rosier, 1985)[37] have, moreover, helped to make this writer's work accessible to a general audience, while his survey of sources in *The Anglo-Saxon Library* (2006) attests to widespread knowledge of the biblical

---

32 Arweiler, *Die Imitation antiker und spätantiker Literatur in der Dichtung*.

33 Hecquet-Noti, ed. and trans., *Avit de Vienne*; see also her article-length studies "La description du déluge," 229–35; "Le corbeau nécrophage, figure du juif," 297–320; and "Ève et le serpent," 2–17.

34 See further Kievits, ed., *Ad Iuvenci Evangeliorum*; van der Laan, *Sedulius, Carmen Paschale Boek 4*; Flieger, "Interpretationen zum Bibeldichter Iuvencus"; Fichtner, *Taufe und Versuchung Jesu*; Mazzega, ed., *Sedulius, Carmen Paschale, Buch III*; Heinsdorf, *Christus, Nikodemus und die Sameritanerin bei Juvencus*; and Deerberg, *Der Sturz des Judas*.

35 Green, review of Heinsdorff, *Christus, Nikodemus und die Samaritanerin Classical Review*, 55.1 (2005), 163–4.

36 See further Lapidge, *Anglo-Latin Literature, 900–1066* and *Anglo-Latin Literature, 600–899*; *The Anglo-Saxon Library*, and in vol. 1, "Aldhelm's Latin Poetry and Old English Verse," 247–70; "Bede the Poet," 313–38; "Bede's Metrical *Vita S. Cuthberti*," 339–56; and "The Study of Latin Texts in Late Anglo-Saxon England," 455–98.

37 Lapidge, and Herren, trans., *Aldhelm: The Prose Works*; Lapidge and Rosier, trans., *Aldhelm: The Poetic Works*.

epics throughout the period.[38] Lapidge's collaboration with Helmut Gneuss in *Anglo-Saxon Manuscripts: A Bibliographical Handlist* (2014) provides a valuable update to an essential book, and it contains a list of all known Anglo-Saxon manuscripts, including those containing biblical poetry.[39] Finally, many of Lapidge's articles touch on the reception of Latin biblical epic in Anglo-Saxon literature, notably "The Study of Latin Texts in Late Anglo-Saxon England" (1982) and "Versifying the Bible in the Middle Ages" (2006), while others treat features of style in Anglo-Latin and Old English poetry that have some bearing on the reception of late antique literature in Anglo-Saxon England.[40]

Andy Orchard's *Poetic Art of Aldhelm* (1994) is the definitive work on this writer's style and sources, and it includes much evidence for his knowledge of Latin biblical epic.[41] So does Orchard's earlier article, "After Aldhelm: The Teaching and Transmission of the Anglo-Latin Hexameter."[42] Peter Godman's *Bishops, Kings, and Saints of York* (1982) provides an edition and translation of Alcuin's York poem, which owes much to the style of late antique verse and alludes directly to the canonical biblical epics.[43] Moreover, his article of the previous year, "The Anglo-Latin *Opus Geminatum* from Aldhelm to Alcuin" (1981), highlights the debt of Anglo-Latin writers to the earlier work of Sedulius in the *Carmen* and *Opus paschale*.[44] So does Gernot Wieland's "*Geminus Stylus*: Studies in Anglo-Latin Hagiography" (1981), published in the same year, and his monograph *The Latin Glosses on Arator and Prudentius in Cambridge University Library, Ms Gg. 5.35* (1983) provides essential context for the study of the biblical epics in this period.[45] Wieland's article with George

---

38 Lapidge, *The Anglo-Saxon Library*.

39 Gneuss and Lapidge, eds., *Anglo-Saxon Manuscripts: A Bibliographical Handlist of Manuscripts and Manuscript Fragments Written or Owned in England up to 1100*; and Gneuss, *Handlist of Anglo-Saxon Manuscripts*.

40 Lapidge, "Some Old English Sedulius Glosses," 1–17; "The Study of Latin Texts in Late Anglo-Saxon England," 99–165; "Surviving Booklists from Anglo-Saxon England," 33–90; "Hypallage in the Old English *Exodus*," 31–9; "An aspect of Old English poetic diction," 153–180; "Old English Poetic Compounds," 17–32.

41 Orchard, *The Poetic Art of Aldhelm*.

42 Orchard, "After Aldhelm," 96–133.

43 Godman, *The Bishops, Kings, and Saints of York*, esp. 124–5.

44 Godman, "The Anglo-Latin *Opus Geminatum* from Aldhelm to Alcuin," 215–29.

45 Wieland, "*Geminus Stylus*: Studies in Anglo-Latin Hagiography," in *Insular Latin Studies*, 113–33; *The Latin Glosses on Arator and Prudentius*.

Rigg, "A Canterbury Classbook of the Mid-Eleventh Century" (1975), initiated a critical debate about the educational potential of certain Anglo-Saxon manuscripts, and the biblical epics figure prominently in this discussion.[46] Emily Thornbury has taken the question up again in *Becoming a Poet in Anglo-Saxon England* (2014), and she provides much new evidence for the reading and adaptation of Latin biblical epic in the period. As she puts it, "the most important genre in the Anglo-Saxon 'curriculum' was undoubtedly the biblical epic ... and in turn the works of Juvencus, Alcimus Avitus, Sedulius, and Arator were quickly integrated into Christian education – a tradition which ... the Anglo-Saxons enthusiastically perpetuated."[47] Finally, Neil Wright's articles "The *Hisperica Famina* and Caelius Sedulius" (1982) and "Imitation of the Poems of Paulinus of Nola in Early Anglo-Latin Verse" provide further context for the insular reception of late antique poetry.[48]

Despite the advances in Anglo-Latin studies confirming the pervasive influence of late antique biblical epic on writers throughout the Anglo-Saxon period, scholarly work on the reception of this literature in Old English poetry has progressed more slowly. As Lapidge has said (2006), "no one, I think, has attempted to read Old English verse in light of the school curriculum which all Old English poets must have studied."[49] That is one of the purposes of this book, and given the obvious learning and Latinity of the authors of *Genesis A* and *Exodus*, for example, it is reasonable to expect that features of the earlier genre inspired writers in the emerging vernacular tradition, especially since both of those poems appear to have been written early in the period, when knowledge of the biblical epics flourished and found new life in the Anglo-Latin verses of Aldhelm, Bede, and Alcuin. Yet the question of any relationship between the two traditions has been muted for the better part of a century, due primarily to a single disagreement.

---

46 See further Rigg and Wieland, "A Canterbury Classbook of the Mid-Eleventh Century (The 'Cambridge Songs' Manuscript)," 113–30; Lapidge, "The Study of Latin Texts," 99–165; Wieland, "The Glossed Manuscript," 153–73; Page, "On the Feasibility of a Corpus of Anglo-Saxon Glosses," 77–95; "Interpreting Interpretation," 59–71; and *Latin Glosses on Arator and Prudentius*.

47 See further Thornbury, *Becoming a Poet in Anglo-Saxon England*, 51.

48 Wright, "The *Hisperica Famina* and Caelius Sedulius," 61–76; see also "Arator's Use of Caelius Sedulius: A Re-Examination," 51–64; and "Imitation of the Poems of Paulinus of Nola in Early Anglo-Latin Verse," 134–51.

49 Lapidge, "Versifying the Bible," 27.

In 1883, Ernst Groth suggested a potential source for the Old English *Exodus* in the *Historia spiritalis* of Avitus,[50] and his view was supported by Mürkens (1899),[51] Brandl (1901–9),[52] and Blackburn (1907).[53] In 1911, however, Samuel Moore published an article, "On the Sources of the Old-English *Exodus*," which challenged that view and argued that every supposed parallel between the poems could be dismissed without much difficulty.[54] He concluded,

> It would not be difficult to show that the differences between these two poems are more remarkable than the resemblances; that the *De transitu Maris Rubri* is notable for the fact that large parts of the narrative are given from the point of view of the Egyptians, whereas in the Exodus the narrative point of view is that of the Hebrew army, or of the poet himself; that Avitus portrays the situation of the Egyptians and Pharaoh with considerable sympathy, whereas to the Old-English poet they are always God's enemies; that Avitus represents the Hebrews as leaving Egypt before dawn, in the moon-light, but that the Old-English poet represents them as leaving by daylight; that in Avitus the pillar first appeared in the evening as a pillar of fire, and that according to the English poet it first appeared as a column of cloud; that in the Latin poem the pillar seems to appear at the first encampment of the Israelites, whereas in the English poem it appears at the third encampment, at Etham: but such an examination would require more space than can be given to it here. The burden of proof is upon those who assert that Avitus is the source of the Old-English poem, and I believe that this burden has not been lifted.[55]

The result of Moore's article was the end of this particular debate and effectively of any further discussion of the biblical epics as potential sources for any poem in the English genre. But many of Moore's arguments themselves can be challenged, as Lapidge has shown, and even if one accepts the differences above, anyone familiar with the Latin genre will recognize the obvious kinship between *Exodus* and numerous poems in the Latin tradition, many of which share the English author's interest in

---

50 Groth, *Composition und Alter der altenglischen Exodus*, 17.
51 Mürkens, *Untersuchungen über das altenglische Exoduslied*.
52 Brandl, "Englische Literatur," in Hermann Paul, ed., *Grundriss der germanischen Philologie*, 2nd edn. (Strasburg 1901–9), vol. 2.
53 Blackburn, *Exodus* and *Daniel*.
54 Moore, "On the Sources of the Old-English Exodus," 83–108.
55 Ibid., 99–100.

heroic dramatization and baptismal imagery. The same interests can be found, for example, in the poetry of Cyprianus, Sedulius, and Arator, not to mention Prudentius.[56] So there is good reason to reconsider the relationship of Latin biblical epic to Old English biblical verse, but because of the general silence of scholars over the last century, my approach to this question in chapter 8 must proceed without much of a scholarly framework, which is why I have relied on the approaches of late antique scholars.[57]

Otherwise, the scholarship on the Old English poems affords the best entrance into the vernacular tradition, especially the editions of the poems. A.N. Doane's two editions of *Genesis A* (1978) and *B* (1991), including a recent revision of the former (2013), provide essential introductions and commentaries on the texts (but see Wright, "*ad Litteram*").[58] The same is true for the editions of *Exodus* by E.B. Irving (1953), Peter Lucas (1977), and J.R.R. Tolkien (1981).[59] Paul Remley's *Old English Biblical Verse: Studies in Genesis, Exodus and Daniel* (1996) offers the most comprehensive survey of the English genre, and Remley provides essential context for the sources and interpretation of these texts.[60] Individual articles are too numerous to count, but preliminary introductions to the genre can be found in *The Poems of MS Junius 11* (2002), edited by Roy Liuzza, and *Old English Literature and the Old Testament* (2012), edited by Michael Fox and Manish Sharma.[61]

---

56 On this point see the early article by Bright, "The Relation of the Caedmonian *Exodus* to the Liturgy," 97–103; and Cross and Tucker, "Allegorical Traditions and the Old English *Exodus*," 122–7.

57 A notable exception is the recent article of Miranda Wilcox, "Creating the Cloud-Tent-Ship Conceit in *Exodus*," which links this image to the *Historia apostolica* of Arator among other works.

58 See further Doane, ed. *Genesis A: A New Edition*; this edition has been revised for the ACMRS; and *The Saxon Genesis: An Edition of the West Saxon Genesis B and the Old Saxon Vatican Genesis*. See, however, Wright, "*Genesis A ad Litteram*," 121–71.

59 See further Irving, ed., *The Old English Exodus*; and Lucas, ed., *Exodus*; Tolkien and Turville-Petre, eds., *The Old English Exodus*.

60 See further Remley, *Old English Biblical Verse*.

61 See further Liuzza, ed., *The Poems of MS Junius 11*; Fox and Sharma, eds., *Old English Literature and the Old Testament*. See also Shepherd, "Scriptural Poetry," 1–36; Greenfield and Calder, eds., *A New Critical History of Old English Literature*, 206–26; Godden, "Biblical Literature: The Old Testament," 206–26; Lawton, "Englishing the Bible," 454–82; Herbison, "The Idea of the 'Christian Epic'," 342–69; Fulk and Cain, eds., *A History of Old English Literature*, 106–19; and Fowler, *The Bible in Early English Literature*, 79–124.

Approach of This Book

My own approach to the Latin and vernacular traditions of biblical versi-fication is based on the work of late antique scholars who have examined the sources of this literature and who have worked to promote the indi-vidual achievement of each author. For example, Carl Springer (*The Gospel as Epic*) compares several accounts of the wedding at Cana in the poetry of Juvencus, Sedulius, Prudentius and Dracontius, and in doing so demon-strates what features of each are common or unique.[62] Likewise, although on a smaller scale, Roger Green considers several descriptions of storms in the poetry of Juvencus, Sedulius and Arator, and in the process he high-lights various similarities and differences among the three renditions.[63] My own approach is similar but much broader in scope. Specifically, each chapter aims, as far as possible, to treat similar episodes in each text, in order to show how different poets approach the same scenes, the purpose being to highlight what is common or unusual in each poem and in the context of the wider genre. As far as I know, no one has attempted to ad-dress the genre as a whole in this way or to consider how the three tradi-tions of late antique, Anglo-Latin, and Old English poetry relate to one another.[64] It is my hope that this book will help students and scholars of the Anglo-Saxon period appreciate better the various ways in which this tradi-tion of writing can enlighten our understanding of Anglo-Saxon literature.

---

62 See further Springer, *Gospel as Epic in Late Antiquity*, 121–7.
63 See further Green, *Latin Epics of the New Testament*, 333–7.
64 A possible exception is the study by Evans, *Paradise Lost and the Genesis Tradition*, which to some extent gauges the progress of Old Testament biblical verse from Latin to the vernacular.

Chapter Two

Juvencus' *Euangeliorum Libri Quattuor* (c. 330 CE)

Ergo age! sanctificus adsit mihi carminis auctor
Spiritus, et puro mentem riget amne canentis
Dulcis Iordanis, ut Christo digna loquamur.

[So, come, Holy Spirit! Be the author of my song, and dip my heart into the pure streams of sweet-singing Jordan, that I may speak things worthy of Christ.]
 – Juvencus, *Euangeliorum libri IV* (*praef.* 25–7)

The Latin tradition of biblical epic begins with the Spanish priest and poet, Juvencus, who wrote a four-book rendition of the Gospels entitled *Euangeliorum libri quattuor* (*Four Books of the Gospels*, hereafter *Euangeliorum libri*) some time around 330 CE.[1] This 3211-line poem is all that remains of the author's work, and although Jerome attests to other compositions "pertaining to the order of the sacraments" (see below) none of these has survived.[2] The standard text of the poem remains that of Johann Huemer (1891), and in it we find neatly assembled what little we know of the author's life and literary activities. Jerome's endorsement of

---

1   The standard text is that of Huemer, ed., *Gai Vetti Aquilini Iuuenci Euangeliorum Libri Quattuor*, CSEL 24. The date of the poem is based on Jerome's reference to Juvencus in his *Chronicon* under the years 329/330. Hence Huemer, v–vi (329/330 CE); Roberts, *Biblical Epic*, 74 (329/330 CE); Green, *Latin Epics*, 7 (329 CE); and Herzog, "Juvencus," in *Handbuch der lateinischen Literatur der Antike* 5, 331–6, at 332 (after 325 but before 329/330).

2   For the flexible sense of the phrase, *ad sacramentorum ordinem*, see further Green, *Latin Epics*, 3–4.

Juvencus in *De uiris illustribus* (*On Famous Men*) is the earliest and most frequently cited source of information:[3]

> Iuuencus, nobilissimi generis Hispanus, presbyter, quattuor euangelia hexametris uersibus paene ad uerbum transferens quattuor libros composuit, et nonnulla eodem metro ad sacramentorum ordinem pertinentia. Floruit sub Constantino principe.

> [Juvencus, a Spanish priest of noblest birth, translating the four Gospels almost word-for-word into hexameter verse, composed four books and many other things in the same metre pertaining to the order of the sacraments. He flourished under the reign of emperor Constantine.]
>
> – *De uiris illustribus* (Ch. 84)[4]

The "very noble birth" of Juvencus (*nobilissimi generis*) must account for the education and learning that are so apparent in his poem, but little else is known about the author's life except that Gaius Vettius Aquilinus Juvencus may have been related to the consul Vettius Aquilinus (286 CE) and that he may have been from Elvira, Spain.[5] The more immediately relevant point is Jerome's statement that Juvencus follows the Bible *paene ad uerbum* ("almost word-for-word"), which suggests a close paraphrase of the Gospels. Scholars have debated the meaning of this phrase, but it is fair to say that *Euangeliorum libri* is a faithful following of the Bible in the eyes of Jerome and the many later poets who emulate the work in approbation of its merit.[6] For them, Juvencus is important, precisely because he takes many of the first steps in the genre, and through careful, conservative choices, he all but validates it in the eyes of the Church. As Deproost says, "L'audace de ce premier projet épique Chrétien, où le prêtre Juvencus héroïse d'emblée la figure centrale du christianisme, a légitimé par avance les futures épopées bibliques qui se succéderont, nombreuses, jusqu'à la

---

3 See Huemer, *Euangeliorum Libri*, v–viii, for a list of early references to Juvencus. See also Green, *Latin Epics*, 1–9; and Sandnes, *Gospel According to Homer and Vergil*, 50–3.

4 Richardson, ed., *De Viris Illustribus*; also Migne, *PL* vol. 23, col. 691.

5 See further Green, *Latin Epics*, 2 and 8–9.

6 For debates on the meaning of the phrase, *paene ad uerbum*, see further ibid., 43–7; Green, "Exegesis by Stealth," 67–8; Colombi, "*Paene ad verbum*," 9–36; Roberts, *Biblical Epic*, 75–6; Fontaine, *Naissance*, 70.

fin de l'antiquité."[7] More than that, Juvencus does not just legitimize the biblical epics to come; he shows all Christian poets how best to make pious use of pagan literature.[8]

Jerome sets the composition of *Euangeliorum libri* within the reign of emperor Constantine ("Floruit sub Constantino principe"), who ruled from 306 to 337 CE, and Juvencus dedicates his work to him at the end of his poem (4.802–12). There he showers Constantine with praise as *terrae regnator apertae* ("ruler of the wide world," 4.407), but says nothing else about his reasons for the dedication.[9] We may suppose that Constantine's conversion had something to do with it and also his subsequent endorsement of Christianity, which opened the way for poems like *Euangeliorum libri*.[10]

Classical Background

The style and diction of *Euangeliorum libri* attest to the author's education and indebtedness to earlier classical writers. Herzog cites Vergil, Ovid, Statius, and Lucan as major influences, among whom Vergil reigns supreme.[11] Ninety-two per cent of the vocabulary in Book 1 of *Euangeliorum libri* is Vergilian in origin, and the *apparatus fontium* of Huemer's edition confirms the poet's deep indebtedness to the *Aeneid*.[12] Huemer lists nearly 300 echoes of Vergil in his edition, the bulk of which (I count 237) point to the *Aeneid*.[13] Thirty-nine echoes of the *Georgics* suggest Juvencus also knew that work well, while a handful of references to the *Eclogues* (perhaps a dozen) fill out the list. Other poets are cited less frequently. Ovid is listed only twenty-three times in Huemer's edition; Statius, twelve; Lucan, three.[14] These findings demand closer scrutiny, but even if most of the

---

7 "The audacity of this first Christian-epic project, in which the priest Juvencus heroizes the central figure of Christianity from the beginning, legitimized in advance the many future biblical epics to come, to the end of antiquity." Deproost, "*Ficta et Facta*," 101–21, at 112.

8 See Roberts, *Biblical Epic*, 74 in note 1 above.

9 See Green, *Latin Epics*, 3–6, who discusses this passage at length. I have adopted his translation of the phrase *terrae regnator apertae* ("ruler of the wide world").

10 See further Fontaine, *Naissance*, 19; Mora-Lebrun, *L'Enéide médiévale*, 68.

11 See further Herzog, "Juvencus," 333.

12 Roberts, "Vergil and Gospels," 50; Borrell, *Las palabras de Virgilio en Juvenco*, 20–2.

13 Allusions to the *Aeneid* are distributed across the four books as follows: 1 (45), 2 (64), 3 (56), 4 (72).

14 Lucan, 1.129, 2.105 (*Ev.* 1.8), 5.331 (*Ev.* 2.315).

Vergilian echoes are discovered to be doubtful, the overall impression will remain: Vergil exerts the single, greatest influence over the language and style of *Euangeliorum libri*.[15]

Dactylic hexameter, the so-called heroic metre, provides *Euangeliorum libri* with its epic framework, and Juvencus is "a purist in the treatment of prosody."[16] He is a skilled imitator of Vergil and favours the spondee (– –) in imitation of the weighted grandeur of the *Aeneid*.[17] To the metre Juvencus adds a host of epic-resounding diction to enhance the essential story of the Bible. The preface abounds with allusions to the fame and glory of epic poets (*famam laudesque poetae*, 8), to Homer and Vergil, and to the deeds of ancient men (*ueterum gestis hominum*, 16), which Juvencus says are nothing next to the "life-giving deeds of Christ" (*Christi uitalia gesta*, 19). The preface also introduces "the hero," who enters the scene in a flame-streaming blaze of glory ("cum flammiuomma descendet nube coruscans / Iudex, althroni genitoris gloria, Christus," 23–4).[18] Later in Book 1, the storm that rocks the Sea of Galilee (2.25–32) rings with echoes of Vergil's tempests in the *Aeneid*, while the star that leads the Magi to the crèche in Book 1 (1.243–51) is based on the comet in Book 2 of the *Aeneid* (2.692–8). When Jesus later warns the people of the pains of Hell (1.759), that vision is a memory of Tartarus (*Aen.* 6.288). At the Crucifixion, the mob mocks Jesus as "the venerable offspring of the Thunderer" (*suboles ueneranda Tonantis*, 4.672), as a man playing god. These and countless other evocations of classical literature draw the action of the poem into the heroic past where, ironically, there is no battle, no conceited death-scene speeches, and no pantheon. There is just the one protagonist, and he is both hero and deity.

---

15 For a fuller discussion of the "epic" nature of *Euangeliorum libri* see further Green, *Latin Epics*, 50–71.

16 Hatfield, *A Study of Juvencus*, 35. Note that there is a general lack of elision in *Euangeliorum libri*, which becomes increasingly common in later Latin verse. Juvencus only elides 105 times in the first 500 lines of his poem, for example, while Vergil does so 232 times in Book 1 of the *Aeneid*. See further Taft, *Study of Juvencus*, 35. See also Longpré, "Aspects de métrique et de prosodie," 128–38; and Longpré, "Traitement de l'élision chez le poète Cyprianus Gallus," 63–77.

17 Taft makes this observation in *Study of Juvencus*, 37–8; but see also Longpré, "Aspects de métrique," 128–38, and Duckworth, *Vergil and Classical Hexameter Poetry*, who notes the prevalence of spondees in the poetry of Vergil and Juvencus.

18 For a list of other words unique to Juvencus, see further Hatfield, *A Study of Juvencus*, 47. For the question of contrast, see further Green, *Latin Epics*, 86.

Biblical Context

Juvencus is conservative in response to the Bible, but *paene ad uersum* ("almost to the verse") would be a better assessment of his style than *paene ad uerbum*. We do not know the precise biblical source of *Euangeliorum libri*, which must have been one of the Old Latin versions of the Bible that Jerome's Vulgate gradually replaced.[19] It is also unclear whether Juvencus' source was from the "European" or "African" branch of the *Vetus*, although the "European" text appears to be closer. Following Green, therefore, I have used it in the analyses below.

Jerome's comment that Juvencus follows the Bible *paene ad uerbum* implies a close rendition of the Gospels, and it is fair to call the author conservative in response to the biblical text, especially in light of the later work of Sedulius, Avitus, and Arator. Still, Juvencus adapts much of what he adopts. Economy of style is a hallmark of his approach, "in the sense of not saying something twice, or not elaborating a point [in the Bible] that is sufficiently clear."[20] Michael Roberts uses the rhetorical term, *abbreviation*, whereby "the paraphrast hoped to achieve the quality of *breuitas*," and *percusio*, "a summarizing style that reduces to a bare minimum outline the events to be described."[21] Whatever the term, economy or abbreviation, Green and Roberts agree that Juvencus condenses the language of the Gospels appreciably, although as Green puts it, "some kind of addition, often combined with adaptation, is pervasive, and an integral part of his method."[22]

---

19   Both versions, "European" and "African," appear in Jülicher, ed., *Itala: Das neue Testament*, 4 vols. For a brief summary of the nature of the "Old Latin" Bible, see further Everson, "The *Vetus Latina* and the Vulgate of the Book of Genesis," 519–36; Gribomont, "Les plus anciennes traductions latines," in *Le monde latin antique et la Bible*, 43–65; Würthwein, *The Text of the Old Testament*, 145–8. Also, for Green's discussions of Juvencus' biblical source, see "Approaching Christian Epic: The Preface of Juvencus," 203–22 at 204–6; Green, "Birth and Transfiguration," 135–71 at 137. For a general discussion of Juvencus' relationship to the Bible, see further Green, *Latin Epics*, 15–134; also Hilhorst, "The Cleansing of the Temple," 61–76; and Fraïse and Michaud, "Pendant ce temps, à la poupe, Jésus goûtait au sommeil," 193–218.

20   See Green, *Latin Epics*, 31–3, but also 25, 35, 79, 108; see also Green, "Some Gospel Episodes," 141; and Green, "Exegesis by Stealth," 70.

21   Roberts, *Biblical Epic*, 108–10, 115, 164, 183, 206. For *percusio* see 115–16 and 167. For other discussions of abbreviation in biblical epic, see further Nodes, *Doctrine and Exegesis in Biblical Latin Poetry*, 84; Roberts, *The Jeweled Style*, 10; Poinsotte, *Juvencus et Israel*, 28–9 and 31; C. Dermott–Small, "Rhetoric and Exegesis in Sedulius' *Carmen paschale*," 223–44, at 224.

22   Green, *Latin Epics*, 36–7.

Juvencus also adds to the biblical narrative in meaningful ways, incorporating adjectives to facilitate the construction of his hexameters, and these "play a major role in what has been called the *Emotionalisierung* or *Psychologisierung* of his narratives," terms used by Fichtner, Flieger, and Thraede, to describe the emotional or psychological intensification of the poetry, which is meant to elicit a stronger response from the reader.[23]

With respect to the four Gospels, Juvencus follows Matthew primarily but makes brief excursions into Mark, Luke, and John, expending about two-and-a-half lines of poetry for each verse of the Bible. In the process, he works to conceal his own voice, a virtue of epic decorum, which means that explicit exegetical commentary in the poem is rare.[24] Generally, Juvencus is more concerned with "*historia*, the literal sense of the Gospels, not allegory or interpretation,"[25] but several commentaries published over the past twenty years have also shown that the addition of a significant word may intimate deeper meaning.[26] In short, the nature of the relationship between *Euangeliorum libri* and the Bible is still evolving.

The Preface (1–27)

The opening of *Euangeliorum libri* is unusual in view of the whole, since it represents an uncommonly spirited response for Juvencus to the conventions of classical epic.[27] He is not normally given to such outpourings, but Juvencus is out to make a strong impression in these first lines and to show that Christ's life and deeds are worthy of epic treatment. For this reason and calling on conventional themes of immortality, fame, and the praise-worthy deeds of men, Juvencus aims to justify his versification of the Bible in the context of his classical-epic predecessors. Invoking Homer, Vergil, and the epic muse, Juvencus betrays a fondness for the sweetness of epic song (*dulcedo*), and he acknowledges the achievements of classical poets, and yet only to a point.[28] For Juvencus, as much for later biblical versifiers, the core values of epic are incompatible with those of Christianity,

---

23 See further Green, "Some Gospel Episodes," 141; also Flieger, *Interpretationen zum Bibeldichter Iuvencus*; Fichtner, *Taufe und Versuchung*; Thraed, "Iuvencus," 881–906.

24 Green describes the relationship between Juvencus and the Gospels in *Latin Epics*, 37.

25 Roberts, *Biblical Epic*, 75.

26 See further Green's review of *Christus, Nikodemus und die Samaritanerin bei Juvencus*, in *Classical Review* 55.1 (2005), 163–4, at 163.

27 See further Green, *Latin Epics*, 16; and Kirsch, *Die lateinische Versepik*, 85–92.

28 See Roberts, *Biblical Epic*, 73; Mora-Lebrun, *L'Enéide* médiévale, 55.

and so they must be adapted for a Christian audience or abandoned altogether (*praef.* 1–27):[29]

> Inmortale nihil mundi conpage tenetur,
> Non orbis, non regna hominum, non aurea Roma,
> Non mare, non tellus, non ignea sidera caeli.
> Nam statuit genitor rerum inreuocabile tempus,
> Quo cunctum torrens rapiat flamma ultima mundum.   5
> Sed tamen innumeros homines sublimia facta
> Et uirtutis honos in tempora longa frequentant,
> Adcumulant quorum famam laudesque poetae.
> Hos celsi cantus, Smyrnae de fonte fluentes,
> Illos Minciadae celebrat dulcedo Maronis.   10
> Nec minor ipsorum discurrit gloria uatum,
> Quae manet aeternae similis, dum saecla uolabunt
> Et uertigo poli terras atque aequora circum
> Aethera sidereum iusso moderamine uoluet.
> Quod si tam longam meruerunt carmina famam,   15
> Quae ueterum gestis hominum mendacia nectunt,
> Nobis certa fides aeternae in saecula laudis
> Inmortale decus tribuet meritumque rependet.
> Nam mihi carmen erit Christi uitalia gesta,
> Diuinum populis falsi sine crimine donum.   20
> Nec metus, ut mundi rapiant incendia secum
> Hoc opus; hoc etenim forsan me subtrahet igni
> Tunc, cum flammiuoma descendet nube coruscans
> Iudex, altithroni genitoris gloria, Christus.
> Ergo age! sanctificus adsit mihi carminis auctor   25
> Spiritus, et puro mentem riget amne canentis
> Dulcis Jordanis, ut Christo digna loquamur.

---

29 The preface to *Euangeliorum libri* is the most frequently discussed passage of the poem.
I will not treat every study associated with the opening, but instead offer a selection of
more recent work. Canali, *Aquilino Giovenco*, 10–17 (comments are those of Santorel-
li); Green, *Latin Epics*, 15–23; Green, "Preface of Juvencus"' 203–22; Roberts, "Vergil
and the Gospels"' 47–61; Gärtner, "Die Musen im Dienste Christi," 424–46; Carruba,
"The Preface to Juvencus' Biblical Epic," 303–12; Evenepoel, "The Place of Poetry in
Latin Christianity," 35–60, esp. 45–6; Ziolkowsky, "Classical Influences on Medieval
Latin Views of Poetic Inspiration," 15–38, esp. 23–4; Costanza, "Da Giovenco a Sedulio," 253–86; van der Nat, "Die Praefatio," 249–57. Witke, *Numen Litterarum*, 199–202.

[Nothing in the world's structure is immortal: not the earth, not the kingdoms of men, not golden Rome, not the sea, not the land, not the fiery stars of the sky. For the Creator of the universe has set an irreversible time in which a final torrent of flame will grip the entire world. Yet illustrious deeds and the distinction of power revisit countless men over the ages, whose fame and praise the poets heap up. Some are celebrated in lofty songs flowing from the font of Smyrna, others by the sweetness of Mincidian Maro. No less does the glory of the prophets themselves run far and wide, lasting like eternity, while the ages fly by and the spinning axis wheels land and sea around the starry heights of heaven in bidden moderation. So even if those songs have earned lasting fame – songs that bind lies to the deeds of ancient men – my sure faith in an eternity of everlasting praise will grant me immortal glory and render me my due reward. For my song will be about the life-giving deeds of Christ, a divine gift among the people without the sin of falsehood. And I will not be afraid that the fires of this world will take my work with them; for perhaps it will spare me from the flames, when the Judge descends, shining in flame-streaming cloud, the Glory of the High-Throned Creator, Christ. So come, Holy Spirit! Be the author of my song and dip my heart into the pure streams of sweet-singing Jordan, that I may speak things worthy of Christ.][30]

The opening words – *inmortale nihil mundi* (1) – are thematically charged. In epic style, they herald the central concern of the poem, which is immortality through Christ's life-giving deeds, a point made explicitly at the end of the preface (*Christi uitalia gesta*, 19). The beginning words also emulate the three-word structure of the openings of both the *Iliad* (Μῆνιν ἄειδε, θεά, 1) and the *Aeneid* (*Arma uirumque cano*, 1), no doubt to infuse *Euangeliorum libri* with an epic aura.[31] But if the theme of the poem is epic in origin, there is no conventional way to embrace it. Immortality may be the ultimate prize, but between it and the mortal world (*mundi*) stands a gulf of nothingness (*nihil*) which cannot be traversed by worldly achievement.[32] It is a reversal of generic expectation, and while classical

---

30 Translations of *Euangeliorum libri* are my own.

31 Monro and Allen, eds., *Homeri Opera*; Mynors, ed., *P. Vergili Maronis Opera*; See also Carrubba, "Preface to Juvencus," 306.

32 Some have seen the influence of Lucretius in the opening lines. See further Arevalo in the *PL* 19, 58, n. 12; Fontaine, *Naissance*, 73–4; Carrubba, "Preface to Juvencus," 306 et passim; also Green, *Latin Epics*, 19: "the Lucretian background of this passage has been overstated"; similar comments appear in Green, "Preface of Juvencus," 211–12.

epic would bridge the gap with heroic deeds, that way is impossible, since, as Juvencus puts it, "nothing in the structure of the world is immortal, not the earth, not the kingdoms of men, not golden Rome," and presumably not the deeds of ancient heroes and the songs commemorating them. In the end, Judgment Day will come to incinerate everything in this world, including the fleeting memories of fame.

This last point covers the essence of lines 4–5, and yet despite their decidedly Christian thrust there is an epic ring to them. The language evokes any number of scenes from classical poetry. Different scholars have suggested different sources of inspiration. I offer Book 10 of the *Aeneid* and the moment Turnus kills Pallas and thus seals his own fate. From Olympus, Hercules looks down in despair, and his father offers the following words of comfort (10.466–9):[33]

> Tum genitor natum dictis affatur amicis:
> "Stat sua cuique dies, breue et irreparabile tempus
> Omnibus est uitae; sed famam extendere factis,
> Hoc uirtutis opus ...

> [Then the father spoke these tender words to his son: "Each man has his day, and the time of life is brief for all and never comes again. But to lengthen out one's fame with action, that's the work of courage ...]

Compare these words to verses 4–5 of *Euangeliorum libri* and consider the linguistic and thematic affinity between the two scenes:[34]

---

33 The translation here is adapted from Fagles, *The Aeneid*.

34 Green, "Preface of Juvencus," 212, has suggested a potential link to Lucan (1.72): "sic, cum compage soluta / Saeculo tot mundi suprema coegerit hora / Antiquum repetens iterum chaos" ("So, when with its structure dissolved its final hour overwhelms the long ages of the universe, seeking primeval chaos once more ..."); see also Kievits, *Commentarius Exegeticus*, 31, who offers a connection to Ovid (*Met.* 1.256–8: "Esse quoque in fatis reminiscitur, adfore tempus, / Quo mare, quo tellus conreptaque regia caeli / Ardeat et mundi moles obsessa laboret" ("He recalled that a time was fated to come, when land and sea and heaven's majestic roof would catch fire, and the foundations of the world would go up in flames"). Trans. from Lombardo, *Metamorphoses* (2010), 12, lines 266–9. Note, too, that Green, *Latin Epics*, 173–4, sees *Aen.* 10.467–8 as the source of inspiration for Sedulius at the opening of Bk. 2 of the *Carmen paschale* (2.10–17).

Nam statuit genitor rerum inreuocabile tempus,
Quo cunctum torrens rapiat flamma ultima mundum.

[For the Creator of the universe has set an irreversible time in which a final
torrent of flame will grip the world entire.]

Just as Vergil names Jupiter *genitor* (466), so does Juvencus name God.
Juvencus also uses the verb *stat* (from *sto*) to emphasize the certainty of
Judgment in the same way Vergil uses *statuit* (from *statuo*) to emphasize
the certainty of death; both poets describe man's ultimate destiny in similar terms and at the same point in the line: *inreuocabile tempus* (467) and
irreparabile tempus (4). But while Jupiter urges "lengthen[ing] out one's
fame with action" (*famam extendere factis*, 468), Juvencus highlights the
futility of doing that in lines 1–3. Furthermore, although epic in tenor,
the lines of *Euangeliorum libri* represent a reversal of the message of the
Vergilian scene – the statement that heroes should pursue fame and glory
at all costs – and he suggests instead that nothing of this world is immortal,
including the praise-worthy deeds of men.

The same idea of extending one's fame through action, "famam extendere factis," continues in lines 6–14 of the preface, and the words *sublimia
facta* in line six, which refer to men's "sublime deeds," are almost certainly
ironic, since Juvencus uses the same adjective elsewhere, only with reference to God, his kingdom, or name.[35] He does not deny the fame and
praise epic heroes have won for themselves (*famam laudesque*, 8), nor does
he rebuke Homer or Vergil for "immortalizing" them. On the contrary, he
appears to admire "the sweetness of Vergil" (*dulcedo Maronis*, 10), which
characterizes much of the poem. But his choice of Vergilian language in the
preface is also used to make a strong Christian statement: Juvencus may
use the diction of classical epic to promote his Christian song, but the glory of ancient heroes and poets (*gloria uatum*, 11) is at best only "like" unto
eternity (*manet aeternae similis*, 12). It is not true immortality.

Even if those heroes and poets have deserved lasting fame ("Quod si
tam longam meruerunt carmina famam," 15), and Juvencus implies they
have not, their achievements are based upon "lies" put to song (*mendacia*,
16) and illusions of immortality. In the closing verses of his preface,

---

35 Of the twenty or so instances of the adjective, most have to do with God's kingdom
    (1.455, 1.544, 1.756, 2.219, 2.795, 3.592. 4.34) or God's person and name (1.515, 2.62,
    4.60, 4.40, 4.134, 4.356, 3.464).

Juvencus repeats two thematically charged words, "fame" (*famam*, 15) and "praise" (*laudis*, 17), which echo *famam laudesque* (8) from the opening of the preface. "The deeds of men" (*gestis hominum*, 16) also figure at this point and echo the words, *homines sublimia facta* (6), ten lines earlier. The full significance of these words now becomes clear. For Juvencus, sure faith in Christ and the afterlife (*certa fides*, 17) will garner the ultimate prize of true immortality (*Inmortale decus*, 18). This glory will not fade but bring eternal praise (*aeternae in saecula laudis*, 17), praise that is truly earned (*meritumque*, 18), unlike the fame of pagan heroes, who have only seemed to earn it (*Quod si … meruerunt*, 15). The repetition of *mereo* through polyptoton at this moment is emphatic.

The difference, then, between the Christian hero, Jesus, and the epic hero, Aeneas, is twofold. Unlike the fictions of epic, Christ's life is true ("Diuinum populis falsi sine crimine donum," 20), and not only does he live a praise-worthy life through his miracles, but he offers eternal life itself. Jesus is therefore the greater hero and *Euangeliorum libri* is the greater epic, because of what they offer Christians – a path to spiritual enlightenment and salvation – and yet both must be presented in secular terms, since classical literature is the gold standard in late antiquity. For this reason, when Christ enters the scene at the end of the preface, he must do so in a blaze of glory, clothed in epic splendour (22–4): "… hoc etenim forsan me subtrahet igni / Tunc, cum flammiuoma descendet nube coruscans / Iudex, altithroni genitoris gloria, Christus" ("for perhaps this will spare me from the flames, when the Judge descends, shining in flame-streaming cloud, the Glory of the High-Throned Creator, Christ"). This dramatic entrance conjures up images of Mercury or Vulcan in the *Aeneid*.[36] Vulcan's fiery descent in Book 8, for example, is especially close (8.423): "Hoc tunc ignipotens caelo descendit ab alto" ("Then the fire-strong god descends from lofty heaven"). Both poets open with the adverb *tunc* and put fiery compounds in the second foot (*flammiuoma*, 23 / *ignipotens*, 423), and the scansion of lines 23 and 423 is identical (SDSS), creating an aural link between the two passages. *Flammiuoma* is a Juvencan coinage, but if not a direct appeal to *ignipotens*, it is at least, as Quadlbauer puts it, in the spirit of epic ("Geist der epischen Tradition").[37] Also, both poets

36   Green, "Preface of Juvencus," 216, also makes a connection with Horace, *Odes* (1.34.6): "Igni corusco nubila diuidens ("Cleaving the clouds with flashing fire"); also, Fontaine, *Naissance* (78–9), notes similar language at 1.357 (*discendit ab alto*), when the Holy Spirit descends on Jesus in the river Jordan.

37   See Quadlbauer, "Zur 'Invocatio' des Iuvencus," 189–212, at 192 n. 14.

use the same verb to describe the descent of the deity (*descendet*, 23/ *descendit*, 423), so that Christ's entrance onto the biblical epic stage is presented in highly conventional terms.

All that remains is to cleanse the way for the new genre by invoking "the muse," and here Juvencus makes his strongest statement yet (25–7): "Ergo age! sanctificus adsit mihi carminis auctor/Spiritus, et puro mentem riget amne canentis/Dulcis Jordanis, ut Christo digna loquamur" ("So come, Holy Spirit, be the author of my song and dip my heart into the pure streams of sweet-singing Jordan"). With a single stroke, Juvencus unseats the pagan muse and redirects the flow of inspiration through the Holy Spirit. The "sweetness" of Maro (*dulcedo Maronis*, 10) now flows from the river Jordan (*Dulcis Jordanis*, 27), and worthy words (*Christo digna loquamur*, 27), a phrase of Vergilian origin (cf. *Phoebo digna locuti*, *Aen.* 6.662), now serve Christ.[38] These brief lines make a powerful, evocative statement about the baptism of classical epic and the beginning of a new literary tradition.[39]

Doing all of this first, it is easy to see why later writers regarded Juvencus with such esteem. His preface makes a convincing argument for the ability of the Bible to inhabit the epic genre, and through a series of carefully selected and repeated words and themes – immortality, fame, glory, praise, the deeds of men – Juvencus assumes the role of Christian epic poet, using Vergilian language to make the transformation convincing. The achievement of the preface – and this must count for the poem's general success among its Christian audiences – is the way Juvencus subtlety adopts, adapts, and subverts the language and themes of classical literature, to promote his song. Without ever criticising Homer or Vergil directly – in fact he seems to admire them – Juvencus manages to be critical of many of the core values of epic poetry. Yet part of the gratification for Christian audiences must undoubtedly have been derived not just from reading a stylistically amplified version of the Bible, but from appreciating the ways in which classical allusions could offer a productive commentary on classical literature.

---

38 Arevalo notes the connection to Vergil in *PL* 19, 62; he also cites Statius *Sat.* 21.5.10. Green mentions the phrase *digna locuti* in *Latin Epics*, 22; see also Quadlbauer, "Zur 'Invocatio'," 190; and Van der Nat, "Die Praefatio des Iuvencus," 253.

39 For a similar assessment of Christian poetry in late Antiquity, see further Springer, *Gospel as Epic*, 71.

The Storm on the Sea (2.25–32)

The poet's rendition of the storm on the Sea of Galilee in Book 2 of *Euangeliorum libri*, based on Mt. 8:23–4, is the other noteworthy passage in the poem (aside from the preface) where Juvencus brings the full force of epic to bear on the Gospels. Michael Roberts, writing of Fortunatus' life of St Martin, has said that "such descriptions [of sea-storms] are so common in late Latin literature that it is hard to maintain the generic affiliation [to epic]," but this is surely an exception.[40] There is no doubt here that Juvencus has Vergil in mind (*Ev.* 2.25–32):[41]

23 Et ascendente eo in nauicula (nauem), secuti sunt eum discipuli eius. 24 Et ecce motus magnus (tempestas magna) factus est in mare, ita ut nauicula (nauis) operiretur (tegetur) fluctibus, ipse uero dormiebat.[42]

Mt 8:23–4

25

Conscendunt nauem uentoque inflata tumescunt
Vela suo, fluctuque uolat stridente carina.
Postquam altum tenuit puppis, consurgere in iras
Pontus et inmissis hinc inde tumescere uentis
Instat et ad caelum rabidos sustollere montes;

30

Et nunc mole ferit puppim nunc turbine proram,
Inlisosque super laterum tabulata receptant
Fluctus disiectoque aperitur terra profundo.

[They board the ship and the sails, propelled by the wind, billow, and the keel soars on with a whistling wave. When the stern reached the deep, the sea

---

40 See Roberts, "The Last Epic of Antiquity," 277. For a description of the same episode in the *Carmen paschale* of Sedulius (2.25–42), see further Green, *Latin Epics*, 199–202. See also Hecquet-Noti, "La description du deluge," 229–35 at 230; Arweiler, *Die Imitation antiker und spätantiker*, 245–9.

41 The parallels: *Vela* (*Aen.* 1.103, *uelum*); *stridente* (*Aen.* 1.102, *stridens*); *Postquam altum tenuit puppis* (*Aen.* 3.192, *Postquam altum tenuere rates*); *ad caelum* (*Aen.* 1.103, *ad sidera*); *sustollere* (*Aen.* 1.103, *tollit*); *montes* (*Aen.* 1.105, *praeruptus aquae mons* (for *rabidos montes*); *ferit* (*Aen.* 1.103, *ferit*); *puppim* (*Aen.* 1.115, *in puppim ferit*); *proram* (*Aen.* 1.104, *prora*); *laterum* (*Aen.* 1.105, *latus*); *fluctus* (*Aen.* 1.107, *fluctus*); *aperitur terra* (*Aen.* 1.107, *terram … aperit*); there are other parallels that I have not cited.

42 Translations of the Bible are adapted from the Douay Rheims. Mt 8:23–4: "And when he entered into the boat, his disciples followed him. And behold a great tempest arose in the sea, so that the boat was covered with waves, but he was asleep."

began to brim with rage and swell with winds that stormed all around them and to raise up furious mountains to the sky. And now it thrashes the stern with its mass, now upon the prow with whirlwind, and the planks take the waves crashing at its sides, and the earth is opened to the sundered deep.]

The still waters of the sea erupt in a tempest of wind and waves, as Juvencus gives rein to his artistic impulses. The biblical language by comparison is mundane and forecasts the change in weather with but a single word, *motus* (var. *tempestas*). Everywhere, the prose resorts to the past tense and passive voice (*factus est, operiretur*), while the action of the poetry is lively and present (e.g., *conscendunt, tumescent,* 25).[43] The drama of the rising swell is more immediate and suspenseful, and the poet's choice of verbs builds a sense of mounting tension (*conscendunt, inflata, tumescunt, consurgere, tumescere, sustollere*). At the same time, the personified sea (*Pontus,* 28), as if Aeolus or Neptune, is roused to fury (*iras,* 27) and bids "rabid mountains" (*rabidos montes,* 29) charge from the sea like rabid dogs with frothy mouths. The metre, too, at the cadence of lines 27–9, propels the storm, and the violence of the words *ferit* (30), *turbine* (30), and *disiecto profundo* (32) add greater fear and commotion. At the breaking point, the very deep (*profundo,* 32) is torn asunder at the caesura by elision (*disiectoque aperitur,* 32), as if the storm would threaten to tear through the very pages of the text. The whole scene, less than ten lines, is a poetic *tour de force* delivering a blast of epic thunder to the comparatively calm waters of the Bible.

The scene also betrays its poetic source of inspiration, and numerous phrases suggest that Juvencus has Vergil in mind.[44] In particular, the words "Postquam altum tenuit puppis" (27) echo "Postquam altum tenuere rates" from Book 3 of the *Aeneid* (3.192), and they appear in the same context as that storm that nearly wrecks the fleet of Aeneas.[45] Line thirty of *Euangeliorum libri* ("Et nunc mole ferit puppim") also points to Vergil and Book 1 of the *Aeneid* ("pontus / In puppim ferit," 1.114–15), where

---

43 Juvencus follows Matthew primarily for this scene, though he does include elements of Mark and Luke, according Fraïsse and Michaud, "Tempête Apaisée," 216.

44 Numerous scholars have given close attention to this scene. See further Green, *Latin Epics,* 61–2; Ratkowitsch, "Vergils Seesturm bei Iuvencus und Sedulius," 40–58; Fraïsse, "Tempête apaisée" 193–218; Canali, *Aquilino Giovenco,* 291–3; Sandnes, *Gospel According to Homer and Vergil,* 59–60. Ratkowitsch and Fraïsse also note that a variant manuscript reading of lines 26–9 contains further parallels to Vergil.

45 See further *Aen.* 3.192–208.

Aeolus all but destroys the Trojan fleet before it ever leaves port. In the Juvencan passage, *pontus* is likewise the implied subject of *ferit*.[46] Line thirty-two of *Euangeliorum Libri* ("Fluctus disiectoque aperitur terra profundo") again echoes Book 1 of the *Aeneid* and that same storm but now at line 107 ("terram inter fluctus aperit"). It is clear, then, that Juvencus takes much of his language from the opening of Vergil's *Aeneid* to boost his own biblical tempest, a suggestion that several other correspondences between the two texts reinforce. The purpose of the amplification is clear: to attract and delight the audience and to intensify the impression of God's power. As Ratkowitsch puts it, it is also "die antiken epischen Seestürme mit dem christlichen zu kontrastieren."[47] It is what Thraede and German scholars term *Kontrastimitation*, whereby an allusion to pagan literature is redirected to suggest a point of contrast with the Christian text. In this case, and ironically, the epic language serves to promote the greater status of God and his omnipotence over pagan deities.

The Nativity (1.243–51)

The poetic adaptation of the storm on the Sea of Galilee is exceptional in the extent it draws upon the "sweetness of Vergil" (*dulcedo Maronis, praef.* 10), but it is not the author's normal *modus operandi*. Sustained reminiscences of that kind are rare in *Euangeliorum libri*. More common are scenes like the nativity in Book 1 (1.243–51), which represents a more understated response to Vergil. It is an episode Juvencus crafts with care, to intensify the magnitude of the moment but also to promote reverence for the occasion. The achievement of the poetry is the harmony of the two (1.243–51):[48]

9 Qui cum audissent regem, abierunt, et ecce stella, quam uiderant in orientem, antecedebat eos, usque dum uenit et stetit supra puerum. 10 Videntes autem stellam gauisi sunt gaudio magno ualde. 11 Et intrantes in domum inuenerunt (uiderent) puerum cum Maria, matre eius. Et procidentes (prostrati)

---

46   Ibid., 1.81–123.

47   Ratkowitsch, "Vergils Seesturm," 49.

48   Colombi, "Paene ad Verbum," 15–16, notes that Tertullian refers to the mystical symbolism of the gifts but in different terms. Origen's earlier *Contra Celsum* (Ch. 1.60) also mentions the symbolism of the gifts. The later *Dittochaeon* of Prudentius also coincides (105–6): "Hic pretiosa Magi sub uirginis ubere Christo / Dona ferunt puero myrraeque et turis et auri" ("Here the Magi bear precious gifts of myrrh, incense and gold to the boy, Christ, beneath the virgin's breast").

adorauerunt eum et apertis thensauris suis optulerunt ei munera (dona),
aurum tus et murram.[49]

– Mt 2:9–11

Ecce iteris medio stellam praecurrere cernunt
Sulcantem flammis auras, quae culmine summo
Restitit et pueri lustrata habitacula monstrat.　　　　　　　　　245
Gaudia magna Magi gaudent sidusque salutant,
Et postquam puerum uidere sub ubere matris,
Deiecti prono strauerunt corpore terram
Submissique simul quaesunt; tum munera trina
Tus, aurum, murram regique hominique Deoque　　　　　　　250
Dona dabant …

[Behold, they see a star coursing before them in the midst of their path,
ploughing the air with flames, which comes to rest at the highest height and
reveals the brightened, humble dwelling of the child. The Magi rejoice with
great joy and hail the star, and as soon as they saw the child at his mother's
breast, they stretched out upon the ground, bodies bent, and, lowered together, beseeched him. Then they made offerings, three gifts – gold, incense,
myrrh, for the king, for the God, and for the man.]

Juvencus attentively preserves the language of the prose in these lines as
well as the order of the words in the Bible. Verse nine of Matthew is echoed
by *ecce* (243), *stellam* (243), *stetit* (in *restitit*, 245), and *puer* ("child," 245,
247), while line ten, "Gaudia magna Magi gaudent" (246), follows the
prose through paronomasia and polyptoton, "gauisi sunt gaudio magno
ualde" (or *gaudium magnum nimis*).[50] Juvencus adds the noun *Magi* to the
scene, which does not appear in the Gospel account but serves to intensify
the sense and sound of the adjective, *magna*, which conveys "great" joy.

49　Mt 2:9–11: "Who having heard the king, went their way; and behold the star they had
　　seen in the East, went before them, until it came and stood over where the child was.
　　And seeing the star they rejoiced with exceeding great joy. And entering into the house,
　　they found the child with Mary his mother, and falling down they adored him: and
　　opening their treasures, they offered him gifts; gold, frankincense, and myrrh."
50　The word "ecce" may aspire to epic ambiance, but it is equally biblical. See further
　　Flieger, *Interpretationen*, 84, and Green, "Episodes," 142, for the epic/biblical nature of
　　this word. See also Green, *Latin Epics*, 56, who mentions the use of other such particles
　　by Juvencus.

So the Magi themselves become vessels of the spirit of joyfulness by virtue of a simple, clever touch. The past tense of the prose also gives way to the present in several places, as it does in the episode of the storm on the Sea of Galilee (2.25–32), and the use of which likewise affords greater dramatic immediacy, so that readers are returned to the moment.

The star ploughing through the sky is also given greater attention in the poetry. Juvencus elevates its status to epic and divine proportions, and yet its celestial splendour ultimately serves to highlight the humanity of Christ. The epic-sounding phrase *sulcantem flammis auras* ("ploughing the air in flames," 244) is probably an allusion to the comet in Vergil's *Aeneid* (2.692–8), but there is little sense that Juvencus borrows much from that context except the visual splendour of the star.[51] His introduction of the participle *lustrata* (245), however, is perhaps significant. In simple terms, the word has to do with "shedding light" on the dwelling of the child, but even in this sense it is revelatory. In classical verse, the verb *lustro* serves a ceremonial function in the context of purification and propitiatory offerings to the deities. It may therefore be that the star has a purifying function in this scene, that it not only reveals the child but sanctifies the moment of his birth. If so, it is a subtle reading of the word and yet in keeping with the kind of close scrutiny Fichtner and Flieger have invited in their studies of Juvencus. It is furthermore significant that the star does not simply come to rest above the "child" (*puer*) as it does in the prose but over his "humble dwelling" (*habitacula*, 245). This diminutive is the first indication that Juvencus aims to place special emphasis on the humanity of Jesus and the tenderness between mother and child (*sub ubere matris*, 247).

The majesty of the star, then, and the lavishness of the three gifts – as yet only symbols of the future man, king, and God – yield to a more earthly,

---

51 Many have recognized this link to Vergil. See further Roberts, "Vergil and the Gospels," 53; Green, *Latin Epics*, 52, who is less convinced; Arevalo, *Evangelicae Historiae Libri IV*, 97; Canali, *Aquilini Giovenco*, 261; Kievits, *Commentarius Exegeticus*, 82; Taft, *Study of Juvencus*, 43–4. Taft lists several verbal links, 44: *stella* (2.694)/*stellam* (1.243), *cucurrit* (2.694)/*praecurrere* (1.243), *cernimus* (2.696)/*cernunt* (1.243), *sulcus* (2.697)/ *sulcantem* (1.244) *culmina* (2.695)/*culmine* (1.244) *summa* (2.695)/*summo* (1.244). See also Lucan, who uses similar language for a star (5.562): "lapsa per altum / aera dispersos traxere cadentia sulcos / sidera"; also, Prudentius later in *Cath.* 12.55 ("qua stella sulcum traxerat"). Roberts elsewhere discusses the verb *sulco* in "Rhetoric and Poetic Imitation," 29–80 at 69–70.

tender moment between mother and child. For now, the reader is spared any thoughts of the Crucifixion and brought instead to feel wonder and joy at the birth, which elicit feelings of devotion. This spirit is personified in the persons of the Magi, whose prostrations Juvencus emphasizes more in the poetry (248–9): "Deiecti prono strauerunt corpore terram / Submissique simul quaesunt" ("they stretched out upon the ground, bodies bent, and, lowered together, beseeched him"). Six of the eight words in these two lines suggest a posture of reverence, an intensification of feeling Kirsch terms the *Emotionalisierung* or *Psychologisierung* of the biblical narrative, through which the poetry elicits deeper thoughts or feelings from the reader.[52] In this case, the changes Juvencus introduces to the Bible enhance the divine essence of the star, which makes an epic entrance, to purify the incarnation and shed light on the humanity of Christ. Humanity and vulnerability lie at the heart of the scene, where feelings of joy and devotion are born and cultivated, while the mystical significance of the three gifts of the Magi invites the reader to contemplate the wonder and paradox of the incarnation, that eternal omnipotence joins to mortality and that meekness is mightiest. By careful, measured choices, Juvencus manages what is one of the most effective and affecting scenes of *Euangeliorum libri*.

The Sermon on the Mount (1.452–68)

The Sermon on the Mount covers nearly half of Book 1 of *Euangeliorum libri*, and the author's handling of the beatitudes offers a good example of the occasional difficulties of translating biblical prose into verse. Much of what is characteristic about Juvencus' versifying style appears in this scene: he follows the Bible closely, but omits two verses for the sake of economy; he uses two lines of poetry for each biblical verse, which is typical, but twice expands a short biblical phrase to an entire line (461, 465), which is also normal; he adopts the essential vocabulary of the Bible as the foundation of his poetic version, but introduces several adjectives (*praecelsa, pulcherrima, magna, plena, larga, puro*) as well as a few abstract nouns (*mansuetudo, insectatio*) to fill out the metre and provoke stronger psychological or emotional responses from his reader; finally, he uses variation to special affect, as a way to capture the rhetorical force of the original sermon, and this too is also a hallmark of Juvencus' style (1.452–68):

---

52 See Green, *Biblical Epics*, 127.

1 Videns autem turbas (populum) ascendit in montem; et cum sedisset, accesserunt ad eum discipuli eius.
2 Et aperuit os suum et docebat eos dicens:
3 "Beati pauperes spiritu, quoniam ipsorum est regnum caelorum.
5 Beati, qui lugunt, quoniam ipsi consolabuntur.[53]
4 Beati mites, quoniam ipsi possidebunt terram.
6 Beati, qui esuriunt et sitiunt iustitiam, quoniam ipsi saturabuntur.
7 Beati misericordes, quia ipsi miserabuntur (misericordiam insequitur).
8 Beati mundo corde, quoniam ipsi Deum uidebunt.
9 Beati pacifici, quoniam fili Dei uocabuntur.
10 Beati, qui persecutionem patiuntur propter iustitiam, quoniam ipsorum
est regnum caelorum.[54]

– Mt 5:1–10

Hos populos cernens praecelsa rupe resedit
Ac sic discipulis gremium cingentibus infit:
"Felices humiles, pauper quos spiritus ambit,
Illos nam caeli regnum sublime receptat,   455
His similes mites, quos mansuetudo coronat,
Quorum debetur iuri pulcherrima tellus.
Hoc modo lugentes solacia magna sequentur.
Pabula iustitiae qui nunc potusque requirunt,
Illos plena manet satiandos copia mensae.   460
Felix, qui miseri doluit de pectore sortem,
Illum nam Domini miseratio larga manebit.
Felices, puro qui caelum corde tuentur,
Visibilis Deus his per saecula cuncta patebit.
Pacificos Deus in numerum sibi prolis adoptat.   465
Felices nimium, quos insectatio frendens
Propter iustitiam premit; his mox regia caeli
Pandetur.

---

53   Note that the *Vetus* places verse 5 before verse 4; Juvencus reflects the later Vulgate (4, 5).
54   Mt 5:1–10: "And seeing the multitudes, he went up into a mountain, and when he was
set down, his disciples came unto him. And opening his mouth he taught them, saying:
Blessed are the poor in spirit: for theirs is the kingdom of heaven. Blessed are the meek:
for they shall possess the land. Blessed are they that mourn: for they shall be comforted.
Blessed are they that hunger and thirst after justice: for they shall have their fill. Blessed
are the merciful: for they shall obtain mercy. Blessed are the clean of heart: for they shall
see God. Blessed are the peacemakers: for they shall be called the children of God. Blessed
are they that suffer persecution for justice's sake: for theirs is the kingdom of heaven."

[Seeing the people, he sat down on a high rock, and with his disciples sitting around him, said: "Blessed are the humble, whom a poor spirit embraces: for the high kingdom of heaven welcomes them. Likewise the meek, whom mildness crowns, are rightly owed the fairest of all lands. So do worthy comforts follow those who mourn. Now, those who seek the food and drink of righteousness, the full abundance of my table awaits their satiety. Blessed is he who grieves the lot of the wretched in his heart, for the bountiful mercy of the Lord awaits him. Blessed are those who look to Heaven with a pure heart: God will ever be visible to them. God receives peacemakers into the fold of his flock. Exceedingly blessed are those whom gnashing persecution haunts in the name of justice: the palace of heaven will soon open unto them.]

Klaus Thraede has treated the first two lines of this passage at length and suggests an epic heritage for the phrase *praecelsa rupe resedit* (452), which may echo Vergil (*Aen.* 3.245): "Una in praecelsa consedit rupe Celaeno, / Infelix uates, rumpitque hanc pectore vocem" ("Only one, Celaeno, sitting atop a high rock, the wicked witch, croaked out a voice from her breast"). The context, though, does not match up with *Euangeliorum libri*, but this may be a case of *Kontrastimitation*.[55]

Even if it is, the language of the Bible and not classical epic forms the core of the poetry here. Each verse of the prose is carefully represented, and each two-line unit of verse covers the essentials of the Gospel account. In line 452, *populos cernens* echoes *Videns ... populum* in Matthew, and although Juvencus makes a minor change from *uidens* to *cernens* – the metre requires the long vowel of the latter – he retains the grammar in the form of the present participle. The total absence of the word *beatus* ("blessed") is notable in this scene, which makes sense, since it cannot not stand as the first word of a hexameter line because of the length of the first syllable (*bĕatus*). Therefore, Juvencus uses *fēlīx*, a word of similar sense ("happy," "fortunate," "blessed"), which also affords greater metrical flexibility as a third declension adjective (*fēlīx* or *fēlīcēs*). It may seem odd that he does not repeat the word as regularly as the Bible does *beatus*, but

---

55 Thraede, "Juvencus," in 377–84, at 380. Thraede cites Vergil's phrase *in rupe resedit* (*Aen.* 5.180) as corroborating evidence, and several other similar phrases, to demonstrate the classical antecedence of this phrase, which he says lends an epic air to the Sermon on the Mount (or at least to the mount).

the insistence of rhetorical "variation" (*uariatio*), or synonymy as Roberts calls it, perhaps directs the poet's preference for synonymic repetition.[56] As a practical solution, which does not diminish the rhetorical force of the original sermon, Juvencus repeats *felix* half as frequently as the prose does *beatus* (454, 461, 463, 466), and he makes up for the absence of the word elsewhere with inflectional rhyme to create the illusion of a near following of the prose. Thus *Similes mites* in line 456 and *lugentes* in 458 share tail-rhyme with the first instance of *felices* in line 454, which Juvencus repeats three more times. He also reinforces the biblical substructure of the poetry by ending each line with a finite verb in the final position (*ambit, receptat, coronat, sequentur, requirunt, manebit, tuentur, patebit, adoptat*). These end-stopped verses help to delineate units of poetry in the way *beatus* does in the prose. The result is the illusion of a *paene ad uerbum* transla-tion of the Bible that is actually a thorough reworking of the original.

Juvencus does a number of other things to capture the aural imprint of the prose. In addition to rhyming and repeating *felix* and preserving the present participial form of *uidens* in *cernens*, he substitutes <u>t</u>erram in verse four with <u>t</u>ellus (457), preserving the alliteration of the source. He also dispenses with the cumbersome con<u>sol</u>abuntur, using <u>sol</u>acia (458) instead, which is still a cognate form. A similar strategy is applied to the translation of *saturabuntur*, which becomes *satiandos* (460), and Juvencus reflects the rhetorical force of *misericordes … miserabuntur* (or variant *misericordi-am*), by introducing similar repetition (*miseri … miseratio*). Finally, al-though he replaces the verb *patiuntur* in verse nine with the more descriptive *premit* (467), not to mention the use of the vivid phrase *insec-tatio frendens* ("gnashing persecution," 466), he does preserve a ghost of the original alliteration in the prose ("<u>p</u>ersecutionem <u>p</u>atiuntur <u>p</u>ropter iustitiam) with his own verse, "<u>P</u>ropter iustitiam <u>p</u>remit; his mox regia caeli/<u>P</u>andetur." Because they are emphatically placed at the beginning of each verse (466 and 467), the words *premit* and *pandetur* effectively cap-ture the sound of the original prose, and *pandetur* is also a passive verb like *patiuntur*. The entire scene reflects the subtlety Juvencus brings to his ver-sification of the Bible, not only in terms of what he says, but how he says

---

56   For rhetorical variation see further Michael Roberts, *Biblical Epic*, 198–9: "The prin-ciple of *uariatio* is one that distinguishes biblical from classical aesthetics. The Bible makes no attempt to avoid repeating the same word; by classical standards, as inter-preted by late Antiquity, such repetition was a stylistic fault."

it. In this case, apart from adopting the essential language of the Bible, he imitates something of its style as well.

The Lord's Prayer (1.589–600)

The reasons for following a particular passage of the Gospels closely vary. Michael Roberts has noted a handful of places in *Euangeliorum libri* where Juvencus tracks the prose methodically, and he points specifically to the Old Testament prophesies, where linguistic signposts mark connections to the New Testament.[57] Roberts also cites the versification of the Lord's Prayer in this context and remarks that Juvencus follows the Bible closely at this point, because the prayer is "of particular doctrinal importance."[58] But if this is a *paene ad uerbum* translation of the Gospels, it is one that admits considerable liberty (1.589–600):

9 Sic ergo orabitis eum: Pater noster qui in caelis es sanctificetur nomen tuum
10 Adueniat regnum tuum. Fiat uoluntas tua in caelo et in terra.
11 Panem nostrum cottidianum da nobis hodie.
12 Et dimitte nobis debita nostra, sicut et nos dimittimus debitoribus nostris.
13 Et ne nos inducas in temptationem, sed libera nos a malo.[59]

– Mt 6:9–13

His igitur uotum placeat concludere uerbis:
Sidereo genitor residens in uertice caeli,   590
Nominis, oramus, ueneratio sanctificetur
In nobis, pater alte, tui: tranquillaque mundo
Adueniat regnumque tuum lux alma reclaudat.
Sic caelo ut terris fiat tua clara uoluntas,
Vitalisque hodie sancti substantia panis   595

---

57 Roberts, *Biblical Epic*, 136, n. 76, cites the following passages as close followings of the corresponding Gospel narrative: 1.141–2, 1.276–7, 1.313–20, 2.535–6, 2.767–71, 2.827–8, 3.144–6, 3.633–5, 4.637–41.
58 Ibid., 136–7.
59 Mt 6:9–13: "Thus therefore shall you pray: Our Father who art in heaven, hallowed be thy name. Thy kingdom come. Thy will be done on earth as it is in heaven. Give us this day our supersubstantial bread. And forgive us our debts, as we also forgive our debtors. And lead us not into temptation. But deliver us from evil. Amen." The reading "supersubstantial bread" (*Panem nostrum supersubstantialem*) follows Jerome's Vulgate, but the *Vetus Latina* reading, "daily bread" (*cottidianum panem*), has been more widely adopted.

> Proueniat nobis; tua mox largitio soluat
> Innumera indulgens erroris debita praui;
> Et nos haut aliter concedere foenora nostris.
> Tetri saeua procul temptatio daemonis absit
> Eque malis tua nos in lucem dextera tollat.   600

[So, it is proper to confine your prayer to these words: "Father residing in the starry height of heaven, may the veneration of your name, we pray, be hallowed – your name, high Father, in us; and may your kingdom come unto this world and your tranquil, nourishing light reveal it. May your bright will be done on earth as it is in heaven and may the life-giving substance of your holy bread be brought to us, daily; may your charity deliver us soon, forgiving the countless sins of our depraved error; and grant, too, that we may forgive the debts that are owed to us. May the vile temptation of the foul demon be gone from us, and may your right hand lift us out of the darkness into the light.]

The essentials of the prose are all here – "hallowed be thy name," "give us this day our daily bread," and so on – but they are intensified by a number of amplifications. The phrase, "the starry height of heaven" ("sidereo … in uertice caeli," 590) does not appear in the prose and is reminiscent of Vergil (*Aen.* 1.225, *sic uertice caeli*), in the scene where Jupiter gazes down from his own lofty throne.[60] The allusion may be meaningful; it certainly elevates the seat of God to epic heights and makes a stronger impression than the prose. To the words, "thy kingdom come" (593), Juvencus adds the line, "may your kingdom come unto this world and your tranquil, nourishing light reveal it" ("tranquillaque mundo / Adueniat regnumque tuum lux alma reclaudat," 592–3), which, together with the adjective *clara* in the following verse, reflects a persistent interest in light motifs throughout *Euangeliorum libri*.[61] It may also be that this "tranquil and nourishing light" ("tranquiliaque … lux alma," 592–3) refers to Christ, who elsewhere in the poem is called the "father of life and light" (*uitae lucisque parentem*, 1.747), who has come to reveal the kingdom of God. The sense of *lux alma* (593) may therefore suggest not only "nourishing," but also "refreshing" or "restoring" with a view to redemption.

---

60 Juvencus uses the phrase *uertice caeli* two other times (1.614, 4.153). Vergil uses it only once in the *Aeneid* (1.225).
61 See further Röttger, *Studien zur Lichtmotivik bei Iuvencus.*

The suggestion that Christ figures in the prayer is supported by the introduction of the adjective *uitalis* ("life-giving," 595), which qualifies "the substance of holy bread" ("Vitalisque hodie sancti substantia panis," 595). This is another meaningful addition, and critics have noted the Eucharistic potential of the word, including Green, Colombi, Kievits, and Herzog, who says, "Juvencus die Brotbitte des Vaterunser 1.595f. spiritualisiert." Given the assertion by Juvencus in the preface that he will sing about "the life-giving deeds of Christ" (*uitalia gesta*, 19), the repetition of the word here is almost certainly connected with the theme of immortality.[62] Colombi cites Tertullian and *orat.* 6–4 as precedence for her own interpretation, arguing that Tertullian invites a dual reading of the prayer (*carnaliter et spiritualiter*), but that he emphasizes the spiritual one ("spiritualiter potius intellegamus").[63] There may be deeper significance as well to the word *largitio* (596) with reference to the bounty of Christ's table, and the line "Innumera indulgens erroris debita praui" (597) as a reference to the forgiveness of sins. The final line, "in lucem dextera tollat" (600), also intimates the promise of salvation. In short, this is a faithful rendering of the original, insofar as it incorporates the language of the biblical text, but the intimation of Christ's role in the prayer, while not at odds with Christian doctrine, does increase the scope of the prose. It is another of the more subtle suggestions of exegesis in *Euangeliorum libri*.

The Centurion's Servant (1.741–66)

Immediately following the Sermon on the Mount comes a series of miracles that highlight the life-giving power and "gifts" of Christ. The story of the centurion's son from Matthew, chapter 8, contains features that are typical of Juvencus' style, and yet as always, a close reading of the scene serves to qualify the *paene ad uerbum* style of *Euangeliorum libri*. In this

---

62 See further Green, *Latin Epics*, 92; Kievits, *Commentarius Exegeticus*, 140; Colombi, "Paene ad Verbum," 19; Herzog, *Die Bibelepik der lateinischen Spätantike* 121. Consider that Juvencus also uses the adjective elsewhere and at key moments in the narrative with reference to Christ's "life-giving table" (*uitali accumbere mensae*, 1.757), his "life-giving grace" (*uitalis gratia*, 2.270), his "life-giving times" ("aduentu proprio uitalia saecula pandet," 2.292), and his "life-giving words" (*uitalia uerba*, 2.452; "dictis pandens uitalibus aures," 2.547; *uitalia dicta frequentat*, 2.725; *uitalia uerba secuti*, 3.255).

63 Colombi, "Paene ad Verbum," 19. Here Columbi also sees depth in Juvencus' choice of the word *substantia* (595) and, looking back to Origen, argues that this word, together with *uitalis*, suggests "the life-giving nourishment of the soul" ("di nutrimento vivificante dell 'anima'").

case, Juvencus introduces language that creates a verbal parallel between the centurion's plea and the response of Jesus. This parallel does not appear in the prose, but is added to the verse for rhetorical emphasis. This language also underlines a didactic message that is not as forcefully made in the Gospel story (1.741–66):

5 Post haec autem cum autem introisset Capharnaum, accessit ad eum quidam centurio rogans (obsecrans) eum. 6 et dicens: Domine, puer meus iacet in domo paralyticus et male torquetur (grauiter poenas dans). 7 Ait (Dicit) illi Iesus: Ego ueniens et curabo eum. 8 Et respondens centurio ait (et dixit) illi: Domine non sum dignus, ut intres sub tectum meum. Sed tantum dic uerbo et sanabitur puer. 9 Nam et ego homo sum sub potestate constitutus, habens sub me milites, et dico huic: Vade, et uadit. Et alio: Veni, et uenit. Et seruo meo: Fac hoc, et facit. 10 Audiens autem Iesus miratus est et sequentibus se dixit: Amen dico uobis: non inueni tantam fidem in Istrahel. 11 Dico autem uobis, quod multi ab oriente et occidente uenient et recumbent cum Abraham et Isaac et Iacob in regno caelorum. 12 Fili autem regni huius ibunt in tenebras exteriores; ibi erit fletus et stridor dentium.13 Et dixit Iesus centurioni: Vade, sicut credidisti, fiat tibi. Et sanatus est puer ex illa hora.[64]

– Mt 8:5–13

Inde recedenti supplex se protinus offert
Centurio et precibus proiectus talibus orat:
"Impubis pueri cruciatur spiritus aeger,
Cuius cuncta repens membrorum munia languor
Dissoluit uitamque tenet iam poena superstes.   745
Sed iussu miserere precor, nam tecta subire

---

64 Mt 8:5–13: "And when he had entered into Capharnaum, there came to him a centurion, beseeching him, 6 and saying, 'Lord, my servant lies at home sick of the palsy, and is grievously tormented.' 7 And Jesus says to him: 'I will come and heal him.' 8 And the centurion making answer, said: 'Lord, I am not worthy that thou shouldst enter under my roof: but only say the word, and my servant shall be healed. 9 For I also am a man subject to authority, having under me soldiers; and I say to this, Go, and he goeth, and to another, Come, and he cometh, and to my servant, Do this, and he doeth it.' 10 And Jesus hearing this, marveled; and said to them that followed him: 'Amen I say to you, I have not found so great faith in Israel. 11 And I say to you that many shall come from the east and the west, and shall sit down with Abraham, and Isaac, and Jacob in the kingdom of heaven. 12 But the children of the kingdom shall be cast out into the exterior darkness: there shall be weeping and gnashing of teeth.' 13 And Jesus said to the centurion: 'Go, and as thou hast believed, so be it done to thee.' And the servant was healed at the same hour."

Crimina nostra uetant uitae lucisque parentem.
Nunc uerbo satis est iubeas remeare salutem.
Subiectos mihi saepe uiros sic nostra potestas
Officiis uerbo iussis parere coegit."   750
Dixerat. Ille uiri motus precibusque fideque
Talia conuersus populo dat dicta sequenti:
"Haut umquam talem memini me gentis auitae
Inuenisse fidem; sed ueris discite dictis,
Quod multos homines diuersis partibus orbis   755
Progenitos caeli regnum sublime uocabit
Cum patribus nostris uitali adcumbere mensae,
Progenies quorum caecis demersa tenebris
Dentibus horrendum stridens fletumque frequentans
Perpetuis poenae cruciatibus acta subibit.   760
At tibi iam, iuuenis, mentis uirtute fidelis,
Vt credis, ueniet fructus cum luce salutis."
Dixerat et dicto citius cum uoce loquentis
Ad puerum celeris transcurrunt munera uerbi,
Ingressusque domum miles properante recursu   765
Praeuenisse Dei laetatur dona medentis.

[As he turned away, a humble centurion offered himself at once to Jesus, and lying prostrate on the ground, begged him with these pleas: "The ailing spirit of my young boy is being tormented, the use of whose limbs has been consumed by a sudden weakness, and now constant pain rules his life. Pity him, I beg, with but a word, for our sins prevent the Lord of life and light from entering into our house. It is enough now for you to command his health to return at a word. My own authority often compels men subject to me to obey their appointed duties at a word." And moved by the pleas and faith of this man, Jesus turned to the people following him and said these words: "I can hardly recall ever finding such faith among my ancestral people; but learn from these true sayings, that the high kingdom of heaven will call many men from various parts of the world to sit down with our fathers at the life-giving table, whose family, sunk in blind shadow, will suffer sentences of punishment, perpetual torture, gnashing their teeth dreadfully, and wailing without end. But to you, young man, by virtue of your faithful heart, because you believe, a blessing will come with the light of salvation." And the gifts of his swift word, the voice of the speaker, hastened to the boy faster than they had been said, and the soldier rushed home with hurried steps and rejoiced to have anticipated the gifts of God the healer.]

Immediately, the posture of the centurion is different in the poetry; it elicits greater sympathy. He offers himself at once to Jesus (*se protinus offert*, 741), supine (*supplex*, 741), and throws himself to the ground (*proiectus*, 742) in humility.[65] The addition of the adjective *impubis* ("young") rouses further pity for the boy, and heavy alliteration intensifies the urgency of the centurion's begging.[66] The first three lines alone express a sense of breathless desperation: "… supplex se protinus offert / Centurio et precibus proiectus talibus orat: / 'Impubis pueri cruciatur spiritus aeger'." Juvencus therefore introduces greater dramatic immediacy and realism to this moment.

Whether for the sake of brevity or to accelerate the pace of the scene, Juvencus omits Jesus' response in verse seven of the Bible and instead folds it into the centurion's speech (746–7). Economy and poetic enhancement are the procedures throughout, even as the author keeps an eye on the prose.[67] In line 755, the clause "quod multi ab oriente et occidente uenient" is deftly converted to a more poetic alternative, "Quod multos homines diuersis partibus orbis / Progenitos," which echoes both the Bible (*quod* + *multus*) and Vergil ("genitos diuersis partibus orbis," *Aen.* 12. 708). Otherwise, several individual words – *Centurio* (742), *pueri* (743), *poena* (745), *tecta* (746), *uerbo* (748), *potestas* (749), *fideque* (751), *Inuenisse fidem* (754), *sequenti* (752), *multos* (755), *caeli regnum* (756), *adcumbere* (757), *tenebris* (758), *dentibus* (759), *fletumque* (759) – reflect the verbal core of the biblical narrative.

Juvencus adds a number of significant details, however, at the end of the scene, to emphasize the didactic message. When the faithful Centurion begs "the father of light and life" (*uitae lucisque parentem*, 747) to restore the health of his boy (*salutem*, 748), Jesus responds with "the blessing of the light of health" ("fructus cum luce salutis," 762), and in doing so echoes the Centurion's own words, *lux* and *salus*. The Centurion's faith therefore becomes an example for the bystanders, and Juvencus is more explicit

---

65   Huemer, *Euangeliorum Libri*, notes a parallel between *miserere precor* in line 746 and *precor, miserere* in *Aen.* 6.117. That may be. The adjective, *supplex*, is also used there (6.115), but the context is different. There, Aeneas begs the Cumaean Sibyl to allow him to see his father, who has been humble in the Underworld (*supplex*). I do not see *Kontrastimitation* here, although the general tone of the Vergilian scene may provide Juvencus with language.

66   See Canali, *Il Poema di Vangeli*, 287–8.

67   See Green, *Latin Epics*, 146.

about the didactic potential of this moment than the Bible is. *Veris discite dictis* (754), he says, "learn from these true words," and Jesus offers this lesson: The Centurion has shown true faith, and so the pain (*poena*, 745) which the boy suffers (*cruciatur*, 743) is relieved, but those who are not as open about their sins (*Crimina nostra*, 747) can expect everlasting torment and suffering (*Perpetuis poenae cruciatibus*, 760). Once again, by repeating the centurion's words, *salus*, *crucio*, and *poena*, Juvencus places greater emphasis on the power of faith. The message to the bystanders is clear: those who believe and confess will receive the gifts of healing and salvation – *fructus salutis* (762), *munera uerbi* (764), *dona medentis* (766) – while those who do not will suffer eternal agony in Hell. The phrase "Dentibus horrendum stridens" ("gnashing their teeth dreadfully," 759) is in all probability adapted from *Aen.* 6.288 and Vergil's image of the Underworld.

The Healing of Two Blind Men (2.408–16)

Similar rhetoric is used by Juvencus in the healing of the two blind men from Matthew, chapter 9. In the episode above, he calls Jesus "the father of life and light" (*uitae lucisque parentem*, 1.747), but that epithet takes on an added dimension here, where both *lux* and *lumen* refer to physical "sight." This scene is handled simply by Juvencus, who introduces a minimum of embellishment to the verse, and although rhetorical variation is a common feature of the poem, these lines show that he may use rhetorical repetition to effect as well. Green has said that Juvencus prefers economy in his rendering of the prose, "in the sense of not saying something twice, or not elaborating a point [in the Bible] that is sufficiently clear."[68] This is generally true, as are Roberts' comments about abbreviation and the rhetorical virtue of *breuitas*: "Repetitions were to be eliminated, redundancies to be pruned."[69] Here, for instance, Juvencus is careful not to repeat the adjective "caecus" more than once, but he does repeat other words, and with good reason (2.408–16):

---

68 See Green, *Latin Epics*, 31–3, but also 25, 35, 79, 108; see also Green, "Some Gospel Episodes," 141; and Green, "Exegesis by Stealth," 70. See also Roberts, *Biblical Epic*, 108, in the context of abbreviation and the virtue of *breuitas*: "Repetitions were to be eliminated, redundancies to be pruned."

69 Roberts, *Biblical Epic*, 108.

27 Et transeunte inde Iesu secuti sunt eum duo caeci clamantes et dicentes:
Miserere nostri, fili Dauid. 28 Et uenit in domum et accesserunt ad eum duo
caeci, et dixit illis Iesus: Creditis, quod possum hoc facere? Dicunt ei: Utique,
Domine. 29 Tunc tetigit oculos eorum dicens: Secundum fidem uestram con-
tingat uobis. 30 Et aperti sunt oculi ipsorum et comminatus est illis Iesus dicens: Videte, ne quis sciat. 31 Illi autem exeuntes diffamauerunt eum in tota
terra illa.[70]

– Mt 9:27–31

Inde reuertenti clamor se protinus offert
Caecorum pariter gressu labente duorum.
Ollis Christus ait: "Quid credunt pectora uestra?   410
Num uirtute mea se reddet lumen ademptum?"
Olli firmato se credere corde fatentur.
Tum Christus fatur: "Credentes cernite lucem
Nec cuiquam nostrum post haec edicite nomen."
Dixit; sed propere per gaudia tanta uidentum   415
Ardor inexpletus famam per cuncta serebat.

[Then a cry from two blind men, both on faltering feet, offered itself at once
to Jesus as he was turning away. Christ said to them: "What do your hearts
believe? That your lost sight will be restored by my power?" They answered
that they believed that with determined hearts. Then Christ said: "See the
light, you who believe! And do not mention my name to anyone after this,"
he said. But soon afterward, their insatiable ardor spread the news everywhere, because of their great joy in their sight.]

The initial appeal of the two men, "Inde reuertenti clamor se protinus
offert" (408), is almost identical to that of the centurion in Book 1 ("Inde
recedenti supplex se protinus offert, 1.741), and both passages focus on
faith. Repetition is also used here to special effect. The verb *credo* appears

---

70 Mt 9:27–31: "And as Jesus passed from thence, there followed him two blind men crying out and saying, 'Have mercy on us, O Son of David.' And when he was come to the
house, the blind men came to him. And Jesus saith to them, 'Do you believe that I can
do this unto you?' They say to him, 'Yea, Lord.' Then he touched their eyes, saying,
'According to your faith, be it done unto you.' And their eyes were opened, and Jesus
strictly charged them, saying, 'See that no man know this.' But they going out, spread
his fame abroad in all that country."

only once in the prose, in verse twenty-eight, but Juvencus uses forms of it three times as part of a rhetorical exchange between Jesus and the blind men. Jesus: "Do your hearts believe?" The men: "We believe." Jesus: "Then, believing, see the light!" The translation is free but the point is clear. Juvencus is underlining the relationship between faith and healing (or salvation). He draws further attention to this theme through alliteration: <u>C</u>aecoroum ... <u>C</u>hristus ... <u>c</u>redunt ... <u>c</u>redere <u>c</u>orde ... <u>c</u>redentes <u>c</u>ernite" (409–13). These aural connections, between "blindness" (409), "Christ" (410), "faith" (410, 412, 413), "the heart" (410, 412), and "sight" (411, 413), contain the message of the scene: seeing is not believing; faith is the path to healing. These gifts are the same as those given to the centurion's son and, as there, the word of Christ is sufficient to release his power (*uirtute mea*, 411), even though he deigns to touch their eyes in the prose (*tetigit oculos eorum*). This show of might also validates the "life-giving deeds of Christ," which are promoted in the preface to *Euangeliorum libri* (*Christi uitalia gesta*, 19), and although *famam* (416) here picks up on *diffamauerunt* in verse thirty-one of the prose, it also serves the epic mission of the poem to present Christ as a "gift among the people," as Juvencus says ("Diuinum in populis falsi sine crimine donum," *praef.* 20), whose *gesta* are greater and truer than the "lies bound to the deeds of ancient men" ("ueterum gestis hominum mendacia nectunt," *praef.* 16).

The Crucifixion (4.642–9)

At the beginning of Book 4, a shift in tone already felt in the latter portions of Book 3 moves inexorably toward the Crucifixion. It is no surprise that Juvencus turns from his earlier focus on gifts and gratefulness to the more bitter offerings of betrayal and death, and the treatment Jesus receives at the hands of the Roman soldiers is a reversal of the homage paid to him at his birth. Unlike the epic overtones that lead the Magi to the crèche in Book 1 (1.243–51), the language here, though lofty enough, is restrained. Juvencus yields now to his more conservative temperament, which is a reminder of the authority he gives to the unembellished deeds of the Gospels over any personal desire to promote his own desire for fame (4.642–9):

27 Tunc milites praesidis susceperunt eum in praetorio et congregauerunt ad eum uniuersam cohortem. 28 Et induerunt eum tunicam purpuream et chlamydem coccineam circumdederunt ei 29 et coronam de spinis posuerunt super caput eius et harundinem in dextram eius et adgeniculantes se ante eum

deludebant eum dicentes: Haue rex Iudaeorum. 30 Et expuentes in faciem
eius acceperunt harundinem et percutietbant caput eius.[71]

– Mt 27:27–30

Traditus est trucibus iustus scelerisque ministris
Militibus: scelerata ludibria corpore praebet.
Purpureamque illi tunicam clamidemque rubentem
Inducunt spinisque caput cinxere cruentis,   645
Inque uicem sceptri dextram comitatur harundo.
Tum genibus nixi regem dominumque salutant
Iudaeae gentis faciemque lauere saliuis
Vertice et in sancto plagis lusere nefandis.

[This righteous man was handed over to the soldiers and savage agents of that
crime – they exposed his body to despicable humiliation. And they led him
out in a scarlet robe and purple tunic, his head crowned with bloody thorns,
and fit his right hand with a reed instead of a sceptre. Then on bended knee
they hailed him as the "king" and "Lord" of the Jewish race, and showered
his face with spit, and abused his holy head with unspeakable blows.]

Although the language of this scene is arranged to accommodate the
metre, it is almost entirely biblical in origin. *Miles* (643), *tunica* (644), *pur-
purea* (644), *chlamys* (644), *spinus* (645), *caput* (645), *dextra* (646), *harundo*
(646), *rex* (647), and *Iudaeus* (648) together tell the story of the Gospels,
and these words appear without adornment in the verse, with the excep-
tions of *trux* ("savage," 642), *sceleratus* ("sinful," 643), and *cruentus*
("bloody," 645). Other turns of phrase that appear to stray from Matthew
are still close synonyms of their Gospel counterparts (*rubentem* for *coccineam*, *inducunt* for *induerunt*, etc.). The only real "poetic" diction is
perhaps the verb *lauere* ("to wash"), which may be an ironic allusion to
Luke 7:38, an image of the "humble" Romans "bathing" Jesus' feet with
tears, but Juvencus channels Matthew for the most part.

---

71 Mt 27:27–30: "The soldiers of the governor taking Jesus in to the hall, gathered together
    unto him the whole band. And stripping him, they put a scarlet cloak about him. And
    platting a crown of thorns, they put it upon his head, and a reed in his right hand. And
    bowing the knee before him, they mocked him, saying: Hail, king of the Jews. And spit-
    ting upon him, they took the reed and struck his head."

There is also a possible allusion to the opening of the poem. It may not seem like much, but the image of the "kneeling" Romans and the appearance of the verb *salutant* (1.245/4.647), in addition to the familiar-sounding structure of *regem dominumque* (4.647) and *regique hominique* in Book 1 (1.25), is enough to evoke the moment when the Magi offer their gifts to the newborn king. The potential link is an effective one, for it evokes the Magi, who hail the star that leads them to the Lord (*sidusque salutant*, 1.245), who cast themselves to the ground in reverence, and offer their gifts "to the man, king, and God ("Tus, aurum, murrham regique hominique Deoque," 1.250). Here, at the end, the Romans offer their own ironic gifts – sceptre, crown, and robe – and hail the "Lord and king" in mock adoration of his divinity (4.647): "Tum genibus nixi regem dominumque salutant" ("Then on bended knee they hailed him as king and Lord"). The allusion to the earlier scene makes the humiliation of the latter all the more poignant, and highlights one of the many and subtle interconnections of thought and word in *Euangeliorum libri*.

The verses that deal with the Crucifixion include an epic flourish here and there, but as Witke puts it, "The death of Jesus on the cross is handled with economic dignity."[72] Apart from the ornamental touch of the epic sunset preceding his death (4.687–91) and the florid language of the Ascension, "Tum clamor Domini magno conamine missus / Aetheriis animam comitem conmiscuit auris" ("Then, after the Lord gave out a cry with great effort / He committed his companion soul to the ethereal airs," 4.701–2), which echoes Ovid (*Met.* 3.60, *magno conamine misit*) and Vergil (*Aen.* 6.761–2, "animam comitem commiscuit auris"), the final moments are handled with reserve (4.662–73):[73]

35 Postquam autem crucifixerunt eum, diuiserunt sibi uestimenta eius sortem mittentes, ut impleretur quod dictum est per prophetam dicentem: Diuiserunt sibi uestimenta mea et super uestem meam miserunt sortem. 36 Et sedentes seruabant eum. 37 Et posuerunt supra cepit eius causam eius scriptam: Hic est Iesus rex Iudaeorum. 38 Tunc crucifixi sunt cum eo duo latrones, unus a dextris et alius a sinistris. 39 Transeuntes autem blasphemabant eum

---

72 Witke, *Numen Litterarum*, 203.

73 See, however, Witke, ibid., 204–6, for a discussion of the epic tenor of the resurrection scene. For the allusions to Ovid and Vergil, see further ibid., 203–4, and Green, *Latin Epics*, 57.

mouentes capita sua 40 et dicentes: Va qui destruebas templum Dei et in triduo illud reaedificabas; libera te, si filius Dei es, et descende de cruce.[74]

– Mt 27:35–40

Iamque cruci fixum pendebat in arbore corpus,
Intactaeque dedit tunicae sub sorte per omnes
Militis unius seruans possessio textum.
Et scriptum causae titulum meritique locarunt,   665
Quod rex Iudaeae plebis gentisque fuisset.
Accidit, ut pariter poenae consortia ferrent
Latrones hinc inde duo; sed caeca furentis
Insultat plebis fixo uaesania Christo:
“Hic est, qui templum poterat dissoluere solus,   670
Hic est, qui trino lucis reparare meatu.
Sed nunc discendat suboles ueneranda Tonantis
Et crucis e poena corpusque animamque resoluat.”

[And now his body hung on the tree, fixed to the cross, and possession of the
tunic went by lot in a single piece to one of the soldiers there, who kept the
fabric. And they set up written notice of his charge and punishment, that he
was king of the Jewish race and people. It also happened that two thieves, on
either side of him, bore together the common grief of his sentence; and the
blind madness of the raving mob cast insults at Christ on the cross: “Here
is the one who brought the temple to ruin by himself; here is the one who
restored it in three turns of the sun. So, let the Venerable Offspring of the
Thunderer come down now and free his body and soul from the torment of
the cross!”]

---

74   Mt 27:35–40: “And after they had crucified him, they divided his garments, casting lots;
that it might be fulfilled which was spoken by the prophet, saying: They divided my
garments among them; and upon my vesture they cast lots. And they sat and watched
him. And they put over his head his cause written: THIS IS JESUS THE KING OF
THE JEWS. Then were crucified with him two thieves: one on the right hand, and one
on the left. And they that passed by, blasphemed him, wagging their heads, and saying:
Vah, thou that destroyest the temple of God, and in three days dost rebuild it: save thy
own self: if thou be the Son of God, come down from the cross.”

Favouring economy, Juvencus does not include the second half of verse thirty-five in the Bible, which repeats the essence of line 663.[75] Elsewhere, the biblical prose forms the core of the scene: *cruci fixum* (662)/*crucifix-erunt*; *scriptum causae* (665)/*causam eius scriptam*; *rex Iudaeae* (666)/*rex Iudaeorum*; *latrones … duo* (668)/*duo latrones*; *qui templum* (670)/*qui … templum*; *trino* (671)/*triduo*; *crucis* (673)/*cruce*. Adaptations for the sake of the metre are few: *tunicae* (663) for the more cumbersome *uestimenta*; and *locarunt* (665) for *posuerunt* in the prose. Noteworthy additions include the phrase *in arbore* ("on the tree," 662), which is nonetheless typical periphrasis for Juvencus and similar to other descriptions of the cross in *Euangeliorum libri*.[76] Canali highlights the significance of *caeca* ("blind," 668), which modifies *uaesania* ("madness") and that elsewhere emphasizes real or spiritual blindness, as it does in the episode of the two blind men (2.408–16).[77] Here the adjective defines the blindness of the Pharisees, who cannot or will not see Jesus as the son of God. As the only real epic embellishment in the scene, Juvencus calls Jesus "Venerable Offspring of the Thunderer" (*suboles ueneranda Tonantis*, 4.672), a nod to Vergil and Jupiter, but the phrase is mock epic in the mouths of those who insult Christ (669–73).[78] With the addition of *poena* to *crucis* in line 673, Juvencus suggests that the bystanders are mocking the healing power of Jesus as well. The word does not just suggest "punishment" but rather "suffering." In fact, they say as much in the following lines (678–80): "Nonne alios quondam trucibus seruare solebat/Morborum uinclis? sese cur soluere poenis/Non ualet?" ("Since he was used to saving others from the savage chains of sickness, can he not free himself from these torments?"). The repetition of *trucibus* (678) in particular is emphatic and picks up on the earlier reference in verse 642 (*trucibus sceleratis*), those "savage humiliations" the Romans inflict upon Jesus.

---

75 Juvencus often reproduces prophetic details in the narrative (see Green, *Latin Epics*, 109); this is an exception but one that falls within the usual parameters of "economy." The later poet Sedulius includes such references less than does Juvencus (Green, *Latin Epics*, 229).

76 See ibid., 98; also, Roberts, *Biblical Epic*, 152.

77 Canali, *Il Poema Dei Vangeli*, 421.

78 See further Hudson-Williams, "Virgil and the Christian Latin Poets," 14.

Conclusion

In the final analysis, to define *Euangeliorum libri* as a "close" rendition of the Bible is to undervalue the author's personal contribution to the enterprise. Although attentive to the prose, Juvencus leaves a strong individual impression on his version of the Gospel-story. He does not often speak out in the way many later biblical poets do, but rather quietly through his choice of words. This may be said of any poet, but there is a sense that Juvencus has much to say himself about the Bible and the life-giving deeds of Christ, and he uses elements of the epic genre to highlight moments that are especially important to him. A richness and depth of meaning will reveal itself to those who linger on the language of this poem, and the more one does so, the more one may raise critical objections to Jerome's *paene ad uerbum* assessment of *Euangeliorum libri*, but only if such objections dismiss the general conservatism of the work and its faithfulness to the spirit of the Gospels.

Chapter Three

Cyprianus' *Heptateuch* (c. 400–425 CE)

Principio dominus caelum terramque locauit:
Namque erat informis fluctuque abscondita tellus
Inmensusque deus super aequora uasta meabat,
Dum chaos et nigrae fuscabant cuncta tenebrae.

[In the beginning the Lord established heaven and earth, for the land was yet
formless and hidden by a flood, and boundless God passed over the vast sea,
as chaos and black shadow darkened all.]

– *Heptateuch* (*Gen.*, 1–4)

Obscurity surrounds the next versification of the Bible from late Antiquity.
The so-called *Heptateuchos* of Cyprianus Gallus (hereafter the *Heptateuch*)
dates to the first quarter of the fifth century, but the date is only a guess,
since the author's true identity remains a mystery. The name we have is the
invention of Rudolf Peiper, who edited the poem for *Corpus Christianorum*
in 1891, and that edition is still the standard text.[1] In it, Peiper mentions
"Cyprianus Gallus" for the first time, although he had already used the
praenomen "Cyprianus" in his 1883 edition of Avitus.[2] On both occasions,
Peiper defers to manuscript catalogues that seem to identify the author by

---

1 The standard edition is that of Peiper, ed., *Cypriani Galli Poetae Heptateuchos*. For a
   recent reassessment of the date, see Pollmann, "Der Sogenannte Heptateuchdichter,"
   490–501. See also Roberts, *Biblical Epic*, 94–5; Roberts, *Jeweled Style*, 9; Nodes, *Doctrine and Exegesis*, 25; Herzog, *Die Bibelepik der lateinischen Spätantike*, 53–60.
2 See further Peiper, ed., *Alcimi Ecdicii Aviti Viennensis Episcopi Opera*, e.g., liii: "Cyprianus dicitur in uetustissimis libris" ("He is called 'Cyprianus' in the oldest books"); also,
   lx–lxiii. See also Roberts, *Biblical Epics*, 93, n. 121.

name, including this one at Lorsch: "Metrum Cypriani super Heptateuchum et Regum et Hester Iudith et Machabaeorum."[3] But this evidence is late, and so may be the attribution of the name.[4] No doubt surrounds the origin of the cognomen "Gallus," however, which appears nowhere in any catalogue or manuscript of the *Heptateuch*, but is coined by Peiper himself on the basis of features of the author's style, which contemporary scholars determined to be "Gallo-" Roman (i.e., French).[5]

Given what we know of the poet's identify, the date of the *Heptateuch* thus depends on internal evidence. The early extreme of 400 CE relies on an allusion in the *Exodus* portion of the narrative (*Ex.* 474–6) to Claudian's panegyric on the third consulate of Emperor Honorius, dated to 397 CE.[6] The poem could not, therefore, have been written before then. At the other extreme, the suggestion of 430 CE is based on echoes of the *Heptateuch* in Claudius Marius Victorius' *Alethia*, a 2000-line versification of Genesis written around that time.[7] But the date of *Alethia* is also an approximation

---

3 The Lorsch catalogue, for example, dates to the tenth century. See Peiper, *Heptateuchos*, i, for a citation of the Lorsch catalogue; and Roberts, *Biblical Epic*, 93, for a summary of the evidence.

4 See Herzog, *Bibelepik*, 56–8.

5 See Roberts, *Biblical Epic*, 93, n. 124: "Lucian Müller, 'Zu Ennius und den christlichen Dichtern,' 127, had already offered that the poet might be from Gaul. His only reason was the extensive literary activity in Gaul in the fourth, fifth and sixth centuries." See also Becker, *De Metris in Heptateuchum*, 18–27.

6 The *terminus a quo* is based on the allusion to Claudius' panegyric in the *Heptateuch* (*Ex.* 474–6): "O nimium felix, celsis cui misit ab astris / Munimenta deus, candens cui militat aether / Et coniuratae ueniunt ad proelia noctes" ("O thou exceedingly blessed, to whom God sent his reinforcement from the lofty stars, / for whom the incandescent ether fights / and allied night comes forth to battle"). The passage refers to Moses moments before he parts the Red Sea, but both the language and imagery point to Claudian, who flatters Honorius in similar terms (*III Cons.* 96–8): "O nimium dilecte deo, cui fundit ab antris / Aeolus armatas hiemes, cui militat aether / Et coniurati ueniunt ad classica uenti" ("O thou exceedingly beloved of god, for whom Aeolus pours out battle-ready winter from its cave, for whom the ether fights and allied winds comes forth to battle at the trumpet call"). See further Roberts, *Biblical Epic*, 94; also, Fontaine, *Naissance*, 246–7; Green, *Latin Epics*, 151; Arweiler, *Die Imitation antiker und spätantiker*, 222.

7 Hovingh, ed., *Alethia*, puts the date of *Alethia* around 420/430, and the usual assumption is that the author is the same "Victorinus" that Gennadius of Marseille mentions in his *De uiris illustribus*, ch. lxi. Gennadius puts the death of Victorius under the reigns of emperor Theodosius (408–50 CE) and Valentinian III (425–55 CE). See further Richardson, ed., *Liber de Viris Illustribus*, 57–97. For echoes of the *Heptateuch* in *Alethia*, see Schenkl, ed., *Claudii Marii Victoris oratoris Massiliensis Alethia*, CSEL 16, 352–3; see also Peiper, *Heptateuchos*, xxv–xxvi and 275–81; and Maurer, *De exemplis quae Claudius Marius Victorius*, diss. 7. Note, however, that some doubt the antecedence of the *Heptateuch* over *Alethia*, a point Roberts addresses in *Biblical Epic*, 94–5.

and so unreliable evidence as well. The only sure testimony seems to be the title of the work itself, which Peiper has based on tenth- and twelfth-century manuscript catalogues referring to the poem as "*Heptateuchos.*"[8] Again, however, this evidence is late, and while the 5550 lines of the extant text do cover the first seven books of the Bible – *Genesis* (1498 lines), *Exodus* (1333 lines), *Leviticus* (309 lines), *Numbers* (777 lines), *Deuteronomy* (288 lines), *Joshua* (585 lines), and *Judges* (760 lines) – that catalogue at Lorsch also attests to versifications of *Kings*, *Esther*, *Judith*, and *Maccabees*, and this poetry has been attributed to Cyprianus.[9] Today these books survive only in fragments, but their existence casts doubt on the original scope of the *Heptateuch*, which appears at one time to have included "all of the historical books of the Old Testament."[10]

Classical Context

Amid such obscurity, it is difficult to say much about the author or his life beyond his work. Fortunately, the *Heptateuch* itself affords plenty of insight. It reveals, for example, that Cyprianus, like Juvencus, maintains strict detachment from his narrative, a virtue of epic decorum. Only rarely does he interrupt events with comments of his own.[11] He is also an ardent imitator of classical poetry, and Peiper cites Vergil as the chief influence – "Vergilium prae ceteris,"[12] as he says – a statement confirmed by nearly 300 citations of Vergil in Peiper's *Auctores Imitatores*.[13] Ovid also figures prominently in the *Heptateuch*, followed by Horace, Persius, Juvenal, Lucan, Statius, and Silius Italicus, while Sallust, Livy, and Tacitus merit honourable mention among prose writers.[14] Juvencus, Prudentius and Paulinus of Nola also figure as Christian influences and show that Christian poetry is now increasingly part of the equation.

---

8 See Peiper, *Heptateuchos*, i. The Nazarius catalogue attests to the name Peiper gives to the poem, as does a twelfth-century catalogue from Cluny.

9 See Peiper, *Heptateuchos*, i and 209–110. See also Roberts, *Biblical Epic*, 95.

10 Roberts, *Biblical Epic*, 95. See also Peiper's opening words in his introduction, i: "Cypriani Galli hominis carmina, quibus Veteris Testamenti historiarum tota series ennaratur …" ("The poetry of Cyprianus Gallus, in which the whole series of the stories of the Old Testament is told …").

11 For Cyprianus' two narrative interventions, see further *Ex.* 1082–6 and *Lev.* 34; see also Nodes, *Doctrine and Exegesis*, 83: "[Cyprianus'] work contains the fewest direct comments of all the biblical epics."

12 See Peiper, *Heptateuchos*, xxiv.

13 Ibid., 275–99.

14 Ibid., xxiv–xxv.

But Cyprianus is less proficient, technically, than his sources of inspiration. In his study of the metre of the *Heptateuch*, André Longpré has shown that Cyprianus knows the rules of dactylic hexameter verse well, but that he is inexperienced: "on sent chez lui l'application du bon élève, non pas l'éclat que confère le génie."[15] Equally alert to the metrical irregularities of the poem, Peiper cites many "deviations" (his word) in the *Index Metricus* of his edition, including several instances when a final syllable is short but should be long.[16] Such and other inconsistencies are enough for Roberts to conclude, "the poem would certainly make it an unsuitable school text,"[17] and that may well have been the case, since Cyprianus does not figure prominently among the biblical poets of the Anglo-Saxon school curriculum, although both Aldhelm and Bede know and cite the *Heptateuch* a fair amount.

Like Juvencus, Cyprianus favours heavily spondaic feet in imitation of the stately measure of epic, but the monotony of his verse again suggests inexperience. So much does Cyprianus prefer the spondee, in fact, that he stands apart from most other late antique writers in this respect, including Prudentius, Paulinus of Nola, Sedulius, Dracontius, and Arator (although not Avitus).[18] Ninety-one per cent of his verses resort to one of eight metrical patterns, and no other Latin poet on record, with the exception of Catullus, is more repetitive in his composition of hexameters than our Gallic poet.[19]

In terms of language, Cyprianus follows in the footsteps of Juvencus, by introducing diction from the stock of classical epic, but echoes of Juvencus and other Christian poets now begin to blur the lines.[20] For example, he

---

15 Longpré, "Structure de l'Hexamètre de Cyprianus Gallus," 75–100, at 100. See also Longpré, "Traitement de l'élision chez le poète Cyprianus Gallus," 63–77.
16 See further Peiper, *Heptateuchos*, 343–8.
17 Roberts, *Biblical Epic*, 96.
18 Duckworth, *Vergil and Classical Hexameter Poetry*, 133.
19 Consider the range of common patterns in the first four feet of Cyprianus' verses (S=spondee; D=dactyl): SSDS, DSSS DDSS/SDSS, DSDS, SDDS, DDDS, SSSS. For a table of these patterns and a few summary conclusions, see further Duckworth, *Vergil and Classical Hexameter Poetry*, 140–1.
20 According to Peiper's appendix, *Auctores imitatores*, Cyprianus echoes Juvencus approximately twenty times, though more echoes may exist, especially among lines that seem to be Vergilian but are filtered through *Euangeliorum libri* (references to Juvencus appear in parentheses): *Gen.* 536 (3.228), 672 (1.469), 713 (1.44), 795 (1.735), 873 (2.422), 916 (2.761), 1287 (3.508), 1370 (3.738), 1432 (3.763); *Ex.* 203 (2.146), 296 (2.523), 375 (3.566), 421 (1.580), 1062 (3.330); *Lev.* 41 (4.104), 195 (1.124); *Num.* 111 (2.293), 695 (4.459); *Iesu naue* 18 (3.315), 40 (1.763), 201 (1.297).

shares with Juvencus an affection for the *Tonans*-epithet, saying, "Atque opifex tali formatur uoce tonantis" ("And now the workman [Adam] is formed by the voice of the Thunderer," *Gen.* 65), and this language originates in classical poetry.[21] Likewise, heavenly messengers come and go from earth in terms that echo both Juvencus and Vergil, so that it becomes difficult to tell whom Cyprianus is following, and the difficulty only increases with the progress of Christian poetry in late Antiquity. As another example, the epic descent of the angel in the *Heptateuch*, which heralds the birth of Isaac ("Nuntius aetherio descendit culmine caeli," *Gen.* 572), may draw inspiration from the descent of Vulcan in the *Aeneid* (8.423) or that of the Holy Spirit in *Euangeliorum libri* (1.357).[22] In other respects, Cyprianus is less guarded in his choice of diction than Juvencus, and his efforts to invest the Bible with an air of epic grandeur can be self-conscious and heavy-handed. Juvencus, for example, does not use the word *Olympus* for "heaven" and for obvious reasons, but Cyprianus does and several times. "I am the great king of Olympus," proclaims God in the *Heptateuch* ("Ego sum rex magnus olympi," *Gen.* 923), and "I am here, having come down from lofty Olympus" ("Atque ideo huc ueni celso degressus olympo," 150). Elsewhere, as in the episode of Abraham and Isaac (*Gen.* 737–54), Cyprianus' introduction of self-consciously poetic adjectives, including *sublimemque deum* ("exalted God," 739), *aetheriis … numen* ("ethereal deity," 741), *tumidi … collis* ("high-rising mountain," 743), or needless periphrasis, such as *cornipedem* ("horn-hoofed," 744, for *asinam* "ass") or *pabula flammarum* ("flame-fodder," 748, for *ligna,* "wood"), suggest youthful exuberance. Even so, there are undoubtedly moments in the poem when the author achieves the effective harmony that more consistently characterizes the style of *Euangeliorum libri*.

Biblical Context

The Latin of the *Heptateuch* suggests a pre-Vulgate model for the poem, and Willy Hass has proposed two related versions of the European text – Lyons, Municipal Library, Ms. 403 and the Würzburg Palimpsest (Mp.

---

21 For other uses of the *Tonans*-epithet in the *Heptateuch*, see further *Genesis*, 141, 168, 325, 793, 930, 1044, 1278; *Exodus*, 134, 728, 1077; *Numbers*, 437; *Deuteronomy*, 52; *Iesu naue*, 465, 491, 500; *Judges*, 236, 412, 437, 503, 522.

22 For another epic description of an angel's descent to earth, see further *Ex.* 992–9.

theol. fol. 64a) – as approximations of the author's source.[23] Whatever his precise model, Cyprianus aims to follow the Old Testament closely and to "produce a metrical version of the whole Heptateuch text, not merely its narrative sections."[24] For this reason, his poem deserves the *paene ad uerbum* assessment of Jerome even more than *Euangeliorum libri*.[25] Moreover, due to the general fidelity of the *Heptateuch* to the Bible and the author's detachment from his narrative, explicit exegesis in the poem is rare. What potential for symbolism exists expresses itself, as in *Euangeliorum libri*, by the addition of a significant word or phrase. Thus a lamb appears in place of the ram at the sacrifice of Isaac, and Christ is the pillar that leads the Israelites through the wilderness in Exodus, prefiguring man's salvation. In short, there is an opening to pursue the deeper meaning of some passages in the poem, but like Juvencus, Cyprianus is more invested in the historical incidents of the Bible themselves.

In versifying the Bible, he uses many of the strategies Juvencus does but on a larger scale. Economy of style plays an even larger role in the *Heptateuch* than it does in *Euangeliorum libri*, and Cyprianus abbreviates the biblical narrative frequently, often dramatically.[26] Much of the ritualistic material in chapter 12 of Exodus is pruned, for example, and there Cyprianus whittles down some fifty-one verses of the Bible to a single line of poetry (*Ex.* 351). The versifications of Leviticus and Deuteronomy are likewise much shorter than they would have been, had the author included such material.[27] Alongside abbreviation, variation (*uariatio*) also plays an

---

23 See further Hass, *Studien zum Heptateuchdichter*, 27–40, who offers a number of comparisons between the text of the *Heptateuch* and versions of the *Vetus Latina*; see also Roberts, *Biblical Epic*, 93–4, and Roberts, *Jeweled Style*, 10, who summarizes these findings. For a text of the Codex Lugdunesis 403, see further Robert, *Pentateuchi Versio Latina Antiquissima e Codice Lugdunensi*. But see also Kriel, "*Sodoma* in Fifth Century Biblical Epic," 7–20, at 9, who disagrees and argues that the poet's rendition of the Gen. 18–19 has more in common with the Vulgate; but his scope is more limited than that of Hass.

24 Roberts, *Biblical Epic*, 119.

25 See further Charlet, "L'inspiration et la forme bibliques dans la poésie latine chrétienne du IIIᵉ au VIᵉ siècle," 613–43 at 638: "… une versification stricte et fidèle des Écritures, connues de lui par une *Vetus Latina*." See also Fontaine, *Naissance*, 247: "Cyprien écrit encore d'une plume agile et claire, mais en se tenant dans les limites étroites d'une stricte paraphrase."

26 See further Roberts, *Biblical Epic*, 183: "brevity dictates the exclusion of unnecessary details."

27 For biblical omissions, see Roberts, *Jeweled Style*, 10; and Roberts, *Biblical Epic*, 183.

important role in resolving the often-repetitive language of the Old Testament.[28] In general, then, the job of the *Heptateuch* poet is much more difficult than that of Juvencus, who chooses material selectively according to a theme (*Christi uitalia gesta*, 19), while Cyprianus wades into Genesis 1:1 and proceeds inexorably through every chapter and verse of the Bible, having to face every textual problem along the way.

The Opening (*Gen.* 1–4)

The absence of any preface to the *Heptateuch* is striking, especially given the length of the work and the effort that must have been involved in producing it.[29] But for whatever reason Cyprianus does not give us one and begins immediately with the "In principio" of Genesis. With his first words, he shows that his poem will be a faithful rendition of the original, allowing for the kind of stylistic enhancements we find in *Euangeliorum libri*. For the sake of comparison with the biblical Latin, I have used Fischer's edition of the *Vetus Latina* with relevant variants in parentheses (1–4):[30]

> In principio fecit deus caelum et terram. 2 terram autem erat invisibilis et inconposita (informis) et tenebrae erant super abyssum et spiritus dei superferebatur super aquas.
>
> – Gen 1:1–2

> Principio dominus caelum terramque locauit:
> Namque erat informis fluctuque abscondita tellus
> Inmensusque deus super aequora uasta meabat,
> Dum chaos et nigrae fuscabant cuncta tenebrae.

> [In the beginning, the Lord established heaven and earth, for the land was yet formless and hidden by a flood, and boundless God passed over the vast sea, as chaos and black shadow darkened all.]

---

28 For a discussion of repetition in the Old Testament and the *Heptateuch*, see Roberts, *Biblical Epic*, 116–17. Roberts also mentions variation on p. 199.

29 See further Charlet, "L'inspiration et la forme bibliques," 638: "L'absence de préface rend difficiles à saisir les intentions du poète: avant tout littéraires, ou édifiantes?"

30 See further Robert, *Pentateuchi Versio Latina*, esp. iv–v. Genesis only begins at chapter 16 and is otherwise fragmentary throughout. Therefore, see Fischer, *Vetus Latina*.

The biblical heritage of these lines is unmistakable. The opening phrase, *In principio* (1) and the two other significant words in the line, *caelum ter-ramque* (1), reflect the language of the prose verbatim, and the substitutions of *dominus* for *deus* and *locauit* for *creauit* are unremarkable; *dominus* appears frequently as a variant of *deus* in the early sections of Genesis. Line four of the *Heptateuch* should follow next, if Cyprianus is tracking the order of the biblical verses, but "boundless God" (*Inmensusque deus*) intervenes instead. The adjective, *inmensus*, in line three finds no correspondence in the prose, but it does appear elsewhere in the Bible about a dozen times, usually with the sense of physical size.[31] Only in Sirach does the word have anything to do with creation, and that passage approaches the context of the *Heptateuch* (16:17–18): "17 in populo mag-no non agnoscar quae est enim anima mea in tam inmensa creatura. 18 Ecce caelum et caeli caelorum abyssus et uniuersa terra et quae in eis sunt in conspectu illius commouebuntur" ("17 In such a multitude I shall not be known: for what is my soul in such an immense creation? 18 Behold heaven and the heavens of heavens, the deep, and all the earth, and things that are in them, shall be moved in his sight"). The Septuagint also reads ἐν ἀμετρήτῳ κτίσει at this point ("in immense/ immeasurable creation"), so it may be that Cyprianus is thinking of God in these terms, as boundless. Daniel Nodes suggests as much and writes that "the substitution [of *in-mensus*] for *spiritus dei* may reflect the poet's desire to interpret Gen. 1:2 as pointing to the immateriality and transcendence of the Creator, rather than to the Holy Spirit."[32]

Peiper cites the *Satisfactio* of Dracontius as a later source for this word in poetry (Nodes echoes him), but numerous earlier examples appear in classical verse, the earliest ones in Lucretius' *De rerum natura*.[33] At the opening of *De rerum natura*, Lucretius says this of Epicurus (1.74):[34] "Atque omne immensum peragrauit mente animoque" ("and he journeyed the whole expanse in mind and spirit"). The word in this context applies to

---

31 See, e.g., Ex. 8:14 (*in inmensos aggeres*), Deut. 17:17 (*inmensa pondera*), Ez. 38:22 (*lapi-dibus inmensis*), Sir 24:41 (*aquae inmensae*), Mac. 2.1:13 (*inmensus exercitus*). Cyprianus uses the word in this context with reference to the land and sea. Thus "Accipit immen-sus errantia litora pontus" (*Gen.* 1.9) and "Germine et immensis errare et pascere terris" (1.24). The adjective appears some twenty times in the *Heptateuch* (*Gen.* 3, 9, 24, 381, 392, 416, 821, 1024, 1338; *Ex.* 8, 20, 170, 437, 452, 493, 660, 1319; *Iue.* 230).

32 Nodes, *Doctrine and Exegesis*, 26, who cites *Ex.* 170 (Ex. 3:15); *Ex.* 425 (Ex. 14:12); *Lv.* 230 (Lv. 24:11); *Nu.* 557 (Nu. 21:17).

33 See ibid. and Peiper, *Heptateuchos*, 275.

34 The Latin text is that of Bailey, *De rerum natura*.

the physical dimensions of the world, but at the end of Book 1, Lucretius uses the adjective again, on his way to statement that nature and the universe are infinite (1.957): "Peruideamus utrum finitum funditus omne / Constet an immensum pateat uasteque profundum" ("Let us see whether everything is utterly finite or extends immeasurably and [is] vastly profound"). *De rerum natura* is the earliest use of the adjective I find in poetry, and although the word has physical dimensions, its meaning in Book 1 of *De rerum natura* points to the infiniteness of the universe. It may therefore be that Cyprianus adopts the adjective as a way to articulate the boundlessness of God, which is more or less what Nodes says.[35]

The Opening Cont. (*Gen.* 5–24)

Whatever the source or meaning of *inmensusque deus* (3), the opening lines of the *Heptateuch* are as close to the Bible as a paraphraser might hope to get. The twenty lines that follow cover the next twenty-five verses of the prose, and it is no small feat that Cyprianus condenses nearly 500 hundred words to 120. *Abbreviation* is the strategy throughout, which begs the question, what does the poet keep or add, when so few words of the Bible are retained? To give a physical impression of just how much material has been omitted, I have included all twenty-five verses of the Bible (5–24):

3 et dixit deus (dominus) fiat lux et facta est lux. 4 et uidit deus (dominus) lucem (lumen) quia bona est et diuisit deus inter lucem et tenebras. 5 et uocauit deus lucem diem et tenebras uocauit noctem et facta est uespera et factum est mane dies unus (primus). 6 et dixit deus fiat firmamentum in medio aquae et sit diuisio inter aquam et aquam et sic est factum. 7 et fecit deus firmamentum et diuisit deus inter aquam quae est super firmamentum et inter aquam quae est sub firmamento. 8 et uocauit deus firmamentum caelum et uidit deus quia

---

35 Peiper cites Lucretius once in his *Auctores Imitatores*, and that allusion also refers to *Genesis* and the death of Adam (*Gen.* 198): "Nongentos igitur postquam complerat Adamus / Ter denosque annos, sopitus morte quieuit" ("Therefore, after Adam had fulfilled nine hundred and thirty years, having been lulled to sleep, he took rest in death"). The corresponding passage in Lucretius describes the death of Homer in similar terms (*sopitus quietest*, 3.1036), though two other near echoes appear earlier in *De rerum natura*, one of them at the opening of the poem. In the preface, Lucretius appeals to Venus to end all wars, to "put them to rest" (*sopita quiescant, praef.* 30), and in Book 3, death is associated with the sleep of the mind and body (3.920): "Cum pariter mens et corpus sopita quiescunt" ("though mind and body rest in sleep").

bonum est et facta est uespera et factum est mane dies secundus. 9 et dixit deus congregetur aqua quae sub caelo est in congregationem unam et uideatur arida et sic est factum et congregata est aqua in congregationem unam. 10 et uocauit deus aridam terram et congregationem aquae uocauit mare et uidit deus quia bonum est. 11 et dixit deus germinet terra herbam pabuli ferentem semen secundum genus et similitudinem et lignum fructuosum (pomiferum) faciens fructum cuius semen sit in se secundum suam similitudinem et sic est factum. 12 et eiecit terra herbam pabuli ferentem semen secundum suum genus et lignum fructiferum faciens fructum cuius semen est in se secundum suam similitudinem et uidit deus quia bonum est. 13 et facta est uespera et factum est mane dies tertius. 14 et dixit deus fiant luminaria in firmamento caeli ita ut luceant super terram et diuidant inter diem et noctem et sint in signis et in temporibus et in diebus et in annis et sint in splendorem in firmamento caeli ita ut luceant super terram et sic est factum. 16 et fecit deus duo luminaria maiora luminare maius in initium diei et luminare minus in initium noctis et stellas. 17 et posuit illas deus in firmamento caeli sic ut luceant super terram. 18 et praesint diei et nocti et diuidant inter diem et noctem et uidit deus quia bonum est. 19 et facta est uespera et factum est mane dies quartus. 20 et dixit deus eiciant aquae reptilia animarum uiuarum et uolatilia uolantia super terram sub firmamento caeli et sic est factum. 21 et fecit deus coetos magnos et omnem animam animalium repentium quae eiecerunt aquae secundum uniuscuiusque genus et omne uolatile pennatum secundum suum genus et uidit deus quia bona sunt. 22 et benedixit illa deus dicens crescite et multiplicamini et implete aquas maris et uolatilia multiplicentur super terram. 23 et facta est uespera et factum est mane dies quintus. 24 et dixit deus eiciat terra animam uiuam secundum unumquodque genus quadrupedum et serpentium et bestiarum terrae secundum genus et pecora secundum genus et omnia reptilia ad genus et sic est factum. 25 et fecit deus bestias terrae secundum genus et pecora secundum genus et omnia serpentia terrae secundum genus et uidit deus quia bonum est.

– Gen 1:3–25

5

Has dum disiungi iussit, a cardine fatur:
"Lux fiat!" et clare nituerunt omnia mundo.
Cum dominus primi complesset facta diei,[36]
Condidit albentem nebulis nascentibus axem.

---

36   Cf. Hrabanus Maurus, *Laudes crucis* (1.15–16): "Principium ut Genesis pie sancto dogmate pandit, / Quod hominem faciens complesset facta creator."

Accipit immensus errantia litora pontus,
Multiplices rapiens ualidis cum tractibus amnes.   10
Tertia lux faciem terrarum fulua retexit.
Arida mox posito narratur nomine terra.
Florea uentosis consurgunt germina campis
Pomiferique simul procuruant brachia rami.
Quarta die generat solis cum lampade lunam,   15
Et stellas tremulo radiantes lumine figit.
Haec elementa dedit subiecto insignia mundo,
Tempora quae doceant uarios mutanda per ortus.
Quinta die accipiunt liquentia flumina pisces
Et uolucres uarias suspendunt aere pinnas.   20
Sexta pater gelidos in spiras lubricat angues
Quadrupedumque greges totos diffundit in agros
Cunctaque multiplici mandauit crescere passim
Germine et inmensis errare et pascere terris.

[These he bade be divided, calling from the threshold: "Let there be light!" and everything shone brightly in the world. When the Lord had finished the deeds of the first day, he made the heavens white with nascent clouds. The boundless sea received wandering shores, drawing many rivers with strong currents. On the third day, tawny light revealed the face of the earth. Soon, "dry land" was spoken, its name established. Flowery buds sprang up on wind-swept fields and branches of fruit-laden boughs bent forward. On the fourth day, he created the moon with the brightness of the sun and set the stars to shine with quivering light. He gave these elements as signs for the world below, that they may teach the changing seasons by their various appearances. On the fifth day, clear streams received fish, and birds set varied wings upon the air. On the sixth day, the Father slid icy serpents into their coils and scattered four-footed herds on all the fields and bade all things everywhere increase with manifold seed, to wander and feed on the boundless lands.]

In favour of economy, the repetition in the prose of the words, *deus*, *lux*, *aqua*, *firmamentum*, *dixit*, *semen*, *secundum genus*, and variations of *et uidit deus quia bonum est* is reduced to a minimum by Cyprianus, and like Juvencus he avoids the periphrastic expression *factum est* altogether.[37]

---

37 Green notes the same omission in *Euangeliorum libri*. See above chapter 2.

Also, while the prose repeats forms of *terra* twelve times, Cyprianus uses it only twice, again to avoid redundancy.[38] The noun, *deus*, likewise appears twenty-five times in the biblical Genesis but not at all in the corresponding lines of the *Heptateuch*. Only once does Cyprianus mention God directly and only then as *dominus* (8). The biblical foundation of the poetry, then, is supplied by other keywords, notably the days of creation.[39] Like Juvencus, who imitates the structure of the biblical prose in his rendition of the Sermon on the Mount (1.452–68), Cyprianus puts the names of the days of creation at intervals and at the same point in the line, to provide similar structure.

In doing so, he reveals some of the metrical irregularities Peiper and others have noticed. For example, line six contains the famous words *Lux fiat* ("Let there be light"), but the line only scans if the two syllables of *fiat* are made to be short (*Lūx fĭăt*, 6). The "i" in *fīo* is long by nature, however, and cannot be short by position, as it is here.[40] Farther down, the adjectives *Tertia* and *Sexta* in verses eleven and twenty-one should be ablatives of time, like *Quarta die* (15) and *Quinta die* (19), but they have to be nominative in order to fit the metre.[41] This results in an unlikely translation of line fifteen: "The third tawny light revealed the face of the earth." What the author means is "On the third day, tawny light revealed the face of the earth," but that is not what the metre dictates. In verse twenty-one, two nominatives compete for subject of the sentence, and further confirm that Cyprianus is being free with his ablatives: "Sexta pater gelidos in spiras lubricat angues." The "a" in *pater* is short by nature and so the "a" in *Sexta* must be short by position (i.e., nominative). The resulting translation

---

38 See above chapter 2 for a discussion of rhetorical variation in *Euangeliorum libri*.

39 Other biblical language here includes *Lux fiat* (6), *dominus* (7), *facta* (7), *diei* (7), *arida* (12), *stellas* (15), *insignia* for *signa* (17), *tempora* (18), *Quadrupedumque* (22), *multiplici* (23), *crescere* (23).

40 In his 1560 edition of the text, Morel says, "the creative *Fiat* as a pyrrhic is wanting in majesty," and so he emends. See further Mayor, *The Latin Heptateuch Published Piecemeal by the French Printer William Morel 1560 and the French Benedictines 1733*, 3. Morel notes Gen. 282 and 429, and adds (rightly), "As I find this license rarely in contemporary poets, or in our poem … and very slight changes are needed to correct … I read without hesitation, *Lux fiat, claro et nituerunt omnia mundo*." He emends on the basis of one ms. reading that contains *laeto* in place of *clare* (i.e., "*lux fiat, et laeto nituerunt omnia mundo*").

41 For other occasions when a long "a" is shortened, see Peiper's *Index Metricus*, 344. The tendency of Cyprianus to shorten vowels at the beginning of lines is also noted by Mayor, *Latin Heptateuch*, xlviii–liii.

makes no sense: "The sixth, the father slipped icy serpents into their coils"; it should read, "On the sixth [day], the father slipped icy serpents into their coils." Also, the two "proper" ablatives of time, *Quarta die* (15) and *Quinta die* (19), scan in the same way. The final syllable of both is short, but it should be long. Other signs in this passage indicate the poet's inexperience, including his dependence on 3rd declension nouns in the 5th foot, which ease the composition of hexameters, as well as a similar choice of third-conjugation verbs in the same position.[42] Cyprianus also relies on a single metrical pattern throughout this passage, DDSS, which appears in 40 per cent of the verses, not to mention other liberties with the quantity of vowels.[43] Collectively, this evidence reinforces the prevailing view that Cyprianus is a less experienced and proficient poet than Juvencus and his classical antecedents.

That being said, much of the language at the opening of the *Heptateuch* aspires to the eloquent style of *Euangeliorum libri* and classical epic. The simple substitution of *fatur* (5) for *dixit* in the prose is telling. The same word appears often in the *Aeneid* as a formula, introducing speeches.[44] In the *Heptateuch*, the word helps to infuse God's words with an air of epic grandeur, a function it also serves in *Euangeliorum libri*.[45] The verb *condidit* (8) also evokes the epic as foundation narrative, which is fitting in the context of Creation. The opening lines of the *Aeneid* point to the ultimate purpose of the hero's journey, to found a city (*conderet urbem*, 1.5), and Aeneas does so by the blood of Turnus in Book 12, plunging his sword into his chest ("ferrum aduerso sub pectore condit," 12.950). It is also noteworthy that Cyprianus does not use the word *gesta* instead of *facta* (7), to describe "the deeds of the [first] day" (*complesset facta diei*, 7). That

---

42 Thus *cardine fatur* (5), *omnia mundo* (6), *litora pontus* (9), *tractibus amnes* (10), *nomina terra* (12), *germina campis* (13), *brachia rami* (14, though not a third-declension noun), *lampade lunam* (15), *lumine figit* (16), *insignia mundo* (17), *flumine pisces* (19), *aere pinnas* (20).

43 For the clustering of the pattern, DDSS, see lines 11–15 and 20–3. For other irregularities in quantity note that both of the vowels in *solis* (15) are made long by position, which is not ideal but acceptable. The "i" in *subiecto* (17) is also made a vowel, but it regularly scans as a consonant, *subjecto*, and *aere pinnas* scans as a dactyl, but the second syllable of *aere* should be long. Also, *errare et pascere* (24) scans as two dactyls with elision of "-e" in *errare*, but *et* should be long by position, given the following "p" in *pascere*.

44 See further *Aen.* 1.131; 1.256; 2.76; 2.107; 2.147; 3.309; 3.385; 3.612 et passim. See Juvencus, 1.348; 1.378; 2.413; 3.138; 3.185; 3.187 et passim.

45 See further *Ev.*, 1.348; 1.378; 2.413; 3.138; 3.185; 3.187 et passim.

would have aligned the creative accomplishments of God with the "life-giving deeds of Christ" (*Christi uitalia gesta*, *praef.* 19) in *Euangeliorum libri* and the *gesta* of epic, but Cyprianus settles on *facio*, perhaps because the meaning of the word ("to make") better suits the context of Creation.

Other language points to earlier classical poetry, even if the precise sources are difficult to isolate. The use of the verb *accipit* in lines nine and nineteen is reminiscent of Ovid's use of the word in the *Metamorphoses*, but may equally originate elsewhere.[46] It is a poetic turn of phrase, however, with no counterpart in the prose.[47] Line thirteen is a golden line, a stylistic hallmark of classical verse: "Florea uentosis consurgunt germina campis,"[48] and line twelve is near golden, but for the appearance of the adverb *mox*. Peiper cites Vergil's *Eclogues* as a potential source for that line (5.25–6), "nulla neque amnem / libauit quadrupes nec graminis attigit herbam" ("nor did any four-footed beast drink from the water or touch a blade of grass"), but it is not a close parallel. Closer is a line from Hilary's *Metrum in Genesin*, a contemporary of Cyprianus (*Met. Gen.*, 101): "Herbarum uaria consurgunt gramina campis." The *Carmen aduersus Marcionitas* also offers a potential link, a poem from which Cyprianus may also borrow the phrase, *inmensus deus* (2.232–4): "Si quaeras, non est: cum uult deus, esse uide-tur. / Arboribus folia, spinis rosa, germina campis / Mortua deficiunt, et rur-sus uiua resurgunt" ("If you look for it, you will not find it. When God wishes it, it appears. Leaves on the trees, the rose with thorns, buds in the fields, dead, they die and, living, they rise again").[49] Note the verbatim use of the phrase *germina campis* (2.233) and the verb *resurgunt* (2.234) at the end of the passage, which nearly matches *consurgunt* in the *Heptateuch* (13). The context is also the same: God's creative power.

Elsewhere, line fourteen begins with a polysyllabic word that can be found in the Vulgate, *pomiferum*, and Cyprianus incorporates it into the poem: "Pomiferique simul procuruant brachia rami" ("the limbs of fruit-laden branches bend forward," 14). The end of the verse, however, is also

---

46 Cf. *Ars amatoria* 2.334 ("multas accipit amnis aquas"); *Heroides* 5.42 ("Caerula ceratas accipit unda rates."); *Met.* 11.475 ("Carbasa deducit uenientesque accipit auras"); *Fasti* 4.472 ("Quaque Symaetheas accipit aequor aquas"). Cf. also *Met.* 1.75 also in the context of creation: "terra feras cepit, uolucres agitabilis aer" ("the land receives beasts, the light air, birds").

47 Cf. Juvencus, *Ev.* 2.31, for similar understatement.

48 Line twelve is near golden: "Arida mox posito narratur nomine terra."

49 The Latin text is taken from Pollmann, ed., *Das Carmen adversus Marcionitas*; see also Thraede, "Epos," 1016.

reminiscent of a passage in Vergil's *Georgics*, "when the almond in the fragrant forests is more deeply clothed in blossom and bends her limbs" (1.187–8: "cum se nux plurima siluis induet in florem et ramos curuabit olentis"). The next verse, line fifteen, "Quarta die generat solis cum lampade lunam," recalls a line from Martial's epigrams, where the poet describes the brightness of a cup in terms of the moon (8.50.7–8): "Materiae non cedit opus: sic alligat orbem, / plurima cum tota lampade luna nitet" ("The work is not inferior to the material; it surrounds the cup, as the moon surrounds the earth, when she shines at the full with all her light").[50] Line 19, "Et uolucres uarias suspendunt aere pinnas," coincides with language in Ovid's *Metamorphoses* at the point where Apollo turns Daedalion into a bird (11.341): "Fecit auem et subitis pendentem sustulit alis."[51] All of this language, whatever its source, serves to elevate the literary status of the *Heptateuch* and give new life to the stories of the Bible.[52] The addition of many colourful adjectives and participles in this scene serves the same purpose, to bring fresh colour and vitality to the prose. Such pairings include, *albentem* ("whitening") with *axem* ("sky"), *nascentibus* ("nascent") with *nebulis* ("clouds," both in line 8), *inmensus* ("vast") with *pontus* ("sea"), *errantia* ("wandering") with *litora* ("shores," both in 9), *multiplices* ("manifold") with *amnes* ("streams"), *ualidis* ("strong") with *tractibus* ("tracts," both in 10), *fulua* ("tawny") with *lux* ("light," 11), *arida* ("dry") with *terra* ("earth," 12), *florea* ("flowery") with *germina* ("buds"), *uentosis* ("windy") with *campis* ("plains," both in 13), *pomiferi* ("fruit-laden") with *rami* ("branches," 14), *tremulo* ("quivering") with *lumine* ("light"), *radiantes* ("beaming") with *stellas* ("stars," both in 16), *liquentia* ("flowing") with *flumina* ("rivers," 19), *uarias* ("variegated") with *pinnas*

---

50 The translation of Martial is that of Bohn, *The Epigrams of Martial*. See also Avienus' *Aratea*: "Desuper in nubes, rutilantis lampada lunae / Pascitur umore et uarias dea lumine formas." See further Taub, "Translating the *Phainomena* Across Genre Language and Culture," 119–38 at 133.

51 Avitus later also alludes to Ovid or Cyprianus in his description of the first-flying birds in *HS* (1.32–4).

52 For other echoes in this scene consider line 17 ("Haec elementa dedit subiecto insignia mundo") and Prudentius' *Contra Symm*. 132–4: "Cuncta equidem quae gignit humus quae continet ipse / Principio institui, nitidoque insignia mundo / Ornamenta dedi speciosaque semina finxi" ("for everything the earth bears, which it itself contains, I have established from the beginning, and I have given great ornaments to the shining world and made wondrous seeds"); or line nineteen, "Quinta die accipiunt liquentia flumina pisces," which may echo Verg. *Aen*. 9.679: "Quales aeriae liquentia flumina circum," which describes Pandarus and Bitias in Book 9, who are like tall oaks by running rivers.

("wings," 20), *gelidos* ("icy") with *angues* ("serpents," 21), *totos* ("all") with *agros* ("fields," 22), and *immensis* ("vast") with *terris* ("lands," 24). These added words, one or two from the Bible, enhance the essential meaning of the scriptural text and intensify the feeling of vitality at Creation, not to mention the impression of God's great power (*immensus deus*, 3), who instils the land and sea with something of his own boundless potential (*immensus pontus*, 9, *immensis terris*, 24).

Adam & Eve (*Gen.* 25–41)

The account of the creation of Adam and Eve in the *Heptateuch* is conflated from incidents in chapters 1 and 2 of Genesis. Such synchronization is not unusual. Cyprianus often rearranges things to reduce apparent inconsistencies in the original or improve the flow of the verse.[53] The lines here cover chapter 1, verses 26–8 of the prose (the creation of Adam), but incorporate chapter 2, 7–8 and the genesis of Eve, which does not come until chapter 2, verses 18–25 of the Bible. Highlighting such minor adjustments shows that Cyprianus does more than simply follow the Scriptures word for word. He rearranges, condenses, and adapts (25–41):

> 1:26 et dixit deus faciamus hominem ad imaginem et similitudinem nostram habeat potestatem piscium maris et uolatilium caeli et omnium pecorum et ferarum et omnis terrae et omnium reptilium quae super terram repunt. 27 et fecit (formauit) deus hominem ad imaginem dei fecit illum masculum et feminam fecit illos.
>
> – Gen 1:26–7

> 2:7 et tunc finxit (fecit) deus hominem (ad imaginem et similitudinem suam) de limo terrae et insufflavit (inspirauit) in faciem eius spiritum uitae et factus est homo in animam uiuentem ... 18 et dixit dominus deus non est bonus hominem solum faciamus illi adiutorium similem sibi ... 21 et inmisit deus soporem (somnium) in Adam et obdormiuit et sumpsit deus unam de costis eius et impleuit locum eius carne 22 et formauit deus costam quam accepit ab Adam in mulierem et adduxit illam ad Adam ut uideret quid eam uocaret 23 et dixit Adam hoc nunc os ex ossibus meis et caro de carne mea haec uocabitur mulier quoniam de uiro suo sumpta est et haec erit mihi adiutorium 24 propter hoc

---

53 See further Roberts, *Biblical Epic*, 128–9, who discusses the poet's rearrangement of the biblical narrative in this scene.

relinquet homo patrem et matrem et adiungetur (adhaerebit) uxori suae et erunt duo in carnem unam 25 et erant ambo nudi Adam et mulier eius et non confundebantur.

– Gen 2:7, 18, 21–5

25

Haec ubi constituit diuina potentia iussu,
Rectorem inspiciens mundanis defore rebus,
Haec memorat: "Hominem nostris faciamus in unguem
Vultibus adsimilem toto qui regnet in orbe."
Et licet hunc solo posset componere uerbo,
Ipse tamen sancta dignatus ducere dextra   30
Inspirat brutum diuino a pectore pectus.
Quem postquam effigie formatum ceu sua uidit,
Metitur[54] solum mordaces uoluere curas.
Ilicet irriguo perfundit lumina somno,
Mollius ut uulsa formetur femina costa   35
Atque artus mixta geminos substantia firmet,
Inditur et nomen, uitae quod dicitur, Aeuua.
Quapropter nati linquunt de more parentes
Coniugibusque suis positis cum sedibus haerent.
Septima luce deus factorum fine quieuit.   40
Sacratam statuens uenturi ad gaudia saecli.

[When divine power established these things according to its bidding, seeing no governor for earthly affairs, He said: "Let us make man perfectly in our own image, that he may rule over all the world." And although He could have fashioned him by word alone, nevertheless deigning to draw him out with His holy hand, He breathed into the lifeless breast from His own divine breast. After He saw him formed in His likeness, He did not suffer him to think on biting cares alone. At once He covered his eyes with pervading sleep, so that woman could be formed more gently from the rib withdrawn, and their combined substance strengthened her limbs. And the name "Eve" was given to her, which means, "of life." So by custom children leave their parents and cleave to their spouses, leaving their own homes. At the seventh light, when He was done creating, God rested, making it a holy day for the joy of future generations.]

---

54 This is the variant reading of *non patitur* in Peiper's edition.

Charles Witke has said of this scene, "there is no place in this text for the poet to stand. He is simply an entrepreneur of a received text, whose data he follows closely ... Cyprian is sober, industrious, but unengaged."[55] It is true, much of the language here leads back to the Bible, and much of it is well known, beginning with the verbatim echo of the prose *faciamus hominem* ("Let us make man") in line twenty-seven. There is no mistaking the context. So, too, the phrase *nostris ... uultibus adsimilem* follows the Bible closely (*similitudinem nostram*), as do several other keywords in the passage: *Inspirat* (30)/*inspirauit* (breathing life into Adam); *formatum* (32)/*formauit* (forming him); *somno* (34)/*somnium* (putting him to sleep); and *costa* (35)/*costa* (removing his rib). These words are markers of the prose, and Cyprianus introduces them as part of the biblical substructure of his poetic narrative. It is certainly fair to call this passage a *paene ad uerbum* translation of the original.

Even so, Cyprianus takes some pains to restructure and abbreviate the Genesis account in the *Heptateuch*, so that it flows more smoothly. The creation of Eve is placed shortly after that of Adam, to resolve language at the end of verse twenty-seven in the Bible which mentions the creation of man and woman before the birth of Eve: "et fecit deus hominem ad imaginem dei fecit illum masculum et feminam fecit illos" ("and God made man in the image of God; he made them man and woman"). Cyprianus also condenses much biblical material in these sixteen lines, whittling down some 600 words to 100, as he works through the end of chapter 1 (26–31) and the whole of chapter 2 (1–25). He does not include the point that Adam is made from "the mud of the earth" (*de limo terrae*, 2:7), however, nor does he mention God's creation of Paradise (2:8), its wondrous trees (2:9), or the four-headed river that flows out of Eden (2:10–15). He says nothing about God's admonition to Adam to avoid the tree of knowledge (2:16–18) but moves briskly from Creation to the Fall. Still, it is hardly fair to call him "unengaged."

The Temptation & Fall (*Gen.* 72–90)

In his rendition of the Fall, Cyprianus loosens the reins somewhat and surrenders to his artistic impulses. He introduces considerable extra-biblical language, to vilify Eve and align her with the green "softness" of Paradise, so that she may be seen as more susceptible to the promptings of

---

55 Witke, *Numen Litterarum*, 191.

Satan. At this moment in the *Heptateuch*, we see Cyprianus at his best (72–90):

3:1 serpens autem erat sapientior (astutior, callidior) omnium bestiarum (animalibus) quae erant super terram quas fecerat dominus deus et dixit serpens ad mulierem quare (cur) dixit deus ne edatis ab omni ligno quod est in paradiso 2 et dixit mulier … 3 … dixit deus ne edamus sed neque tangamus (contingetis) ne moriamur 4 et dixit serpens mulieri non morte moriemini 5 sciebat enim deus quoniam qua die ederitis ex illo aperientur oculi uestri et scientes bonum et malum 6 et uidit mulier quia bonum (dulcis, suaue) est lignum in escam et quia bonum (pulchrum) est oculis ad uidendum et (speciosum est ad intuendum) cognoscendum et sumpsit fructum de ligno illo et manducavit et dedit uiro suo et accepit Adam et manducauit 7 et aperti sunt oculi eorum et tunc scierunt (uiderunt) quia nudi erant et suerunt sibi folia fici et fecerunt sibi tegimenta.

– Gen 3:1–7

Has inter sedes et bacis mitibus hortos
Spumeus astuto uincens animalia sensu
Serpebat tacite spiris frigentibus anguis;
Liuida mordaci uoluens mendacia sensu   75
Femineo temptat sub pectore mollia corda:
"Dic mihi, cur metuas felicia germina mali?
Numquid poma Deus non omnia nata sacrauit?
Atqui si studeas mellitos carpere uictus,
Aureus astrigero ridebit cardine mundus."   80
Illa negat uetitosque timet contingere ramos;
Sed tamen infirmo uincuntur pectora sensu.
Ilicet ut niueo iam mitia dente momordit,
Adfulsit nulla maculatum nube serenum.
Tum sapor inlecebram mellitis faucibus indens   85
Perpulit insueto munus deferre marito.
Quod simul ac sumpsit, detersa nocte nitentes
Emicuere oculi mundo splendente sereni.
Ergo ubi nudatum prospexit corpus uterque
Quae pudenda uident, ficulnis frondibus umbrant.   90

[Among these seats and gardens with their ripened berries, a seething serpent, surpassing other animals in cunning wit, silently slithered on icy coils. Mingling jealous lies with mordant wit, he tempted the soft heart beneath the womanly breast: "Tell me, why do you fear the fruitful buds of the apple? Did not God hallow all the fruits He made? Besides, if you seek to pick this honey-sweet food, the golden world will smile down from the starry heights." The woman refused and feared to touch the forbidden boughs, and yet her heart was overcome by a feeble mind. And as soon as she bit the ripened fruit with a snowy tooth, clarity untainted by a single cloud dawned upon her. As the taste poured the bait down her honey-sweet throat, it urged her to extend this gift unto her innocent husband. And as soon as he tasted it, darkness disappeared and, shining with clarity, their eyes widened at the radiant world. Then when each saw the naked body of the other, which now seemed shameful, they shaded themselves with fig leaves.]

The fruitful, pleasant groves of Paradise stand in sharp contrast to the image of the malevolent serpent, whose cold, soundless movement through the garden is illicit.[56] The repetition of *sensus* (73, 75) from the outset highlights Satan's uncommon cunning, which accounts for his success, and his wit is "conquering" (*uincens*, 73) and "biting" (*mordaci … sensu*, 75) – double-edged puns that foreshadow his viciousness and Eve's coerced consumption of the fruit. Satan's lies are "livid" (*liuida mendacia*, 75), which means "spiteful" or "malicious" but also "bruised" or "discoloured" in the context of over-ripened fruit. The potential for both senses is effective among Eden's more mellow berries (*bacis mitibus*, 72), which are wholesome, ripe, and ready to eat. Satan's words, on the other hand, are rotten.[57]

Eve is the unwitting victim in all of this, but she is (as always) the more compelling character than Adam. Like the garden berries themselves (*bacis mitibus hortos*, 72), Eve is *mollis*, "soft" or "mild," as if to say, ripe for the picking. So the fruit slides easily down her "soft," pliant throat ("Femineo temptat sub pectore mollia corda," 76), again to imply that her resolve is weaker than that of Adam, and yet he fares no better in the crisis and falls from grace in less than a line ("Quod simul ac sumpsit," 87). Cyprianus says nothing about his conscience or his heart, but lavishes attention on Eve and the rhetoric of Satan. The serpent's question, "Dic mihi, cur metuas felicia germina mali?" ("Tell me, why do you fear the fruitful buds of the apple?"), contains a pun that appears often in Christian poetry, in which

---

56 Note, however, that Cyprianus describes the creation of serpents in similar terms (*Gen.* 21): "Sexta pater gelidos in spiras lubricat angues."

57 Cf. Sedulius, *Carmen paschale* (1.51–4), who describes paganism in similar terms and aligns it with Satanism.

malum means "apple" or "evil," depending of the length of the vowel. It must be "apple" here, given its position in the line (*mālum*), but it is hard to ignore what the ear can detect and the eye can see on the page. Innocent Eve, although she knows the branches of the tree are forbidden (*uetitosque … ramos*, 81), is disadvantaged by a weak wit, and the repetition of *sensus* in line eighty-two punctuates this point (82): "Sed tamen infirmo uincuntur pectora sensu" ("and yet her heart is conquered by her feeble mind"). Cyprianus repeats both the verb *uinco* (82, 73) and *sensu* (73, 75, 83) from the opening of the passage – both of which appear in the same position of the line – to re-emphasize the fact of Satan's superior guile and Eve's inescapable gullibility. She can do nothing but succumb, and so she bites the apple with a snowy tooth ("Ilicet ut niueo iam mitia dente momordit," 83), a token of her innocence and the loss of it. It is also an echo of the biting wit of Satan (*mordaci … sensu*, 75). It may or may not be going to far here to suggest an echo of *mors* ('death') in the verb *momordit*.

In general, little of the significant language in this passage links it to the Bible or supports the assumption that Cyprianus is either literal or conservative in his response to the scriptural text. There is an artist's hand at work in this scene that aims not just to versify the prose but offer something more. Specific traces of the Bible appear in the words *astuto* (73), *animalia* (73), the *serp-* in *serpebat* (74), *dic* (77), *cur* (77), *omnia* (78), *contingere* (81), *sumpsit* (87), *nudatum* (89), and *ficulis* (90), none of which is especially emphatic. All of the meaningful words in the scene come from Cyprianus: the initial, bucolic description of Paradise (72); the emphatic repetition of *sensus*, which highlights Satan's cunning and Eve's susceptibility (73, 75, 82); the lively characterization of the serpent as *spumeus* (73) and *uincens* (73), and his biting, treacherous wit (75); the portrayal of Eve as soft-hearted (*mollia corda*, 76); her infirmity of sense (*infirmo sensu*, 82); and her snowy-toothed innocence (*niueo dente*, 83), a possible echo of the teeth-torn lover's letter in Ovid's *Heroides* ("Forsitan admotis etiam tangere labellis, / Rumpere dum niueo uincula dente uolet" ("Perhaps to be touched by her enclosing lips as she resolves to tear the seal with a snowy tooth," 18.17–18). Overall, this is a thoughtfully crafted scene in which Cyprianus condenses the biblical source and introduces new drama to one of the most famous passages in the Bible.

The Flood (*Gen.* 287–321)

In versifying the account of the Flood and Noah's ark, Cyprianus likewise adapts the prose appreciably, by eliminating repetition and contradictions that appear in the prose.[58] Economy is again the practice throughout, and Cyprianus rearranges the verses of the Bible to suit the poetic rendition. Much extra-biblical language is also introduced, to intensify the drama of the Deluge. Note that I, too, have rearranged the verses of the Bible, to accord with the narrative sequence of the poetry (*Gen.* 287–310):

> 7:11 … proruperunt omnes fontes abyssi et cataractae caeli patefactae sunt. 12 et factae sunt pluuiae diluuii super omnem terram quadraginta diebus et quadraginta noctibus.
>
> 7:21 et mortua est omnis caro quae mouebatur super terram, uolatilium (uolucrum), pecorum et iumentorum, et ferarum et omnis serpens qui mouetur super terram et omnis homo 22 et omnia (cuncta) quaecumque habent spiritum uitae et omnis qui erat super aridam mortuus est. 23 et deleta est omnis suscitatio quae erat super faciem omnis terrae, ab homine usque ad pecudem et repentium et uolatilium caeli et deleta sunt de terra. et derelictus est solus Noe in arca cum iis qui cum ipso erant.
>
> 7:18 Vehementer inundaverunt et omnia repleverunt in superficie terrae porro arca ferebatur super summum aquarum.
>
> 8:1 et memor fuit dominus Noe et bestiarum et iumentorum qui cum illo erant et tunc misit dominus spiritum super terram et abstinuit aquam. 2 et conclusi sunt fontes abyssi (aquarum) et cataractae caeli et detenta est pluuia de caelo. 3 cessauit aqua de terra euntes et redeuntes et coeperunt minui post centum quinquaginta dies. 4 et sedit arca in mense septimo septima et uicensima mensis super montes Ararat. 5 aqua autem minuebatur (decrescebant) usque ad undecimum mensem in undecimo autem mense prima die mensis apparuerunt capita montium. 6 post quadraginta dies aperuit Noe ostium arcae quod fecit 7 et emisit coruum ut uideret utrum cessasset aqua et exiens non est reuersus (rediit) donec siccaret aqua a terra. 8 et emisit columbam post eum ut uideret si cessasse(n)t aqua(e) super faciem terrae. 9 non inueniens columba requiem pedibus suis reuersa est (rediit) ad eum in arca et extendit manum suam accepit eam et induxit eam semetipsum in arcam 10 tenuit septem diebus aliis et iterum dimisit columbam ex arca 11 et reuersa est columba ad eum sub uespera(m) habens ramum oleae (folium oleae et ramum, portans ramum oliuae uirentibus foliis) in ore suo et cognouit Noe quia defecit aqua a terra.
>
> – Gen. 7:11–8:11

---

58 See further Roberts, *Biblical Epic*, 130–1, who discusses the poet's handling of repetition and contradiction in the Bible.

Interea totos laxarunt nubila nimbos,
Atque abyssus riguos dimisit in aequora fontes.
Iamque quater denis stagnantur cuncta diebus.
Non uolucres leuibus suspendunt corpora pinnis,   290
Nec fera celsiiugo deuitat marmora colle,
Omnia conduntur pelago, mors omnibus una est.
Nec minus interea tumidum suspensa per aequor
Arca fluens clausum munibat pendula uatem
Venturisque parens seruabat semina saeclis   295
Naufragio secura suo. Mox rarior aether
Nubibus in piceis coepit constringere nimbos.
Iamque relabenti decrescit in aequore pontus
Ac, postquam modico fluitabat flumine cumba,
Emittit senior nigrantem pectora coruum,   300
Qui leuibus pinnis uolucri dum flamine fertur,
Non rediit, iusti suspendens uota prophetae.
Post hunc albentem mittit per stagna columbam,
Quae super aequoreum campum defessa uolatu,
Nusquam nancta solum, uati se reddidit almo.   305
Cumque recurrentis fulgerent septima solis
Lumina, dimittit pinna plaudente uolucrem,
Quae nemore inuento ramis praepinguis oliuae
Ora referta tulit, cum iam per sidera uesper
Surgeret ac tremulo noctem praecurreret igni.   310

[Meanwhile the clouds unleashed the rains, and the abyss released flowing springs into the oceans. And already within forty days everything was flooded. Birds did not suspend their bodies on light wings, nor did the beasts of the heaven-touching hills escape the marbled deep. Everything was brought together by the sea, one death for all. Meanwhile, floating over the swelling ocean, the pendulous ark protected the prophet shut therein and the father saved the seeds of future generations, safe from its own destruction (shipwreck). Soon, a clearer sky began to bind the rains to the pitch-black clouds. And now the water receded with the ebb of the sea, and when the boat floated on the calm waters, the old man sent out a black-breasted crow that, while borne on light wings by the swift breeze, did not return, prolonging the prayers of the just prophet. Afterwards, he sent out a white dove over the watery plain that, wearied from flight and having found land nowhere, returned to the nurturing prophet. And when the seventh light of the returning sun shone, he sent out the bird on beating wings, which, when it found a forest, brought back in its mouth the branches of a lush olive tree, and then evening rose among the stars and preceded night with its flickering fire.]

Given the prominence classical poetry in biblical epic, one might expect to find echoes of Ovid's account of the flood in the *Metamorphoses* here (esp. *Met.* 1.260–347). But that is not the case, at least insofar as it would involve the kind of sustained reminiscence we find in Juvencus' rendition of the storm on the sea of Galilee in *Euangeliorum libri* (2.25–32), which borrows heavily from Vergil's tempests in the *Aeneid*. There are only a few potential, scattered echoes of Ovid in these lines. Verse 287 of the *Heptateuch* contains the verb *laxo*, which describes the initial release of the rain ("Interea totos laxarunt nubila nimbos"), and this word coincides with a cognate form at the same point in the *Metamorphoses*, where Jupiter commands the rivers let loose their waters (1.281): "Iusserat; hi redeunt ac fontibus ora relaxant" ("He commanded; they return and loose their streams from their mouths"). Cyprianus also uses the noun *fontes* in the next line, which may echo *fontibus* in the *Metamorphoses* (1.281), but it may equally echo the Bible, where it also appears (*omnes fontes*). In fact, Peiper cites this verse of the *Heptateuch* (288) as a potential source for the later *Alethia* of Victorius (2.467): "[de abysso] atque nouos pandit fontes torrentibus aequos" (2.467); but the only two words in common, *abyssus* and *fontes*, also appear in the Bible and therefore do not originate in the *Heptateuch*.

The alliterative doublet, *nubila nimbos* (287) may come from the account of the flood in the *Metamorphoses*. The words do appear in close proximity at the end of Ovid's sequence, where Jupiter calms the storm ("Nubila disiecit nimbisque aquilone remotis / Et caelo terras ostendit et aethera terris" ("He parts gloom from scattered cloud with the north wind and reveals earth to the heavens, heavens to the earth," 1.328–9). A few lines earlier, Ovid also uses the verb *stagno* to describe the inundated land – "Iuppiter ut liquidis stagnare paludibus orbem … uidet" ("When Jupiter sees the world flooded by clear waters …" 1.324–6). It is the same verb that appears at the opening of Cyprianus' account (289): "Iamque quater denis stagnantur cuncta diebus" ("And already in forty days everything is flooded"). Likewise, the verb *demittere* in verse 288 of the *Heptateuch* echoes Jupiter's resolve to flood the world in the first place ("Poena placet diuersa, genus mortale sub undis / Perdere et ex omni nimbos demittere caelo" ("A different punishment pleases him, to destroy the mortal race beneath the waves and send down pouring rains from all heaven," 1.260–1), and the phrase "totos … nimbos" in Cyprianus (287) may be adapted from Ovid's words, "ex omni nimbos … caelo" (1.261); but that is reaching, and so is the suggestion that Cyprianus adopts the adjective *piceus* ("pitch-black") in 297 from Ovid's scene ("Terribilem picea tectus caligine uultum" ["covering his dread face with pitch-black gloom," 1.265]), a word that describes Jupiter and not the weather. The only other suggestive link between the two episodes is the description of the weary bird in the *Metamorphoses*, which falls into the water, too tired fly on (1.307–8): "Quaesitisque diu terris, ubi sistere possit, / In mare lassatis uolucris uaga decidit alis ("Having looked for land for too long, somewhere to rest, the wandering bird falls upon weary wings into the sea"). In the *Heptateuch*, the dove barely manages to get back to the ark (304–5): "Quae super aequoreum campum defessa uolatu, / Nusquam nancta solum, uati se reddidit almo" ("Which, weary from its flight over the watery plain, finding land nowhere, returns to the nurturing prophet"). There may be an echo there, but overall there is little in these lines, apart from a few potential echoes, to suggest that Cyprianus models himself on Ovid in any meaningful way. In fact, much of the more vivid imagery of the *Metamorphoses* is absent, including the frightening scenes of doomed creatures swimming through the water.

In response to the Bible, Cyprianus abbreviates dramatically in favour of economy and eliminating redundancy (e.g., in 7:21–3). Remnants of Genesis survive in some twenty-five words of the 150 of poetry, and these track the order of the biblical prose closely, even matching the inflectional forms of the original (allowing for differences in tense). Such correspondences suggest that Cyprianus is working through the prose methodically, as he often does: *abyssi/abyssus* (288), *fontes/fontes* (288), *quadraginta diebus/quater denis … diebus* (289), *cuncta/cuncta* (289, though biblical *omnis* is more common), *uolucrum/uolucres* (290), *ferarum/fera* (291), *omnia/omnia* (292), *mortua est omnis/mors omnibus una est* (292), *arca/arca* (294), *coeperunt/coepit* (297), *decrescebant/decrescit* (398), *emisit coruum /emittit … coruum* (300), *non rediit/non rediit* (302), *emisit columbam/mittit … columbam* (303), *redit/reddidit* (305), *dimisit/dimittit* (307), *ramum oliuae/ramis … oliuae* (308), *in ore suo/ora* (309), *sub uespera(m)/uesper* (309). The sum of the poetic account therefore aims to represent the *facta* of the Bible over a florid adaptation of classical verse or a pathway to figural associations between the Flood and Baptism. The reference to the "seeds" stored up in the ark (295) is probably only a metaphor for the animals and family of Noah, meant to re-populate the world after the Flood. It does not suggest rebirth or redemption through Christ in any appreciable way.

Nonetheless, rhetorically and stylistically, Cyprianus is invested in the composition of this scene, even if the final product appeals primarily to the essential deeds of the Bible. Poetic variation throughout aspires to classical standards and helps to offset the repetitive prose of Genesis. Cyprianus uses as many synonyms for "water" as he can (e.g., *aequor, fons, pelagus, pontus, flumen, stagnum*, and *aequoreus campus*). On the other hand, some repetition in this scene may be emphatic. In verse 290 ("Non uolucres leuibus suspendunt corpora pinnis"), Cyprianus echoes Book 11 of the *Metamorphoses* and the scene in which Apollo turns Daedalion into a bird (11.341): "Fecit auem et subitis pendentem sustulit alis." More to the point, he also echoes himself and the opening of Genesis and the first creation of birds (*Gen.* 19–20): "Quinta die accipiunt liquentia flumina pisces / Et uolucres uarias suspendunt aere pinnas" ("On the fifth day, clear rivers receive fish and birds raise variegated wings upon the air"). So there is a potential connection in the mind of the poet between the birth of the world out of Chaos and its return to a primordial state at the Flood, leading to a rebirth of the world thereafter. Although it is tempting to connect these moments to salvation history, there is little explicit in the text to invite such an interpretation, although it may be in the back of the poet's mind.

The Destruction of Sodom & Gomorrah (*Gen.* 661–7)

The account of the destruction of Sodom and Gomorrah is even more dramatic than the Flood. While God forgoes the use of fire in the first case, he shows no restraint here in what is one of the most spectacular episodes of the Old Testament. Cyprianus takes special pains to elevate the prose to epic heights, in particular by channelling Vergil and Statius (*Gen.* 661–7):

> 24 Et pluit dominus super Sodomam et Gomorram sulphur et ignem a domino de caelo 25 et ciuitates illas euertitet omnem regionem et omnes inhabitantes in ciuitatibus et quae nascebantur de terra.[59]
>
> – Gen 19:24–5

> Mox fragor horrisono de sidere fulmina torquet
> Sulpureaeque ruunt olido cum turbine flammae,
> Quae pariter muros atque ardua culmina lambunt.
> Omnibus in cinerem celeri cum labe reuulsis

---

59   Gen. 19:24–5: "And the Lord rained upon Sodom and Gomorrah brimstone and fire from the Lord out of heaven. 25 And he destroyed these cities, and all the country about, all the inhabitants of the cities, and all things that spring from the earth."

Cernebat rutilo surgentes uertice flammas   665
Eminus Abramus, memori cum pectore tractans
In uerbis domini numquam se adiungere mendum.

[Soon a crash hurls lightning down from the dread-sounding sky, and sulphurous flames fell in a putrid swirl that lapped walls and towering peaks. As everything fell to ashes in the swift devastation, Abraham watched from the distance as the flames rose up, golden-red, to the heights, reflecting with a mindful heart on the words of the Lord, never to yoke oneself to sin.]

Evidence of the biblical language appears in only two words of the *Heptateuch*, *sulpur* (662) and *omnis* (664). If not for the reference to "Abraham" (666), there would be little to indicate the source of the poetry. God's agency, which is explicit in the prose ("Et pluit dominus ... a domino"), is attributed to nature now, to an anonymous "crash" and "sulphurous flames" ("fragor ... sulpureaeque ... flammae," 661–2) that might as well refer to Jupiter's thunderbolts. Many of the poetic turns of phrase in the *Heptateuch* have an epic ring about them. The self-consciously florid adjective, *horrisono* ("dread-sounding," 661), is rare and probably Vergilian (cf. *Aen.* 6.573, 9.55) or Statian (cf. *Theb.* 6.232).[60] The phrase *fulmina torquet* (661) also points to Vergil (*fulmina torques, Aen.* 6.208) or Ovid (*fulmina torquet, Ex ponto* 3.27), while other expressions echo similar language in Book 10 of the *Thebaid*, including *uertice flammas* (*Gen.* 665)/*uertice flammas* (*Theb.* 10.675), *pectore tractat* (*Gen.* 666)/*pectore tractans* (*Theb.* 10.934), and *ardua culmina* (*Gen.* 663)/"*Ardua* mox toruo metitur culmina uisu" (*Theb.* 10.840). None of these allusions, however, fits precisely with the context of the *Heptateuch*, and Cyprianus appears not to model his description on any particular episode from either the *Thebaid* or the *Aeneid*. Even so, it is clear that his creative sensibility will not content itself with the mere *facta* of the Bible in this case, as Cyprianus aspires to accommodate the more refined literary expectations of his time. The result is a scene that looks less like the Bible and more like epic.

Abraham & Isaac (*Gen.* 737–54)

That is not the case with the episode of Abraham and Isaac, which reflects the events of the Bible with little added thunder. It is a close rendition of

---

60 For the text of Statius, see further Hall et al., eds., *P. Papinius Statius*, 3 vols. See also Joyce, *Statius, Thebaid.*

the prose. One word does give pause, however, and it may hint at typology, but the core of the scene coincides with the incidents of Genesis (*Gen.* 737–54):

21:33–4 … Abraham uero plantauit nemus in Bersabee et inuocauit ibi nomen domini dei aeterni. 34 et habitauit Abraham in terra Philistinorum diebus multis. 22:1 et factum est post haec uerba temptauit deus Abraham et dixit ad illum Abraham Abraham et ille dixit ecce ego et dixit ei accipe filium tuum illum unicum quem dilexisti illum Isaac et uade in terram altam et inpones illum ibi hostiam in uno ex montibus de quo tibi dixero. 3 exsurgens autem Abraham mane strauit asinam suam et adhibuit secum duos pueros et Isaac filium suum et concidit ligna in holocaustum et surgens abiit et uenit ad locum quem dixit illi deus die tertia et respiciens Abraham oculis uidit locum a longe. 5 et dixit Abraham pueris suis sedete hic cum asina ego autem et puer pertransibimus usque illuc et cum adorauimus reuertemur ad uos. 6 accepit autem Abraham ligna ad holocaustum et inposuit Isaac fillio suo accepit autem et ignem in manu sua et gladium et abierunt ambo simul dixit autem Isaac ad Abraham patrem suum dicens pater qui dixit quid est fili et dixit ecce ignis et ligna ubi est ouis ad holocaustum. 8 dixit Abraham deus prouidebit sibi ouem ad holocaustum fili euntes ambo simul. 9 uenerunt ad locum quem dixerat illi deus et aedificauit Abraham altare (aram) et inposuit ligna et alligauit pedes Isaac filio suo et inposuit eum in altare super ligna. 10 et extendit Abraham manum suam ut acciperet gladium et iugularet filium suum. 11 et uocauit eum angelus domini de caelo et dixit illi Abraham Abraham ille autem dixit ecce ego … 13 et respiciens Abraham oculis suis uidit et ecce aries (ouis) unus (post tergum eius) tenebatur in uigulto Sabech cornibus et abiit Abraham et accepit arietem et obtulit eum (in) holocaustum pro Isaac filio suo.

Inde senex curuo terram dum sulcat aratro,
Ingentem laetis compleuit messibus aulam
Sublimemque deum supplex per uota precatus
Philistinorum placidus consedit in aruis.   740
In quibus aetherii temptatur numinis orsis,
Vnicus ut natus gladio decumbat ad aram.
Nec mora, cum tumidi conscendit culmina collis,
Cornipedem ducens famulis natoque uadentem.
Tertia iamque die, cum sol candentior axe   745
Fulgeret medio, totas dum contrahit umbras,
Dimittit pueros senior natumque capessit,
Vt sarmenta gerens, flammarum pabula, collo

Scanderet oppositi pariter fastigia collis.
Iamque adeo flammis surgentibus altar ad ipsum   750
Sistitur, euinctus manibus posterga retortis.
Dumque pater natum properat diffindere cultro,
Eminus albentem prospectat sedulus agnum,
Qui melius fuso compleret sacra cruore.

[Then, as the old man tilled the ground with a curved plough, he finished the great palace at the blessed time of harvest, and when he had humbly invoked the high Lord in prayer, he settled peacefully in the land of the Philistines. In the course of the ethereal Deity's work, Abraham was tested, to the end that his only son should die on the altar by the sword. Without delay, he climbed the peaks of a high-reaching hill, while leading a horn-hoofed beast in stride with servants and the boy. On the third day, as the sun shone more brightly in the midst of the sky, where it reined in all the shadows, the aged man dismissed his servants and seized the boy, so that, bearing wood (fodder for flames) he might ascend the ridge on the top of the opposite hill with him. Once there, with the flames rising up, the boy was taken to the altar, hands bound behind his back. And just when the father hastened to sacrifice his son with a knife, the diligent man saw a white lamb nearby, whose bloodshed better served the sacrificial rights.]

The language of the prose is reflected in the words *deum* (739), *Philistinorum* (740), *temptatur* (741), *unicus* (742), *gladio* (742), *aram* (742), *tertia iamque die* (745), *pueros* (747), *altar* (750), and *posterga* (751), which are enough to announce the source of the poetry, even without further context. As is often the case in the *Heptateuch*, these words are introduced in succession and track the sequence of the prose, to provide a scriptural foundation for the verse. Throughout the passage, there is a strong affinity with the text of Genesis, despite the abbreviating style of Cyprianus, who omits all of the direct speech, for example, including the whole address to Abraham by the angel in verses 11–13 of the Bible.

Amplifications are for the most part predictable, even self-consciously poetic. There is little advantage to having the harvest be a "happy" one (*laetis … messibus*, 738), unless, together with *placidus* (740), these words suggest an emotional counterpoint to the difficulties to come, but Cyprianus adds no further psychological dimension to the scene, and Abraham goes about his "test" (*temptatur*, 741) with clinical efficiency and apparent indifference, so that any emotional context introduced by these adjectives has nowhere to go and dissipates. The elevation of *deus*

("God") to "the ethereal divinity" (*aetherii numinis*, 741) adds little more than window dressing, although the earlier juxtaposition of God's loftiness and Abraham's lowliness is effective (*Sublimemque deum supplex*, 739). The description of the mountain as *culmina collis* (743) originates in a familiar classical collocation, *culmina caeli* (cf. also *fastigia collis* in line 249), and with it Cyprianus sets out to raise the hill to epic heights. That the mountain is *tumidus* (743) is absurd. Of natural phenomena, the word normally applies to wind and waves, and even if the sense is "rising high" or "protuberant" here, the more usual sense of "swollen" or "puffed up" is hard to ignore. Finally, the periphrastic expressions, *cornipedem* ("horn-footed" or "hoofed," 744), for the unassuming *asina* ("ass"), and "fodder for flames" (*flammarum pabula*, 748) for "firewood," beg for attention as poetry, but these and other additions do not infuse the story with new vitality so much as overburden it with timeworn classicisms.[61] In this case, there is no real organic design behind the versification of the scene. It is as if Cyprianus looked at the prose and systematically upgraded everything he could with more "poetic" language.

The only meaningful addition appears in verses 752–3: "Eminus albentem prospectat sedulus agnum, / Qui melius fuso compleret sacra cruore" ("And as the father quickened to cut his son with the knife, the zealous man saw a white lamb nearby, whose bloodshed better served the sacrificial rights"). The choice of the noun *agnus* ("lamb," 753) is noteworthy, because it does not appear in the Vetus (though *ouis* is a variant) or in the Vulgate, and so it may be a typological allusion to Christ. The Septuagint reads κριὸς, "ram," and *aries* is a common variant in the Vetus and the standard reading in the Vulgate, but *agnus* does not appear in either, nor does the reference to the whiteness of the lamb (*albentem*, 753), which may suggest the purity of Christ. The added reference to bloodshed (*cruore*, 754) furthermore invites the context of the Crucifixion, but if there is a link between Isaac and Christ here, it is a subtle one. The author says nothing himself.

The Pillar of Cloud & Fire (*Ex.* 412–17)

The crossing of the Red Sea is among the most famous symbolic moments in the Old Testament, and Christian poets regularly highlight the baptismal

---

61 The phrase *flammarum pabula* (748) perhaps echoes Lucan, *Phar.* 7.5 (*non pabula flammis*).

significance of the episode.[62] It is also one of the most dramatic sequences in the Bible and thus one that poets often amplify. For his part, Cyprianus acknowledges the symbolic significance of the moment, if only with a word, but his primary impulse is to promote the dramatic potential of the anxious flight of the Israelites, the incessant pursuit of the Egyptians, and the dangerous passage through the waters.[63] Consider first the departure of the Israelites from Succoth (*Ex.* 412–17):

20 Profectique de Soccoth castrametati sunt in Etham in extremis finibus solitudinis. 21 Dominus autem praecedebat eos ad ostendendam uiam per diem
in columna nubis et per noctem in columna ignis ut dux esset itineris utroque
tempore. 22 Numquam defuit columna nubis per diem nec columna ignis per
noctem coram populo.[64]

– Ex. 13:20–2

Sochotumque dehinc ueniunt Othumque relinquunt,
Ignotas monstrante uias per deuia Christo.
Qui cum mane nouo lucem pandebat ab astris,
Ante uolans niuea sulcabat sidera nube   415
Candentemque iubar fuscata per aethera solem
Nocte tegens, claro fulgebat crine cometae.

[Then they leave Succoth and come into Etham, with Christ showing them hidden pathways through the wild – he cast light from the stars with the new morn and, flying before them, ploughed the stars in snowy cloud, and when night covered over candescent day, his brilliance spread throughout the heavens and shone with the bright tail of a comet.]

---

62 For discussions of the spiritual symbolism of Exodus and other parts of the Bible, see
    further de Lubac, *Exégèse médiévale*; an English translation is available by Sabanc and
    Macierowski, *Medieval Exegesis: The Four Senses of Scripture*. See also Danielou, *From
    Shadows to Reality*; *The Bible and the Liturgy*; "Déluge, baptême, jugement chez les
    pères de l'église," 69–94.
63 The Crossing of the Red Sea is one of the most appealing episodes to Christian poets, and
    versions of the story can be found not only in the *Heptateuch* but also in the poetry of Pru-
    dentius, Paulinus, Sedulius, *Carmen de Resurrectione*, *De martyrio Maccabaeorum*, Sidonius
    Apollinaris, and Dracontius. See further Roberts, "Rhetoric and Poetic Imitation," 73.
64 Ex. 13:20–2: "And marching from Succoth, they encamped in Etham, in the utmost
    coasts of the wilderness. 21 And the Lord went before them to show the way, by day
    in a pillar of a cloud, and by night in a pillar of fire; that he might be the guide of their
    journey at both times. 22 There never failed the pillar of the cloud by day, nor the pillar
    of fire by night, before the people."

Cyprianus begins with the essentials of the Bible, echoing *Soccoth* and *Etham* with *Sochotumque* and *Othumque* (412). He then combines two phrases from Genesis, "in extremis finibus solitudinis" ("the extremes ends of the wilderness") and *ostendendam uiam* ("showing the way") into a single verse ("Ignotas monstrante uias per deuia Christo," 413). The prepositional phrase, *ante uolans* (415), registers the biblical verb, *praecedebat*, while the temporal construction, *cum mane nouo* (414), follows *per diem* in the prose. Collectively, this language shows that Cyprianus is keeping an eye on the Bible, as he always does, to produce a more or less faithful rendition of the original.

A few stylistic amplifications of the scene are to be expected. This is an important moment in the Bible and one that already stands out in the prose, and so it is not surprising that the pillar should do more than simply "precede" the Israelites, but "ploughed through the stars in snowy cloud" ("niuea sulcabat sidera nube," 415). This imagery is reminiscent of the comet in Book 2 of the *Aeneid*, which heralds the death and destruction of Troy (2.693–8), and an allusion to Vergil would explain the choice of *cometae* at the end of this passage (417). But this pillar of fire brings life and not death, and so it has more in common with the star in Book 1 of *Euangeliorum libri*, which leads the Magi to the crèche and the newborn child (*Sulcantem flammis auras*, 1.244). The significance of that scene is also comparable. In both instances, a celestial body leads the people to the site of a new birth and salvation, and in the *Heptateuch*, one word, *Christo* (413), brings the weight of the New Testament to bear on the meaning of the passage; and although Cyprianus is generally silent about the mystical sense of Scripture, his intervention at this moment speaks volumes. Christ comes to lead all faithful souls from their spiritual wandering, to be saved and enlightened by the waters of Baptism. So the significance of *ignotas uias* ("unknown paths," 413) and *deuia* ("secluded" or "wandering paths," 413) extends in the *Heptateuch*, potentially to include the metaphorical journey from spiritual deviation to salvation in Christ. That being said, despite the obvious and explicit symbolism of this passage, it is not necessarily the case that Cyprianus intends his readers to pursue the deeper meaning of the Old Testament at every turn in the *Heptateuch*.

Pharaoh's Call to Arms (*Ex.* 426–33)

The sudden vision of Christ among the Israelites is a fleeting one, and Cyprianus is obviously more invested in the heroic tenor of the moment. In the Bible, Pharaoh's preparations for war amount to a single verse

(14:7): "Tulitque sescentos currus electos quicquid in Aegypto curruum fuit et duces totius exercitus" ("And he took six hundred chosen chariots, and all the chariots that were in Egypt: and the captains of the whole army").[65] In that case, there is some impression of the size of the army, but little emotional intensity and no sense of movement or expectation. Here is what Cyprianus brings to his rendition of the scene with the help of Vergil (*Ex.* 426–33):

> Ergo alacris in bella ciet ceu parua phalanges
> Ferratos agitans currus, quos axe uolante
> Trinus miles agit, uolucrem dum surgit in hastam,
> Nunc humilis, nunc uentosas sublimis in auras,
> Terroris fraudisque capax, quia uerbere crebro   430
> Pulsati sternunt acies, quae comminus obstant,
> Cornipedes pulsumque rotis feruentibus addunt,
> Incita quas uariis adsultibus ungula uersat.

[Eager, then, he mobilizes his troops as if for a small war, spurring his iron-clad chariots, driven by a three-man team over the spinning axis, who raise their winged spears, now low, now high into the blustery air. They can terrify and harm, since, driven by the steady whip, they scatter battle lines that stand before them, and the horses' hoofs intensify the pounding from the rage of the wheels, which agile steeds lead into charge after charge.]

This breathless eight-line sentence brings a level commotion which is absent in the prose, and the poet's amplifications serve to intensify the drama of the scene, promoting excitement and anticipation. Cyprianus does not mention "Egypt" or the number of its troops. Instead, he channels a passage from Vergil's *Georgics*, which describes the thrill of chariot racing, in order to promote the action of his own account. His phrase, *axe uolante* (427), "the flying axis," echoes "uolat ui feruidus axis" in the *Georgics* (3.107), as does *rotis feruentibus* (432). Lines 428–9 follow Vergil more closely still, and the image of the racers in the *Georgics* reflects that of the chariot riders in the *Heptateuch*. Vergil writes, "And now low, now

---

65 Cf. Septuagint: "καὶ λαβὼν ἑξακόσια ἅρματα ἐκλεκτὰ καὶ πᾶσαν τὴν ἵππον τῶν Αἰγυπτίων καὶ τριστάτας ἐπὶ πάντων" ("And he took six hundred choice chariots and all the cavalry of the Egyptians and the third-ranked officers over them all"). The translation is that of Perkins, *A New English Translation of the Septuagint*, ed. Pietersma and Wright 52–81 at 61. The online edition of the NETS is available at http://ccat.sas.upenn.edu/nets.

lifted high, they seem to be carried through the emptiness and raised into the air" ("iamque humiles iamque elati sublime uidentur / aera per uacuum ferri atque adsurgere in auras," 3.108–9). Cyprianus echoes Vergil with a similar construction, *nunc … nunc* (429) for *iamque … iamque* (108), and then *humilis* (429)/*humiles* (108), *sublimis* (429)/*sublime* (108), *in auras* (429)/*in auras* (109), all in the same order. His choice of the verb, *surgit*, (428) also approximates *adsurgere* (109) in the *Georgics*. The final verse in the *Heptateuch*, "Incita quas uariis adsultibus ungula uersat" (433), contains another Vergilian allusion, a simile borrowed from Book 5 of the *Aeneid* that compares boxing to "various assaults" on a fortress ("uariis adsultibus inritus urget," 5.422). Cyprianus uses these words to describe the charging chariots (*uariis adsultibus*, 433) with greater detail and emotion. In all, the passage is a clear case of close imitation, like the echoing of Vergil's storms in Book 1 of *Euangeliorum libri*. There, Juvencus evokes the power of Vergil's poetry to heighten the drama of the moment, but also to suggest a point of contrast, by putting the power of the storm into the hands of God. There is no such *Kontrastimitation* here, however. This is a more straightforward case of ecphrasis for the emotional value it can afford. Cyprianus is here after that Vergilian "sweetness" (*dulcedo*), to attract and delight his readers, not to educate them.[66]

Egypt Enters the Sea (*Ex.* 459–66)

In the same vein, the crossing of the sea itself and the passage through the waters does not highlight a spiritual message or the suggestion of baptismal meaning, but stages the destruction of the Egyptians in martial-heroic terms. In the Bible, God addresses Moses and tells him what to do and what will happen (14:15–18). Cyprianus omits that speech and introduces instead an apostrophe to the hero and the personification of nature, both of which enhance the martial tenor of God's intervention (474–6): "O nimium felix, celsis cui misit ab astris / Munimenta deus, candens cui militat aether / Et coniuratae ueniunt ad proelia noctes!" ("O most blessed man, to whom God has sent his defences from the high stars, for whom the shining ether fights and night bands together"). These words, in particular *munimenta* ("defences," "fortifications," "ramparts"), *militat* ("to serve as a soldier" or "wage war"), and *coniuratae* ("to band together by oath," "to unite"), appeal to martial-heroism, and not one of them appears in the Bible.

---

66 For a succinct definition of ecphrasis in biblical epic, see further Roberts, "Rhetoric and Imitation," 42.

The final destruction of Pharaoh and his army is described in similar terms, to amplify the emotional drama of the original more than anything else (*Ex.* 488–515):

Quod licitum credens Pharao, dum comminus instat,
Ingreditur calcatque salum; sed tarda repente
Plaustra gemunt totoque in terram pectore proni   490
Cornipedes genibus nequiquam pondera trudunt,
Quae penitus uincto nequibant axe moueri.
Illicet exsangues immensaque compede uincti
Festinam temptare fugam rursumque reuerti
Nitentes uano stimulant terrore iugales.   495
His aliud maius miseris multoque tremendum
Ingeritur magis et sensus affligit inertes.
Namque fretum dubios solitum collidere fluctus
Discretas coniunxit aquas undasque tumentes
Miscuit et totam fundo demersit Aegyptum.   500

[Pharaoh, looming near and thinking all was safe, advanced and tread into the deep, but suddenly the sluggish carts groaned and the horn-hoofed steeds, chests right down to the ground, knees bent, heaved their loads in vain, which they could hardly move, because of the crippled [lit., fettered] axels. Exhausted and shackled by an immeasurable bond, they tried to turn back and make a hasty retreat. Struggling, the men cracked their whips in vain terror. But something far more terrifying rushed down upon those wretched men and crushed their dumb senses all the more. For the sea, no stranger to the crash of the shifting tides, rejoined the parted waters and mingled the swelling waves, and plunged the whole of Egypt to the bottom.]

The interjection of the adverb *repente* (489), "suddenly," heightens the anticipation, as Pharaoh's army advances into the sea, and the following verse adds a vivid sense of sound, with the "groaning" carts (*gemunt*, 490) and heavy alliteration – "P̲laustra gemunt t̲ot̲oque in t̲erram p̲ectore p̲ro-ni" (490) – which re-enacts the frantic panting of the helpless horses. Alliteration carries on throughout the sentence (*Cornip̲edes … p̲ondera … p̲enitus*, 491–3), and chain-imagery adds to the scene, as axels, horses, and men are "fettered" in place by the power of God (*uincto axe*, 492 and *com-pede uincti*, 493), who hinders their escape. There is plenty of movement, as horses pull and riders whip – yet to no avail. This frustration leads to hopeless panic (*uano terrore*, 495) and the threat of something even worse (*aliud … tremendum*, 496). This last line is borrowed from Book 2 of the

Aeneid (2.199–200), "Hic aliud maius miseris multoque tremendum / obicitur magis atque improvida pectora turbat," where it precedes the death of Laocoon, who dares to oppose the will of the gods. Visually dramatic, the focus of the scene in *Exodus* moves from the threatening sight of Pharaoh, to his stalled chariots, the struggling horses, and finally the men, who crack their whips in vain, just moments before their deaths. The whole is a poetic *tour de force* by Cyprianus, who shows potential in this scene to rival his fellow Christian poets.

Conclusion

Reinhart Herzog wrote that Cyprianus was from the beginning not among the canonical biblical epic poets of late Antiquity, presumably because of the technical and stylistic inconsistencies of the poem, but also because of the author's determination to follow the Bible so closely, even at the expense of poetic artistry. It is also true that other twentieth-century critics, few though they are, disparaged the poem.[67] Eleanor Shipley Duckett believed "the literary value of the narrative is negligible, as it lacks both originality and poetic grace," and F.J.E. Raby was no more flattering: "The picture of Paradise, which with its trees and rivers offered an opportunity for at least rhetorical digression, is formal and bare."[68] Fair enough: Cyprianus is sparing in his description of the garden; however, his characterizations of Satan and Eve are not devoid of "poetic grace," and many episodes in *Exodus* are lively and entertaining, especially the incidents at the Red Sea. The problem, then, is not so much with the author's poetic shortcomings, but the artistic shortcomings of the source itself and the author's ill-considered plan to try and include everything. It is no accident that the most compelling moments of the *Heptateuch* are also some of the most engaging moments of the Bible, and had Cyprianus chosen to focus on those episodes only, he might have had an easier time and found a wider, more enduring audience. In his defence, this epic project is perhaps beyond the skill of any poet, if the goal is to make a literary work of the whole Old Testament.

---

67 Roberts is the exception here; he has worked to show many virtues of the *Heptateuch* and its author in *Biblical Epics* and *The Jeweled Style*.

68 Duckett, *Latin Writers of the Fifth Century*, 65; Raby, *History of Christian-Latin Poetry*, 76.

Chapter Four

Sedulius' *Carmen Paschale* (c. 425–450 CE)

Cognoscite cuncti,
Mystica quid doceant animos miracula nostros.

[Let us all recognize what these mystical miracles teach our souls.]
– *Carmen paschale* (4.263–4)

The *Carmen paschale* (*Paschal Song*) of Sedulius is a versification of the Gospels in five books and 1770 hexameters (384/300/339/309/438), dating roughly between the years 425 and 450 CE.[1] In addition to this poem, Sedulius also wrote two hymns and a later, longer prose rendition of the *Carmen* called the *Opus paschale*.[2] That was penned at the

---

1 The standard text is that of Huemer, ed., *Sedulii Opera Omnia*, CSEL 10. It has been revised by Panagl to include new indices, readings, and an updated bibliography. For a recent re-evaluation of the manuscript evidence, see Springer and *The Manuscripts of Sedulius: A Provisional Handlist*. For the title of the poem, see Sedulius' letter to Macedonius (Huemer, 12, 8–10): "Huic autem operi fauente Domino *paschalis carminis* nomen inposui, quia pascha nostrum immolatus est Christus" ("So, with the help of the Lord, I have given this work the name *Carmen paschale*, since Christ was sacrificed at Easter"). For the date of the *Carmen paschale*, see Green, *Latin Epics*, 140–3; and Springer, *Gospel as Epic*, 1, 23–6 and 42–3.

2 The text of the *Opus paschale* and hymns appear in Huemer, *Sedulii Opera*, 163–303. The title of *Opus paschale* is given by Sedulius (Huemer, 173, 16–19). For the relationship of the *Carmen* to the *Opus paschale*, see further Di Berardino, *Patrology*, 324–5. See also Springer, who treats the *Carmen* and *Opus* in *Manuscripts of Sedulius*. Springer notes that the *Opus* never achieved the popularity of the *Carmen* (11–12), though the hymns were popular (12–13). A loose translation of the *Carmen paschale* is that of Sigerson, *The Easter Song*. Better is the translation of Springer, *Sedulius: The Paschal Song and Hymns*. All translations of the *Carmen paschale* here are my own.

request of his friend and mentor Macedonius, about whom we know very little.[3]

No one would call this a *paene ad uerbum* translation of the Bible.[4] The *Carmen paschale* is much freer in style than either *Euangeliorum libri* or the *Heptateuch*, although like Juvencus, Sedulius offers a thematically driven poem that highlights the miracles and manifest omnipotence of Christ. But the *Carmen paschale* moves beyond the work of Cyprianus and Juvencus in the way it incorporates symbolic connections between the Old and New Testament. Words like *figura* and *signum* become more common, as poets of the fifth and sixth centuries break the silence imposed by the epic conventions of distance and detachment.[5] Now they pause more often and at greater length to comment on the underlying meaning of the Word. What does the Flood signify? Why is the Crossing of the Red Sea important for Christians? What does Moses have to do with Christ? With one eye on their predecessors and one hand on the Bible, the poets of the sixth century venture out into the deeper signification of the Scriptures.[6]

Little is known about the life of Sedulius, and though a brief surviving inscription provides some clues, it offers little more than what we gain from Jerome's evaluation of *Euangeliorum libri* in his *De uiris illustribus*. The inscription reads:[7] "Sedulius uersificus primo laicus in Italia philosophiam didicit; postea cum aliis metrorum generibus heroicum metrum Macedonio consulente docuit. In Achaia libros suos scripsit tempore imperatorum Theodosii et Valentiniani" ("The poet Sedulius first studied philosophy as a layman in Italy; he later taught the heroic metre among

---

3 For a suggestion that the *Carmen paschale* was originally unfavourably received by Macedonius, see Roberts, *Biblical Epic*, 79–80, esp. n. 69 at p. 79. It was at the request of Macedonius that Sedulius wrote the *Opus paschale* after the *Carmen* (Huemer, 171, 3–5).

4 See, e.g., Green in "Birth and Transfiguration," 158: "Coming from Juvencus to Sedulius we have crossed a boundary; and this boundary approximates to the boundary between biblical text and biblical commentary." Also, Green, *Latin Epics*, 185: "Sedulius generally gives himself more freedom than Juvencus did, and it is seldom that Jerome's formula of *paene ad uerbum* could be applied."

5 See further Dermott-Small, "Rhetoric and Exegesis"; and van der Laan, "Imitation créative dans le *Carmen Paschale* de Sedulius," 135–66 at 139.

6 On the point that Sedulius goes beyond Juvencus in his response to soteriological and eschatological meaning, see Roberts, *Biblical Epic*, 168; and Green, *Latin Epics*, 146–53, who discusses the important role of Paulinus of Nola in the gradual movement away from strictly literal renditions of the Bible.

7 For details on the life of Sedulius, see further Green, *Latin Epics*, 135–43; also Di Berardino, *Patrology*, vol. 4, 321–6; and Raby, *A History of Christian Latin Poetry*, 108–10.

other kinds of metre with the encouragement of Macedonius. He wrote his books in Greece at the time of the emperors Theodosius and Valentinian").[8] There is little here about the origins of Sedulius, but the references to Valentinian III (425–55 CE) and Theodosius II (408–50 CE) at least help to fix the date of the poem between 425 and 450 CE.

More relevant to our reading of the *Carmen paschale* is a prefatory letter Sedulius addresses to his friend and mentor, Macedonius, which offers no biographical information, but does speak to his fondness for poetry and belief that it can serve the devotional needs of a Christian audience under the proper circumstances:[9]

... multi sunt quos studiorum saecularium disciplina per poeticas magis delicias et carminum uoluptates oblectat. Hi quicquid rhetoricae facundiae perlegunt, neglegentius adsequuntur, quoniam illud haud diligunt: quod autem uersuum uiderint blandimento mellitum, tanta cordis auiditate suscipiunt, ut in alta memoria saepius haec iterando constituant et reponant. Horum itaque mores non repudiandos aestimo sed pro insita consuetudine uel natura tractandos, ut quisque suo magis ingenio uoluntarius adquiratur Deo. Nec differt qua quis occasione inbuatur ad fidem, dum tamen uiam libertatis ingressus non repetat iniquae seruitutis laqueos, quibus ante fuerat inretitus. Hae sunt, pater egregie, nostri operis causae, non superuacuae, sicut didicisti, sed commodae.

[... there are many who prefer an education in secular studies through the delights of poetry and the pleasures of song. Whatever rhetorical eloquence they read, they tend to heed less, since they do not enjoy it. But whatever poetry they read [lit. "see"], sweetened with charm, they take up with such eagerness of heart that it sticks and stays in the front of their minds by frequent repetition. So I think the practice of these people is not to be rejected but taken in response to each one's innate experience or nature, so that he may be drawn more voluntarily to God according to his disposition. As long as he is on the path to freedom, it does not matter how he is drawn to the Faith, provided he does not fall into the same snares of iniquitous servitude that entangled him before. These, eminent father, are the reasons for my work, which are not superfluous, as you can see, but advantageous.]

---

8 Huemer, *Sedulii Opera*, viii. See also Green, *Latin Epics*, 136; and Springer, *Gospel as Epic*, 23–4.

9 Green provides a discussion of the two letters to Macedonius in *Latin Epics*, 154–61; he also notes the anonymity of Macedonius at 154.

Whatever Macedonius may think, Sedulius appears to be serious about the potential of poetry to stir the faith of his readers. Such literature, he argues, is only dangerous to the soul, if it is already in peril and therefore more liable to stray. The problem is not in the book but the reader. It is not a very convincing argument, but swayed as he is by the profits of pleasure, Sedulius plays down the spiritual dangers of verse, allowing only that the weakness of the medium is proportional to the inner weakness of the individual, who must govern himself according to his own faith. The greater virtue of poetry, above and beyond prose, is that the reader will remember better what he has read. Sedulius therefore defends "poetic delights" (*poeticas delicias*) and "the pleasures of song" (*carminum uoluptates*), honeysweetened with charm (*blandimento mellitum*), because he believes that Vergil's sweetness (*dulcedo*) may serve to instruct the faithful.[10] That may be true, but there is a sense here that the language of Sedulius is as much a special plea as a strong rhetorical argument. Moreover, many of these words offer a foretaste of his banquet-themed preface, which is not not just a defence of poetry but proof of the author's susceptibility to its charms.

Classical Context

Sedulius' love of classical lore and his predilection towards sumptuous literary allusion permeate the *Carmen paschale*. Like Juvencus and Cyprianus, he admires Vergil a great deal. In fact, he has been called "the Christian Vergil," and his poem, "the Christian *Aeneid*."[11] Van der Laan effectively captures the relationship between the two poets: "Le *Carmen paschale* avec son abondance de réminisences virgiliennes donne une réponse claire à la question pathétique de Jérôme: *Quid cum euangeliis Maro?*"[12] In short, Sedulius has everything to do with Vergil. Well over 300 echoes have been identified in the *Carmen paschale* by Huemer and others, as well as dozens of allusions to Juvencus, Prudentius, Ovid, Lucan, Ausonius, and Paulinus of Nola, showing that Sedulius is well versed in

---

10 Roberts comes to the same conclusion in *Biblical Epic*, 85, where he discusses this passage.

11 See Green, *Latin Epics*, 209: "Among the classical authors used by Sedulius Vergil is supreme." Green cites several episodes where the language is evocative of Vergil and other classical poets, esp. 213–26. See also Roberts, *Biblical Epic*, 78: "Sedulius was the Christian Vergil"; the same comment appears in Roberts, "The Last Epic of Antiquity," 265. See also Springer, *Gospel as Epic*, 76, who calls the *Carmen paschale* the "Christian *Aeneid*." Springer, *Gospel as Epic*, 78, also comments on the influence of Vergil.

12 van der Laan, "Imitation créative," 141.

both classical and Christian literature.[13] Sixth-century tastes differ from those of the fourth, however, and with the increasing popularity of the Vulgate, Christian readers no longer need and are no longer satisfied with epic aggrandizements of the Bible in the way Juvencus' audiences were. They want that, but also "moral and spiritual commentaries to encourage or sustain faith" ("commentaires moraux et spirituels pour encourager ou soutenir leur foi").[14] Therefore, Sedulius and subsequent biblical poets entertain the deeper spiritual significance of the Scriptures alongside the essence of the Word and the aesthetics of Vergil, and as a result, the blending of the two traditions, classical and Christian, becomes more sophisticated than it was in the hands of Juvencus or Cyprianus.[15]

For example, the description of Elijah's fiery ascent in Book 1 of the *Carmen paschale* is typical of the kind of nuanced fusion of Christian and classical literature we find throughout the poem.[16] Here, Sedulius uses double-entendre and wordplay as a path to deeper meaning (1.179–87):[17]

Aurea flammigeris euectus in astra quadrigis,
Qua leuis aerios non exprimit orbita sulcos,   180
Sidereum penetrauit iter curruque corusco
Dexteriora petens spatio maiore triumphum
Duxit et humani metam non contigit aeui.
Quam bene fulminei praelucens semita caeli
Conuenit Heliae! meritoque et nomine fulgens   185
Hac ope dignus erat: nam si sermonis Achiui
Vna per accentum mutetur littera, sol est.

[And borne to the stars in a flaming chariot, whose gentle trail left no airy tracks, he struck a starry road and in his glimmering cart (seeking better things

---

13   Huemer only lists classical echoes in his notes. For a more recent and comprehensive list of sources, with Vergil at the top, see Green, *Latin Epics*, 419–31. See also van der Laan, "Imitation créative," 141, n. 39 and 142–7 for specific references to Vergil, Ovid, and Lucan; also Gao, *Vergil and Biblical Exegesis in Early Christian Latin Epic*, 185.

14   Ibid. See also De Nie, *Poetics of Wonder*, 373 and 427–8.

15   See further Gao, *Vergil and Biblical Exegesis*, 185–93, for some sensitive readings of this process in his dissertation. See also van der Laan, "Imitation créative," 154–64.

16   See Juvencus' similar handling of the scene (3.265ff.) and Green's reference to it in *Latin Epics*, 86.

17   See also Green, *Latin Epics*, 286–9, who treats 1.672–84 and 687–90 of Arator's *Historia apostolica*; that scene is obviously based on this one, though Green does not mention it.

on a greater course), drove to victory and did not pass the post of human life. How well that brilliant path to gleaming heaven suits "Elijah," who, shining in merit and name earned that help; for if one letter [of his name] is changed according to the accent of the Greek tongue, it becomes "sun" ["helios"]].

Figuratively speaking, *maiore spatio* ("a greater space," 182) refers to "heaven," although *spatium* is also the word for a racetrack like the Circus Maximus in Rome. That means "metam" in the following line alludes both to the point of death and the turning post of the course, and the word *triumphum* implies both earthly "victory" and eternal salvation. In Book 5 of the *Carmen paschale*, Christ takes leave of his disciples in similar terms, and they are worthy to witness his own "triumph" (5.423–5): "coramque beatis / Qui tantum meruere uiris spectare triumphum, / Aetherias euectus abit sublimis in auras" ("And in the presence of those blessed men, who were worthy to behold so great a triumph, he was carried off, sublime, into the ethereal airs and departed"). The underlying message in both scenes is that Christ and his faithful disciples can achieve greater "heights" than any glory-seeking mortal in pursuit of earthly fame.[18] The allusion to a race is therefore playfully derisive, and it shows that Sedulius can evoke the grandeur of the classical world without being a servant to it. Like Juvencus, he depends on his knowledge of pagan poetry for some measure of that "sweetness," but he does not celebrate underlying values that are at odds with Christianity.

Sedulius takes a similar stance at the end of his poem, where he finds another use for the image of the chariot. The classical allusions here to Vergil and Ovid (and perhaps Statius), are meant to be understated, even undermined, but it may be that Sedulius loses rein of his sources at this moment (4.291–302):[19]

Vtque caduca uagi contemnens culmina saecli
Monstraret se rite Deum, non curribus altis,
Qui pompae mortalis honor, rapidisque quadrigis

---

18   The last two lines of this passage may suggest knowledge of the Latin or Greek riddle tradition (186–7): "nam si sermonis Achiui / Vna per accentum mutetur littera, sol est" ("for, if one letter of his name is changed according to the accent of the Greek tongue, it becomes 'helios' ["sun"]"). The change-a-lettter type of riddle is a common variation in the *enigmata* of Symphosius, for example. See Behrens, ed., *Poetae latini minores*, vol. iv.

19   Green, *Latin Epics*, 216, mentions this scene briefly. Van der Laan provides a more thorough analysis in "Imitation créative," 160–2.

Puluereum sulcauit iter nec terga frementis
Ardua pressit equi, faleris qui pictus et ostro   295
Ora cruentatum mandentia concutit aurum:
Sed lento potius gestamine uilis aselli
Rectori suffecit honos ...

[And spurning the teetering heights of this transitory world, that he might show that he is rightly God, he did not plough the dusty road in some lofty chariot, an honour reserved for mortal pomp, nor [did he ride] in swift four-horse carts, seated atop some tall, champing steed draped in purple garb and metal regalia, tossing its head and biting its bloodied, golden bit; but to be the languid burden of a lowly ass was honour enough for the Lord ...]

This is the "victorious" entrance of Jesus into Jerusalem, and Sedulius takes considerable pains to suggest what he is *not* doing, that is, entering the scene like a triumphant Roman general, surrounded by pomp and glory. Yet it is hard to ignore the very image of a purple-robed Messiah, riding into Jerusalem in a golden chariot. In fact, it is one of the persistent ironies of the genre of biblical epic that some of the most compelling moments represent condemnations of secular values in the very language of that tradition. In this case, the image of the horse and lavish garb evoke Dido's steed in the *Aeneid* or that of Minos in Ovid's *Metamorphoses*, as a way to elevate the emotional intensity of the scene.[20] It is a textbook case of what German scholars call *Kontrastimitation* and the *Psychologisierung* of the biblical narrative. For Sedulius, there is a thin line here between censure and admiration, but many Christian poets before and after him revel in this kind of ornamental pageantry, even if the point is to emphasize the opposite.

Cecrops as Satan (1.38–44)

A more overt allusion to classical mythology for the sake of censure involves the images of Cecrops and Daedalus in Book 1 of the *Carmen*

---

20 See further van der Laan, 160–2, who points to Vergil, *Aen.* 4.134–5 ("ostroque insignis et auro stat sompes ac frena ferox spumantia mandit") and Ovid, *Met.* 8.33–4. ("purpureusque albi stratis insignia pictis terga premebat equi spumantiaque ora regebat"). Green, *Latin Epics*, 216, offers the same allusions to Vergil and Ovid but adds the following: *Aen.* 12.82 (*equos ... frementis*); *Aen.* 5.310 (*phaleris insignem*); and *Aen.* 7.279 (*fuluum mandunt sub dentibus aurum*).

paschale, which Sedulius manipulates in order to condemn paganism and spiritual delusion (1.38–44):[21]

> Hanc constanter opem laesis adhibete medullis,
> Quos letale malum, quos uanis dedita curis
> Attica Cecropii serpit doctrina ueneni,   40
> Sectantesque magis uitam spirantis odorem
> Legis Athenaei paedorem linquite pagi.
> Quid labyrintheo, Thesidae, erratis in antro
> Caecaque Daedalei lustratis limina tecti?

[Keep using this balm for wounded hearts [i.e., the worship of God], into which deadly evil creeps, the Attic doctrine of Cecropian poison, which is given over to vain cares; and following instead the scent of the law that breathes life, give up the stench of the Athenian countryside. Why, children of Theseus, do you wander in that labyrinthine cave and roam the blind thresholds of the Daedalean hall?]

In this passage, Sedulius aligns paganism with the mythical founder of Athens, Cecrops, who now leads Christians into a Daedalean maze of delusion and sin, at the heart of which lurks Satan himself.[22] The words, *letale mălum* (39), must mean "deadly evil," given the demands of the metre, but one cannot help but see *letale mālum*, "deadly apple," especially in the context of the verb *serpo* ("to creep," 40) and the word *uenenum* ("poison," 40), both of which conjure up images of the serpent and fruit in Eden.[23] In fact, just a few lines later, Sedulius says that Christ "has renewed man dying from the sweetness of the forbidden apple with the better food and drink of sacred blood through which he has dispelled the poison spread by the serpent" ("Qui pereuntem hominem uetiti dulcedine pomi / Instauras meliore cibo potuque sacrati / Sanguinis infusum depellis ab angue uenenum," 1.70–2). It therefore appears that the Fall is on his

---

21 See further 1.242–81 in the *Carmen paschale* for a digression on various pagan practices. See also Springer, *Gospel as Epic*, 35–7, for other examples of Sedulius' polemical and didactic tendencies.

22 Springer comments briefly on this passage, calling Sedulius a "latter-day Paul" who addresses the Athenians with reference to paganism (*Gospel as Epic*, 30). Springer also provides a discussion on the serpentine imagery and there mentions this passage, 93–5.

23 For other uses of the word *uenenum* in the *Carmen paschale*, see 1.40, 1.72, 2.186, 3.190, and 5.64 (the last example refers to Judas as the "poison" to Christ's "honey").

mind at this point, and he is not the only one.[24] A century later, the poet Avitus echoes this same passage in the context of the temptation of Eve in *Historia spiritalis* (2. 220): "Dis tamen esse cupit similis, serpitque uenenum / Ambitione nocens" ("but she wanted to be like God, and so the poison crept in, wounding her with ambition").[25] The words, *serpitque uenenum*, echo this passage of the *Carmen paschale* and suggest that Avitus comes to the same conclusion as Sedulius, who aligns Cecrops with the devil and so links paganism with Satanism. This suggestion becomes more likely if one considers that Cecrops is often depicted in classical art as a serpent below the waist. So there is plenty of evidence in these passages alone to suggest that Sedulius is interested in much more than the historical incidents of the Bible, which nevertheless remain the keystones of his versification.[26]

Biblical Context

Jerome's Vulgate was by this time in wide circulation, and yet Sedulius appears to have used a European version of the *Vetus Latina* as his biblical model.[27] Working through the narrative of the Old Testament in Book 1, he proceeds chronologically from Genesis to Daniel (see Appendix 1), and the whole book contains roughly eight sections: prefatory matter (1.1–37); a condemnation of paganism (1.38–59); emphasis on God's omnipotence over creation, especially personified Nature (1.60–102);[28] fifteen miracles

---

24 See further 2.186: "The devil readies another attack with his viperous poison" ("Altera uipereis instaurans arma uenenis"); and 3.189–92: "Look! That slippery serpent is up to his old tricks, envious with the bile of black venom and loving to fatten himself on human suffering" ("En iterum ueteres instaurans lubricus artes / Ille chelydrus adest, nigri qui felle ueneni / Liuidus humano gaudet pinguescere tabo"). Note how the word is also used of Judas in Book 5 (5.64) and of the acerbic thief crucified next to Christ (5.216).

25 See further Nodes, ed., *The Fall of Man*. Avitus uses the plural form of *deus* here as a simple classicism or perhaps as *Kontrastimitation*.

26 For serpentine depictions of Cecrops in classical literature by Pausanias and Ovid, see further Jones and Ormerod, *Pausanias, Description of Greece*, 5 vols., Loeb (New York, 1918), 9.33; see also Magnus, ed., *Metamorphoseon Libri XV* (Berlin, 1914), 2.55.

27 See further van der Laan, *Sedulius, Carmen Paschale Boek 4*, 204–12; Green, *Latin Epics*, 187. But Mayr, *Studien zu dem Paschale carmen des christlichen Dichters Sedulius*, 95, and Springer, *Gospel as Epic*, 110, favour the Vulgate. Pieri, "Sulle fonte evangeliche di Sedulio" 125–234, suggests that Sedulius may have used a harmony of the Gospels as his source. Green, *Latin Epics*, 183–4, is not convinced and assumes that "Sedulius worked directly from the gospels themselves."

28 See further Dermott-Small, "Rhetorica and Exegesis," 226–7.

from the Old Testament, offering proof of God's past and future might (1.103–219; see Appendix 2); a lively recapitulation of those miracles (1.220–41); a lengthy and at times light-hearted digression on various forms of paganism (1.242–81); a discussion of the Trinity, including a condemnation of Arianism and Sabellianism (1.282–333); and an appeal to Christ for favour and salvation (1.334–68). Books 2–5 then proceed from Matthew to John, and when Sedulius runs out of material on Matthew at the beginning of Book 4 (line 82), he moves to Mark (Mk 1:23) for the remainder of the book and to the end of what may be called the miracle-sequence of the *Carmen paschale*. Book 4 ends with the death and resurrection of Lazarus, which prefigures the events of Book 5 and, appropriately enough, the poem concludes with the final chapter and verse of John (21:25). In all, Sedulius maintains a close eye on the Bible, however free his rendition is at times.

While the *Carmen paschale* includes many comments from the author on the interpretation of the Gospels, his procedural approach to individual episodes is comparable to that of Juvencus (more than Cyprianus).[29] Carl Springer's assessment of the poet's *modus operandi* in Book 3 of the *Carmen paschale* in the context of the wedding feast at Cana provides a succinct appraisal of his work, which could be applied to all of the biblical versifiers, who "retain, omit, condense, expand."[30] Like Juvencus, Sedulius adopts keywords from his biblical source as the authenticating voice of his poem, and then omits whatever material does not suit his purpose. He shares with Juvencus a thematic focus on the deeds of Christ (*Christi uitalia gesta*, *Ev. Praef.* 19), specifically his miracles (*miracula Christi*, 1.26), but chooses more selectively than Juvencus which episodes to include. Thus "incidents that do not center around Christ are excluded from Books 2–5."[31]

Rhetorical amplification also plays a more significant role in the *Carmen paschale* than it does in either *Euangeliorum libri* or the *Heptateuch*. Nowhere is that clearer than in Book 1, which does not involve the Gospels directly but incidents from the Old Testament that prefigure Christ's deeds in the New. While crucial to the meaning of the *Carmen paschale*, the free rendition of several miracles from the Old Testament is far from the *paene ad uerbum* approach of Juvencus and Cyprianus. Springer goes so far as to say that Book 1 is not rhetorical *amplification* at all, since it appears to cover the whole of the

---

29 Green, *Latin Epics*, 189, even remarks how Sedulius' approach is formulaic in the handling of miraculous episodes.
30 Springer, *Gospel as Epic*, 111. Green also cites Springer in *Latin Epics*, 185.
31 Springer, *Gospel as Epic*, 23–48, but esp. 44–5.

Old Testament; if anything, it is extreme *abbreviation*.[32] Book 1 also makes it clear that Sedulius is more willing than his predecessors to explore and discuss the underlying meaning of the Bible. Thus Christ appears at the banks of the Red Sea in Book 1 as a figural Moses.[33] Such exegetical links are inspired by earlier commentaries on the Bible, including those of Clement of Alexandria, Origen, Jerome, and Augustine, but a systematic study of Sedulius' patristic sources remains to be done.[34] Even so, it is clear that Sedulius intends his audience to do more than sit back and enjoy the paschal banquet. Several times, he addresses them directly and enjoins them to take action. For this reason, interpreting the *Carmen paschale* is a more complicated process than it is for earlier biblical epics, since the audience must not only consider the depth and meaning of allusions to classical literature, but now the depth and meaning of allusions to the Bible and scriptural exegesis as well. As an intellectual and devotional exercise, Sedulius is modest in his preface, when he calls his poem "meagre greens from a poor garden" (15–16).

The Preface (1–16)

The opening of the *Carmen paschale* also suggests there is no conventional way to begin a versification of the Bible in late Antiquity. The opening of *Euangeliorum libri* approximates but transforms the traditional *proemium* of classical epic, and Cyprianus begins immediately with the "In principio" of Genesis. For his part, Sedulius introduces something different altogether – sixteen lines of elegiac distiches (and not hexameters) that transform the image of a Roman banquet into a dual metaphor for the Holy Eucharist and the spiritual consumption of literature (1–16):[35]

---

32 Ibid., 15.

33 For the poet's tendency to comment on the theological significance of Old and New Testament passages, see further Springer, *Gospel as Epic*, 60–2. See also Green, *Latin Epics*, 220–44.

34 For the influence of biblical commentary on the *Carmen paschale*, see further van der Laan, "Imitation créative," 139–41. See also Green, *Latin Epics*, 160, who links the form of the preface not to Prudentius or Claudian, but to "certain prefaces of Ausonius and Martial; the tone is naturally rather different."

35 See further Dermott-Small, "Rhetoric and Exegesis," 242–4. More than one scholar has passed over the preface for the opening of the main narrative (1.17ff) and often for the sake of comparisons with Juvencus. E.g., Mayr, *Studien zu dem Paschale Carmen*, 7–8; Gärtner, "Musen im Dienste," 436–44; Costanza, "Giovenco a Sedulio," 253–86. For the association of hexameter verse ("heroic metre") with epic, see further Springer, *Gospel as Epic*, 72. For his discussion of the opening, see 77–8. For the general significance of the Eucharist in the *Carmen paschale*, see Green, *Latin Epics*, 238.

Paschales quicumque dapes conuiua requiris,
   Dignatus nostris accubitare toris,
Pone supercilium si te cognoscis amicum,
   Nec quaeras opus hic codicis artificis:
Sed modicae contentus adi sollemnia mensae   5
   Plusque libens animo quam satiare cibo.
Aut si magnarum caperis dulcedine rerum
   Diuitiasque magis deliciosus amas,
Nobilium nitidis doctorum uescere cenis,
   Quorum multiplices nec numerantur opes.   10
Illic inuenies quidquid mare nutrit edendum,
   Quidquid terra creat, quidquid ad astra uolat.
Cerea gemmatis flauescunt mella canistris
   Conlucentque suis aurea uasa fauis.
At nos exiguum de paupere carpsimus horto,   15
   Rubra quod adpositum testa ministrat, holus.

[You who seek this paschal banquet as a guest, having deigned to recline at our couches, put aside your arrogance, if you think yourself a friend, and do not look here for the work of an artful book. But come contently to the rites of a modest table and be sated happily in spirit more than with food. Or if you are taken by the sweetness of great things and, being dainty, love richness more, then feast on the lavish fare of learned nobles, whose manifold wealth cannot be counted. There you will find whatever the sea provides for food, whatever the land creates, whatever soars to the stars. Waxen honey turns to gold in gem-covered cups, and golden vessels gleam in their honeycombs, but we have picked meagre greens from a poor garden, which are put before you in an earthen-red pot.]

This is an invitation to a metaphoric meal, a paschal banquet (*pascales dapes*) whose main course is food for the soul.[36] As readers, we are guests at this feast, called to recline on couches after the Roman fashion and to

---

36   Compare Book 5, lines 405–8, another paschal meal to which the apostles come. See
    also Springer for a discussion of that passage in *Gospel as Epic*, 107. See also Green,
    Latin Epics, 60, who discusses the feeding of the multitudes in Juvencus and the phrase,
    "opimis dapibus" (3.87), which "underlines the point that through Christ they make
    an excellent meal, both physically and spiritually."

enjoy the spiritual nourishment of biblical verse. "Biblical banquets and feasts," says Michael Roberts, "frequently take on the colours of or make allusion to the rhetorical *conuiuium luxuriosum*" of Antiquity, and Sedulius is appealing to that world, much as Juvencus appeals directly to the sweetness of Maro in his preface to *Euangeliorum libri*.[37] Sedulius lavishes similar attention on the wedding feast at Cana at the opening of Book 3 (3.1–11), where "sweet cups blush with wine not born of nature" ("Dulcia non nato rubuerunt pocula musto," 7), but the meal here is more figurative than literal, and Sedulius tries to say that his poetry is less than "the epitome of dining luxury."[38]

The whole preface unfolds in a series of double-entendres involving literal and figurative forms of consumption. Sedulius says that his guest may be *deliciosus* in the sense of "dainty" or "pleasure-loving," but the added sense of "delicious" is hard to ignore and suits the culinary focus. The dainty guest, he adds, may favour "the sweetness of grand things" (*magnarum … dulcedine rerum*), by which he means food and related luxuries but also the enjoyment of great literature. Again, *dulcedo* is a loaded word, and Juvencus uses it in his preface to evoke the "sweetness" of classical verse and Vergil in particular (*Ev. Praef.* 10, *dulcedo Maronis*).[39] Therefore, the meals of "learned nobles" ("Nobilium nitidis doctorum uescere cenis") are not just feasts for the stomach but metaphorical allusions to the poetry of Homer and Vergil among others, whose "food" is offered up in golden cups filled with honeyed eloquence. In contrast and with feigned humility, Sedulius pretends to offer only "meagre greens from [the] poor garden" of his wit.[40] We are not deceived, but Sedulius is earnest about the wholesome "food" of the Bible, and his language recalls the similar fare Prudentius recommends in his "Hymn before Eating" in the *Cathemerinon* (3.63–5):[41]

---

37   See further Roberts, "Vergil and the Gospels," 51, who provides an example from Book 2 of Juvencus' *Euangeliorum libri*, the versification of John 2:1–11, the setting of Christ's first miracle at the wedding feast of Cana. There, Juvencus adopts imagery from Dido's splendid banquet in Book 1 of the *Aeneid*.

38   Ibid.

39   For the significance of *dulcedo* here, see further Springer, *Gospel as Epic*, 77–8 and ch. 2 above.

40   For a discussion of the humility topos, see further Tunberg, "Prose Styles and Cursus," 111–21 at 114; see also Roberts, *Biblical Epic*, 80; and Green, *Latin Epics*, 160–1; Curtius, *European Literature*, 83–9.

41   For a discussion of this hymn, see further Evenepoel, "Prudentius' *Hymnus Ante Cibum* (*Cath.* 3)," 125–37.

> Nos holeris coma, nos siliqua
> Feta legumine multimodo
> Pauerit innocuis epulis.   65

[As for us, the leaves of greens, the pod that swells with varied beans, will nourish us with an innocent banquet.]

So it may be a humble meal, but the Bible and the verses based on it offer real substance. For Sedulius, biblical poetry is the healthier choice, and although epic is undoubtedly sweeter, it cannot compare with the real "richness" and "good taste" of the New Testament.

Following his preface, Sedulius expresses contempt for classical verse at the opening of the main narrative, and he is less forgiving at this moment than Juvencus, though also less convincing (1.17–26):

> Cum sua gentiles studeant figmenta poetae
> Grandisonis pompare modis, tragicoque boatu
> Ridiculoue Geta seu qualibet arte canendi
> Saeua nefandarum renouent contagia rerum   20
> Et scelerum monumenta canant, rituque magistro
> Plurima Niliacis tradant mendacia biblis:
> Cur ego, Dauiticis adsuetus cantibus odas
> Cordarum resonare decem sanctoque uerenter
> Stare choro et placidis caelestia psallere uerbis,   25
> Clara salutiferi taceam miracula Christi?

[Since pagan poets are eager to parade their fictions in pompous rhythms and, with their tragic wailing, foolish Geta or whatever other kind of singing, to renew the heathen blights of impious things and sing memorials of sins, offering further lies in their papyri books with custom as their teacher, why should I, who am used to resounding odes of ten chords in David's songs and standing devoutly in the holy choir, chanting calmly to the heavens, be silent of Christ the Saviour's famed wonders?]

In the same way Juvencus rebukes the "lies bound to the deeds of ancient men" ("Quae ueterum gestis hominum mendacia nectunt," *Ev.* 1.16), Sedulius rejects classical poetry as purely fictitious (*figmenta poetae*), and he likewise uses the word *mendacia* ("lies," 22) to refer to the pagan books of Antiquity.[42]

---

42 See further De Nie, *Poetics of Wonder*, 379.

In the process, he imitates what he considers to be the "pompous" style of classical poetry through a series of long, open vowels ("Grandisonis pompare modis, tragicoque boatu," 18).[43] His use of the phrase *scelerum monumenta* ("memorials of sins," 20) is also deliberately grandiose, and like Juvencus he offers the miracles of Christ as a wholesome alternative to those stories. In fact, his later words, "haec mihi carmen erit" ("this will be my song," 37), are almost certainly a direct allusion to *Euangeliorum libri* and represent a desire to set the *Carmen paschale* within the same tradition of biblical epic.[44]

Old Testament Miracles in Book One

The condemnation of paganism in Book 1 of the *Carmen paschale* (1.38–59) leads into a series of Old Testament miracles that highlight God's omnipotence over man and nature. As Sedulius puts it, "Te duce difficilis non est uia; subditur omnis / Imperiis natura tuis, rituque soluto / Transit in aduersas iussu dominante figuras" ("With you as leader, the way is not hard; all nature is subject to your commands, and freed of its routine, nature changes into opposite forms by your indomitable will," 1.85–7). Many of the Old Testament scenes in Book 1 prefigure Christ's miraculous deeds in the New Testament part of the poem, and so God's ability to overturn the laws of nature here is bound to Christ's healing gifts and resurrection in the latter portion of the *Carmen paschale*. In all likelihood, the Easter vigil provides a source for many of the episodes of Book 1. The first of these, the story of Enoch, is also among the second series of readings in the Easter vigil (*Gen* 5, 6, 7 and 8) and the second, Abraham's offering of Isaac, is the third reading in the vigil (*Gen* 22.1–19). The account of the Crossing of the Red Sea is both the fourth miracle in the poem and the fourth reading in the vigil (Ex 14.24–31 and 15.1), and the

---

43 In particular, Sedulius criticises tragedy and comedy; the reference to Geta is an allusion to the comedies of Terence. See Green, *Latin Epics*, 163; Green also mentions Springer in the same passage, whom he says wrongly attributes Geta to Hosidius Geta, the writer of a cento called the *Medea*. See further Springer, *Gospel as Epic*, 77. The *Opus paschale* gives no indication of Geta's identity ("seu ridicule Getae comica foeditate"), but Remigius' commentary does (Huemer, 321): "Getae, persona comica est apud Terentium."

44 Green, *Latin Epics*, 164; and Roberts, "The Last Epic of Antiquity," 264, who note the connection to the sibyl.

tenth reading in the vigil, the story of Jonah, is the thirteenth miracle in the *Carmen paschale*, while the story of the three youths from the book of Daniel figures in the vigil as the twelfth reading and the fourteenth miracle in the *Carmen paschale*.[45] So it would appear that the twelve readings of the vigil provide a loose framework for the selection of miracles in the first book of the *Carmen paschale* and a basis for many of the connections between the Old and New Testament.[46] It should also be said that Prudentius' *Cathemerinon* contains similar passages related to the readings of the vigil, and it may be that Sedulius has him in mind as much as the liturgy.

Three Miracles from Exodus

The central meaning of Book 1 is contained in three consecutive miracles from the book of Exodus: the Crossing of the Red Sea (1.136–47), the image of the heaven-falling manna (1.148–51), and the drawing of water from the rock (1.152–9). These episodes are linked by figural symbolism that highlights the paschal theme of the poem.[47] The episode of the Crossing of the Red Sea comes first (1.136–47):

> Peruia diuisi patuerunt caerula ponti
> In geminum reuoluta latus, nudataque tellus
> Cognatis spoliatur aquis, ac turba pedestris
> Intrat in absentis pelagi mare, perque profundum
> Sicca peregrinas stupuerunt marmora plantas.   140
> Mutauit natura uiam, mediumque per aequor
> Ingrediens populus rude iam baptisma gerebat,
> Cui dux Christus erat, clamat nam lectio: multas
> Vox Domini super extat aquas; uox denique uerbum est.
> Verbum Christus adest, geminae qui consona legis   145
> Testamenta regens ueterem patefecit abyssum,
> Vt doctrina sequens planis incederet aruis.

[A road lay open through the cerulean waters of the parted sea, which rolled back into a double flank, and the naked earth was stripped of its usual waters, as

---

45 See further Schmidt, *Hebdomada Sancta 2 Vols.* (Rome, 1956), vol. 2, 143–53.

46 It may also be that Sedulius has Prudentius in mind, and Hymns 3–12 of *Cathemerinon* cover many of the same episodes with reference to the vigil. See further Green, *Latin Epics*, 168.

47 These episodes are based on Ex 14:21–25, Ex 16:13–16, and Ex 17:1–7.

a host of footmen entered a sea without water, and throughout the deep the dry bedrock marvelled at the foreign prints. Nature changed its way, and the people, walking into the midst of the sea, experienced a rudimentary Baptism with Christ as their leader; for the scripture proclaims: the voice of God stretches over many waters; in the end, the voice is the Word. The Word is Christ, who, reigning over the Testaments united in twofold law, laid open the old abyss, so that a following doctrine might stretch forth over the open plains.]

In the *Heptateuch*, Cyprianus only hints at the significance of the crossing, saying, "Ignotas monstrante uias per deuia Christo" ("with Christ showing the way through the unknown wilderness"), but Sedulius puts symbolism above the deeds themselves and he lavishes attention on the poetry.[48] The waters are "cerulean blue" (*caerula ponti*) and the sea, like a fallen warrior, is "despoiled" of its precious "armour" (*spoliatur*), while the personified seabed marvels at the foreign footprints now appearing on its surface. The real significance of the passage, however, lies with the figural implications of the crossing as a metaphorical Baptism.[49] It is no mistake that Sedulius echoes the words from the beginning of his miracle sequence and his earlier emphasis on God's ability to make nature "change its way" and "cross over" into different "forms" (*natura … Transit in aduersas … figuras*, 1.86–7). In those earlier passages, nature changes its form with "God as its leader" (*Te duce*, 1.85), and Sedulius uses that language here again to reinforce the fact of God's omnipotence and to show precisely how nature can change its way at His biding (*Mutauit natura uiam*, 1.141). More than that, as the Israelites "cross over" the dry seabed with "Christ as their leader" ("cui dux Christus erat," 1.143), the sea changes the nature of its surface (*figura*), literally and figuratively, to deliver a message of Baptism.

The two miracles that follow likewise point to the New Testament. In describing Moses and the feeding of the Israelites in the wilderness (Ex 16.13–16) and the story of drawing water from the rock (Ex 17.1–7), Sedulius deliberately avoids naming Moses (1.148–51), because he wants to emphasize the agency of Christ first at the Sea and now here (1.159): "His igitur iam sacra tribus dans munera rebus, / Christus erat panis,

---

48 See further Green, *Latin Epics*, 238, who refers to the episode as a "history or prehistory of baptism." For a fuller discussion of Sedulius' "authorial intrusions," see Springer, *Gospel as Epic*, 90–2.

49 See further Danielou, *The Bible and the Liturgy*, esp. 86–98; Dermott-Small, "Rhetoric and Exegesis in Sedulius' *Carmen Paschale*," 227; and Roberts, *Biblical Epic*, 185–6.

Christus petra, Christus in undis" ("Therefore, granting His sacred gifts on these three occasions, Christ was the bread, Christ was the rock, Christ was in the water").[50] Together, these three miracles form a symbolic unit, whose full significance is revealed at the end of the *Carmen paschale*.

In Book 5, in the context of the Crucifixion, Sedulius considers the symbolism of the wound in Christ's side. In the process, he echoes language from those three miracles in Book 1 (5.288–92):

> Vulnere purpureus cruor et simul unda cucurrit.
> Haec sunt quippe sacrae pro religionis honore:
> Corpus sanguis aqua tria uitae munera nostrae.   290
> Fonte renascentes, membris et sanguine Christi
> Vescimur atque ideo templum deitatis habemur

[Crimson blood and water flowed at the same time from the wound. Surely these things stand for the honour of our sacred religion – body, blood, water – three gifts for our life. Reborn at the font, we are fed on the limbs and blood of Christ, and so held to be the temple of His deity.]

With this passage in mind, consider again the words at the end of the threefold sequence in Book One (1.158–9): "His igitur iam sacra tribus dans munera rebus, / Christus erat panis, Christus petra, Christus in undis" ("Granting sacred gifts on these three occasions, / Christ was the bread, Christ was the rock, Christ was in the water"). Those three miracles or "gifts" prefigure man's redemption through Christ by Baptism and participation in the Eucharistic gifts of body and blood. As Prudentius puts it, it is through Christ that we are fed, "nourishing our hearts with mystic feasts" ("Cuius subsidio nos quoque uescimur / Pascentes dapibus pectora mysticis").[51] So the words *fonte renascentes* (5.291) at the end of the *Carmen*

---

50   Here Sedulius is channelling Paul and 1 Corinthians (10:1–4): "Nolo enim uos ignorare fratres quoniam patres nostri omnes sub nube fuerunt et omnes mare transierunt et omnes in Mose baptizati sunt in nube et in mari; et omnes eandem escam spiritalem manducauerunt; et omnes eundem potum spiritalem biberunt bibebant autem de spiritali consequenti eos petra petra autem erat Christus" ("For I would not have you ignorant, brethren, that our fathers were all under the cloud and all passed through the sea. And all in Moses were baptized, in the cloud and in the sea. And did all eat the same spiritual food. And all drank the same spiritual drink and they drank of the spiritual rock that followed them and the rock was Christ"). See also O'Daly, *Days Linked by Song*, 158, who also mentions Corinthians in the context of Prudentius' *Cathemerinon* and similar imagery there.

51   *Cathemerinon*, "Hymn before Eating" (5.107–8).

paschale refer not just to Baptism in general but to the figural signification of the Crossing of the Red Sea in Book 1. Also, the words, "membris et sanguine Christi uescimur" (5.291–2), recall not only the heaven-falling manna and the water from the rock but symbolically Christ's body and blood. So the climax of the *Carmen paschale* returns us to the beginning of the poem and the emphasis on God's power over nature and death. This passage also serves to bring unity to the narrative as a whole, reinforcing the meaningful relationship between the Old and New Testaments.[52]

Abraham & Isaac (1.114–20)

Book 1 contains a number of other episodes that evoke the New Testament in similar ways. These stories, as Carl Springer puts it, are "designed to instruct the faithful, not only to dazzle them with virtuosity," but dazzling is surely part of it.[53] The story of Abraham and Isaac is one of the more famous figural episodes from the Old Testament, and Sedulius approaches it with catechism in mind (1.114–20):[54]

Mactandumque Deo pater obtulit, at sacer ipsam
Pro pueri iugulis aries mactatur ad aram.   115
O iusti mens sancta uiri! pietate remota
Plus pietatis habens contempsit uulnera nati
Amplexus praecepta Dei, typicique cruoris
Auxilio uentura docet, quod sanguine Christi
Humana pro gente pius occumberet agnus.   120

[And the father offered his son to be sacrificed to God, but [instead] a sacred ram was sacrificed on the altar in the place of his boy's throat. Oh, the holy heart of that righteous man! Putting pity aside and having more piety, he considered his child's wounds of little importance, having embraced the

---

52 Springer also notes the connection between the opening and closing portions of the *Carmen paschale*, and mentions God's omnipotence and ability to overturn the laws of nature in Book 1 (1.85–92) and in connection with Christ's resurrection in Book 5 (5.276–84). See further Springer, *Gospel as Epic*, 68–70.

53 Springer treats several such episodes, which he says are "filled with shadows, types, and references, all of them pointing to Christ and the events of his life, passion, and death" (ibid., 35). See also Dermott-Small, "Rhetoric and Exegesis," 227.

54 See also Sedulius' rendition of the Jonah story (1.192–6), which bears figural significance. Springer mentions the typal significance of the episode in *Gospel as Epic*, 35.

precepts of God! And with the help of figural bloodshed he teaches what is to come, that a pious lamb would die for the human race by the blood of Christ.]

For Cyprianus, this episode is important mainly as part of the historical incidents of the Old Testament, but not without a hint of typology. In place of the ram Abraham sees in the thicket (*arietem*), Cyprianus offers "a white lamb" (*albentem agnum*, *Gen.* 753), whose bloodshed better fulfills the sacrifice ("Qui melius fuso compleret sacra cruore," *Gen.* 754). Cyprianus says nothing else, but it is meaningful that Sedulius uses similar language here to highlight the typological significance of the event. Specifically, he uses the words *typicique cruoris* (118), *pius agnus* (120), and *docet* (119) as a way to teach his audience how the episode is important for Christians. As added touches of devotion and intimacy, Abraham "embraces" the commandments of God over his son (*Amplexus praecepta Dei*, 118), and the sense of *pietas* (116, 117) refers both to fatherly "duty" in the classical sense of the word and "pity" or "piety" from a Christian point of view.

The Nativity (2.89–101)

Another episode of figural significance is one Juvencus treats as well (1.243–51), and Sedulius is well aware of *Euangeliorum libri*, but he is more willing than Juvencus to distance himself from the biblical narrative for the sake of spiritual commentary. Green makes the point that Sedulius seems not to have been trying to replace Juvencus, but that he is out to do more according to his theological agenda.[55] This passage, like the treatment of Abraham and Isaac, suggests as much and serves an instructive function (2.89–101):

9 Qui cum audissent regem, abierunt, et ecce stella, quam uiderant in orientem, antecedebat eos, usque dum uenit et stetit supra puerum. 10 Videntes autem stellam gauisi sunt gaudio magno ualde. 11 Et intrantes in domum inuenerunt puerum cum Maria, matre eius. Et procidentes adorauerunt eum et apertis thensauris suis optulerunt ei munera, aurum tus et murram.[56]

– Mt 2:9–11

---

55   See further Green, *Latin Epics*, 153 and 174–5, for a discussion of this episode.

56   Mt 2:9–11: "Who having heard the king, went their way; and behold the star which they had seen in the East, went before them, until it came and stood over where the child was. 10 And seeing the star they rejoiced with exceeding great joy. 11 And entering into the house, they found the child with Mary his mother, and falling down they adored him: and opening their treasures, they offered him gifts; gold, frankincense, and myrrh."

Ergo alacres summo seruantes lumina caelo
Fixa magi sidusque micans regale secuti   90
Optatam tenuere uiam, quae lege futura
Duxit adorantes sacra ad cunabula gentes.
Thensaurisque simul pro religione solutis,
Ipsae etiam ut possint species ostendere Christum,
Aurea nascenti fuderunt munera regi,   95
Tura dedere Deo, myrram tribuere sepulchro.
Cur tria dona tamen? quoniam spes maxima uitae est
Hunc numerum confessa fides, et tempora summus
Cernens cuncta Deus, praesentia, prisca, futura,
Semper adest semperque fuit semperque manebit   100
In triplici uirtute sui.

[Therefore, keeping their eyes fixed on the heights of heaven, and following
the star shining regally, the hastening Magi held the chosen course that by
future law led the adoring folk to the sacred crèche. At once they spread out
treasures in devotion, so that their images might symbolize Christ: They gave
golden gifts for the newborn king, incense for God, and myrrh for the tomb.
But why three gifts? Because our greatest hope of life, faith, revealed this number, and because the highest God, who sees through all time, present, past, and
future, always is, always was, and always shall be in threefold power.]

Like Juvencus, Sedulius aligns the gifts of the Magi with stages in
Christ's life ("Aurea nascenti fuderunt munera regi/Tura dedere Deo,
myrram tribuere sepulchro," 95–6), but he does not stop there. Sedulius
addresses his audience directly, "But why these three gifts?" ("Cur tria
dona tamen?" 1.97).[57] He then explains to them that their number symbol-
izes the Holy Trinity, and in doing so shows that he is more interested in
the doctrinal implications of the gifts than the incarnation itself. Unlike
Juvencus, who uses the language of epic to intensify the revelatory nature
of the star, which ploughs through the sky in flames (*Sulcantem flammis
auras*, 1.244) and leads the Magi to a scene of human intimacy, Sedulius is

---

57 See further Springer, *Gospel as Epic*, 85. Springer also treats the end of this episode
    (2.101–61) in terms of the author's interest in the figural significance of biblical epi-
    sodes. "Like the wise men," he says, who do not return to Herod, "Sedulius' readers are
    to shun the path of evil and stick to the narrow road which leads to salvation" (p. 87).

more concerned with what that moment means for "future law" (*lege futura*, 1.91), for "the reverence of God," and "for religion" (*pro religione*, 1.93). The phrase *pro religione* is almost certainly a pun, meaning both "devotion" in the context of the incarnation and "religion" more broadly as a reference to the birth of Christianity. Carl Springer also suggests in his translation of the poem that the words, "Duxit adorantes sacra ad cunabula gentes" ("led the adoring folk to the sacred crèche" 92), may be taken broadly to mean "[the star/faith] has led adoring gentiles to the holy cradle," meaning pilgrimages to the Holy Land.[58] For Sedulius, then, "faith" (*fides*, 1.98) is the main focus, as it applies to God's "threefold power" (*In triplici uirtute sui*, 1.101), while Juvencus, who says nothing, offers a more personal scene with greater feeling.

The Lord's Prayer (2.231–48)

The verse rendition of the Lord's Prayer in the *Carmen paschale* is the lengthiest interpolation in the early part of the poem, and Sedulius expands the original account to seventy lines of poetry (2.231–300).[59] Eight interconnected sections build upon a single word or phrase of the prose and introduce spiritual commentary. The context is not, as one might expect, the Sermon on the Mount (Mt. 5–7), but the inculcation of the apostles to be "fishers of men" (Mt. 4:19) or, as Sedulius puts it, men who "fish for human souls" (1.220–21). Given the length of the amplified prayer, I offer only an excerpt here, to show how Sedulius amplifies the Bible, and because the language diverges markedly from that of the Gospel, I include echoes of the biblical *Pater noster* only in italics (2.231–48):[60]

> Quin etiam celerem cupiens conferre salutem
> Orandi praecepta dedit, iudexque benignus
> Indulgenda peti breuiter iubet, ut cito praestet,
> Sic dicens: orate patrem, baptismate nostrum,
> Iure suum; propriumque homini concessit honorem   235

---

58 See further Springer, *Paschale Song and Hymns*, 51, 69.
59 For another discussion of this passage, see Green, *Latin Epics*, 179.
60 For Sedulius' catechetic impulse, see further Mazzega's edition of book 3, 30–2.

Et quod solus habet cunctos permisit habere.
Qui dominum *caeli patrem* memoramus, in ipso
Iam fratres nos esse decet nec origine carnis
Germanum tractare odium, sed spiritus igne
Flagrantes abolere doli monumenta uetusti   240
Atque nouum gestare hominem, ne forsan ab alto
Degenerent terrena Deo, cui nos duce Christo
Fecit adoptiuos caelestis gratia natos.
Sanctificetur ubi *Dominus*, qui cuncta creando
Sanctificat, nisi corde pio, nisi pectore casto?   245
Vt mereamur eum nos *sanctificare* colendo,
Annuat ipse prior, sicut benedicier idem
Se iubet a nobis, a quo benedicimur omnes.

[Moreover, wanting to bring swift salvation, he gave instructions for prayer, and that benevolent judge bids our requests be sought briefly, that he might readily grant them: "Beseech the father, who is ours through baptism, his own by right," he said, "he gave his own honour to men, and what he alone has, he allowed all men to have. It is right for those of us who are mindful of the Lord Father in heaven to be brothers in him and not to draw fraternal hate from the origin of the flesh. But rather, enflamed with the fire of our spirits, we should destroy the monuments of ancient wickedness and make a new man, that we of the earth may not be unworthy of the Lord; for with Christ as our leader, God's celestial grace makes us his adopted children. Where else should the Lord be hallowed, who hallows all things through creation, but in the pure breast, in the pious heart? He first instructed so that we deserve to sanctify him by worshipping him, just as he ordered that he be blest by us, by whom we all are blest.]

The first reference to the prayer appears at line 237 with the words *caeli patrem*, which allude to the initial words of the prose ("Pater noster qui in caelis es"). The echo of the second verse, "hallowed be thy name" (*sanctificetur nomen tuum*), does not come for another seven lines (*sanctificetur ubi Dominus*, 244), and the intervening material offers an exhortation to love God with the soul and not the flesh, the implication being that the weakness of the flesh is what led to the Fall and the subsequent discord between Cain and Abel. A second exhortation to overcome sin and follow "Christ as a leader" comes next. The phrase *duce Christo* reaffirms the agency of Christ in the salvation of man, although it requires him to worship God through his actions and not just his prayers. The opening of this version of the *Pater noster*, then, moves beyond paraphrase of the Bible to spiritual-didactic commentary. It is a much freer and lengthier rendition than what we find in *Euangeliorum libri*, and the biblical exegesis and homiletic tone that attach themselves to the *Pater noster* in the *Carmen paschale* are undoubtedly more "biblical" than "epic."

The rest of the prayer (lines 249–300) builds upon the biblical narrative in similar ways. To the words, "thy kingdom come," Sedulius adds commentary on the brilliance and eternal nature of God's kingdom, emphasizing the primacy of Christ (*principe Christo*, 1.252). To the phrase, "thy will be done," he adds that God's "will" is chiefly to protect us from the devil (1.255–62). The "daily bread" is a metaphor for the body of Christ, as it almost certainly is in *Euangeliorum libri* ("Vitalisque hodie sancti substantia panis / Proueniat nobis, 1.595–6), but Sedulius refers to Christ more explicitly, saying (1.263–5)

Annonam fidei speramus pane diurno,
Ne mens nostra famem doctrinae sentiat umquam
A Christo ieiuna, suo qui corpore et ore   265
Nos saturat simul ipse manens uerbumque cibusque.

[*With our daily bread we hope for a harvest of faith,*
Lest our minds should ever hunger for the doctrine,
Being starved of Christ, who feeds us with his own
Body and voice, being at once food and the word.]

In the next section, the words "forgive us our sins as we forgive those who sin against us" (1.269–78), lead to a digression from the Gospel of Matthew emphasizing man's accountability to God. The words, "lead us not into temptation" (1.279–87) become a short sermon on the indulgence of worldly pleasures, and finally, "deliver us from evil" (1.288–300) becomes an exhortation to pursue "good" ("debemus adire / Sectarique bonum"). So Book 1 ends with the final words of the prayer, or rather, it ends with Sedulius exhorting his reader to pursue the same path of liberty (*bona libertas*, 1.299) he mentions in his letter to Macedonius (*uiam libertatis*), and "to avoid the grim jaws of the savage wolf and enjoy life in Christ's pastures" ("euadere torua cruenti / Ora lupi uitaque frui per pascua Christi, 1.299–300). More could to be said about the precise ways in which Sedulius builds upon the essential language of the prose in this case, but it is clear in that the *Pater Noster* for Sedulius is not just a petition to the Father but to the Son as well. He also takes some pains to assert that, while the will of God is to answer our prayers, ours must be to live in accordance with the tenets of the Faith.

Three Blindness Miracles

So the message often in the miracle sequence of the *Carmen paschale* is that Christ rewards the faithful.[61] This point is reinforced in several miracles involving the healing of the blind, the first of which is based on Matthew 9:27–30 and appears halfway through Book 3, well into the poem (3.143–51):

> 27 Et transeunte inde Iesu secuti sunt eum duo caeci clamantes et dicentes: Miserere nostri, fili Dauid. 28 Et uenit in domum et accesserunt ad eum duo caeci, et dixit illis Iesus: Creditis, quod possum hoc facere? Dicunt ei: Utique, Domine. 29 Tunc tetigit oculos eorum dicens: Secundum fidem uestram contingat uobis. 30 Et aperti sunt oculi ipsorum et comminatus est illis Iesus dicens: Videte, ne quis sciat. 31 Illi autem exeuntes diffamaverunt eum in tota terra illa.[62]
>
> – Mt 9:27–31

> Inde pedem referens duo conspicit ecce sequentes
> Caecatos clamare uiros: fili inclite Dauid,
> Decute nocturnas extinctis uultibus umbras   345
> Et clarum largire diem. quam credere tutum,
> Quam sanum est cognosse Deum! iam corde uidebant
> Qui lucis sensere uiam; tunc caeca precantum
> Lumina defuso ceu torpens ignis oliuo

---

61 For a full list with cross-references to Sedulius' treatment of NT miracles, see Green, *Latin Epics*, 180–3.

62 Mt 9:27–31: "And as Jesus passed from thence, there followed him two blind men crying out and saying, 'Have mercy on us, O Son of David.' 28 And when he was come to the house, the blind men came to him. And Jesus saith to them, 'Do you believe that I can do this unto you?' They say to him, 'Yea, Lord.' 29 Then he touched their eyes, saying, 'According to your faith, be it done unto you.' 30 And their eyes were opened, and Jesus strictly charged them, saying, 'See that no man know this.' 31 But they going out, spread his fame abroad in all that country."

Sub Domini micuere manu, tactuque sereno   350
Instaurata suis radiarunt ora lucernis.

[Then, retracing his steps, behold, he saw two blind men following him and calling out: "Noble son of David, dispel these dark shadows from our light-deprived faces and grant them the brilliance of day." Oh, how prudent to believe, how sensible to know God! Those two men, already seeing with their hearts, sensed the path of light; and then the blind eyes of those entreating men, like a dying flame given new oil, pulsed beneath the hand of the Lord; and with his bright restorative touch, light shone from their eyes.]

The first two lines follow the Vulgate closely with the verbs *sequor* and *clamo* and the adjective *caecus*; the third line, however, introduces a sustained play on words involving images of light and darkness. The blindness of the men is called "nocturnal shadow" (*nocturnas ... umbras*, 345), and their eyes are "extinguished" (*extinctis*, 345) like the flames of a fire. It is as much spiritual blindness as physical.[63] The word *lumina* ("lights") in line 349 offers a poetic alternative to the biblical *oculus*, and it serves to emphasize more strongly the light imagery of the scene. The word *lumen* never appears in the Bible in this sense. In fact, beyond a word or two, there is little to connect the diction of the poetry to that of the prose. What Sedulius does instead is use synonymic substitution and poeticisms to echo the Bible indirectly. This is clear in the climax of the episode, where he compares the rekindling of sight to the flame of a waning lamp. When Christ touches the eyes of the blind men, sight returns at once, and the "lamps" burst into flame.[64] Inner faith, therefore, makes the two men worthy of healing. In the same way, Juvencus stresses the internal health of the soul against outward signs of physical infirmity.

In Book 3 of the *Carmen paschale*, Christ heals the centurion's son, because the man puts his faith in God's far-reaching power (3.121–8). Christ heals the woman of her issuing blood for the same reason, for the "wealth of faith that flows in her healthy heart" ("Ast ubi credentis iam sano in pectore coepit / Diues adesse fides" 120–1) and, in Book 1, the three youths are saved from the fiery furnace by virtue of their ardent souls (1.204–5): "O quanta est credentum gloria! flammis / Ardentis fidei

---

63 De Nie touches on this significance of light imagery in *Poetics of Wonder*, 397–8.
64 See Green, *Latin Epics*, 218, who attributes the poetry here to the epic heritage of the *Carmen paschale*.

restincta est flamma camini" ("Oh, how great is the glory of those believers! With the flames of ardent faith, the flame of that furnace was checked"). Often in the *Carmen paschale*, Sedulius makes a point of saying that Christ does not deny or withhold his gifts from those who believe ("Credenti quae nulla negat nec dona retardat," 3.16), and the miracles that highlight the healing of the blind and lame almost always emphasize the spiritual health of the physically infirm.

At the opening of Book 4, Christ again restores the sight of two blind men, and here Sedulius refines his approach to this kind of miracle while not abandoning the focus on inner faith (4.31–9):

30 Et ecce duo caeci sedentes secus uiam audierunt, quod Iesus transit et cla-mauerunt dicentes: Miserere nobis fili Dauid. 31 Turba autem increpabat eos, ut tacerent. At illi magis clamabant dicentes: Domine, miserere nobis, fili Dauid. 32 Et stetit Iesus et uocauit eos et ait: Quid uultis, ut faciam uobis? 33 Dicunt illi: Domine, ut aperiantur oculi nostri. 34 Misertus est autem illis Iesus tetigit oculos eorum et confestim uiderunt et secuti sunt eum.[65]

– Mt 20:30–4

Praeterea geminos Dominus considere caecos
Dum quoddam transiret iter comitante caterua
Conspicit, extinctae poscentes munera formae
Flebilibusque uagas implentes uocibus auras.
Nec cunctata solens pietas inferre salutem,   35
Quae sentit flagrare fidem, mox lumina tangens
Euigilare iubet, quae somnus presserat ingens,
Atque diu clausas reserans sub fronte fenestras
Ingrediente die fecit discedere noctem.

[Afterward, when the Lord was crossing a road crowded with people, he saw two blind men sitting there, begging for the gifts of their lost sight and filling the wandering airs with tearful voices. And accustomed to bestowing

---

65 Mt 20:30–4: "And behold two blind men sitting by the way side, heard that Jesus passed by, and they cried out, saying: 'O Lord, thou son of David, have mercy on us.' 31 And the multitude rebuked them that they should hold their peace. But they cried out the more, saying: 'O Lord, thou son of David, have mercy on us.' 32 And Jesus stood, and called them, and said: 'What will ye that I do to you?' 33 They say to him: 'Lord, that our eyes be opened.' 34 And Jesus having compassion on them, touched their eyes. And immediately they saw, and followed him."

his aid, his unwavering pity sensed their ardent faith, and touching them, he bade their eyes be wakeful, eyes that great sleep had overcome; and opening the long-shut windows beneath their brows, he made the night vanish with the coming of day.]

The words *caeci* and *considere* (for *sedentes*) pick up on the biblical prose in the first line; so does *transiret* for *transit* in verse 32, but the remainder of the scene departs from the Gospel narrative appreciably. As with the scene in Book 3, the men's sight is "extinguished" (*extinctae*, 33), while the fire of their inner faith burns brightly (*flagrare fidem*, 36). The word *lumina* (36) again describes the "eyes," but two new ideas separate this miracle from the last. Blindness is now compared to a heavy sleep ("quae somnus presserat ingens," 37), like the sleep of death lying over the girl Christ "awakens" earlier (3.103–42), and their eyes are likewise bidden to rouse and be watchful (*Euigilare iubet*, 4.37), like drowsy sentinels at their post. A new metaphor also compares blindness to shuttered windows now opened by the hand of God, so that the light of day and faith may shine in. All of this imagery builds upon the essential Gospel narrative, to emphasize the importance of cultivating personal faith and the rewards that brings.

Of the three other miracles in the *Carmen paschale* involving the healing of the blind, the last is the most elaborate and significant.[66] In Book 4, Christ opens "the gateways of a blind man's cheeks" at the waters of Siloah (4.251–70):[67]

1 Et praeteriens uidit hominem caecum a nativitate. 2 Et interrogauerunt eum discipuli eius dicentes: Rabbi, quis peccauit hic aut parentes eius, ut caecus nasceretur? 3 Respondit Iesus: Neque hic peccauit (deliquid) neque parentes eius, sed ut manifestetur opera Dei in illo. 4 Me oportet operari opera eius qui me misit dum dies est; ueniet nox, cum nemo potest operari. 5 Cum sum in hoc mundo, lux sum mundi. 6 Haec cum dixisset, expuit in terram et fecit lutum de sputamento et superlinuit lutum super oculos eius. 7 Et dixit ei: Vade in natatoria Siloae (Siloam), quod interpretatur Missus. Et abiit et lauit et uenit uidens.

– Jn 9:1–7

---

66 A brief account of healing blindness appears at 4.99–105 and then at 4.106–8.

67 See also O'Daly, *Days Linked by Song*, who mentions this episode with reference to Prudentius and *Cathemerinon* 9, where much of the same imagery and interpretation appears.

Inde means genitum cernit considere caecum,
Qui male praegnantis dilapsus uentre parentis
In lucem sine luce ruit. Tunc sanguinis ille
Conditor humani mundique orientis origo,
Inperfecta diu proprii non passus haberi   255
Membra operis, natale lutum per claustra genarum
Inliniens hominem ueteri de semine supplet.
Nec uisum tamen ante capit, quam uoce iubentis
Accepta Domini Siloam uenisset ad undam
Et consanguinei tutus medicamine limi   260
Pura oculos fouisset aqua. mox ergo gemellae
Vultibus effulgent acies tandemque merentur
Ignotum spectare diem. cognoscite cuncti,
Mystica quid doceant animos miracula nostros.
Caeca sumus proles miserae de fetibus Euae,   265
Portantes longo natas errore tenebras.
Sed dignante Deo mortalem sumere formam
Tegminis humani, facta est ex uirgine nobis
Terra salutaris, quae fontibus abluta sacris
Clara renascentis reserat spiramina lucis.   270

[As he was walking along, Christ saw a man born blind sitting nearby, who
had fallen from his poor mother's pregnant womb, rushing into the light
without light. Then the Creator of human blood and the Origin of the world's
beginning – not long allowing the limbs of his own work to be imperfect –
smeared natal mud upon the gates of his cheeks and made that man whole
again from his ancient seed. But he did not regain his sight until he heard the
voice of God commanding him to come to the pool of Siloah, and the pure
water had healed his eyes, made whole by the remedy of the kindred mud. So
his two pupils soon shone from his face and earned at last to see the unknown
day. Let all recognize what these mystic miracles may teach our souls! We are
the blind offspring of Eve's wretched womb, who bear a darkness born of
longstanding sin; but since God deigned to take on mortal form, the human
coil, this land has been made wholesome for us by the Virgin, washed by sacred fonts, so that it might open the shining paths of light reborn.]

The essence of the biblical story underlies the poetic narrative, and there
is sufficient language from the prose to authenticate the verse, but Sedulius
also uses the story to introduce baptismal imagery. The blind man stands
for all of humankind, and with a view to Adam and Eve, blindness is the

result of man's failure in Eden.[68] That much is suggested by "the fall" in line 252, but more explicit allusions to Genesis begin with the epithets for Christ as "founder of humankind" and "origin of the nascent world" ("Conditor humani mundique orientis origo," 4.254). These epithets situate Christ at the moment of Creation, so that Sedulius offers a virtual re-enactment of Adam's birth in the mud smeared on the blind man's cheeks. That is an allusion to Genesis 2:7 "formauit igitur Dominus Deus hominem de limo terrae" ("And the Lord God formed man of the slime of the earth"). The "slime" (*limus*) there is like the mud used to heal the blind man, and that it is "natal mud" (*natale lutum*, 4.256) announces a connection to man's rebirth in Christ. Sedulius then alludes to Adam and Eve explicitly with reference to the "ancient seed" (*ueteri de semine*, 4.257) and by Christ's refusal to let his "own work" suffer imperfection ("Inperfecta diu proprii non passus haberi/Membra operis," 255–6). As the miracle draws to a close, the blind man cleans his eyes in the pool of Siloah, an allusion to Baptism, and Mary enters the narrative as the vessel of man's redemption. Her appearance also echoes the opening of the poem, where Sedulius describes Mary as the new Eve, through whom the human race is renewed by the birth of Christ (2.33–4): "Christo nascente renasci/Possit homo et ueteris maculam deponere carnis" ("Man can be reborn with the birth of Christ and put aside the stain of ancient flesh"). But Sedulius does not leave his readers to connect these symbolic dots by themselves. He intervenes directly and says, *cognoscite cuncti*! (4.263), much as he does at the opening of his poem (*mentes huc uertite cuncti*, 1.37), proclaiming that we are "the blind offspring of Eve's wretched womb" (4.265) and that this story is a metaphor for our own fallen condition, but that Christ may renew us, if we cultivate our faith.

Conclusion

Sedulius is the first writer in the genre to make biblical epic an important source of biblical commentary. In this respect, he is as much a path-breaker as Juvencus, who shows how to make good and pious use of pagan literature. Obviously, Sedulius knows *Euangeliorum libri*, and when he sits down to versify a particular episode, there is a sense that Juvencus is a touchstone for his own work. But he parts company with Juvencus (and Cyprianus) in terms of his greater predilection towards sumptuous

---

68 See further Dermott-Small, "Rhetoric and Exegesis," 233.

elocution – "poetic delights" as he calls them (*poeticas delicias*) – and symbolism, through which the historical events of the Bible assume greater spiritual significance. Biblical epic therefore becomes more sophisticated in this period, as poets like Sedulius add exegesis to the already complex blend of classical and Christian literature. But Sedulius is more than equal to the task, and a close reading of many passages of the *Carmen paschale* reveals layers of meaning that mingle classical allusion with Christian doctrine. There is good reason to call Sedulius the Christian Vergil.

Chapter Five

Avitus' *Historia Spiritalis* (c. 500 CE)

Et tamen adueniet tempus, cum crimina ligni
Per lignum sanet purgetque nouissimus
Adam Materiamque ipsam faciat medicamina uitae.

[And yet there will come a time when a new Adam will cleanse and purge the sins
of the tree by the cross and make his body the remedy of life.]

– Historia spiritalis (3.20–2)

Alcimus Ecdicius Avitus of Vienne was the son of Hesychius and Audentia
and one of four children. His father was bishop of Vienne, and Avitus
assumed that position upon his father's death around 490 CE.[1] Avitus
himself died between 517 and 519.[2] His biblical poem, *De spiritalis*

---

1 See Shanzer and Wood, *Avitus of Vienne*, 14; Hecquet-Noti, ed. and trans., *Avit de Vienne*, 24–5; Nodes, ed., *The Fall of Man*, 1; Roberts, *Biblical Epic*, 99–100. Roberts cites the *Vita* of Avitus for the date of the poet's succession to the episcopal see, "in or shortly before 491" (p. 99), but we cannot be sure, say Shanzer and Wood, 7. The reference to the *Vita* can be found in the edition of Morrica *Storia della letteratura latina cristiana*, vol. 3, 139. For Avitus' family ties, see Mathisen, "Epistolography, Literary Circles and Family Ties in Late Roman Gaul," *TAPA* 111 (1981), 100, and the introduction to Avitus' letters in Shanzer and Wood, *Avitus of Vienne*, 4–6.

2 See further Roberts, "The Latin Literature of Late Antiquity," in *Medieval Latin* 537–46. Avitus was present at the council of Epao (517) but absent from the council of Lyon (519), hence the suggestion of 518 for his death. Furthermore, his feast day is 5 February and his *Vita* puts his death within the reign of emperor Anastasius, who died in 518; so 5 February 518 is a probable date. See also Shanzer and Wood, *Avitus of Vienne*, 10.

historiae gestis (*On the Events of Spiritual History*), hereafter *Historia spiritalis*, is a five-book rendition of episodes from Genesis and Exodus, written in 2552 hexameters (325; 423; 425; 658; 721), and its date of composition lies somewhere between 497 and 500.[3] Like the *Carmen paschale*, *Historia spiritalis* is a thematically driven versification of the Bible, and each of the five books of the narrative relates to the general theme of salvation history. The five books include[4] *De initio mundi* (*On the Beginning of the World*), *De originali peccato* (*On Original Sin*), *De sententia Dei* (*On God's Judgment*), *De diluuio mundi* (*On the Flood on the World*), *De transitu maris rubri* (*On the Crossing of the Red Sea*). This, then, is no *paene ad uerbum* translation of the Old Testament in the style of the *Heptateuch* but, as the title suggests, a spiritual commentary on the incidents of the Bible.[5]

Classical Context

Avitus' writings show extensive knowledge of classical literature, and as a member of the highest social class, he would have had an excellent education.[6] As Shanzer and Wood remark in their edition of his letters, "his was perhaps the last generation for which the full Roman pattern of education was available in Gaul, and he certainly took immense pride in the correctness of his pronunciation," for example.[7] Predictably, Vergil exerts the greatest influence upon the language of the poem, although Avitus also echoes "Lucan, Silius Italicus, Valerius Flaccus, Martial, and Claudian, among pagan authors, and Prudentius, Marius Victorius, Cyprianus Gallus,

---

3 I have used Hecquet-Noti's edition of Avitus for the text, but I have also consulted Peiper throughout.

4 Avitus himself names the work in a letter to his cousin Apollonaris, bishop of Auvergne. See Shanzer and Wood, *Avitus of Vienne*, 51.

5 See further Wood, "Avitus of Vienne: The Augustinian Poet," 262–77 at 274: "Avitus' biblical epic is therefore not simply a piece of narrative writing: inspired by Augustine, it is primarily biblical exegesis, pursuing in particular two of the approaches to scriptural exposition set out by the bishop of Hippo: *historia* and *allegoria*."

6 Shanzer and Wood, *Avitus of Vienne*, 58; Goelzer, *Le Latin de Saint Avit*, 3–4; Hecquet-Noti, *Avit de Vienne*, tome I, 25–6; and Deproost, 'La mise en oeuvre du merveilleux épique dans le poème De deluvio mundi d'Avit de Vienne," 88–103 at 88.

7 Shanzer and Wood, *Avitus of Vienne*, 7. See esp. Avitus' Letter 57 in the same edition, 270–3.

and Dracontius, among Christian."[8] Avitus also mentions his close relative, Sidonius Apollinaris, who is another important influence.[9]

Much of *Historia spiritalis* rings with echoes of earlier classical poetry. Jonah is "buffeted on land and sea" in precisely the same terms as Aeneas ("Multum ille et terris iactatus et alto," 4.359), and Avitus describes the great storm at the Flood (4.429–40) with an epic zeal rivaling earlier biblical poets.[10] God descends to earth in terms that echo the movements of the deities in Vergil's *Aeneid*,[11] and Nicole Hecquet-Noti identifies Adam, Noah, and Moses as the "heroes" of the work; the latter two are both called *heros* in the poem.[12] Hecquet-Noti also connects the *gesta* of *Historia spiritalis* to the glorious deeds of epic and suggests that the three-part movement of the narrative bears a resemblance to the general shape of the *Aeneid*: a peaceful interval (Eden/Carthage), a new land (Flood/Latium, etc.), and a final battle (Exodus/Turnus).[13] That battle on the banks of the Red Sea becomes the staging ground for a conflict of epic proportions, in which heroes take up arms against their foes and deliver magniloquent speeches.[14] "Such speeches," as Michael Roberts remarks, "were felt to be one of the glories of epic,"[15] and they serve to "intensify the emotional force of the narrative."[16]

---

8 This list is from Wood, "Avitus of Vienne," 263, who cites also Costanza and Arweiler in his notes. See further Costanza, *Avitiana I* and Arweiler, *Die Imitation antiker und spätantiker Literatur*. Goelzer provides his own list in his extensive analysis of *Historia spritalis* (p. 5), including Vergil, Ovid, Claudian, Horace, Seneca, Catullus, Juvenal, Silius, Statius, Propertius, Martial, and Ausonius. Hecquet-Noti offers the following in her edition as "les principales sources d'inspiration d'Avit" (p. 67): Vergil, Lucan, Ovid, Statius, Silius Italicus, but also more broadly Cicero's *De natura deorum* and Pliny's *Naturalis Historia*.

9 See further, Wood, "Avitus of Vienne," 264 and Goelzer, "Ovid et saint Avit," in *Mélanges* 275–80. Goelzer credits Sidonius as an important intermediary for the influence of Ovid on *Historia spiritalis*, including the episode of the Flood. See also Deproost, "Mise en oeuvre," 88, n. 3.

10 See further Hecquet-Noti *Avit de Vienne*, tome I, 67–73.

11 Ibid., 68, where Hecquet-Noti refers to *Aen.* 4.276–8, "la disparition de Mercure, ou *Aen.* 9.656–8, celle d'Apollon."

12 See ibid., 38. Hecquet-Noti also links Adam, Moses, and Noah with Christ, and promotes typology as a unifying feature of the poem.

13 Ibid., 45.

14 See further Roberts, "Rhetoric and Poetic Imitation in Avitus." For uses of the word *heros* in the narrative as a classicism see, e.g., 4.222 (Noah) and 5.67 (Moses). For martial-heroic scenes in the Exodus section of the poem, see also 5.373–83 and 5.501–25.

15 Ibid., 31.

16 Roberts, *Biblical Epic*, 194. Also, Hecquet-Noti, *Avit de Vienne*, tome I, 52.

Above the earth, *Olympus* stands for heaven, and the name of "God" appears in the plural form, *dei/di*, as a deliberate classicism.[17] Below, on earth, Satan "arms" for war (*armat*, 2.125) and enters Eden, having covered his "airy body" (*aerium corpus*, 2.121) with a serpent's skin. It is perhaps no coincidence that the adjective *aerium* sounds like *aereum* ("bronze"), the stuff of epic battle-gear. Elsewhere, in response to the epic simile, Avitus lavishes detail on comparisons of all kinds, so that untended souls grow to be as unruly as abandoned fields (4.37–53) and sin, like a surging river (4.62–75), ruins all in its path.[18] Everywhere, Avitus amplifies the original language of the Bible, adding lofty diction and imagery from his classical sources of inspiration,[19] and yet Roberts has cautioned that Avitus is also careful, even conservative in his use of classical-poetic diction, and can be critical of classical mythology.[20]

Biblical Context

By this time, Jerome's Latin translation of the Bible had been available for almost a century, and yet Avitus appears to have used the Vulgate and *Vetus Latina* in his poem and without much recourse to the Greek Septuagint.[21] "Avitus was the first of the Old Testament poets to introduce a thematic principle of selection" to the versification of the Bible (although New Testament poets had already broken that ground), and because he limits his focus to "spiritual history," he is "able to circumvent many of the problems his predecessors had encountered," notably Cyprianus.[22] Like Sedulius, Avitus depends in many places on symbolism to support his theme, so that, for example, the wood of the tree of Paradise comes to symbolize the cross and the forgiveness of sins (3.20–2): "Et tamen adueniet tempus, cum crimina ligni/Per lignum sanet purgetque nouissimus Adam/Materiamque ipsam faciat medicamina uitae" ("A new Adam will

---

17 For other examples of the plural form of *deus* see, e.g., 2.202, 209, and 220.

18 In the last instance, compare Juvencus (1.687), who, in versifying Mt. 7:13–14, refers to evils that may sweep one away like the current of a river ("arripit hos pronoque trahit uelut impetus amnis").

19 On amplification in Avitus, see Roberts, *Biblical Epic*, 193–8.

20 See Roberts, "Preface to Avitus," 405, where he suggests that the use of the *tonans* epithet serves as *Kontrastimitation*, offering critical commentary on the pagan gods.

21 See Hecquet-Noti, *Avit de Vienne*, tome I, 74–7. See also Deproost, "Mise en scène," 44, n. 5, who favours parallels with the Vulgate over the Vetus. Peiper's edition also offers a list of citations at 297–9.

22 Roberts, *Biblical Epic*, 123.

clean and purge the sins of the tree by the cross and make his body the remedy of life").[23] Noah's Ark also serves as an emblem for the redemptive power of the cross in the context of Judgment Day (4.323–5): "Effugiet tunc ille malum quicumque paratus, / Construat ut ualidam praeduri teg-minis arcam: / Per lignum uitale crucis seruatus ab undis" ("He will then escape evil, whoever is prepared to build a sturdy ark of powerful protec-tion, so that he may be saved from the waves by the life-giving wood of the cross"). This last example coincides with imagery in Book One of the *Carmen paschale* (1.70–8), where Sedulius describes Jonah's whale as a *uitale sepulchrum* ("a life-giving tomb"), much like the *uitale lignum* of Avitus' ark. There is no doubt, then, that Avitus views the incidents of the Old Testament as much more than literal events. For him the collected books of the Bible are a spiritual history of Christianity.[24]

For this reason, Avitus amplifies the original stories of the Bible with all manner of embellishments. Some of these provide subtle commentary; oth-ers involve extended excursus. In Genesis, for example, Avitus creates a sexually charged image of Eve fondling the forbidden fruit (2.215–16), and this striking image neatly weds pride and desire. Later on, in the wake of satiety, the woeful pair contemplate suicide (3.32–40) in what is a realistic drama about the pain and guilt of newborn sin. Both scenes contain star-tling departures from the biblical text that add greater psychological and emotional depth to the story of the Fall. As a touching scene in this con-text, the couple weep for the first time, and "unbidden moisture pours down their attentive cheeks" (3.209–19). Their cheeks, surprised at this, take note of the event, in what is a powerful statement about the loss of innocence. Many other additions populate the narrative of *Historia spirit-alis*, and these intensify a variety of thoughts and feelings awoken by the prose and often intimate deeper meaning. Thus "the burning bush signifies the ardour of the pious heart (5.37–9); the Passover sign ... looks forward to the sign of the Cross, for Christ is the lamb (5.247, 254); the manna in

---

23 In associating Christ and the redemptive power of the cross with the tree of life in the Garden of Eden, Avitus no doubt chooses the word *materia*, which refers to wood or some other building material, as a pun on the wood of the tree (*lignum*); the notion of redemption as a medication (*medicamina*) is probably a reference to a healing salve made from the bark of trees. The substance of Christ, therefore, in opposition to the substance of the tree, forms the essential ingredient in the remedy for mortal life: eternal salvation.

24 See Deproost, "Mise en oeuvre," 89, who mentions the role of imagination and com-mentary in the context of Book 4 of *Historia spiritalis*, which involves the Flood.

the desert foreshadows Christ born without the involvement of semen (5.458–61); the water from the rock shows the thirst-quenching qualities of Christ's wounds (5.462–6)," and so on.[25] Signs and symbols abound in pursuit of spiritual signification, and these are coloured by classical allusions and poetic interpolations that add tremendous depth to the narrative.

The Opening (1.1–13)

The opening of *Historia spiritalis* does not offer a preface in the epic tradition of the *praefatio*. Avitus delivers no grand invocation of the muse, Christian or otherwise, nor is there much homage paid to Homer or Vergil, such as we find at the opening of Juvencus' *Euangeliorum libri*. Instead, "the deeds of ancient parents" (*priscorum facta parentum*, 4), of Adam and Eve, provide a sense of "antiquity" with reference to the Old Testament, and their sins – not those of distant heroes – earn the poet's censure. Avitus' emphasis on original sin carries throughout the whole of *Historia spiritalis*, and the various hardships which the human race has had to endure since the expulsion from Eden (*uarios ... labores*, 1) begin here with the failed first father (1–13):[26]

> Quidquid agit uarios humana in gente labores,
> Vnde breuem carpunt mortalia tempora uitam,
> Vel quod polluti uitiantur origine mores,
> Quos aliena premunt priscorum facta parentum.
> Addatur quamquam nostra de parte reatus, 5
> Quod tamen amisso dudum peccatur honore,
> Ascribam tibi, prime pater, qui semine mortis
> Tollis succiduae uitalia germina proli.
> Et licet hoc totum Christus persoluerit in se,
> Contraxit quantum percussa in stirpe propago: 10
> Attamen auctoris uitio, qui debita leti
> Instituit morbosque suis ac funera misit,
> Viuit peccati moribunda in carne cicatrix.

---

25 Wood, "Avitus of Vienne," 265.

26 See also Shea, *Poems of Alcimus Ecdicius Avitus*, 14: "It [the first poem] begins and ends by focusing on sin and death." Also, throughout my discussion of Avitus, I have consulted the English translations of Shea, *The Poems of Alcimus Ecdicius Avitus*, and the French translation and edition of Hecquet-Noti, *Avit de Vienne*, tomes I and II.

[Whatever brings various hardships down on the human race, from which mortal seasons pluck brief life, or to whatever extent our nature is tainted and soiled by its origins, burdened by the distant deeds of ancient parents – although guilt is also owing on our part – but what has been committed since the long loss of that glory, I blame on you, first father, who with the seed of death destroyed the life-giving buds of future generations. And although Christ has paid for the sum of this on his own – all that our progeny contracted on its beaten stock – nonetheless, it is by the inventor's vice, who established the penalty of death and brought disease and decay, that the scar of that sin lives in our death-ridden flesh.]

Bitter memory marks the opening of *Historia spiritalis*. Channelling Juvenal's *Satires* (1.85–6) and that poet's censure of vice in the world (1.85–6), Avitus links the burdens of his own time to the birth of original sin in Paradise.[27] The verb *carpere* (2), whereby "mortal times pluck brief life" ("Vnde breuem carpunt mortalia tempora uitam," 2), is also an allusion to that first crime in Eden. Cyprianus puts this same word into the mouth of Satan in the same context (*Hept. Gen.* 79–80): "Atqui si studeas mellitos carpere uictus,/Aureus astrigero ridebit cardine mundus" ("But if you strive to pluck the honey-sweet food, the golden world will smile from the starry heights"). Later in Book 1 of *Historia spiritalis*, the verb applies to the wholesome fruit God has set aside for the nourishment of Adam and Eve, but even that moment is filled with foreboding (1.307): "Sumite concessas fruges et carpite poma" ("Take the allotted fruit and pluck those apples"). That food, says God, nourishes long life and pleasant toil (1.308–9): "Hic operis dulci studio secura quiescat/Deliciisque fruens longaeuo in tempore uita" ("Here may life rest easy in pursuit of sweet labour and enjoy delights in long life").[28] Adam, however, forfeits that "sweet labour" out of ambition, and thereby condemns man to the various hardships that now burden mortal life ("uarios humana in gente labores," 1). So the first line of *Historia spiritalis* is a reminder of Adam's punishment for his disobedience (Gen. 3:17): "… in laboribus comedes ex ea cunctis diebus vitae tuae" ("… in labour and toil shall you eat [of the earth] all the days of your life"). The only consolation for this hardship is *Christus* (9), who figures in this context as a

---

27 Cf. Juv. *Sat.* 1.85–6: "Quidquid agunt homines, uotum, timor, ira, uoluptas,/Gaudia, discursus, nostri farrago libelli est."

28 The phrase *operis dulci studio* (1.308) is hypallage. It is not the pursuit that is sweet, but the labour.

promise of future redemption. He will be a new Adam for the world (*nouissimus Adam*, 3.21), and he will succeed where the first father failed. That is the essential message of the opening to *Historia spiritalis*.

The Creation of the World (1.14–29)

Without any further word about Adam, Avitus turns abruptly at line fourteen to Creation, introducing sudden light and beauty in stark contrast to the gloom of the preceding lines.[29] Everywhere the language of the Bible is omitted or upgraded for the sake of a visual portrait, and this language is much indebted to earlier classical verse. As one critic puts it, "Avitus' structure is clearly graphic; it pictures the Christian cosmic vision as if it might have been pictured in later centuries in stained glass."[30] So distant is this tableau from the narrative of the Bible that it suffices to include references to the scriptural prose in the context of analysis only (1.14–29):

> Iam Pater omnipotens librantis pondere uerbi
> Vndique collectis discreuerat arida lymphis   15
> Litoribus pontum constringens, flumina ripis.
> Iam proprias pulchro monstrabat lumine formas
> Obscuro cedente die uarioque colore
> Plurima distinctum pingebat gratia mundum.
> Temporibus sortita uices tum lumina caelo   20
> Fulsere alterno solis lunaeque meatu.
> Quin et sidereus nocturno in tempore candor
> Temperat horrentes astrorum luce tenebras.
> Actutum suaui producens omnia fetu
> Pulchra repentino uestita est gramine tellus.   25
> Accepere genus sine germine iussa creari
> Et semen uoluisse fuit. Sic ubere uerbi
> Frondescunt siluae: teneris radicibus arbor
> Durauit uastos paruo sub tempore ramos.

[Now the Almighty Father, with the weight of a measured word, parted dry land from the waters that pooled all around, binding sea to shores, rivers to banks. He then revealed individual forms in the shining light and, as darkness

---

29 This sudden transition may suggest that the preface was added late to the narrative.
30 Shea, *Poems of Alcimus Avitus*, 20.

left the day, profuse splendour painted a world adorned with rich colour. Then lights, allotted in turn to times in heaven, shone by the alternating paths of sun and moon. Even at night, starry brilliance softened the dreadful shadows with the light of the stars. Bringing everything to life at once in sweet birth, the beautiful earth was suddenly clothed in grass. Seedless creations were assigned species and their seed was His will. Thus by the fertility of the word, forests grew leaves and the wood of delicate roots hardened great limbs in no time.]

These sixteen lines cover the first twenty verses of Genesis, and Avitus reduces some three hundred words to one hundred. He does not so much as name "heaven" or "earth," and other anticipated language is missing as well. There is no *Fiat lux* ("Let there be light"), no *firmamentum* or *abyssus*, and little sense that God is pleased with his efforts (i.e., "*et uidit Deus quod esset bonum*").[31] The biblical noun *aqua* is abandoned for the more poetic *lympha* (15), and the prose *lux* is replaced by the more lyrical alternative, *lumen* (17, 20).[32] Only later in the scene, and only once, does the poet resort to the former (*luce tenebras*, 23). The days of Creation are not mentioned at all, which provide Cyprianus with a structural framework for his account of Creation in the *Heptateuch* (*Gen.* 1–24), and most of the repetition in the prose is eliminated in the poem, including the ubiquitous phrase *factum est* which gives structure to the biblical narrative. Direct speech is also omitted, and only two references to the word of God appear in this passage, one at the beginning (*pondere uerbi*, 14) and one at the end (*ubere uerbi*, 27).[33] These frame the initial moments of Creation within the scope of God's omnipotent and fertile word, and yet nothing is named explicitly, as it is in the Bible.

Traces of the prose that do survive are unremarkable. They begin in the second verse (15): "Vndique collectis discreuerat arida lymphis." This line adapts Genesis 1:4, "and he divided light from the darkness" ("et diuisit lucem a tenebris"), but in *Historia spiritalis* God divides land and sea, which does not happen in the Bible until later in verse nine: "Dixit uero Deus: Congregentur aquae, quae sub caelo sunt, in locum unum: et appareat arida. Et factum est ita" ("God also said: Let the waters that are under

---

31   Note, however, Hecquet-Noti, *Avit de Vienne*, tome I, 132, n. 3, who mentions the phrase *uidit Deus quod esset bonum* at the end of this section.

32   Avitus uses the phrase *arida lymphis* again at the end of the Flood, connecting this moment with the recreation of the world (4.562): "Libera subductis nituerunt arida lymphis."

33   The phrase *ubere uerbi* is rare, but see Arator, *Hist. Apost.* (*uberibus uerbis*, 1.577).

the heaven, be gathered together into one place: and let the dry land appear. And it was so done"). Avitus therefore rearranges things as Cyprianus does in the *Heptateuch*. Verse nine of the Bible is also where the word *arida* ("dry") first appears, and Avitus adopts it and the reference to the "gathered waters" in line fifteen of his poem (*collectis ... lymphis*, 15). His use of the participle *collectis* is probably guided by *colligatur* in the *Vetus Latina*, where it appears as a variant for *congregetur*. Likely, too, the verb *discreuerat* (15) is an echo of *discreuit*, another variant in the *Vetus*, which sometimes appears instead of *diuisit* in verse four of the Bible ("et diuisit deus inter lucem et tenebras").[34] Otherwise, Avitus includes a handful of biblical words, including references to the shadows (*tenebras*, 23), the day (*Obscuro cedente die*, 18), the time (*temporibus*, 20), the first species (*genus*, 26), and their seeds (*semen*, 27). All of this is biblical diction, as is the verb *creo* (i.e., *creauit Deus caelum et terram*), which does not make an appearance until line twenty-six and then only with passing reference to the things bidden to be made (*iussa creari*, 26). In short, the scriptural language of the scene does not provide much of an authenticating voice for the poetry. Avitus could have chosen from any number of well-worn words and phrases from the Bible, but instead he prefers to stand at a distance, like an impressionist painter, since close proximity to the prose is no longer needed, no longer in tune with the literary tastes of his time.

The remarkable language in this portrait is therefore non-biblical, including several phrases at the cadence of the line, which harkens to earlier classical and Christian poetry. The doublet *pondere uerbi* (14), for example, which is rare, appears almost verbatim in Juvencus' *Euangeliorum libri* in the context of Jesus' words to Mary (1.303): "Nec genetrix tanti persensit pondera uerbi" ("And his mother did not perceive the weight of his words"). It may be that Avitus borrows this phrase as a way of expressing the weight of God's utterance in the first moments of Creation. The phrase *flumina ripis* (16), or variants of it, also shows up frequently in classical poetry, such as in the works of Vergil (*Ecl.* 7.52; *Georg.* 4.527), Horace (*Carm.* 1.20.6), Ovid (*Met.* 2.241), and Statius (*Theb.* 4.313), but also in the Christian poetry of Cyprianus (*Ios.* 108) and later in Fortunatus (*Carm.* 6. 5. 327). The effective juxtaposition of *luce tenebras* can be found in Ovid

---

34 See also Hecquet-Noti, *Avit de Vienne*, Tome I, 129, n. 6, who mentions this reading in the *Vetus Latina*, and Ambrose, who uses it himself to describe the separation of the waters on the second day (*Hex.* 2.3.8).

(*Am.* 3.8.36), Lucan (*Phar.* 8.58), and Silius Italicus (*Pun.* 6.150), but also in Juvencus (1.624), Paulinus (*Carm.* 18.273, 19.419, 32.218), Cyprianus (*Gen.* 536), and Dracontius (*Laud. Dei* 1.419, 2.12). Avitus himself uses the phrase again, twice (5.518, 6.455). But Dracontius and *De Laudibus Dei* leave a strong impression on the closing verses of this scene.[35] The words *frondescunt siluae* (28) appear verbatim in Dracontius' *De Laudibus Dei* in the context of God's creative power (2.223–4): "Per te fetat humus, per te, Deus, herba uirescit,/Frondescunt siluae, spirat flos, germinat arbor" ("Through You the earth is fruitful, through You, God, the grass grows green, forests gain leaves, the flower breathes, the tree buds"). So, too, *radicibus arbor* (28) at the end of the line resonates with an earlier passage from Book 1 of Dracontius (1.627): "Maior et ex truncis surgit radicibus arbor/Et foliis uestita uiret redeuntibus annis" ("And a greater tree arises from the stricken roots and, clothed in leaves, grows green for the returning years"). Note the use of *uestita* ("clothed") as well, which describes the grass in this passage of Avitus ("uestita est gramine tellus," 25). In short, Avitus appears to know Dracontius and several other Christian poets, which speaks to the influence of both Christian and classical verse on *Historia spiritalis*.

The purpose of all this added language is to embellish the biblical vision of Creation, by introducing fresh colour.[36] Thus the light that reveals the new land is "beautiful" (*pulchro … lumine*, 17), and God "paints" it with "varied colour," like an artist (*uarioque colore … pingebat*, 19). The grass is "beautiful" and clothes the ground like raiment ("pulchra repentino uestita est gramine tellus," 25). The interplay of light and darkness also adds degrees of shade to the scene in accordance with the passage of time. Shapes are first revealed by light (*lumine formas*, 17), and then darkness yields to day (*obscuro cedente die*, 18). "Lights" are set in heaven (*lumina caelo*, 20), and their brightness shines against the blackness of night ("sidereus nocturno in tempore candor," 22), as shadows are tempered by the light of the stars (*astrorum luce tenebras*, 23). To these sights, Avitus adds sound. Alliteration abounds, including a significant link between *pater* (14) and *pondere* (14) in the first verse, which bind God and the weight of His word. Tailing alliteration connects the waters (*lymphis*, 15) to their shores *litoribus* (16), and paronomasia joins alliteration in several places: *flumina*

---

35 See Hecquet-Noti, *Avit de Vienne*, tome I, 128–9, who notes other echoes of Dracontius.

36 See also Wood, "Avitus of Vienne, the Augustinian Poet" 264, who highlights the *locus amoenus* theme and names Sidonius' panegyric on the emperor Anthemius as an important source for Avitus here.

(16)/*lumine* (17); *lumina* (20)/*lunae* (21)/*luce* (23); *tempore* (23)/*temperat* (24)/*tenebras* (24); and *gramine* (25)/*germine* (26). These aural effects show that Avitus is not simply concerned with the verbal relationship of his poem to the Bible, but with the sound of the poetry as well, which is also part of the artistry of *Historia spiritalis*. Looking forward, we may consider that Anglo-Saxon poets learned much from their late antique predecessors, including an appreciation for such aural pyrotechnics.

Creation of Adam (1.44–72)

The account of the creation of Adam and Eve in *Historia spiritalis* is much longer than it is in the *Heptateuch*, to which Cyprianus affords but thirteen lines (25–37). Avitus uses ten times as many and mostly for the sake of Adam (1.44–169), but like Cyprianus he omits a great deal, eliminating redundancies and rearranging the biblical narrative to refine and stylize the original. At the opening of the poem, Avitus introduces Adam as the primogenitor of spiritual history and the failed first father (*prime pater*, 7). Adam was meant to tend the earth and its inhabitants, and to honour God, but his disobedience brought only toil (*labores*, 1) and death into the world (*semine mortis*, 7). All of the optimism expressed in this scene, then, is tinged with irony, knowing what we do of Adam's future. That being said, God's intimate involvement in the creation of man and His ambition to see him rise to his potential, despite knowledge of his failures, offers a positive message to the reader, who may see in these lines God's affection for and commitment to humankind (1.44–72):[37]

> 2:1 Igitur perfecti sunt caeli et terra, et omnis ornatus eorum …
> 2:15 Tulit ergo Dominus Deus hominem et posuit eum in paradiso uoluptatis ut operaretur et custodiret illum.
> 1:26 Et ait faciamus hominem ad imaginem et similitudinem nostram et praesit piscibus maris et uolatilibus caeli et bestiis uniuersaeque terrae omnique reptili quod movetur in terra. 27 Et creauit Deus hominem ad imaginem suam …
> 2:20 Appellauitque Adam nominibus suis cuncta animantia et uniuersa uolatilia caeli et omnes bestias terrae Adae vero non inueniebatur adiutor similis eius.

---

37 I have rearranged the biblical narrative to match the narrative sequence of the poetry.

Ergo ubi completis fulserunt omnia rebus,
Ornatuque suo perfectus constitit orbis,   45
Tum Pater omnipotens aeterno lumine laetum
Contulit ad terras sublimi ex aethere uultum
Illustrans quodcumque uidet: placet ipsa tuenti
Artifici factura suo laudatque Creator
Dispositum pulchro, quem condidit, ordine mundum.   50
Tum demum tali Sapientia uoce locuta est:
"En praeclara nitet mundano machina cultu;
Et tamen impletum perfectis omnibus orbem
Quid iuuat ulterius nullo cultore teneri?
Sed ne longa nouam contristent otia terram,   55
Nunc homo formetur, summi quem tangat imago
Numinis, et nostram celso donatus honore
Induat interius formonsa in mente figuram.
Hunc libet erectum uultu praeponere pronis,
Qui regat aeterno subiectum foedere mundum,   60
Bruta domet, legem cunctis ac nomina ponat,
Astra notet caelique uias et sidera norit
Discat et inspectis discernere tempora signis.
Subiciat pelagus saeuum ingenioque tenaci
Possideat quaecumque uidet: cui bestia frendens   65
Seruiat et posito discant mansueta furore
Imperium iumenta pati iussique ligari
Festinent trepidi consueta in uincla iuuenci.
Quoque magis natura hominis sublimior extet,
Accipiat rectos in caelum tollere uultus: 70
Factorem quaerat proprium, cui mente fideli
Impendat famulam longaeuo in tempore uitam."

[So, when the work was done, everything shone and the earth stood complete
in its adornment. Then the Almighty Father turned His face, joyful with eternal light, from lofty heaven toward the land, enlightening all that it beheld.
That handiwork pleased its Maker looking on, and He praised the world He
had made, so well arranged in comely order. Then at last Wisdom spoke with
a fair voice: "Behold, this brilliant frame shines with earthly cultivation, and
yet what further good is this world, filled with all these finished things, without a guardian to tend to it? But lest prolonged inactivity should darken this
new land, let man now be made, let the image of highest Divinity touch him
and, since he has been granted lofty honour, let him assume our figure deep
within his finely fashioned mind. It pleases me to put this man, upright in

countenance, before the lowly, who should rule over the world subjected to our eternal covenant, that he should tame the beasts, establish the law and names for all things, observe the stars and pathways of heaven, know the constellations and, having read the signs, learn to follow the seasons: Let him subject the savage sea to his steadfast nature and let him be master of whatever else he beholds. Let the grazing beast serve him and, when their wildness has been subdued, let tamed cattle learn to heed his bidding and, when commanded, let restless bulls hasten to be bound in familiar bonds. Also, let the higher nature of man stand out all the more; let him be given to bear proper regard to heaven. Let him seek his own Maker and with a faithful heart live a long, dutiful life."]

Language from the prose Genesis is scattered over several lines throughout this scene and represented not only by verbatim echoes but synonyms as well. The words that more or less correspond to the Vetus or Vulgate include *ornatusque* and *perfectus* (45), which track the opening of Genesis, chapter 2, and *ergo* (44) is a close counterpart for *igitur* in the same verse. Avitus goes to chapter 2:1 before Genesis 1:26, to provide a direct transition from Creation to the birth of Adam. Cyprianus uses the same tactic in the *Heptateuch* (*Gen.* 25–8):

Haec ubi constituit diuina potentia iussu,   25
Rectorem inspiciens mundanis defore rebus,
Haec memorat: "Hominem nostris faciamus in unguem
Vultibus assimilem. Toto qui regnet in orbe."

[When Divine Power had established these things according to His bidding, seeing no ruler for earthly matters, He said: "Let us make man perfectly in our image, that he may rule over all the world."]

Like Avitus, Cyprianus makes a transition between the completed world and the creation of Adam, and uses an abstract noun of the first declension instead of "God." So *Diuina Potentia* ("Divine Power," 25) appears in the *Heptateuch*, and *Sapientia* ("Wisdom," 51) in *Historia spiritalis*.[38] The stylistic kinship is striking, and so is God's active recognition in both scenes that earth needs a keeper – a *rector* (26) in the first case and a

---

38 Avitus uses *sapientia* again in this way at line 73, where God deigns to form Adam with his hands: "Haec ait et fragilem dignatus tangere terram" ("This he said and deigning to touch the fragile earth …").

cultor (54) in the second. Other evocations of the biblical prose in this passage appear mainly in verses 55–7 with reference to Genesis 1:26 and the words *homo* (56), *imago* (56), and *nostram* (57); *formetur* (56) is a variant of *creauit* in the *Vetus* in verse twenty-seven. In addition, the references to the beasts (*bestia*, 65) and their names (*nomina*, 61) provide additional connections to the biblical prose.[39]

Despite Adam's imminent failure, hence the inescapable irony behind the optimism of this scene, the dominant tone is one of hopefulness. Things are going well. The earth is made and beautifully so. It shines with God's divine light, and affairs are set in order (*ordine mundum*, 50). The machine is finely tuned ("En praeclara nitet mundano machina cultu," 52), and God's desire for man is that he will incline towards the divine essence within him (*formonsa in mente*, 58). As part of his eternal pact with God (*aeterno … foedere*, 60), Adam is set to rule over the earth and its creatures but, above all, to raise his eyes to heaven and honour God ("accipiat rectos in caelum tollere uultus," 70), just as God has deigned to look upon the earth ("contulit ad terras sublimi ex aethere uultum," 47). The juxtaposition of *ex aethere uultum* (47) and *in caelum tollere uultus* (70) is emphatic and almost certainly represents an allusion to Ovid and the creation of man in Book 1 of the *Metamorphoses*.[40] If it is, the purpose of the allusion appears not to be *Kontrastimitation*. There is no apparent censure of Ovid or pagan deities at this point. In fact, the creation of man immediately precedes the golden age in the *Metamorphoses*, which is precisely what God desires for Adam, that is, a long and fruitful life in service to the Lord ("famulam longaeuo in tempore uitam," 72).

The Creation of Adam Cont. (1.73–84)

God's deference towards Adam above His other creations is clear from His personal involvement in man's creation. As Cyprianus puts it, God could have formed man with a word ("Et licet hunc solo posset componere uerbo," *Gen.* 29), but He deigns to touch him with His hands. In *Historia spiritalis*, this process is described with clinical precision and

---

39 The phrase *placet ipsa tuenti* (48) captures the spirit of "uidit Deus quod esset bonum" in the Bible.

40 Cf. Ovid, *Met.* 1.84–6: "Pronaque cum spectent animalia cetera terram, / Os homini sublime dedit caelumque tueri / Iussit et erectos ad sidera tollere uultus" ("While other prone animals look to the earth, he gave man an uplifted face, bidding him look to heaven and bear their upward faces to the stars").

detail, and Ian Wood has identified Augustine's commentary on Genesis as a potential source for Avitus at this moment (1.73–130).[41] I offer only a brief excerpt from the lines immediately following God's speech in the previous section (1.73–84):

2:7 formauit igitur (finxit) dominus deus hominem de limo terrae et inspirauit in faciem eius spiraculum uitae et factus est homo in animam uiuentem.

– Gen. 2:7

… Haec ait et fragilem dignatus tangere terram
Temperat umentem consperso in puluere limum
Orditurque nouum diues Sapientia corpus.   75
Non aliter quam nunc opifex cui est artis in usu
Flectere laxatas per cuncta sequacia ceras
Et uultus implere manu seu corpora gypso
Fingere uel segni speciem componere massae,
Sic Pater omnipotens uicturum protinus aruum   80
Tractat et in lento meditatur uiscera caeno.
Hic arcem capitis sublimi in uertice signat,
Septiforem uultum rationis sensibus aptans
Olfactu, auditu, uisu gustuque potentem.

[This He said and, deigning to touch the fragile earth, mixed damp mud with the scattered dust, and His abundant wisdom began a new body. It was no different than an artist's work today, whose customary craft it is to shape supple wax into all manner of malleable things and fill out faces with his hand, or mold bodies from plaster, or sculpt the image of a statue from a block. In this same way the Omnipotent Father at once took the nascent soil in His hand and designed organs in the thick mud. Here He marked out the peak on the crown of his lofty head, fitting the face with seven holes for the senses of reason, the power of smell, hearing, sight, and taste.]

The opening extra-biblical verses evoke Cyprianus at the same moment in the *Heptateuch* (*Gen.* 29–30), and the alliterative triad, *dignatus ducere dextra* ("deigning to draw him out with his hand") is comparable to Avitus' wording, *dignatus tangere terram* ("deigning to touch the earth"), which contains the same participle, followed by an alliterative doublet; the

---

41 See further Wood, "Avitus of Vienne," 265–6.

following line of *Historia spiritalis* also begins with *temperat*, offering a third instance of alliteration to match the number in Cyprianus. Like Avitus, Cyprianus also puts the main verb at the beginning of the following verse ("Inspirat brutum diuino a pectore pectus," 31), so that there is a general stylistic affinity between the two poets at this point.

But perhaps Avitus has more in common with Hilary of Arles than Cyprianus. Hilary's *Metrum in Genesin* also involves the hand of God in the creation of Adam ("manibusque meis procedat in aeuum," 120), and other language further links the two works.[42] In particular, Hilary also describes the creation of Adam in terms of a sculptor's work (121–2): "Inde, opifex rerum, assumis mollia terrae / Atque uirum formas" ("Then, Artisan of the World, You took up supple bits of earth / and formed man"). Avitus begins his epic simile in lines 76–9 with the very same word, *opifex* (76), and so perhaps Hilary's use of that, *mollia*, and *formas* was enough to prompt the extended conceit in *Historia spiritalis*.[43] Moreover, despite the intervention of Augustine's commentary in the creation of Adam, it must be said that Hilary describes the particulars of anatomy in similar terms (139–40): "Et pecus obtinuit, uentrem, praecordia, neruos. / Venarum riuos et sparsum corpore sanguem" ("… and he received a chest, stomach, heart, nerves, streams of veins, and blood spread throughout the body"). Hilary also offers spiritual commentary on the incidents of Genesis, and so it may be that Hilary is the initial impetus for Avitus' interest in symbolism. Be that as it may, the apparent kinship with Cyprianus and Hilary, not to mention Augustine, serves as a reminder of the difficulty of isolating the precise sources of texts in this period.

The Creation of Eve (1.146–57)

The creation of Eve is much shorter than that of Adam, only twenty-five lines out of the nearly one hundred-and-twenty-five, and while he lavishes attention on Adam, Avitus does not so much as say why Eve needs to be

---

42 Hilary also introduces direct speech for the first time at this moment and with the same words, "Faciamus, ait hominem" (*Met. Gen.* 116), and other passages mention the hand of God (e.g., "O felix animal, summi cui dextra tonantis / Est pater" ("O blessed being, whose father is the hand of the high Thunderer," 125).

43 Note, however, Ovid, who uses the same epithet in the *Metamorphoses* (1.79) and in the context of man's creation (1.78–9): "Natus homo est, siue hunc diuino semine fecit / Ille opifex rerum, mundi melioris origo …" ("Man was born. Either the artisan of things, source of a better world, made him of divine seed …").

created. Nor is there any criticism of her at this point, a striking omission given the upbraiding of Adam at the beginning of *Historia spiritalis* (1.1–13). There, Avitus calls Adam the "author of vice" (*auctoris uitio*, 11) and blames him almost exclusively for the fall of man. Here, in contrast, Eve comes quietly into existence (146–57):

> Immisit (iniecit) ergo Dominus Deus soporem in Adam cumque obdormisset tulit unam de costis (costam de latere) eius, et repleuit (posuit) carnem pro ea 22 Et aedificauit (formauit, figurauit) Dominus Deus costam quam tulerat de Adam in mulierem et adduxit eam ad Adam.
>
> – Gen. 2:21–2

Dumque petunt dulcem spirantia cuncta quietem,
Soluitur et somno laxati corporis Adam.
Cui Pater omnipotens pressum per corda soporem
Iecit et immisso tardauit pondere sensus,
Vis ut nulla queat sopitam soluere mentem: 150
Non si forte fragor securas uerberet aures,
Nec si commoto caelum tunc intonet axe,
Sed nec pressa manu rupissent membra quietem.
Tum uero cunctis costarum ex ossibus unam
Subducit laeuo lateri carnemque reponit.   155
Erigitur pulchro genialis forma decore
Inque nouum subito procedit femina uultum.

[And as everything that breathed sought sweet silence, Adam too, relaxing in body, was overwhelmed by sleep. The Father Almighty cast a deep sleep over his breast and, releasing a weight, dulled his senses, so that no power could stir his slumbering mind, not even if by chance some crash should ring his tranquil ears, nor if heaven should thunder from its shaken vault, but his limbs, held down by God's hand, could not disrupt his rest. Then He took one of his ribs from all of the bones and restored the flesh on his left side. A nuptial form of lovely grace was made and suddenly woman put forth her new countenance.]

Eve cannot be made without "Adam," "sleep," "his bones," and "one of his ribs," and these words give away the biblical source (*Adam, soporem, costarum ex ossibus unam*). Adam himself refers to Eve in the Bible as "bone of my bone" ("os ex ossibus meis," 2:23), and that later phrase is echoed here. The verb *iecit* (149) is a Vetus variant of *immisit* (Gen. 2:21), along with *lateri* (155 "for costam de latere") and *reponit* (155 for *posuit*), so that there appears to be an affinity with the Old Latin Bible. The choice of *forma* ("beauty," 156) is a thought-provoking vestige of *formauit* in the *Vetus Latina* ("he formed"), and it evokes God's creative agency as well as the physical beauty of His work. Forgetting for the moment that Eve is to be blamed for her seduction of Adam, there is no censure in this scene of her beauty or allure. In fact, her loveliness accords with the beauty of all God's creations, and the adjective *pulcher* in particular (*pulchro ... decore*, 156) appears numerous times in the lead-up to this scene. The first light God sheds upon the earth is beautiful ("Iam proprias pulchro monstrabat lumine formas," 17), and so is the nascent earth (*pulchra ... tellus*, 25), and the whole order of creation (*pulchro ... ordine mundum*, 50). When God commits the world to Adam's care, he is superlative about the beauty of his work: "Haec ... cernis pulcherrima" (133), "These most lovely things you see ..." Therefore, Eve is lovely because she is part of the natural order of the world, and there is no need to see in her fairness a token of more dangerous *uoluptas* ("desire"). Like Adam, she is as yet untainted by the first promptings of sin.

The Creation of Eve: Spiritual Meaning (1.158–74)

No doubt the favourable description of Eve's entrance into the world is owing in large measure to the spiritual significance of her birth. For Avitus, she is not only the first woman but a symbol of the nascent Church, and so he can hardly fault her at this point (1.158–74):

> Quam Deus aeterna coniungens lege marito
> Coniugii fructu pensat dispendia membri.
> Istius indicium somni mors illa secuta est, 160
> Sponte sua subiit sumpto quam corpore Christus.
> Qui cum passurus ligno sublimis in alto
> Penderet nexus, culpas dum penderet orbis,
> In latus extensi defixit missile lictor.
> Protinus exiliens manauit uulnere lympha, 165
> Qua uiuum populis iam tum spondente lauacrum
> Fluxit martyrium signans et sanguinis unda.
> Inde quiescenti, gemina dum nocte iaceret,
> De lateris membro surgens ecclesia nupsit.
> Principio Rector tanti sacrare figuram 170
> Disponens uincli nectit conubia uerbo:

"Viuite concordi studio mundumque replete,
Crescat longaeuum felici semine germen,
Non annis numerus uitae nec terminus esto."

[Joining Eve to her husband by eternal law, God repaid the loss of that rib with the blessing of marriage. Adam's sleep was a symbol of the death that followed, which Christ freely endured when he assumed human form, the exalted one, who would suffer and be hanged, bound on the high cross. And while he atoned for the sins of the world, a soldier pierced his exposed side with a spear. Immediately bursting forth, blood flowed from the wound, and signifying martyrdom, his flowing blood even then promised life-giving Baptism for the people. And in his stillness as he lay there for two nights, the ascending Church was wed to the wound at his side. The Lord, the Supreme Ruler, determined from the outset to consecrate the symbolism of so great a union, bound the marriage with these words: "Live in the pursuit of harmony and fill the world. May your offspring, blessed in seed, live long and may there be no number to your years nor end to your life."]

Nuptial, legal, and monetary allusions populate the scene, as Eve is bound to her husband by eternal law ("aeterna coniungens lege marito," 160) and Adam is repaid the wound at his side with the blessing of marriage (*coniugii fructu pensat*, 161). So, too, Christ, who pays for the sins of the world on the cross ("culpas dum penderet orbis," 163), is recompensed through marriage to the Church (*ecclesia nupsit*, 169), which proceeds symbolically from the wound at his side (*De lateris membro*, 169).[44] Avitus' choice of *membrum* ("limb,"169) in this context may seem peculiar, but it is an echo of Adam's lost rib (*dispendia membri*, 159) and the literal stimulus for spiritual meaning. The birth of faith and its bond to Christ is therefore a re-enactment of the birth of Eve and her marriage to Adam. All of this is a *figura*, says Avitus (170), which appears at the beginning of time, *principio* (170), a word that neatly hearkens back to Genesis 1:1 and now signals the end of the work begun there. So the marriage of Adam and Eve is a keystone, God's culminating achievement, and yet only moments into their union, the threat of death already looms near – those short, difficult days that trouble Avitus at the opening of his poem ("Vnde breuem carpunt mortalia tempora uitam," 1.2). God does not want the end

---

44 See Fontaine, *Naissance*, 257, who also mentions the connection of Eve to the Church in this scene: "… la création de la femme et celle de l'Église."

of time (*nec terminus esto*, 174), and it is not *His* will but the will of Adam and Eve and the will of the serpent that brings pain and death into existence; and yet God's reference to it here is filled with foreboding.

God has not set Adam and Eve up for failure. Eden was His wedding gift and the world, a dowry (1.191–2): "Pro thalamo paradisus erat mundusque dabatur/In dotem et laetis gaudebant sidera flammis" ("Paradise was their marriage-bed and the world their dowry, and the stars rejoiced in joyous flames"). Everything is as yet untainted by original sin, and the heavens attend the wedding in joyful observance of the moment. The words "laetis gaudebant sidera flammis" (192) even look forward to the birth of Christ and the adoration of the Magi (cf. Juvencus, *Ev.* 1.246): "Gaudia magna Magi gaudent sidusque salutant" ("The Magi rejoice with great delight and hail the star"). But this scene and the attendance of nature also recalls a darker union, that of Dido and Aeneas, whose illicit "marriage" in the cave contrasts with the public, pious ceremony of Adam and Eve here in the presence of God (4.165–72):

Speluncam Dido dux et Troianus eandem   165
Deueniunt. Prima et Tellus et pronuba Iuno
Dant signum; fulsere ignes et conscius aether
conubiis summoque ulularunt uertice Nymphae.
Ille dies primus leti primusque malorum
Causa fuit; neque enim specie famaue mouetur   170
Nec iam furtiuum Dido meditatur amorem:
Coniugium uocat, hoc praetexit nomine culpam.

[Dido and the Trojan leader come to the same cave. Primal Earth and nuptial Juno give the sign. Fires shone and heaven bore witness to their union, and the nymphs cried out from highest peak. That day was the first cause of death and evil; and no more is Dido moved by looks or reputation, no more does she think of secret love: she calls this marriage and with this name conceals her fault].

Juno is the goddess of marriage, and so her vindictive manipulation of this situation in the *Aeneid*, meant to thwart the mission of Aeneas, stands in contrast to God's nurturing support of Adam and Eve. As in *Historia spiritalis* (*sidera flammis*, 192), the stars attend the union of Dido and Aeneas (*fulsere ignes*, 167), and *prima tellus* ("primal earth," 166) is a counterpart to the nascent world in Genesis. Dido herself calls this a marriage (*Coniugium uocat*, 172), and yet she is deceived. Much as the serpent dupes Eve, Juno misleads Dido and brings her to her doom. Like Eve, she is a victim in this drama, caught between Juno and Aeneas, just as Eve is caught between Satan and God; both moments lead to destruction and death (169–70): "Ille dies primus leti primusque malorum / Causa fuit" ("That was the first day of death and the cause of evil"). These are Vergil's words, but Avitus, writing of the Fall, could not have put it better, especially given the connection in biblical epic between the "apple" and "evil" (*mălum/mālum*). The day in which Adam and Eve take that fruit is also their first day of death and that of all humankind.

Satan's Defiant Complaint (2.89–116)[45]

The end of Book 1 comes with a clear admonition from God (1.302–15), which serves to conclude the Creation sequence of *Historia spiritalis* and foreshadow the Fall. In many respects, Book 2 is the heart of the poem.[46] There, God encourages Adam and Eve to enjoy the fruits of Paradise ("Sumite concessas fruges et carpite poma" ["Take the allotted fruit and pick the apples"], 1.307), just not those from the one tree (1.310–12): "Est tamen in medio nemoris, quam cernitis, arbor / Notitiam recti prauique in germine portans: / Huius ab accessu uetitum restringite tactum" ("There is however one tree, as you know, in the middle of the grove, that bears knowledge of right and wrong in its seed: keep your hands from that forbidden touch"). The instructions are clear, and so are the consequences. Obedience, says God, will bring eternal life; disobedience will bring death (1.318–19): "Non immensa loquor: facilis custodia recti est. / Seruator uitam, finem temerator habebit" ("What I am saying is not impossible; perseverance in what is right is easy. The follower will have life, the trespasser, death").

That is how things stand when the devil arrives on the scene. As Avitus puts it, "continuere bonis, donec certamine primo / Vinceret oppressos fallacem culpa per hostem" ("they kept to right until, in their first battle, wrong overcame them, [and] they were overwhelmed by a deceitful foe").[47] Innocence as much as pride is the weakness of Adam and Eve, and

---

45 Hecquet-Noti, *Avit de Vienne*, tome I, 68ff., aligns Satan with Turnus.

46 See Deproost, "Mise en scène," 43.

47 Deproost, "Mise en scène," 44, notes extensive amplification in the treatment of Satan, and that the 423 lines of this episode cover only eight verses of the Bible (Vulgate). He also says (p. 54) that Satan echoes Juno's wrathful speech in the *Aeneid* (7.293–322); See further Abbolito, "Avito e Virgilio," 49–72 at 59–60; Hecquet-Noti, *Avit de Vienne*, tome I, 199.

their enemy knows how to exploit it, having recently fallen himself. Satan's jealously towards Adam in particular, who is God's new favourite, offers a strong incentive for the devil's vengeful plan (2.90–116):

"Pro dolor hoc nobis subitum consurgere plasma
Inuisumque genus nostra creuisse ruina!   90
Me celsum Virtus habuit, nunc ecce reiectus
Pellor et angelico limus succedit honori.
Caelum terra tenet, uili compage leuata
Regnat humus nobisque perit translata potestas.
Non tamen in totum periit: pars magna retentat   95
Vim propriam summaque cluit uirtute nocendi.
Nec differre iuuat: iam nunc certamine blando
Congrediar, dum prima salus experta nec ullos
Simplicitas ignara dolos ad tela patebit.
Et melius soli capientur fraude, priusquam   100
Fecundam mittant aeterna in saecula prolem.
Immortale nihil terra prodire sinendum est
Fons generis pereat, capitis deiectio uicti
Semen mortis erit. Pariat discrimina leti
Vitae principium. Cuncti feriantur in uno: 105
Non faciet uiuum radix occisa cacumen.
Haec mihi deiecto tantum solacia restant.
Si nequeo clausos iterum conscendere caelos,
His quoque claudantur. Leuius cecidisse putandum est,
Si noua perdatur simili substantia casu.   110
Sit comes excidii, subeat consortia poenae
Et, quos praeuideo, nobiscum diuidat ignes.
Sed nec difficilis fallendi causa petetur:
Haec monstranda uia est, dudum quam sponte cucurri
In pronum lapsus; quae me iactantia regno   115
Depulit, haec hominem paradisi limine pellet."
Sic ait et gemitus uocem clausere dolentis.

["For shame that this clay has suddenly risen in my place and that a loathsome race has flourished in my ruin! Power once held me high. Now look! I am an outcast, a reject, and this mud succeeds my angelic honour. Earth rules heaven. Dirt, raised in squalid form, reigns, and power passed from me is lost. But it has not been lost entirely. A great part retains its strength and it is famed for its high power to harm. No more waiting: I shall at once begin my battle of seduction, and while their nascent prosperity is still untested, their innocence, ignorant of guile, will be open to my darts. And better they be taken alone in deceit, before they send offspring into the eternal ages. Nothing immortal can be allowed to come of this earth; let the source of this race perish. The seed of death will be the downfall of their vanquished line. Let the beginning of life open the threshold unto death. Let them all be cut down at once: the severed root will bring forth no living bud. It is the only comfort that remains for me, since I have been banished. If I cannot rise back up to the heavens that are barred to me, then let them be barred as well. It will feel lighter to have fallen, if this new creature suffers a similar fate. Let us be comrades in ruin, companions in punishment. And these fires I see before me? Let them share those as well. The cause of their fall will not be hard to find: I will show them the way I once freely ran, falling headfirst. The pride that drove me from the kingdom will cast man from the threshold of Paradise." Thus he spoke and sighs of grief broke off his speech.]

Satan's wounded pride betrays both the source of his ambition and the cause of his ruin. He cares only for might (*uirtus*, 91), stature (*celsum*, 91), glory (*honori*, 92), ruling (*regnat*, 94), and the transfer of power (*translata potestas*, 94), and nothing for the well-being of the world or its inhabitants, which would qualify him to rule. He is an angry, petulant child, who resorts to name-calling. Knowing Adam's origins in the "earth," which is what his name means, Satan insults him with a series of bitter puns – *Plasma* (89), *limus* (92), *terra* (93), *uili conpage* (93), *leuata ... humus* (93–4). The best of these is his complaint that "earth" or "dirt" (i.e., Adam) will rule heaven (*Caelum terra tenet*, 93) and that the lowest will be exalted.[48]

Satan therefore vows to attack Adam and Eve with the power he has left, "the power to harm" (*uirtute nocendi*, 96), and waging a martial-heroic battle of seduction (*certamine blando*, 97), he plans to use verbal spears (*tela*, 99) against the happy couple, to strike them at their weakest point, their innocence (*simplicitas*, 99). Knowing full well how to fall, Satan aims to lead Adam and Eve down the path to destruction (114–16): "Haec monstranda uia est, dudum quam sponte cucurri / In pronum lapsus; quae me iactantia regno / Depulit, haec hominem paradisi limine pellet" ("I will show them the path I once freely ran, falling head-first. The pride that drove me from the kingdom will cast man from the threshold of Paradise").

---

48 Compare also *plasma* (89)/*ruina* (90); *celsum* (91)/*reiectus* (91); *limus* (92)/*angelico ... honori* (92); *uili compage* (93)/*leuata ... humus* (93–4).

Therefore, while Adam may sow the seeds of death in his disobedience ("prime pater, qui semine mortis / Tollis succiduae uitalia germina proli" ["you, first father, who with the seed of death, deprived future generations of life-giving buds"], 7–8), Satan is the one who offers the seeds to Adam in the first place and plants the first thoughts of pride in his heart. As the devil says, "Semen mortis erit" ("The seed of death will come to be," 2.104).

The Temptation (2.145–65)

Given Satan's resentment towards man and God, the temptation of Adam and Eve is undertaken with single-minded purpose, and Eve first is beset by a flurry of rhetorical language, which is precisely what the devil has planned to use in this battle of seduction (*certamine blando*, 2.97). His first words to Eve make a well-aimed appeal at her pride, at her beauty and status, which allow the first seeds of doubt to swell (2.145–65):[49]

"O felix mundique decus pulcherrima uirgo,   145
Ornat quam roseo praefulgens forma pudore,
Tu generi uentura parens, te maximus orbis
Exspectat matrem, tu prima et certa uoluptas
Solamenque uiri, sine qua non uiueret ipse;
Vt maior, sic iure tuo subiectus amori   150
Praedulcis coniunx,[50] reddes cui foedere prolem.
Vobis digna datur paradisi in uertice sedes,
Vos subiecta tremit famulans substantia mundi:
Quod caelum, quod terra creat, quod gurgite magno
Producit pelagus, uestros confertur in usus.   155
Nil natura negat, datur ecce in cuncta potestas.
Non equidem inuideo; miror magis ut tamen una
Contineat liber dulci super arbore tactus.
Scire uelim: quis dura iubet, quis talia dona
Inuidet et rebus ieiunia miscet opimis?"   160
Haec male blanditam finxerunt sibila uocem.
Quis stupor, o mulier, mentem caligine clausit?

---

49   See further Homey, "Evas Schuld," 474–97.

50   Unlike Hecquet-Noti and Shea, I take *praedulcis coniunx* (151) to refer to Eve, given the context and appearance of similar adjectives referring to her, including *praefulgens* (146). Moreover, Satan is already addressing her through apostrophe.

Cum serpente loqui, uerbum committere bruto
Non pudet, ut uestram praesumat belua linguam?
Et monstrum pateris, responsumque insuper addis?   165

["O blessed, fairest maiden, gift to the world, whom outstanding beauty adorns with rosy-cheeked modesty, you will be the bearer of a race; a boundless world awaits you as its mother. You are the first and sure pleasure of man, his solace, without whom he could not live. You are greater, so he is rightly subject to your love, sweet wife, to whom you will bear offspring by your union. A worthy seat is given you at the summit of Paradise. Subjected to you, the servile substance of the world trembles. Whatever heaven and earth creates, whatever the sea yields from its great gulf is given to your use. Nature denies you nothing. Look! Power is given to you in all things! I am not jealous, but I am amazed that the freedom of your touch withdraws from that one, sweet tree. I would like to know who is ordering you around so harshly? Who is it that jealously guards such gifts, mingling starvation with abundance?" Wickedly his hissing assumed a beguiling voice. What dullness, woman, clouds your mind with fog, to make you speak with a snake, trade words with a brute? Are you not ashamed that a beast is using your language? And you listen to this monster, and then, on top of that, you answer?]

Satan's words to Eve are guilefully chosen. He puts the focus on her and repeats the pronouns, *tu* and *uos* several times (*tu … te … tu … tuo … uobis … uos … uestros*). It is an appeal to pride, and so are the superlative compliments he heaps upon her: *pulcherrima* ("most beautiful," 145): *praefulgens* ("shining very brightly," 146); *praedulcis* ("most sweet," 152); even *prima* ("first") pays tribute to her special status. Satan's offering of *potestas* ("power," 156) flatters Eve and leads her into a false sense of her own importance in the world.[51] The very substance of the earth, he says, is subject to her will ("Vos subiecta tremit famulans substantia mundi," 153), and Adam, too, is subject to her love ("tuo subiectus amori," 150); both serve and worship her, and the earth trembles at her feet (*tremit*, 153). She is a god, and yet the alleged acquiescence of the world (*substantia mundi*, 153), like everything else in this speech, is a lie, since "nothing in the structure of the world," says Juvencus, "is immortal" ("Inmortale nihil mundi conpage tenetur," *Ev. Praef.* 1), but Eve does not know that. She is as yet still subject to that innocence, *simplicitas*, which Satan perceived at once

---

51 See Deproost, "Mise en scène," 58.

(2.99). So the "initial" or "first state" (*prima salus*, 98) of Adam and Eve is their weak point, and Lucifer works carefully to entice Eve to move beyond that first condition.[52]

The whole scene is thoughtfully orchestrated by Avitus. All that Satan offers Eve is born of his own desires. As the devil acknowledges in his first speech, he knows full well how to fall and how to lead others to similar ruin (2.114–16). That lofty seat he promises to Eve is the very one he would occupy (*in uertice sedes*, 152). He would also see the substance of the world serve him and not her (*famulans substantia mundi*, 153), and have heaven and earth at his disposal ("caelum ... terram ... uestros confertur in usus," 154–5). "Everything," he says to Eve, is given into her power ("datur ecce in cuncta potestas," 156), and although he claims not to envy her (*Non equidem inuideo*, 157), the opposite is true. That power lost and given to Adam is precisely what Satan laments and envies (*perit translata potestas*, 94). Moreover, even though Avitus berates Eve for her naivety – "Quis stupor, o mulier, mentem caligine clausit" ("What dullness, woman, clouds your mind with fog," 162) – her shortcoming is not so much wilful ignorance as it is pure innocence. Furthermore, Avitus has already sympathized with Eve, by characterizing her favourably as a symbolic vessel of the Church, and so despite his final words here, she appears to be less the villain and more the victim.

The Fruit (2.208–16)

As an added touch, Avitus presents the forbidden tree not just in terms of the knowledge to be gained, a point the Bible makes, but also in terms of the allure of the fruit itself, which looks and smells delicious. Eve does not simply surrender to curiosity, to a desire for insight; she yields to corporeal pleasure (*uoluptas*). Nicole Hecquet-Noti has made the point that the language of the temptation evokes classical erotic poetry, and this passage in particular is suggestive (2.208–16):[53]

> Ille ut uicino uictam discrimine sensit,
> Atque iterum nomen memorans arcemque deorum
> Vnum de cunctis letali ex arbore malum   210

---

52 See further Nodes, "Avitus of Vienne's Spiritual History," 185–95 at 176–7, who emphasises the inability of Adam and Eve to withstand temptation without divine assistance.
53 See further Hecquet-Noti, "Ève et le serpent," 2–17 at 7.

Detrahit et suaui pulchrum perfundit odore.
Conciliat speciem nutantique insuper offert,
Nec spernit miserum mulier male credula munus,
Sed capiens manibus pomum letale retractat.
Naribus interdum labiisque patentibus ultro   215
Iungit et ignorans ludit de morte futura.

[When he sensed that she was beaten by the impending crisis, remembering again that name and the citadel of celestial beings, he plucked a single, lovely apple from the deadly tree and imbued it with a sweet scent. He commended its appearance and offered it to the wavering girl, and the trusting woman did not meanly spurn the hapless gift, but taking the lethal apple in her hands, she drew it in. She raised it to her nose and then to her open lips and, ignorant of impending death, she played with it.]

The word *discrimen* (208) marks the point of no return, and Satan has used it already in his first speech (104–5): "Pariat discrimina leti / Vitae principium" ("Let the beginning of life open the threshold unto death"). That moment has now come to fruition (as it were) and once again Satan's action is prompted by a memory of his former life in heaven (209). Hecquet-Noti has remarked that Satan's earlier promise of the sweet tree, "dulci ... arbore" (158), has been cast aside for the plain, deadly truth (210): "Vnum de cunctis letali ex arbore malum / Detrahit" ("he picked one of the fruits from the lethal tree"). Although the word *mālum* must mean "apple," there is a strong sense of "evil" here (*mălum*), just as there is in the *Heptateuch* at the same moment (77):[54] "Dic mihi, cur metuas felicia germina mali" ("Tell me, why do you fear blessed buds of the apple?"). Those seeds are as much the seeds of "evil" as they are of "fruit," and Cyprianus adds further irony by including the adjective *felix*, which means "auspicious" or "lucky" as well as "fruitful." Seeing "evil" in the "apple," then, creates a meaningful bit of commentary on Satan's offer of "good-omened" fruit, which only lightly conceals the deadly truth.

Of course, none of this is in the Bible, and Eve stands innocently at the centre of this revised human drama, which is more complex, more compelling, and more visually realistic than the original narrative in Genesis.

---

54 See also Hequet-Noti, "Ève et le serpent," 6 and 9, who also notes this pun. Hecquet-Noti, *Avit de Vienne*, tome I, 214, n. 1, also comments on the pun here and in Cyprianus' *Heptateuch*.

There is a sense in verse 214 that what Eve should do is spurn the fruit and the evil it represents ("nec spernit miserum mulier male credula"), and the repetition there of *male* points to the danger of the apple (*malum*), while the heavy alliteration on "m" suggests that the fruit is more deliciously appealing to her than not. These are sounds of self-contained delight, and her fondling of the fruit is highly suggestive. Curiosity leads her down a dangerous path on the way to illicit *uoluptas* ("pleasure"), and Avitus' choice of the verb *ludo* ("to play") in this scene is effective, since it implies both innocent "play," to complement Satan's earlier emphasis on the *simplicitas* (99) of Adam and Eve, but also hints at Eve's sexual awakening. In short, Eve is bombarded by mental, emotional, and physical suggestions, and so, given her innocence, it is inevitable that she will give in.

The Fall (2.231–4)

The tipping point is pride.[55] Eve decides "she wants to be like God, and the poison creeps in, harming her with ambition" ("Dis tamen esse cupit similis serpitque uenenum / ambitione nocens," 2.220–1).[56] That "power to harm" is the one bit of might Satan still owns, and he has already promised to use it against the couple in his first speech (*uirtute nocendi*, 2.96). That being said, while Eve is unaware of the intricacy of Satan's stratagems, she does struggle with the choice, and the inner contest of fear and love is psychologically realistic ("Hinc amor, inde metus ... proelia fluctus," 2.222). But Satan cannot be deterred from his singular purpose. Incessantly, he puts the fruit in Eve's face and chips away at her resolve ("Ostentatque cibum dubiae queriturque morari," 226). In the end, she can do nothing but relent (2.231–4):

> Adnuit insidiis pomumque uorata momordit.
> Dulce subit uirus, capitur mors horrida pastu.
> Continet hic primum sua gaudia callidus anguis
> Dissimulatque ferum uictoria saeua triumphum.

---

55 See further Wood, "Avitus of Vienne," 272, who cites "ambition or arrogance," as the cause of the Fall. There he also mentions Augustine and his emphasis on "*iactantia* when discussing the Fall." Variations of that word appear more than once in this scene.

56 These lines are probably inspired to some extent by Book 1 of the *Carmen paschale*, where Sedulius uses similar language to describe the dangerous influence of paganism.

[She gave in to his guiles and bit into the apple, devouring it. The sweet venom spread, and horrid death came from that food. The guileful serpent at first contained his joy, and savage victory concealed cruel triumph.]

The fall is swift. Eve's first bite heralds death, and the internal rhyming of *momordit* ("she bites," 231) and *mors* ("death," 232) is emphatic and effective; so is the oxymoron *dulce ... uirus* ("sweet ... venom," 232). In the end, despite her innocence (*simplicitas*), the failing of Eve must be a conscious decision to give in to the devil's promptings (*adnuit*, 231), and that can be seen as an exercise of free will.

Adam, meanwhile, is blissfully unaware, as he returns from a walk in the garden ("Ignarus facti diuersa parte reuertens / Adam diffusi laetus per gramina campi," 235–6). He is still enjoying the liberty that comes from faithfulness, a point Avitus makes at the opening of the book (2.1–3): "Vtitur interea uenturi nescia casus / Libertas secura bonis fruiturque beata / Vbertate loci" ("Meanwhile, carefree liberty, knowing nothing of the fall to come, enjoys the goods and blessed abundance of that place"). That is exactly what Adam is up to, and when he sees Eve, he offers only "chaste kisses" (*oscula casta*, 237), while she meanwhile is suffering the first pangs of temerity (238–9): "Occurrit mulier, cui tunc audacia primum / flabat femineos animosa in corda furores" ("He runs to her, and for the first time brazenness rouses the feminine passion within her beating chest"). Exhilarated, but as yet blind to the truth of Satan's guile, Eve can only see the fruit as "life-giving" (*cibum ... uitali ex germine*, 242). This and everything else she says to Adam is highly ironic. She says that he, too, will be like God (*similem ... tonanti* ["like ... the Thunderer"], 243).[57] She knows this, because she is not "ignorant" (*non ... nescia*, 244). The fruit is a "gift" (*donum*, 243), and using the same rhetoric Satan just used on her – for he has taught it to her – she questions Adam alluringly (2.250–1): "Why are you looking down? Why do you resist this blessed gift and delay future glory?" ("Lumina cur flectis? Cur prospera uota moraris / Venturoque diu tempus furaris honori?"). Her words imitate the earlier rhetoric of Satan in the temptation of Eve. This glory (*honor*, 251) is what Satan, too,

---

57 See further Roberts, "Prologue to Avitus," 404, who suggests a critical reading of *tonans* here (2.243), which may serve to criticize paganism. If so, such usage is akin to the poet's earlier choice of *dis* (2.220). Also, note that Eve is echoing her own earlier desire ("Dis tamen esse cupit similis," 2.220).

desires, and it is what led to his fall and that of Eve. Knowing this, he guilefully plants it in her heart. Adam's fall is even quicker than Eve's, since it comes from someone he knows and trusts and, when he bites, the same poison creeps in (*uenenum*, 259), and the same death draws near (*letum*, 253, 270).

Again, all of this is carefully orchestrated by Avitus, who creates a realistic and revealing drama, in which Adam and Eve are led to embrace the desires of Satan, which corrupt the line of man. The devil's poisonous influence explains how man's nature became corrupted in the first place (*polluti ... origine mores*, 1.3) and justifies the metaphors of contamination Avitus uses in his preface. Still, given the devil's determination to destroy humankind and the poet's emphasis on their innocence (*simplicitas*, 2.99), one may fairly ask who is the true "author of vice" (*auctoris uitio*, 1.11), Adam or Satan?

The Opening of Book Four (4.1–10)

The Fall is the central drama of *Historia spiritalis* and it carries into Book 3, *De sententia Dei*, where God passes judgment on the unhappy pair.[58] Book 4, *De diluuio mundi*, involves the Flood, by which God cleanses the sins of the world that have taken root since the birth of evil in Paradise (*semine mortis*, 1.7). In Book 1, Avitus calls Adam "the author of vice" (*auctoris uitio*, 1.11), and because of his failure as "first father" (*prime pater*, 1.7) and *cultor* of the world ("cultivator," 1.54), earth's souls have grown as unruly as untended fields (4.37–53). Thus the first word of Book 4 is, emphatically, *infectum* (4.1–10):

> Infectum quondam uitiis concordibus orbem
> Legitimumque nefas laxata morte piatum
> Diluuio repetam; sed non quo fabula mendax
> Victuros lapides mundum sparsisse per amplum
> Deucaliona refert, durum genus unde resumpti   5
> Descendant homines cunctisque laboribus apti
> Saxea per duram monstrent primordia mentem.
> Sed ueri compos fluctus nunc prosequar illos,
> Per quos immissus rebus uix paene creatis
> Lactantem uelox praeuenit terminus orbem.   10

---

58 Hecquet-Noti, *Avit de Vienne*, tome II, 41, isolates the hymn at the end of Book 3 as central to the message of the whole poem.

[I shall retrace how the world was once infected by common sin and how lawful sin was purged by the Flood and unfettered death, but not that false tale of how Deucalion scattered stones over the spacious earth, which came to life – a hard race from which new men descended and, ready for any labour, showed their stony origins in their hardened minds – instead, wielding truth, I shall now pursue the waves that brought a swift end to the inveigled world, which had only just been made].[59]

This beginning is the closet thing to an epic *praefatio* in *Historia spiritalis*. As in epic, the significant words are set first, in this case *infectum*, and like Vergil, Avitus uses the first person to announce himself as poet (*repetam*, 2), which is also conventional. Not since Juvencus and *Euangeliorum libri* has there been so clear a line in biblical epic to the traditional invocation. Like Juvencus, who acknowledges Vergil and Homer in his preface, Avitus likewise cites Ovid and the story of the flood in the *Metamorphoses*.[60] He also emphasizes the falsehood of that tale in opposition to the truth of his own narrative (*ueri compos*, 8), and his condemnation of "that false story" (*fabula mendax*, 3) is now stereotypical in the Christian genre. Juvencus scorns the "lies" of ancient songs (*mendacia*, 16) versus the truth of Christ's deeds, who is "without the sin of falsehood" (*falsi sine crimine*, 20), and Sedulius rebukes the same "lies" at the beginning of his *Carmen paschale* (*mendacia biblis*, 1.22), which he calls *figmenta* ("fictions," 1.17), *contagia* ("contagions," 1.20), and *scelerum monumenta* ("memorials of sins," 1.21).[61] Avitus is therefore in familiar waters at this moment.

---

59 Although *lactantem ... orbem* may refer to the world as "milky" and therefore "nascent," the sense of *lactare* is also to "delude" or "deceive." Hecquet-Noti, *Avit de Vienne*, tome II, 35, n. 6, favours the former sense ("Le participe *lactans* signifie *qui est au sein*"), as does Shea in *The Poems of Alcimus Avitus*, 100 ("the fair and fertile earth"), but I have chosen "deluded" because *rebus uix paene creatis* ("things scarcely even made") already accounts for the idea of "nascence," while "deluded" accounts for what is almost certainly a pun by Avitus, whereby the world is both "nascent" and recently "deceived" by Satan.

60 But see Goelzer, "Ovid et saint Avit," who cites Apollonius as an important influence on Avitus in *De deluuio mundi*.

61 Avitus continues his diatribe against mythology in the context of giants (1.86–122). See also Deproost, "Mise en oeuvre," 89, who discusses the preface to Book 4 and the place of *fabula mendax*. Wood, "Avitus of Vienne," 269, suggests that Avitus resorts to this conventional opening because he can no longer use Augustine's commentary on Genesis, which serves as his intellectual model for the earlier books of *Historia spiritalis*. He therefore suggests that the lack of such a model may explain what he calls "the alleged decline in quality of the last books of the SGH."

Forebodingly, his use of *terminus* in the last line hearkens back to God's final words to Adam and Eve at their wedding (1.174): "Non annis numerus uitae nec terminus esto" ("May there be no number to the years of your lives and no end"). At that moment, God tacitly acknowledges the potential for any future, good or ill, depending on their exercise of will, and it is no mistake that Avitus alludes to these words at the Flood (4.164): "Haec clades uiuis carnique hic terminus esto" ("This is death for the living, and here is an end to flesh"). Adam and Eve have brought this on themselves and the human race through their disobedience. In this context, Ian Wood has made a number of connections in *Historia spiritalis* that highlight God's law as an important theme, including the beginning of Book 4, where giants rule the earth according to their own will and in neglect of God's law ("propria ualuit pro lege uoluntas" ["each one's will prevailed over law"], 4.13).[62] In the same passage, Avitus says that men have advanced in the world by virtue of their power to harm (*uirtute nocendi*, 4.18), and this is the very same power they learned from Satan, who first used it against Adam and Eve (*uirtute nocendi*, 2.96). With it, he poisoned the world and brought it once again to the brink of ruin. That is to say, Satan's poisonous influence on humankind in the garden, which tainted the blood of man, has been passed down through the ages. Only the Flood can wash it from the world.

The Flood: Spiritual Signification (4.323–6)

At the opening of Book 3, *De sententia Dei*, Avitus offers Christ as a consolation for the Fall (3.20–2): "Et tamen adueniet tempus, cum crimina ligni / Per lignum sanet purgetque nouissimus Adam / Materiamque ipsam faciat medicamina uitae" ("And yet there will come a time when a new Adam (Christ) will clean and purge the sins of the tree with the cross, who makes his body the remedy of life"). At the end of Book Three, he invokes Christ again, this time to restore what Adam has lost (3.390): "Sed famulis tu redde tuis quod perdidit Adam ("But you, Christ, restore to your servants what Adam squandered"). Book Four presents another promise of man's redemption in the person of Noah, a figure for Christ, who saves mankind with the wood of the ark (the cross), and cleanses the world in a

---

62 See further Wood, "Avitus of Vienne," 271.

flood of baptismal water and blood, foreshadowing the Crucifixion and man's future salvation.[63] Leading up to the Deluge, Avitus says (4.323–6),

Effugiet tunc ille malum quicumque paratus,
construat ut ualidam praeduri tegminis arcam:
per lignum uitale crucis seruatus ab undis
tunc cernet quanto contempserit otia fructu.

[Then will that man escape evil, whoever has prepared to build a mighty ark with a hard exterior. Saved from the waves by the life-giving wood of the cross, he will then know what good his condemnation of indolence has won him].

Even before the dramatic narrative account of the Flood, therefore, Avitus has already indicated the spiritual significance of the episode, and throughout Book 4 he offers additional commentary. Like the ark, he says, "the true Church weathers many storms" ("Non aliter crebras Ecclesia uera procellas / sustinet," 4.493–4), and we must bend like the ark on the waves, "lest an unyielding mind feel a slackening within and let any sin enter in" ("Sed sic cedamus, fluxum ne sentiat intus / Peccatumue trahat mens impenetrabilis ullum," 4.508–9). Avitus then says that the Jews did not yield, and like the raven that abandoned its master and the ark (the cross), so that it might feed on the flesh of the fallen, "so do you not know, Judea, how to keep your master's faith and, leaving Him, you love the flesh" ("Sic nescis, Iudaee, fidem seruare magistro / Sic carnem dimissus amas," 4.569–70). "Therefore the Lord," he says, "sanctified this one baptism [the Flood], vowing that, although he had cleansed the world in the purging waters, the guilty should not expect a second such washing" ("Sic unum Genitor iurans baptisma sacrabat: / Vt semel ablutum lymphis purgantibus orbem, / Sic sperare reos lauacrum non posse secundum," 4.618–20). God's rainbow is a promise that no second flood will overwhelm the world, but Avitus hints ominously at other punishments. The rainbow, he says, is also a standard for all of the symbols of the Bible: "for Christ," as he puts it, "the giver of life, sent those signs on ahead of him" ("Namque dator uitae praemisit talia Christus," 4.641).

---

63   Hecquet-Noti, *Avit de Vienne*, tome II, 43 and 44, also highlights this spiritual connection. In particular, she links the term *opifex salutis* (4.341) with Christ elsewhere in Christian literature. See also Wood, "Avitus of Vienne," 273.

The Flood: Epic Amplification (4.429–40)

The description of the Flood is therefore secondary to its spiritual significance, and yet Avitus lavishes considerable attention on the literary image of the Deluge, which spans over one hundred-fifty lines (429–584).[64] In them, Avitus draws upon his knowledge especially of Vergil, Ovid, and Silius Italicus, but also of Cyprianus and Sidonius Apollinaris.[65] Echoes of Cyprianus are noteworthy, given the repeated metrical missteps of the *Heptateuch* and Avitus' apparent concern for "good" Latin, but given the small number of Old Testament biblical poems available at the time, it should not be surprising that Avitus would read and echo it. Unlike Cyprianus, however, Avitus all but abandons the narrative of the Bible, with the first drops of rain (4.429–40):[66]

> 7:11 … rupti sunt omnes fontes abyssi magnae et cataractae caeli apertae sunt.
> 12 et facta est pluuia super terram quadraginta diebus et quadraginta noctibus.
>
> – Gen. 7:11–12

Ilicet obtegitur caelum nimiisque tenebris	
Victa repelluntur fuscati lumina solis.	430
Insanas hominum mentes uix tangere terror	
coeperat, insuetus mox profluus aethere nimbus	
Et ualido primum similis demittitur imbri.	
Arida terrarum pariter maduere per orbem,	
Vna fuit toto facies et nubila caelo.[67]	435
Aegyptus tunc ipsa nouas expauit ad undas	
Alsit et infusus Garamans dudumque calentes	
Vmida Massylas tetigerunt frigora Syrtes.	
Nec longum pluuiae species, non denique guttae	
Stillant, sed rupto funduntur flumina caelo.	440

---

64 See Roberts, *Biblical Epic*, 131ff, who treats Avitus' account in detail. See also Hecquet-Noti, "La description du déluge dans Avit," 229–35.

65 Hecquet-Noti provides the specific details in her edition of Avitus, *Avit de Vienne*, tome II, 84–6.

66 Hecquet-Noti, "Le corbeau nécrophage," 297–300, at 297.

67 See Arweiler, *Die Imitation antiker*, 77, who cites a potential echo of Ovid *Ars.* 2.468: "unaque erat facies sidera terra fretum."

[At once, the heavens were hidden by all-consuming shadow. The vanquished light of the darkened sun was thrust back. Barely had fear begun to take the maddened minds of men, when a strange, outpouring rain came down, at first like a great storm. All at once around the world, dry lands were drenched. There was but one dark face for all of heaven. Egypt then shuddered before the new waters, the flooded land of the Garamantes, suffused with warmth a short time ago, shivered, and damp cold touched the Massylian Syrtes. No longer did the semblance of rain, nor mere raindrops, trickle down, but rivers poured down from the sundered heavens.]

Only four words lead back to the scriptural prose in Genesis, 7:11–12 – *caelum* (429), *terrarum* (434), *pluuiae* (439), and *rupto* (440) – and only one of these (*pluuiae*) provides any biblical anchorage for the outpouring of verse. Avitus' approach at this moment is akin to that of Cyprianus in the *Heptateuch* at the destruction of Sodom and Gomorrah (*Gen.*, 661–7), whose initial words build dramatically upon a single word of the Bible, *sulphur* (*Gen.*, 661–3): "Mox fragor horrisono de sidere fulmina torquet/ Sulpureaeque ruunt olido cum turbine flammae,/Quae pariter muros atque ardua culmina lambunt ..." ("Soon a crash hurls lightning from the dread-sounding sky, and sulphurous flames rush down in noxious swirls that licked at the walls and towering peaks alike").[68] Avitus may also have Cyprianus in mind with the image of the falling shadows and the darkened sun ("nimiisque tenebris/... fuscati lumina solis"), which accord with the image of Chaos at the opening of the *Heptateuch* ("dum chaos et nigrae fuscabant cuncta tenebrae" ["while chaos and black shadow darkened all"], *Gen.* 4).

But Avitus and Cyprianus part company in the distance each is willing to put between himself and the Bible. Where flashes of flamboyance are localized in the *Heptateuch*, Avitus does not feel bound to the scriptural narrative at all, and so (as it were) "No longer does the semblance of rain, nor mere raindrops, trickle down, but rivers pour from the sundered heavens" ("Nec longum pluuiae species, non denique guttae/Stillant, sed rupto funduntur flumina caelo," 4.439–40). In particular, Avitus lingers on the grizzly deaths of earth's sinful inhabitants, straying far from the text of the Bible to dispatch them (4.473–87):

---

68 A further connection between the two scenes is baptismal: both signify a cleansing of the world, one by fire and one by water, both of which "rain" down from heaven (cf. Gen. 19:24: "Et pluit dominus super Sodomam et Gomoram sulphur et ignem" ("And the Lord rained down fire and sulfur on Sodom and Gomorrah")).

Tum maior strepitu tanto mortalibus aegris
Fit metus, ascendunt turres et celsa domorum[69]
Culmina praesentemque iuuat uel tempore paruo   475
Sic differre necem. Multos, dum scandere temptant,
Crescens unda trahit, quosdam montana petentes
Consequitur letoque fugam deprendit inanem.
Ast alii longo iactantes membra natatu
Defessi expirant animas, aut pondere nimbi   480
Obruta flumineas commixta per aequora lymphas
In quocumque bibunt morientia corpora monte.
Aedibus impulsis alii periere ruina
Inque undas uenere simul dominique domusque.
It fragor in caelum sonitu collectus ab omni   485
Quadrupedumque greges humana in morte cadentum
Augent confusos permixta uoce tumultus.

[Then an even deeper fear with a tremendous uproar fell upon those accursed
mortals, who climbed the towers and high rooftops of their homes, desperate
to postpone imminent death, if only for a moment. Many, as they tried to
climb, were dragged off by the heaving water; some, heading for the mountains, were hunted down by death and robbed of futile flight. Still others,
limbs flailing in endless swimming, exhaled their last breaths in exhaustion,
or under the weight of the rain, their bodies, commingled with the seas, were
submerged as they choked down rivers of water and died on whatever mountain they could find. Others perished in the ruins of their fallen homes. Lord
and land alike were immersed in water. A din, drawn up from every recess,
was raised up to the heavens, and amidst the human dead, the drowning herds
of four-footed beasts added to the jumbled clamour.]

This scene intensifies the fear and commotion of the Flood dramatically.
The purpose, presumably, is not to delight but to disturb, and to instruct:
God does not take wanton disobedience lightly, and none will escape His
judgment. Perhaps the poetry falls on the side of self-indulgence as an exercise of art for its own sake, but that seems unlikely, given Avitus' stated
objectives elsewhere, which include "not squandering further days on a
work that charms a few knowledgeable people by preserving a metrical

---

69 See Arweiler, *Die Imitation antiker*, 99, who notes a connection in this line to Vergil,
    Aen. 2.445–6: "Dardanidae contra turris ac tota domorum / culmina convellunt."

pattern, but instead composing a work that serves many readers with its measured instruction in faith" ("… tempus insumere nec in eo inmorari, quod paucis intellegentibus mensuram syllabarum seruando canat, sed quod legentibus multis mensurato fidei adstructione deseruiat"). Such measured instruction does not exclude the use of emotion, which can elicit a particular response from the reader, in this case a dose of fear, to urge amending one's ways. In fact, Avitus makes this point explicitly in Book 3, *De sententia Dei*, when he says, "But while life remains, while we still thrive in the light, let the message of fallen Adam who died long ago frighten us, while there is still a place for weeping" ("Nos autem, dum uita manet, dum luce uigemus, / Olim defuncti perterret nuntius Adam, / Dum locus est flendi," 3.307–9). That may be the unstated message here as well, although, since Avitus does not offer any explicit guidance, one may rightly demand some justification for the graphic nature of these images.

The Opening of Book Five (1–18)

The final book of *Historia spiritalis* serves the same function as the story of the Flood. Both *De diluuio mundi* and *De transitu maris rubri* (*The Crossing of the Red Sea*) offer snapshots of the Bible in dramatic terms, and both promote spiritual messages in terms of Baptism.[70] Like the Flood, the waters of the Red Sea cleanse the sins of God-defying Egypt and lead a chosen people through "the streams of sweet-singing Jordan" ("amne canentis / Dulcis Jordanis, *Ev. Praef.* 26–7), as it were, to arrive safely in the promised land. The individuality of Book 4 expresses itself mainly in its martial-heroic tenor, and here Avitus takes full advantage of the inherent drama of Exodus. He lingers on the arms of the Egyptians, adds magniloquent speeches on both sides, and brings the full force of his poetic powers to bear on the conflict between Pharaoh and Moses, whose mortal struggle ends with the dramatic intervention of God. Thus, while Avitus says that the symbolism of the book is more important than the story itself (*maiorque figuris*, 17), he expends considerable energy on this spectacle, ranging farther from the Bible in the process than any of his predecessors. Here is how Book 5 opens (5.1–18):

---

70 For a detailed reading of this section of the poem, see further Roberts, "Rhetoric and Poetic Imitation in Avitus," 29–80. Hecquet-Noti, *Avit de Vienne*, tome II, 118, also emphasizes the role of earlier poets, including Cyprianus, as sources of inspiration for Avitus.

Hactenus in terris undas patuisse canenti
Terram inter fluctus aperit nunc carminis ordo.
Illic diluuium quos perderet, ante petiuit,
Nunc ad diluuium pleno succensa furore
Sponte sua current periturae milia gentis.   5
Sed non ut dignum tanti praeconia facti
Eloquium captent: diuina in laude uoluntas
Sufficit et famulo monstrari munere uotum.
Quod si quis nequeat uerbis persoluere grates,
Non minimum uirtutis habet uel credere gestis,   10
Signa per electos quae porrexere priores.
In quibus excellit longe praestantius illud,
Quod pelago gestum rubro celeberrima perfert
Scriptorum series, in cuius pondere sacro
Causarum mage pignus erat pulchramque relatu   15
Pulchrior exuperat praemissae forma salutis,
Historiis quae magna satis maiorque figuris
Conceptam grauido peperit de tegmine uitam.

[Singing till now about waters overspreading the land, the sequence of my song now unfolds the land between the waves. There, the Flood destroyed those it first pursued; now, thousands of people, a doomed and desperate race, filled with madness, will run freely to the flood. But I do not sing so that my words may capture eloquence worthy of so great a tale. My will to praise the Divine is enough for me, and my vow is made manifest by this humble tribute. And if one cannot give thanks in words, he has not the least bit of virtue or belief in the deeds that the chosen elders have handed down as signs. Among them, one stands out by far, which a most renowned series of writers relates as the deeds of the Red Sea, in whose sacred weight the pledge was more important than the causes, so that the fairer image of promised salvation outshines the beauty of the story itself which, great enough in fact and greater still in figures, gives life born beneath the pregnant veil].

The word *diluuium* ("flood") in lines three and four serves as a bridge between Books 4 to 5, and allows Avitus to extend his earlier symbolism to this book. The parting of the Red Sea, although a reversal of the descending deluge, nonetheless carries the same baptismal meaning. Marius Victorius makes a similar transition in Book 2 of his *Alethia*, and Avitus may have that in mind (*Aleth*. 1.1–2): "Hactenus arcanam seriem, primordia mundi, / Vt sincera fides patuit, sine fraude cucurri …" ("To this point, I have recounted that mysterious sequence, the origins of the world, as my pure faith without deceit has shown …").[71] That said, it is hard not to think of Sedulius at this point, who highlights the dual meaning of the crossing in the *Carmen paschale* (1.145–7): "Verbum Christus adest, geminae qui consona legis / Testamenta regens ueterem patefecit abyssum, / Vt doctrina sequens planis incederet aruis" ("Christ is the word who, ruling the harmonious testaments of a twin law, laid open the old abyss, so that a following doctrine might go forward over the open plains"). Through double-entendre, Avitus offers a pun on *aperio* ("to lay open" or "reveal," 2) in the same way Sedulius uses *patefacio* ("to lay open" or "expose," 146), as a means to uncover the deeper significance of the passage. The symbolism, says Avitus, is but one of the "signs" the ancient prophets handed down in the Old Testament ("Signa per electos quae porrexere priores," 11), which lies beneath the surface, beneath "the pregnant veil" ("grauido peperit de tegmine," 18). Much of this imagery relates to Baptism and rebirth through Christ; hence the "sacred weight" which is pregnant with meaning (*pondere sacro*, 14), and the "pledge" or "symbol" of the episode (*pignus*, 15), which can refer both to a "child" and "figures" born beneath the pregnant covering or veil ("figuris … Conceptam grauido peperit de tegmine uitam," 17–18).[72] The "image" or "beauty" of promised salvation (*praemissae forma salutis*, 16) brings additional wordplay, since *praemissae salutis* can refer both to the "deliverance" of the Israelites in literal terms, that is, their earthly delivery to safety (*salus*), but also man's "promised salvation" through Christ (*praemissae salutis*). The use of *forma* is also a pun, which conveys both "beauty" and "meaning," which come together to outshine the attractiveness of the story itself ("pulchramque relatu / Pulchrior exuperat," 15–16). Given the energy Avitus expends on building such richness into his narrative here, it seems clear that he is trying to raise the status of this story to the point where it may outshine the pre-eminence of epic.

---

71   Note that Hecquet-Noti, *Avit de Vienne*, tome II, 147, n. 2, emends *potuisse* (1) to *patuisse* on the basis of sense and kinship to the *Alethia*, which Avitus may be following here. *Potuisse* is the reading in the principal manuscripts, however, and with the sense of *praeualeo*, I have retained it.

72   See ibid., 149, n. 4, in which Hecquet-Noti cites Apollinaris, *Epist.* 9.2.2, as a potential source for the birth imagery here.

Pharaoh's Call to Arms (5.501–6 and 519–25)

Certainly, the elaborate description of the Egyptian host aspires to rise above the original story of the Bible. This is ecphrasis on an epic scale, inspired by the vivid images of shields and armaments in classical poetry.[73] Cyprianus expends such energy in his account of the Egyptian force in the *Heptateuch*, although on a smaller scale, and Avitus appears to emulate something of that work here.[74] Both poets begin with the single verse of the Bible on which the following lines are loosely based (14:7): "Tulitque sescentos currus electos quicquid in Aegypto curruum fuit et duces totius exercitus" ("And he took six hundred chosen chariots, and all the chariots that were in Egypt: and the captains of the whole army"). It is a humble beginning for the poetry to follow (5.501–6 and 519–25):

> Ergo bella rogant, feruens rapit arma iuuentus,
> spumantes ducuntur equi phalerisque potentes
> suspendunt alacres splendentia frena iugales.
> Pugnax pompa nitet, subiectos curribus axes
> aurato temone trahunt: tum cetera pubes   505
> induitur chalybe aut fuluo circumdatur aere.
>
> ...
>
> Progreditur collecta manus: rex ipse frementes
> Curru cogit equos, telis tamen undique saeptus   520
> Delituit, densam reddunt hastilia siluam.
> Concutitur pulsata rotis et pondere tellus,
> Angustauit humum latam stipata iuuentus
> Conclusitque uias. Quidquid uirtutis habere
> Aegyptus potuit, totum mors proxima ducit.   525

[They cry out for war. The fervent youth takes up arms. The battle-ready horses are brought out, foaming at the mouth and mighty in arms, they stand poised, yoked with resplendent bridles. The martial procession gleams and draws chariot-axels joined beneath by a golden rod. Then the rest are clad in steel or gird in tawny brass ... The gathered host advances. The king himself drives raging steeds from his cart, and, although surrounded by spears on all

---

73 See further Deproost, "L'épopée biblique," 26–7; Hudson-Williams, "Virgil and the Christian Latin Poets," 15; Roberts, "Rhetoric and Imitation," 29.

74 Compare lines *Ex.* 426–33 of the *Heptateuch*, and note that Avitus describes the "army" of Moses in terms of martial-heroism (5.371–83).

sides, still he hides. The shafts create a dense forest, and the pounded earth shudders beneath the weight and wheels. The youths, pressed together, narrowed the breadth of the land and blocked the roads. Whatever power Egypt held, imminent death drew it all unto itself.]

The style of the poetry in this scene is asyndetic, which hastens the action. Only *que* ("and" 520), *tum* ("then" 505), and *aut* ("or" 506) link the thoughts of the first several lines, and both Peiper and Hecquet-Noti have used commas to punctuate this passage, where periods might have served the shifting focus better: thus in the first lines, "[the Egyptians] cry for war" (501). Then the camera turns (as it were) to the men: "the fervent youth takes up arms" (501). Then "foaming steeds are led out" (502). Three changes in the first two lines and several more promote a sense of anticipation. In verses 504–6, the same process draws the reader's attention inward from a view of the whole "procession" (*pompa*, 504) to the "carts" (*curribus*, 504), and then to the "men" (*pubes*, 505). The same focus narrows inward from line 519 from the whole army (*collecta manus*, 519) to the one man at the centre of it all (*rex ipse*, 519). These shifting points of view add realism and new vitality to the biblical account.

Nothing better captures the author's dramatic aspirations at this moment than the phrase *Pugnax pompa nitet* ("the martial procession shines," 504), with which Avitus beats the epic drum triumphantly. Sedulius has something to say about such poetry: "Cum sua gentiles studeant figmenta poetae / Grandisonis pompare modis ... cur ego ... Clara salutiferi taceam miracula Christi" ("Since pagan poets are eager to parade their fictions in big-sounding rhythms ... why should I ... be silent of Christ the Saviour's famed wonders?" 17–18). Of course Avitus is not a pagan poet, but his exuberance in this scene verges on the pompous side of that "sweetness" (*dulcedo*) that biblical poets love and struggle at times to dilute. The catena of technical language and complicated syntax – especially in lines 510–13 (not given here) – even aim to match the intricacies of the links and fastenings of the armour themselves, and one may reasonably wonder what greater value such description yields beyond an impression of the author's virtuosity. That is to say, if Juvencus restrains his personal enthusiasm for classical poetry, to serve the essential words and deeds of the Gospels, Avitus suffers from no such compunction.

Pharaoh's Final Speech (5.671–82)

Several speeches end the final book of *Historia spiritalis* and these are delivered not just by Pharaoh but by his men, Moses, and God. Pharaoh believes that the Israelites are running to the sea out of cowardice (605–8), but his determination to pursue them at any cost is not shared by his soldiers, one of whom speaks out against the folly of opposing the Lord (620–35). "What is the cause of this monstrous path?" ("Monstriferae quae causa uiae?" 623), he says, and "No one would go down into that dry deep, with me as leader" ("Non duce me quisquam siccum descenderit aequor," 629). This last statement is revealing in light of God's stated power in the *Carmen paschale* (1.85–7): "Te duce difficilis non est uia; subditur omnis / Imperiis natura tuis, rituque soluto / Transit in aduersas iussu dominante figuras" ("With you as leader the way is not hard. All nature yields to your commands and, freed of its daily ritual, nature changes into opposite forms by your ruling will"). At the crossing of the Red Sea, Sedulius says that nature did indeed change its way ("Mutauit natura uiam," 1.141) and, with Christ as leader, the Israelites underwent a rudimentary Baptism ("Ingrediens populus rude iam baptisma gerebat, / Cui dux Christus erat" (1.142–3). This context of Sedulius emphasizes the ignorance of the Egyptians in *Historia spiritalis* and especially of the Pharaoh, who ignores God's power and how easily he wields it.

All that remains is for the sentence of death to be carried out (*sententia leti*, 637), and by the time Pharaoh has realized his mistake, it is too late. In the *Heptateuch* (*Ex.* 459–66), Cyprianus lavishes attention on this moment, as the chariot wheels stick in the mud and men and horses struggle in vain to escape. Avitus does not do this, not yet. His lead-up to the death of Pharaoh and his army is slower. The waters surround the Egyptians, and they should die at this point, but time suddenly stops like the walls of water themselves (5.665–70), and Pharaoh is granted a moment's reprieve to lament his fate. Given its place in the narrative, this final speech should be counted as the most significant (5.671–82):

> Ille, ferus semper, iam mitis morte sub ipsa:
> "Non haec humanis cedit uictoria bellis;
> Expugnamur, ait, caeloque euertimur hoste.
> Effuge quisque potes uictusque euade satelles
> Nec iam tela Deo conatibus ingere cassis."   675
> O si compunctas humana superbia mentes
> Ante obitum mutare uelit! Quid denique prodest
> Tunc finem posuisse malis, cum terminus urget,
> Praesentis uitae spatium dum ceditur aeuo?
> "Confitearis!" ait, "sanus" Scriptura "ualensque."   680
> Si tunc peccatum quisquam dimittere uouit,
> cum peccare nequit, luxu dimittitur ipse.

[That man, ever wild, now tame in the face of death, spoke: "This victory is not lost by human contest. We are beaten," he said, "and overthrown by a celestial foe. Take flight whoever can and escape, my conquered friends; do not raise arms in vain effort against God." Oh, if only human pride had wanted to change its stubborn mind before this moment of death! In the end, what good is it to put an end to evil deeds when the end itself presses down on us, as the course of mortal life gives way to time? "Let the hale and hearty confess," say the Scriptures. If anyone has vowed to renounce sin, he will be released from the pleasures of the world, when he decides to sin no more.]

This is not the Pharaoh of the Bible, and no such words of warning come from Moses. The Pharaoh of Exodus charges wordlessly to his doom, but Avitus takes full advantage of the moment to suggest regret on the part of Egypt's leader and to emphasize the vanity of human pride (*superbia*, 676), which originates in the Fall and leads man to his destruction.[75] For Avitus, this speech is a homiletic moment and, even though he is resigned, Pharaoh is still unrepentant. Therefore, Avitus offers his wilful determination as a warning to the reader. Repent now (*Confitearis*, 680), while there is still time.

The Destruction of Egypt (5.683–97)

The final destruction of Pharaoh and his army immediately follows his speech and it comes in a tumult of beaten armour and blood. This visual imagery is characteristic of *Historia spiritalis*, and the scene hearkens back to the poet's earlier depiction of the Flood. The message is certainly similar, that the waters of the Sea wash away the sins of the world and those of Egypt, just as the Flood purges the corruption of Noah's generation (5.683–97):[76]

---

75 Romans 10.9: "Quia si confitearis in ore tuo Dominum Iesum et in corde tuo credideris quod Deus illum excitauit ex mortuis saluus eris" ("For if thou confess with thy mouth the Lord Jesus and believe in thy heart that God hath raised him up from the dead, thou shalt be saved"). See also Roberts, "Rhetoric and Imitation," 38, who attributes the opening words to Vergil: "non haec humanis opibus, non arte magistra /Proveniunt" (*Aen.* 12.427–48); and "frangimur heu fatis" inquit "ferimurque procella" (7.594). On the same page, Roberts links the imperatives to "the standard pattern for short battlefield speeches in epic."

76 Notably, Hecquet-Noti, *Avit de Vienne*, tome II, 231 n. 4, highlights the perhaps unusual use of the adjective *exaltatis* (683) in this scene with reference to *undis* ("exalted" or lit. "raised" waters) and suggests a potential allusion to the Crucifixion. Such imagery is not persistent throughout the passage, at least not overtly, but the use of a single word may bear significance on its own. Together with *pendens* and the death/ birth symbolism of the crossing, the suggestion is appealing.

15:8 Et in spiritu furoris tui congregatae sunt aquae stetit unda fluens congregatae sunt abyssi in medio mari. 9 Dixit inimicus Persequar et comprehendam
dividam spolia implebitur anima mea evaginabo gladium meum interficiet eos
manus mea 10 Flavit spiritus tuus et operuit eos mare submersi sunt quasi
plumbum in aquis vehementibus.

– Ex. 15:8–10

Ergo exaltatis pendens sustollitur undis
Mox mergenda phalanx: lympharum monte leuata
Pondere telorum premitur, fundoque tenaci   685
Indutum reuehunt morientia corpora ferrum.
Pars exarmatis cum primum libera membris
Implicuit nantes miseris complexibus artus,
Auxilio decepta perit pariterque tenentes   690
Alterno sub fasce ruunt nexique necantur.
Ast alii, lassata diu dum brachia iactant,
Incurrunt enses iaculisque natantibus haerent,
Concolor et rubro miscetur sanguine pontus.
Quin et conspicuus princeps Memphitidis aulae,   695
Candentes ducens nigro rectore iugales,
Inspector cladis propriae gentisque superstes
Vltimus ingressis per currum naufragat undis.

[Hovering before imminent death the host is tossed onto the looming waves.
Hoisted on a mountain of water, they are burdened by the weight of their
spears, and their iron armour drags their dying bodies down to the relent-
less deep. Some, when their limbs were at last freed of their armour, were
entangled in the desperate flailing of other swimmers and, helplessly holding
on together, weighed down by their baggage, they sink and die. Others, con-
tinuously throwing their weary arms around, are thrust onto the swords and
spears of other swimmers, and the like-coloured sea is mingled with crimson
blood. Even the illustrious prince of the Memphian palace, leading his team
gleaming with a black steersman, a final witness to his own destruction and
that of his people, is drowned by his chariot in the onrush of waves.]

The poetry of this lively scene is based loosely on Exodus 15:8–10 and
primarily on verse ten, but there is little in common with the prose.[77] The

---

77 The words *pendens* and *undis* in line 687 may refer to *unda fluens* in the prose of verse
   eight.

panic and mayhem do, however, have much in common with the depiction of the Flood in Book 4, *De diluuio mundi* (4.473–87), where Avitus captures the commotion and chaos, by moving abruptly from image to image ("Multos ... quosdam ... Ast alii ... alii" ("Many ... some ... still others ... others," 4.476–83).[78] Each of these adjectives or pronouns offers a different view of death somewhere in the Flood, and in the Red Sea, the uproar is the same, as "some" are tangled in a mix of flailing limbs (*Pars*, 5.687), and "others" are stabbed in a mangle of swords and spears (*Ast alii*, 5.692). The first group to die in the Flood attempts to clamber out, but they are pulled back down by the rising waters ("Multos, dum scandere temptant,/Crescens unda trahit," 4.476). Likewise, the first to die in the Red Sea are dragged to the bottom by their heavy armour ("fundoque tenaci/Indutum reuehunt morientia corpora ferrum," 5.686). At the Flood, some head for the mountains in hope of finding safety (*quosdam montana petentes*, 4.477), but their "bodies die" on whatever slope they manage to find ("In quocumque bibunt morientia corpora monte," 4.482). In a reversal of this image, a towering mountain of water pursues the Egyptian host (*lympharum monte leuata*, 5.684) and draws their "dying bodies" into the deep (*reuehunt morientia corpora*, 5.686). The phrase, *morientia corpora*, is identical to that of the earlier scene and the comparable mountain imagery is striking. Still others in the Flood, "limbs flailing in endless swimming, exhale their last breath in exhaustion" ("Ast alii longo iactantes membra natatu/Defessi expirant animas," 4.479–80). In the same way, "still others" in the sea perish in the confusion of swords and spears, "relentlessly throwing their weary arms about" ("Ast alii, lassata diu dum brachia iactant," 5.692). Both lines begin in the same way (*Ast alii*) and contain similar language throughout (*iactantes/iactant, longo/diu, membra/brachia, lassata/defessi*), and Pharaoh's men are drowned by the weight of their spears (*pondere telorum*, 5.685), just as the victims of the Flood are drowned by the "weight of the storm" (*pondere nimbi*, 4.480). Pharaoh himself dies soon thereafter, title intact – *conspicuus princeps Memphitidis aulae* ("Illustrious prince of the Memphian palace," 5.695). The reference is surely ironic, given that his power is nothing next to the omnipotence of God. He is like all such men who die indiscriminately in the Flood, whose name and worldly possessions sink to the bottom of the sea ("Inque undas uenere simul dominique domusque" ["And lords and

---

78 See Arweiler, *Die Imitation antiker*, 101, who notes the use of *alii ... alii* as a mark of epic style that Christian poets adopt.

land (lit. homes) alike went into the Flood"], 4.484). Therefore, whatever classical models Avitus may have in mind for the individual words and phrases of this passage, it appears that his greatest source of inspiration is himself.[79] If so, one may wonder about the effective advantage of repeating such similar action in the context of what is essentially the same message. In all likelihood, Avitus could not escape covering both scenes, which are so prominent in the Old Testament and so important to the spiritual history of the Bible. Yet one may argue that *Historia spiritalis* would be a stronger work without one or the other.

Epilogue and Conclusion (5.711–21)

At the close of Book 5, Avitus offers an epilogue that returns the reader to the beginning of the book and to the beginning of the poem, where he first offers a promise of redemption: "hoc totum Christus persoluerit in se" ("All of this Christ paid for through himself," 1.9). This final passage brings structure and unity to the book and to the work as a whole, and here Avitus aims to leave his audience with a strong sense of the mystical meaning of the crossing and of *Historia spiritalis*, generally (5.711–21):

> Si quid triste fuit, dictum est quod paupere uersu,
> Terserit hic sacri memorabilis unda triumphi,
> Gaudia quo resonant, crimen quo tollitur omne
> Per lauacrum uiuitque nouus pereunte ueterno:
> Quo bona consurgunt, quo noxia facta necantur,   715
> Israhel uerus sacris quo tingitur undis;
> Consona quo celebrat persultans turba tropaeum,
> Quo praecurrentes complentur dona figurae,
> Quas pius explicuit per quinque uolumina uates.
> Nosque tubam stipula sequimur numerumque tenentes   720
> Hoc tenui cumbae ponemus litore portum.

[If anything spoken in this meagre song was sad, the great wave of holy victory wipes it clean here, in which joys resound, by which all sin is removed and, with the death of the old, a new man lives in Baptism, by which good things come to pass; evil deeds are checked, and true Israel is bathed in its

---

79 For a summary of classical and Christian sources for various turns of phrase in this passage, see further Hecquet-Noti, *Avit de Vienne*, tome II, 230–3.

sacred waves; by its virtue, an exultant crowd harmoniously celebrates victory and the ancestral gifts of symbolism are fulfilled, which the holy prophet unfolded in five books. And we follow his horn with our reed, echoing their number, and we will make a port for our small boat upon this shore.]

With the same humility Sedulius expresses at the opening of the *Carmen paschale*, who offers his poem as "meagre greens from a poor garden" (*paupere ... horto*, 14), Avitus ends with a comparable, self-deprecating reference to his "poor verse" (paupere uersu, 5.711), and his use of *tristis* ("sad") in the same line may refer to the woeful tale but also to his "pathetic" talent. A pun seems likely, especially since there is nothing truly sad about the demise of Pharaoh, and the tone is victorious. Invoking Moses, Avitus offers his five-book "history" as a small "pipe" (*stipula*) next to the grandeur of the great "horn" (*tuba*) of the Pentateuch, and he brings his little boat into port ("Hoc tenui cumbae ponemus litore portum"), signalling the end of the poem.[80]

It is a humble ending for what is obviously a rich and complex work. There is nothing meagre about *Historia spiritalis* in scale or presentation. Avitus amplifies each of the biblical stories in his poem to dramatic proportions and goes far beyond the kind of subtle exegesis we find in earlier biblical epic. More than Juvencus and Cyprianus, Sedulius and the writers of his generation become stepping stones for Avitus, whose statement in Book 5, "Tu cognosce tuam saluanda in plebe figuram" ("You, [reader], recognize your own figure in that people who will be saved," 5.254), originates in similar exhortations in earlier verse and perhaps in the *Carmen paschale* (4.263–4): "Cognoscite cuncti, / Mystica quid doceant animos miracula nostros!" ("Let all recognize what these mystical miracles teach our souls!").

In contrast to earlier biblical epics, especially *Euangeliorum libri* and the *Heptateuch*, whose proximity to the biblical narrative makes it easier to see how the authors meld classical and Christian literature, there are fewer textual traces in *Historia spiritalis* to ground the narrative in the language of the Scriptures. This poem, then, bears a much stronger individual imprint than earlier biblical epics, because it expresses more clearly the author's personal thoughts and feelings on original sin and man's path towards redemption, however filtered these views may be by extra-biblical literature, such

---

80 As Green also remarks, the reference to a small or humble boat in this context is a classical trope that appears elsewhere in Horace (*Odes*, 4.15.3–4), Vergil (*Georgics*, 2.41), Statius (*Thebaid*, 12.809), etc. See further *Latin Epics*, 155, n. 1.

as Augustine's commentary on Genesis. In other words, even if Avitus' thoughts are mediated by the orthodox teachings of the Church, they are complicated by a strong sense of personal emotion that comes from the author's internalization of classical and Christian poetry. Determining the register of these thoughts and feelings, their significance in the interpretation of a given scene, will be important work in the future.

Chapter Six

Arator's *Historia Apostolica* (c. 544 CE)

Versibus ergo canam quos Lucas rettulit Actus,
   Historiamque sequens carmina uera loquar.
Alternis reserabo modis quod littera pandit
   Et res si qua mihi mystica corde datur.

[So I shall sing in verse the Acts Luke related, and following that story, I shall speak true poetry. In turns, I shall set out what the letter reveals and whatever mystical sense is given to my heart.]

– Arator's *Letter to Pope Vigilius* (19–22)

Born in the region of Liguria, Italy, at the end of the fifth century, Arator was a rhetorician and politician before entering the Church as subdeacon.[1] His biblical epic, *Historia apostolica* (*The Apostolic History*), is a two-book rendition of Acts written in 2326 hexameters (1076; 1250) and was dedicated to Pope Vigilius (537–55) in the spring of 544 CE.[2] Little else is known about the poet's life before or after this date, but according to a brief inscription, Arator read his work to Pope Vigilius on delivery and publicly on three subsequent readings in front of the Church of St Peter in

---

1 See Wright, "Arator's Use of Caelius Sedulius," 39–64 at 39; Green, *Latin Epics*, 253.

2 For the title of the poem, see further Orbán, ed., *Aratoris Subdiaconi Historia Apostolica*, 2 vols., CCSL 130, 3 and 221; Schrader, *Acts of the Apostles*, 15, n. 1; see also Green, *Latin Epics*, 251, n. 2. For the date of 544 CE, see further Orbán, *Historia apostolica*, 5; Green, *Latin Epics*, 252; Schwind, *Arator Studien*, 9.

Chains in Rome.[3] These performances, if they can be called that, attest to the contemporary appeal of *Historia apostolica*, and the popularity of the poem endured well into the Middle Ages. In Anglo-Saxon England, it was read for centuries and imitated by England's most famous scholars, who adapted its language and style to their idiosyncratic compositions in Anglo-Latin.[4] There is no question, then, that this was a well-liked work.

Arator's Letter to Florianus

A few verse letters attached to *Historia apostolica* provide a sense of Arator's reasons for undertaking his versification of Acts.[5] The first of these is addressed to one abbot Florianus, and it offers a foretaste of the author's style and predilection for wordplay. Florianus must have groaned at the pun on his name (*florem*, 1), but Arator's intention is not mockery; it is endearment. The double-entendre, not the last example here, affords a *pro forma* entrance into the epistle, but it also speaks to the poet's general interest in the deeper meaning of words, and that is a defining feature of *Historia apostolica* (1–28):[6]

> Domino sancto, uenerabili et in Christi gratia spiritaliter erudito Floriano abbati, Arator subdiaconus S.

> Qui meriti florem, maturis sensibus ortum,
>   Nominis ore tui iam, Floriane, tenes –
> Nam, primaeuus adhuc, senibus documenta dedisti,
>   E quibus in caelum uita pararet iter –
> Ad carmen concurre meum pedibusque labanti   5
>   Porrige de placido saepe fauore manum!
> Ieiuno sermone quidem, sed pinguia gesta

---

3 Arator read from *Historia scholastica* first on 6 April, then 17 April, 8 May, and 30 May. See further Orbán, *Historia apostolica*, 5–6; Green, *Latin Epics*, 251; De Nie, "Whatever Mystery May be Given to my Heart," 3; Martin, "The Influence of Arator in Anglo-Saxon England," 75–81 at 75; Hillier, *Arator on the Acts of the Apostles* , 1; see also Hillier, "Arator and Baptism," 112.

4 See further Orbán, *Historia Apostolica*, 14–17, and the *Testimonia*, 108–54.

5 See ibid., 1, n. 1, for the importance of these letters in the absence of other biographical information.

6 For a full translation of the poem, see Schrader, *Arator's on the Acts of the Apostles*. Translations of *De actibus apostolorum* are my own, although I have consulted Schrader.

Scripsimus, ac pelagi pondere gutta fluit.
Inter grandiloquos per mille uolumina libros
　　Maxima cum teneas, et breuiora lege!　　　　　　　　　　　10
Naturaeque modo, quam rerum condidit Auctor,
　　Concordent studiis celsa uel ima tuis.
Quae genuit tigres, quae nutrit terra leones,
　　Formicis, apibus praebuit ipsa sinum.
　Et si respicias, dispenset ut omnia rector,　　　　　　　　　　15
　　Ingenium mites, uim meruere truces.
Ipsaque continuum uirtus infracta laborem
　　Deserit et uarias quaerit habere uices.
Loricam solitus membris imponere miles
　　Gymnasii gaudet nudus adire locum.　　　　　　　　　　　20
Et, qui ferratas acies atque agmina uincunt,
　　Imbelles feriunt per sua tela feras.
Ergo gradum retinens et prisca uolumina linquens,
　　Cede dies operi quod pia causa iuuat.

[To the holy, venerable lord Florianus, spiritually instructed in the grace of Christ, subdeacon Arator sends greetings.

You, Florianus, who already bear the flower of merit in your name, born of mature sense – for, though young, you have taught the old, so that life might prepare to make its way to heaven – hasten to my song, and with gentle, frequent favour extend your hand to me, stumbling on my feet. My speech is poor, to be sure, but these deeds are rich, and a single drop [of water] flows from the depth of the sea. Although you have truly great things in your grandiloquent books, those thousands of volumes, read lesser things as well. Like nature, which the Author of the world established, let high and low unite in your studies. The earth itself, which bears tigers and feeds lions, also offers her bosom unto ants and bees. And if you think how the Ruler distributes everything, the meek get the brains, and the brutes, the brawn. And that very brawn, if weakened, forsakes continuous work and seeks some other way. The soldier, used to arming his limbs, is happy to go to the exercise field unarmed. And those who conquer battle lines and ironclad ranks also bear their spears against unwarlike beasts. Therefore, slowing your pace and abandoning those ancient volumes, give your days to work that a pious cause supports.]

As an added touch to the pun in the first line, the *-or-* in "Florianus" repeats not just in *florem* (1) but *ortum* (1) and *ore* (2) as well, so that each line – beginning and end – rings with the sound of the recipient's name, feeding flattery. As a playful invocation of "the muse," Arator begs the favour of Florianus, his deity, to hasten to his song and "lend him a hand" (*porrige ... manum*, 6). The reference to the poet's "stumbling feet" is, no doubt, is another pun alluding to the author's awkward skill as well as the metre of his poem, which is measured in "feet."[7]

The following references to "hand" and "foot" lead the author into a series of juxtapositions promoting the virtue of lowliness against the apparent vice of loftiness. In these lines, Arator aims to convince Florianus that *Historia apostolica* and similar Christian literature is of greater spiritual value than those classical tomes. Thus strong hand/weak feet (5), poor speech/rich deeds (7), small drop/big sea (8), great books/lesser ones (10), lofty/low (12), tigers and lions/bees and ants (13–14), mind/might (16). Collectively, these images promote the value of Christian poetry, despite its humble origins in prose, while the "grandiloquent books" (*grandiloquos ... libros*, 9) refer to the written achievements of Antiquity. Recall that Sedulius uses similar language to rebuke "the fictions" that "pagan poets parade with big-sounding rhythms" ("... gentiles studeant figmenta poetae / Grandisonis pompare modis," 1.16–17), not to mention the preface to his *Carmen paschale*, which offers a striking image of classical literature in terms of a lavish Roman feast. Like Arator, Sedulius recommends the meagre food of Scripture. So at the end of his letter, Arator tells Florianus to put aside his ancient tomes and to attend to a work (his work) that serves the more pious cause of Christianity ("prisca uolumina linquens, / Cede dies operi, quod pia causa iuuat," 23–4). The epistle to Florianus, then, sets Arator firmly within the ranks of his fellow biblical-epic predecessors, who likewise appreciate the sweetness of classical literature but also question its compatibility with Christianity.

Arator's Letter to Pope Vigilius

A letter to Vigilius joined the text of *Historia apostolica* when Arator delivered it to the pope. In it, Arator speaks more plainly about his approach

---

7   See further Green, *Latin Epics*, 278: "in matters of meter [Arator] is quite inventive" and "happy to scan words in an unusual way." Green offers the examples of *Samaria* (1. 626) and *Aquila* (2. 511), and points further to McKinlay's edition, 154 and 215 (i.e., *Index grammaticus, s.v. prosodiaca*). It may therefore be that Arator is exposing a measure of genuine anxiety here; otherwise, we may attribute these words to the conventional humility topos.

to the Bible and his interest in the mystical sense of Scripture.[8] Like the letter to Florianus, this letter offers context for our reading of the poem, but it also provides a sense of the author's journey into the stewardship of the Church during a very turbulent time. As such, it is of special interest for historical and literary purposes, and so I have included the whole of it here (*Epist. ad Vigilium*, 1–26):[9]

Domino sancto beatissimo atque apostolico et in toto orbe primo omnium sacerdotum, papae Vigilio, Arator subdiaconus S.

Moenibus undosis bellorum incendia cernens,
  Pars ego tunc populi tela pauentis eram.
Publica libertas, sanctissime papa Vigili,
  Aduenis incluso soluere uincla gregi.
De gladiis rapiuntur oues pastore ministro   5
  Inque humeris ferimur te reuocante piis.
Corporeum satis est sic euasisse periclum,
  At mihi plus animae nascitur inde salus.
Ecclesiam subeo dimissa naufragus aula;
  Perfida mundani desero uela freti.   10
Transferor ad niueas Petri sine turbine caulas
  Et fruor optati iam statione soli.
Litoris ille sinus ad carbasa nostra parauit,
  Fluctibus in mediis cui uia sicca fuit.
Esse reus potero, grates si reddere cessem.   15
  Vnius officio displicuere nouem.
Sensibus ardor inest horum celebrare labores,
  Quorum uoce fides obtinet orbis iter.
Versibus ergo canam quos Lucas rettulit Actus,
  Historiamque sequens carmina uera loquar.   20
Alternis reserabo modis quod littera pandit
  Et res si qua mihi mystica corde datur.
Metrica uis sacris non est incognita libris:
  Psalterium lyrici composuere pedes;

---

8 For the chronology of this letter, see further Orbán, *Historia apostolica*, 4–5.
9 For the text of *Historia apostolica*, see McKinlay, ed., *Aratoris Subdiaconi De Actibus Apostolorum*, CSEL 72, xxviii; see also the recent edition of Orbán, ed., *Aratoris Subdiaconi Historia Apostolica*, 2 vols., CCSL 130. My citations follow Orbán.

Hexametris constare sonis in origine linguae   25
  Cantica, Hieremiae, Iob quoque dicta ferunt.
Hoc tibi, magne pater, cum defero munus amoris,
  Respice, quod meritis debita soluo tuis!
Te duce tiro legor, te dogmata disco magistro;
  Si quid ab ore placet, laus monitoris erit.   30

[To the holy, most blessed and apostolic Pope Vigilius, foremost of all priests in the entire world, Arator subdeacon sends his greetings.

Seeing the fires of war atop the billowing walls, I was then among those terrified at the spears. You come, holiest Pope Vigilius as liberty for all to loosen the bonds of a captive flock. With the shepherd at hand, the sheep are spared from the sword and, reclaiming us, you bear us on your pious shoulders. It is enough to have escaped mortal danger, but for me the safety of the soul has come to mean more. Having left the palace, I have come to the Church as a castaway. I flee the faithless sails of the worldly sea. I am brought over to the snow-white and storm-free [sheep]folds of Peter, and now enjoy the anchorage of this longed-for land. He for whom there was a dry path in the midst of the sea has made a strip of shore for these sails. I will be guilty, if I ever stop giving thanks to him. The nine [lepers] displeased him [Jesus] by the courtesy of one of them. There is a burning in my heart to celebrate the labours of the men by whose voice faith finds a path in the world. So I shall sing in verse the Acts Luke related, and following that story, I shall speak true poetry. In turns, I shall set out what the letter reveals and whatever mystical sense is given to my heart. The power of metre is not unknown to sacred books. Lyrical feet make up the Psalter. They also say that the Song of Songs, the sayings of Jeremiah, and Job were written in hexameter in their original language. As I give this gift of love to you, great father, know that I am repaying the debts I owe to your merit. I was recruited under your guidance; by your teaching, I have learned the doctrine. If anything from my lips is pleasing, the praise goes to the teacher.]

The letter opens ominously with an allusion to the siege of Rome by the Gothic King Vitiges in 537/8 CE. Apparently, Arator saw it unfold.[10] Reading as this does like another fall of Troy, Orbán cites three epic sources for the phrase *bellorum incendia* ("the fires of war," 1) in his edition, including Vergil (*Aen.* 1.566), Valerius Flaccus (*Arg.* 6.739), and Silius

---

10 See further Green, *Latin Epics*, 257; also, Schrader, *Acts of the Apostles*, 3.

Italicus (*Pun.* 2.358).[11] The Vergilian connection is the most appealing, since it aligns the fall of Rome with the fall of Troy and introduces epic drama to the events of Arator's situation; for "who does not know the city of Troy," proclaims Dido to Aeneas, "its might, men, and the fires of so great a war?" ("quis Troiae nesciat urbem, / Virtutesque uirosque aut tanti incendia belli," 565–6). Her last words here, *incendia belli*, may be Arator's source of inspiration, or perhaps they come from Flaccus or Italicus. On the other hand, they may originate in the poetry of Juvencus, whose *Euangeliorum libri* offers another potential source (*Ev.* 4.99): "Discurrent cunctis bellorum incendia terris" ("The fires of war shall run through all the lands"). These are Jesus' words to his apostles at the end of the poem, and they are based on Matthew 24:6: "Audituri enim estis praelia, et opiniones praeliorum" ("And you shall hear of wars and rumours of wars"). The context is the end of the world, and perhaps Arator thought it was at hand, seeing the walls of Rome burning before him, and if he was remembering the end of *Euangeliorum libri*, he would have known its beginning – "Inmortale nihil mundi conpage tenetur" ("Nothing in the structure of the world is immortal," *praef.* 1), not even "golden Rome" (*aurea Roma*, 2). As Juvencus says, "the Creator of the universe has set an irreversible time in which a final torrent of flame will grip the entire world ("Nam statuit genitor rerum inreuocabile tempus, / Quo cunctum torrens rapiat flamma ultima mundum," 4–5). Seeing the fires before him and fearing death, Arator may indeed have felt that time was at hand, and a connection with Juvencus would neatly align the fall of Rome with the coming of Judgment Day. Even if Arator did not believe it was the end of time, he would have appreciated the poetry of the connection. In any event, there is no need to exclude Vergil in favour of Juvencus. In all likelihood, Juvencus had Vergil's passage in mind anyway, and so an echo of *Euangeliorum libri* is still an echo of the *Aeneid*. Finally, those simple words, *bellorum incendia*, may be said to herald the end of Latin biblical epic itself, since Arator is the last such writer in Antiquity. Those fires, even if they did not bring about the end of time, were enough to see the "final flame" of the genre (*flamma ultima, Ev. Praef.* 5). Thus the tradition of Latin biblical epic begins with water, with the streams of "sweet-singing Jordan" (*Ev. Praef.* 27), and ends here in the mid-sixth century with the fires of Rome (*bellorum incendia cernens*, 1).

---

11 See Orbán, *Historia Apostolica*, 213.

At this moment, Pope Vigilius is a source of great comfort to Arator. He is the shepherd of Christ, who comes to the rescue of his lambs ("De gladiis rapiuntur oues pastore ministro, 5), to "loosen the chains of his captive flock" ("Aduenis incluso soluere uincla gregi," 4) and he has played a personal role in Arator's spiritual education. Interestingly, the phrase *soluere uincla* is probably Sedulian, and it appears in the *Carmen paschale* in the context of the Lord's Prayer and the forgiveness of sins (2.269–72):

> Debita laxari qui nobis cuncta rogamus,
> Nos quoque laxemus; proprii nam cautio uerbi   270
> Spondentes manifesta tenet, grauiusque soluti
> Nectimur alterius si soluere uincla negemus:

[We beg that all our trespasses be forgiven and that we, too, may forgive; for a clear verbal obligation keeps us to our promises, and we are more gravely bound in freedom, if we refuse to loose the chains of another.]

The metaphorical chains in Arator's poem may therefore be linked to redemption, since Vigilius tends to the salvation of Christian souls. Note, too, that Arator expresses a need to repay the good merits of Vigilius ("Respice, quod meritis debita soluo tuis!" ["Know that I am repaying the debts I owe to your merits"], 28),[12] and though he is not talking about the forgiveness of sins, there is a sense of *quid pro quo*, given that Vigilius comes to safeguard the poet's physical and spiritual liberty (*libertas*, 3). It therefore makes sense that all of the fame and praise pagan poets heap on their heroes, as Juvencus puts it – "Adcumulant quorum famam laudesque poetae" (*praef.* 8) – now go to Pope Vigilius, who is the pious fulfilment of those values (30): "Si quid ab ore placet, laus monitoris erit" ("If anything from these lips is pleasing, the praise goes to the teacher").

In the lines that follow, Arator again resorts to his knowledge of Sedulius, when he says, "Sensibus ardor inest horum celebrare labores, / Quorum uoce fides obtinet orbis iter" ("There is a burning in my heart to celebrate the labours of these men, by whose voice faith obtains a path in the world," 17–18). Arator means Peter and Paul, but Sedulius offers similar words

---

12 Avitus uses the same language in his dedication to Parthenius (64–5): "Iam stimulat promissa dies, ut debita tandem / Contractusque meos soluere, docte, uelim" ("Now the promised day impels me, learned one, that I should wish to repay my debts and contracts").

with reference to the Gospels at the beginning of the *Carmen paschale* (1.27–8): "Dominumque tonantem / Sensibus et toto delectet corde fateri" ("I love with all my heart and soul to praise the Lord-Thunderer"). Moreover, just as God is the way to salvation for Sedulius (*uia namque salutis*, 1.35), the one who "leads firm steps to the paschal gifts" ("Haec firmos ad dona gradus paschalia ducit," 1.36), Peter and Paul are the means by which faith finds a path in the world ("Quorum uoce fides obtinet orbis iter," 18). Although Arator says he will follow in the footsteps of Luke and his account of Acts, he is more like Sedulius and Avitus in his determination to enhance the literal events of the story (*historiam sequens*, 20) with mystical meaning (*res mystica*, 22). As he puts it, he will follow "what the letter reveals" (*quod littera pandit*, 21) and whatever mystical sense is given to his heart ("Et res si qua mihi mystica corde datur," 22). The poetry of *Historia apostolica* is guided by these two principles: the letter (*littera*) and the heart (*cors*), but the counsel of the heart does not weaken Arator's faithfulness to the letter of Acts, which he follows attentively in his way.

Arator's Letter to Parthenius, Part 1

The author's letter to his friend and mentor, Parthenius, is the longest of the three surviving verse epistles. It is also the most personal.[13] In it, Arator expresses more than *pro forma* affection for his teacher, whose instruction he recalls with fondness. Arator remembers in particular the occasions when he would sit and listen to Parthenius read classical poetry, "in which there was false art and arrogant pomp" ("In quibus ars fallax, pompa superba fuit," 42), but Arator loved it.[14] In fact, he wanted to write such poetry himself, but his teacher encouraged him to turn his talents towards the praise of God, to direct "his will," as Avitus would say, "towards

---

13 For Arator's relationship with Parthenius, see further Green, *Latin Epics*, 254–5.

14 Green, *Latin Epics*, 267, writes, "There is a passing condemnation of *ars fallax* and *pompa superba*, but in the context of his long-gone education, not the present poem." However, it could be argued that Arator is using his memory of the past as present commentary. Rhetorically, that would free him from blaming Vergil directly, but allow him to join the ranks of earlier poets in their condemnation of epic *mendacia* ("lies"). As Green suggests, Arator probably assumed this letter would accompany the poem, which means the context of his long-gone education takes on renewed life for the general reader. So also Green, *Latin Epics*, 322, where he writes, "Christ's triumph is a very important theme in the poem" and especially the phrase *noua pompa triumphi* ("a new celebration of triumph"). That passage invites comparison with this one.

divine praise" ("diuina in laude uoluntas," 5.7). This is what Parthenius means in the following re-enacted speech (53–68):

> Quae cum nostra tibi fragilis cecinisset arundo
> Et mihi, care, tuus saepe faueret amor,
> "O utinam malles" dixisti "rectius huius   55
>   Ad Domini laudes flectere uocis iter,
> Vt, quia nomen habes, quo te uocitamus, Arator,
>   Non abstrusa tibi sit sed aperta seges!"
> Constitui, fateor, si quando forte mererer
>   Ingenii fructus ad meliora sequi,   60
> Quo te cumque loci contingeret esse, uirorum
>   Maxime, transmitti, quod modularer, opus.
> Iam stimulat promissa dies, ut debita tandem
>   Contractusque meos soluere, docte, uelim.
> Sume, quod ex nitido libauimus aequore carmen   65
>   Et licet exiguas suscipe gratus aquas!
> Oceanus rerum spatio manet altus in illo,
>   De quo uix laticem traximus ore breuem.

[And when my fragile reed had sung those songs to you, dear [friend], your affection often spoke supportively to me: "Oh, would that you would bend the path of your voice straighter to the praise of God," you said, "so that, since you bear the name Arator, as I call you, a harvest may not be hidden from you but revealed." I determined, I must say, that if ever I by chance became worthy of pursuing the fruits of my talent to those better things, the work I put to song would find you, greatest of men, wherever you might be. Now that promised day compels me at last to repay those debts and contracts, teacher. Take this song that I have skimmed from the shining surface of the sea and, although it is but a trickle, receive its waters graciously. A deep ocean rests in its measure, from which I have scarcely drawn a brief drop with my lips.]

There is real affection in the juxtaposition of Arator's words *mihi, care, tuus* (54), which puts a term of endearment, *care* ("dear"), between the two men, and "love" (*amor*, 54) at the end of the line. There are also elegiac strains to the literary apostrophe, "O utinam malles" dixisti "rectius huius / Ad Domini laudes flectere uocis iter!" ("Oh, would that you would bend the path of your voice straighter to the praise of God"). Similar words in a different context can be found in the *Elegies* of Propertius, where a young man longs to reach his lover's heart with his pathetic voice (1.16.27–8): "O utinam traiecta caua mea uocula rima / Percussas dominae uertat in auriculas!" ("Oh, would that my soft voice would cross through some hollow cleft, and enter into my lady's startled ears!").[15] On some level, Arator's sentiments represent a transformation of such elegiac poetry.

The pun on Arator's name in lines 57–8 appeals to the same spirit as that in his letter to Florianus, but deeper meaning resides here. "Arator" means "ploughman" in Latin, and the successful "harvest" (*seges*, 58) refers to his Christian poem. Parthenius wants Arator to plough straight lines of verse, and to sow them with holy seeds, avoiding, as Sedulius would put it, "the sterile sweeps of land where arid earth does not know how to bear fruit" ("Et steriles habitare plagas, ubi gignere fructum / Arida nescit humus," 1.50–1); in other words, paganism and pagan literature. All that comes of that land, says Sedulius, is "damned as the food of Tartarus" ("Tartareo damnata cibo," 1.53). Parthenius, professing to know better, therefore encourages Arator "to direct the fruits of his talent to better things" ("Ingenii fructus ad meliora sequi," 60), where *fructus* refers both to the "benefits" of good work and the "fruit" that comes of the ploughman's share.

Not done with double-entendre, Arator closes this section with a burst of wordplay. The words *spatium*, *altus*, and *breuis*, are all metrical puns: *spatium* refers to the physical "space" or extent of the poem as well as the "measure" or "quantity" of metre; and *altus* means not only "deep" with reference to the sea, but "high" literature and perhaps "the profound ocean" of epic. The "brief" spring or trickle (*laticem*) that he draws from this ocean suggests Arator's humble work (conventional modesty) but also the dactyl as the "brief" measure of quantity in hexameter poetry, as opposed to the spondee, which may be viewed as "high" or "deep," like the ocean (*altus*). It is a game of words for the benefit of a teacher who fostered Arator's faith and talent.

Arator is like Sedulius when he says that "a deep ocean resides in [his poem's] measure, from which I have scarcely drawn a brief drop with my lips" ("Oceanus rerum spatio manet altus in illo, / De quo uix laticem traximus ore breuem," 1.68). Referring to a forest, Sedulius says much the same thing of his own efforts in the *Carmen paschale* (1.96–8): "Ex quibus audaci perstringere pauca relatu / Vix animis conmitto meis, siluamque patentem / Ingrediens aliquos nitor contingere ramos" ("Of such things I

---

15 Trans. is that of Kline: www.yorku.ca/pswarney/3110/Propertius.htm#_Toc498857579.

can barely lift my soul to touch upon a few in this bold recital, and entering an open wood, I strive to touch a branch or two"). Considering the kinship of these two poems, it is noteworthy that many of the similarities between them relate to Book 1 of the *Carmen paschale* and affinities appearing in the space of just fifty lines (1.50–100), suggesting that Arator is very familiar with the opening book of Sedulius' poem.

Arator's Letter to Parthenius, Part 2 (69–82)

Turning from his memories of youth to nearer times, Arator now recollects his entrance into the Church, and in this context begins to talk about *Historia apostolica*. He says that he wishes to approach the versification of Acts by blending his knowledge of the Old and New Testaments, that is, by following the letter of the Bible (*littera*) and his heart (*corde*). In describing this approach, Arator once again reveals his debt to early biblical epic and especially the *Carmen paschale* (*Epist. Parth.* 69–82):[16]

> Namque ego, Romanae caulis permixtus amoenis
> > Ecclesiae, tonso uertice factus ouis,   70
> Pascua laeta uidens et aprica uolumina Christi
> > Quaerebam gustu tangere cuncta meo
> Et nunc Dauiticis assuetus floribus odas
> > Mandere, nunc Genesim mens cupiebat edax.
> Cumque simul uiolas et lilia carpere mallem,   75
> > Quae uetus atque nouus congeminauit odor,
> Incidit ille mihi, quem regula nominat Actus,
> > Messis apostolicae plenus in orbe liber,
> In quo nos Dominus Petro piscante leuauit
> > De gremio salsi caeruleique maris   80
> Ostensaque dedit caelestis imagine nauem
> > Gentibus assumptis exsaturare famem.

[And so, drawn into the pleasant [sheep]folds of the Roman Church – made a sheep by my tonsured head – seeing the joyful pastures and sunlit tomes of Christ, I wanted to taste everything. At one moment, being accustomed to the flowers of David, I wanted to consume his songs, and at another moment my ravenous mind hungered for Genesis. And because I would rather graze

---

16 For another discussion of this letter, see further Green, *Latin Epics*, 260.

on violets and lilies at the same time, in which the scent of the Old and New Testaments combine, I fell on the book the canon calls "Acts," a book filled with the Apostles' harvest in the world, in which the heavenly Lord, with Peter as his fisherman, raised us up from the bosom of the salty, cerulean sea, and – with clear symbolism – the celestial [Lord] brought a ship to satisfy the hunger of the nations taken up therein.]

The same pastoral imagery appears in Arator's letter to Vigilius. In fact, all of his letters contain such imagery. In this instance, the word *amoenus* (69) leads to the floral imagery to follow, and the poet's view that the pasture of the Church is a *locus amoenus* in the classical tradition of such scenes. At the opening of the *Carmen paschale*, Sedulius says that he, too, is accustomed to singing David's songs ("Dauiticis adsuetus cantibus odas," 1.23), by which he means the Psalms, and Arator echoes him, saying that he is "accustomed to consuming the odes of David's flowers" ("Dauidicis assuetus floribus odas," 73). The single difference of *floribus* (73) is owing to Arator's emphasis on floral imagery, but this too originates with Sedulius, who compares the Old and New Testaments to the "scent" (*odor*, 76) of "violets and lilies" (*uiolas et lilia*, 75). Arator therefore harmonizes two passages from Book 1 of the *Carmen paschale*, which include Sedulius' reference to his song as "soft lilies" and "violets of the purple field" ("Lilia, purpurei neu per uiolaria campi," 1.278), and the scriptures as roses (*rosis*, 1.46). Sedulius also calls the Old Testament the "scent" of the law that "breathes life" ("uitam spirantis odorem / Legis," 1.41), and Arator's agricultural imagery echoes both of these passages, while his reference to the "cerulean sea" (*caeruleique maris*, 80) is yet another familiar Sedulian phrase (*caerula ponti*).[17]

Arator chooses Acts as the subject of his poem, therefore, in part because it allows him to explore the significant relationships between the Old and New Testaments, which he wants to do, but also because he is, like his audience, already "accustomed" (*assuetus*) to earlier versifications of the Gospels, specifically those of Juvencus and Sedulius, which is why he goes farther afield.[18] The Gospels have been done and done well, and so

---

17 See further *Carmen paschale* (1.136, 2.222, and 3.219).

18 A manuscript of the tenth century supports this assumption (ms. Orléans 295, fol. 36ᵛ) and that Juvencus and Sedulius had already written the evangelical acts, so there was no need to go over them again. See McKinlay's edition (p. xxx): "Qui, considerans Iuuencum et Sedulium scripsisse actus euangelicos, noluit eos iterum rescribere sed totum se contulit ad actus Apostolicorum describendos"; see also Green, *Latin Epics*, 259.

his choice of Acts is logical, given that it has not been versified before and that it will allow Arator to take up where Juvencus and Sedulius left off, that is, after the Gospel of John.

Classical Context

Arator was educated in Milan, Pavia, and Ravenna,[19] and that training contributed to his knowledge of the many classical authors he echoes in *Historia apostolica*, notably Vergil, Ovid, Lucan, Valerius Flaccus, Silius Italicus, Statius, Martial, Juvenal, and Claudian,[20] but also Prudentius and Sedulius, among Christian poets.[21] Vergil is usually the preeminent source of inspiration for all of the biblical versifiers of the period, and he does play a prominent role in *Historia apostolica*, but Green has made a good case for the equal or greater importance of Lucan, who contributes a wealth of language to Arator.[22]

Whatever the chief source of influence, it is clear that the bulk of Arator's diction is classical in origin, and various scholars highlight their favourite turns of phrase to show it. Orbán provides a summary list in his edition, citing "heaven" as *Olympus*, *Tartarus* as "Hell," and God (predictably) as *Tonans*, "the Thunderer."[23] Schrader notes that "Peter advises the Jews to flee their sins" ("Sed fugite, o miseri") in words used long before to warn against the Cyclops (1.188; *Aeneid* 3.639),[24] and he highlights two allusions to the famous flight of *fama* in the *Aeneid*, "fama uolat per urbem" (cf. 2.662–3 and *Ad Parthenium*, 27–8), without which, he says, "it would almost not be an epic of any sort."[25] To that point, Green cites several arguments that challenge the classification of *Historia apostolica* as "epic" at all,

---

19   Orbán, *Historia apostolica*, 1; Green, *Latin Epics*, 254; Schrader, "Arator: Reevaluation," 64–77 at 65.

20   This list is taken from Orbán, *Historia apostolica*, 9.

21   See further Green, *Latin Epics*, 329–30; Orbán emphasizes the strong influence of Sedulius on *Historia apostolica*, 9; also, Deproost, *L'Apôtre Pierre dans une épopée de VIe siècle*, esp. 280–3. For the later reception of Arator in Anglo-Saxon England, see Orchard, *Poetic Art of Aldhelm*, 166–7; Wright, "Arator's Use of Caelius Sedulius," esp. 38; Wright has re-evaluated many of the parallels in McKinlay's edition and concludes that several of McKinlay's connections between Arator and Sedulius are tenuous.

22   Green, *Latin Epics*, 329. See also Orbán, *Historia apostolica*, 411–60, for a running list of echoes.

23   Orbán, *Historia apostolica*, 10. Schrader, *Acts of the Apostles*, 5, offers a similar list.

24   Schrader, *Acts of the Apostles*, 6.

25   Ibid.

but he himself concludes in the interest of harmony, saying, "Laetitiat poeta cum theologo" ("The poet rejoices with the theologian").[26] Elsewhere, Michael Roberts provides good evidence to suggest that "Arator's language shows the continuing creation of a Christian poetic idiom," in which "pagan locutions are given a new, specifically Christian connotation."[27] Broadly speaking, this practice follows Arator's predecessors in the genre, who adopt and adapt that which they take from their predecessors.

Much of the style of *Historia apostolica*, language aside, resorts to the conventions of epic, though usually not without some kind of adaptation. The heroic metre is a hallmark of the prior genre, and in using dactylic hexameter Arator follows Juvencus, Cyprianus, Sedulius, and Avitus.[28] Arator also converts the pagan Muse for the purpose of his song, just as Juvencus did two hundred years before him, and he calls on the Holy Spirit several times.[29] Numerous speeches also yield epic strains, as Green has shown,[30] although Roberts has noted that many speeches from the biblical Acts are also "prime candidates for elimination," since "they are rarely an integral part of an episode."[31]

Classical Context: Storm on the Sea (2.1067–81)

Arator's description of the storm on the sea in book 2 of *Historia apostolica* (2.1067–81) is characteristic of the kind of epic enhancement readers of the genre had come to expect. Much of what Arator does here harkens back to Juvencus and his description of the storm on the Sea of Galilee in *Euangeliorum libri* (2.25–32), not to mention the works of Lucan and Vergil.[32] The poetry of the episode is based on chapter 27 of Acts, verses

---

26 See further Green, *Latin Epics*, 350. Green reviews the epic question on 337–50; see also Hillier, "Arator and Baptism," 313.

27 See further Roberts, *Biblical Epic*, 178.

28 See further Schrader, *Acts of the Apostles*, 5. But also see Green, *Latin Epics*, 338, who is right to point out that dactylic hexameter is used by a number of Christian poets outside the genre of epic.

29 See further Roberts, *Biblical Epic*, 178. Roberts points out several invocations of the Holy Spirit in the poem (1.142, 225–8, 2.577–83) and Peter (1.771–2, 896–8).

30 See further Green, *Latin Epics*, 291–8.

31 Roberts, *Biblical Epic*, 114.

32 For commentary on this scene, see further Green, *Latin Epics*, 333–7; Schrader *Acts of the Apostles*, 11.

13–20, and in rendering it Arator draws deeply from the well of pagan poetry (2.1067–81):[33]

27:13 Aspirante autem austro, aestimantes propositum se tenere, cum sustulissent de Asson, legebant Cretam. 14 Non post multum autem misit se contra ipsam ventus typhonicus, qui vocatur Euroaquilo. 15 Cumque arrepta esset navis, et non posset conari in ventum, data nave flatibus, ferebamur … 20 Neque autem sole, neque sideribus apparentibus per plures dies, et tempestate non exigua imminente, jam ablata erat spes omnis salutis nostrae.[34]

– Acts 27:13–20

Soluerat Eoo classem de litore uector	
Austri nactus opem, cuius spiramine laeta	
Crebrescente uia uelique patentibus alis	
Aequora findebat puppis. Sed mite quid umquam	1070
Ventorum tenuere doli? Mox flatibus Euri	
Rupta quies pelagi, tumidisque incanduit undis	
Caerulei pax ficta maris; furit undique pontus	
Attollensque suas irato gurgite moles	
Denegat abreptae uestigia certa carinae,	1075
Quae suspensa polis deiectaque iungitur aruis	
Terrarum caelique sequax. Caret artis amicae	
Praesidiis manus apta rati, gelidoque pauore	
Deponunt animos nigroque sub aere caeci	
Naufragium iam iamque uident, clausoque profundo	1080
Mortis imago patet.	

[The captain launched the fleet from the eastern shore with the help of a southerly wind, whose breath drove the joyful ship to plough the deep, as the road opened up and the wings of the sail unfurled. But what mildness do the faithless winds ever have? Soon, with a gust from the east, the calmness of the sea

---

33 Since no *Vetus Latina* version of Acts is yet available, I have (following Green) used the Vulgate for quotations of the Bible. See Green, *Latin Epics*, 283, n. 168.

34 Acts 27:13–20: "And the south wind gently blowing, thinking that they had obtained their purpose, when they had loosed from Asson, they sailed close by Crete. 14 But not long after, there arose against it a tempestuous wind, called Euroaquilo. 15 And when the ship was caught, and could not bear up against the wind, giving up the ship to the winds, we were driven … 20 And when neither sun nor stars appeared for many days, and no small storm lay on us, all hope of our being saved was now taken away."

erupted, and the sculpted stillness of the cerulean water began to boil with swelling waves. The ocean raged all about them and, heaving up its mass from the seething abyss, denied sure path to the battered ship, which, raised up to the heavens and thrown down, was joined to sky and land like an attendant of heaven and earth. The crew assigned to the ship had not the protection of loving knowledge, and in cold fear abandoned their souls. Blind beneath the blackened cloud, they saw the shipwreck at that moment, and the image of death was revealed, as the deep closed all around them.]

This dramatic scene is equivalent in magnitude to the storm on the Sea of Galilee in *Euangeliorum libri* (2.25–32), and, like it, the biblical heritage of the poetry is audible throughout, despite departures from Acts. Thus Arator's *austri … spiramine* (1068) echoes *aspirante autem austro* in the prose, while the simple word for "wind" appears in both scenes (*uentus/uentorum*, 1071). The poetic turn of phrase, *flatibus Euri* (1071), economically adapts the source, *Euroaquilo … flatibus*, thanks in large part to Vergil and the *Georgics* (2.339): "… et hibernis parcebant flatibus Euri" ("… and the east winds spared their wintry gusts"). Just as the ship is "caught" by the storm in the prose (*arrepta esset nauis*), so it is here (*abreptae … carinae*, 1075), and Arator's terse phrase *Deponunt animos* (1079) condenses the longer biblical verse, "… ablata erat spes omnis salutis nostrae" ("all hope of our being saved was now taken away"), even without a precise overlap in diction.[35] It may also be that Arator's choice of *animus* (1079) is guided by Paul's assurances to the crew in verse 22 of Acts: "Et nunc suadeo uobis bono animo esse: amissio enim nullius animae erit ex uobis, praeterquam nauis" ("And now I exhort you to be of good cheer. For there shall be no loss of any man's life among you, but only of the ship"). Even without it, there is sufficient biblical subtext to show that Arator is attentive to the biblical prose, even if the epic tenor makes the stronger impression.

Orbán, Green, and others have discussed the classical origins of this scene in detail, and so a summary will suffice with a few additions of my own.[36] As Green says, "the description of the storm is a rich intertextual mosaic, with Vergil and Lucan again prominent."[37] Arator deploys every

---

35 Orbán, *Historia apostolica*, suggests a link to Vergil (*Deponunt, animos*, 5.751), but syntax eliminates the likelihood of an echo, since *deponunt* belongs to the previous verse (5.750–1): "Transcribunt urbi matres populumque uolentem / Deponunt, animos nil magnae laudis egentis."

36 See further Orbán, *Historia apostolica*, 287–8; Green, *Latin Epics*, 333–7.

37 Ibid., 335.

word for "sea" or "water" he can muster, and it is a testament to his skill that he does not repeat himself once: *aequor* (1070); *pelagus* (1072); *unda* (1072); *mare* (1073); *pontus* (1073); *gurges* (1074); and *profundus* (1080). This same strategy applies to ships: *classis* (1067); *puppis* (1070); *carina* (1075); and *ratis* (1078). This display of rhetorical variation is a virtue of classical decorum that can be found in all of the biblical epics, and it shows that Arator is conscious of that style in general terms alongside more specific echoes of secular verse. These include the words *Soluerat Eoo ... uector* (1069), which recall Vergil (*uictor soluebat Eoo*, *Aen.* 11.4) and the moment when Aeneas mourns Pallas.[38] Arator's turn of phrase, *rupta quies pelagi* (1072), appeals to language in Lucan's storm in the *Pharsalia* (*saeua quies pelagi*, 5.442), and other echoes confirm the classical origins of these words.[39] The triad, *furit undique pontus* (1073) bears close resemblance to another moment in Lucan's storm (*ferit undique pontus*, *Phar.* 5.570), though similarities can be found elsewhere, including Vergil's storm in the *Aeneid* ("caelum undique et undique pontus," *Aen.* 3.193). The pair, *incanduit undis* (1072), probably originates in Catullus ("Tortaque remigio spumis incanduit unda," 64. 13), which appears nowhere else, and other linguistic affinities with Catullus suggest that the nautical imagery in *Carmen* 64 may be a general source of inspiration for Arator here. The rising and falling of the ship on the waves (1076) probably comes from Vergil, as Green notes (1.106–7),[40] who also suggests that *manus apta* (1078) may echo Statius (*manus apta*, *Theb.* 3.306), allowing that the context is different. Green also highlights the word *abreptae* (1075), which coincides with *abreptas* in Vergil's storm in Book 1 (1.108), but it may also be an adaptation of *arrepta* in the Bible ("Cumque arrepta esset navis," 27:15). All in all, Arator draws much of his language and imagery from earlier classical sources, and he uses these, much as does Juvencus, to boost the literary register of his poetic rendition.

It should also be noted that Arator draws upon his knowledge of Christian poets for this scene. Consider, for example, how his storm compares to that in Juvencus' *Euangeliorum libri*. Both ships set out in similar terms: *Conscendunt navem* (*Ev.*1.25)/*Soluerat classem* (*Hist. apost.* 2.1067). Juvencus then fills the sails of his ship with wind, which "flies with a

---

38 Cf. also Valerius Flaccus, whose words appear in the same point in the line ("Numen et eoo surgentes litore currus," *Arg.* 5.245).

39 In citing this echo, Green notes Lucan, 1.239, *rupta quies populi*. Orbán also cites Statius (*rupta quies*, *Theb.* 2.125) and Valerius Flaccus (*rupta quies*, *Arg.* 3.46).

40 Green, *Latin Epics*, 336.

groaning surge" ("uentoque inflata tumescent/Vela suo, fluctuque uolat stridente carina"), and likewise Arator unfurls his own sails, and though his ship does not "fly," it does have wings ("uelique patentibus alis," 1069). In the following lines of both poems, Arator and Juvencus refer to their ships with the same word, *puppis* ("Postquam altum tenuit puppis," *Ev.* 1.27; "Aequora findebat puppis," *Hist. Apost.* 1070), and the subsequent uprising of the sea is described in similar terms. Juvencus says it (*pontus*, 1.28) "raised up furious mountains to the sky" and "now it thrashes the stern with its mass, now upon the prow with whirlwind" ("ad caelum rabidos sustollere montes;/Et nunc mole ferit puppim nunc turbine proram," 1.29–30). Compare that with Arator, who says that the sea (*pontus*, 1073) "rages around them" and "raises up its mass from the seething abyss" ("furit undique pontus/Attollensque suas irato gurgite moles"). Both he and Juvencus personify the sea, probably with Aeolus or Neptune in mind, and both use similar verbs (*sustollere/ attollens*) to raise up a mass of water (*nunc mole/moles*). Simply put, there is every reason to consider that Arator's epic sources of inspiration include biblical epics as well as classical ones.

Biblical Context

Like its biblical counterpart, *Historia apostolica* falls into two main sections. The first deals with Peter and the events of Acts 1–12, and the second involves Paul and Acts 13–28.[41] Schrader suggests that the poem would have "demanded of its hearers a good knowledge of Acts and of the Bible generally," and analysis of any number of scenes confirms this observation, but neither Acts nor the Bible is a precise model for *Historia apostolica* in the way it is for Juvencus or Cyprianus. This is no *paene ad uerbum* rendition of Acts, but it must be said that Arator is closer to his biblical source than Avitus is in *Historia spiritalis*, although he is not as faithful to the letter as Sedulius is in the *Carmen paschale*. Omission or economy figures prominently among the tools Arator uses to versify the Bible, much as it does for his predecessors.[42] Roberts has shown that much is omitted in favour of highlighting the acts of Peter and Paul, "and details are often reduced to a bare minimum, sufficient only to supply a narrative outline for the poet's interpretive reflections."[43] For Arator, Acts is more of a source for "searching out spiritual meaning," and his narrative alternates between literal

---

41 For the importance of Peter especially, since further Hillier, "Arator and Baptism," 113.
42 See further Green, *Latin Epics*, 278–82; Roberts, *Biblical Epic*, 113–15.
43 Roberts, *Biblical Epic*, 114–15.

episodes and allegorical interpretations of them.[44] In this respect, and "unlike Sedulius, who does not separate narration from interpretation … the regular alternation between literal narrative and mystical interpretation becomes a principle of composition" in *Historia apostolica*.[45] Acts is a starting place for biblical commentary, as Orbán puts it ("als Ausgangsbasis für kommentierende Ausführungen"),[46] and given Arator's constant interventions in the narrative – not a virtue of epic decorum – the poet ceases to be just a narrator and becomes a *praedicator* ("preacher") as well.[47] His work is therefore "a cross between traditional epic, the persuasive techniques formulated for forensic oratory, and the exegetical methods of the Christian sermon."[48] That said, Green has argued persuasively that Arator's handling of many episodes (he mentions 1.754–64, 2.156–73, 1.672–84, 1.687–90, and 2.1156–60, specifically) shows that "the original [biblical account] is not ignored, or quickly passed over," and that there is in these episodes "an underlying fidelity to the original."[49] This reassessment sounds a lot like the productive analyses of *Euangeliorum libri* over the last twenty years, which have sought and succeeded to qualify generalizations about that poet's *paene ad uerbum* approach to the Bible. The same level of scrutiny pays dividends in *Historia apostolica*.

Biblical Context: Storm at Sea, Part II (2.1131–51)

There can be no doubt as to the exegetical tenor of *Historia apostolica*, which promotes baptismal meaning above all. Richard Hillier has suggested that the delivery of the poem in the Easter season of 544 CE may have had something to do with the author's focus on Baptism, adding that many of the biblical readings for the season would have allowed audiences to follow the often allusive nature of Arator's verse. Consider, for example, the interpretation that follows the poet's lively account of the storm on the sea which has just preceded (2.1131–51):[50]

---

44 Schrader, *Acts of the Apostles*, 4. For a fuller discussion of Exegesis in the poem, see further Green, *Latin Epics*, 298–321; and Hillier, *Arator on the Acts of the Apostles*.
45 Roberts, *Biblical Epic*, 172.
46 Orbán, *Historia apostolica*, 7.
47 Roberts, *Biblical Epic*, 176.
48 Schrader, *Acts of the Apostles*, 179.
49 See further Green, *Latin Epics*, 286–9.
50 See further Hillier, "Arator and Baptism," 114.

... Memoranda figurae
Sacramenta piae ualeant, qua lege probemus:
Tempore quo primi fulserunt lumina mensis,
Hoc numero currente die de carnibus agni
Turba iubetur ali, quarum munimine tacto   1135
Libera Niliacas meruit uitare tenebras.
Hinc spatio simili Paulus de gurgite mundi,
Quos auferre cupit, secum conuiuere suadet
Et sacrum libare cibum, uestigia Moysi
Obseruata legens. Quorum speculantibus actum   1140
Haec duo sunt diuersa locis sed proxima causis,
Et repetita salus uno de fonte leuatur:
Agnus Christus inest, panis quoque Christus habetur
De caelo, quod et ipse docet; qui corpore Iesum
Sumpserit hoste caret nec iam sua iura Pharao   1145
Aegyptusque tenet. Mox omnia daemonis arma
His merguntur aquis, quibus ille renascitur infans,
Qui captiuus erat. Salsae quoque fluctus abyssi
Linquitur, et tetri superantur stagna draconis
Ereptoque gregi largitur pascua Christus,   1150
Nominibus propriis, pastor iam uerus edenti.

[Let us examine by what law the memorable secrets of holy symbolism
may prevail. When the light of the first month shone forth, and on the day
proceeding from this number [i.e., fourteen], the people were ordered to be
fed on the flesh of the lamb, and after they had tasted of that protection,
they deserved to escape the shadows of the Nile, as free men. So Paul in
the same measure persuades those whom he wants to take out of the abyss
of the world to eat with him and taste of the sacred food, following in the
esteemed steps of Moses. Those who consider the deeds of these two men
will see that they are different in space of time but alike in cause, and that
their duplicate salvation is drawn from one source: Christ, the lamb; Christ
is also the bread of heaven, a fact he himself explains. He who partakes of
Christ in body will have no enemy, just as Pharaoh and Egypt do not now
have power. Soon, all of the demon's weapons will be sunk in these waters
where the once captive child is reborn. The stream of the salty abyss is also
left behind, and the swamps of the foul serpent are overcome, and Christ
gives pastures to his delivered flock, in their own names; he is a true shepherd to those who eat.]

This exegetical commentary on the events of the storm (2.1067–1131) adds a wealth of wordplay and allusion to the literal narrative. The opening lines combine exegesis and the language of jurisprudence. Like a lawyer, Arator sets out "to prove" (*probemus*) by which "law" (*qua lege*) the "cause" (*sacramenta*) of holy symbolism may "prevail" (*ualeant*).[51] He wants to show how the "law" of the Old and New Testaments can reveal the holy sacraments and in particular Baptism. This meaning is apparent, he says, in the various figures (*figurae*), by which he means Paul (1137), Moses (1139), and Christ (1143), but also figuratively the symbolic connections that link Exodus, Acts, and Christ. Translation of these lines strains to fit it all in, and the degree of wordplay almost overburdens the literal sense of Acts with the semantic weight of symbolism. That being said, it could be argued that such weight is the effective substance of *Historia apostolica* and the strength of the poem, if the purpose and inclination is to linger on such meaning.

In this case, Arator links Paul with Moses, since both men lead hosts through the waters of the sea towards salvation, and both provide their people with nourishment. Such food makes them worthy of salvation, and one cannot help but think of the significant figures in Book One of the *Carmen paschale*, including Enoch (*meritis uiuacibus Enoch*, 1.103), Elijah ("meritoque et nomine fulgens," 1.185), and Elisha ("meritisque suis succedere dignum," 1.177), all of whom earn God's help by virtue of similar merits. The very point that Christ is the source of the connection between the delivery of both Moses and Paul ("salus uno de fonte leuatur," 1142) originates in Book 1 of the *Carmen paschale*, where Sedulius names Christ as the source of the heaven-falling manna, the water-pouring rock, and the crossing of the Red Sea: "Christus erat panis, Christus petra, Christus in undis" ("Christ was the bread, Christ was the rock, Christ was in the water," 1.159). Arator does the same thing (2.1143–4): "Agnus Christus inest, panis quoque Christus habetur / De caelo" ("Christ is the lamb, Christ is also the bread from heaven"). Consumption of the body of Christ therefore offers deliverance from the abyss of worldly pleasures (*de gurgite mundi*, 1137), and Baptism in the waters of the Church drowns the weapons of the demon ("mox omnia daemonis arma / His merguntur aquis," 1146–7), just as God once sunk the weapons of Egypt in the baptismal waters of the Red Sea ("nec iam sua iura Pharao / Aegyptusque tenet," 1145–6). This last point, that neither Pharaoh nor Egypt has any remaining

---

51 Cf. Cic. *Fam.* 13.16.3: "apud te ueritas ualebit."

power, echoes the prediction of Avitus in *De transitu maris rubri* (5.524–5): "Quidquid uirtutis habere / Aegyptus potuit, totum mors proxima ducit" ("Whatever power Egypt had, imminent death drew unto itself"). In this scene, one begins to see the potential weight of meaning that inhabits the text of *Historia apostolica* and which challenges the reader to explore it. If Arator is a preacher (*praedicator*), his readers must be more than attentive congregants; they must themselves become interpreters of the Bible.

So the audience of *Historia apostolica* would indeed have needed more than mere knowledge of Acts to interpret this text, and following the thread of spiritual meaning is complicated further by poetic elocution and rhetorical variation. So, for example, the biblical prose resorts to the verb *sumere* ("to eat") throughout Acts 27:33–8, but the poetry requires more varied diction – *alo* (1135), *conuiuo* (1138), *libo* (1139), *sumo* (1145), *edo* (1151). Each of these words introduces shades of meaning to the passage and complicates our understanding of it. Double-entendre and concise allusions to other books of the Bible also make interpreting the episode an active process, the full depth of which is only revealed through several readings. It is moreover hard to imagine that Arator's audience, standing in front of the Church of St Peter in 544 CE, caught all of these allusions on the fly, however much they may have enjoyed the performance of the poem.

Opening of the Poem

Historia apostolica begins not with the first chapter of Acts, which is taken up in subsequent lines (1.21–68), but with an *in medias res* allusion to the Gospels and Christ's resurrection as articulated by Sedulius. A possible link to Avitus also connects the opening of the poem to spiritual history and the redemption of man, but Arator's primary concern is with the divinity of Christ, God's omnipotence over creation, and Christ's victory over darkness and death. His triumph opens a way in the world for the Acts of the Apostles. As Arator says of the souls of the saved, "Omnipotens parat ipse uias ("The Almighty himself prepares the way," 1.20), and this work includes the deeds of his disciples, whose charge it is to spread the word of God throughout the earth (1–20):[52]

---

52 See Green, *Latin Epics*, 268; see also Schrader, *Acts of the Apostles*, 56: "This highly abstract opening refers to the consequences of the crucifixion. Christ descended into hell to free the just; there was darkness, the earth quaked, and the dead awoke (Mt. 27:45, 51–4). Christ returned, having made it possible for Adam's children to enter paradise; there, it is promised the saved will reign with Him (Tim. 2:12)."

Vt sceleris Iudaea sui polluta cruore,
Ausa nefas, compleuit opus rerumque Creator
Hoc, quod ab humanis sumpsit sine semine membris,
Humana pro stirpe dedit, dignatus ut ima
Tangeret inferni, non linquens ardua caeli,   5
Soluit ab aeterna damnatas nocte tenebras
Ad Manes ingressa dies; fugitiua relinquunt
Astra polum comitata Deum; cruce territa Christi
Vult pariter natura pati, mortisque potestas
Se uincente perit, quae, pondere mersa triumphi,   10
Plus rapiens nil iuris habet; diuinaque uirtus
Rursus membra ligans animata cadauera mouit;
Ad uitam monumenta patent cineresque piorum
Natalem post busta nouant. Lux tertia surgit;
Maiestas cum carne redit speciemque coruscam   15
Vmbrarum de sede refert, ut ab exsule limo
Interclusa diu patriae repetatur origo.
Omnipotens parat ipse uias et corpora secum
Post tumulos regnare iubet; moriente ueneni
Semine, florigero sua germina reddidit horto.   20

[When Judea, polluted by the blood of its atrocity, had dared to do unspeakable wrong and carried out its work, and when the Creator of the universe gave on behalf of the human race what he took without seed from human limbs, deigning to touch the depths of hell without abandoning the heights of heaven, then daylight, having shone upon the dead, freed damned shadows from eternal night. Fugitive stars left heaven in the company of God. Nature, terrified by the cross of Christ, wanted to suffer too, and the power of death died in its victory. Being overwhelmed by the weight of that triumph and too greedy, death had no authority, and divine strength, reconnecting limbs, roused animated corpses. Tombs stood open to life and the ashes of pious men found new birth after the grave. The third light arose. Majesty returned with flesh and brought back from the seat of shadows a face of shining light, so that the origin of the fatherland, long sealed off, might be sought once more by exiled man (Adam). The Almighty himself prepared the way and commanded bodies to rule with him after death; and when the poisonous seed died, he returned his own seeds to the flower-bearing garden.]

Avitus begins his poem on *Spiritual History* in similar terms, when he says that the whole human race is "polluted" by its origins (*polluti* ...

origine, 1.3) and guilty of sin by way of Satan's influence ("nostra de parte reatus," 1.5). Arator puts Judea in the same context. Adam is the source of contamination, as the "originator of vice" (*auctoris uitio*, 1.11), but there, as here, Christ brings redemption through death. The original "seed of death" (*semine mortis*, 1.7) is born of Adam, whose disobedience leaves the "stalk" of human kind corrupted and "stricken" by sin (*percussa*).[53] Christ pays for all of that on the cross, as Avitus says (1.9–10): "hoc totum Christus persoluerit in se, / Contraxit quantum percussa in stirpe propago" ("Christ has paid for all of this in his person – all that our line committed in its stricken stock"). As a corollary, Arator highlights the point that Christ is born of man but "without seed" ("ab humanis sumpsit sine semine membris," 3), and so not of the "stricken stalk" polluted by the blood of Adam and the "seed of death" (*semine mortis*). Christ is, as Juvencus would say, "Diuinum in populis falsi sine crimine donum" ("A divine gift among the people without the crime of falsehood," *Ev. Praef.* 20), and so his holy and untainted blood can cleanse the polluted line or stalk of man. Christ does all of this, Arator says, *humana pro stirpe* ("for the sake of the human race" or "stalk," 1.4), and at the end of this section, he adds, "with the death of the poisonous seed, Christ returns his buds to the flowery garden," by which he means heaven but also a state of existence worthy of reentering that first paradise ("moriente ueneni / Semine, florigero sua germina reddidit horto," 19–20).[54] It is noteworthy that the only use of the adjective *floriger* in the *Carmen paschale* refers to the garden of Eden and man's expulsion from it, which may suggest that Christ in *Historia apostolica* intends to lead humanity back to that prelapsarian state (2.1): "Expulerat primogenitum saeuissimus anguis / Florigera de sede" ("A most savage serpent drove first-born man from his flowery seat"). Sources or not, Avitus and Sedulius offer valid context to articulate the allusive and floral imagery of Arator's opening, which presents salvation in terms of original sin and the first seed of disobedience, which was sown by Adam. Furthermore, Arator's choice of language in these lines

---

53 Cf. Sedulius, 2.9–10: "Crescere posquam / Coepit origo, perit clademque a semine sumpsit" ("after their origin grew to maturity, it withered and plucked death from its seed").

54 Note that Sedulius sees Mary in these terms, who atones for the sins of Eve (1.30–1): "Sic Euae de stirpe sacra ueniente Maria / Virginis antiquae facinus noua uirgo piaret" ("So with blessed Mary coming from the stock of Eve, / a new virgin atones for the sin of the old virgin").

suggests that he believes that the Jews are retracing Adam's steps, by crucifying Christ and polluting their own bloodline.[55]

That being said, the Crucifixion is part of God's greater plan, which appears to be the sense of the words, "compleuit opus rerumque Creator" ("the creator of the universe completed his work," 2), which return the reader to any number of points in the Bible, including the beginning of time, Creation. It may also be that Arator is thinking of the Incarnation in the *Carmen paschale*, where analogous language appears (*Carm. Pasch.* 1.37–9): "uterumque puellae/Sidereum mox implet onus, rerumque creator/Nascendi sub lege fuit" ("A celestial weight soon filled the young girl's womb, and the Creator of the Universe came into being by mortal law"). The words, "implet onus, rerumque creator" sound a lot like Arator's phrase, "compleuit opus rerumque Creator" (2), which Arator may adopt to connect the two moments as part of God's plan, that is, birth and death. Again, the richness of intertextuality is one of the strengths of biblical epic, which allows readers to roam freely from work to work by way of echoed diction. In other words, the identification of direct sources may not be as significant as the function of memory in reading this literature.

Other turns of phrase suggest that Arator has Sedulius in mind throughout this scene, including the language of the harrowing (4–5): "dignatus ut ima/Tangeret inferni, non linquens ardua caeli." Although not precisely the same, compare Sedulius' words in the same context (2.214): "… Inferiora petens et non excelsa relinquens" ("… Seeking the lower depths but not relinquishing the heights"). Certainly, Arator's reference to the oxymoronic defeat of death, which kills itself (*Se uincente perit*, 10), is akin to that of Sedulius, even if the language originates with Lucan (*te uincente perit*, *Phar.* 5.267). The conquest of death is a key theme at the opening and the end of the *Carmen paschale*. In Book 5, Sedulius denounces the power of death, which, given Christ's return from the grave, has failed to achieve victory (5.276–7): "Dic ubi nunc tristis uictoria, dic ubi nunc sit/Mors stimulus horrenda tuus" ("Tell me, where is your sad victory now? Speak up, horrid death, where is your sting now?"). This apostrophe, originating in I Corinthians 15:55, provides a structural and thematic link to Book 1 of the *Carmen paschale*, where Sedulius recapitulates a series of Old Testament miracles (1.220–1) and concludes in similar terms: "Dic, ubi sunt, natura, tuae post talia leges?/Qui quotiens tibi iura tulit?" ("Tell me, Nature, where are your laws after this? Who has overthrown your laws so many times?"). As a close parallel to the passage in Book

---

55 Arator returns to his invective against Judea later in Book 1 (1.188): "Sed fugite, o miseri, funesta piacula gentis" ("But flee, you wretches, the deadly sins of your race"). Trans. adapted from Schrader.

5, the rhetorical question in Book One foreshadows Christ's victory over nature and death, and brings unity of thought and purpose to the whole *Carmen paschale*. This fact appears not to have escaped Arator's eye, who, by echoing Sedulius, finds powerful language and a context to emphasize Christ's ability to renew mankind through His death and resurrection.

Peter Heals a Lame Man, Part I (1.244–61)[56]

While the opening lines of *Historia apostolica* do not provide the opportunity to consider how the poet goes about versifying the Bible, they do offer an important context for the events to follow, by inviting the reader to pursue the spiritual links between the Old and New Testaments. A better test of Arator's relationship to the New Testament narrative is afforded by an analysis of other scenes in the poem, which facilitate comparisons with the earlier biblical versifications. Consider, for instance, how Arator handles the healing of a lame man in Book 1 (1.244–61):

1 Petrus autem et Iohannes ascendebant in templum ad horam orationis nonam 2 et quidam uir qui erat claudus ex utero matris suae baiulabatur quem ponebant cotidie ad portam templi quae dicitur Speciosa ut peteret elemosynam ab introeuntibus in templum 3 is cum uidisset Petrum et Iohannem incipientes introire in templum rogabat ut elemosynam acciperet 4 intuens autem in eum Petrus cum Iohanne dixit respice in nos 5 at ille intendebat in eos sperans se aliquid accepturum ab eis 6 Petrus autem dixit argentum et aurum non est mihi quod autem habeo hoc tibi do in nomine Iesu Christi Nazareni surge et ambula 7 et adprehensa ei manu dextera adlevauit eum et protinus consolidatae sunt bases eius et plantae 8 et exiliens stetit et ambulabat et intrauit cum illis in templum ambulans et exiliens et laudans Dominum.[57]

– Acts 3:1–8

---

56   A similar episode is recounted in Book 2 of the poem, 2.156–241.

57   Acts 3.1–10: "1 Now Peter and John went up into the temple at the ninth hour of prayer. 2 And a certain man who was lame from his mother's womb, was carried: whom they laid every day at the gate of the temple, which is called Beautiful, that he might ask alms of them that went into the temple. 3 He, when he had seen Peter and John about to go into the temple, asked to receive an alms. 4 But Peter with John fastening his eyes upon him, said: Look upon us. 5 But he looked earnestly upon them, hoping that he should receive something of them. 6 But Peter said: Silver and gold I have none; but what I have, I give thee: In the name of Jesus Christ of Nazareth, arise, and walk. 7 And taking him by the right hand, he lifted him up, and forthwith his feet and soles received strength. 8 And he leaping up, stood, and walked, and went in with them into the temple, walking, and leaping, and praising God."

Claudus erat, cui prima dies exordia uitae
Membrorum cum strage dedit, languore coaeuo   245
Octo lustra gerens, ad quem comitante Iohanne
"Respice" Petrus ait; uotum spes lusit auarum
Cumque negat, meliora parat. Quam saepe grauatos
Desperata iuuant, et semine nata sinistro
Prosperitas, celans maestis confinia laeta   250
Principiis, ad uota uenit! Gaudebit egenus
Plus uacua meruisse manu, qui munera poscens
Est datus ipse sibi. "Nulla hic mihi uena metalli"
Respondit "quae fundat opes; ego ditior aegro
Pauper ero; progressus abi!" De uoce iubentis   255
Exiluit medicina potens, atque hospite gressu
Conuixere pedes. Cunabula longa relinquens
Calcauit ueteranus humum plantisque nouellis
Materies se prisca mouet: cui praepete cursu
Protulit incessus, quicquid non edidit ortus.   260
Stat facti manifesta fides.

[There was a lame man, whose first day gave him the beginnings of life with
decrepit limbs, suffering forty years with a languor of the same age; accompanied by John, Peter said to him, "Look at us." Hope misled that man's
greedy prayer, but when hope denies, it has better things in store. How often
hopeless moments help the oppressed, and good fortune born of inauspicious
seed – concealing its joyful nearness by woeful beginnings – comes in answer
to prayer! The needy man will rejoice in earning more from an empty hand
if, in begging for wealth, he is given to himself. "I have no vein of metal here,"
said Peter, "to dole out money. Still, though poor, I will be of greater benefit
to the infirm. Go. Walk." Powerful healing sprang from the voice of the one
commanding him, and the lame man's feet rejoiced in renewed step. Leaving
his litter at last, the grown man tread upon the earth and his old frame went
forward on fledgling soles: his steps in nimble stride showed what birth had
refused. Faith in this matter stood manifest.]

Despite apparent consensus that Arator departs from the biblical narrative in eager pursuit of exegetical commentary, this part of the episode at
least, the part concerning the narrative of Acts 3:1–8, is faithful to the original. Not only does Arator retain much of the prose language, but he reproduces elements of the direct speech there, including Peter's imperatives,
respice ("look at us!" 247), which he takes verbatim from the Bible ("dixit

respice in nos"), and *abi* ("go!" 255), which follows *surge et ambula* in Acts 3:6. Arator is therefore invested not only in the diction of the Bible but the style of it as well, which he endeavours to reproduce in some measure.

So the initial words of the passage, *Claudus erat, cui* (244), imitate the prose (*qui erat claudus*, 3:1), and both "Petrus" (245) and "Iohannus" (246) are strong markers of the original (*Petrum et Iohannem*). Other words likewise give away the biblical source, including *plantis* in line 258 for *plantae* (3:7), and the words *Nulla hic mihi* (253) for *non est mihi* (3:6). More subtle signs include the phrase, "prima dies exordia uitae," which aims to recapture the expression *ex utero matris* ("from his mother's womb," 3:1), while the poet's choice of *spes* ("hope," 247) echoes *sperans* in Acts 3:5, not to mention the following participle, *desperata* (249), a participle of the same root. That being said, even with the helping context of *spes*, only someone very familiar with Acts would appreciate how Arator's elliptical phrase, "uotum spes lusit auarum" ("hope deceived the greedy prayer," 247), refers to verse five of the Bible: "at ille intendebat in eos sperans se aliquid accepturum ab eis" ("But he looked earnestly upon them, hoping that he should receive something of them"). Arator takes for granted fairly precise knowledge of the original narrative, or else he is assuming that his rendition is clear enough to stand on its own and make sense. The former seems more likely, since he is echoing the Bible and therefore alluding to it.

The only notable departure in these opening lines comes in the middle of the passage (1.248–53), where Arator pauses to comment on the nature of wishes or prayers, which may be answered in times of hardship. Arator aims to make a distinction between the lame man's plea for physical wealth (*uotum ... auarum*, 247) and the spiritual "prosperity" (*prosperitas*, 250) that comes of a longing for Christ (*ad uota uenit*, 251). The word is the same, *uotum*, but the nature of simply wanting something is different from the nature of prayer. Hence the rather convoluted moral (1.251–3): "Gaudebit egenus / Plus uacua meruisse manu, qui munera poscens / Est datus ipse sibi" ("The needy man will rejoice in having earned more from an empty hand if, in begging for wealth, he is given to himself"). Put differently, the lame man receives a better gift than wealth, because the gift of his restored limbs leads to faith, which in turn leads firm steps to the paschal gift of salvation, as Sedulius would say. It is a point Arator makes explicit in his later commentary on the episode, where he says, "Pete dona salutis! / Non fragiles secteris opes, quas spernere debet, / Cum Domino qui diues erit" ("Seek the gifts of salvation! Pursue not fleeting wealth, which one should spurn who wants to be rich in the Lord," 1.286–92).

Paul Raises a Dead Man (2.753–81)

In chapter 20 of Acts there is a briefly mentioned incident in which a
young man falls from a third-story window, and Paul revives him. This
youth, Eutychus, has the misfortune of falling asleep during one of Paul's
late-night lessons on the top floor of a house, where lanterns afforded better light and space than the room below. Unlike the healing of the lame
man in Book 1, the separation of biblical narrative and biblical commentary is not so discrete here. Long before Arator declares his intention to
pursue the mystical significance of the episode ("Quae gloria facti / Instruit
ad ueterem causas aperire figuram" ["The glory of this event instructs one
how to reveal the causes according to ancient symbolism"], 2.801–3), he
has already engaged in interpretation, beginning with the early geographi-
cal reference to Troas in the biblical narrative, which he feels begs interpretive commentary (2.757–71):

6 nos uero nauigauimus post dies azymorum a Philippis, et uenimus ad eos
Troadem in diebus quinque, ubi demorati sumus diebus septem. 7 Una autem
sabbati cum conuenissemus ad frangendum panem, Paulus disputabat cum
eis profecturus in crastinum, protraxitque sermonem usque in mediam
noctem. 8 Erant autem lampades copiosae in coenaculo, ubi eramus congre-
gati. 9 Sedens autem quidam adolescens nomine Eutychus super fenestram,
cum mergeretur somno graui, disputante diu Paulo, ductus somno cecidit de
tertio coenaculo deorsum, et sublatus est mortuus. 10 Ad quem cum de-
scendisset Paulus, incubuit super eum: et complexus dixit: Nolite turbari,
anima enim ipsius in ipso est.

– Acts 20:6–10

Tu quoque signa ferens titulos in carmine nostro,
Troia, repone tuos et laudibus adde triumphos,
Qui magis ex uero fulgent tibi clarius actu 755
Quam quae pomposo reboant tua bella cothurno!
Lingua colona Dei cum semina feta saluti
Spargeret, in seram produxit tempora noctem
Plus animis factura diem; micuere coruscae
Lampades, ut uerbi lucerent igne fideles. 760
Solus ab excubiis uiuacibus Eutychus exul
Mersa sopore graui commisit membra fenestrae.
O male parta quies! O semper dedita somno
Pectora, nuda bono! Quantis patet ille ruinis,

Quem nox sola tenet numquamque resuscitat aegrum   765
Ad meliora caput! Nescit uigilare periclo,
Qui patitur dormire Deo. Quid inane fenestrae
Quaeris, adulte, chaos quidue hac in parte quiescis,
Qua ruiturus eris? Res est inimica saluti
Pendula celsa sequi furtiuaque somnia prono   770
Carpere uelle toro.

[You too, Troy, who bear standards in our song, put aside your banners and add to your praises triumphs that shine more brightly from true action than those wars of yours, which bellow in a pompous, tragic style. While the tongue of God's servant was spreading the fruitful seeds of salvation, he lengthened into the late-night hours that would make more day for the souls. Glimmering lanterns shone so that the faithful might shine with the fire of the Word. Eutychus alone, banished from the ones keeping vigilant watch, settled on the window and fell into a deep sleep. O badly gotten rest! O hearts ever given to slumber, despoiled of good! How open to ruin is he whom only night holds and who never rouses his weary head to better things! He does not know how to be wakeful for danger who allows himself to rest from God. Why, man, do you pursue the empty chaos of the window and sleep in a place where you will fall to your ruin? It is a threat to one's salvation to seek out high, overhanging places and to want to seek furtive sleep on a precipitous bed.]

Arator must have assumed that some members of his audience would have heard the audible connection between Troas and ancient Troy, and so he addresses the word at the beginning of this scene, using it to make some generic exhortations about "good" and "bad" literature. Thoughts of Troy lead Arator inevitably to thoughts of fame and glory, war and banners, and these provide him with some predictable language (*signum, titulus, laus, triumphus, pomposus, bellum*). Arator is self-consciously clever, when he says that Troy not only "bears signs" in his song ("signa ferens titulos in carmine nostro," 753), meaning "battle-standards" (*signa*), but also figuratively the indelible traces epic has left on *Historia apostolica*. The *signa* of Troy in the latter sense refer to the style and diction of classical poetry that provide as much of a subtext for interpreting the poem as the underlying *signa* or "symbols" of the events of Acts themselves. In fact, the words, "Tu quoque signa ferens titulos in carmine nostro, / Troia" could be viewed as a general standard for the way in which biblical poets combine the two traditions, classical and Christian, to create hybrid compositions.

Like Juvencus, who highlights the "sublime deeds of men" in his preface to *Euangeliorum libri* (*homines sublimia facta*, *Ev. Praef.* 5), "whose
fame and praise the poets heap up" ("Adcumulant quorum famam
laudesque poetae," *Ev. Praef.* 8), Arator feels that he must address the
proper place of "triumph" and "praise" (*laudibus adde triumphos*, 754) in
his own poem, since he has now invoked them with the context of Troy. In
generic terms, and like Juvencus and other biblical poets, Arator says that
the deeds of his poem, *actu* (755) – almost certainly a pun on "Acts" –
shine more brightly than those of epic, because they are true (*uero*, 755)
and not just pompous tales of fiction ("Quam quae pomposo reboant tua
bella cothurno," 756). Arator makes a similar statement in his letter to
Parthenius about "false art" and "arrogant pomp" ("In quibus ars fallax,
pompa superba fuit," 42), and Sedulius says much the same thing at the
beginning of his *Carmen paschale* ("Cum sua gentiles studeant figmenta
poetae / Grandisonis pompare modis, tragicoque boatu" ["Since pagan poets are eager to parade their fictions in big-sounding rhythms and with
their tragic wailing ..."], 1.17–18). Arator's reference to the "pompous,
tragic style" (*pomposo reboant ... cothurno*, 756) is almost certainly an
echo of Sedulius' phrase "pompare ... tragicoque boatu." In short, Arator's
condemnation of classical epic is stereotypical.

The biblical heritage of the scene is contained in a few unmistakeable
words and phrases from the prose, and as long as Arator is concerned with
the narrative events, he remains close to the Bible. The initial digression on
"Troy" is prompted by the biblical context of "Troas," despite the digression. The next explicit point of contact does not come until line 758, with
the line "in seram produxit tempora noctem." This refers to verse seven of
the prose, allowing for minor changes ("protraxitque sermonem usque in
mediam noctem"). Otherwise, the words, *lampades* (760), *Eutychus* (761),
fenestra (762) and the phrase *Mersa sopore graui* (for *mergeretur somno
graui*, 20:9), evoke the language of the biblical Acts. Even so, much of this
diction from the first mention of Troas becomes a platform for Arator to
introduce his own metaphorical commentary. Thus the "lamps" (*lampades*, 760) are not simply lights for the sake of brightness, but symbols of
enlightenment for the faithful (*fideles*, 760), who are inspired by the fire of
the Holy Spirit (*uerbi ... igne*, 760). Sleep is not just "rest," but a spiritual
slumber that can shut and blind the eyes of the soul to the awareness of
God. Like the poetic descriptions of physical blindness in the poetry of
Juvencus or Sedulius, the absence of light in sleep is a potential metaphor
for spiritual imperception, just as light may signal illumination. On the
other hand, blindness can also be a sign of spiritual (in)sight, since faith

does not enter through the eyes, but the heart. Arator's digression on inner wakefulness and vigilance finds expression elsewhere in Christian poetry and notably in the miracle sequence of the *Carmen paschale* (4.35–9):

Nec cunctata solens pietas inferre salutem,   35
Quae sentit flagrare fidem, mox lumina tangens
Euigilare iubet, quae somnus presserat ingens,
Atque diu clausas reserans sub fronte fenestras
Ingrediente die fecit discedere noctem.

[Not used to withholding his help, his unwavering pity sensed ardent faith, and touching them, he bade their eyes be wakeful, eyes that great sleep had overcome; and opening the long-shut windows beneath their brows, he made night vanish with the coming of day.]

Unlike Sedulius, Arator is not nearly so single-minded in response to chapter 20 of Acts, no doubt because of his will to pursue the mystical sense of the scene. So Arator begins with his digression on Troy and the proper place of praise, and then moves on to a spiritual interpretation of sleep, all of which precedes a direct interpretation of the episode later that runs for another twenty-five verses (2.801–25). There, Arator equates the three levels of the house with the three stories of Noah's ark, saying that Eutychus falls down to the lowest one, which is inhabited by wild animals (i.e., hell, *Tartareum*, 815), until he is raised up to the top floor (through Paul's intervention), where he joins Noah and other "lofty things" (*alta*, 813). The three floors also represent salvation in the mystical significance of the number three, which refers to the Holy Trinity. Even without a closer analysis of those lines, it is clear that Arator is asking a lot of his audience in this passage, which is expected to follow the underlying narrative of Acts, its epic undertones, and the author's abrupt interjections of spiritual meaning, which may attach themselves at any moment to any given word or image.

Crossing of the Red Sea, Part I (2.40–52)

This final example is based on chapter 13 of Acts and verses 14–17, in which Paul enters the synagogue in Antioch to preach, among other things, about the exodus of the Israelites and the miracles of Moses in the wilderness. Verses 1–26 of Acts outline Paul's work in Seleucia, Cyprus, Salamina, and Paphos, including an incident in which Paul encounters a sorcerer named Elymas, whom he blinds for "perverting the right ways of the Lord" ("non desinis subuertere uias Domini rectas," 13:10), but none of this is of primary interest to Arator, who is more concerned with the crossing of the Red Sea as a path to baptismal commentary, while the miracles of Moses prefigure Christ's deeds in the New Testament. It is clear from Arator's choice of language and imagery in this scene that the miracle sequence of Book 1 of the *Carmen paschale* (1.103–219) once again plays a central role in Arator's spiritual interpretation of Acts (2.40–69):[58]

14 Illi uero pertranseuntes Pergen, uenerunt Antiochiam Pisidiae: et ingressi synagogam die sabbatorum, sederunt. 15 Post lectionem autem legis, et prophetarum, miserunt principes synagogae ad eos, dicentes: Viri fratres, si quis est in uobis sermo exhortationis ad plebem, dicite.16 Surgens autem Paulus, et manu silentium indicens, ait: Viri Israelitae, et qui timetis Deum, audite 17 Deus plebis Israhel elegit patres nostros et plebem exaltauit cum essent incolae in terra Aegypti et in brachio excelso eduxit eos ex ea. 18 et per quadraginta annorum tempus mores eorum sustinuit in deserto.

– Acts 13:14–18

Antiochi dictam de nomine uisitat urbem	40
Paulus et extemplo properat dare uerba cateruis	
Quas synagoga tenet dextraque silentia mandans,	
"Nostis" ait "patribus tellus Aegyptia nostris	
Qua posuit feritate iugum, crudelibus aruis	
Quos rapuit per signa Deus. Quibus omnia cedens	45
Mutauit natura uices, cum uirga fugauit	
Terga maris fluctusque suis stetit exul ab oris	
Puluereo de calle placens pontique facultas	
Obsequio est subiecta pedum, redeunte profundo	
Naufragium factura reis, quae uertere iussa	50
Per uarios sua iura modos his strauit arenas,	
His cumulauit aquas; iustis uia, sontibus unda.	

[Paul visits a city called Antioch by name and hastens to speak at once to the crowd in the synagogue, and commanding silence with his hand, he spoke: "You know with what savagery the land of Egypt placed a yoke on our fathers. God rescued them from those cruel fields by way of miracles, by which

---

58 I am indebted to Schrader's translation of this scene, which I have followed closely.

nature, allowing everything, changed her course, when the staff put the sea to flight and the flood stood as an exile from its own shores, welcoming [the Israelites] on its dusty path, and the power of the sea was made to indulge their feet; when the deep returned, its might shipwrecked the guilty, and being commanded to change its laws by various means, it stretched out sand for them [the Israelites], but for these [Egyptians] it heaped up waters: a road for the righteous, a wave for the guilty.]

The opening verses cover Acts 13:14–17, which provide Arator with a starting point. At first, he follows the language of the Bible intently (2.40–3): *Antiocham/Antiochi* (40); *synogogam/synagoga* (42); *manu silentium indicens/dextraque silentia mandans* (42);[59] *ait/ait* (43); *patres nostros/patribus … nostris* (43); and *terra Aegypti/tellus Aegyptia* (43). These connections are enough to authenticate the biblical verse and show that Arator is doing precisely what he says he will do in his letter to Vigilius (21–2): "Alternis reserabo modis quod littera pandit/Et res si qua mihi mystica corde datur" ("In turns, I shall set out what the letter reveals and whatever mystical sense is given to my heart"). The difference between Arator and his predecessors, however, is the measure of the two, that is, how much attention he gives to the letter versus how much he gives to the mystical sense. But to say that Arator does not follow the Bible closely is to over-simplify things, since he does pay close attention to the narrative of Acts, when he is following it. What is more, many of his departures from the text of the New Testament betray connections to earlier biblical epics, so that they are not so much spontaneous responses to his heart, as he would have us believe, but conscious recollections of earlier Christian poetry.

In this case, Arator diverges from Acts in describing the parting of the waters, but not without Avitus and Sedulius in mind. He says that "nature changes its course when the staff [of Moses] put flight to the sea" ("Mutauit natura uices cum uirga fugauit /Terga maris"), and Avitus uses the same words in *De transitu maris rubri* to describe the pillar of fire and cloud that leads the Israelites through the desert ("Mutauit natura uices," 5.445). The context may be different, but it is still Exodus and only moments before the crossing. Moreover, Avitus himself is probably echoing Sedulius and his description of the crossing of the Red Sea in Book 1 of the *Carmen paschale* (1.141–2): "Mutauit natura uiam, mediumque per aequor/Ingrediens populus rude iam baptisma gerebat" ("Nature changed its path, and going into

---

59 Cf. Lucan, *dextraque silentia iussit* (*Phar.* 1.298).

the midst of the sea, the people experienced a rudimentary Baptism"). That passage of Sedulius is essential for what Arator is trying to say: that the miracles of Moses prefigure those of Christ, who comes to cleanse the world.

Arator follows Sedulius again, when he mentions the water from the rock and the manna from heaven (2.53–65). These two miracles appear in the *Carmen paschale* (1.148–59) immediately after the episode of the Red Sea (1.136–47), and all three form a symbolic unit with reference to Baptism, a theme of central importance in *Historia apostolica*. With reference to Christ, Sedulius says that He was "already granting His sacred gifts on these three occasions; Christ was the bread, Christ the rock, Christ was in the water" ("His igitur iam sacra tribus dans munera rebus, / Christus erat panis, Christus petra, Christus in undis," 1.158–9). Arator likewise links these episodes in his own narrative and conceives of the "three gifts life" that foreshadow the coming of Christ (2.89–92):

> Consule signa maris, quae mystica dona susurrant
> Temporibus uentura crucis, cum sanguine Iesus   90
> Tinxit aquas laterisque uno de uulnere fluxit
> Quod uitae tria dona daret!

> [Look at the signs of the sea, which whisper the mystical gifts to come at the time of the Cross, when Jesus coloured the waters with his blood, and from the single wound at his side there flowed that which gave three gifts of life!]

On the one hand, Arator credits Paul as the one who "sings these precepts of Baptism, mixing the Old and New" ("Quam bene uox Pauli cecinit praecepta lauacri / Permiscens antiqua nouis!"), and this is what Arator himself aims to do, as he says in his letter to Parthenius (75–7): "Cumque simul uiolas et lilia carpere mallem, / Quae uetus atque nouus congeminauit odor, / Incidit ille mihi, quem regula nominat Actus" ("And since I would rather graze on violets and lilies at the same time, in which the scent of the Old and New Testaments combine, I fell upon the book which the canon calls Acts"). What Arator does not say is that he is actually following Sedulius, who is as much his source of inspiration in this scene as Paul is.

Conclusion

Objectively speaking, Arator's poem may be the richest of all the biblical epics, since it allows the audience to immerse itself in both the epic swell of the storm in Book 2, for example, but also the ensuing spiritual interpretation of the episode. If we fail to appreciate the literary achievement of

Historia apostolica in modern times, it is because we cannot connect with the contemporary tastes of late Antiquity, when audiences took great pleasure in the subtle and insistent interactions of these two textual traditions.

At the beginning of the genre of biblical epic in the early fourth century, Juvencus focuses on "Christ's *dicta* or *doctrina*, as well as his *facta*," but for the most part he is determined to let the *facta* speak for themselves.[60] A century later, Sedulius "occupies a middle ground between Juvencus and Arator," following the Bible closely but interjecting doses of spiritual commentary.[61] By the time of Sedulius, as Michael Roberts has said, biblical versifiers had become conduits, even preachers, for the *facta* of the Bible.[62] Avitus is the freest of them all in terms of his desire to elaborate on biblical episodes, and his *Historia spiritalis* only loosely recounts the literal events of the Scriptures. Moreover, his style is so overblown at times that his poetry is more inaccessible than that of earlier biblical poets for whom the Bible is a constant guide. Even so, the vitality and drama Avitus infuses into his characterizations of Satan and Eve, not to mention the speeches he introduces to elevate the literary drama of the Fall, add great depth and interest to the original biblical narrative. By comparison, Arator is not nearly so invested in that level of poetic embellishment, for whom the flowers of the Old and New Testaments are attractive not simply for their sweetness (that *dulcedo*) but for the richness of mystical meaning that lingers in the scent.

Generally speaking, there is a development in the genre of biblical epic throughout late Antiquity in terms of the author's response to the Bible and his personal involvement in the narrative. It is easy to suggest that writers over time move away from the *paene ad uerbum* style of Juvencus towards greater stylistic liberty and spiritual commentary, but such a generalization discounts any number of scenes in which later poets follow the Bible closely or those earlier instances where they depart from it appreciably.

The question now remains, how do later Christian poets and their audiences, specifically those of Anglo-Saxon England, inherit this literature and respond to it in their own writings? What is the nature of the Anglo-Latin debt to late antique biblical epic, and is there a connection between the Latin genre and its re-genesis in Old English biblical verse? What can we learn by comparing these two literary traditions?

---

60 Green, *Latin Epics*, 84.
61 Springer, *Gospel as Epic*, 86.
62 Roberts, *Biblical Epic*, 179.

Chapter Seven

Reading Biblical Epics in Anglo-Saxon England: Aldhelm, Bede, Alcuin

Quamobrem non est spernenda haec [metrica ratio], quamuis gentilibus communis ratio, sed quantum satis est perdiscenda, quia utique multi euangelici uiri, insignes libros hac arte condiderunt, et Deo placere per id satagerunt, ut fuit Juvencus, Sedulius, Arator, Alcimus, Clemens, Paulinus et Fortunatus, et caeteri multi.

[So the use of metre is not to be rejected, even if it is common to pagans as well as ourselves, but to be learned thoroughly as much as necessary, since many evangelical men without a doubt have written famous books in this style and strove to please God by them. Such were Juvencus, Sedulius, Arator, Avitus, Prudentius, Paulinus, Fortunatus, and many others.]

– Hrabanus Maurus[1]

The biblical epics of late Antiquity entered England in the seventh century with the coming of Christianity and the foundation of monastic schools. There, Juvencus, Sedulius, and Arator especially played important roles in

---

1 *De institutione clericorum*, *PL* 107, col. 0293–0420A at 0396a. Hrabanus Maurus (c. 776–856) was the student of Alcuin. As abbot and headmaster of the abbey of Fulda, an Anglo-Saxon foundation established by Sturm (744) at the instigation of St Boniface (680–754), Hrabanus passed on the curriculum of biblical poetry inherited from Alcuin and his teaching. It is therefore not surprising that he mentions many of the same authors Alcuin names in his York poem (lines 1551–4). See further Godman, ed., *Alcuin: The Bishops, Kings and Saints of York*, xxxiii–ix and lx–lxxv.

a programmed study of Latin literature.[2] Pious and practical, their versifications of the Bible offered suitable devotional reading and technical-sty-
listic knowledge of how to compose hexameter verse. Rhetorical patterns
and a host of classical-poetic diction, earlier adopted and transformed by
the Christian poets of late Antiquity, further inspired imitative works beyond the normal boundaries of the prior genre.[3]

Biblical Epics in Monastic Settings

The initial venue for the teaching and transmission of late antique Latin
biblical epic in Anglo-Saxon England was the monastic classroom, though
no classbooks, teachers' manuals, or drawings of schools survive, and so
we cannot be sure about the procedures of the time or even the physical
spaces in which such learning took place.[4] Ælfric Bata's tenth-century
Colloquies offer some lively glimpses into the classrooms of the time, but
these scenes of students working away, pen and tablet in hand, provide
little sense of a program for the whole period.[5] It is, moreover, hard to
imagine, as Michael Lapidge notes, how students would have memorized
thousands of lines of poetry from wax tablets capable of holding little
more than thirty lines of text.[6] That might have sufficed for the preface to

---

2 See further Lapidge, "Versifying the Bible in the Middle Ages," 11–40 at 12; Steen,
   Verse and Virtuosity, 18; Stenton, *Anglo-Saxon England*, 96–129. For the foundation
   of Anglo-Saxon schools, see further Lapidge, *Anglo-Latin Literature 600–899*, 1–168;
   Lapidge, *Anglo-Latin Literature 900–1066*, 1–48; Wilson, *Christian Theology and Old
   English Poetry*, 30–7; Orbán, *Historia Apostolica*, vol. 1, 14. Also, for a recent list of
   "core curriculum" poetic texts, which seem to have been "remarkably stable throughout
   the Anglo-Saxon period" and which includes Sedulius, Juvencus, and Arator at the top of
   the list (and then Prosper of Aquitane, Prudentius, Symphosius, Vergil, Aldhelm, Bede,
   Beothius, "Cato," Martianus Capella, Avitus, Cyprianus, Lactantius, Paulinus of Nola,
   and Persius) see further Thornbury, *Becoming a Poet in Anglo-Saxon England*, 49.
3 Evidence that the Anglo-Saxons were formally versed in Latin rhetoric is inconclusive.
   For recent studies, see further Steen, *Verse and Virtuosity*, 9, who writes, "there is no direct
   evidence that the progymnasmata (the preliminary rhetorical exercises) were ever taught
   in the monasteries of Anglo-Saxon England"; also Knappe, *Traditionen der Klassischen
   Rhetorik im angelsächsischen England*; Knappe, "Classical Rhetoric in Anglo-Saxon England," 5–29, esp. 6, 13, 28; and Lapidge, "Hypallage in the Old English *Exodus*," 31–9.
4 Lapidge, "The Study of Latin Texts in Late Anglo-Saxon England," 99–165, at 100; also
   Riché, "La vie quotidienne dans les écoles monastiques d'après les colloques scolaires,"
   417–26.
5 See further Porter, "The Latin Syllabus in A-S Monastic Schools," 463–82.
6 See Lapidge, "The Study of Latin Texts," 101.

Euangeliorum libri but not the whole of it (3219 lines), which would have taken over a hundred sessions to copy and commit to memory. In practical terms, it is more likely that students studied and memorized parts of these texts in schools and gained broader knowledge of them in later private reading, for which the monastic schedule afforded plenty of time.[7]

Even that process, though, is hard to imagine. Many of the surviving manuscripts that contain biblical epics are large anthologies of literature filled with hundreds of pages; not the sorts of things you would curl up with. More likely they were school books of some kind.[8] Cambridge, University Library (CUL) Gg. 5. 35 (s. xi med) and Paris, Sainte- Geneviève 2410 (s. x/xi) attest to such collections, and they are packed with pages of Latin for readers of all levels.[9] Not deluxe manuscripts, these are functional compendia marred by all manner of scribbles, stains, and scratches penned by generations of readers. They are just the sort of books from which Latin teachers would have taught their students, or else they were library books that served the private hours of monks. In all likelihood, they were both.[10]

Many of the texts in CUL Gg. 5. 35 contain suitable passages for basic Latin instruction, including the anonymous preface to Juvencus' *Euangeliorum libri*. It is the first item in the manuscript (fol. 1r) and, at only eight lines, it offers a nice set piece of a suitable length for a single lesson.[11] It is also heavily glossed with cues for the elementary reader, and so it must

---

7　Ibid., 126: "According to the stipulations of the Benedictine Rule, private reading held a substantial place in the monastic life: three hours each morning in winter, two hours each afternoon in summer, nearly all day every Sunday throughout the year – an average of 20 hours per week."

8　See further Rigg and Wieland, "A Canterbury Classbook," 113–30; Lapidge, "The Study of Latin Texts," 99–165; Wieland, "The Glossed Manuscript," 153–73; Page, "On the Feasibility of a Corpus of Anglo-Saxon Glosses"; Wieland, "Interpreting Interpretation," 59–71. For a more extensive treatment of how glosses may indicate "classbooks," see also Wieland, *The Latin Glosses on Arator and Prudentius*.

9　Despite its shelfmark, Paris, Sainte-Geneviève 2410 (s. x/xi) was written in late Anglo-Saxon England in the second half of the tenth century (based on paleographical evidence), attesting to the endurance of *Euangeliorum libri IV* in later Anglo-Saxon England. It was donated to the Sainte-Geneviève Library in the eighteenth century. See further Lapidge, "The Study of Latin Texts," 114; Springer, *Manuscripts of Sedulius*, 10.

10　For the distinction between "classbook" and "library book," see further Lapidge, "The Study of Latin Texts," 126–7; see also Wieland, "The Glossed Manuscript," 153–73.

11　On the authorship and style of this preface, see further Green, *Latin Epics*, 15.

have been somebody's idea of an exercise at some point, even if many of the glosses were inherited from continental exemplars.[12] The following text is edited from CUL Gg. 5. 35, fol. 1r (marginal glossing has been omitted for the most part):

       .i. docuit
Mattheus instituit uirtutum tramite mores

Et bene uiuendi iusto dedit ordine leges.

    b   a   d   d   e   c
Marcus amat terras inter caelumque uolare

 f uel ueniens g g   i   f .s. iura h i uolatu
Et uehemens aquila stricto secat omnia lapsu.

    facundius   conflicta
Lucas uberius describit praelia Christi,   i. genelogiam Christi
                                   ab ioseph usque
                       .i. prima   adam. auita .i. ab aeuo
Iure sacer uitulus, quia uatum menia fatur auita.

b nuntiat b uel −e gratia dei   .i. uociferenti
Ioannes fremit ore leo, similis rugienti

a .i. sonat
Intonat aeternae pandens misteria uitae.

[Matthew taught morals by way of virtues and gave laws for living well in due order. Mark loves to fly between the earth and sky, and, a soaring eagle, cuts everything in his strict flight. Luke describes the struggles of Christ more fully, a sacred calf by right, for he utters the office of the ancient prophets. John, the lion, roars from his mouth, booms like thunder, laying bare the mysteries of eternal life.]

The elementary glosses of this short poem appeal to a reader who is approaching the text from the point of view of a beginner. The syntactical-alphabetic glosses in lines 3 and 4, for example, are functional and direct the reader through the syntax of the Latin in stages.[13] Only a novice or a teacher of novices would need to show such basic steps – *Amat* (a) *Marcus*

---

12 See further Lapidge, "The Study of Latin Texts," 124–5. See also Lendinara, "Was the Glossator a Teacher?" 1–27, esp. 26.

13 For further discussion of alphabetic and syntactical glosses in Anglo-Saxon manuscripts, see further Robinson, "Syntactical Glosses," 443–75.

(b) *uolare* (c) *terras inter* (d) *caelumque* (e), *et* (f) *secat* (f) *uehemens aquila* (g) *omnia* (h) *stricto lapsu* (i). Other glosses likewise focus on the beginner, providing basic synonyms for verbs (*instituit*, .i. *docuit* or *intonat*, .i. *sonat*), while the glossing over *fremit* in the second-to-last line (*uel –e*), shows the reader that the word can also be spelled *fremet*, as a second conjugation verb. This is yet another note for the novice.

Versifications of the Lord's Prayer

Another indication that the poems of CUL Gg. 5. 35 were model *exempla* for Anglo-Latin students is offered by a series of items at the end of the manuscript. Folios 421a–3b contain several Christian poems and texts of a didactic nature, including two anonymous versifications of the Lord's Prayer.[14] A brief lesson on the Greek alphabet with interlinear glosses precedes these texts, and it spells out the "alpha" and "omega" of the Greek in Latin. These are elementary notes for someone. The alphabet is also preceded by several heavily glossed riddles, a genre with strong ties to education (fols. 418b ff.).[15] Enigmata offer all kinds of material for the instruction and delight of young readers. Not only are they entertaining, but riddles offer bursts of exemplary Latin vocabulary and metre, not unlike that poem at the head of *Euangeliorum libri*, and many are of an ideal length for instructional purposes.

The two verse renditions of the *Pater noster* that follow this material themselves appear to be experiments in poetic composition, and both are heavily indebted to the earlier renditions of the prayer in the biblical epics of Juvencus and Sedulius.[16] Other stylistic features suggest that these are also Anglo-Latin compositions linked to the school of Alcuin and perhaps the work of one or more of his students in England or on the continent. Echoes of Alcuin set the date of composition for both poems between the

---

14 These two versifications of the PN are followed by the *Gloria in Excelsis* and *Credo*, both of which appear in Greek and the second of which is heavily glossed in Latin. Several short enigmata then pick up (fol. 422b) and herald in more verses, this time on the *Te Deum* (423a). More riddles then follow (423b).

15 For the connection of the riddles in CUL G.g. 5. 35 to educational programming in Anglo-Saxon England and Latin instruction, see further Thornbury, *Becoming a Poet*, 52–65.

16 The two versifications of the *Pater noster* in this section of CUL Gg. 5. 35 were printed in 1851 by Giles, "Anecdota Bedae, Lanfranci et aliorum," *Publications of the Caxton Society* 12 (1851), 47. They were reprinted by Walther in "Versifizierte *Pater Noster* und *Credo*," 45–64.

birth of Alcuin (c. 735) and the date of CUL Gg. 5. 35 (mid-eleventh century). A date in the ninth century would not be unreasonable, but there is nothing to prevent a later one.[17]

For ease of analysis, I have put the scansion of the two poems on the left, and I have underlined echoes of the biblical *Pater noster* as well. I have also included echoes of other Latin poems in bold-faced type, whose works I have italicized in the line below. All of this markup may seem excessive, but it serves as a reminder of the richness of intertextuality in this period, something that is frequently awkward to demonstrate in writing:

Pater noster a (CUL Gg. 5. 35 fol. 421^b):

[DSSS] Sancte Pater, summa **celi** qui **sedis** in aula,
        (*Juv. 1.590 residens … caeli*)
[DDDD] **Sanctificetur** honore tuum uenerabile nomen,
        (*Sed. 2.244; Juv. 1.591*)
[SSSS] **Emundans** neuis seruorum corda tuorum.
        (*Ald. virg. 1637 emundans crimina*)
[SDSD] Nobis adueniat regnum, tua **magna potestas**,
        (*Alc. Carm. 50.15 magna potestas*)
[SDDS] Quondam qui tenuit regimen nunc **hoste repulso**,
        (*Sed. 2.217 hoste repulso*)
[DSSS] Filius ut regnet semper per tempora pacis.
[SDDD] In celis ueluti colitur tua **cara uoluntas**,
        (*Juv. 1.595 clara uoluntas*)
[SDSD] Sic dignos faciant fructus tibi **corpora nostra**,
        (*Sed. 2.258 corpora nostra*)
[DSSS] Impleat et sanctus nostri **precordia flatus**.
        (*Bede, Cuth. 1.211 praecordia flatu*)
[DSSS] Pauperibus potum nobis panemque ministra,   10
[DDDS] Semper ut esuriem superes estusque laborem,
[DSSS] Atque tuos pascat panis uictoribus aptus.
[DDSS] Te, **genitor**, petimus, dimittas **crimina nostra**,
        (*Juv, 1.590 genitor; Alc. Carm. 90.4. crimina nostra*)
[DSDS] Fratribus ut culpe ueniam poscentibus ante
[DSSS] Viscere perfecto pacis indulsimus alme.   15

---

17 Godman, *Bishops, Kings, and Saints*, xxxvii, puts Alcuin's date of departure for the
    continent at 781 or early in 782. Bullough, *Alcuin*, 336–46 and esp. 337, puts it closer to
    786. If these poems are continental in origin, a date in the early to mid-ninth century
    would makes some sense, but the poems themselves offer no conclusive evidence.

[DSSD]   Nonque sinas seruos uinci, pater, **hoste maligno,**
          (*Alc. Carm. 69.193 & 124.10*)
[SSSS]   Olim qui **primoplastum** detrusit ab Eden.
          (*Prud. Cath. 9.17*)
[DDSS]   **Eripe** sed, genitor, agnos de **faucibus** hostis,
          (*Alc. Rhythm. 2.4.2 same expression*)
[SDSS]   Vt possint Domino semper seruire superno.
[DSSS]   Quod petimus fiat Christo fiatque uolente!   20

[Holy Father, you who sit in heaven's highest hall, may your venerable name
be hallowed honourably, cleansing the hearts of your servants of their sins.
May your kingdom come to us, your great power – the enemy has been repelled, who once held dominion! – so that your son may ever reign over times
of peace. As your beloved will is honoured in heaven, so may our bodies
yield worthy fruit unto you, and may the Holy Spirit fill our hearts. Give
bread and drink to us poor, that you may ever overcome hunger, heat and
toil, and may your bread, fit for victors, feed your own. You, Father, we beg,
forgive us our sins, as we have indulged our brothers, seeking pardon for
previous offences with a perfect heart nourishing peace. And let not your
servants be overcome by the wicked foe, who once drove first-made man
from Eden. But snatch up your sheep, Father, from the jaws of the enemy,
that they may ever serve the supernal Lord. May that which we ask be done
and be done by the will of Christ.]

Pater noster b (CUL Gg. 5. 35 fol. 422[a]):

[DSSS]   **O genitor nostri, <u>celi</u> qui sede moraris,**
          (*Nam genitor noster, Juv. 1.567; 2.216*)
[DSSS]   Rite tuum **in nobis** <u>nomen</u>, rogo, **<u>sanctificetur</u>,**
          (*Juv. 1.591–2; Sed. 2.244 1st word*)
[DDSS]   **Adueniatque <u>tuum</u>** jam sceptrum **hoste repulso.**
          (*Juv. 1.594; Sed. 2.249*)
[DDSS]   Vendicet et sibi nos seruos **conseruet in euum.**
          (*Alc. Carm. 24.15; 103.2.4; 104.4.2; 107.1.9*)
[DDSS]   Inque polo tua ceu persistet **sancta <u>uoluntas</u>,**
          (*Alc. Carm. 45.65 & 109.11.4*)
[DSSS]   Sic maneat clemens <u>in terris</u> **munere claro.**
          (*Ald. Enig. 85.5*)
[SSSS]   **Qui panis uite es pascens doctrina fideles;**
          (*cf. Sed. .264–6; 5.34; 5.366; 5.403*)

[SSDS]   Quo semper <u>panem</u> tribuas, poscamus, in orbe.
[DSDS]   Et pariter nobis uitiorum <u>debita</u> laxa,
[DSSS]   Sicut eis, qui in nos peccant, <u>dimittimus</u> ipsi.   10
[SSSS]   Et **saeua**, ne nos fallat **tentatio** torui,
              (*Juv. 1.602*)
[SSSS]   Sed cunctis in te fidentes **eripe noxis**. Amen
              (*cf. Ven. Fort. 2.5 latera 1, eripe credentes*; Bede *libell.* 283 &
              569 & *Hymn* 10.13.4; *Alc. Carm.* 62.37 & *Rhythm.* 2.4.2; Raba-
              nus *Carm.* 9.7 & 13.29 & 18.1.23, etc.)

[Our Father, you who linger on heaven's seat, may your name, I pray, be duly
hallowed in us, and may your power come, now that the enemy has been
repelled. May it claim us as its servants and keep us safe forever. And just as
your holy will persists in heaven, so may it remain merciful on earth in that
bright gift. You who are the bread of life and the teaching that feeds the faithful. So may you ever grant bread, we ask, on earth. And equally release the
debts of our sins, as we ourselves forgive those who sin against us. And may
the savage temptation of the merciless one not deceive us, but may you snatch
those trusting in you from all harm. Amen.]

Unlike the poetry of most classical and late antique authors, who choose
(or are able) to vary their metrical patterning from line to line, both of these
compositions are highly repetitive, and this is a feature of later Latin verse.
There is also little elision in either poem, with the exception of the two instances in the second text (lines 7, 10), and this again suggests a later date.
The individual verses in each poem are also composed, for the most part, of
end-stopped lines with a fixed cadence; such regularity points to a beginner's proficiency, allowing that the Prayer itself is composed of discrete
units of sense, which only affirms its value as a model for basic-Latin students. In each poem, the distribution of dactyls and spondees betrays metrical monotony and therefore inexperience: the first version of the Prayer
repeats the pattern DSSS seven times in just twenty lines. That is almost
50 per cent, and only seven patterns are not repeated elsewhere, so that
thirteen of the twenty lines contain patterns repeated somewhere else in the
text. This metrical monotony applies to the second poem as well, where the
same pattern (DSSS) is used four times in just twelve lines. The pattern
SSSS is used three times, and so is DDSS. Only two patterns are not repeated in this case, so that ten of the twelve lines contain recycled metrical
patterning. Compare such tendencies against those of Juvencus, who does
not repeat a single pattern in the first twelve verses of *Euangeliorum libri*,

for example, to say nothing of poets like Vergil and Ovid, who repeat patterns much less frequently.[18] On the other hand, the reliance on spondaic feet in this instance may also represent an effort to emulate Juvencus, whose poetry is heavily spondaic in imitation of the weighted grandeur of epic. If so, the preponderance of spondees over dactyls may reflect a desire to introduce similar *grauitas* to this versified Prayer.

Be that as it may, there is no doubt that both poems are modelled on the poetry of Juvencus and Sedulius, and not in a general way but specifically on their versifications of the Lord's Prayer in *Euangeliorum libri* (1.590–600) and the *Carmen paschale* (2.237–97). Like Juvencus and Sedulius, these Anglo-Latin poets retain the essential elements of the prose (in the underlined words), but the words in bold show that they do so at times according to their late antique models. That is to say, some of the biblical phrasing reflects the very syntax and diction of Juvencus and Sedulius, which means that the Anglo-Latin poets are not following the Bible but these intermediary sources. This serves as a reminder of the complexity of textual transmission in the Anglo-Saxon period, especially in the case of poetry.

The most frequent points of contact between the Anglo-Latin and late antique traditions appear at the cadence of the lines. In the first poem, the phrase *hoste repulso* originates in the *Carmen paschale* of Sedulius (2.217), and no earlier author uses this expression, which also appears in line three of the second poem. Moreover, the phrase *corpora nostra* in line eight of the first poem appears verbatim in the *Carmen paschale* and again in the context of Sedulius' versification of the Prayer (2.258). The words *eripe … faucibus* in line eighteen of the first poem, "snatch us from the jaws of the foe," appear in Alcuin (*Rhythm* 2.4.2) but also in Sedulius' version of the Prayer at the same point in the line, but in a different context. In the *Carmen paschale*, Sedulius says, "Dulcia nam Domini nostris in faucibus haerent" ("For the sweetness of the Lord lingers in our throats," 2.267). This context is different from the Anglo-Latin poem, where the sweetness of God's word resists the venom of Satan's wolfish maw. That being said, and allowing for the difference of context, it is possible to see how an Anglo-Saxon student working through the text of the *Carmen paschale* (or his memory of it) could adapt Sedulius to suit his own rendition of the Prayer. On the other hand, it is also true that Alcuin's phrasing is closer in this case than that of Sedulius, as are several turns of phrase in both poems. Alcuin, for

---

18 See further Duckworth, *Vergil and Classical Hexameter*, for statistical analyses of the heroic metre.

example, is the only Anglo-Latin poet to use the phrases *hoste maligno* (*Alc. Carm.* 69.193 and 124.10) and *conseruet in aeuum* (*Alc. Carm.* 24.15, 103.2.4, 104.4.2, 107.1.9). It is therefore likely that these poems owe a debt to Alcuin's work, blurring further the lines of transmission between late antique and Anglo-Saxon literature. Still, there is no doubt that the form and content of the two Anglo-Latin poems are indebted directly to the biblical epics of Juvencus and Sedulius in what is a clear example of the pervading influence of that literature upon Anglo-Saxon writing.

The second poem only strengthens this assumption, and it contains several phrases that echo Juvencus and *Euangeliorum libri*. Thus in the second half of line one, the words "celi qui sede moraris" appear in Book 2 of Juvencus' poem as "celi qui sede moratur" with reference to Christ (2.216). Also, even though the Anglo-Latin poet quotes the Bible throughout his versification of the *Pater noster*, many of his words appear in the same position of the line as those in the version of Juvencus. This is true for the words *Sanctificetur* and *adueniatque* in line 3, as well as *sancta uoluntas* in line 5, which resonates with *clara uoluntas* in Juvencus; the phrase *cara uoluntas* in line 7 of the first poem is even closer.

The coincidence of imagery is also noteworthy, in particular the "bread of life" motif in the second poem, which is something Sedulius highlights in his rendition of the Prayer. In the second poem, the author calls Christ "the bread of life, the doctrine that feeds the faithful" (7), and this passage is reminiscent of poetry in the *Carmen paschale* (2.264–6), where Sedulius calls the daily bread a "portion of faith" for those who hunger for the doctrine of Christ (*doctrina*). The figural associations in the second poem explain the significance of the bread in the first rendition of the Prayer, which the author calls *aptus uictoribus*, "fit for victors" (12); in other words, for those who receive salvation through Christ, "the bread of life." Like the late antique versifications of the Lord's Prayer, the Anglo-Latin renditions are therefore petitions to both the Father and the son. Simply put, these two anonymous poems offer good evidence that Anglo-Latin authors made good use of their remembered reading of late antique literature, in this case the writings of two of the most famous biblical versifiers, Juvencus and Sedulius. What is more, the preservation of these texts in an eleventh-century manuscript, poems whose style owes an appreciable debt to the much earlier poetry of Alcuin, Bede and Aldhelm, attests to the influence of that path-breaking work of the seventh and eighth centuries and the enduring popularity in Anglo-Saxon England of Christian-Latin verses in the "classical" style. In this case, these imitative versifications of the Lord's Prayer were of sufficient value or interest to someone to have merited preservation in CUL Gg. 5. 35 as minor addenda to the canonical biblical epics and Christian poetry that pack the pages of the codex.

Evidence of Verbal Echoes in Anglo-Latin Verse

Myriad echoes of Juvencus, Sedulius, and Arator attest to the wide-ranging influence of Latin biblical epic on Anglo-Latin literature. Numerous allusions appear in the margins of scholarly editions, and although many of these require contextualization, they provide valuable clues for one author's knowledge of another. Surviving booklists and manuscripts provide additional evidence, and all of this together offers a sense of how well a particular writer's work was known throughout the period. The following pages, therefore, offer a summary of evidence for knowledge of Latin biblical epic in Anglo-Saxon England, beginning with Juvencus. Throughout, I have used the evidence contained in Michael Lapidge's *Anglo-Saxon Library*, adding evidence of my own. It is also true that many passages discussed later in this same chapter add to the evidence below.

Knowledge of Juvencus

Evidence for knowledge of *Euangeliorum libri* in Anglo-Saxon England, aside from six surviving manuscripts containing the poem and a reference to it in an inventory of books given to the church of Saint-Vaast in Arras by Sæwold of Bath (c. 1070),[19] depends on echoes in the writings of Aldhelm, Bede, Alcuin, Lantfred, Wulfstan, and Byrhtferth.[20] Based on Lapidge's citations in *The Anglo-Saxon Library*, I count 123 echoes of *Euangeliorum*

---

19 See further Lapidge, *Anglo-Saxon Library*, 136. The poem also appears in an eighth-century Würzburg inventory from the area of the Anglo-Saxon mission in Germany; see ibid., 148.

20 For a list of Anglo-Saxon manuscripts containing *Euangeliorum libri IV*, see further Gneuss and Lapidge, eds., *Anglo-Saxon Manuscripts*, items 7, 12, 87, 489, 540, 903. See also Lapidge, *Anglo-Saxon Library*, 319, from which the following summary is taken: Cambridge, UL, Ff. 4. 42 (Wales, s. ix²; prov. England, s. ix²); Cambridge, UL, Gg. 5. 35 (St Augustine's, Canterbury, s. xi^med); Cambridge, CCC 304 (Italy, s. viii¹; prov. England, s. ix/x); London, BL, Royal 15. A. XVI (N. France, s. ix/x; prov. Canterbury, s. x²); Oxford, BodL, Barlow 25 (? England, s. x); Paris, Bibliothèque Sainte-Geneviève 2410 (Christ Church, Canterbury, s. x/xi). Lapidge provides a summary overview of these manuscripts in "The Study of Latin Texts," 99–165. There he also mentions a possible early fragment from seventh-century England in Cues, Hospitalbibliothek, MS 171 (108); the fragment appears in Lowe, *CLA*, VIII, no. 1172.

libri in the works of the above-named authors:[21] Lantfred (1), Alcuin (2), Wulfstan (3), and Byrhtferth (2) echo Juvencus only seven times collectively, while Aldhelm (84) and Bede (31) account for the majority of citations (115). Lapidge cites only two references to the poem in Alcuin's writings – one in his York poem (line 1551) and another in his collectaneum *De laude dei,* where the whole of the preface appears.[22] But Alcuin also alludes to the *Euangeliorum libri* several times in his correspondence with reference to Judgment Day (*praef.* 22–4), the Incarnation (*Ev.* 1. 60–3), and, like Jerome, the gifts of the Magi (*Ev.* 1. 250–1).[23] Also, in the index to his edition to Alcuin's York poem, Peter Godman lists seventeen echoes of the *Euangeliorum libri* not listed in *The Anglo-Saxon Library.*[24] This brings the total number of citations to at least 140. The more important point, however, is that all these echoes suggest knowledge of Book 1 of *Euangeliorum libri* above all, and the preface in particular. Thirty-seven of Aldhelm's eighty-four citations allude to Book 1, as do fourteen of Bede's thirty-four;[25] and both Bede and Aldhelm cite Book 1 in their respective metrical treatises more than any other portion of the poem.[26] The early portion of the text is also often the most regularly and heavily glossed part of the poem in manuscripts, which also suggests greater familiarity with that section of

---

21 See also Ogilvy, *Books Known to the English, 597–1066.* My own calculations are based on Lapidge's citations for each author, each of whom appears alphabetically in *The Anglo-Saxon Library.*

22 See Lapidge, *Anglo-Saxon Library,* 231–2. For a discussion of the *collectaneum,* see further Constantinescu, "Alcuin et les 'Libelli precum' de l'époque Caroligienne," *Revue de l'histoire de la spiritualité* 50 (1974).

23 For citations of *Euangeliorum libri* in Alcuin's correspondence, see Norton, "Prosopography of Juvencus," 114–20. References to the preface of the *Euangeliorum libri* appear in Alcuin's *Epistula* 126 (*ad Arnonem*) and 166 (*ad Theodulfum*); Alcuin refers to the incarnation in *Contra Felicem Urgellitanum Episcopum libri septem* II.6 (*PL* 101, 152) and in *Aduersus Elipandum (Toletanum) libri quattuor,* II.8 (*PL* 101, col. 266); the reference to the Magi in *Euangeliorum libri* appears in Alcuin's *De diuinis officiis,* Ch. 5 (*PL* 101, col. 1179).

24 See Godman, *Bishops, Kings and Saints,* 149 (references in parentheses are to Alcuin's poem): i. 7 (222), 96 (497), 281 (757), 341 (921), 737 (1379); ii. 112 (855), 153 (194), 177 (147), 412 (491), 575 (217); iii. 1 (13), 79 (1098–9), 480 (43), 492 (1293), 556 (226); iv. 49 (251), 150 (976).

25 Cf. Aldhelm's citation of other books of *Euangeliorum libri* (Bk2, 8; Bk3, 22; Bk4, 17) and Bede's (Bk2, 3; Bk3, 8; Bk4, 6). Note that Lantfred quotes 2.625, and Wulfstan, 1.404, 2.177, 4.353.

26 See further Lapidge, *Anglo-Saxon Library,* 178–9 and 219.

the work.[27] In other words, if *Euangeliorum libri* was part of a larger curriculum of Christian reading – and collections such as CUL Gg. 5. 35 suggest that it was – it stands to reason that teachers might only cover a portion of each text with their students. As both the beginning of the poem and the genre of biblical epic, Book 1 of *Euangeliorum libri* is a logical choice for close study, and it is tempting to think that part of the reason why Aldhelm and Bede are so familiar with Book 1 is that they were themselves reading it and teaching it to their students year after year. We can only guess how different Anglo-Saxon schools and teachers introduced students to such literature, but there is little doubt that Book 1 of *Euangeliorum libri* played a significant role in the Latin education of the period.

Knowledge of Cyprianus

The *Heptateuch* of Cyprianus survives in Anglo-Saxon England in a single manuscript, Cambridge, Trinity College B. I. 42 (St Augustine's, Canterbury, s. x²), which contains *Genesis, Exodus, Leviticus, Numbers,* and *Deuteronomy*.[28] The manuscript, however, is later than the two authors who knew Cyprianus best, Aldhelm and Bede, who cite the *Heptateuch* some twenty-five times, collectively. No other writer of the period appears to quote the poem at all, though I suspect further evidence awaits discovery. For his part, Aldhelm cites the *Heptateuch* eighteen times and alludes to *Genesis* (2), *Exodus* (5), *Numbers* (2), *Judges* (8), and *Kings* (1). His wide-ranging familiarity with the poem suggests more than a passing acquaintance with the narrative of the *Heptateuch*, which he quotes frequently in his *Carmen de uirginitate* (ten times), four times in his metrical treatises, and four times in his riddles (92.3, 72.1, 96.4, 46.4).[29] Note, too, that *Judges* and *Kings* do not appear in the Trinity College manuscript, so that Aldhelm's text could not have been an earlier version of Cambridge, Trinity College B. I. 42 but a different codex altogether. The same appears to be true for Bede, who likewise quotes *Judges* (1), *Genesis* (2), *Exodus* (2), and *Deuteronomy* (1). Bede also cites Jerome's endorsement of Juvencus in his *Commentary on Matthew* and promotes the

---

27 See Lapidge, "The Study of Latin Texts," 125.

28 See Gneuss and Lapidge, eds., *Anglo-Saxon Manuscripts*, item 159. See also Orchard, *Poetic Art of Aldhelm*, 162–3.

29 See Lapidge, *Anglo-Saxon Library*, 180. The citations of *De metris* are from pp. 80 and 92 of Ehwald's edition, *Aldhelmi Opera*; those from *De pedum regulis* likewise appear at 158 and 189.

orthodoxy of the *Heptateuch*, by citing it in his *Commentary on Genesis*.[30] He furthermore reproduces a large section of *Exodus* in *De arte metrica* (lines 507–21), in which he cites the Canticle of Moses in order to exemplify the use of hendecasyllabic metre.[31] Obviously, then, Bede was familiar with Cyprianus' version of the Crossing of the Red Sea, but neither he nor Aldhelm shows any preference for a particular part of the *Heptateuch*. Instead, their echoes of the text range widely from *Genesis* to *Judges* throughout their writings, which suggests broad familiarity with the *Heptateuch* rather than with a fragment or a small part of the text. Granting that the *Heptateuch* is not as popular or readily available as the other canonical versifications of the Bible at this time, the poem nevertheless leaves a notable impression on two of the most influential writers of the Anglo-Saxon period.

Knowledge of Sedulius

Sedulius is easily the most popular and influential biblical poet of the Anglo-Saxon period, judging from manuscript evidence and echoes of the poem in Anglo-Latin. Eight manuscripts of the *Carmen paschale* survive plus four references to the author in various booklists:[32] "Sedulium" appears on the inventory of an otherwise unknown grammarian named Æthelstan (s. x²);[33] and item 27 on a list of books donated to Saint-Vaast by Sæwold of Bath names Sedulius alongside Juvencus ("Iuuencus, Sedulius in

---

30 Bede quotes *Genesis* 1–4 of the *Heptateuch* in his commentary on Genesis; for the Latin text, see Jones, ed., *Comm. in Genesin*, CCSL 118.

31 See Kendall, ed., *De Arte Metrica*, CCSL 123A, 81–141.

32 A list of the eight Anglo-Saxon manuscripts of Sedulius' poem can be found in Gneuss and Lapidge, eds., *Anglo-Saxon Manuscripts*, items 12, 53, 253, 491, 652f, 824.5, 890, 903. I quote Lapidge's summary in *Anglo-Saxon Library*, 331: Cambridge, UL, Gg. 5. 35 (St Augustine's, Canterbury, s. xi^med); Cambridge, CCC 173, fols. 57–83 (S. England, s. viii²; prov. Winchester, Canterbury); Edinburgh, NLS Advocates 18. 7. 7 (s. x^ex; prov. Thorney); Evreux, BM, 43 (?England, s. x); London, BL, Royal 15. B. XIX, fos. 1–35 (Christ Church, Canterbury, s. x²); Oxford, BodL, Lat. theol. c.4 (?Worcester, s. x²) (frg.); Paris, BNF, lat. 8092 (England, s. xi²/⁴); Paris, Bibliothèque Sainte-Geneviève 2410 (Christ Church, Canterbury, s. x/xi). Lapidge also notes two continental manuscripts in Anglo-Saxon script (pp. 157 and 160) from the area of the Anglo-Saxon mission in Germany: Basle, UB, O. IV. 17 (possibly Fulda, s. viii/ix); and Gotha, Landesbibliothek, Mbr. I. 75, fols. 1–22 (S. England or Anglo-Saxon centre on continent, s. viii^ex). These manuscripts attest to the wider transmission of the poem by Anglo-Saxons beyond England.

33 Lapidge, *Anglo-Saxon Library*, 133.

uno uolumine");[34] Bishop Leofric's catalogue of books for the Church of Exeter mentions, in Old English, "Sedulies boc";[35] and one list, perhaps from Worcester, contains "Sedulius" as the second and ninth items, both being copies of the poem, in addition to a copy of Remigius' prose commentary on the text (item 13).[36] Elsewhere, Alcuin names Sedulius as one of the poets available at York ("Quid quoque Sedulius, uel quid canit ipse Iuuencus," 1550), and both Bede and Aldhelm cite Sedulius as a model for the composition of Latin verse in their respective metrical treatises.[37] Taken together, the *Carmen* and *Opus paschale* also constitute an *opus geminatum*, a literary tradition that inspired imitative works in England in the form of Aldhelm's prose and verse *De uirginitate*, Bede's two lives of Cuthbert and Alcuin's two lives of Willibrord.[38] Bede mentions Aldhelm's "twin work" in his *Historia ecclesiastica* and acknowledges the debt to Sedulius (*HE* V., 18): "Scripsit et de uirginitate librum eximium, quem in exemplum Sedulii geminato opere et uersibus exametris et prosa conposuit" ("He also wrote an excellent book on virginity both in hexameter verse and in prose, producing a twofold work after the example of Sedulius").[39] There is no doubt, then, that Sedulius was among the favourite poets of the Anglo-Saxon period and that his *Carmen paschale* was the most influential biblical poem from late Antiquity. I count 354 echoes of the *Carmen paschale* in the Latin works of the period, which is almost three times as many as the number for *Euangeliorum libri* (122), and I am sure that others can add to this number.[40] The distribution of these references again favours Aldhelm, due mainly to the length of *De uirginitate*: Aldhelm (189), Bede (45), Alcuin (30), Asser (1), Lantfred (1), Abbo (1), Wulfstan (82), Aelfric (1), and Byrhtferth (4). As with the references to *Euangeliorum libri*,

---

34   Ibid., 137.

35   Ibid., 139.

36   Ibid., 141.

37   See further Godman, *Bishops, Kings, and Saints*, line 1550; see also Ehwald, ed., *Aldhelmi Opera*; and Jones, ed., *Opera Didascalica*, CCSL 123A.

38   See further Godman, "The Anglo–Latin *Opus Geminatum* from Aldhelm to Alcuin," 215–29; and Wieland, "*Geminus Stylus*," 113–33.

39   See further Colgrave and Mynors, eds., *Bede's Ecclesiastical History of the English People*, 114–15. The translation is based on that edition.

40   I have added the twenty-five citations listed in Godman's edition of Alcuin's York poem, which Lapidge does not cite in *Anglo-Saxon Library*. Godman's citations follow, with the numbers in parentheses referring to the lines of Alcuin's York poem: praef. 11–12 (1536); i. 55 (82), 67 (1310), 82–3 (672), 85 (1591), 96 (742), 136 (1322), 146 (1449), 302 (932), 312 (1), 337 (1497), 341 (990, 1245); ii. 14 (836), 97 (1589), 206 (1247); iii. 78 (1231), 91 (865), 100 (1149), 226 (1365, 1370), 227 (1370), 293 (793), 301 (1617); iv. 8 (1379); v. 120 (466), 328 (630).

Aldhelm's echoes of Book 1 of the *Carmen paschale* outweigh those of all the other books of the poem (81).[41] The same is true for Bede, who appears to be much less familiar with the end of the *Carmen paschale* than the beginning.[42] Wulfstan is the exception here. He cites Book 3 twenty-six times, significantly more than any other book of the poem. That particular section of the *Carmen paschale* deals with Christ's miraculous deeds in the New Testament, and perhaps Wulfstan uses those miracles as models for his rendition of the deeds of St Swithun.[43] Apart from this textual evidence, several Sedulian manuscripts are heavily glossed in Latin (and some in Old English) and accompanied on three occasions by the Carolingian commentary of Remigius of Auxerre.[44] All of this collateral material lends credence to the assumption that Sedulius' *Carmen paschale* was studied closely and consistently throughout the Anglo-Saxon period.

Knowledge of Avitus

No manuscript of Avitus' *Historia spiritalis* survives from the Anglo-Saxon period, but evidence for knowledge of the poem exists in the writings of the Anglo-Saxons themselves. "Alcimi Auiti" appears on a list of books donated by Bishop Æthelwold of Winchester to the monastery of Peterborough, refounded in 970,[45] and Alcuin names "Alcimus" among the authors available in the library at York (*Alcimus et Clemens, Prosper, Paulinus, Arator,* 1552).[46] Aldhelm and Bede also provide textual evidence for knowledge of the author in their verse and prose writings: four echoes of *Historia spiritalis* appear in Aldhelm's poetry, three in the *Carmen de uirginitate* and one in

---

41 Aldhelm's echoes of the different books of the *Carmen paschale* are as follows: Bk.1 (81); Bk.2 (28); Bk.3 (29); Bk.4 (24); Bk.5 (27).

42 Bede's echoes of the different books of the *Carmen paschale* are as follows: Book 1 (23); Book 2 (9); Book 3 (6); Book 4 (1); Book 5 (6).

43 Wulfstan's citations of the different books of the *Carmen paschale* include the following: Bk.1 (18); Bk.2 (13); Bk.3 (26); Bk.4 (16); and Bk.5 (9).

44 For known Old English glosses to these manuscripts, see further Napier, *Old English Glosses: Chiefly Unpublished*, Anecdota Oxoniensia 4, Medieval and Modern Series, Pt. 11 (1900), no. 51; Meritt, *Old English Glosses (A Collection)*, nos. 28, 29, 30, 31; Page, "Anglo-Saxon Scratched Glosses," 209–15 at 210–13; Page, "More Old English Scratched Glosses," 43–5; Ker, *Catalogue of Manuscripts Containing Anglo-Saxon*, 418; Lapidge, "Some Old English Sedulius Glosses from Bn Lat. 8092," 1–17. For the Latin glosses to these manuscripts, see further Lapidge, "The Study of Latin Texts," 114–17; and Wieland, "The Glossed Manuscript."

45 See further Lapidge, *Anglo-Saxon Library*, 134–5.

46 See Lapidge, *Anglo-Saxon Library*, 230; and Godman, *Bishops, Kings and Saints*, 124–5.

the *Carmen ecclesiastica*;[47] and Bede cites Avitus nine times, six in his metrical life of St Cuthbert and twice in his poem on Judgment Day (*Versus de die iudicii*), in addition to a single reference in his *Commentary on Genesis*, which again attests to the orthodoxy of biblical verse in the minds of prominent Christians like Bede and Jerome.[48] Despite the poverty of manuscript evidence, therefore, the distribution of verbal echoes suggests broad familiarity with Avitus' *Historia spiritalis*, which is to say the whole of it was available at some point. Moreover, the kinship of certain episodes of *Historia spiritalis* with poetry in Anglo-Latin and Old English invites further speculation as to the possible connections between Avitus and Anglo-Saxon literature. Michael Lapidge has argued that Samuel Moore's rejection of Avitus as a source for the Old English *Exodus* is not as conclusive as some might think, and I agree.[49] "Moore's 'demolition,'" as he puts it, "(which on inspection turns out to be more special pleading than demolition) has steered scholarship away from the obvious inspiration of the Old English *Exodus*, namely the curriculum of Christian Latin poets which were studied in all Anglo-Saxon schools."[50] The tradition of Latin and vernacular verse in the period therefore stands to owe much to Avitus, and we should not hesitate to reconsider potential connections.

Knowledge of Arator

Knowledge of Arator in Anglo-Saxon England is extensive, far more so than knowledge of Avitus. Eight manuscripts of *Historia apostolica* have survived,[51] and two booklists cite him by name, one in Bishop Leofric's

---

47 See further Lapidge, *Anglo-Saxon Library*, 179. The passages in question are i. 25 (*CdV* 1584), ii. 358 (*CdV* 846), vi. 223 (*CE* iv.6.7), and vi. 512 (*CdV* 1912).

48 See further Lapidge, *Anglo-Saxon Library*, 204.

49 See further Moore, "On the Sources of the Old-English Exodus," in *Modern Philology* 9 (1911); see also Lapidge, "Versifying the Bible in the Middle Ages," 27–8.

50 Ibid., 28.

51 See further Lapidge, "The Study of Latin Texts," 116–24. The eight surviving manuscripts of Arator's poem are listed in Gneuss and Lapidge, eds., *Anglo-Saxon Manuscripts*, items 12, 175, 280f, 488, 523.5f, 620.6f, 660f, 890f. I list Lapidge's summary in *Anglo-Saxon Library*, 281: Cambridge, UL, Gg. 5. 35 (St Augustine's, Canterbury, s. xi^med; London, BL, Royal 15. A. V, fos. 30–85 (s. xi^ex); London, Westminster Abbey Library, 17 (England, s. xi/xii) (frg.); Oxford, BodL, e Mus. 66 [offsets] (?N Italy, s. vi or vii); Oxford, BodL, Rawlinson C. 570 (St Augustine's, Canterbury, s. x²); Paris, BNF, lat. 8092 (England, s. xi¹). On whether London, BL, Royal 15. A. V is Anglo-Saxon or not, see Wieland, "British Library, Ms. Royal 15. A. V: One Manuscript or Three?" 1–25.

inventory of books donated to Exeter and another in an unidentified list from Worcester.[52] Alcuin also mentions Arator as one of the poets available at York (line 1552), and a bulk of evidence comes from verbal echoes in Anglo-Latin literature. I count 139 allusions to Arator's poem in Anglo-Latin, including citations by Aldhelm (42), Bede (31), Alcuin (26), Lantfred (3), Wulfstan (32), and Byrhtferth (5).[53] Not surprisingly, Aldhelm cites *Historia apostolica* mostly in his *Carmen de uirginitate* (22), followed by a fairly even distribution of echoes in his *Carmina ecclesiastica* (8), *Enigmata* (5), *De metris* (5), and *De pedum regulis* (2).[54] What is more, just as Aldhelm cites Book 1 of *Euangeliorum libri* and *Carmen paschale* more than any other book of the poem, so does he echo Book 1 of the *Historia apostolica* twice as frequently as Book 2.[55] Bede likewise cites Book 1 more often than Book 2, though not significantly so (Bk.1, 18; Bk.2, 12).[56] He also acknowledges a debt to Arator's poem in his prose commentary on the Acts of the Apostles (*Expositio actuum apostolorum*):[57]

In quo me opusculo, cum alii plurimi fidei catholicae scriptores, tum maxime iuuauit Arator, sanctae romanae ecclesiae subdiaconus, qui ipsum ex ordine librum heroico carmine percurrens nonnullos in eodem metro allegoriae flores admiscuit, occasionem mihi tribuens uel alia ex his colligendi uel eadem planius exponendi.

---

52 See Orchard, *Poetic Art*, at 167–8. See also Lapidge, "Surviving Booklists from Anglo-Saxon England." Arator's name appears twice on the Worcester booklist (two copies of his poem).

53 I have added twenty-one citations of Arator's *Historia* from Godman's edition of Alcuin's York poem: i. 52 (664), 54 (1628), 99 (34), 227 (4), 234 (629), 404 (1405), 528 (1379), 553 (35), 777 (1318), 801–2 (427ff), 953 (1208), 989 (57); ii. 78 (267), 106 (429), 123 (1246), 183–4 (159ff), 520 (1364), 624 (365), 928 (282), 939 (1166), 1167 (1036).

54 See further Lapidge, *Anglo-Saxon Library*, 178–9.

55 Aldhelm cites Book 1 of *Historia apostolica* 28 times and Book 2, 14.

56 Bede's distribution of quotations of *Historia apostolica* include *Ep. ad Vigilium* (1); Bk.1, 18; Bk.2, 12.

57 See further Laistner, ed., *Expositio Actuum Apostolorum et Retractatio*. Lawrence Martin also emphasizes the importance of Arator for Bede in "Knowledge of Arator in Anglo-Saxon England," noting (p. 80) that "Laistner's edition of Bede's *Commentary* credits Augustine for the symbolism of the lame beggar, but Augustine does not develop the full four points of the symbolic structure of Bede's *Commentary* on the story. Every feature of Bede's allegorical structure is, however, found in Arator (1.244–92)."

[In this small work, although many other writers of the Catholic faith [have helped me], Arator has helped me the most, a sub-deacon of the Holy Roman Church, who went through that book in order and in heroic verse; he added many flowers of allegory in the same metre, giving me the occasion to take other things from it or explain the same things more plainly.]

It is clear from this quotation that Bede read Arator's letter to Parthenius, in which Arator refers to the "flowers" of the Psalms (*Dauidicis assuetus floribus*, 73) and "violets" and "lilies" of the Old and New Testaments (*uiolas et lilia*, 75) that commingle in the Acts of the Apostles ("uetus atque nouus congeminauit odor"). Bede's reference to the mingling of flowers as allegories for the symbolism of the Testaments (*allegoriae flores admiscuit*) coincides with Arator's emphasis, and this is only the beginning of Bede's debt to Arator. Lantfred of Winchester cites the *Historia apostolica* as a way to elevate the tone of his preface in his life of Saint Swithun,[58] and Wulfstan of Winchester does the same in his preface to the versification of Lantfred's prose ("Narratio metrica de Sancti Swithuno").[59] Byrhtferth of Ramsey cites Arator in his life of St Ecgwine ("Vita sancti Echwini") and quotes lines 1.226–7 of the poem in his *Enchiridion*.[60] Like Juvencus and Sedulius, then, Arator enjoyed enduring popularity throughout the Anglo-Saxon period, from the time of Aldhelm to Wulfstan, and his poem is among the three most popular biblical versifications of the period.

Summary Conclusions

So what do we learn from all of this empirical evidence? For one, it is clear that Juvencus, Sedulius, and Arator are the most popular biblical poets of the time, though manuscript and textual evidence also points to knowledge of Cyprianus and Avitus among other Christian writers, notably Prudentius. It also appears that many of the biblical poems circulated together in compendia or with groups of books donated to various institutions by generous benefactors. This is especially true of Juvencus, Sedulius, and Arator, who show up as the first three items in CUL Gg. 5. 35 and on a number of other

---

58   See Lapidge, *Anglo-Saxon Library*, 240.

59   See ibid. For Wulfstan's poem, see Lapidge, *The Cult of St. Swithun*, 371–551.

60   See further Baker and Lapidge, eds., *Byrhtferth's Enchiridion*, 2.3. 265. The text of *Vita s. Ecgwini* is also in Lapidge's edition of the *Enchiridion*.

booklists as well.[61] Such collections suggests an awareness of a genre of biblical epic as well as a general program of reading. What is more, based on the distribution of echoes in Anglo-Latin, it is clear that the first books of *Euangeliorum libri*, *Carmen paschale*, and *Historia apostolica* were the best-known sections of the poems, which suggests a selective program of reading focused on the early portions of the texts. As for the glosses accompanying them, many are inherited from the continent, as Michael Lapidge has shown; but even if they are not the *ad hoc* responses of a teacher or student to the text, they still offer ready-made pedagogical aids for Latin teachers, who could have used them in their classrooms. Glossed passages like the one at the opening of *Euangeliorum libri* in CUL Gg. 5. 35 (fol. 1r) provide exemplary evidence for the kinds of problems encountered by basic Latin students, and there is no reason why English teachers could not have used such passages in their own lessons.

The question remains, what is the context of this verbal evidence in Anglo-Latin literature? Do these echoes count for more than disparate strands of remembered reading? Certainly, there are times when a given word or phrase from biblical epic enters Anglo-Latin without special significance. This is true of much of the Christian-poetic diction Juvencus and other biblical poets adopt from their classical sources, such as the *Tonans* epithet, or the phrase *culmina caeli* ("the heights of heaven"), and there are practical reasons for adopting and repeating such phrases, which can fill out the metre of a hexameter line, for example.[62] Latin was not the native language of the Anglo-Saxons, and writing hexameter poetry always presented challenges. As Neil Wright has said, "Aldhelm was one of the first Germanic speakers to compose Latin hexameter verse," and "he was therefore working in a poetic tradition completely foreign to that of his own native oral verse; hence he was faced with the daunting task of mastering not only alien systems of prosody, quantitative metre, and

---

61 Juvencus and Sedulius also both appear in Paris, Bibliothèque Sainte-Geneviève 2410 (Christ Church, Canterbury, s. x/xi) (Gneuss and Lapidge, item 903), and both Arator and Sedulius in Paris, BNF, lat. 8092 (England, s. xi²/⁴) (Gneuss and Lapidge, item 890). Juvencus and Sedulius appear as item 27 on Sæwold's list of books donated to Bath ("Iuuencus, Sedulius in uno uolumine"); and Arator and Sedulius appear one after the other in the list of books donated to the Church of Exeter by Leofric (19. *Sedulius boc*/20. *liber Aratoris*); likewise, both Sedulius and Arator appear on an inventory from an unidentified centre, possibly Worcester (s. xi^ex), in double copies (Sedulius, 2/9; Arator 15/26).

62 Juvencus uses the phrase *culmina caeli* in the *Euangeliorum libri*, 3.456 ("Sic uobis faciet genitor, qui culmina caeli"). The phrase is ubiquitous in Aldhelm's verse.

poetic diction, but also a canon of poetic themes and motifs quite different from that familiar to him."[63] It is easy, therefore, to imagine how a stock of ready phrases could be used to facilitate poetic composition in a second language, which is to say that Anglo-Latin poets did resort to simple imitation and repetition, "as much of the conventions and commonplaces of Christian-Latin verse, as of its vocabulary and phraseology."[64] There are nevertheless moments when an Anglo-Latin writer such as Aldhelm borrows more than just a word or phrase from some formulaic word-hoard, but alludes to whole scenes that bring with them thematic significance from their source.

Aldhelm (d. 709 CE)

Aldhelm (c. 640–709) has been called "the best read man of his time," with a "capacious memory for the works of his predecessors."[65] While details of Aldhelm's life are scarce, we do know that he was well educated and that he studied at the famous school of Theodore and Hadrian in Canterbury, probably between 670 and 675,[66] and the extent of his surviving work highlights Aldhelm's interest in poetry, especially. His surviving writings include the *Carmina ecclesiastica*, a series of dedications to various churches; the *Epistola ad Acircium*, a lengthy work to King Aldfrith of Northumbria that contains a metrical treatise on hexameter verse, *De metris*, a hundred riddles that exemplify poetic composition; and a second metrical treatise, *De pedum regulis*, which provides a list of words to fit lines of hexameter verse.[67] Aldhelm also wrote a treatise on virginity in prose and verse, *De uirginitate*, in imitation of the *opus geminatum* established by Sedulius' *Carmen* and *Opus paschale*. Finally, Aldhelm has left an octosyllabic poem, *Carmen rhythmicum*, as well as a dozen or so letters, and these are printed in Ehwald's edition.

The date of Aldhelm's death is recorded in the *Anglo-Saxon Chronicle* under the year 709, but the pervasive influence of his work spans the

---

63 See further Wright, "Imitation of the Poems of Paulinus of Nola in Early Anglo-Latin Verse," 134–51 at 140.

64 Ibid.

65 Orchard, *Poetic Art of Aldhelm*, 281.

66 See further Lapidge and Rosier, *Aldhelm: The Poetic Works*, 1; and Orchard, *Poetic Art of Aldhelm*, 4.

67 Aldhelm's works are collected in Ehwald, ed., *Aldhelmi Opera*. My summary follows Andy Orchard, *Poetic Art of Aldhelm*, 6–7.

Anglo-Saxon period and extends beyond England to the continent in the hands of Christian missionaries.[68]

Scattered Memories of Biblical Epic

Everywhere in his writings, Aldhelm shows knowledge of his prior Latin reading, including the Latin biblical epics. Even a cursory survey of his poetic corpus reveals language and imagery overlapping with episodes from late antique verse. In *Poem 3* of his *Carmina ecclesiastica*, for example, which contains a verse dedication to the Church of St Mary built by Bugga, daughter of Centwine, King of the West-Saxons, there appears a description of the ascension of Christ in terms that are reminiscent of the departure of Elijah in Book 1 of the *Carmen paschale* (1.170–87). Of Jesus, Aldhelm writes, "Inde petit superas meritis splendentibus arces / Angelicis turmis ad caeli culmina ductus" ("from there he sought the higher citadels by his shining merits, borne to the heights of heaven by angelic throngs" (3.14–15). In the *Carmen paschale*, Sedulius describes the departure of Elijah in similar terms, saying, "he was carried to the stars" (*euectus in astra*, 1.179), and Aldhelm's phrase, "ad caeli culmina ductus" (15) is comparable; both poets also use a past participle (*euectus/ductus*). Elijah then "seeks better things" (*Dexteriora petens*, 1.182) in heaven in the same way Jesus "seeks higher citadels" ("inde petit superas ... arces," 14), and both poets use a form of *petere* to describe it ("to seek"). Just as Elijah "shines in merit and name" ("meritoque et nomine fulgens," 1.185), Jesus ascends by way of his own "shining merits" (*meritis splendentibus*, 14). The word *splendentibus*, if inspired by the context of Sedulius, suggests not only "splendid" but "glittering" or "shining," given the fiery way in which Elijah leaves the world (*flammigeris quadrigis*, 179; *curruque corusco*, 181; "fulminei praelucens semita caeli," 184).

In the same poem, shortly after this moment, Aldhelm says that "we are nourished by the body and sacred blood of Christ" ("Corpore nam Christi sacroque cruore nutrimur," 3.76), and in particular, he highlights the golden chalice (*aureus atque calix*, 72) and silver paten of Bugga's new basilica (*argento ... fabricata patena*, 74), which he calls bearers of the "medicine of life" (*medicina uitae*, 75). This last phrase is likely an echo of Avitus, who, at the opening of Book 3 of *Historia spiritalis*, alludes to the salvation of man in the following terms (3.20–2): "Et tamen adueniet tempus, cum

---

68 See further Orchard, *Poetic Art of Aldhelm*, 1–5.

crimina ligni / Per lignum sanet purgetque nouissimus Adam / Materiamque ipsam faciat medicamina uitae" ("And yet there will come a time when a new Adam (Christ) will clean and purge the sins of the tree by the cross, and he makes his body the remedy of life"). Aldhelm takes this image from *Historia spiritalis* and applies it to the body and blood of Christ, which is precisely what Avitus means by *materiam* ("substance"). It is also worth noting that that passage of *Historia spiritalis* is not an unimportant one, but key to the whole poem and linked to the central message of salvation history. It is an important passage and one that draws attention, so it is not surprising that Aldhelm would have known it.

In poem 4 of *Carmina ecclesiastica*, entitled *In duodecim Apostolorum Aris* (*On the Altars of the Twelve Apostles*), Aldhelm provides a series of short but lively tableaux treating each of the twelve apostles. Given his usual sources of inspiration, it is not difficult to imagine where Aldhelm looks for illustrations of these exemplary lives. Sedulius is a master of the short scene and he is Aldhelm's favourite Christian poet. In the context of Paul, Aldhelm versifies the incidents of Acts 28:8, in which the father of Publius suffers from a fever and dysentery. In describing these events, Aldhelm becomes something of a biblical poet himself, and so I include the context of Acts for comparison (4.20–3):

Contigit autem patrem Publii febribus et dysenteria vexatum jacere. Ad quem Paulus intrauit: et cum orasset, et imposuisset ei manus, saluauit eum.[69]

– Acts 28:8 ·

Sic patrem Pupli, quem febris torsit anhela,   20
(Torridus atque calor frigus brumale coquebat
Nec non extales multauit poena pudenda)
Curauit citius Domino tribuente medelam.

[So with God's help he quickly administered a cure to Publius' father, who reeled with a panting fever, as torrid heat and wintry cold burned him up, and an embarrassing ailment afflicted his bowels.]

The language of the Bible survives in the words *Publi* and *febris* ("fever," 20), which in the context of Acts are enough to evoke that scene in

---

69 Acts 28.8: "And it happened that the father of Publius lay sick of a fever, and of a bloody flux. To whom Paul entered in; and when he had prayed, and laid his hands on him, he healed him."

chapter 28. Note that Aldhelm finds no inspiration from Arator's *Historia apostolica* at this point, where only two lines report the same incident (2.1207–8): "Multiplicem dat Paulus opem Publiique parentem / Finitima de clade leuatur" ("Paul gives manifold help to Publius' father and raises him from the brink of death"). The *Carmen paschale*, on the other hand, contains a similar episode in Book 3, where Jesus heals Peter's mother-in-law, who is also suffering from a fever, though not dysentery (*Cp.* 3.33–6):

> Forte Petri ualidae torrebat lampadis aestu
> Febris anhela socrum, dubioque in funere pendens
> Saucia sub gelidis ardebat uita periclis,   35
> Immensusque calor frigus letale coquebat.

> [As it happened, Peter's mother-in-law was being consumed
> By a scorching fever that was like the heat of an intense lamp,
> And hanging on the brink of death, her ailing life burned
> Beneath ice-cold chills, as an intense heat cooked up a lethal cold.]

There is no question that Aldhelm's juxtaposition of hot and cold, "calor frigus brumale coquebat" is based on the phrasing of Sedulius, "calor frigus letale coquebat," not to mention Aldhelm's first words, "febris torsit anhela / Torribus …" (20), which echo "torrebat … febris anhela" (33–4) in the same episode of the *Carmen paschale*.

Elsewhere, in Riddle 88, Aldhelm treats the Basilisk in terms that recall the opening of Avitus' *Historia spiritalis*. In the first line, Aldhelm describes the creature in the following terms (88.1): "Callidior cunctis aura uescentibus aethrae" ("More cunning than all creatures breathing air").[70] The adjective *callidior* gives away the biblical source, being one of the variants describing the serpent's cunning (3:1): "serpens autem erat sapientior (astutior, callidior) omnium bestiarum." What is more, Aldhelm says the serpent "Late per mundum dispersi semina mortis" ("spread the seeds of death broadly throughout the world"). That phrase, *semina mortis* (2), echoes Avitus, who at the opening of *Historia spiritalis* rebukes Adam as the failed first father, "who with the seed of death deprive[d] future generations of life-giving buds" ("qui semine mortis / Tollis succiduae uitalia germina proli"). That "seed of death" is vital to the imagery of man's stricken stalk at the beginning of Avitus' poem, and Aldhelm borrows it,

---

70 The translation here is taken from Juster's translation of the riddles, *Saint Aldhelm's Riddles*, 55.

linking the Basilisk to the devil and apparently blaming the serpent as much as Adam for the Fall of man.

Opening of *Carmen de Virginitate* (1–16)

For the Anglo-Saxons, then, late Antiquity was a font of Christian-poetic inspiration, and the biblical verses of Juvencus, Sedulius, and Arator were enormously influential, as they were held to be more spiritually wholesome than the pagan songs of Vergil and his predecessors.[71] At the opening of Aldhelm's hexameter poem on virginity, there is much to suggest that his characterization of *Omnipotens Deus* ("Almighty God") in lines 1–16 is indebted to similar language in Sedulius' *Carmen paschale* (esp. lines 1.60–78).[72] Ehwald has noted some of these allusions in his edition, but many of the finer points have not been drawn out.[73] Consider the two passages side by side:

Carmen de uirginitate (1–16)		*Carmen paschale* (1.60–78)[74]
Omnipotens genitor mundum dicione gubernans,		Omnipotens aeterne Deus, spes unica mundi,
Lucida stelligeri qui condis culmina caeli,		Qui caeli fabricator ades, qui conditor orbis.
Necnon telluris formans fundamina uerbo,		Qui maris undisonas fluctu surgente procellas
Pallida purpureo pingis qui flore uirecta;		Mergere uicinae prohibes confinia terrae,
Sic quoque fluctiuagi refrenans caerula ponti,	5	Qui solem radiis et lunam cornibus imples
Mergere ne ualeant terrarum litora limphis,		Inque diem ac noctem lumen metiris utrumque,
Sed tumidos frangant fluctus obstacula rupis,		Qui stellas numeras, quarum tu nomina solus,

---

71 For Vergil as the most cited author in Aldhelm's poetry, see further Orchard, *Poetic Art*, 164; and Wright, "Imitation of Paulius of Nola," 141; ultimately, see Manitius, *Zu Aldhelm und Baeda* (1886), 574–9.

72 See also Green, *Latin Epics*, 165–7, who highlights the influence of Ausonius' *Oratio* on Sedulius at this point in the *Carmen paschale*.

73 For the edition of Aldhelm's *Carmen de uirginitate*, see Ehwald, ed., *Aldhelmi Opera*.

74 "Almighty eternal God, single hope of the world, who are the maker of heaven, founder of earth, who keep the wave-crashing winds of the flood-surging sea from drowning the banks of the neighbouring land, who fill the sun with beams and moon with crescent horns, and measure out the light for each day and night, who number the stars, whose names, signs, powers, courses, places, times are known to you alone, who shaped the new land into various forms and gave living limbs to the sluggish earth, who restore men dying from fruit's forbidden sweetness with better food and with the drink of sacred blood dispel the poison poured in by the serpent, who rebuild the human race – those once shut within the ark, buried by the swift force of the foaming flood – from one stalk, so that your mystic strength might show that it is possible, with the cross as protector, to renew in flowing waters what sins of the flesh kill and thereby wash the whole world in one Baptism."

Aruorum gelido qui cultus fonte rigabis
Et segetum glumas nimbosis imbribus auges;
Qui latebras mundi geminato sidere demis: 10
Nempe diem Titan et noctem Cynthia comit;
Piscibus aequoreos qui campos pinguibus ornas
Squamigeras formans in glauco gurgite turmas;
Limpida praepetibus sic complens aera cateruis,
Garrula quae rostris resonantes cantica pipant   15
Atque creatorem diuersa uoce fatentur:[75]

Signa, potestates, cursus, loca, tempora nosti,
Qui diuersa nouam formasti in corpora terram
Torpentique solo uiuentia membra dedisti,
Qui pereuntem hominem uetiti dulcedine pomi
Instauras meliore cibo potuque sacrati
Sanguinis infusum depellis ab angue uenenum,
Qui genus humanum praeter quos clauserat arca
Diluuii rapida spumantis mole sepultum
Vna iterum de stirpe creas, ut mystica uirtus,
Quod carnis delicta necant, hoc praesule ligno
Monstraret liquidas renouari posse per undas,
Totum namque lauans uno baptismate mundum.

The general structural symmetry of these two passages is apparent. Both are built on a series of anaphoric *qui*-clauses that emphasize God's omnipotence over Creation. In the first line of Aldhelm's poem, his apostrophe to *Omnipotens genitor* (1) reflects Sedulius' invocation of *Omnipotens aeterne Deus* in line sixty of the *Carmen paschale*.[76] Aldhelm also situates God's power in relation to the human world (*mundum … gubernans*, 1), just as Sedulius does (*spes unica mundi*, 60).[77] Aldhelm's second line begins with a nod to the corresponding line of the *Carmen paschale* (61), but he makes several changes. First, he adopts the Sedulian focus on the "Founder,"

---

75   The translation is that of Lapidge and Rosier, *Poetic Works*, 103: "Almighty Progenitor, guiding the world by Your rule, Who are the Creator of the shining heights of the star-filled heaven, (Who) also formed the foundations of the earth by Your Word; You Who paint the pale greensward with purple blossom, and restrain the azure surface of the wave-wandering sea so that the shores of the lands are not submerged by water, but rather that obstacles of rocks may break the swollen waves; Who water the crops of the ploughed fields with a cool spring and swell the husks of corn by rain from cloudbursts, Who remove the hiding places of the earth by a two-fold radiance – namely, Titan [i.e., the sun] that adorns the day and Cynthia [i.e., the moon] (that adorns) the night; Who ornament the expanses of ocean with plump fish, forming scaly squadrons in the greyish waters; Who similarly fill the clear air with swift-flying flocks of birds which, chirping with their beaks, pipe chattering songs and proclaim the Creator with their diverse voices."

76   Aldhelm uses the *Omnipotens* epithet in eight other verses of *Carmen de uirginitate*: 506, 679, 1606, 1678, 1761, 1915, 2019, 2107; see also his *Carmen ecclesiastica* 4.1. 36 ("Arbiter omnipotens ad caeli culmina uexit"); and *Enig.* 91.1 ("Omnipotens auctor, nutu qui cuncta creauit"). Note, too, that Aldhelm closely echoes the second verse of the *CdV* on two later occasions in the poem: *CdV* 1445 ("Lucida stelligeri scandentes culmina caeli"); and 2816 ("Limpida stelligeri scandentes culmina caeli").

77   See also line 35 of the *Carmen de uirginitate*: "Quo pater omnipotens per mundum cuncta creauit"; also Riddle 100.7: "Nam Deus ut propria mundum dicione gubernat."

but uses a verbal form of *condo* (*condis*, 2) instead of the nominal *conditor* (61), which appears in the *Carmen paschale*. He then replaces *caeli fabricator* with *culmina caeli*, which is nonetheless a common Sedulian phrase.[78] Aldhelm's second verse is also a golden line, and that is a hallmark of Sedulian style. As Neil Wright has shown, thirty-one of the first 368 verses of the *Carmen paschale* are golden lines,[79] and it makes sense that Aldhelm, who quotes Book 1 of the *Carmen paschale* more than any other part of the poem, would also imitate this point of style. Thus twenty-four of the first 368 verses of the *Carmen de uirginitate* are also golden lines, in addition to another 22 verses which are "near golden," as Andy Orchard defines them, or "closely modelled on the golden line form."[80] The only other poem of the period with as many golden lines is the *Hisperica famina*, a contemporary Hiberno-Latin text that Aldhelm may have known, but whose ultimate model is the *Carmen paschale* anyway, and so Aldhelm owes a debt to Sedulius one way or another.[81]

In verses three and four of *Carmen de uirginitate*, Aldhelm deepens his debt to Sedulius, moving beyond the level of verbatim echoing. As Orchard has said, Aldhelm not only refines inherited diction, making it his own, but "transformed almost everything he transmitted."[82] So his fourth verse is a golden line ("Pallida purpureo pingis qui flore uirecta") that diverges from Sedulius to comment on the creative power of "the Word" (*formans fundamina uerbo*), but this emphasis is not at odds with the focus on God's omnipotence in the *Carmen paschale*.[83] Sedulius himself comments on the

---

78 Note that like his predecessors, Aldhelm places this phrase at the cadence of the line. Cf. Juvencus, *Euangelia*, 3.456 ("Sic uobis faciet genitor, qui culmina caeli"); Sedulius, *Carmen paschale*, 4.94 ("Ille nocens anguis, deiectus culmine caeli"); and Cyprianus, *Heptateuch*, *Gen.* 592 ("Nuntius aetherio descendit culmine caeli"); see also Aldhelm *CdV* 1445 and 2816, as well as *Enig.* 100, which also begins with an apostrophe to God, the Founder, *Conditor* (1), who supports the world "while the hanging heights of broad heaven revolve" ("Pendula dum patuli uertuntur culmina caeli," 3).

79 See Wright, "The *Hisperica Famina* and Caelius Sedulius," 61–76, at 75–6; see also Orchard, *Poetic Art of Aldhelm*, 96–7.

80 Ibid., 97.

81 See further Wright, "The *Hisperica Famina*," 76: "on closer examination they [the sections of *De oratione* and *De gesta re* of B-text] reveal a surprising level of literary borrowing and imitation, principally of the *Carmen paschale* of Sedulius."

82 Orchard, *Poetic Art of Aldhelm*, 281.

83 Aldhelm's focus on "the Word" anticipates his theme later in the preface ("uerbum de uerbo peto," 33).

miraculous power of the Word in Book 1.[84] Moreover, Aldhelm's focus on the Word anticipates his own invocation to the muse at lines 30–1, where he declares, "I shall strive with prayers to move the Thunderer, Who grants us the divine declaration of his gentle Word. I seek the word from the Word" ("Sed potius nitar precibus pulsare Tonantem, / Qui nobis placidi confert oracula uerbi; / Verbum de uerbo peto: hoc psalmista canebat"). Even though Aldhelm appears to digress from lines 62–3 of the *Carmen paschale* at this point in line four, his language suggests otherwise. Specifically, his third and fourth verses form a grammatical unit composed of a present participial phrase (*formans fundamina*) and a medial finite verb in the following line (*pingis*). This is precisely what Sedulius does in lines 62–3 of the *Carmen paschale*, where he uses a present participial phrase (*fluctu surgente*) and a medial finite verb (*prohibes*). What is more, if Aldhelm's choice of *pingis* represents a deliberate alliterative imitation of Sedulius' *prohibes*, the allusion to the *Carmen paschale* represents a degree of virtuosity that can only be appreciated by someone who is very familiar with the earlier poem. Consider, finally, that there is a correspondence in line three of Aldhelm's poem between *telluris fundamina* and *confinia terrae* in line sixty-four of the *Carmen paschale*. Both phrases contain third-declension neuter accusative plural nouns (*fundamina/confinia*) followed by a genitive singular word for "earth" (*telluris/terrae*), which again suggests that Aldhelm is imitating not just the content of the *Carmen paschale* but its very style. There is even a coincidence of alliteration between the two phrases, *fundamina/confinia* and *telluris/terrae*. All this to say, however deliberate Aldhelm's choice of imitative words may be, the consequence of the synonymic phrasing, coupled with the imitative grammar and alliteration, leads the reader's ear to acknowledge aural connections between the two passages. So transformed is the original language and context of the *Carmen paschale*, that readers may not even appreciate why this is such a Sedulian-sounding passage, even if they recognize it to be so.

---

84 *Cp.* (1.144–6): "Vox Domini super extat aquas; uox denique uerbum est. / Verbum Christus adest, geminae qui consona legis / Testamenta regens ueterem patefecit abyssum" ("The voice of God stretches over many waters; in the end, / The voice is the Word and the Word is Christ, who rules / The harmonious Testaments of a twin law and has laid open the old abyss").

In lines five and six of *Carmen de uirginitate*, Aldhelm picks up the thread of the corresponding passage from the *Carmen paschale*, echoing lines 62–3 closely. The links here remove any doubt about Aldhelm's source of inspiration, and he imitates Sedulius' two-line structure of participle (*surgente*, 62) and finite verb (*prohibes*, 63) with *refrenans* (5) and *frangant* (7), including two close verbal echoes in *mergere* (6/64) and *fluctus* (7/62). With Sedulius in mind, he renders the whole of *undisonas fluctu … procellas* (62) with a single compound word, *fluctiuagi* (5), and then ends the line with an unmistakeable Sedulian phrase, *caerula ponti* (5), which he puts at the cadence of the verse, as he does with *culmina caeli* in line two.[85] Both phrases constitute a tri- and disyllabic pair, or a 3 + 2 unit, a combination Aldhelm resorts to frequently.[86] Note, too, that Aldhelm substitutes *confinia terrae* in line sixty-three with *terrarum litora* (6), another variation comparable to the form and meaning of *telluris fundamina* in line two. In light of these correspondences, it is clear that Aldhelm is not simply remembering his earlier Latin reading in a general way but recalling specific passages, to the point where he can emulate Sedulius' style more or less organically.

Following the series of anaphoric "qui" clauses in lines 1–16 of the *Carmen de uirginitate*, Aldhelm turns again to God for inspiration. Grammatically, his invocation of the muse begins with the imperative form, *da* ("give," 17), followed by a purpose clause (17–18): "Da pius auxilium clemens, ut carmine possim / Inclita sanctorum modulari gesta priorum" ("Grant help, merciful, pious [Lord], that I may sing the deeds of former saints in song"). After his own series of anaphoric *qui*-clauses in the *Carmen paschale* (1.60–78), Sedulius likewise begs the help of God with an allusion to Psalm 119, where he uses the imperative *da*, followed by a purpose clause (79–82):

> Pande salutarem paucos quae ducit in urbem
> Angusto mihi calle uiam uerbique lucernam   80
> Da pedibus lucere meis, ut semita uitae
> Ad caulas me ruris agat …

---

85 Sedulius uses the phrase three times in the *Carmen paschale*, always at the cadence (1.136, 2.222, 3.219); Aldhelm likewise uses it three times in the *Carmen de uirginitate* (5, 423, 1736).

86 See Lapidge, *Aldhelm: the Poetic Works*, 21. The alternative for Aldhelm in most other cases is an inversion of this syntax, so, 2+3, as in *fonte rigabis* in line 8.

[Stretch out a road for me along the narrow path that leads but few to the city of salvation, and grant the lantern of your word to light my feet, that the road of life may lead me to the sheepfold in the country ...]

In fact, the whole opening section of the *Carmen paschale* (17–102), which proclaims God's omnipotence and ability to redeem the frail and infirm, sounds a lot like Aldhelm, or rather, Aldhelm sounds a lot like Sedulius, whose first words after his preface are "Hanc constanter opem laesis adhibete medullis" ("Continually grant help to wounded hearts," *Cp.* 1.38). Aldhelm addresses God with the same emphasis: "Auxilium fragili clementer dedere seruo" ("Mercifully grant help to a frail servant," 37). What is more, Aldhelm's emphasis on "the renowned deeds of saints" (*inclita gesta sanctorum*) originates in the opening of *Euangeliorum libri*, where Juvencus resolves to sing of "Christ's life-giving deeds" (*Christi uitalia gesta*, 19), or the beginning of the *Carmen paschale*, where Sedulius heralds "the renowned miracles of Christ" (*Clara miracula Christi*, 1.26). Or perhaps Aldhelm has another Christian poet in mind, Prudentius, and the "renowned deeds of Christ" in the *Cathemerinon* (*gesta Christi insignia*, 9.2). Whatever his precise source or sources, it is clear that Aldhelm is channelling his knowledge of Latin Christian literature, especially Sedulius, whose work he obviously admires.

The Opening Sections of the *Carmen de Virginitate*

Many other allusions to the Latin biblical epics appear in the opening sections of *Carmen de uirginitate*. Some of these are close verbal parallels; others are more subtle reminiscences. The following examples are noteworthy: the reference to the "Thunderer" in line 31 (*Tonantem*), a calling-card of the biblical poets despite its classical origins; Aldhelm's show of disdain for the "unspeakable verses" of pagan Antiquity, "uersibus infandis non umquam dicere dignor" (28), a statement made stereotypical by Juvencus, Sedulius, and Arator, among others;[87] the definition of the Trinity as "simplex" and "triplex" (38–41) is an allusion to the *Carmen paschale* ("Quod simplex triplicet quodque est triplicabile simplet," 1.298);

---

87 Juvencus likewise opposes songs that "bind lies to the deeds of ancient men" ("Quae ueterum gestis hominum mendacia nectunt," *Ev.* 20), and Sedulius rebukes classical poets who "saeua nefandarum renouent contagia rerum" ("renew the savage contagions of unspeakable things," *Cp.* 1.20).

the Prudentian tenor of lines 47–52 and 138–9[88] evokes the mystical gar-
lands and "strophes" of the *Cathemerinon* (3.17–20), a poem that resides
on the edges of the genre;[89] the statement that nothing is "difficult" for
God in line 54 ("Nec tibi difficile"), who "relaxes" the laws of nature
("Qui crebris uicibus naturae iura relaxas"), is a clear allusion to lines 85–7
of the *Carmen paschale* and the central theme of Book 1;[90] and Aldhelm's
adaptation of the miracle of the talking ass from the *Carmen paschale*
(1.160–2) is Sedulian, which he applies to his own meagre talent after the
manner of Sedulius' self-deprecating preface.[91] In general, a pattern begins
to emerge vis-à-vis Sedulius, and it appears that Aldhelm is not simply
incorporating disparate strands of the *Carmen paschale*, but following the
progress of the poem step by step, so that the first two hundred and fifty
lines of *Carmen de uirginitate* track the narrative progress of Book 1 of
the *Carmen paschale*. This level of indebtedness supports the suggestion
that Sedulius is Aldhelm's favourite Christian poet, apart from myriad
other echoes of him in his work.

As if more proof were needed, Aldhelm's exemplary lives of chaste men
and women in *Carmen de uirginitate* reveal further affinities with the
Carmen paschale and the miracle-sequence of Book 1. The group of fifteen Old Testament miracles in Sedulius' poem (1.103–219) and others
elsewhere in the *Carmen paschale* offer brief but saintly images of faithful
disciples, and these provide easy sources of inspiration for Aldhelm and
other Anglo-Latin writers. Specifically, four of his first five stories, those
of Elijah, Elisha, Jeremiah, and Daniel and the three youths (248–90), are

---

88 See *CdV*. 138–9: "Nunc igitur raros decerpant carmina flores / E quis uirgineas ualeant
    fabricare coronas!" ("Now, then, let these songs gather rare flowers from which virgin
    crowns may be made").

89 Prudentius also declares his disdain for the pomp of the pagan muse in the same passage
    ("Sperne, camena, leues hederas," *Cath.*, 3.16).

90 See further *Carmen paschale*, 85–7: "Te duce difficilis non est uia; subditur / Imperiis
    natura tuis, rituque soluto / Transit in aduersas iussu dominante figuras" ("All nature is
    subject to your commands, / and freed of its ritual, / Nature changes to contrary forms
    by your dominating will"). Compare *CdV* (53–4): "Nec tibi difficile prorsus quicquam
    arbitror esse, / Qui crebris uicibus naturae iura relaxas" ("I do not, of course, think
    anything difficult for you, who relax the laws of nature with frequent changes").

91 See further *Cp*. 1.160–2: "Angelicis tremefacta minis adfatur asella / Sessorem per uerba
    suum, linguaque rudenti / Edidit humanas animal pecuale loquellas" ("Frightened by
    angelic threats, an ass addressed / Its rider in words and with braying tongue / [And] the
    barnyard beast made human speech"). Aldhelm adapts this passage to portray himself
    as the lowly ass.

adapted from Sedulius, to fit with Aldhelm's emphasis on chastity. Unlike Sedulius, who focuses more on faith, Aldhelm's rendition of Daniel's story emphasizes purity: "Scriptorum ueterum liquido monumenta testant-ur,/Quod Daniel semper uirgo florescet almus" ("The monuments of ancient writings attest clearly that blessed Daniel ever thrives as a virgin"). Sedulius says nothing about Daniel's chastity, only that he is "the innocent glory of the Hebrews" ("Hebraeumque decus Danihel decernitur insons," 1.214) and "a just man" (*iustus uir*, 215). Aldhelm's description of the three youths in the furnace, on the other hand, emphasizes how they "preserve the rights of chastity" ("Tres pueri partier seruarunt iura pudoris," 368), a point not made by Sedulius. Even so, they overcome the flames of the furnace by means of "faith" in much the way they do in the *Carmen paschale* ("Ardentis fidei restincta est flamma camini," 1.205), despite the fact that Aldhelm gives virginity the power to fight these fires (384–7):

O mirum dictum, pueros quod flamma camini,
Torribus innocuis diro sub carcere coxit,   385
Verum uirginitas spreuit tormenta rogorum
Scintillante fide dum feruent corda uirorum.

[It is incredible to say that the flame of the furnace cooked those youths in a cruel prison of harmless brands; in fact, virginity scorned the torments of that pyre, while the hearts of those young men seethed with scintillating faith.]

Contiguity with Sedulius includes the reference to the furnace itself (*flamma camini*, 384), which is taken from the same scene in the *Carmen paschale* (*flamma camini*, 1.205), as is the image of the furnace as a pyre (*rogus*, 386) which "dares do nothing" against the youths ("Nil audente rogo," *Cp.* 202). Aldhelm's emphasis on the "harmlessness" of the "innocuous brands" (*Torribus innocuis*, 385) is a composite of images taken from Sedulius' fourth Old Testament miracle, the burning bush, where "innocuous flames" (1.127) yield to God's will, as the bush resists the "torrid harm" of the fire ("nec torrida uiuens/Sensit damna frutex"). This last example shows that Aldhelm sometimes draws various scenes together from his broader memory of a source. In this instance, the two episodes are not far apart; the story of the burning bush (1.127–31) is less than a hundred lines from the episode of the three youths (1.195–205) and fits into the same narrative sequence. It is therefore easy to imagine how the two scenes could have come together in Aldhelm's imagination.

The Birth of John the Baptist (414–25)

The transition to New Testament material at line 391 of the *Carmen de uirginitate* offers a final example of how Aldhelm works from his memory of Sedulius. In this scene, Aldhelm treats the birth of John the Baptist, a man filled with the Holy Spirit (*sacro spiramine plenus*, 396), like the three youths or Elijah in the *Carmen paschale* (*Plenus at ille Deo*, 1.176; *spirante Deo*, 1.197). Even though John is a model for virgins (*Virginibus … exempla*, 395), the miraculous account of his birth evokes a different episode in the *Carmen paschale*. Here is Aldhelm's account (414–20):

> Sic fulsit felix uirgo baptista Iohannes
> Nuntius et domini dictus praecursor in aeuum;   415
> Quem genuit sero patris ueneranda propago,
> Quamuis fecundo caruisset corpore mater
> Iamdudum et sterili matrix algesceret aluo.
> Nullus erat potior muliebri uiscere natus
> Ni medicus mundi, proles generata Tonantis;   420

[So the blessed virgin John the Baptist shone, the messenger and spoken precursor of the Lord forever; he was born late from his father's venerable lineage, though his mother had lacked a fruitful womb, a parent long since cold in her sterile belly. No other child born of woman's womb was more important than this except the healer of the world, the begotten son of the Thunderer.]

In these lines, Aldhelm bases his description of John's birth on that of Isaac in the *Carmen paschale*. There is no mistaking the characterization of John's mother and her barren, icy womb ("sterili matrix algesceret aluo," 418) as anything but an allusion to Sara and the birth of another late arrival (1.107–13):

> Saucia iam uetulae marcebant uiscera Sarrae
> Grandaeuo consumpta situ, prolemque negabat
> Frigidus annoso moriens in corpore sanguis:
> Cum seniore uiro gelidi praecordia uentris   110
> In partum tumuere nouum tremebundaque mater
> Algentes onerata sinus, spem gentis opimae
> Edidit et serum suspendit ad ubera natum.

[The stricken womb of poor old Sara had already withered away, consumed by aged neglect, and her icy blood, dying in an old body, kept denying her a child; her husband was older than she was when the insides of her frigid womb swelled to new birth, and the trembling mother, burdened by a cold belly, brought forth the hope of a fertile race, as she held the late-come child to her breast.]

The language of Sedulius makes the connection to Aldhelm clear, and the following baptismal imagery in the *Carmen de uirginitate* with reference to John offers Aldhelm the opportunity to incorporate the central theme of the *Carmen paschale* into his own narrative (421–5):

Idcirco mundus mundum sine labe piacli
Abluit et laticis Christum sub flumine tinxit
Humida fluctiuagi sacrantem caerula ponti
Fontibus et uitreis donantem munera partus,
Dum uetuli redeunt iterum ad cunabula uitae.   425

[So being pure of sin and without fault, he washed a pure man and dipped Christ into the waters of the river, sanctifying the wet, cerulean streams of the wave-wandering sea and giving the gifts of birth in the vitreous springs, as the old return once more to the beginnings of life.]

In effect, Aldhelm combines two passages from Book 1 of the *Carmen paschale* in this scene, both of which involve Baptism. In the first instance and through polyptoton in line 421 – another of Sedulius' favourite rhetorical devices – Aldhelm refers to a clean man (*mundus*) washed by another (*mundum*). The sense of "mundus" is arresting, since the word normally refers "the world," but Aldhelm's choice of diction may be explained by his memory and appropriation of Sedulian language in a scene that describes the Flood as a figural Baptism (1.73–9). At the end of that episode, Sedulius says Christ "washes the whole world in one Baptism" ("Totum namque lauans uno baptismate mundum," 78), and Aldhelm adapts this passage in line 421 of the *Carmen de uirginitate*. Also, the language of the phrase, *caerula ponti* (423), in Aldhelm's poem is Sedulian and appears in the context of Book 1 at the crossing of the Red Sea, another figural moment. As Sedulius says, "the people underwent a rudimentary Baptism," walking into the Red Sea ("Ingrediens populus rude iam baptisma gerebat"). Finally, the "gifts of birth" which Aldhelm mentions at the birth of John the Baptist (*donantem munera partus*, 424) are almost certainly connected to a corresponding passage in the *Carmen paschale* that ends the Old Testament miracle sequence in Book 1, where Sedulius identifies Christ as the source of the mystical gifts in the Old Testament ("His igitur iam sacra tribus dans munera rebus,/Christus erat panis, Christus petra, Christus in undis" ["So, granting his sacred gifts on these three occasions, Christ was the bread, Christ the rock, Christ was in the water," 1.159]). Note the similarity of the Sedulian phrase, *dans munera* and the Aldhelmian, *donantem munera*. In short, Aldhelm's memory of Sedulius is so insistent that he recalls the language and contexts of the poem at every turn, which he is able to incorporate into his own narrative seamlessly.

Bede (c. 673–735 CE)

A Northumbrian monk and scholar, the Venerable Bede spent much of his life reading and writing about the Bible, and like Aldhelm he knew the literature of late Antiquity well. What little we know of Bede's life is reported by the author himself at the end of his most famous work, *Historia Ecclesiastica Gentis Anglorum* (*The Ecclesiastical History of the English People*), where he surveys the course of his life.[92] At the age of seven, Bede entered the twinned monasteries of Wearmouth-Jarrow, where he was ordained as deacon at nineteen and priest at thirty. In his own words (*HE* 5.24), "I have spent all my life in this monastery, applying myself entirely to the study of the Scriptures ... it has always been my delight to learn or to teach or to write."[93] The consequence of that life is an eclectic body of work, including biblical commentaries, metrical treatises, scientific writing, and of course, poetry.[94]

Even a cursory reading of Bede's verse reveals knowledge of the late antique versifiers.[95] In the first of his *Hymns*, *De Opere Sex Dierum*

---

92 For the Latin text of *Historia ecclesiastica*, see further Lapidge, ed., *Beda Storia Degli Inglesi* (*Historia ecclesiastica gentis Anglorum*), 2 vols. See also the earlier edition of Colgrave and Mynors, eds., *Bede's Ecclesiastical History of the English People*, for an English translation. For an introduction to Bede's life, see further Brown, *A Companion to Bede*, 1–16, and his *Bede the Venerable*, 1–23; Ward, *The Venerable Bede*, 1–18; Whiting, "The Life of the Venerable Bede," 1–38.

93 Colgrave and Minors, *Ecclesiastical History*, 566–7.

94 Bede surveys his own work in this same passage, *HE* 5.24.

95 For a discussion of Bede's library and his knowledge of classical and Christian poetry, see further Laistner, "The Library of the Venerable Bede," 237–66.

Primordialium et de Sex Aetatibus Mundi (*On the Work of the First Six Days and the Six Ages of the World*), Bede assumes the role of biblical poet and, despite his attendant focus on the six ages, tracks the language of Genesis observantly.[96] Bede obviously knows that verbal links to the original authenticate the scriptural voice of his poetry, and he could have had no better teacher in this respect than the biblical epics of late Antiquity, which also provide ample language to intimate the mystical sense of the Scriptures. Consider the first stanza of the hymn, accompanied by the text of the Vulgate Genesis for comparison (1.1–4):

> In principio fecit deus caelum et terram. 2 terram autem erat invisibilis et inconposita et tenebrae erant super abyssum et spiritus dei superferebatur super aquas.
>
> – Gen 1:1–2

> Primo Deus caeli globum
> Molemque terrae condidit,
> Terram sed umbris abditam
> Abyssus alta texerat.

> [At first, God created the sphere of heaven and the bulk of the earth, but a deep abyss covered the earth hidden by shadows.]

Even in this short stanza, it is clear that Bede is following the language of the Bible and its narrative sequence of events (the prose is given second): *primo* (1)/*Principio, deus* (1)/*deus, caeli* (1)/*caeli, terrae* (2)/*terram, terram* (3)/*terram, umbris* (3)/*tenebrae, abyssus* (4)/*abyssum*. Bede also uses the epic-resounding *condidit* ("he founded") in place of the verb *fecit* ("he made") or *creauit* ("he created"), a choice Cyprianus and other biblical poets make in the same context. Hence the opening of the *Heptateuch* (*Gen.* 8): "Condidit albentem nebulis nascentibus axem" ("He established the sky, white with nascent clouds," *Gen.* 8).[97] Bede's use of this verb, like Cyprianus, is meant to elevate the literary status of the hymn and to introduce an air of epic grandeur. A few lines later, in stanza six, Bede describes

---

96 The Latin text is from Fraipont, ed., *Bedae Venerabilis Opera*, CCSL 122.

97 The word is ubiquitous in Latin biblical epic, but see, e.g., Avitus' account of creation (1.48–50): "Placet ipsa tuenti / Artifici factura suo laudatque creator / Dispositum pulchro, quem condidit, ordine mundum" ("That creation pleases the onlooker, and the Creator lauds the world he established, which was set in such lovely order").

the Flood and refers to Noah's ark as *arca mystica* ("the mystical ark," 6.2). In so doing, he intimates the underlying baptismal significance of the vessel, and such meaning figures prominently in the work of his favourite Christian poet, Arator. As Arator himself says, he is fond of pursuing whatever mystical sense is given to his heart ("Et res si qua mihi mystica corde datur," *Ad Parth*. 22), and he is just one of the late antique writers who passes this inclination on to Bede.[98]

Other Hymns contain similar links, such as *Hymn 5, Resurrectione Domini* (*The Resurrection of the Lord*), where Bede refers to the redemptive power of the wood of the cross as a remedy for the sins of the original wood (tree) of Paradise (3.1–4):

Crux namque sacratissima
Ligni prioris uulnera
In patre nostri seminis
Sanauit hostem saucians.

[For the most sacred cross cleansed the wounds of the prior wood in the father of our seed, crippling the enemy].

Bede's language in these hymns is often concise and therefore difficult to interpret, and this is a point Michael Lapidge has observed, but the context of Avitus in this case can help to unfold the sense.[99] Specifically, the opening of Book 3 of *Historia spiritalis* alludes to the coming of Christ as a cure for the crimes of man, a scene Aldhelm also echoes in his dedication to the Church of St Mary in *Poem 3* of *Carmina Ecclesiastica*. Here again are Avitus' words (3.20–2): "Et tamen adueniet tempus, cum crimina ligni / Per lignum sanet purgetque nouissimus Adam / Materiamque ipsam faciat medicamina uitae" ("And yet there will come a time when a new Adam [i.e., Christ] will cleanse and purge the sins of the tree by the cross and make his body the remedy of life"). Note the phrase, *crimina ligni* ("sins of the wood/tree," 22), which accords with *ligni prioris uulnera* ("wounds of the former wood/tree," 2) in Bede's hymn; both are references to the crime of taking the forbidden fruit. Like Bede, Avitus also uses the superlative (*nouissimus Adam*, 23) to refer to Christ, just as Bede personifies the cross

---

98 The hymns of Prudentius in the *Cathemerinon* also provide a host of similar mystical interpretations, and these may equally inspire Bede.

99 See further Lapidge, *Anglo-Latin Literature*, vol. 1, 329.

(*crux sacratissima*, 1), and both *Adam* and *crux* "cleanse" the sins of the world in similar terms (*sanauit* (4)/*sanet purgetque* (23). The reference to "the father" (*In patre*, 3) and the "seed" (*nostri seminis*, 3) in Bede's hymn may also be explained by similar references to Adam at the opening of *Historia spiritalis*, where Avitus invokes Adam as "the first father" and blames him for introducing the seed of death into the world (1.7–8): "Ascribam tibi, prime pater, qui semine mortis/Tollis succiduae uitalia germina proli" ("I blame you, first father, who with the seed of death destroy the life-giving buds of future generations"). In the following verse of this same scene, foreshadowing Book 3 of *Historia spiritalis*, Avitus alludes to the redemption of man through Christ, who "has paid for all of this on his own – all that our line has contracted on its stricken stalk" ("Et licet hoc totum Christus persoluerit in se,/Contraxit quantum percussa in stirpe propago," 9–10). This language emphasizes the connection between the birth of sin in Adam and its purgation through Christ. Therefore, even if Avitus is not a direct source for Bede here, there is little doubt that his allusive style is indebted to the poetry of late Antiquity and that that context can help to decode Bede's use of language and imagery.

The Opening of Bede's *Vita Cuthberti*

Following in Aldhelm's footsteps, Bede composed an *opus geminatum* on the life and deeds of St Cuthbert around 705 CE.[100] This poem offers Bede wider scope than do his *Hymns* to exercise his poetic creativity.[101] In a prefatory letter, Bede dedicates his poem to a priest named John, who was preparing for a journey to Rome.[102] It would appear that the poem was

---

100 For a general introduction to the person and life of St Cuthbert, see further Bonner, "Saint Cuthbert: Soul Friend," 24–41; Bonner et al., eds., *St. Cuthbert*; Stranks, *The Life and Death of St. Cuthbert*. For an introduction to the prose life of Cuthbert, see further Eby, "Bringing the Vita to Life," 316–38; and Stancliffe, "Disputed Episcopacy," 7–39.

101 For a discussion of the *opus geminatum* in general, see further Godman, "The Anglo-Latin *opus geminatum* from Aldhelm to Alcuin"; Wieland, "*Geminus Stylus*: Studies in Anglo-Latin Hagiography." For the date of Bede's verse life of Cuthbert, see further Lapidge, *Anglo-Latin Literature*, vol. 1, 340.

102 Yaager, ed., *Bedas metrische Vita sancti Cuthberti*, 56–7: "Vnde tibi uel ad memoriam meae deuotionis uel ad tuae peregrinationis leuamentum beati Cuthberti episcopi, quae nuper uersibus edidi, gesta obtuli" ("So I offer this life of blessed bishop Cuthbert, which I have recently set to verse, to you or in memory of my devotion, or as a way to lighten your journey"). See also, Lapidge, *Anglo-Latin Literature*, vol. 1, 341.

meant to give him some comfort and entertainment along the way.[103] Like Aldhelm's *Carmen de uirginitate*, the verse *uita* of Cuthbert is not biblical epic, though features of its structure and style reflect the work of Arator in particular and that of other late antique poets as well. Michael Lapidge has already linked the allusive nature of the poem to Arator's *Historia apostolica*, which likewise includes prose capitula at the head of each narrative episode, which are then followed by a section of verse and a bit of exegesis.[104] Everywhere, as Lapidge says, "Bede's metrical *uita* is permeated with verbal reminiscences of Arator," but Bede is drawing on his memory of Juvencus and Sedulius as well, especially in his preface (1–10):[105]

> Multa suis Dominus fulgescere lumina saeclis
> Donauit, tetricas humanae noctis ut umbras
> Lustraret diuina poli de culmine flamma.
> Et licet ipse deo natus de lumine Christus
> Lux sit summa, deus sanctos quoque iure lucernae   5
> Ecclesiae rutilare dedit, quibus igne magistro
> Sensibus instet amor, sermonibus aestuet ardor;[106]
> Multifidos uarium lichinos qui sparsit in orbem,
> Vt cunctum noua lux fidei face fusa sub axem
> Omnia sidereis uirtutibus arua repleret.   10

---

103 According to Lapidge, "Bede's Metrical *Vita S. Cuthberti*," in *Anglo-Latin Literature*, vol. 1 (339–55), both the letter and revised rendition of *Vita Cuthberti*, surviving in some twenty manuscripts, is later than the original date of the poem, perhaps by fifteen years, so the earlier version in Besançon, Bibliothèque municipale 186 likely represents the work of a younger Bede in his thirties. If so, that means Bede was revising his earlier writing, as his skill developed. See further Thornbury, *Becoming a Poet*, 192.

104 Lapidge, "Bede's Metrical *Vita*," 351. See, however, Green, *Latin Epics*, 270–3, who echoes others in arguing that the prose capitula were not written by Arator: "This person, working at the latest in the early ninth century, sometimes misread the text, or hastily added elements from his memory of Acts, or even elsewhere." But if the capitula date to the ninth century, that is much later than Bede, who died in 735. On this basis, then, we may push the composition of Arator's capitula back to the eighth century, when Bede would have read a copy of Arator with capitula. Orbán, *Historia apostolica*, 6, n. 35, sets the date of the capitula more broadly, between the seventh and ninth centuries.

105 Ibid. Also, textual citations of Bede's *Vita sancti Cuthberti* are based on Jaager's edition, *Bedas metrische Vita sancti Cuthberti*.

106 Cf. Arator *Epist. Vigilium* (17–18): "Sensibus ardor inest horum celebrare labores, / Quorum uoce fides obtinet orbis iter" ("There is a burning in my heart to celebrate the labours of these men, by whose voice faith finds a path in the world").

[God has given many lights to shine in their own time, that their holy flame might enlighten the dark shadows of human night from the height of heaven. And though Christ himself – born of God's light – is the highest radiance, God has duly given his saints to shine as beacons for the Church, through whom, with fire as their teacher, love instils their hearts and flame burns from their words; that has spread many lamps throughout this flickering world, so that, under each sky, a new light of faith shed by that torch may fill every field with starry power.]

Light imagery abounds in these opening verses and with an enthusiasm worthy of Juvencus.[107] Similar passages appear throughout *Euangeliorum libri*, including the description of Simeon's first sight of Christ (*Ev.* 1.205–6): "En splendida nostros / Lux oculos tua circumstat radiisque renidet" ("Behold, your glittering light besets my eyes and glistens with its beams"). Bede uses no fewer than fifteen different words for "light" and "fire" in this passage – *fulgesco, lumen* × 2, *lustro, flamma, lux* × 3, *lucerna, rutilo, ignis, aestuo, ardor, lychnus, sidereus* – and this deliberate show of rhetorical *uariatio*, in addition to the complexity of the seven-line sentence spanning verses 4–10, represent an earnest effort on his part at poetic virtuosity. Thematically, the contrast between the light of faith and darkness of ignorance and sin represents the enlightenment Christ's disciples have brought into the world.

Aldhelm may also play a role in the opening emphasis on God's agency (*deus, dominus, Christus*), whose "supreme light" ("Lux sit summa," 5) and "starry strength" (*sidereis uirtutibus*, 10) support his disciples. The scope of God's omnipotence in the world (*cunctum … axem / omnia … arua*, 9–10) is also reminiscent of Aldhelm's focus on the creative power of God at the beginning of the *Carmen de uirginitate* ("Omnipotens genitor mundum dicione gubernans," 1ff.), where he channels Sedulius. Bede's favourite biblical poet, however, is not Sedulius but Arator. That is clear from the outset of his *Vita Cuthberti*. Consider the following passage from the beginning of Arator's versifications of Acts (1.119–23):

Spiritus aetherea descendens sanctus ab aula
Irradiat fulgore locum quo stemma beatum   120
Ecclesiae nascentis erat, quibus igne magistro
Imbuit ora calor dictisque fluentibus exit
Linguarum populosa seges.

---

107 See further Röttger, *Studien zur Lichtmotivik Bei Iuvencus*, 122.

[The Holy Spirit, descending from the ethereal palace, lit up that blessed place with radiance, where the origin of the nascent Church was, for whom [apostles], with fire as their teacher, heat imbued their mouths and a populous crop of tongues left them with fluent speech.]

The similarity to Bede's Latin at the opening of *Vita Cuthberti* is striking, which contains the same emphasis on rhetorical variation and numerous words for "light" – *irradio, fulgor, ignis, calor* – as well as a close verbal parallel between Bede's sixth line, "Ecclesiae rutilare dedit, quibus igne magistro," and line 121 of Arator's poem: "Ecclesiae nascentis erat, quibus igne magistro." The kinship of diction and context suggests strongly that Bede is borrowing directly from Arator and, like Aldhelm, is doing so beyond the level of precise verbal echoing.

Line eleven begins with another echo of Arator (*Petri Paulique*, 2.1233), but the mid section of Bede's preface draws more heavily on his memory of Juvencus, and lines 13–24 in particular suggest a close affinity to that anonymous preface that heads up *Euangeliorum libri*. The brief eight-line description of the apostles there is thought not to be the work of Juvencus, on the basis of style, but Bede probably did not question that it was, especially since manuscripts identify it as *PRAEFATIO IVVENCI*.[108] In style and subject matter, the simple, passing allusions to the four apostles offers Bede an entrance into his own narrative, and his adaptation of the Juvencan poem suggests not some vague reminiscence of the genre but a specific memory of that particular text. Consider the two passages side by side:

Euangeliorum libri (praef. 1–8)	*Vita Cuthberti* (13–24)
Mattheus instituit uirtutum tramite mores	Ast Asiae lucem uerbi serit ore Johannes,
Et bene uiuendi iusto dedit ordine leges.	Hauserat e domini quae pectore mystica ructans.
Marcus amat terras inter caelumque uolare	Bartholomaeus eoa uolat per regna triumphans, 15
Et uehemens aquila stricto secat omnia lapsu.	Indomitosque armis lingua domat inclitus Indos.
Lucas uberius describit praelia Christi, 5	Tu quoque Niliacos componens, Marce, furores,
Iure sacer uitulus, quia uatum munia fatur.	Sicca euangelicis satias de nubibus arua.
Ioannes fremit ore leo, similis rugienti	Affrica Cypriani dictis meritisque refulget,

---

108 See further Huemer's edition, *Euangeliorum Libri*, just above p. 1 (the page itself is
unnumbered).

Intonat aeternae pandens mysteria uitae.[109]   Spernere delicias fuso qui sanguine suasit.   20
Pictauis Hilario multum radiata magistro
Discutit errorum uera iam luce tenebras.
Constantinopolim Chrysostomus ille Joannes.
Aurato nitidae lustrat fulgore loquelae.[110]

As with Aldhelm's adaptation of Sedulius at the opening of *Carmen de uirginitate*, the above passages involves similar subject matter, in this case the evangelical efforts of faithful Christians. Specific verbal parallels begin with the phrase, "serit ore Ioannes," in line 13 of the *Vita Cuthberti*, which echoes "Ioannes fremit ore" in line 7 of the Juvencan poem. "John" is the subject in both cases and each phrase is composed of a disyllabic finite verb in the present tense (*serit/fremit*), followed by verbatim use of the word *ore* in the ablative. The difference is that John "roars from his mouth" in the Juvencan poem and "sows light with it" in Bede's.[111] John literally "belches out" the mysteries of the Faith in Bede's narrative (*pectore mystica ructat*, 14), which appears to be an odd reference to John 13.23, but the choice of language is more likely due to the characterization of John as a lion in

---

109 "Matthew taught morals by a path of virtues / And gave laws for living well in due order. / Mark loves to fly between the earth and sky, / And, a soaring eagle, clips all in his strict flight. / Luke describes more fully the battles of Christ. / A sacred calf by right, since he speaks the office of the prophets. / John, the lion, roars from his mouth, booms like thunder, / Revealing the mysteries of eternal life."

110 "And in Asia John sows the light of the word with his lips [lit. mouth], belching out the mysteries he had imbibed at the Lord's breast. Bartholomew flies, triumphant, through the eastern kingdoms, and conquers the Indians with his words [lit. tongue], renowned for their arms. You too, Mark, calming the savagery of the Nile, water the dry lands with your evangelical rain-clouds. Africa beams by the words and merits of Cyprian, who, by shedding blood, persuaded us to shun pleasure. Poitiers, lit much with Hilary as its teacher, now scatters the shadow of sin with true light. John Chrysostom enlightens Constantinople with the golden brilliance of his polished speech." See further Steen, *Verse and Virtuosity*, 22–8, whose translation I have adapted and who offers a discussion on the rhetorical devices of this passage, several of which Steen attributes to late antique biblical epic.

111 The agrarian imagery in Bede's poem, the idea that the light of faith is sown or scattered throughout the world, appears persistently in Alcuin's verse life of Willibrord as well, who says, for example, "sparsit euangelicae radios per pectoral lucis" ("he spread beams of evangelic light throughout their breasts," ii.5). Moments earlier, Alcuin also refers specifically to "spreading the seeds of celestial life" (i.9–10): "Semina perpetuae cupiens caelestia uitae / Spargere, qua rarus fuerat prius accola uerbi" ("wishing to spread the seeds of perpetual life, where the inhabitant of the Word was rare before").

the Juvencan poem, where he "intones the mysteries of life" (*intonat ... mysteria uitae*, 8), as if "roaring" or "bellowing" (*leo, similis rugienti*, 7). Bede may therefore choose *ructat* as an alliterating counterpart to *rugienti*, a move that coincides with Aldhelm's *modus operandi* vis-à-vis his source in the *Carmen de uirginitate*.

In line fifteen, Bede describes Bartholomew as "flying triumphantly through the kingdoms of the world" ("Bartholomaeus Eoa uolat per regna triumphans," 15). Why is Bartholomew "flying"? Again, the reason is likely the description of Mark in the Juvencan poem, where his anamorphic form, the mighty eagle (*uehemens aquila*), "loves to fly between heaven and earth" (*Marcus amat terras inter caelumque uolare*, 3–4). In this case, Bede retains *uolare* as evidence of his source and condenses *terras inter caelumque* to *per regna*, exchanging *uehemens*, a third-declension adjective, for a similar-sounding present participle, *triumphans*. The result is a Juvencan-sounding passage that bears the stamp of Bede's renovating ingenuity. When he comes to St Cuthbert in line twenty-nine of his preface, Bede says that he "taught the English how to follow in his steps and ascend to the heights" ("Scandere celsas suis docuit iam passibus Anglos," 29). With the same emphasis, Juvencus says that "Matthew established morals on a path of virtue" ("Mattheus instituit uirtutum tramite mores, 1), leading Christians along the road to heaven. This is precisely what Cuthbert does, teaching Christians how to live faithfully on their journey towards salvation.

At the closing of his preface, Bede all but acknowledges his debt to Juvencus and the wider tradition of biblical epic. It is no coincidence that he writes a thirty-eight-line preface of the same style and scope as that of *Euangeliorum libri* or that he alludes to the language of Juvencus several times. Bede is doing exactly what Aldhelm did before him and what Alcuin will do in the next century, that is, looking for inspiration among the best, most suitable models at his disposal, the very works that played a role in his own education and the same works he read, re-read and recommended to others throughout his life. This particular moment, the invocation of "the muse," aims to situate *Vita Cuthberti* within the tradition of biblical epic, and Bede draws upon his knowledge of Juvencus and Arator to align his life of Cuthbert with the prestige of the earlier genre. A reading of these authors in the same context puts this debt out of doubt:

1. *Euangeliorum libri* (*praef.* 23–7):

Tunc, cum flammiuoma descendet nube coruscans   [...Then, when he descends, shining in flame-
Iudex, altithroni genitoris gloria, Christus.   spewing cloud, the Judge, the Glory of the

Ergo age! sanctificus adsit mihi carminis auctor   25
Spiritus, et puro mentem riget amne canentis
Dulcis Jordanis, ut Christo digna loquamur.

High-Throned Creator, Christ. So come,
Holy Spirit! Be the author of my song and dip
My heart into the pure streams of sweet-singing
Jordan, that I may speak things worthy of Christ.]

2. *Historia apostolica* (1.223–7):

    … post missus ab astris
Nescia uerba uiris facundus detulit ignis.
Ne quid inexpertum studio meditemur inani,   225
Spiritus alme, ueni! Sine te non diceris umquam;
Munera da linguae qui das in munere linguas.

[…After the fluent (Spirit) was sent from
the stars, flames brought down words
unknown to men. Come nourishing
Spirit, that nothing may be
judged unskilled in vain attempt!
Grant your gifts to this tongue, you who
grant tongues by your gift.
Without you, you cannot be called;]

3. *Vita Cuthberti* (*praef.* 35–8):

Tu, rogo, summe, iuua, donorum spiritus auctor,   35
Te sine nam digne fari tua gratia nescit;
Flammiuomisque soles dare qui noua famina linguis,
Munera da uerbi linguae tua dona canentis.

[You, I beg, Highest Spirit, Author of
gifts, help me: for without you, your grace
cannot be worthily told. You who are
used to giving new speech to flame-
spewing tongues, grant the gifts of the word
to me, the tongue to sing your blessings.]

Note that Bede adopts the unmistakable compound *flammiuoma* from the preface to *Euangeliorum libri* (23), a word that appears nowhere else in verse and so effectively announces his debt to Juvencus. In *Euangeliorum libri*, this word engulfs the cloud that carries Christ to earth at Judgment Day. That scene is also evocative of Vulcan's descent to earth in the *Aeneid* (*Aen.* 8.423), but the fiery language here aims to raise the poetry to biblical epic proportions. Bede's invocation of the Holy Spirit, *donorum spiritus auctor* (35–7), also coincides with that of Juvencus, *carminis auctor spiritus* (25–6), and both expressions appear in the same place at the end of the preface. The difference of *donorum* in Bede simply redirects the emphasis towards the "gifts of speech" and the praise of Cuthbert instead of Christ. Juvencus aspires to sing things worthy of Christ ("ut Christo digna loquamur," 27), and Bede says much the same thing with his words, *digne fari* ("to speak worthily," 36), a phrase he almost certainly adapts from the final words of Juvencus' preface (*ut Christo digna loquamur*, 27). Moreover, the words *dona canentis* (38), are probably based on the phrase *amne canentis* (26) in the same passage at the end of the preface to Juvencus' poem, where they describe the "sweet-singing waters" of the Jordan. In short,

Bede is borrowing and adapting several Juvencan phrases in this passage – all of them from the preface to *Euangeliorum libri* – in order to align his work with the prestige of the earlier tradition.

His choice of *donum* ("gift," 35, 38) and *munus* ("gift," 38) represents a fusion of language and themes from Juvencus and Arator. In particular, lines 36–8 of Bede's preface are a composite of lines 226–7 of Arator's cry for the "gifts of the tongue" in his preface to *Historia apostolica* (*munera da linguae*, 227), which he echoes verbatim (*munera da linguae*, 38), though even these words find a source in Juvencus (*munera linguae*, 2.420). Bede also borrows from Arator the pun on "spiritus," which means both "breath" and "spirit," without which one cannot speak. Arator says, "Sine te non diceris umquam" ("without you, you cannot be called," 226), and Bede echoes him closely (36): "Te sine nam digne fari tua gratia nescit" (36). Jan Ziolkowsky writes that

> Medieval poets had at least three compelling reasons for connecting the Holy Spirit with inspiration: first, because the *Spiritus Sanctus* was easily coordinated with the widespread conception of in*spir*ation as a breathing that comes upon a poet; second, because the Holy Spirit was associated with an intensely verbal form of spiritual inspiration; and third, because the Holy Spirit had been shown repeatedly in the Bible to be capable of filling men with the powers of poetry and prophecy.[112]

But a fourth reason, perhaps the most compelling one for Bede, is that he connects the Holy Spirit with inspiration because Arator does. He is not so much concerned with the significance of the Holy Spirit in the process of inspiration as the legacy of the words themselves in the tradition of great Christian poetry. Knowing Juvencus well and many other Christian poets, Bede understands the significant role of the Holy Spirit in place of the pagan muse as an impulse for creativity. But his choice of words here is guided more by a desire to emulate Arator himself, out of affection for his work and knowledge that doing so will promote his own stature as a poet.

Miracles in *Vita Cuthberti*

In the *Carmen de uirginitate*, Aldhelm echoes Sedulius at every turn, and he adapts scenes from the *Carmen paschale* for characterizations of his model virgins. At times, these allusions constitute verbatim echoes; at

---

112 Ziolkowsky, "Classical Influences," 25.

others, the borrowing is more subtle, owing to innate knowledge of an earlier work. The same is true for Bede, who knows Sedulius well (though not as well as Aldhelm does) and for whom the *Carmen paschale* is a source of inspiration for some of the miraculous deeds of Cuthbert.[113] Michael Lapidge has made a strong case for the influence of Arator on *Vita Cuthberti*, and it is clear that Bede prefers Arator to Sedulius. That being said, while Arator provides the framework of the poem – the prose capitula and exegetical reflections that bookend the events of Cuthbert's life – Sedulius offers additional support.[114] For one, Bede, like Aldhelm, appears to recall particular episodes of the *Carmen paschale* and combine them in his life of Cuthbert (171–84):

> Diuinis horam dum sacrat laudibus almus,
> Cernit equum subito ipsius decerpere morsu
> Tecta casae, fenique fluunt in fasce cadentis
> Missa pio iuueni summo conuiuia dono,
> Qualia siccato meruisti gramine quondam,   175
> Flammeus aetherias, uates, qui scandis ad auras.
> Ergo sacer calidi panis carnisque superna
> Iam dape pastus, agit grates positisque procellis
> Carpit iter gaudens, Christo comitante, serenum.
>
> VII
>
> Quomodo angelum hospitio suscipiens dum panem quaerit ministrare
>   terrenum, caelesti ab eodem remunerari meruerit.
> Hinc maiora petens monachis Hrypensibus almus   180
> Corpore, mente, habitu, factisque adiungitur et mox
> Ponitur hospitibus famulus …[115]

---

113 On the credibility of the miracles in *Vita Cuthberti*, see further Berlin, "Bede's Miracle Stories," 434–43.

114 See further Lapidge, "Bede's Metrical *Vita S. Cuthberti*," in *Anglo-Latin Literature*, vol. 1, 339–55, esp. 351–5.

115 "While that nurturing man was devoting the hour to the divine praises [of God], he suddenly saw his horse biting a morsel out of the walls of the building, and, in a bundle of falling hay, a banquet sent as a gift from on high to the pious youth flowed out, which food you once earned on that arid grass, O prophet, who scaled the ethereal airs in flame. Therefore, that holy man, now fed on that supernal feast of warm bread and meat, gave thanks in the wake of the storm, [and] rejoicing strikes a shining road with Christ as his companion. *Chapter VII: How accepting an angel into his hospitality, as he sought to serve earthly bread to him, he deserved to be rewarded by that same celestial being.* From here seeking greater things that nurturing man was joined to the monks of Ripon in body, mind, dress, and deeds, and soon is placed as servant to guests."

This episode, which Lapidge discusses in the context of the Besançon version of Cuthbert's life, "occurs in chapter six, where Cuthbert seeks shelter from a rainstorm in a shippon. He ties his horse to the wall and sets about praying; and the horse, biting into the thatched roof, dislodges a warm loaf of bread miraculously hidden there."[116] The language of Bede's Latin is allusive and difficult, not just in terms of the literal narrative, but the literary allusions underlying the scene. If Bede intends his audience to appreciate these references, his readership must be very familiar indeed with biblical epic. Even Jaager, who edited the poem, appears to overlook the fullness of Bede's debt to Sedulius here.

This particular chapter of Cuthbert's life finds a source in the anonymous prose *uita* of Cuthbert, but the language of the poetry shows a debt to Sedulius as well.[117] The whole section moves from Bede's memory of Elijah's fiery ascent to heaven in Book 1 of the *Carmen paschale*, which is based on 1 Kings 17 of the Bible. Bede alludes directly to Sedulius in lines 175–6 of the *Vita*, when he says, "you once earned that kind of food on the dry grass, prophet, you who scaled the ethereal airs in flame" ("Flammeus aetherias, uates, qui scandis ad auras"). This is an allusion to Elijah in 1.179 of the *Carmen paschale*, who is "carried to the stars in a flame-borne chariot" ("Aurea flammigeris euectus in astra quadrigis"). In the *Carmen paschale*, Elijah is fed in the wilderness by heaven-sent ravens, who fetch bread and meat, and it would seem that the *morsu* ("bite") that the horse takes from the side of the building in *Vita Cuthberti* spurs a memory for Bede of the *morsibus* ("bites of food") that the ravens offer to Elijah in the wild ("Tradidit inlaesam ieiunis morsibus escam," ["they handed over food unharmed in tiny bites"], 1.173). For Bede, the isolation of Cuthbert and his hunger leads to a recollection of Elijah in the *Carmen paschale*, so that the "banquets" sent to Cuthbert from heaven, *conuiuia* (173) – elaborate for a feast of bread – are connected to the central theme of the *Carmen paschale*, which is the Eucharistic meal of Christ's body and blood. These gifts of bread in the *Vita Cuthberti* thus coincide with the figural significance of food in the *Carmen paschale*, including the *dapes* here ("sacrificial feast or meal," 178), a word of special significance to Sedulius from the

---

116 Lapidge, *Anglo-Latin*, vol. 1, 341. See also Rambridge, "Alcuin, Willibrord and the Cultivation of Faith," 15–32, esp. 21.

117 See further Lapidge, *Anglo-Latin Literature*, vol. 1, 339. Lapidge cites the following chapters as unique to the verse life and probably made aware to Bede by oral report: 3, 5, 17, 20, 25, 33, 34, 39, 42, 44, 45, and 46.

beginning of his poem (*Cp. praef.* 1–3): "Paschales quicumque dapes conuiua requiris / Dignatus nostris accubitare toris, / Pone supercilium si te cognoscis amicum" ("You who seek this paschal banquet as a guest, put aside your pride, if you think yourself a friend").

This is not the only link to the *Carmen paschale* in this scene. Apart from the obvious allusion to Elijah in lines 175–6 and the figural nature of the bread, Bede borrows from Sedulius the reference to Elijah's worth and the manner of his departure. In Book 1 of the *Carmen paschale*, Sedulius makes much of worthiness according to one's "merits" (*meritis*). It is a word he emphasizes in his first miracle, where Enoch is "first from the chaos with long-lived merits" ("Primus abusque chao meritis uiuacibus Enoch," 1.103), and Sedulius continues to emphasize this virtue in the person of Elisha, who is "worthy to follow [Elijah] according his own merits" ("Plura dedit meritisque suis succedere dignum," 1.177) and in the context of Elijah himself, who "shines in merit and name" ("meritoque et nomine fulgens," 1. 185). This insistence on "merit" almost certainly leads Bede to use *meruisti* in line 175 of the *Vita Cuthberti*, which betrays a further debt to Sedulius.

In the end, when the storm passes and Cuthbert is able to venture out into the weather, he strikes a bright (or cheerful) path in the dawn of the new day ("Carpit iter gaudens, Christo comitante, serenum," 179). Here is yet another reference to Elijah, whose path is likewise bright ("Sidereum penetrauit iter" ["he struck a starry road"], 1.181]), and like Elijah, who "seeks greater things" in heaven ("Dexteriora petens," *Cp.*, 1.182), Cuthbert heads to Ripon in search of "greater things" there ("Hinc maiora petens," 180). In this, it is clear that Bede continues his train of thought on the departure of Elijah right into the next chapter of Cuthbert's life, showing that the whole episode in chapter 6 of Bede's versified *vita* is crafted not according to a mechanical recollection of earlier Latin poetry, but by a natural and organic memory of something he had read. The episode is proof that much remains to be said about the ways in which medieval poets incorporated their prior reading into their own compositions. Even here, where the allusion to Sedulius is clear in line 176, the language of that allusion is different from that of the original context, showing that the evidence of verbatim echoing can only tell part of the story.

Alcuin (735–804 CE)

Like Bede and Aldhelm, Alcuin of York (c. 735–804) was the product of an education that promoted the study of Christian poetry, and his surviving writings show that he is part of the same Anglo-Latin pedigree.[118] Unlike Bede, however, who seldom ventured far from the cloister, Alcuin spent much of his life travelling.[119] During his early education under his friend and mentor, Ælbert, future Archbishop of York (773–8), Alcuin journeyed to the continent on several occasions and mingled there with the social and intellectual elite of his time. None of these encounters was more consequential than those with Emperor Charlemagne, who invited Alcuin to join his Frankish court after a meeting in Parma in 781.[120] Alcuin accepted that offer and left England some time thereafter, returning only twice in his lifetime (786 and 790–3). In the years that followed, Alcuin became a leading scholar in the Carolingian Renaissance, directing Charlemagne's palace school, and retiring to Tours in 796 as abbot of St Martin's. He died there in 804.[121]

Before leaving England, Alcuin was master of the school at York and keeper of its library.[122] That library contained a wealth of writings from England and the continent, and Alcuin names several of them in his York poem, including the works of the most famous biblical versifiers (1551–2): "Quid quoque Sedulius, uel quid canit ipse Iuuencus, / Alcimus et Clemens, Prosper, Paulinus, Arator, / Quid Fortunatus, uel quid Lactantius edunt" ("... what Sedulius or Juvencus himself sings, Alcimus and Clemens, Prosper, Paulinus, Arator, what Fortunatus or Lactantius relate").[123] A careful reading of Alcuin's poetry reveals a debt to each one of these poets, and when Alcuin invokes Christ at the opening of his York poem (*Christe deus*, 1), he is responding in one way or another to the biblical epics of late Antiquity, beginning with Juvencus' *Euangeliorum*

---

118   For an overview of Alcuin's poetic oeuvre, see further Stella, "Alkuins Dichtung," 107–28. For a more general assessment of his work, see Bullough, "Alcuin's Cultural Influence," 1–26.

119   For a brief biography of Alcuin, on which this section is based, see further Godman, *Alcuin: Bishops, Kings, and Saints*, xxxv–ix. For Alcuin's tutelage under Ælbert and his travels with him, see further Alcuin's *Epitaphium Ælberti*, MGH PLAC 1, 206–7, which is dedicated to his teacher.

120   Godman, *Bishops, Kings, and Saints*, xxxvii, puts Alcuin's date of departure at 781 or early in 782. See, however, Bullough, *Alcuin: Achievement and Reputation*, 336–46 and esp. 337, who puts the date closer to 786.

121   Ibid., 18.

122   See Story, *Carolingian Connections*, 5; Godman, *Alcuin: Bishops, Kings, and Saints*, xxxvi. For a summary of Alcuin's writings, see further Lapidge, *Anglo-Latin Literature 600–899*, 21–4.

123   See further Godman, *Alcuin: Bishops, Kings, and Saints*, lxxi. The reference to "Clemens" is to Prudentius.

libri (*Ev. Praef.* 25–7): "Ergo age! sanctificus adsit mihi carminis auctor/Spiritus, et puro mentem riget amne canentis/Dulcis Jordanis, ut Christo digna loquamur" ("Therefore come, Holy Spirit! Be the author of my song and dip my heart into the pure streams of sweet-singing Jordan, that I may speak things worthy of Christ"). In the lines that follow his invocation, Alcuin begs the Lord for the gifts of the tongue and channels Arator in doing so (3–4): "unica lingua Dei, donorum tu dator alme;/munera da mentis, fragili da verba poetae" ("only voice of God, kindly bestower of gifts,/grant inspiration, grant words to this feeble poet"). Compare Arator's plea in *Historia apostolica* (1.226–7): "Spiritus alme, ueni! Sine te non diceris umquam;/Munera da linguae qui das in munere linguas" ("Come, nourishing Spirit! Without you, you cannot ever be called; grant the gifts of the tongue, you who grant tongues as a gift!"). It may also be that Alcuin is echoing Bede and the opening of his verse *Life of Cuthbert*, which is likewise indebted to Arator.

We know, then, that Alcuin promotes and imitates the Christian poetry of late Antiquity and that he admires Vergil as much as Juvencus does, even if his attitude towards the classics is at times ambiguous. Gernot Wieland has highlighted Alcuin's letter to Archbishop Ricbod of Treves, in which the poet complains of not having heard from his friend in a year.[124] He blames Vergil and laments, "Would that the four gospels and not the twelve of Aeneas filled your heart ("Utinam euangelia quattuor, non Aeneadis duodecim, pecus compleat tuum").[125] Apparently, a fondness for epic poetry was distracting Ricbod from his more important duties, including the one to his friend.

In any event, Alcuin appears to change his tune elsewhere, when he calls Vergil "propheta" and "praeclarus uates." He also refers to classical literature nostalgically in many of his letters and poems, and uses a classical tag for his own signature, "Flaccus."[126] "All of this," says Wieland, "adds up to praise for Vergil on the one hand, condemnation on the other," but while Alcuin may seem to contradict himself, it may also be that he is showing the two sides of his public face: one for the Church, to frown on pagan verse, and one for the court, to flaunt his erudition.[127]

---

124 See further Wieland, "Alcuin's Ambiguous Attitude Towards the Classics," 84–95. See also Alberi, "'The Better Paths of Wisdom'," 896–910, esp. 907, which mentions "Ricbod's misdirected *amor saeculi*." See also Springer, "The Biblical Epic," 119.

125 Ibid. The letter itself can be found in Dümmler, ed., MGH Epistulae 4:39, letter 13.

126 Wieland, "Alcuin's Ambiguous Attitude," 85–6.

127 Ibid., 86 and 88.

Biblical epic offers something of a solution to this problem, being "classical" without being too "pagan," and as such suitable devotional reading. Alcuin's own student, Hrabanus Maurus (c. 776–856), recommends biblical epic in his *De institutione clericorum*, and while acknowledging its pagan heritage, he argues that biblical verse is the product of men who were themselves teachers of the gospels (*euangelici uiri*) and eager to please God ("Deo placere per id satagerunt").[128] Their poetry, he says, should not be rejected, "non est spernenda," but learned thoroughly as a path to greater faith (*perdiscenda*). Hrabanus' admiration for Christian poetry is no doubt owing in part to the influence of Alcuin, who introduced his continental students to the virtues of biblical epic, including the writers he mentions in his York poem.

Scattered Echoes

Other evidence of Classical and Christian poetry can be found especially in Alcuin's longer poems.[129] His 240-line narrative on the sack of Lindisfarne, which was attacked in 793 by the Vikings, draws heavily on his knowledge of earlier Christian verse as a way to articulate the vicissitudes of life and the need for constant prayer.[130] Alcuin opens with a reference to Adam and the "various calamities" (*per uarios casus*) man has had to endure since his expulsion from Eden. Apparently, the sack of Lindisfarne was meant to be seen as one such tragedy, and Alcuin offers the context of man's long mortal suffering as a source of comfort and perspective to the monks of Lindisfarne. In so doing, he channels several of his favourite poets (1–5):

> Postquam primus homo paradisi liquerat hortos,
>   Et miseras terras exul adibat inops,
> Exilioque graui poenas cum prole luebat,
>   Perfidiae quoniam furta maligna gerit,
> Per uarios casus mortalis uita cucurrit,   5
>   Diuersosque dies omnis habebat homo.

---

128 *De institutione clericorum* of Hrabanus Maurus appears in *PL* 107, col. 0293–0420A.

129 For the most part, the short poems of Alcuin contain few references to the biblical epics, probably because they are mainly bursts of praise directed at various individuals.

130 The text here is that of Dümmler, ed., *Poetae Latini Aevi Carolini* 1, MGH, 229–35.

[After the first man gave up the gardens of Paradise, and ventured out into the wretched lands, a destitute exile, and paid the price for his grim banishment along with his offspring – because he carries that spiteful scheme of faithlessness – mortal life has run into various calamities, and each man has unpredictable days.]

In his 1881 edition of this poem, Ernst Dümmler offers Vergil's *Aeneid* (1.204) as a source for the phrase *per uarios casus* ("into various calamities," 5) and that is likely, ultimately. *Historia spiritalis* offers a possible intermediary source, however, with similar language in the same context. The beginning of *Historia spiritalis* has several points in common with Alcuin's language here (1.1–2 and 7): "Quidquid agit uarios humana in gente labores, / Vnde breuem carpunt mortalia tempora uitam ... Ascribam tibi, prime pater" ("Whatever brings about various hardships on the human race, from which mortal seasons pluck brief life ... I blame on you, first father"). Like Alcuin, Avitus singles out Adam, "the first father" (*prime pater*, 7) as the source of the "various hardships" (*uarios ... labores*, 1) that humankind has had to suffer since the Fall, and Alcuin's language is comparable, who refers to Adam as "the first man" (*primus homo*, 1) and the cause of "the various calamities" (*uarios casus*, 5) of life since then. Both poets single out "mortal life" (*mortalis uita*, 5, and "breuem ... mortalia tempora uitam," 2) as the most significant consequence of man's disobedience, and both promote Christ as source of consolation.

Five lines later, Alcuin adapts Juvencus, when he says that "No one holds guaranteed happiness for himself forever and "Nothing is eternal under heaven's high axis" ("Nemo sibi semper gaudia certa tenet. / Nil manet aeternum, celso sub cardine caeli," 10–11). With these words, Alcuin echoes the preface to *Euangeliorum libri* (1): "Inmortale nihil mundi conpage tenetur" ("Nothing in the structure of the world is immortal"). Offering further proof of the impermanence of the world, Alcuin highlights the fall of several empires, including Babylon, Persia, and Rome (9.37–8): "... Roma, caput mundi, mundi decus, aurea Roma, / Nunc remanet tantum saeua ruina tibi" ("Rome, head of the world, glory of earth, golden Rome, only savage ruin now remains for you"). The reference to "golden Rome" is a verbatim echo of Juvencus' preface (1–2): "Inmortale nihil mundi conpage tenetur / Non orbis, non regna hominum, non aurea Roma" ("Nothing in this world's structure is immortal: not the earth, not the kingdoms of men, not golden Rome").

Alcuin then pursues the theme of worldly transience and urges devotion to God as the only sure path to salvation from mortal suffering. In this context, he reviews the lives of several famous men who have triumphed by their merits, including Moses and "Ezekiah, king of a pestilent people, to whom benevolent God added fifteen years" ("Ezechiae regis pestiferi populi / Huic quoque ter quinos clemens deus addidit annos," 9.162–3). The biblical souce of this allusion is 2 Kings 20:1–6, but Alcuin's direct source is more likely Book 1 of the *Carmen paschale*, where Sedulius treats the same episode in similar terms (1.88–9): "Vltima labentis miseratus tempora lucis / Ter quinos quondam regi Deus addidit annos" ("Pitying the final hours of his fading light, / God once gave fifteen more years to a king"). The correspondence between line 163 of Alcuin's poem and eighty-nine of the *Carmen paschale* is too close to be coincidence, and no doubt the exemplary lives in Book 1 of the *Carmen paschale* inspire this echo. Together, these three allusions provide some evidence for how Alcuin incorporates his memory of late antique verse into his Anglo-Latin poetry.

Alcuin's Life of Willibrord (1–12)

Like Bede and Aldhelm, who must have felt it had been done by Juvencus, Sedulius, and Arator, Alcuin did not produce a versification of the Bible. Instead, like them, he wrote poetry in the style of late antique and Anglo-Latin verse, including an *opus geminatum* dedicated to the life and deeds of Saint Willibrord (*Vita Willibrordi*), who died in 739 CE.[131] The poem, in thirty-four chapters and 377 verses, was written around 796 at the request of Beornrad (d. 797), archbishop of Sens and former abbot of Echternach, to whom the poem is dedicated.[132] Echternach was the final resting place of Willibrord, who founded the monastery.[133]

In style, *Vita Willibrordi* reveals a debt to Bede's *Vita Cuthberti* in how Alcuin organizes the life around a series of episodic chapters. Unlike Bede, however, Alcuin does not offer exegetical commentary on the events of

---

131 For the Latin text, see MHG *Scriptorum rerum Merovingicarum* 7:81–141. See also *PL* 101, 693–724; Wattenbach and Dümmler, *Monumenta Alcuiniana*, 39–79; Reischmann, *Willibrord*. An English translation of the prose appears in *Soldiers of Christ*, 189–211. For biographical details on Willibrord, see further Schäferdiek, "Willibrord," 107–9.

132 For introductory details on *Vita Willibrordi*, see further Talbot, "The Life of Saint Willibrord," 189–91; Wood, "An Absence of Saints?," 335–52 at 347; Mayr-Harting, "Alcuin, Charlemagne and the Problem of Sanctions," 207–18 at 212. For the date of the death of Beornrad, see further Wampach, *Geschichte der Grundherrschaft Echternach im Frühmittelalter*, 184.

133 Talbot, "Life of Willibrord," 190.

the saint's life, and most of the incidents are reported briefly and without much elaboration. In fact, on average, each episode is only ten lines long.[134] Even so, there is ample evidence to suggest that Alcuin is indebted not only to the Christian poets of late Antiquity but the two most prominent writers of his own period, Aldhelm and Bede. A sample from his preface will suffice to show how this is so (1–12):

Ecce tuis parui uotis, uenerande sacerdos,
    Cor quia de uero feruet amore mihi,
Pontificis magni Wilbrordi et praesulis almi
    Percurrens titulis inclyta gesta citis.
Sit licet inferior, strepitans cum murmure rauco,   5
    Illius egregiis sermo meus meritis:
Protulit ad templum Christi, Wilbrorde sacerdos,
    Nostra fides uestrum parua minuta tamen,
Quae, rogo, suscipias clementer mente benigna,
    Criminibusque meis posce, precor, ueniam.   10
Non sunt digna tuis meritis mea munera, praesul,
    Qui regnas summi diues in arce poli:

[So I have obeyed your request, reverent priest, because my heart burns with genuine affection for the blessed prelate and noble bishop Willibrord, as I hasten through his celebrated deeds with short titles. Although my speech, prattling on with a grating hum, may be inferior to the eminent merits of that man, still my faith, Father Willibrord, has born these petty, paltry offerings to the temple of Christ, which, I beg you to accept mercifully with a gracious heart and grant forgiveness of my sins, I pray. My offerings are not worthy of your merits, bishop, you who reign glorious in heaven's citadel.]

Alcuin's opening words, "Ecce tuis parui uotis, uenerande sacerdos" ("So I have obeyed your request, reverent priest," 1), coincide with a similar

---

134 Preface (24 lines); Ch. 1 (14 lines); Ch. 2 (8 lines); Ch. 3 (7 lines); Ch. 4 (13 lines); Ch. 5 (7 lines); Ch. 6 (10 lines); Ch. 7 (6 lines); Ch. 8 (8 lines); Ch. 9 (5 lines); Ch. 10 (6 lines); Ch. 11 (9 lines); Ch. 12 (9 lines); Ch. 13 (10 lines); Ch. 14 (10 lines); Ch. 15 (9 lines); Ch. 16 (13 lines); Ch. 17 (8 lines); Ch. 18 (14 lines); Ch. 19 (14 lines); Ch. 20 (30 lines); Ch. 21 (15 lines); Ch. 22 (24 lines); Ch. 23 (11 lines); Ch. 24 (10 lines); Ch. 25 (7 lines); Ch. 26 (4 lines); Ch. 27 (9 lines); Ch. 28 (6 lines); Ch. 29 (10 lines); Ch. 30 (14 lines); Ch. 31 (19 lines); Ch. 32 (14 lines); Ch. 33 (18 lines); Ch. 34 (84 lines).

statement in the six-line preface to Hilary's *Metrum in Genesin* (1–2): "Paruimus monitis tua dulcia iussa secuti,/Antistes Christi" ("Following you sweet bidding, I have obeyed your request, priest of Christ"), and Alcuin's next words, *uenerande sacerdos* ("reverent priest," 1), are used frequently and primarily by Venantius Fortunatus in his *Carmina* and always at the same point in the line.[135] Alcuin then appears to echo Hilary again, when he refers to his unfitness to praise the merits of Willibrord, worried that he may be "strepitans cum murmure rauco" ("prattling on with a grating hum," 5), and Hilary says much the same thing in *Metrum in Genesin* ("Rauca quidem stridens," 3). It may also be, however, that Alcuin has Aldhelm in mind, whose language in the final line of *Riddle 21* (a carpenter's file) is notably close to that of Alcuin, allowing for the rearrangement of the words ("Garrio uoce carens rauco cum murmure stridens," ["Speechless myself, I screech a raucous shriek"]).

In line two, Alcuin's burning desire to sing about the life and deeds of Willibrord sounds a lot like many similar declarations elsewhere in the poetry of late Antiquity and the early Middle Ages. In his prefatory letter to Pope Vigilius in *Historia apostolica*, for example, Arator proclaims, "There is a burning in my heart to celebrate the labours of these men" ("Sensibus ardor inest horum celebrare labores," *Epist. Vigilium* 17–18), and Bede echoes that passage at the opening of his *Vita Cuthberti* with reference to luminaries of the Church (7): "Sensibus instet amor, sermonibus aestuet ardor" ("Love instils their hearts and a flame burns from their words"). At the opening of the *Carmen paschale*, Sedulius defiantly proclaims his determination to celebrate the Lord-Thunderer with all his heart and soul ("Dominumque tonantem/Sensibus et toto delectet corde fateri," 27–8), and his thematic emphasis on the "merits" (*merita*) of various Old Testament figures bleeds into the poetic hagiography of Anglo-Latin literature. All of these allusion have two things in common: first, they appear at the beginning of their respective poems, which means Alcuin may be looking for a good way to begin his own work; and second, they are all potentially and simultaneously echoes of Anglo-Latin or late antique poetry, which shows just how influential that earlier literature is.

A final example: Alcuin uses the phrase *inclyta gesta* (4) to describe the "celebrated deeds" of Willibrord. Such deeds, says Michael Roberts, are "the characteristic subject matter of epic," and Juvencus draws on them for "the life-giving deeds of Christ" in *Euangeliorum libri* (*Christi uitalia*

---

135 See further *Carm.* 3.3.3, 3.22.1, 3.24.5, 3.25.1, 34.21, and 4.136.

gesta, praef. 19), and so it may be that Alcuin is trying to imbue his hagiographical poem with a similar epic aura. On the other hand, the only other place where Alcuin uses this phrase is *Carmen* 9, that same poem that he wrote for the monks of Lindisfarne after the attack of the Vikings in 793. There he uses it in a direct allusion to Bede's *Vita Cuthberti*, since Cuthbert is one of the famous saints of Lindisfarne (*Carm.* 9.175–7): "Non opus est nostris dicere uersiculis./Dum prius heroicis praeclarus Beda magister/Versibus explicuit inclita gesta patris" ("It is not necessary for me to speak about him in verse, since the great master Bede set out the renowned deeds of father [Cuthbert] before in heroic poetry"). It is therefore likely that Alcuin's evocation of those *inclyta gesta* is a nod not to Vergil and classical epic, but to "master Bede" and earlier late antique poets, who had already revised the definition of that phrase to include the glorious deeds of Christ.

Opening Chapters of *Vita Willibrordi*

Following his prefatory address to Beornrad and his appeal to Willibrord himself, Alcuin sets out in the first two chapters of his poem to introduce the saint, whose piety and virtue are presented in conventional, hagiographical terms. Like many such openings in medieval literature, Willibrord is praised as "strong in virtue, full of divine love, keen of word, sharp of mind, [and] ardent in action ("uir uirtute potens, diuino plenus amore,/Ore sagax et mente uigil, et feruidus actu," 1.2–3). Like Enoch in Book 1 of the *Carmen paschale* ("meritis uiuacibus Enoch," 1.104), Willibrord is also famous for his own "lively merits" ("meritis uiuacibus almus," 1.7), and this near-verbatim echo is but one of several allusions to Sedulius in this passage. Thus Alcuin borrows from Sedulius language to describe Willibrord's far-ranging travels, and that language helps him to elevate the literary status of his work and to align the deeds of the saint with the paragon of virtue and good action, Christ (2.1–8):

> Ille deo plenus, lumen de lumine Christo,
> Iam quascumque piis peragrauit gressibus urbes,
> Vel castella, casas, uel conpita, semper ubique
> Sparsit euangelicae radios per pectora lucis.
> Multorum donec fidei pia flamma reluxit,   5
> Et nox caeca procul illo discessit ab orbe,
> Cotidieque ruunt idolorum fana profana,
> Et populi Christus resonabat in ore fidelis.

[That man, full of God, light of Christ's light, whatever city he visited with his pious steps, be it castle, cottage, or cross-road, spread the beams of evangelical light at every turn and always from his breast, until the pious flame of faith rekindled in the hearts of many, and blind night left the world, and the impious sanctuaries of idols fell daily to the ground, and Christ echoed from the lips of the faithful.]

The initial phrase, *Ille deo plenus* ("that man, full of God ..." 1) may seem odd, but it is not uncommon in Christian verse.[136] It appears early on in the *Carmen paschale* with reference to Elijah, moments after the story of Enoch (1.176–7): "Plenus at ille Deo postquam miracula terris / Plura dedit" ("That man, full of God, later performed many miracles on the land"). Willibrord, too, performs many miracles, and the language Alcuin uses to describe his journeys (2.2–3) evokes the peregrinations of Christ in Book 3 of the *Carmen paschale* (3.23–5): "Inde salutiferis incedens gressibus urbes, / Oppida, rura, casas, uicos, castella peragrans, / Omnia depulsis sanabat corpora morbis" ("Then, heading out with health-bringing steps to the cities, and traveling through towns, the countryside, farms, villages and forts, he healed everyone, driving off their ailments"). Anaphora makes this scene stand out, and the memory of it leads Alcuin to adopt several words from Sedulius, including *peragrauit* (2)/*peragrans* (24), *gressibus urbes* (2)/ *gressibus urbes* (23), and *castella, casas* (3)/*casas ... castella* (24). Also, in chapter 6 of *Vita Willibrordi*, just forty-two lines later, Alcuin once again alludes to the same passage, when he says that Willibrord "filled the cities, villas, towns, and countryside with an awarenes of God" ("impleuerat urbes / Agnitione dei, uillas, atque oppida, rura" 6.9–10). The last two words, *oppida, rura* (6.10), echo the same language in the Sedulian passage (*oppida, rura* ... 3.23). Unlike Christ, however, whose steps are "health-bringing" (*salutiferis ... gressibus*, 3) and directed at healing, Willibrord's journeys have a more general, holy purpose (*piis ... gressibus*, 2): to spread the light of the Gospels or, as Alcuin puts it, "the beams of evangelical light from his breast" ("Sparsit euangelicae radios per pectora lucis," 4). Persistent light imagery pervades verses 4–8 of this scene, and though it is ubiquitous in Christian literature, Alcuin may be following Bede and the opening of *Vita Cuthberti*. Like Willibrord, Cuthbert "spread many lamps throughout the flickering world" ("Multifidos uarium lichinos qui sparsit in orbem," 8); note the common verb *sparsit* (8)/*sparsit* (4). Bede also uses a metaphor

---

136 Cf. early example in Lucan, *Phar.* 9.564. See also Prudentius, *Psych. Praef.* 26; Paulinus, *Carm.* 16.127, 19.179; Bede, *Cuth.* 1.126; Wulfstan, *Swith. Praef.* 220.

to equate night with ignorance and sin: "donauit, tetricas humanae noctis ut umbras / Lustraret ("God has given many lights [i.e., disciples] to enlighten the black shadows of human night," 2–3). In the same way, Alcuin says that "blind night departed at once from the world" at the hands of Willibrord ("Et nox caeca procul illo discessit ab orbe," 6). Darkness is sin in both cases, although Alcuin is more specific about the role of paganism and idolatry, *idolorum fana profana* ("the impious sanctuaries of idols," 2.7), words he borrows from Sedulius (*fana profana*, 1.47). In all, it is clear that Alcuin's approach to the life of Willibrord here is similar to that of Bede in *The Life of Cuthbert*: both organize their narratives around a series of episodes, and both rely heavily on the poetic diction of late antique verse to articulate their praise of the saint.

Miracles in *Vita Willibrordi*

Many of the miracles of St Willibrord show that Alcuin is emulating Bede and channelling episodes and language from earlier Christian poetry, especially Sedulius.[137] As a case in point, chapter 30 of *Vita Willibrordi* combines two Sedulian miracles in a way that is similar to Bede and Aldhelm's style. The narrative also unfolds according to the sequence of his late antique model (30.1–14):

Interea mulier totis paralitica menbris,	
Continuis semper septenis languit annis,	
Tabida nec ualuit quicquid sibi menbra mouere:	
Vltima uix moriens suspiria corde trahebat.	
Ante dei sancti corpus portata iacebat,	5
Effundens lacrimas fessa cum uoce tepentes.	
Sola fides uiguit, posse sperare salutem	
Per famulum Christi, nec se spes ipsa fefellit.	
Ecce repente salus leuiter per membra cucurrit,	
Igneus atque calor uenas afflauit apertas,	10
Ossibus et neruis uirtus redit inclita cunctis.	
Surrexit mulier toto mox corpore sospes,	
Atque domum propriis gaudens se currere plantis,	
Quae prius alterius languens portatur ab ulnis.	

---

137 On the broader function of miracles in *Vita Willibrordi*, see further Mayr-Harting, "Alcuin, Charlemagne and the Problem of Sanctions," 207–18.

[Meanwhile, a woman paralyzed throughout her limbs languished continually for seven endless years, and nothing prevailed to stir her wasting limbs. Dying, she could barely draw her last gasps from her breast. When she was brought before the body of God's saint, she lay there shedding warm tears with a weary voice. Only her faith grew in strength, so that she might have the power to hope for a cure through God's servant; and that faith did not disappoint. Behold! healing at once ran nimbly through her limbs, and a fiery warmth infused her open veins, and glorious strength returned to her bones and nerves. Before long, the woman was up, whole of body, and rejoicing to run herself home on her own two feet, she who was once languished and was carried in the arms of another.]

The language of this scene is based on two consecutive miracles in the *Carmen paschale*, that of "the sleeping girl" and of "the wasting woman" (3.103–28). In the Bible, these miracles are also consecutive (Mk. 5), and it is one of the longer sequences for Sedulius. In the *Carmen paschale*, the young girl has just died and given up her last breath ("Functa die superas moriens amiserat auras," 3.104). Alcuin adopts the language of those final exhalations for his account of the paralytic woman in *Vita Willibrordi* (30.4): "Vltima uix moriens suspiria corde trahebat" ("Dying, she could barely draw her last gasps from her breast"). Then, Alcuin takes from Sedulius the emphasis on the healing-power of faith, which, for the ailing woman in the *Carmen paschale*, is the only thing she is "rich" in, having lost all of her wealth (3.119–20): "Ast ubi credentis iam sano in pectore coepit / Diues adesse fides mediis immersa cateruis …" ("But when a wealth of faith began to flow into the healthy heart of that believer, as she dove into the midst of the crowd …"). Only the strength of faith captures the attention of Jesus, and this is what distinguishes the woman in Alcuin's poem as well (30.7–8): "Sola fides uiguit … nec se spes ipsa fefellit" ("only her faith grew in strength … and that hope did not let her down"). Moreover, when the paralytic woman yields to that faith and prays to the Lord for healing, "a fiery warmth infuses her open veins, and glorious strength returns to her bones and nerves" ("Igneus atque calor uenas afflauit apertas, / Ossibus et neruis uirtus redit inclita cunctis," 10–12). This is the same warmth of life that re-enters the body of the "sleeping girl" in the *Carmen paschale* (3.138–9): "Dixerat et gelida constrictum morte cadauer / Spiritus igne fouet, uerboque immobile corpus" ("He spoke, and the body bound in cold death was warmed with the fire of the spirit"). Admittedly, the language of these two scenes is not the same and the connection is more subtle, but numerous similarities between the two episodes invites comparison and consideration that Anglo-Latin poets adapt their models in a variety of ways, beyond the level of verbatim emulation.

Summary Conclusions

In short, the evidence for verbal echoes cited by Lapidge and various editions of late antique poetry provides a general sense of which books the Anglo-Saxons preferred or seemed to know best, but the fact of synonymic allusions and more subtle adaptations of such literature better characterizes its reception in Anglo-Latin. Aldhelm, Bede, and Alcuin do not simply borrow scattered words from their remembered reading without some care for the context; often, they model particular scenes on whole passages of those poems, in order to elicit a particular effect or response from the reader. Reflexes to conventional invocations of the muse offer a case in point, in which Anglo-Latin poets appeal to the earlier tradition as a way to elevate the status of their own works by association. As far as they are concerned, that is the best way to begin a Christian poem. The result is not a continuation of biblical epic but a transformation of it to promote the spread of Christian literature now for English audiences.

Therefore, the question remains, what is to be gained from a reading of the Latin biblical epics alongside Old English biblical verse? How do English poets go about versifying the Bible? What books are important to them? Do they pursue the same allegorical and figural connections that we so often find in the poetry of Sedulius, Avitus, and Arator, or are they more like Cyprianus and Juvencus, who tend to favour the historical deeds of the Bible above all else? Does knowledge of the one tradition enlighten our reading of the other, or is there little sense of kinship between the two, and so little point in comparing them? These are questions to be answered in the next chapter.

Chapter Eight

Old English Biblical Verse:
Genesis A, Genesis B, Exodus

Nu sculon herigean   heofonrices weard,
meotodes meahte   and his modgeþanc,
weorc wuldorfæder—   swa he wundra gehwæs,
ece drihten,   or onstealde!
He ærest sceop   eorðan bearnum   5
heofon to hrofe,   halig scyppend;
þa middangeard,   moncynnes weard,
ece drihten,   æfter teode
firum foldan, frea ælmihtig.[1]

[Now we should praise the Guardian of the Kingdom of Heaven, the might of the
Maker and his purpose, the work of the Glorious Father, the Eternal Lord, who
established a beginning for each wonder. He first created heaven as a roof for the
children of the earth, the Holy Creator. Then, the Guardian of Mankind, Eternal
Lord, made land for men, this middle-earth.]

– *Caedmon's Hymn* (c. 670)

The English tradition of biblical verse begins with the story of Caedmon
in Bede's *Ecclesiastical History (Historia Ecclesiastica)*.[2] This important
work is the only surviving witness to the life and writings of this unusual

---

1 The text is based on the West-Saxon archetype in O'Donnell, *Cædmon's Hymn: A
   Multimedia Study, Archive and Edition*, 208. See also the earlier edition of Dobbie, ed.,
   The Anglo-Saxon Minor Poems, ASPR 6, 106.

2 For the Latin text of *Historia ecclesiastica*, see further Lapidge, ed., *Beda Storia Degli
   Inglesi*, 2 vols. An English translation can be found in Colgrave and Mynors, eds.,
   Bede's Ecclesiastical History, iv. 24, 416.

poet;[3] unusual because, unlike his Latin counterparts in late Antiquity, who tend to be noble-born, well-educated, and eager to voice their praise of God, Caedmon begins as an illiterate cowherd with no apparent will or ability to sing.[4] Faced with the opportunity to perform or run out of the room, Caedmon chooses the latter and hides in a cowshed. The Latin poet Arator, on the other hand, goes out to meet crowds of eager listeners at the Church of St Peter in Chains in Rome, to give encore readings of his *Historia apostolica*, and before him Sedulius boldly declares (1.26–8), "Why should I be silent of Christ the Saviour's famed wonders, when I can speak the truth and love to praise the Lord-Thunderer with all my heart and soul?"[5] Caedmon is not nearly so self-assured, and in many other ways the tradition of English biblical poetry stands a world apart from the earlier Latin genre.

Caedmon's story is also unusual, because it is miraculous in nature and involves actual divine inspiration. When he falls asleep in that shed, Caedmon is visited in a dream by a heavenly messenger who grants him the gift of song. The birth of Latin biblical epic by comparison is mundane. There is nothing otherworldly about the talent of Juvencus, however good a poet he may be, and Juvencus can only hope "to speak things worthy of Christ" ("ut Christo digna loquamur, " *praef.* 27). Arator, too, must beg the Holy Spirit for inspiration, for the "the gifts of the tongue" (*Munera da linguae*, 1.227), while Caedmon has this gift thrust upon him in his sleep and effectively against his will. "I do not know how to sing," he protests, trying to escape yet another performance, but heaven's answer comes with imperative finality: "Be that as it may, you must sing to me ... Sing of Creation" ["At tamen" ait, "mihi cantare habes" ... "Canta" inquit "principium creaturarum"].[6] Like it or not, Cædmon opens up and out comes the hymn for which he is now known: "Nu sculon herigean heofonrices weard" ["Now we should praise the Guardian of the Kingdom of Heaven ..."]. When he awakens the next morning, that gift remains intact, and for

---

3 For the relationship between the Latin and Old English texts of *Cædmon's Hymn*, see further Orchard, "Poetic Inspiration and Prosaic Translation," 402–22; O'Brien O'Keeffe, *Visible Song*, CSASE 4, 23–46; and Kiernan, "Reading Caedmon's 'Hymn' with Someone Else's Glosses," 157–74; See also O'Donnell, *Cædmon's Hymn: A Multimedia Study*, 2–4 and 233–48 for a recent bibliography.

4 As the full story of Caedmon's experience has been rehearsed many times, I will not do so here.

5 "Cur ego ... Clara salutiferi taceam miracula Christi? / Cum possim manifesta loqui, Dominumque tonantem / Sensibus et toto delectet corde fateri" (*CP*, 1.23–8).

6 Colgrave and Mynors, *Ecclesiastical History*, 416.

the rest of his life Caedmon knows with enviable assurance that all his songs will be pleasing to the Lord.

This sanction helps to validate the English tradition of biblical verse, which did not enjoy the prestige of the Latin genre. Nothing like biblical epic had been attempted before in English, and though Juvencus had long since taken many of the first steps in Latin, Latin was not the native language of the Anglo-Saxons, and they were not, like their continental neighbours, direct inheritors of a tradition of literature that evolved over the course of several centuries. Latin writing came to England only after the coming of Christianity (c. 600), and biblical epic arrived as a collection of work that had already run its course. Therefore, even if Old English poets were familiar with the prior Latin tradition, they had to struggle with its language as non-native speakers and to retake many of the first steps, to establish the vernacular genre for native audiences. Bede's narrative, then, is not only important because it provides an origin story for English poetry, but because it helps to justify its merit, which God himself has sanctioned. Put differently, despite the prestige of Latin writing, the Old English poets of the Anglo-Saxon period could set out with confidence, knowing that God was behind them.

Old English Biblical Poems

Unfortunately, despite Bede's testimony that Caedmon went on to sing about "the whole creation of the world, the origin of the human race, and the whole history of Genesis, of the departure of Israel from Egypt and the entry into the promised land and many other stories taken from the sacred Scriptures," Caedmon remains – unless one counts the *Hymn* – a biblical poet without a biblical poem.[7] Today, the surviving corpus of Old English biblical verse amounts to a single codex and a few scattered poems, all of which are unique, anonymous, and untitled in their native manuscripts.[8] Even so, the very existence in this period of such a collection in

---

7   The translation here is from Colgrave and Mynors, *Ecclesiastical History*, 418.

8   For a brief introduction to Old English poetry, see further Scragg, "The Nature of Old English Verse," 55–70. For a recent introduction to Old English biblical verse, see Fox and Sharma, eds., *Old English Literature and the Old Testament*, 8–15; see also Shepherd, "Scriptural Poetry," in *Continuations and Beginnings*, 1–36; Greenfield and Calder, eds., *A New Critical History of Old English Literature*, 206–26; Godden, "Biblical Literature: The Old Testament," 206–26; Lawton, "Englishing the Bible," 454–82; Herbison, "The Idea of the 'Christian Epic'," 342–69; Fulk and Cain, eds., *A History of Old English Literature*, 106–19; and Fowler, *The Bible in Early English Literature*, 79–124.

the vernacular is remarkable. According to Paul Remley's definition of biblical verse as "compositions which maintain reasonable fidelity to biblical narratives while evincing their own distinctive poetical identities,"[9] a handful of poems meet the criteria, and most of them (save *Judith*) appear in the so-called Junius manuscript, Oxford, Bodleian Library, Junius 11.[10] They are: *Genesis A* (2318 lines) and *Genesis B* (618 lines), which cover the events of the Bible through Genesis 22:13 (the Offering of Isaac); *Exodus* (590 lines), which builds to the Crossing of the Red Sea (Ex 13:20–14:31) but alludes to other books of the Bible; *Daniel* (764 lines), which deals with the first five chapters of the biblical text and overlaps with lines of a poem entitled *Azarias* in the Exeter Book; and *Judith* (348 lines), which appears in the *Beowulf Manuscript* and features the struggle between the heroine and the drunken Holofernes (Jud. 12:10–51).[11] The poetic renditions of Psalms 51–150 in the *Paris Psalter* also qualify as biblical verse, but because they are "determinedly literalistic renditions from the Scriptures reflecting a minimal artistic intervention on the part of their translators" and do not for the most part accord with the *modus operandi* of Latin biblical poets, they are beyond the scope of this study.[12]

So are the many "amorphous" texts (Remley's term) that reside at the edges of the genre and correspond more loosely to the Bible.[13] Such poems include *Christ and Satan* (729 lines), the last poem in the Junius manuscript and a free rendition of the Fall of angels (ll. 1–365), Harrowing of Hell (ll. 366–662), and Temptation of Christ in the wild (ll. 663–729);[14] *Christ I, II, III* (439, 426, and 797 lines), which form the first piece in the *Exeter Book* and present a spirited account of the Advent (*I*), Ascension (*II*), and Doomsday return of Christ (*III*);[15] Cynewulf's *Fates of the*

9　See Remley, "Biblical Translation: Poems," 66–7. The *Judith* poem appears in Dobbie and Krapp, eds., *Beowulf and Judith*, ASPR 4.

10　See Krapp, ed., *The Junius Manuscript*, ASPR 1.

11　All of these poems appear in Krapp, ed., *The Junius Manuscript*, 3–132; and Dobbie and Krapp, eds., *Beowulf and Judith*, ASPR 4, 99–109. *Azarias* appears in the *Exeter Book*, ed. Dobbie and Krapp, 88–94; see also the edition of Farrell, *Daniel and Azarias*.

12　Krapp, ed., *The Paris Psalter and the Meters of Boethius*, ASPR 5, 3–150. Much, however, remains to be said about the artistic achievement of the poetic psalter, as Jane Toswell has demonstrated in *The Anglo-Saxon Psalter*. See, e.g., 319–39, where Toswell examines the textual relationship between prose and poetic translations of the psalms in Old English and highlights the individuality of each.

13　Remley uses the term "amorphous" in "Biblical Translation," 67.

14　Krapp, *Junius Manuscript*, 135–58; see also Clubb, ed., *Christ and Satan: An Old English Poem*; and Finnegan, ed., *Christ and Satan: A Critical Edition*.

15　All three poems appear in Krapp and Dobbie, eds., *The Exeter Book*, ASPR 3, 3–49.

Apostles (122 lines), which appears in the *Vercelli Book* and offers a short but energetic meditation on the deaths of the apostles;[16] and three poetic versions of the Lord's Prayer, *Lord's Prayer I, II, III*, (11, 123, and 37 lines, respectively), the second of which compares in scope and style to the versified *Pater noster* in the *Carmen paschale* of Sedulius (2.231–300).[17] Each of these poems relates to the Bible in one way or another, as do many other poems in the corpus, including *Caedmon's Hymn*, but since *Genesis A, B,* and *Exodus* are anthologized in the Junius Manuscript, which is recognized as a collection of biblical poetry, and since they contain a number of scenes that overlap with those in earlier chapters of this book, I have chosen to focus my attention on them, as a way to compare the general *modus operandi* of the Old English poet against that of the Latin.

Genesis A&B (8th and 9th c.)

The 2936-line versification of Genesis from the Anglo-Saxon period appears in the Junius Manuscript (Oxford, Bodleian Library, Junius 11) and covers the incidents of the Bible through Genesis 22:13 (the Offering of Isaac). Modern editors have given the extant text two titles, however, *Genesis A* (lines 1–243 and 852–2935) and *Genesis B* (lines 235–851), because it is actually the work of two different poets, even if the scribe who copied it makes no such distinction in the narrative.[18] The manuscript itself is also divided into two parts, "Liber I" (*Genesis A, B, Exodus,* and *Daniel*), which includes several illustrations, and "Liber II" (*Christ and Satan*), which was added to the codex at a later date.[19] On the basis of an integrated re-examination of the "codicology (methods of pricking, folding, and ruling), paleography, initials, and the style of the first artist," Leslie Lockett has provided convincing evidence to set the date of "Liber

---

16 Krapp, ed., *The Vercelli Book*, ASPR 2, 51–4.

17 *Lord's Prayer I* appears in *The Exeter Book*, 223–4; *Lord's Prayer II* and *III* appear in Dobbie, ed., *The Anglo-Saxon Minor Poems*, ASPR 6, 70–4, 77–8.

18 For a description of the Junius Manuscript, see further the introduction in Gollancz, ed., *The Cædmon Manuscript*; Ker, *Catalogue of Manuscripts Containing Anglo-Saxon*, no. 334; Remley, *Old English Biblical Verse*, 18, n. 26; Doane, *Genesis A* (2013), 1–31. A digital facsimile of Junius can be found online at http://image.ox.ac.uk, "Early Manuscripts at Oxford University"; see also the CD Rom edition of Muir, ed., and Nick Kennedy, *MS. Junius 11*. The text of *Genesis A* is edited by Krapp, *The Junius MS*, ASPR 1, though I have used Doane's text in *Genesis A: A New Edition, Revised* (2013), which replaces his earlier edition, *Genesis A: A New Edition* (1978).

19 Doane, *Genesis A* (2013), 19, suggests, "as much as a generation" later; also Lockett, "An Integrated Re-Examination of the Dating of Junius 11" 141–74, at 142, n. 4, and 158.

I" to between 960 and 990. This provides a rough *terminus ante quem* for the poetry in the collection.[20] The original dates of composition for *Genesis A* and *B*, however, are considerably earlier.

Dating Old English verse is complicated by the general anonymity of the surviving poetic corpus. Even so, scholars have gained much from internal analyses of the texts. Traditionally, and on the basis of linguistic evidence, *Genesis A* has been dated to the seventh or eighth century, since "in style, vocabulary and meter, it closely resembles *Beowulf*, *Exodus*, and *Daniel*," poems thought to be early, "and differs from the poems known to be late."[21] Since the middle of the last century, however, many prominent scholars began to challenge the reliability of such linguistic testing, preferring instead the evidence of historical, cultural and paleographical studies.[22] More often than not, these debates have surrounded the text of *Beowulf*, but uncertainty has spilled into rest of the corpus, destabilizing traditional arguments for the dating of all Old English poetry. If *Beowulf* is late, where does that put *Genesis A*, which shares so many features?

More recently, applying his own integrated re-examination of the evidence, R.D. Fulk has renewed support for linguistic and metrical testing by re-evaluating the findings of earlier scholars on a much larger scale. His study of West Germanic parasiting, contraction, contraction in negated verbs and indefinite pronouns, compensatory lengthening for loss of *h*, analogical lengthening in diphthongal stems, and in particular instances of Kaluza's law, have yielded persuasive evidence to reaffirm the traditional arguments for the dating of Old English poetry.[23] Thus Fulk reasserts an early date for *Beowulf* not after around 725, if Mercian (which he favours),

---

20 Doane, *Genesis A* (2013), 32 and 51, pushes the *terminus ante quem* to before 900 on the basis that *Genesis B* was introduced near that time; see also Lockett, "An Integrated Re-Examination," 172.

21 Doane, *Genesis A* (1978), 36. See also Sievers, "Caedmon und Genesis," in *Britannica* 57–84; Hofmann, "Untersuchungen zu der altenglischen Gedichten Genesis und Exodus," 1–34; Menner, "The Date and Dialect of *Genesis A*," 285–94; Irving, "On the Dating of the Old English Poems *Genesis* and *Exodus*," 1–11; and Remley's summary in *Old English Biblical Verse*, 2, note 3.

22 See esp. Whitelock, *The Audience of Beowulf*, 26–8; Sisam, *Studies in the History of Old English Literature*, 119–39; Crandall Amos, *Linguistic Means of Determining the Dates of OE Literary Texts*; Kiernan, *Beowulf and the Beowulf-Manuscript*; and the essays in Chase, ed., *The Dating of Beowulf*.

23 See further Fulk, *A History of Old English Meter*, 348–51; this summary is taken from Blake's review in *Modern Philology*, 92.2 (1994), 220–4 at 222; see also Momma, *MLN* 35.1 (1997), 79–83, for a statement on the contribution of Fulk's study; and Donoghue, *Speculum*, 69.4 (1994), 1164–6.

and not after around 825, if Northumbrian.[24] By the same criteria, he sets the composition of *Genesis A* after *Beowulf* and around 750, if Mercian, or around 825, if Northumbrian.[25] Doane, who edits *Genesis A* and *B*, agrees with this chronology.[26] *Daniel* and *Exodus* then follow *Genesis A* and *Beowulf*, with a terminal date of around 825.[27] Fulk's findings are by no means absolute, but the collective weight of his evidence lends reasonable probability to the chronology.

Setting the date of *Genesis B* is somewhat less involved, since it is a translation of a ninth-century Saxon versification of the Bible.[28] In 1875, Eduard Sievers put forward compelling evidence to suggest that the language and style of *Genesis B* were too different from that of *Genesis A* to be the work of the same author, and that it was more likely the product of a Saxon poet writing in the style of the *Heliand*.[29] His theory turned out to be true, when a fragment of a Saxon Genesis was discovered in the Vatican library in 1894 containing lines (1–26a) that coincided with verses of *Genesis B* (790–817). Given the kinship of the Saxon poem to the *Heliand* (ca. 821–40), *Genesis B* has also been assigned to the mid-ninth century.[30] As for its inclusion in the Junius Manuscript, it is likely that *Genesis B* was introduced into the text to replace lost pages in *Genesis A* where the original account of the Fall had once been.[31] In other words, it was meant to fill a gap.

Biblical Context

According to A.N. Doane, "What we have in *Genesis A*, in its present form copied shortly before the year 1000, is an apparently continuous text

---

24 Ibid., 390: "Whether *Beowulf* is Northumbrian or Mercian in origin cannot be determined with assurance, but what evidence there is suggests that it is Mercian."

25 Ibid., 349.

26 Doane, *Genesis A* (2013), 55.

27 Fulk, *History of Meter*, 391–2.

28 Old Saxon biblical poetry is represented by two works, the *Heliand* (6000 lines) and *Genesis* (337 surviving lines). See further Sievers, ed., *Der Heliand und die Angelsächsische Genesis*; and Sievers, *Heliand*, Germanistische Handbibliothek; see also Doane, ed., *The Saxon Genesis*; Derolez, "*Genesis*: Old Saxon and Old English"; and Behaghel, ed., *Heliand und Genesis*, 10th ed.

29 The story of this discovery has been well rehearsed. See, e.g., Krapp in *The Junius Manuscript*, xxv; and Fulk and Cain, *History of OE*, 112.

30 Lockett, "Integrated Re-Examination," 171; Doane, *Genesis A* (1978), 51–2.

31 See further ibid., 10 and 30, n. 78; Fulk and Cain, *History of OE*, 122; and Doane, *Genesis A* (2013), 6.

of Genesis, showing plenty of evidence of a mixed Vulgate/Old Latin text, numerous exegetical interventions, some sections reminiscent of liturgical lections, and an oral style."[32] That leaves plenty of room for qualifications about the proximity of the poem to the Bible, even if most critics agree that *Genesis A* is a faithful rendition of the Old Testament. In fact, Doane all but reiterates Jerome's *paene ad uerbum* assessment of Juvencus' *Euangeliorum libri*, when he says that the *Genesis A*-poet "has systematically, virtually phrase by phrase, reproduced in traditional poetry the essential meaning of the Latin Genesis," and that "few if any episodes are omitted altogether."[33] That assessment would suggest that the style of *Genesis A* is nearer to the versifying methods of Juvencus and Cyprianus than those of Sedulius, Avitus, or Arator, who tend to be freer in their responses to the Bible.[34]

In fact, the omissions and additions to the scriptural prose in *Genesis A* do bear closer resemblance to the general *modus operandi* of Juvencus and Cyprianus. Like them, the English poet aims to reproduce the biblical narrative faithfully and in the process to exclude repetitive and obscure features of the original.[35] As Doane puts it, "The poet's main principle of selection seems to be that material must be new, and must not retard the advance of the narrative by repetition or obscurity; if material is difficult but important, it must be clarified so that it serves to explain the central

---

32 Doane, *Genesis A*, 78. For the Latin scriptural basis of *Genesis A*, see also Remley, "The Latin Textual Basis of *Genesis A*," 163–89, and *Old English Biblical Verse*, 114 and n. 56.

33 Ibid., 61 and 63. Doane effectively reiterates this statement in his revised edition of *Genesis A*, 86. See also Huppé, *Doctrine and Poetry*, 148 and 177. The Latin biblical source for *Genesis A* is unknown, but the consensus is that it is a mixed text, combining elements of the Vulgate and *Vetus Latina*. See further Remley, "The Latin Textual Basis of *Genesis A*," 163–90. For a general discussion of the Old Testament in Anglo-Saxon England, see also Marsden, *The Text of the Old Testament in Anglo-Saxon England*, CSASE 15. See also Godden, "Biblical Literature," 209: "*Genesis A*, a long fairly faithful rendering of the book of Genesis into lively, often magniloquent verse, reflects many of the ways in which the Old Testament interested the Anglo-Saxons. Its structure is narrative and literal, following the sequence of the biblical book closely"; see also Huppé, *Doctrine and Poetry*, 142.

34 See also Thornbury, *Becoming a Poet*, 52, who likewise says, "Other [Old English] poets, like those of *Genesis A, Daniel, Andreas*, and *Judith*, preferred more straightforward narrative modes, akin to the amplifying but essentially linear form of Juvencus."

35 Doane, *Genesis A*, 87–8. See also p. 77: "many changes, omissions, and conflations are in evidence, apparently made so as to avoid the repetitiveness which marks biblical style and structure." See also Fulk and Cain, *History of Old English*, who cite Genesis 3–5, 8–22 as examples and refer to Remley, *Old English Biblical Verse*, 439.

meaning of the episode in which it appears."[36] This practice reflects the approaches of Juvencus and Cyprianus, both of whom make the same decisions for the same reasons: to bring greater clarity and economy to the poetic narrative.[37] Additions also accord with the general style of the *Heptateuch* and *Euangeliorum libri*, whose authors tend to be conservative in their amplifications of the Bible. So the use of classical-poetic diction by Juvencus and Cyprianus introduces an air of "antiquity" to the poetic text, just as the use of Germanic-heroic language does in *Genesis A*, and like them, the Old English poet does not use such language without cause. This can be seen, for example, in the approach to the story of Creation (112–40), which introduces several extra-biblical epithets to enhance the literary value of the original account and intensify the impression of God's far-ranging power.

The one significant difference between the author of *Genesis A* and Juvencus and Cyprianus is his occasional tendency towards homiletic commentary, which "relate[s] the events of the narrative to the moral life of the audience."[38] Juvencus and Cyprianus in contrast tend to observe epic decorum and remain detached from their narratives. That being said, the Old English poet also favours the essential deeds of the Bible over any interpretation of them. The addition of a significant word or phrase may intimate deeper meaning in a particular scene, just as it does in the poetry of Juvencus and Cyprianus, and Fred Robinson has shown that "name-etymologizing," for example, may suggests a kind of subtle commentary in *Genesis A*.[39] On the other hand, Wright is right to urge caution in the reading of what is ultimately a literal translation of the Bible: "It is one thing to say that the poem allows for extra-literal interpretation by a reader so inclined, and quite another to say that the poet deliberately or consistently encourages it."[40] In other words, only a reader familiar with the interpretation of the Old Testament, be it through literature like the Latin biblical epics or the liturgy, will be more inclined to perceive and indeed pursue symbolism in the events of *Genesis A*. But by and large, the

---

36 Doane, *Genesis A*, 88.

37 Ibid., 88–9.

38 Ibid., 93.

39 See further Robinson, "The Significance of Names in Old English Literature," 14–58, esp. the pun on Seth's name at 29–32, and Noah, 33. See also Fulk and Cain, *History of Old English*, 114, for a summary of other exegetical moments.

40 See further Wright, "*Genesis A ad Litteram*," in *Old English Literature and the Old Testament*, 121–71.

author's primary objective is to provide a *paene ad uerbum* translation of the Bible that brings vitality to the essential deeds of Genesis.

Germanic-Heroic Context

Broadly speaking, much of what is true for the "heroic" nature of Latin biblical epic is true for Old English biblical verse. Just as the Christian-Latin poets turn to Vergil for a measure of the sweetness that his poetry affords (*dulcedo*), so English writers see the potential of Germanic-heroic verse to enhance their own renditions of the Bible. Latin versifiers use dactylic hexameter, "the heroic metre," to create an epic framework for their Latin poems, and likewise Old English writers use the alliterative metre of the Germanic tradition, to afford their work a similar air of "antiquity" and to add vigour to the stories of the Bible. In particular, Doane isolates "the long expansions and additions in the translation of Genesis 14:1–6 (1960–2101),"[41] and he says the account of the "war of the kings" is "the result of the natural pressure of the verse medium itself, allowing the poet to indulge in some free 'heroic' composition according to the traditional themes and formulas and suggesting that he was indeed an experienced and competent poet at home in the traditional oral-written medium, even if he was no match for the *Beowulf*-poet."[42] In addition, the epic-resounding diction of the Latin genre, through which God becomes the "Thunderer" (*Tonans*) and heaven, *Olympus*, finds similar expression in the way Old English poets adopt notions of kingship and vassalage to articulate the relationship between God and man. Thus "the Lord" is *drihten*, a term that applies elsewhere to the "lords" of men, including *Beowulf*'s *Geata dryhten* ("Lord of the Geats," 1484), and the servants of the king or prince are his "thanes" (*þegnas*), which is exactly what the *Genesis A*-poet calls the angels of heaven (15): "Ðegnas þrymfæste þeoden heredon" ("the mighty thanes praised their prince"). Adam, too, is called a "thane" in *Genesis B* (705), and the word, *hæleð* ("hero"), is used several times in both *Genesis A* and *B*, to describe "warriors" in those poems. Thus in *Genesis B*, Satan boasts of his rebel angels, "Strong comrades stand around me, hard-minded heroes, and they will not fail me in the

---

41 Doane, *Genesis A*, 93. Doane makes the point that *Genesis B* serves to provide "an external homiletic comment on the Fall of Man, appropriate in the context of a vernacular Genesis story in the literal mode."

42 Ibid. In particular, Doane makes a distinction between the poetry before line 1982, which is more or less close to the Bible, and after 1982, which is considerably freer.

fight. They have chosen me as their lord, brave warriors" ("Bigstandað me strange geneatas, þa ne willað me æt þam striðe geswican, / hæleþas heard-mode. Hie habbeð me to hearran gecorene, / rofe rincas," 284–6b). Satan himself dons the "hero's helm" (*hæleðhelm*, 444) and arms for battle in Eden (*Gen. B* 441–5). In many instances, language such as this could apply equally to kings or warriors in a more secular context, and examples of what late classical scholars call *Kontrastimitation* in Latin biblical epic appear throughout *Genesis A* and *B*. Again, the characterization of God at Creation in *Genesis A* (112–40) does precisely this and shows how God's might and influence extend above and beyond the range of any mortal ruler.

Opening of *Genesis A* (1–14)

While much of the narrative of *Genesis A* follows the biblical prose obser-vantly, the first one hundred lines do not. In the *Heptateuch*, Cyprianus begins without any preamble, repeating the first words of Genesis nearly verbatim (*Gen.* 1): "Principio dominus caelum terramque locauit" ("In the beginning God established heaven and earth").[43] The author of *Genesis A*, in contrast, opens with an exhortation to praise the Lord (1–14), followed by a lengthy account of the apocryphal fall of angels (15–111), which be-comes a negative *exemplum* for the audience on the consequences of pride and failing to do what the poet exhorts from the beginning. The theme of disobedience is taken up again in *Genesis B*, where Satan's determination to defy God passes on to His newest creations, Adam and Eve, who then follow in Lucifer's footsteps. The initial exhortation, then, to do what is "right" (*riht*, 1) and to love and praise the Lord is relevant to the immedi-ate context of Lucifer's fall and to the subsequent demise of Adam and Eve, but all of it is absent in the Bible (1–14):[44]

---

43   For a dated but accessible introduction to *Genesis A* and *B*, see further Gurteen, *The Epic Fall of Man*, esp. 93–127.

44   Compare Juvencus, *Ev.* 1.27 ("ut Christo digna loquamur"); Sedulius, *Cp.* 1.28 ("Sen-sibus et toto delectet corde fateri"); Arator, *Hist. apost.* 1.229–30 ("Vt duo iussa colant tabulis conscripta duabus: / Dilige mente Deum feruenti plenus amore"); Aldhelm, preface to *Cdv.* 9–10 with reference to the saints ("qui laude perenni / Rite glorificant moderantem regna Tonantem"); Bede, *Vit. Cuth.* 38 ("Munera da linguae, uerbi tua dona canentis"); and Alcuin, *Carm.* 1.6 ("Vt mea lingua queat de te tua dicere dona").

Us is riht micel   ðæt we rodera weard,
wered wuldorcining,   wordum herigen,
modum lufien.   He is mægna sped,
heafod ealra   heahgesceafta,
frea ælmihtig.   Næs him fruma æfre,   5
or geworden   ne nu ende cymþ
ecean drihtnes,   ac he bið a rice
ofer heofenstolas   Heagum þrymmum,
soðfæst and swiðfeorm   sweglbosmas heold.
Ða wæron gesette   wide and side   10
þurh geweald Godes   wuldres bearnum,
gasta weardum.   Hæfdon gleam and dream
and heora ordfruman   engla þreatas,
beorhte blisse.   Wæs heora blæd micel!

[It is very right that we should praise the Guardian of heaven, the Glory-King
of hosts, with words and love him in our hearts. He is the essence of power,
the head of all noble creatures, the Lord Almighty. There is no beginning to
Him, nor will there now be an end to the Eternal Lord, but He sits forever
mighty over heaven's seats. With high power, just and prolific, He has held
heaven's embrace, which was established far and wide by God's might for the
children of glory, the guardians of souls. They had joy and happiness, those
angelic hosts, and bright bliss in their Creator. Great blessedness was theirs!]

Much of the language in this opening passage reflects the author's fondness for the world of Germanic heroism, just as poets of the Latin tradition
seek out features of classical-poetic diction to align their work with the
epic genre. At the opening of *Euangeliorum libri*, Juvencus takes great
pains to transfer the useable words and values of the pagan system to the
person of Christ, who enters the narrative, "shining in flame-streaming
cloud, the Glory of the High-Throned Creator" ("flammiuoma descendet
nube coruscans / Iudex, altithroni genitoris gloria, Christus," 23–4). In
Genesis A, God likewise appears to English readers as "the Glory-King of
Hosts" (*wereda wuldorcining*, 2a), and "the head of all high Creation, the
Lord Almighty" ("heafod ealra heahgesceafta, / frea ælmihtig," 4–5a).
From the beginning, the vernacular poet places strong emphasis on God's
power, which is also a virtue of secular kings in the Germanic-heroic tradition – *mægna sped ... frea ælmihtig ... a rice ... Heagum þrymmum ...
geweald Godes*. Each of these words testifies to the incommensurate might
of God, which justifies his right to rule as "keeper of heaven" (*rodera*

weard, 1b) and "eternal Lord" (*ecean drihtnes*, 7a). In turn, since he provides all things, his devoted angels enjoy "bright bliss" (*beorhte blisse*, 14a) and "great blessedness" in heaven (*blæd micel*, 14b). That word, *blæd*, can mean both "glory" or "blessedness" as well as "fruit," and given the obvious connections between the Fall of angels and that of man, it is tempting to suggest a pun here, even if the usual word for "fruit" in *Genesis B* is *ofet*.

No less allusive are the opening words of *Genesis A*, which appear to echo the Latin liturgy and language in the Holy Eucharist. In 1914, Ferdinand Holthausen suggested a source for the opening words of *Cædmon's Hymn* (*Nu sculon herigean …*) in the preface to the Canon of the Mass, and in 1947 Bernard Huppé extended the context to include to the opening of *Genesis A*.[45] "Even more clearly than the *Hymn*," he wrote, "the lines [of *Genesis A*] reflect the Latin words of the Preface to the Mass."[46] Huppé then cited the relevant passage from the liturgy, which I will quote here: "Vere dignum et iustum est, aequum et salutare, nos tibi semper et ubique gratias agere: Domine sancte, Pater omnipotens, aeterne Deus" ("Truly it is fitting, right and proper that we should give praise and thanks to God everywhere and at all times").[47] The correspondence in language is self-evident, but the words, "Vere dignum … nos … gratias agere" coincide with "Us is riht micel ðæt we … herigen," while the epithets, *Domine sancte*, *Pater omnipotens*, and *aeterne Deus* find expression in the Old English, *rodera weard* (1b) and *wereda wuldorcining* (2a). The significance of this potential allusion is its connection to the broader context of salvation history, and yet because *Genesis A* is primarily a literal retelling of the Old Testament, it is unlikely that these words invite a spiritual reading of the poem similar to Avitus' *Historia spiritalis*. More likely than not, the Old English poet simply means that we should praise and love God for creating the world and that his own inclination to do so is made manifest by his poem. In this respect, he shares with Avitus a "will toward divine praise" ("diuina in laude uoluntas," 5.7).

Genesis A: Creation (112–40)

When the poet turns directly to the versification of the Bible at line 112 of *Genesis A*, his initial approach suggests an attentive eye to the

---

<hr>

45 See further Holthausen, ed., *Die ältere Genesis*, 91; Huppé, *Doctrine and Poetry*, 134–5; also Michel, "*Genesis A* and the *Praefatio*," 545–50, at 546. Klaeber also made the connection before Holthausen in "Die christlichen Elemente im *Beowulf*," 111–36.

46 Huppé, *Doctrine and Poetry*, 134. See also Doane, 225, n. 1–3a.

47 Ibid.

original.[48] Not only does he account for every verse of the corresponding scriptural text but the narrative order of the Vulgate as well: 112–15a (Gen. 1:1); 115b–21a (Gen. 1:2); 121b–5b (Gen. 1:3); 126–30a (Gen. 1:4); 130b–40a (Gen. 1:5). He also imitates the Latin grammar in several places and chooses language that nearly matches the prose.[49] This latter point is more difficult to show, given the distance of Old English and English poetic idiom from biblical Latin. Verbatim links do not as easily present themselves in English as they do in Latin biblical epic, but there is some help to be had. Although later, Aelfric's prose translation of Genesis (late 10th c.) is a faithful translation of the Bible, and it is striking how many of his words overlap with *Genesis A*.[50] I have therefore included it alongside the Vulgate, as a way to bridge the gap somewhat between the two traditions, knowing well how much time separates the two. I have also included relevant variants from the *Vetus Latina* (in parentheses), since many Anglo-Saxons continued to use the Old Latin Bible or encounter readings from it in the liturgy or biblical commentaries (112–40):[51]

1 In principio creauit (fecit) Deus caelum et terram. 2 Terra autem erat inanis (rudis) et uacua et tenebrae super faciem abyssi et spiritus Dei ferebatur super aquas. 3 Dixitque Deus fiat lux et facta est lux. 4 Et uidit Deus lucem quod esset bona et diuisit lucem ac tenebras 5 appellauitque lucem diem et tenebras noctem factumque est uespere et mane dies unus.[52]

---

48   See Doane, *Genesis A*, 295: "at 112 the poet is free to take up the paraphrase in a literal manner, without slighting the traditional meaning or becoming excessively complex."

49   See further ibid., 77: "notably faithful to the ordering and wording of the Latin Genesis, so much so that elements of almost every sentence in the poem can be related precisely to elements of the meaning, diction, and even grammar found in the textual traditions of the Latin Bible."

50   For commentary on Aelfric's close proximity to the Bible see further Minkoff, "Some Stylistic Consequences of Aelfric's Theory of Translation," 29–41; Greenfield and Calder, *A New Critical History of Old English Literature*, 85; Marsden, "Aelfric as Translator," 319–58. See also *The Old English Hexateuch*.

51   The text of the prose Genesis is that of Marsden, ed., *The Old English Heptateuch and Aelfric's Libellus de Veteri Testamento et Novo*, EETS 330; Fulk and Cain, *History of Old English*, 108. Also, for the persistence of the *Vetus Latina* in Anglo-Saxon England, see further Doane, *Genesis A*, 79.

52   Gen. 1:1–5: "1 In the beginning God created heaven and earth. 2 And the earth was void and empty, and darkness was upon the face of the deep, and the spirit of God moved over the waters. 3 And God said: Be light made. And light was made. 4 And God saw the light that it was good, and he divided the light from the darkness. 5 And he called the light Day, and the darkness Night; and there was evening and morning one day."

1 On anginne gesceop God heofenan and eorþan. 2 Seo eorðe soþlice
wæs ydel and æmtig and þeostru wæron ofer þære niwelnisse bradnisse, and
Godes gast wæs geferod ofer wæteru. 3 God cwæþ þa: "Geweorðe leoht,"
and leoht wearþ geworht. 4 God geseah þa þæt hit god wæs, and he todælde
þæt leoht fram þam þeostrum 5 and het þæt leoht dæg and þa ðeostra niht. Ða
wæs geworden æfen and morgen, an dæg.

– Gen 1:1–5

Her ærest gesceop   ece drihten,
helm eallwihta,   heofon and eorðan,
rodor arærde   and þis rume land
gestaþelode   strangum mihtum,
frea ælmihtig.   Folde wæs þa gyt
græsungrene.   Garsecg þeahte
sweart synnihte   side and wide,
wonne wægas.   Ða wæs wuldortorht
heofonweardes gast   ofer holm boren
miclum spedum.   Metod engla heht,
lifes brytta,   leoht forð cuman
ofer rumne grund.   Raþe wæs gefylled
heahcininges hæs.   Him wæs halig leoht
ofer westenne   swa se wyrhta bebead.
Ða gesundrode   sigora waldend
ofer laguflode   leoht wið þeostrum,
sceade wið sciman.   Sceop þa bam naman
lifes brytta.   Leoht wæs ærest
þurh drihtnes word   dæg genemned,
wlitebeorhte gesceaft.   Wel licode
frean æt frymðe   forþbæro tid,
dæg æresta.   Geseah deorc sceado
sweart swiðrian   geond sidne grund.
   Ða seo tid gewat   ofer timber[53] sceacan
middangeardes.   Metod æfter sceaf
scirum sciman,   scippend ure,
æfen ærest.   Him arn on last,
þrang þystre genip,   þam þe se þeoden self
sceop nihte naman.

115

120

125

130

135

140

---

53 I have followed Krapp's emendation, *timber* (135); cf. Doane, *Genesis A*, 149 and 298,
who retains *tiber*.

[Here the eternal Lord, Helm of All Living Things, first created heaven and earth, raised up the sky and established this broad land through His strong powers, the Lord Almighty. The earth was not then green with grass. Far and wide the sea, the dark waves, were covered by black, unending night. Then, gloriously bright, the spirit of the Guardian of Heaven was borne over the water in great haste. The Creator of Angels, the Giver of Life, bade light come forth over the broad earth. Hastily was the High King's hest fulfilled. Holy light came for him across the desolation, as the Maker commanded. Then the Ruler of Victories parted light from darkness, shadow from brightness, over the ocean-flood. The Giver of Life then gave names to both. Through God's word light was first named "day," a wondrously bright creation. Well did that first day, that fruitful time, please the Lord at the beginning. He saw dark, black shadows vanish over the wide land. Then, as time hastened forth over the framework of the earth, the Creator, the Maker, made the first night appear in the clear brightness. Hastening in behind Him, a cloud of dark rushed in, to which the Prince himself gave the name, "night."]

Like poets of the Latin genre, the Old English versifier authenticates his work with verbal links to the prose. In the first line, the adverb *ærest* ("first," 112) corresponds to the prose *in principio*, and the verb *gesceop* ("he created," 112) renders the Latin *creauit*; numerous glosses of the period link *scieppan* and *creo*.[54] The whole phrase, *ærest gesceop*, moreover approximates Aelfric's wording, *On anginne gesceop*, and it is a verbatim echo of *Caedmon's Hymn* (*He ærest gesceop* 5a), reinforcing the kinship between the English verse and the Bible.[55] The pairing of *heofon and eorðan* (113) also neatly reflects the diction, syntax, and grammar of the original (*heofenan and eorþan / caelum et terram*), so that no one would mistake this for anything but the opening of Genesis. Such thoughtful fidelity compares in particular to the initial approach of Cyprianus in the *Heptateuch*.

Close parallels to the Bible continue at every turn and provide a solid scriptural foundation for the poetry.[56] Again, this approach is similar to

---

54 Aelfric uses it in his grammar: *creo* (*ic scyppe*). The cognate form *scyppend* regularly appears for Creator, and *creatura* is *gesceaft* (both here are Ael. Glosses in Zupitza). The glosses to the Psalms regularly use *scieppan* for *creo*, etc.

55 The *Beowulf* poet also sings a version of the Creation-story (lines 92–8). As Godden, "Biblical Literature," 215, notes, "the minstrel invites the audience ... to see a parallel between the building of Heorot and God's building of the world ... Old Testament allusion here is used to suggest the satanic aspects of Grendel and the Edenic aspects of Heorot."

56 Doane, *Genesis A*, 82, highlights another link between the phrase *idel and unnyt* (105) and the Vulgate (*inanis et uacua*, 1:2).

that of the Latin versifiers, though the *Genesis A*-poet is more repetitive than his late antique counterparts, who tend to favour rhetorical variation (*uariatio*). Thus the word *leoht* ("light") appears four times in close proximity (122b, 124b, 127b, 129b) in response to the four instances of *lux* ("light") in the Latin, which means the poet is perhaps redundant but also respectful of the original: "Fiat lux et facta est lux" (1:3) / "heht ... leoht ... wæs ... leoht"; "diuisit lucem ac tenebras" (1:4) / "gesundrode ... leoht wið þeostrum" (126–7); and "appellauitque lucem diem" (1:5) / Leoht wæs ... dæg genemned" (129b–30). Other close links to the prose include the word *gast* ("spirit," 120a), which reflects Aelfric's language (*gast*, 1:2) as well as the Latin (*spiritus*), while references to the first "day" (*dæg*, 130b, 133a), "evening" (*æfen*, 138a), and "night" (*nihte*, 140a) coincide with the Old English (*dæg, æfen, niht*, 1:5) and the Latin (*diem, uespere, noctem*).

Other turns of phrase track the language of the Bible more loosely. These include the rendering of the Latin phrase, *spiritus Dei* ("the spirit of God"), as *heofonweardes gast* (120a) in Old English, which is not as close as Aelfric's translation (*Godes gast*), but the poetry nonetheless appeals to the basic sense and grammar of the prose. The noun, *folde* ("earth," 116a), does not reflect Aelfric's language either (*eorðe*, 1:2), who repeats the same word from Gen. 1:1 (*eorðan*), but the poet's alternative nonetheless conveys the essential meaning of the Latin (*terra* 1:2), and it enters the poem out of the need for alliteration, variation, or both. In the *Heptateuch*, Cyprianus makes the same choice, selecting *tellus* ("land") in the second instance (*Gen.* 2), since he had already used *terra* in the first line ("Principio dominus caelum terramque locauit," *Gen.*, 1). Both he and the Old English poet use variations to reduce redundancy in the original. Therefore, while the Old English poet is more repetitive in this scene than his late antique predecessors would be, he is still sensitive to the need for variation. In this case, the emphasis on light in the prose may govern the poet's decision to follow the Bible closely and repeat *leoht* in response to *lux*.

Elsewhere, the phrase *ofer holm boren* ("carried over the sea," 120b) is comparable to Aelfric's prose *geferod ofer wæteru* ("carried over the waters," 1:2), and both expressions reflect the general meaning and grammar of the Latin (*ferebatur super aquas*, 1:2). The poet does not use Aelfric's verb, *todælde* ("parted," 1:4), to describe how God "parted light from the shadows" ("Ða gesundrode ... leoht wið þeostrum," 126–7), but the basic sense of the poetry is the same as the prose ("diuisit lucem ac tenebras"). Moreover, the poet's phrasing of *leoht wið þeostrum* (127b) is almost identical to Aelfric's wording ("leoht fram þam þeostrum," 1:4). Finally, the poet's statement that the first day pleased the Lord (*Wel licode / frean*,

131b–2a) appears to reflect the same feeling in the Bible, "Et uidit Deus lucem quod esset bona" ("And God saw the light that it was good," 1:4), even if the wording is different. In short, there is plenty of language here to suggest that the author of *Genesis A* is following the narrative of the Vulgate closely and taking pains to imitate its language and grammar. This approach approximates the *paene ad uerbum* style of Juvencus in *Euangeliorum libri* or that of Cyprianus in the *Heptateuch*, allowing that *paene ad uerbum* means following the basic narrative of the Bible through selective verbal and grammatical allusions, while introducing poetic language to intensify the emotional and psychological appeal of the original. That is what we find in the poetry of Juvencus and Cyprianus, and that is what we find at the beginning of *Genesis A*.

Additions to the biblical narrative in this scene, which are extensive, are governed by several factors. While the prose account of Creation contains some sixty (Latin) or seventy (Old English) words, the poetic rendition has twice as many, nearly one hundred and fifty. The greater length of *Genesis A* is owing in part to the Old English appositive style, through which the author introduces apposite language to qualify previous statements.[57] So the essence of Gen 1:1 ("creauit Deus caelum et terram") is repeated by two separate but roughly equivalent statements in *Genesis A*: "gesceop ... heofon and eorðan" ("he created ... heaven and earth," 112–13); and "rodor arærde, and þis rume land gestaþolode" ("he raised up the sky and established this broad land," 114–15a). The same process governs the expansion of lines 116b–19a, where *garsecg* ("sea," 117b) and *wonne wægas* ("dark waves," 119a) are broadly analogous, or *sceade wið sciman* (128a) and *leoht wið þeostrum* (127b). This stylistic hallmark of Old English poetry marks a point of contrast with Latin biblical epic, which tends to promote economy of style in response to the conventions of classical rhetoric. So Cyprianus uses a single verse to capture the essence of Gen 1:1 and then moves on, while the Old English poet lingers, adding shades of meaning. This is not to say that Latin poets are immune to

---

57 For a discussion of the appositive style in Old English, see further Robinson, *Beowulf and the Appositive Style*; see also Orchard, *A Critical Companion to Beowulf*, 57–61. The appositive style can also be found in many Latin Christians poems. E.g., Prudentius' *Cath.* (3, 1–2): "O crucifer bone, lucisator, / Omniparens, pie, uerbigena"; Augustine's *Precatio ad Christum* (1–2): "Spes mea Christe Deus, hominum tu dulcis amator, / Lux, uia, uita, salus, pax et decus omne tuorum"; Paul the Deacon (*Carm.* 49, 1–7): "Christe, deus mundi, qui lux es clara diesque ... omnipotens ... conditor alme"; Hrabanus Maurus (*Carm.* 85, 13): "Christe deus, hominum saluator, rector et auctor."

expansion of various kinds, but the persistence of the appositive style in Old English poetry means that Anglo-Saxon biblical verse will always be more expansive in this respect.

The most marked use of the appositive style in this passage involves a series of epithets for "God" or *deus*, which are introduced as a way to resolve repetition in the original and to add greater psychological depth to the narrative.[58] Ironically, what seems to be a repeated reference to the same word (*deus*) is not so different from rhetorical variation in Latin biblical epic, since the English author must use different phrases for the same noun.[59] As Michael Roberts says of the Latin tradition, "the principle [of variation] can be seen at work in all the biblical poets. It is perhaps most marked in the *Heptateuch* poet, because of the peculiar difficulties of giving a close version of the Heptateuch text."[60] The author of *Genesis A* faces the same challenge and so refers to "God" as *ece drihten* ("Eternal Lord," 112b), *helm eallwihta* ("Protector of all living things," 113a), *frea ælmihtig* ("Lord almighty," 116a), *heofonweardes gast* ("Spirit of the heavenly Guardian," 120a), *metod engla* ("Ruler of angels," 121b), *lifes brytta* ("Giver of life," 122a, 129a), *heahcyning* ("High King," 124a), *se wyrhta* ("the Maker," 125b), *sigora waldend* ("Ruler of victories," 126b), and *scippend ure* ("our Maker," 137b).[61] These epithets serve not only to resolve the issue of repetition, but to deepen the reader's impression of God's far-ranging power. Kirsch would call this the *Emotionalisierung* or *Psychologisierung* of the biblical narrative.[62]

Moreover, these epithets also introduce context from the tradition of Germanic-heroic verse, just as expressions such as *Tonans* ("the Thunderer")

---

58 See also Griffith, "The Register of Divine Speech in *Genesis A*," *ASE* 41 (2012), who suggests (at p. 63) that "the poet made a concerted attempt to differentiate between the spoken language of God and that of mortal speakers. In particular the analysis shows that divine language is highly patterned, alliteratively ornate and unusually hypermetric."

59 So when the author describes how God creates the sea, he uses the words *garsecg* (117b), *wonne wægas* (119a), *holm* (120b), and *laguflode* (127a).

60 Compare Roberts, *Biblical Epic*, 198–9, who says, "characters that appear frequently are variously identified. Thus Abraham is *propheta* (Gen. 440), *procer* (Gen. 444), *pater* (Gen. 455), *senex* (Gen. 460), and *uates* (Gen. 486); Noah is *senex* (Gen. 283), *uates* (Gen. 294), *senior* (Gen. 300) and *propheta* (Gen. 302)."

61 Woolf comments on "the habit of variation in Anglo-Saxon poetic style" with reference to *The Dream of the Rood*, where the "richness of synonyms" likewise contributes to the artistry of that poem. See further "Doctrinal Influences on *The Dream of the Rood*," 137–53, at 151–2.

62 See Green, *Biblical Epics*, 127.

do in Latin Christian poetry. Thus the noun *drihten* ("lord") is ubiquitous in Old English verse with reference to a "lord of men" (e.g., *eorla drihten*), while the "Eternal Lord" (*ece drihten*, 112b) in *Genesis A* outlives any earthly king, who must suffer the decay of age and strength.[63] Secular warrior-kings put great store in their physical prowess, and the "Almighty Lord" (*frea ælmihtig*, 116a) has an abundance of it, who creates the world not only by virtue of words (*þurh drihtnes word*, 130) but through physical might (*strangum mihtum*, 115b). Being eternal and almighty, and protecting all living creatures as *helm eallwihta* ("Protector of all living things," 113a), God is therefore the supreme "Lord of victories" (*sigora waldend*, 126b), unmatched and undefeated, even by the rebel angels of heaven. The implied suggestion is that neither the *helm Scyldinga* of *Beowulf*, for example, nor any other man can compete with such a king.[64] How could the generosity of earthly lords, of "ring-givers" (*beaga brytta/sinces brytta*), compare with the very "Giver of Life" (*lifes brytta*, 122a, 129a)?[65] So the poet's additions to the Bible in this scene offer a vivid and thought-provoking translation of the original story, incorporating the secular-heroic values of physical strength, authority, protection, and generosity, and making God "the high king" of all (*heahcininges*, 124), who creates the world. By engaging secular poetry in these terms, the Old English versifier sets out to entertain and teach his audience in much the same way Juvencus, Sedulius, and Arator do, that is, by blending features of the two traditions, Christian and non-Christian, to promote the greater virtues of the latter.

Creation of Eve (169a–89a)

There is no account of the creation of Adam in *Genesis A*, since the manuscript is missing pages where that episode should appear (after line

---

63 See, e.g., *eorla drihten* in *Beowulf* (1050). See also Doane, *Genesis A*, 99, who mentions *ece drihten* and *leofne drihten* in the context of formulaic language.

64 *Helm Scyldinga* appears in *Beowulf* at lines 371, 456, 1321.

65 At the opening of *Beowulf*, Scyld Scefing is called *beaga brytta* ("distributor of rings," 35) and Wealhtheow refers to Hrothgar as *sinces brytta* ("distributor of treasure," 1170); the Wanderer also longs to find a new treasure-giver (25): "sohte sele dreorig sinces bryttan." See also Scragg, "Nature of OE Verse," 61–2, who discusses variations of the kenning, *sinces brytta* ("distributor of treasure"); and Gardner, *The Construction of Old English Poetry*, 21: "God wins battles, deals out treasures to those who have earned them, gives his thanes a safe place to live, and so forth."

168a).[66] In treating Eve, the Old English versifier, like Cyprianus, combines the two references to her in Genesis 1:27 and 2:18–22 to create a smoother and more logical narrative.[67] As with the *Heptateuch*, there is no suggestion here that we should read beyond the literal sense of the text for any deeper meaning. Eve does not, as she does in Avitus' *Historia spiritalis* (1.146–57), represent the birth of the Church, nor does the poet blame her at this point for her role in the expulsion from Paradise. Allowing for minor points of difference, the representation of Eve in *Genesis A* is a straightforward following of the Bible (169a–89a):[68]

18 Dixit quoque Dominus Deus: "Non est bonum esse hominem solum. Faciamus ei adiutorium similem sui." 19 Formatis igitur Dominus Deus de humo cunctis animantibus terrae et uniuersis uolatilibus caeli, adduxit ea ad Adam ut uideret quid uocaret ea; omne enim quod uocauit Adam animae uiuentis, ipsum est nomen eius.

20 Appellauitque Adam nominibus suis cuncta animantia et uniuersa uolatilia caeli et omnes bestias terrae. Adam uero non inueniebatur adiutor similis eius. 21 Inmisit ergo Dominus Deus soporem in Adam, cumque obdormisset tulit unam de costis eius et repleuit carnem pro ea. 22 Et aedificauit Dominus Deus costam quam tulerat de Adam in mulierem et adduxit eam ad Adam.[69]

18 God cwæð eac swilce: "Nis na god þisum men ana to wunienne. Uton wircean him sumne fultum to his gelicnisse." 19 God soþlice gelædde þa nitenu þe he of eorþan gesceop, and þære lyfte fugolas, to Adame, þæt he foresceawode hu he hig gecigde. Soðlice ælc libbende nyten, swa swa Adam hit gecigde, swa ys hys nama. 20 And Adam þa genamode ealle nytenu heora

---

66   See further Doane, *Genesis A*, 151 and esp. 9, which gives an account of what these missing pages may have contained, including an account of "Gen 2:7 creation of Adam."

67   See Remley, *Old English Biblical Verse*, 127, who cites Raw and her discussion of the sources of this episode, which is a conflation of the 2 references to Eve in Genesis.

68   *Pace* Doane, *Genesis A*, 300: "The episode is greatly augmented by traditional material of the most eclectic sorts."

69   18 And the Lord God said: "It is not good for man to be alone: let us make him a help like unto himself." 19 And the Lord God having formed out of the ground all the beasts of the earth, and all the fowls of the air, brought them to Adam to see what he would call them: for whatsoever Adam called any living creature the same is its name. 20 And Adam called all the beasts by their names, and all the fowls of the air, and all the cattle of the field: but for Adam there was not found a helper like himself. 21 Then the Lord God cast a deep sleep upon Adam: and when he was fast asleep, he took one of his ribs, and filled up flesh for it. 22 And the Lord God built the rib which he took from Adam into a woman: and brought her to Adam.

namum and ealle fugelas and ealle wilddeor. Adam soþlice ne gemette þa git
nanne fultum his gelican. 21 Ða sende God slæp on Adam and þa þa he slep,
þa genam he an ribb of his sidan and gefilde mid flæsce þær þær þæt ribb
wæs, 22 and geworhte þæt ribb þe he genam of Adame to anum wifmen and
gelædde hig to Adame.

– Gen 2:18–22

Ne þuhte þa gerysne   rodora wearde
þæt Adam leng   ana wære   170
neorxnawonges   niwre gesceafte
hyrde and healdend.   Forþon him heahcyning,
frea ælmihtig   fultum tiode
wif, aweahte   and þa wraðe sealde,
lifes leohtfruma,   leofum rince.   175
He þæt andweorc   of Adames
lice aleoðode   and him listum ateah
rib of sidan.   He wæs reste fæst
and softe swæf,   sar ne wiste,
earfoða dæl   ne þær ænig com   180
blod of benne   ac him brego engla
of lice ateah   liodende ban,
wer unwundod.   Of þam worhte God
freolice fæmnan,   feorh in gedyde,
ece saula.   Heo wæron englum gelice.   185
þa wæs Adames bryd
gaste gegearwod.   Hie on geogoðe bu
wlitebeorht wæron   on woruld cenned
meotodes mihtum.

[It did not then seem right to the Guardian of Heaven that Adam should be
alone any longer, the shepherd and keeper of this new creation, Paradise. So
the High King, Lord Almighty, Bright Source of Life, brought forth woman
for him as a help, awakened her, and gave her quickly to the dear warrior. He
separated her substance from Adam's body, skilfully drew a rib from his side.
He was fast asleep. He rested softly and knew no pain, not one bit of woe,
nor did any blood come from the wound, but the King of Angels drew forth
living bone from the body, and the man was unwounded. From it, God made
noble woman, put life in her, an eternal soul. They were like angels. Then
Eve, Adam's bride, was given a soul. They were both beautifully bright in
their youthfulness, born into the world by God's might.]

Like Cyprianus, the Old English poet omits much of verses nineteen and twenty of the biblical book, where Adam names the animals. That moment diverts the focus from Adam and his need for a helpmate, and so it is omitted. Close links to the Bible begin with the word *gerynse* ("fitting," "proper," 169), which provides a loose tie to the prose (OE *god*, "good," and Lat. *bonum*). Structurally, the word also comes at the beginning of the scene, as it does in the original, suggesting that the poet is following the text of the Bible observantly. The epithet, *rodera wearde*, is a florid substitution for *God* in verse eighteen of Genesis, but it leads back to the prose nonetheless. The upgrade is also similar to those made in the Creation sequence (112–40), where *deus* ("God") appears several times and must be adapted for the sake of the poetry. The reference to Adam in line 170 provides a strong link to the original scene, and so does *ana* ("alone"), which echoes the English prose (*ana*) and the Latin (*solum*). The alliteration between *Adam* and *ana* also highlights the disadvantage of Adam's unique status. In the wider context of Old English verse, the theme of solitude figures prominently in elegiac poetry as one of the worst fates a warrior can suffer, and that is what the *Genesis A*-poet calls Adam (*leofum rince*, "dear warrior," 175). It may therefore be that the poet imagines a thematic connection between the two traditions at this point in the hero's common need for fellowship.

Although it does not appear in the corresponding prose, the word "Paradise" (*neorxnawonges*, 171) does show up in the wider context of this section and provides additional scriptural footing for the poet. The reference to Eve as a helpmate (*fultum*, 173b) is the same word Aelfric uses (*fultum*), and it also corresponds to the Latin *adiutorium*.[70] The peculiar use of the verb *teon* in this scene (*fultum tiode*, 173b) is perhaps best understood as a pun anticipating the removal of Adam's rib in lines 177b–8a ("ateah / rib of sidan" ["he plucked the rib from his side"]) and 182 ("of lice ateah liodende ban" ["he plucked the living bone from his body"]).[71] That moment also provides the clearest signal of the source, and it echoes the English prose closely (*rib of his sidan*) in response to the Latin ("unam de costis eius").[72] The reference to "sleep" (*swæf*, 179a) also corresponds to the prose

---

70 See further Doane, *Genesis A*, 299–300, for the suggestion that *adiutorium* is a *Vetus Latina* reading.

71 See ibid., 300. Recall that Avitus offers a similar pun in the creation of Eve with *dispendia membri* (1.159) and *de lateris membro* (1.169).

72 It is noteworthy that Adam's "side" is not mentioned in either the Vulgate or *Vetus Latina* but cited in both the verse and prose Old English.

(*soporem/slæp*), even though the latter is a verb. Sleep also explains the poeticism of line 174, *wif aweahte* ("he awoke the woman"), which is to say that Eve is awoken unto life. Doane raises the question of Adam's pain at this point, and notes that it is a commonplace in Christian literature that he feels none. He cites Augustine and Jerome among prose exegetes and also Cyprianus.[73] Finally, the phrase "Of þam worhte God / freolice fæmnan" (173a–4b) covers the Old English "geworhte … to anum wifmen" ("he made that [rib] into a woman") with reference to the Latin *aedificauit … mulierem*, and the additional adjective *freolice* ("noble," "beautiful") is complimentary. The word *fæmne* ("woman") also appears later in the context of verse twenty-three of the Old English prose ("þeos bið geciged fæmne" ["Let her be called woman"]), and so that, too, finds some correspondence in the later English Bible. In short, there is more than enough language in this scene to suggest the author of *Genesis A* is following the Bible closely, and that his method of embedding scriptural echoes into the poetry coincides with the general *modus operandi* of the Latin biblical poets.

Satan's First Speech (*Genesis B*, 271b–91)

At the point where *Genesis B* intervenes in the text of *Genesis A* at line 235, the poet says that Adam and Eve "were dear to God, so long as they chose to uphold his holy words" ("Heo wæron leof Gode / ðenden heo his halige word healdan woldon," 244b–5b). So long as they were loyal, "they knew not a whit of sorrow" (*nyston sorga wiht*, 242).[74] In the context of *Genesis A*, it is hard to forget the similar stance of God's angels at the beginning of the poem (15–16a): "the mighty thanes exalted their Lord, [and] spoke his praise in gladness" ("Þegnas þrymfæste þeoden heredon, / sægdon lustum lof"). So long as they were loyal, "they knew no sin nor how to commit evil" ("Synna ne cuþon, / firena fremman," 18b–19a). Like Adam and Eve, they were innocent and joyful, until the devil seduced and corrupted them. Misled by Lucifer, they turned away from God and "chose not to honour his words anymore ("noldon alwaldan word weorþian," 328b–9a). That also becomes the will of Adam and Eve in *Genesis B*, and so when the author of *Genesis A* says moments before that

---

73 See further Doane, *Genesis A*, 300.

74 The author of *Genesis A* says much the same thing moments before, that "they did not know how to do or commit sin, but kept ardent love for the Lord in their hearts" ("Man ne cuðon / don ne dreogan, ac him drihtnes wæs / þam on breostum byrnende lufu," 189a–91).

they were "like angels" ("Heo wæron englum gelice," 185) it is hard not to perceive a sense of irony and foreboding, despite the different authorship of the two poems.[75]

In *Genesis B*, God creates Lucifer with the expectation that, like Adam and Eve, who "bowed their heads to the heavenly king ... and spoke thanks for everything ("Hnigon þa mid heafdum heofoncyninge ... and sædon ealles þanc," 237–8), he would praise and thank the Lord (256b–7): "Lof sceolde he drihtnes wyrcean ... and sceolde his drihtne þancian" ("He had to fulfill God's praise ... and thank his Lord"). But Lucifer refuses to bow his head, enticed by pride to do "something worse" ("to wyrsan þinge," 259a).[76] Pride (*ofermod/oferhygd*) is the impetus for Lucifer's disobedience in *Genesis A* and *Genesis B*, and pride gives birth to the ambitions that lead him to his ruin. Despite his inexorable failure, however, Lucifer learns from that defeat (like his counterpart in *Historia spiritalis*) how best to seduce the innocent pair, by having them retrace his steps. Granted, Satan in *Genesis B* sends a subordinate to do his dirty work in Eden, but that devil goes with his instructions and shares in Lucifer's fall, having been seduced by the same ambition and pride.[77] Therefore, many of the words in this speech reappear later in the temptation of Adam and Eve, as tokens of the devil's own disastrous experience. At this point, however, Lucifer is as yet ignorant of God's omnipotence and so he is defiantly optimistic. In my own analysis of Satan's fall and his subsequent temptation of Adam and Eve, I would like to acknowledge the earlier work of Eric Jager in "Tempter as Rhetoric and Teacher: The Fall of Language in the Old English *Genesis B*."[78] My own discussion arrives at similar conclusions, but I have tracked the narrative sequence along a slightly different route (271b–91):

Feala worda gespæc

se engel ofermodes.   Þohte þurh his anes cræft
hu he him strenglicran   stol geworhte,
heahran on heofonum;   cwæð þæt hine his hige speone þæt
he west and norð   wyrcean ongunne,   275
trymede getimbro;   cwæð him tweo þuhte

---

75 See further Biggs, "'Englum gelice'," 447–52.
76 "He had to give praise ... and thank his Lord." The head-bowing motif can be found in the *Heliand*. See further Sievers at this point, *Heliand und die Angelsächsische Genesis*.
77 See further Doane, *Genesis B*, 277.
78 See further Jager, "Tempter as Rhetoric and Teacher: The Fall of Language in the Old English *Genesis B*," 99–118.

þæt he gode wolde   geongra weorðan.
"Hwæt sceal ic winnan," cwæð he.   "Nis me wihtæ þearf
hearran to habbanne.   Ic mæg mid handum swa fela
wundra gewyrcean.   Ic hæbbe geweald micel   280
to gyrwanne   godlecran stol,
hearran on heofne.   Hwy sceal ic æfter his hyldo ðeowian,[79]
bugan him swilces geongordomes?   Ic mæg wesan god swa he.
Bigstandað me strange geneatas,   þa ne willað me æt þam striðe geswican,
hæleþas heardmode.   Hie habbeð me to hearran gecorene,   285
rofe rincas;   mid swilcum mæg man ræd geþencean,
fon mid swilcum folcgesteallan.   Frynd synd hie mine georne,
holde on hyra hygesceaftum.   Ic mæg hyra hearra wesan,
rædan on þis rice.   Swa me þæt riht ne þinceð,
þæt ic oleccan   awiht þurfe   290
gode æfter gode ænegum.   Ne wille ic leng his geongra wurþan."

[That arrogant angel spoke many words. He considered how, by his own power, he might make a stronger throne for himself, higher in heaven. He said that his heart enticed him to begin work in the west and north, to prepare structures. He said it seemed doubtful to him that he would be a servant to God. "Why must I toil?" he said. "I have no need of a lord, not one bit. I can work as many wonders with my hands. I have great might to make a diviner throne, higher in heaven. Why must I serve to win His favour, bow to Him in such service? I can be God as much as He. Strong comrades stand around me, hard-minded heroes who will not fail me in the fight. They have chosen me as their lord, brave warriors. With such allies as these one can take counsel and act on it, with such comrades. They are my eager friends, faithful in heart. I can be their lord, rule in this realm. So it does not seem right to me that I should have to pay court to Him one bit for any good. I will not be His servant anymore."]

Se engel ofermodes ("the angel of pride," 272a) is a fitting epithet for Lucifer, and the poet already singles out his arrogance as a failing ten lines earlier (262): "his engyl ongan ofermod wesan" ("his angel began to be proud").[80] For Lucifer, the birth of pride begins with his determination to

---

79 This turn of phrase can be found in the *Heliand* 1472. See Sievers, ibid., 12, "mer sculun gi aftar is huldi thionon."

80 The focus on pride is persistent in *Genesis A* and *B*. Thus *oferhygde* (22), *oferhygd* (29), *oferhidig* (66), *ofermod* (262), *ofermodes* (272), *ofermede* (293), *oferhygd* (328), *ofermetto* (332), *ofermetto* (337), *ofermoda* (338), *ofermetto* (351), and then not again in *GenB* or *GenA*.

build a kingdom apart from God's (274b–6a): "cwæð þæt hine his hige speone þæt/he west and norð wyrcean ongunne,/trymede getimbro" ("He said that his heart enticed him to begin work in the west and north, to prepare structures").[81] It is his heart (*hige*, 274), the poet says, that first entices him to betray God, and the verb in this context, *speone* (274), from *spanan* ("to allure" or "entice"), appears for the first time in *Genesis B* and nowhere else in *Genesis A* or *B* but in the context of the Fall (350b as *forspeon*, 575b, 588b, 684b, 687b, 720b).[82] This word, therefore, is thematic in *Genesis B* and, appearing as it does here, suggests an origin for Satan's seductive power in his own self-delusion. This is the angel's first lesson in the corruptive influence of desire, and he will pay for it, but not without putting that lesson to good use in Eden.

Seduction is the key to Lucifer's *cræft* (272a) or "power," another word the author introduces in this passage. Nowhere does it appear in *Genesis A* or *B* before this moment, and nowhere does it describe God's might in either poem. The heart of the devil's *cræft* is his capacity to deceive, which may originate in the biblical description of the serpent as "more cunning" than other creatures (Gen 3:1; *Vetus Latina* variants in parenthesis): "Sed et serpens erat callidior (astutior, sapientior) cunctis animantibus (ominium bestiarum) terrae quae fecerat Dominus Deus" ("Now the serpent was more subtle than any of the beasts of the earth which the Lord God had made"). Of the ten uses of the word in *Genesis B*, most refer to the devil's malevolent guile, notably *feondes cræft* (449, 453) and *deofles cræft* (492, 823), and by introducing the word in this first speech, the poet highlights a qualitative difference between the power of God, which is creative and nurturing, and the craftiness of the devil, which is malevolent and destructive.[83] Given its primary function to deceive, Lucifer's *cræft* is also illusory, which means that the angel's confidence in his own might is misguided,

---

81 The situation of Satan's kingdom in the northeast is conventional. Note, too, the passage in *Genesis A* (31b–4a): "þa he worde cwæð, niþes ofþyrsted, þæt he on norðdæle/ham and heahsetl heofena rices/agan wolde." Also, note the location of God's seat in the southeast ("þæt is suð and east," 667).

82 Note 720, *deofles gespon*, the nominal form (devil's lure), which is nonetheless based on the verb. Also, the verb *spanan* does not appear in the extant narrative of *Genesis A* at all and so it is particular to the Fall in *Genesis B*. Sievers, *Heliand und Genesis*, also points to *Judith* 294 for a similar turn of phrase.

83 The ten occurrences of *cræft* in *Genesis B* are at 269, 272, 402, 416, 449, 453, 492, 500, 618, and 823.

since he is deluded by the very nature of *cræft* to deceive. Put differently, the first victim of Satan's seductive guile is not Adam or Eve but Lucifer.

Moments before this first speech, the narrator takes some pains to anticipate much of what the angel will say, thereby diffusing the force of his self-righteous indignation.[84] When Lucifer boasts, "I have much power to make a diviner throne, higher in heaven" ("Ic hæbbe geweald micel / to gyrwanne godlecran stol, / hearran on heofne," 280b–2a), he is echoing not only his earlier thought, "þohte þurh his anes cræft / hu he him strenglicran stol geworhte, / heahran on heofonum" ("He considered how, by his own power, he might make a stronger throne for himself, higher in heaven," 272b–4a), but the narrator's prior comment that he "began to raise up conflict against the highest Lord of heaven, who sits on the holy throne" ("ongan him winn up ahebban / þone hehstan heofnes waldend, þe siteð on þam halgan stole," 259–60). Satan's assumption that "much power" (*geweald micel*, 280b) is sufficient against the highest power in heaven (*þone hehstan heofnes waldend*, 260a) is therefore deluded, and because the poet has already emphasized God's superlative might, *se alwealda* ("the all-powerful," 246), Lucifer's speech is highly ironic.[85] In fact, the narrator makes a point of saying that God allowed Lucifer "to wield much" in the kingdom of heaven (*micles wealdan*, 253b), even to be "highest next to the Lord" ("hehstne to him on heofone rice," 254a), but "much power" is not omnipotence, and "highest next to God" is not highest of all.[86] Satan's idea of divinity is also narrower. God's throne is a "holy" one, and much of his energy is devoted to the creation and nurturing of the world ("þe siteð on þam halgan stole," 260). Satan, on the other hand, wishes only to build a "stronger throne" (*strenglicran stol*, 273) and to surround himself with

---

84 Cf. Robinson's comments about repetition in *Beowulf* in "Two Aspects of Variation in Old English Verse," 144: "A more specifically pointed use of repetition may be seen in the Unferth intermezzo of *Beowulf*, where the hero's repetition of Unferth's own words in his reply to the hostile *þyle* gives force and sting to the rejoinder."

85 For other connections between the narrator's preamble and Lucifer's first speech, compare the following: *mid handum* (279): *stod his handgeweorc* (241b); *þurh handmægen halig drihten* (247); and *mid his handum gesceop, halig drihten* (251). The noun *handmægen* is uncommon and only appears elsewhere in *Andreas* in a similar context and otherwise in *Heliand* 730, 1445. See Sievers, *Heliand und Genesis*, 25. Also, *Hwy sceal ic æfter his hyldo ðeowian* (282); *nolde Gode þeowian* (264b); *Ne meahte he æt his hige findan þæt he gode wolde geongerdome, þeodne þeowian* (266b–8a); *geongordomes* (283a); *giongorscipe* (249a); *geongordome* (267b); *folcgesteallan* (287a); *folcgestælna* (271a); *Ic mæg hyra hearra wesan* (288b); *ahof hine wið his hearran* (263a).

86 Note the pun on *Waldend* and *geweald*.

"strong companions" (*strange geneatas*, 284b). There is no creative or nurturing impulse to his desire to rule. Therefore, even though he says he can be like God ("Ic mæg wesan god swa he," 283b) and build "a diviner throne" (*godlecran stol*, 281a), Lucifer's idea of divinity appears to be limited to the abuse of brute force.

A large envelope pattern emerges at the end of Lucifer's speech, which serves to enclose the whole sequence from the angel's birth to the narrator's final thoughts on his monologue (246–99). The poet's conclusion is meant to provide heaven's perspective and some commentary on the consequences of ingratitude and overweening pride (292–9a):[87]

> Ða hit se allwalda   eall gehyrde,
> þæt his engyl ongan   ofermede micel
> ahebban wið his hearran   and spræc healic word
> dollice wið drihten sinne,   sceolde he þa dæd ongyldan,   295
> worc þæs gewinnes gedælan,   and sceolde his wite habban,
> ealra morðra mæst.   Swa deð monna gehwilc
> þe wið his waldend   winnan ongynneð
> mid mane wið þone mæran drihten.

[When the Almighty heard all of that, that his angel began to uplift great pride against his Lord and speak haughty words rashly against his ruler, he had to repay the deed, share the work of war, and have for his punishment the worst of all miseries. So does each man who sets out to contend against the renowned Lord.]

The envelope pattern is marked by the repetition of *se allwalda* in line 292a, which echoes *se alwalda* in line 246a. At this point, God hears "that his angel has begun to raise up much pride against his Lord" ("þæt his engyl ongan ofermede micel ahebban wið his hearran," 293–4a), and these words reflect the narrator's earlier comment "þæt his engyl ongan ofermod wesan, / ahof hine wið his hearran" (262–3a). It is significant that God does not at all recognize the angel's supposed "great power" ("geweald micel," 280), only his "great pride" (*ofermede micel*, 293). The repetition of the word, *eall* ("all") in line 293b ("Ða hit se <u>all</u>walda <u>eall</u> gehyrde," 292) offers a final statement on the matter: God is omnipotent and omniscient; in short, unbeatable. Through paronomasia, the poet then slights

---

87 I have followed Krapp's punctuation of this passage in *The Junius Manuscript*, 12.

the devil's attempt to surpass his Lord (*hearran*, 294) with nothing but "lofty language" (*healic word*, 294). The pun suggests that Lucifer's "high/haughty words" (*healic word*) are insignificant next to his "higher" Lord (*heahran/hearran*). The minor addition of the adverb *dollice* is also meant to highlight the "foolishness" of Lucifer.

The passage ends with a warning to the reader, that the punishment Lucifer receives at the hands of God awaits any who "sets out to contend against the renowned Lord" ("þe wið his waldend winnan ongynneð," 298). The whole sequence, from the first creation of Lucifer to the author's final admonition to the reader, is carefully constructed to expose the fallacy of Lucifer's ambitions, which are based on a false assumption of power and a narrow vision for its use. He is both inferior to the superlative might of God and ill-suited to replace Him. Even so, the devil is possessed of enough might to be destructive, and as his counterpart says in Avitus' *Historia spiritalis*, "A great part [of my power] retains its own strength and that is renowned for its high power to harm" ("pars magna retentat / Vim propriam summaque cluit uirtute nocendi," 95–6).

The Temptation of Adam (495–521)

The temptation of Adam in *Genesis B* is unusual in the genre, and the author's source is probably the corresponding lines of the *Saxon Genesis*, which have not survived.[88] Leading up to this moment, Lucifer delivers a second speech from Hell (356–441a), in which he resolves "to turn Adam from God's will" ("onwendan him þær willan sines," 400a), and to see him forfeit His grace ("þæt hie his hyldo forlæten … ahwet hie from his hyldo," 404b–6b). These two words, *willa* ("will") and *hyldo* ("favour" or "grace"), are repeated throughout the Temptation sequence of *Genesis B*, and they play a crucial part in the devil's plan. Lucifer's new ambition (having failed himself) is to turn man from the praise of God to more personal desires. By replacing God's words (*word*) and counsel (*lar*) with his own, the devil aims to undermine man's loyalty to the Lord. In particular, and like his counterpart in Avitus' *Historia spiritalis*, Satan is incensed that Adam, "who was made of earth, should assume [his] mighty throne" ("þæt

---

88 See Doane, *Genesis B*, 282: "There is no known direct source, and the motif is rare: it occurs in the Anglo-Norman *Mystère d'Adam* (twelfth century) and in Hugo Grotius' *Adamus Exul* (see Evans, RES n.s. 14.9–10, and Woolf, 'Fall of Man,' 188.) Murdoch, *MÆ* 45.72, points out a minor fifteenth-century poem of 581 lines in MS Karlsruhe 408 in which a devil sent as a messenger approaches Adam first."

Adam sceal, þe wæs of eorðan geworht, / minne stronglican stol beheal-
dan," 365–6).[89] That same onomastic pun appears in Avitus' poem, where
the devil complains that "earth succeeds my angelic honour" ("angelico
limus succedit honori," 2.90).[90] Given that Adam is the source of the devil's enmity only after God, it makes sense that he focuses his initial
attack on him and not Eve (491–510):

Wearp hine þa on wyrmes lic   and wand him þa ymbutan
þone deaðes beam   þurh deofles cræft.
Genam þær þæs ofætes   and wende hine eft þanon
þær he wiste handgeweorc   heofoncyninges.
Ongon hine þa frinan   forman worde   495
se laða mid ligenum: "Langað þe awuht,
Adam, up to Gode?   Ic eom on his ærende hider
feorran gefered,   ne þæt nu fyrn ne wæs
þæt ic wið hine sylfne sæt.   Ða het he me on þysne sið faran,
het þæt þu þisses ofætes æte,   cwæð þæt þin abal and cræft   500
and þin modsefa   mara wurde
and þin lichoma   leohtra micle,
in gesceapu scenran,[91]   cwæð þæt þe æniges sceates ðearf
ne wurde on worulde.   Nu þu willan hæfst,
hyldo geworhte   heofoncyninges,   505
to þance geþenod   þinum hearan,
hæfst þe wið drihten dyrne geworhtne.
Ic gehyrde hine þine dæd and word
lofian on his leohte   and ymb þin lif sprecan

---

89 Sievers long ago noted several correlations between *Genesis A* and Avitus. They appear
in *Der Heliand und die Angelsächsische Genesis*, 18–23. For a discussion of the pre-
eminence of God's *lar* in *Genesis B*, see further Ehrhart, "Tempter as Teacher: Some
Observations on the Vocabulary of the Old English *Genesis B*," 435–46.

90 See further Sievers, *Der Heliand* (1875), 19.

91 See Doane, *Genesis B*, 282, who takes *gesceapu* to mean "condition" or "destiny," on
the basis that Old Saxon *giskapu* never has the sense of "form" or "shape," which the
Old English *gesceap* does. I have taken the word as an equivalent to the Latin *forma*,
nonetheless, on the basis of sense (that it agrees with *lichoma*) and in response to the
Old English appositive style, allowing that the sense of "condition" may have applied
to the original Saxon audience. Also, I have taken *sceattes* in the same line as a reference
to "wealth" or "property" and not clothing, as Doane suggests. It seems to me that the
normal sense is in keeping with the misguided ambitions of Satan, who promises Adam
and Eve the world and everything in it (cf. 813, *sceattes wiht*).

swa þu læstan scealt   þæt on þis land hider
his bodan bringað."   510

[He then cast himself into the body of a serpent and wound about the tree of death through devil's craft. There he took the fruit and turned back to where he knew the handiwork of Heaven's King would be. With his first word, the hateful creature began to question him with lies: "Do you long for anything from God above, Adam? I am here on His errand, having journeyed from afar, and it was not long ago that I sat with God himself. He commanded me to make this journey and He commanded you to eat this fruit. He said your strength and power, your understanding, would grow greater, and your body, far brighter, your form, more radiant. He said you would have no want of wealth in the world. You have now gained the good will, the grace of the King of Heaven, served to the satisfaction of your Lord, made yourself dear to Him. I have heard Him in His brightness praise your words and deeds, speak about your life. So you have to carry out what His messengers bring here into this land."][92]

Now the devil puts his *deofles cræft* (492) to good use, possessing a serpent and plucking the fruit from the tree, just as Satan does for Eve in *Historia spiritalis* (2.210–11):[93] "unum de cunctis letali ex arbore malum / Detrahit et suaui pulchrum perfundit odore" ("He plucks a single, beautiful apple from the deadly tree and imbues it with a sweet scent"). Both poets emphasize the "deadliness" of that tree (*deaðes beam / lethati ex arbore*), though Avitus more so with the added pun, *mālum / mălum* ("apple" / "evil"). The narrator of *Genesis B* is also more explicit about the danger to Adam, and he makes a point of saying that the serpent's words are full of "lies" ("*mid ligenum*," 496). As with Lucifer's first speech, the narrator's interjection at this point is meant to undermine the devil's

---

92 I have used Doane's translation of lines 504–5 at p. 282 of his edition ("You have now gained the good will, the grace of the king of heaven, served to the satisfaction of your lord") and Klaeber's translation, line 506 ("served to the satisfaction of your lord"), in *The Later Genesis*, 51.

93 See Doane, *Genesis B*, 281: "The orthodox explanation of the biblical serpent was that it was a natural animal suffering diabolical possession, rather than a phantasmic appearance of a disguised devil (cf. Augustine, *De ciu. Dei*, 14.11). Most commentators on *GB*, supposing that the devil appears to Adam and Eve in the form of an angel, regard the mention of the snake here and at 590 as either an irrelevant traditional element or some confusion in the text (see Woolf, 'Fall of Man,' 190, and Vickrey's ed., 198–203)."

credibility and the rhetorical force of his words. It is as if he does not wish the reader to become too immersed in the serpent's guile.

The whole speech is driven by the devil's hatred for God and man (*lað*). Only moments before, Satan declares his wish "that [Adam and Eve] should become hateful to God" themselves ("þæt hie wurdon lað gode," 452),[94] and as the personification of enmity (*se laða*, 489b, 496b), his servant is well qualified for the task.[95] He knows that Adam, like God's prelapsarian angels, will be loyal to the Lord, and so he appeals first to his sense of responsibility: "God commanded me ... and he has commanded you to eat the fruit..." ("Ða het he me ... het þæt þu þisses ofætes æte," 499–500). The repetition of the verb *hatan* (*het*) is meant to ring in Adam's ears as a reminder of his subservience to the Lord. The devil ends his speech with similar words, saying, "[Adam] must carry out what [God's] messengers bring" ("swa þu læstan scealt þæt ... his bodan bringað"). Therefore, the first assault on Adam is mainly intellectual in nature.

Satan's herald also appeals to Adam's emotional faculties, especially with his first words, "Do you long for anything, Adam, from God above?" ("Langað þe awuht/Adam, up to Gode?" 496b–7a).[96] It is a searching question, meant to foster doubt and desire in Adam's heart, the kind of longing that led Lucifer himself to his demise. As specific prompting, the serpent lays out all that Adam can expect to gain from a taste of the fruit: "strength and power" (*abal and cræft*, 500b); intellectual enhancement ("þin modsefa mara wurde," 501); greater physical beauty ("þin lichoma leohtra micle,/þin gesceapu scenran," 502–3a); and wealth in the world (*sceattes ... on worulde*, 503b–4a). These are all things Lucifer himself has coveted and still covets. It is also noteworthy that he, like the devil in *Historia spiritalis*, who puts the focus on Eve as a way to soften her up (*tu ... te ... tu ... tuo ... uobis ... uos ... uestros*, 2.145–55), uses the same rhetoric on Adam (*þu ... þin ... þin ... þin ... þe ... þu ...*, 500–10). The promise of greater *cræft* ("power") also raises alarms, knowing as we do that it has

---

94 Renoir, "The Self-Deception of Temptation," 47–67, at 48.

95 See also 429b, where Satan enquires of his fellow angels (428–9): "Gif hit eower ænig mæge/gewendan mid wihte þæt hie word Godes/lare forlæten, sona hie him þe laðran beoð" ("If any of you can devise it in any way ... that they abandon God's word ... they shall at once become the more hateful to him").

96 Cf. in contrast Lucifer's first speech (289–90) and his declaration that he no longer needs anything from God: "Swa me þæt riht ne þinceð,/þæt ic oleccan awiht þurfe gode æfter Gode ænegum" ("So it does not seem right to me that I should have to pay court to Him one bit for any good").

led Lucifer to his downfall. Finally, Satan begins here to put his ultimate plan into motion, by subverting the "will" and "favour" of God. So his servant tells Adam that he has now fulfilled those things to the satisfaction of the Lord ("Nu þu willan hæfst, / hyldo geworhte heofoncyninges," 504a–5b), and so he may begin to think about his own desires. It is a lie, of course, along with the exhortation to heed God's commands ("het þæt þu þisses ofætes æte"), and both promptings are meant to deceive Adam, by using God's own language against him.

The Temptation of Eve I (564–87)

But Adam is not fooled: "I know what God himself commanded me ... he bade me honour his words and hold them well, and follow his counsel" ("Ic wat hwæt he me self bebead, / he het me his word weorðian and wel healdan, / læstan his lare," 535b–8a). The devil's original question, then, "is there a whit of anything you need from God" (*wuht*, 496), is plainly answered by Adam (533b–5a): "No, I cannot acknowledge a whit of your business, not your words, not your wisdom, the errand, or your utterances" ("Hwæt, ic þinra bysna ne mæg, / worda ne wisna wuht oncnawan, / siðes ne sagona"). Unlike Satan, who in his first speech says that he does not want "any good from God" ("gode æfter gode ænegum," 291), Adam reaffirms his faith by saying that he does: "He mæg me of his hean rice / geofian mid goda gehwilcum" ("He can provide me with every good from his high kingdom," 545b–6a).

Eve is another matter.[97] To be fair, the devil's initial approach to her is mainly an appeal to her love for Adam and her fear that God will punish them both for disobeying His divine messenger (551a–63). Only later does he turn to more subversive tactics, and his words to Eve in these lines are similar to those he speaks to Adam, showing that the essence of Satan's plan does not change, only his target (564–87):

Æt þisses ofetes.   Ðonne wurðað þin eagan swa leoht
þæt þu meaht swa wide   ofer woruld ealle   565
geseon siððan   and selfes stol

---

97 For some character analyses of Eve in *Genesis B*, see further Woolf, "The Fall of Man in *Genesis B* and the Mystère d'Adam," 187–99, esp. 196–7; Klinck, "Female Characterization in Old English Poetry," 597–610; Renoir, "Eve's I.Q. Rating," 262–72; Overing, "On Reading Eve," 35–64.

herran þines   and habban his hyldo forð.
Meaht þu Adame   eft gestyran
gif þu his willan hæfst   and he þinum wordum getrywð.

        ...

               Span þu hine georne   575
þæt he þine lare læste   þy læs gyt lað Gode,
incrum waldende   weorðan þyrfen.
Gif þu þæt angin fremest,   idesa seo betste,
forhele ic incrum herran   þæt me hearmes swa fela
Adam gespræc,   eargra worda,   580
tyhð me untryowða,   cwyð þæt ic seo teonum georn,
gramum ambyhtsecg,   nales Godes engel.
Ac ic cann ealle swa geare   engla gebyrdo,
heah heofona gehlidu.   Wæs seo hwil þæs lang
þæt ic geornlice   Gode þegnode   584
þurh holdne hyge,   herran minum,
drihtne selfum.   Ne eom ic deofle gelic.'

["Eat this fruit. Then will your eyes be so clear that you will be able to see over all the world, even the throne of the Lord himself, and you will hereafter hold his favour. You will then be able to rule Adam, if you have his will and if he believes your words ... Entice him eagerly to follow your counsel, so that you two do not become hateful to God, your Ruler. If you accept this undertaking, best of women, I will conceal from the Lord that Adam spoke so many injuries to me, evil words. He accuses me of untruths, says that I am eager for wrong, a servant to the malignant, not at all God's angel. But I know all the angels' origins, heaven's high vaults. For a long time, I eagerly served God with a faithful heart, my master, the Lord himself. I am not like a devil!"]

The serpent's first words, *Æt þisses ofetes* ("eat this fruit," 564) were spoken to Adam (*þisses ofætes æte*, 500), while the promise of greater sight is biblical in origin ("Scit enim Deus quod in quocumque die comederitis ex eo, aperientur oculi vestri ..." ["For God knows that on the day you eat of that, your eyes shall be opened"], 3:5). The narrator has already made the point that the devil's words are lies ("se laða mid ligenum" 496a), and so when he tells Eve that greater sight will earn God's favour ("habban his hyldo forð," 567), the reader can recognize the irony. Lucifer himself forfeited God's grace out of personal ambition, and so he was cast down to Hell (301–4): "hyldo hæfde his ferlorene ... Acwæð hine þa fram his hyldo and hine on helle wearp" ("he had forsaken His favour ... God cast him from his favour and threw him into hell," 301–4). That fate answers plainly Lucifer's question in his first speech (282): "Hwy sceal ic æfter his hyldo ðeowian" ("Why must I serve to win His favour?" 282). Satan therefore knows the consequences of falling from grace, which is why he makes it a part of his plan in his second speech ("his hyldo forlæten ... ahwet hie from his hyldo," 404–6). The repetition, twice, of that word (*hyldo*) in close proximity in two separate passages, makes the reappearance of it here highly ironic.

Satan cannot bend Adam to his devilish "will" (*willa*) or "counsel" (*lar*), and so he turns to Eve to do it for him. When the serpent first approaches Adam, he tries to convince him that he has fulfilled God's "will" and "favour" ("Nu þu willan hæfst,/hyldo geworhte heofoncyninges"). That plan does not work, and so he uses Eve as an intermediary, to gain access to Adam's will, so that he will follow her words and counsel instead ("gif þu his willan hæfst and he þinum wordum getrywð ... þine lare," 569). Whomever Adam believes, Satan or Eve, he is doing the devil's work. Moreover, when the serpent tells Eve to "entice" or "seduce" Adam eagerly ("Span þu hine georne," 575) he uses the verb *spanan* which has not been seen since that lead-in to Satan's first speech, where the narrator tells how ambition first seduced Lucifer to prepare his own kingdom in heaven (273–4a). He says, "hine his hige speone" ("his heart seduced him," 274b). Thus Satan's experience offers knowledge of the power of desire, and the devil believes that Eve can do to Adam what he could not achieve. Put differently, even though Adam rebukes the serpent, by saying he will only follow God's counsel (*læstan his lare*, 535–8), that is not strictly speaking true. He is also likely to follow Eve's advice (*þine lare læste*, 576).

The Fall of Eve (588–600)

The moment of Eve's fall has been carefully orchestrated by the devil (and the poet), although his plans are less successfully deployed than in *Historia spiritalis*, where he does not have to contend with Adam. The fact that much of Satan's earlier language reappears here suggests that the author has thoughtfully anticipated this scene and the whole of the Temptation sequence. On the one hand, Eve's pliability is to be expected, as a conventional feature of Latin biblical epic, but the unfolding of the Old English drama is in large part due to the author's own design, which is to some extent indebted to the original Saxon poet (588–600):

Lædde hie swa mid ligenum   and mid listum speon
idese on þæt unriht,   oðþæt hire on innan ongan
weallan wyrmes geþeaht,   hæfde hire wacran hige   590
metod gemearcod,   þæt heo hire mod ongan

lætan æfter þam larum.   forþon heo æt þam laðan onfeng
ofer drihtnes word[98]   deaðes beames
weorcsumne wæstm.   Ne wearð wyrse dæd
monnum gemearcod.   Þæt is micel wundor   595
þæt hit ece god   æfre wolde
þeoden þolian,   þæt wurde þegn swa monig
forlædd be þam lygenum   þe for þam larum com.
Heo þa þæs ofætes æt,   alwaldan bræc
word and willan.   600

[So he led her on with lies, seduced that woman toward wrong with his schemes, until the serpent's advice began to well up within her. The Lord had marked her with a weaker mind, so that her thoughts began to heed his counsel. Therefore, against the word of God, she took the toilsome fruit of the deadly tree from the hateful creature. No worse deed has been marked for men. It is a great wonder that eternal God, our King, ever allowed so many of His thanes to be so utterly misled by the lies that came of that counsel. She then ate the fruit, broke the will and word of the Almighty.]

What the devil cannot achieve through Adam by lying ("se laða mid li-genum," 496a), he accomplishes through Eve ("Lædde hie swa mid lige-num," 588, and "forlædd be þam lygenum," 598a). These are also the same lies Satan uses to tempt Eve in Cyprianus' *Heptateuch* (75): "Liuida mor-daci uoluens mendacia sensu / Femineo temptat sub pectore mollia corda" ("Mingling jealous lies with mordant wit, he tempts the soft heart beneath the woman's breast").[99] That same, soft heart, weaker than Adam's (*hire wacran hige*, 590b), is a mark upon Eve often in Latin Christian poetry, and the failing here is by God's design (*metod gemearcod* ["the Lord marked her out"], 591a).[100] The verb, *mearcian* ("to mark" or "stain") is

---

98 See Klaeber, *Later Genesis*, 51, for the transgressive sense of *ofer* (593).

99 See also *Hept., Gen.* 81–2, in the same scene: "The woman refuses and fears to touch the forbidden boughs, and yet her heart was overcome by a feeble mind" ("Illa negat uetitosque timet contingere ramos; / Sed tamen infirmo uincuntur pectora sensu"). The same weakness (*wifes wac geþoht* ["the woman's weak thought"], 649a) is hightlighted again in *Genesis B*, when Eve bears the fruit to Adam (647–9).

100 For a discussion of Eve's "weaker mind" and other women in Old English, see further Belanoff, "The Fall (?) of the Old English Female Poetic Image," 822–31. Vickery, "The Vision of Eve in *Genesis B*," 86–102; and Vickery, "*Micel Wundor* of *Genesis B*," 245–54; also, Hill, "The Fall of Angels and Man in the Old English *Genesis B*," 279–329, at 282.

undoubtedly pejorative, and it recalls the opening of *Historia spiritalis*, where Avitus says, "our nature is tainted, soiled by its origins, [and] burdened by the distant deeds of our ancient parents" ("uel quod polluti uitiantur origine mores, / Quos aliena premunt priscorum facta parentum," *Hist. spirit.* 1.3–4). According to most biblical poets, Latin and English, humanity bears the mark of Eve's vulnerability, and the author of *Genesis B* repeats this word in the same scene, saying, "no worse deed has been marked out for man" ("Ne wearð wyrse dæd / monnum gemearcod," 594b–5a). Later, in the aftermath of the Fall, Adam uses it himself: "Hwæt, þu Eue, hæfst yfele gemearcod / Uncer sylfra sið" ("So, Eve, you have evilly marked our path," 791–2). The onomastic pun *Eue/yfele* (Eve/evil) offers a new and ironic etymology for Eve's name, which in origin means "of life" ("Et uocavit Adam nomen uxoris suae, Heua eo quod mater esset cunctorum uiuentium," Genesis 3:20).[101]

The verb *spanan* (*speon*, 588a) also reappears in this scene, as a way to emphasize the insistent role of seduction in the Fall. Satan tells Eve to entice Adam eagerly ("Span þu hine georne," 575a), until he will heed her counsel (*þine lare læste*, 576a), and that is precisely what happens to her, as the devil seduces her with his schemes ("and mid listum speon," 588), until her mind begins to heed his counsel ("þæt heo hire mod ongan / lætan æfter þam larum," 591b–2a). The thematic noun *lar* ("counsel" or "teaching"), which should refer to God's instructions, is once again co-opted by the devil in this passage. Here the poet understatedly calls Eve's actions *unriht* ("unright"), and when she eats the fruit ("Heo þa þæs ofætes æt," 599a), she fulfills the devil's earlier exhortation (*Æt þisses ofetes*, 564a) and his plan to have Adam and Eve break the "will" and "word" of the Almighty ("alwaldan bræc / word and willan," 599b–600a). The key for the reader in all of this is to recognize the use of recurrent language in *Genesis B* and to interpret its significance. Although such repetition may seem redundant, the context changes with the shifting focus on Lucifer, Adam, and Eve, adding new and different levels of meaning at each moment. This insistent use of thematic repetition is unlike what we find generally in Latin biblical epic, where important words are often repeated, but nothing comparable to the style of *Genesis B*.

---

101 Gen. 3.20: "And Adam called the name of his wife Eve: because she was the mother of all the living."

The Fall of Adam (selections, 626ff.)

Having eaten the fruit, Eve now seeks out Adam, and the scene replays once more. Eve is now close to fulfilling her part in the devil's plan, which will end with the corruption of Adam. She has already been "misled by lies" (*forlæd mid ligenum*, 630a), the same lies that failed to work on her husband (*se laða mid ligenum*, 496a), and now unknowingly she follows in the footsteps of Satan. Like the serpent ("genam þær þæs ofætes," 493a), she plucks the fruit from the tree herself and offers it to Adam, bearing within her the piece she has already eaten (636): "Sum heo hire on handum bær, sum hire æt heortan læg" ("One she bore in her hands, one in her heart"). Eve does exactly what the devil has instructed her to do, and in this respect she is unlike her biblical counterpart, who "is primarily motivated by her desire to be 'as God, knowing good and evil' while in *Genesis B* the poet alters this aspect of the narrative and depicts Eve as deceived by the devil."[102] It is also important and more realistic, psychologically, that Eve "sins not from ignorance and not from pride ... but from genuine concern" for her husband (684–5):[103]

Hio spræc him þicce to   and speon hine ealne dæg
on þa dimman dæd   þæt hie drihtnes heora   685
willan bræcon.   Stod se wraða boda,
legde him lustas on   and mid listum speon,
fylgde him frecne.

[She spoke to him insistently and tempted him all day to that dark deed, that they should break the Lord's will. The savage messenger stood by, instilling him with desires, tempting him with tricks, hounding him fiercely.]

The first verse, "þicce to and speon hine ealne dæg" reflects·the devil's earlier counsel that Eve should "Entice him eagerly, to follow [her] advice" ("Span þu hine georne/þæt he þine lare læste," 575a–6a). Ironically, Eve thinks she is fulfilling the will of God, not breaking it (*willan bræcon*, 686a). Adam, on the other hand, because he has proven to be difficult, requires additional prompting, and so the devil joins Eve, "tempting him

---

102 Hill, "The Fall of Angels and Man," 280. Hill concludes that "Eve is in effect subjectively innocent" because "she acted *þurh holdne hyge*."
103 Klinck, "Female Characterization," 599.

with his tricks" (*mid listum speon*, 687b). This last phrase is repeated ver-batim from Satan's counsel to Eve as to how best to sway Adam ("and mid listum speon," 588b). The repetition serves to emphasize the devil's relent-less determination to destroy man, which is done as much through persis-tence as guile.

Worn down, Adam falls from grace in much the same way Eve does, but the consequence of their collective downfall is more catastrophic. Once again, the poet intervenes with commentary, but this time of a more meta-phorical nature (704–23a):

<pre>
Heo spræc ða to Adame,   idesa sceonost,
ful þiclice   oð þam þegne ongan   705
his hige hweorfan   þæt he þam gehate getruwode
þe him þæt wif   wordum sægde.
Heo dyde hit þeah þurh holdne hyge,   nyste þæt þær hearma swa fela,
fyrenearfeða   fylgean sceolde
monna cynne   þæs heo on mod genam   710
þæt heo þæs laðan bodan   larum hyrde
ac wende þæt heo hyldo   heofoncyninges
worhte mid þam wordum   þe heo þam were swelce
tacen oðiewde   and treowe gehet
oð þæt Adame   innan breostum   715
his hyge hwyrfde   and his heorte ongann
wendan to hire willan.   He æt þam wife onfeng
helle and hinnsið   þeah hit nære haten swa
ac hit ofetes noman   agan sceolde.
hit wæs þeah deaðes swefn   and deofles gespon,   720
hell and hinnsið   and hæleða forlor,
menniscra morð   þæt hie to mete dædon,
ofet unfæle.
</pre>

[She then spoke to Adam ceaselessly, fairest of women, until that servant's heart began to turn, so that he trusted in her bidding, in the words his wife spoke to him. She did it, however, with a faithful heart – she did not know that so much pain, so much terrible suffering, would persecute mankind, all because she got it into her head to follow the counsel of that hateful messen-ger; but she thought she was fulfilling the favour of the heavenly king with her words, which she revealed to that man as proof, and vowed them to be true, until his thoughts, the heart within his breast, began to bend to her will. He accepted hell and exile from that woman, although it was not called that;

it bore the name of "fruit." Nonetheless, it was the sleep of death, the devil's lure, hell and exile, the ruin of men, the death of humankind, that they made that unholy fruit their food.]

There are undertones of sympathy for Eve at this moment, owing mainly to her innocence, which is also the focus of Satan's assault in Avitus' *Historia spiritalis*. Eve is ignorant of the danger before her, as the poet says (*nyste*, "she did not know," 708b), and she acts out of a "faithful heart" (*þurh holdne hyge*, 708a), which she believes to be in tune with God's favour (*hyldo*, 712a), even though the opposite is true. What is more, Eve is still the "fairest of women" (*idesa sceonost*, 704b) at this point, a phrase the poet uses earlier, when Eve seeks out Adam, having just eaten the fruit. There, the poet likewise calls her *idesa scenost* (626b) and "the brightest of all women to have come into the world" ("wifa wlitegost þe on woruld come," 627), not because she has eaten the fruit, but "because she was the handiwork of the heavenly king, / even though she was then secretly undone, misled by lies" ("forþon heo wæs handgeweorc heofoncyninges / þeah heo þa dearnenga fordon wurde, / forlæd mid ligenum," 628–30b). Her beauty, then, is a gift of the Maker's touch and not a gift from the devil. The fact that she still bears some measure of that heavenly grace is tragic.

Still, the wanton disobedience of Adam and Eve cannot be dismissed. Adam has put his trust in Eve's bidding (*þam gehate getruwode*, 706b), in her words (*wif wordum sægde*, 707), when the benefit of God's grace depends on his commands alone, as the poet says from the beginning (244b–5): "Heo wæron leof gode / ðenden heo his halige word healdan woldon" ("They were dear to God, so long as they chose to keep his holy words"). Adam is adamant in his rejection of the devil's initial offer, saying, "Ic wat hwæt he me self bebead" ("I know myself what God commanded me," 535b), and so he can hardly be entirely innocent. His fall, then, and the fall of Eve are cautionary tales for the audience on the corruptive influence of desire. Just as the heart of Lucifer is enticed to challenge God in heaven ("cwæð þæt hine his hige speone," 274b), so this same mental or emotional faculty is the weakness of Adam and Eve on earth (*his hige hweorfan*, 706a; *his hyge hwyrfde*, 716a), and Satan exploits that weakness, knowing full well what the consequences will be.

Summary Conclusion to the Fall

The whole of *Genesis B* offers a thoughtful meditation on the inner workings of ambition and pride, and there is much in the Old English narrative to consider about the nature of desire and how it affects man's relationship to God. Through Satan, the poet leads the audience through a dramatic re-enactment of the Fall, which is entertaining but also instructive as a warning about Satan's guile and the consequences of sin. At many moments, the author also interjects, like Sedulius or Arator, to expand on or elucidate a particular point, and these asides offer productive guidance for the reader. For example, Satan's fall ends with an exhortation not to challenge God's authority (292–9a), while Eve's belief in her own faithfulness does not change the fact that she fails to recognize the promptings of the devil in the first place. Adam is also blinded, and he fails to perceive the stratagems of the devil in the voice of the one he loves. Their ignorance coincides with the *simplicitas* ("innocence") of Adam and Eve in Avitus' *Historia spiritalis*, and additional comparisons with that and other Latin biblical epics will no doubt further enrich our reading of the Fall in *Genesis B*.

The Flood 1371–91

The account of the Flood in *Genesis A* spans about three hundred lines (1248–1554) and covers the events of the Bible roughly from Genesis 6:2 to 9:20. By this point in literary history, the figurative signification of the story was well known, as the example of Latin biblical epic attests.[104] So the ark, being made of wood, could symbolize the cross or the Church, which offer redemption through Baptism, signified by waters of the Flood. The ark could also represent the tomb of Jesus, as an enclosure, and Noah could prefigure Christ, as an agent of salvation. Numerous Latin poets treat the episode or accompanying individuals in these terms. Cyprianus is not among them – he favours the literal narrative in the *Heptateuch* (*Gen.* 287–310) – but Sedulius presents the ark as a vessel of redemption. God's "mystical power," he says (*mystica uirtus*, 1.75), shows that it is possible "to renew by flowing waters what the sins of the flesh kill, so bathing the whole world in one Baptism" ("liquidas renouari posse per undas, / Totum namque lauans uno baptismate mundum," 1.77–8). Avitus of Vienne dedicates a whole book of his *Spiritual History* to the Flood (*De diluuio mundi*), in which he emphasizes the symbolic meaning of the story over the literal account. The author of *Genesis A* is more conservative, though many words here invite closer consideration and suggest that he is aware of the exegetical potential underlying the biblical narrative, even if the pursuit of such meaning is not his primary goal.

---

104 Doane, *Genesis A*, 325ff., takes for granted the baptismal significance of the episode.

For example, the Flood represents a re-genesis of the world, and the *Genesis A*- poet is attuned to this symbolism, since he echoes language and imagery from the earlier Creation sequence.[105] On each occasion, he calls God *lifes leohtfruma* ("Bright Source of Life," 175, 1410), an epithet he reserves mainly for God's creative agency. This word appears for the first time when God completes his work on the sixth day. In the later context of the Flood, God (1410) suddenly remembers Noah and the ark, and so puts an end to the deluge. It is as if, His anger appeased, God now returns to His more creative proclivity, restoring light and life to the world. God also tells Noah and his kin to go forth and multiply ("Tymað nu and tie-drað," 1512), just as he does to Adam and Eve ("Temað nu and wexað," 196),[106] and Andy Orchard has argued that "the poet of *Genesis A* had in mind the second biblical passage even as he rendered the first."[107] Other echoes link the Flood and Creation in *Genesis A*, and suggest that the English author, like Cyprianus, aligns the two events, to emphasize the new beginning at each moment. Less explicit is any suggestion that we should view the Flood as a symbol of Baptism, however. Given the length of this episode, I offer only an excerpt of it here (1371b–91):[108]

7:11 … rupti sunt omnes fontes abyssi magnae et cataractae caeli apertae sunt. 6 … diluuii aquae inundauerunt super terram …12 et facta est pluuia super terram quadraginta diebus et quadraginta noctibus. 19 et aquae praeualuerunt nimis super terram opertique sunt omnes montes excelsi sub uniuerso caelo. 17 Factumque est diluuium quadraginta diebus super terram et multiplicatae sunt aquae et eleuauerunt arcam in sublime a terra.[109]

---

105   Griffith provides an excellent side-by-side comparison of God's speeches to Adam and Eve (196–205) and Noah (1512–17, 1532–8), showing several other correspondences in style and diction, though he does not discuss the thematic connection. See further Griffith, "The Register of Divine Speech in *Genesis A*," 69.

106   Lines 1532–5 repeat this command and contain language that also overlaps with lines 196–205.

107   Orchard, "Intoxication, Fornication, and Multiplication," 333–54, at 339.

108   I have rearranged the order of the biblical narrative to match the narrative sequence of the poetry.

109   Gen. 7:11: "… all the fountains of the great deep were broken up, and the flood gates of heaven were opened. 6 … the waters of the flood overflowed the earth. 12 And the rain fell upon the earth forty days and forty nights. 19 And the waters prevailed beyond measure upon the earth: and all the high mountains under the whole heaven were covered. 17 And the flood was forty days upon the earth, and the waters increased, and lifted up the ark on high from the earth."

7:11 ða asprungon ealle wyllspringas þære micclan niwelnisse, and þære heofenan wæterþeotan wæron geopenode. 6 ... þa þæs flodes wæteru yþedon ofer eorðan. 12 and hit rinde þa ofer eorðan feowertig daga and feowertig nihta on an. 19 and þæt wæter swiðrode swiþe ofer eorðan; wurdon þa behelede ealle þa heahstan duna under ealre heofenan. 17 Wæs þa geworden micel flod, and þa wæteru wæron gemenigfilde and ahefdon upp þone arc.

– Gen 7:11–19 (selectively)

... Drihten sende

regn from roderum and eac rume let	
willeburnan on woruld þringan	
of ædra gehwære, egorstreamas	
swearte swogan. Sæs up stigon	1375
ofer stæðweallas. Strang wæs and reðe	
se ðe wætrum weold, wreah and þeahte	
manfæhðu bearn, middangeardes,	
wonnan wæge, wera eðelland.	
hof hergode, hygeteonan wræc	1380
metod on monnum. Mere swiðe grap	
on fæge folc feowertig daga,	
nihta oðer swilc. Nið wæs reðe,	
wællgrim werum. Wuldorcyninges	
yða wræcon arleasra feorh	1385
of flæschoman. Flod ealle wreah,	
hreoh under heofonum, hea beorgas	
geond sidne grund and on sund ahof	
earce from eorðan and þa æðelo mid.	
þa segnade selfa drihten,	1390
scyppend usser, þa he þæt scip beleac.	

[The Lord sent down rain from the heavens and from every vein, far and wide, let wellsprings press upon the world, let ocean-streams roar darkly. The seas rose up over the shore-walls. Strong He was and fierce who wielded the waters; He covered and consumed earth's children of wickedness with a black wave, the homeland of men. The Lord ravaged their homes, avenged on man their willful crimes. The sea gripped fiercely onto the doomed people for forty days and as many nights. The punishment was fierce, deadly grim for men. The waves of the King of Glory drove the lives of the faithless from their carcasses. The Flood covered everything, fierce under heaven, the high mountains over the wide ground, and it raised the ark on the water from the

earth and the nobility with it. Then the Lord himself, our Maker, blessed
them, who sealed that ship.]

The biblical heritage of the poetry is clear. The inevitable noun, *regn*
("rain," 1372a), finds precedence in the Latin *pluuia* (7:12), and resonates
with the verbal form *rinde* ("it rained") in the later English prose, while
the prepositional phrase, *from rodorum* ("from the heavens," 1372a), reflects, albeit with greater enthusiasm, the original *caeli* (7:11). In place of
the more lively verb *rupti sunt* ("[the fountains] were broken up"), the
Old English poet uses a humbler word, *sende* ("he sent," 1371b), though
he may be hearkening back to the Latin (*rupti sunt*) by way of alliteration
(*regn from roderum*). If so, he is tracking the Bible to the point of style,
which would match Aldhelm's emulation of Sedulius in the *Carmen de
uirginitate*. The coincidence of another alliterative doublet in the same
verse of the Bible, *cataractae caeli* (7:11), lends some credence to this possibility, but since alliteration must appear in every line of Old English
verse, the connection may be purely coincidental.

Doane points to the Latin *fontes abyssi* (7:11), as the source of the Old
English compound *willeburnan* ("wellsprings," 1373a), which is comparable to *wyllspringas* in the English prose, reinforcing Doane's suggestion.
Verses 1375b–6a ("Sæs up stigon / ofer stæðweallas") loosely render Genesis
7:6 ("diluuii aquae inundauerunt super terram"),[110] while the duration of the
Flood ("feowertig daga, nihta oðer swilc," 1382b–3a) clearly identifies the
source ("quadraginta diebus et quadraginta noctibus, 7:12). The Old English
prose is also similar ("feowertig daga, and feowertig nihta," 7:12), but note
that the poet neatly eliminates repetition by substituting the phrase *nihta
oðer swilc* ("as many nights"). The covering of the world and the mountains
in the biblical Genesis, 7:19 ("et aquae praeualuerunt nimis super terram
opertique sunt omnes montes excelsi sub uniuerso caelo") is the subject of
lines 1386b–8a of *Genesis A* ("Flod ealle wreah, / hreoh under heofonum,
hea beorgas / geond sidne grund"), and the uplifting of the ark on the waters
("et eleuauerunt arcam in sublime a terra," 7:17) is the focus of lines 1388a–
9a of the poem ("and on sund ahof / earce from eorðan"). In this case, the
poetry is closer to the Bible than the Old English prose ("and ahefdon upp
þone arc"), insofar as the latter does not render the final phrase *a terra*
("from the earth"). In all, there is plenty of language here to link the poetry
of *Genesis A* to the Bible.

---

110 Doane, *Genesis A*, 468.

Much of the accompanying diction also suggests a connection to the opening of *Genesis A*. When the poet says, "drihten sende / regn from roderum and eac rume let ... " (1371a–2), he loosely echoes the first moments of creation (112–14): "Her ærest gesceop ece drihten ... rodor arærde and þis rume land ("Here the eternal Lord first created ... raised the heavens and this broad land"). The difference is that the first moment marks the rise of the world, while the second heralds its fall. The noun *willeburnan* (1373) also appears elsewhere only in *Genesis A* at that earlier moment, where it describes the bright and rainless beauty of the earth (208b–14a):

>   Neorxnawang stod
> god and gastlic,   gifena gefylled
> fremum forðweardum.   Fægere leohte   10
> þæt liðe land   lago yrnende,
> wylleburne.   Nalles wolcnu ða giet
> ofer rumne grund   regnas bæron,
> wann mid winde ...

[Paradise stood good and godly, filled with gifts, with enduring benefits. Pleasantly the well-spring washed the peaceful land with running water. No clouds as yet bore rains over the ample ground, dark with wind ...]

Upon second reading, that calm, clear time appears to foreshadow the Flood, and the four rivers that stately flow from Eden (*eastreamas ... feower*, 216), which God has sent out into the world with their gloriously-bright waters ("[Drihten] wætre wlitebeorhtum, and on woruld sende," 220), now return in this darker time to consume it ("Drihten sende ... on woruld ... egorstreamas swearte swogan," 1371–5a).[111] Here may be another echo, and if the *egorstreamas* of the Flood recall the *eastreamas* of Paradise, the phrase "of ædra gehwære" ("from every rein," 1374a) may refer to the rivers of the world as well as the oceans, which makes good sense.

The falling of darkness at the Deluge also returns the world to a primordial state of chaos. In the beginning, "far and wide, the sea, the dark waves, were covered by black, unending night" ("Garsecg þeahte / sweart synnihte side and wide, / wonne wægas," 117b–19a). Before the Flood, God

---

111 The echo of *drihten* appears in the earlier scenes as an instrumental *drihtnes mihtum* (218b).

warns Noah (1300a–2a): "Ic wille mid flode folc acwellan ... ðonne sweart wæter, / wonne wælstreamas werodum swelgað." ("I will kill the people with a flood ... when dark water, black slaughter-streams swallow the multitudes"). Those dark waves (*wonne wægas*, 119a) now return (*wonnan wæge*, 1379a, 1462a), and the black shadows God first "saw vanish over the wide land" at Creation ("geseah deorc sceado / sweart swiðrian geond sidne grund," 133b–4) come again to consume the world ("Flod ealle wreah ... geond sidne grund," 1386b–8a, and 1429–30). Both phrases, *wonn wæg* and *geond sidne grund*, appear nowhere else in *Genesis A* but at these two moments, and the recurrence of the same language and similar imagery suggests strongly that there is a connection between Creation and the Deluge in the mind of the poet. Similar repetition is also used by Cyprianus in the same context, who says that "birds did not suspend their bodies on light wings" ("Non uolucres leuibus suspendunt corpora pinnis" 290). That line, which echoes Ovid (*Met.* 11.341), also echoes Cyprianus himself and his description of Creation (*Gen.* 19–20): "Quinta die accipiunt liquentia flumina pisces / Et uolucres uarias suspendunt aere pinnas" ("On the fifth day, clear rivers receive fish and birds raise varied wings upon the air"). The repetition, then, in both poems suggests that God undoes the light and life he brings at the beginning of time, and it is in no small part thanks to the recurring imagery in the *Heptateuch* that I thought to consider the thematic relationship between Creation and the Flood in *Genesis A*. That is to say, here is a good example of how knowledge of Latin biblical epic can enlighten one's reading of the Old English genre.

Turning to the ark, the poet calls the ship a great "sea-chest" (*micle merecieste*, 1317) and the "greatest of sea-houses" (*geofonhusa mæst*, 1321) or "ocean-houses" (*holmærna mæst*, 1422), but there is no clear indication that the vessel is anything but a storehouse for the creatures of the earth. The poet does not say explicitly that the ark is the tomb of Christ or that it represents the redemption of man, as Sedulius does, though he does call God "the redeemer" or "saviour" on several occasions (*nergend*), and the use of this word may indicate the conventional symbolism, especially since it appears disproportionately in the context of the Flood (1285b, 1295a, 1314b, 1327b, 1356b, 1367a, 1483b, 1497b, 1504a).[112]

Also, the potential for baptismal meaning is strengthened by the poet's use of the verb *segnian* (1390) in this context. That verb is used earlier

---

112 Then only 1924 and in the context of purging of Sodom and Gomorrah, 2435, 2634, 2864.

(1365b), when God seals up the ark and blesses it. Doane suggests that "baptismal significance is evoked by *segnade*," which means he "made the sign of the cross over [the ark]."[113] He also says that "the epithets for God recall the regenerative aspect of Baptism by setting the Flood beside the Creation, for the Flood is a figure of the new creation of Baptism. The use in passing of the second person (*nergend usser, scyppend usser*) further establishes an immediate moral tone." Doane therefore takes for granted the baptismal significance of the episode, and he offers yet another example to invite a symbolic interpretation. Thus lines 1320–6 describe the pitch (or *bitumen*) that seals the ark, and Doane, citing Bede, Isidore, and the *Pentateuchal Commentary*, interprets the *bitumen* as faith, in part because the poet lingers on his description of the substance.[114] Wright, however, argues that nothing in that passage suggests necessarily a spiritual subtext for the *bitumen*, and he says it is "the literal information about pitch as a waterproofing substance that fascinated the *Genesis A*-poet."[115]

Clearly, there is some disagreement about how far we are meant to pursue the Christian message of the Flood and other episodes in *Genesis A*, and this is due mainly to the literal, silent approach of the author, which inclines more towards the kind of subtle exegesis we find in the poetry of Juvencus and Cyprianus than the more overtly spiritual renditions of Sedulius, Avitus, and Arator. That being said, we should not hesitate to pursue symbolic interpretations in *Genesis A*, where the text appears to invite them, since poets of the Latin tradition include such allusive language even in the most literal of renderings. I would add in this particular instance that Avitus describes the ark in comparable terms, saying, "Then will that man escape evil, whoever has prepared to build a mighty ark of an impenetrable exterior. Saved from the waves by the life-giving wood of the cross, he will then know what good his condemnation of indolence has won him" ("Effugiet tunc ille malum quicumque paratus, / Construat ut ualidam praeduri tegminis arcam: / Per lignum uitale crucis seruatus ab undis / Tunc cernet quanto contempserit otia fructu," 4.323–6). This passage does not concern the *bitumen* directly, but it does present the solid construction of the ark as a metaphor for faith. It is but one example of how a word or two, in this case *ualidam* and *praeduri*, may lead the poet into a moment of deeper reflection.

---

113 Doane, *Genesis A*, 332.
114 Ibid., 329–30. See also Utley, "The Flood Narrative," 207–26, esp. 210.
115 Wright, "*Genesis A ad Litteram*," 137.

Abraham & Isaac (2887–907)

The offering of Isaac is another episode in biblical epic that frequently invites a typological interpretation. Latin poets seldom fail to hint at the symbolic links between God and Abraham, and Isaac and Jesus. Sedulius, for one, is explicit about this symbolism (1.114–20):

Mactandumque Deo pater obtulit, at sacer ipsam
Pro pueri iugulis aries mactatur ad aram.   115
O iusti mens sancta uiri! pietate remota
Plus pietatis habens contempsit uulnera nati
Amplexus praecepta Dei, typicique cruoris
Auxilio uentura docet, quod sanguine Christi
Humana pro gente pius occumberet agnus.   120

[And the father gave his child to be sacrificed to God, although a ram was sacrificed in place of the boy's throat. Oh, the pious heart of that righteous man! Putting pity aside and having more piety, he ignored the [potential] wounds to his child, embracing God's commands, and with the help of figural bloodshed, teaches what is to come, that a pious lamb would die for the human race by the blood of Christ.]

The *Genesis A*-poet, on the other hand, treats the scene literally and with no apparent reference to any underlying meaning, which is to say he follows Genesis, chapter 22, closely (2897–907):

Veneruntque ad locum quem ostenderat ei Deus in quo aedificauit altare et desuper ligna conposuit cumque conligasset (conligatis manibus et pedibus) Isaac filium suum posuit eum in altari super struem lignorum. 10 Extenditque manum et arripuit gladium ut immolaret filium.[116]

Hig comon þa to þære stowe þe him geswutelode God, and he þær weofod arærde on þa ealdan wisan, and þone wudu gelogode, swa swa he hyt wolde

---

116   Latin: "And they came to the place which God had shown him, where he built an altar, and laid the wood in order upon it; and when he had bound Isaac his son, he laid him on the altar upon the pile of wood. And he put forth his hand, and took the sword, to sacrifice his son."

habban to his suna bærnytte syþþan he ofslagen wurde. He geband þa hys sunu. 10 and his swurd ateah, þæt he hyne geoffrode on þa ealdan wisan.[117]

– Gen 22:9–10

Gestah þa stiðhydig   steape dune
up mid his eaforan   swa him se eca bebead
þæt he on hrofe gestod   hean landes
on þære stowe   þe him se stranga to,   2900
wærfæst metod,   wordum tæhte.
Ongan þa ad hladan,   æled weccan,
and gefeterode   fet and honda
bearne sinum   and þa on bæl ahof
Isaac geongne   and þa ædre gegrap   2905
sweord be gehiltum.   Wolde his sunu cwellan
folmum sinum,   fyre scencan
mæges dreore.

[Then, resolute, he climbed the steep hill with his child, as the eternal One had bidden him, so that he stood at the height of the high land in the place where the Mighty One, the Righteous Creator, had led him with words. He then began to load a funeral pyre, to kindle fire, and bound his son's hands and feet, then raised young Isaac onto it; he then quickly grabbed his sword by the hilt. He meant to kill his son by own hand, to quench the fire with the blood of his child.]

The direct allusion to Isaac in line 2905 betrays the biblical source of the episode, and the poet includes other, specific links. The reference to the mountain (*steape dune*, 2897b) can be found in Genesis 22:2 (*super montium*), and the emphasis on God's command ("swa him se eca bebead," 2898b) coincides with Gen. 22.3 ("ad locum quem praeceperat ei Deus" ["to the place which God had commanded him"]). That same passage is echoed in verses 2900–1 through the appositive style ("on þære stowe þe …wærfæst metod, wordum tæhte"), and the phrase "on þære stowe þe" is close to the Latin prose (*ad locum quem*), not to mention the Old English

---

117 Old English: "They then came to that place which God had shown him, and where he built an altar in the old way, and laid the wood on it, so as he would burn his son after he was slain. He bound his son, 10 and drew his sword, to offer him in the old way."

(*to þære stowe*). When Abraham binds "the hands and feet of his son" ("and gefeterode fet and honda bearne sinum" 2903–4), he once again echoes the language of the Bible and apparently the *Vetus Latina* ("conligatis manibus et pedibus Isaac filium suum"). The perfunctory English prose does not mention the hands or feet ("He geband þa hys sunu" ["He then bound his son"]). Finally, the description of the sword, "gegrap sweord be gehiltum" ("He grabbed the sword by the hilt," 2905–6), is reflected by *swurd ateah/arripuit gladium* in both the English and Latin Bible, while other words for the "pyre" and "sacrifice" leave no doubt as to the biblical source of the scene.

But while the poet calls Isaac "his eaforan" (2898a), "bearne sinum" (2904a), "Isaac geongne" (2905a), "mæges" (2908a), and "his sunu" (2906b) there is no insistence that he must symbolize Christ or that Abraham must represent God; and while it may be true, as Huppé suggests, that literate audiences would have taken for granted the figural significance of the episode, no such assumption takes precedence over the literal events here.[118] Like Wright, I see no reason to take the description of Isaac's wood-gathering (*wudu bær sunu*, 2887b) as a reference to Jesus and the cross, even if the suggestion is a tempting one.[119] Ultimately, the focus of the passage does not appear to be symbolic in nature, but bound more to the poem's central theme of obedience.[120] As Larry McKill has shown, the *Genesis-A* poet emphasizes the importance of obedience with the repetition of numerous clauses in this sequence: "hæfde on an gehogod/þæt he gedæde swa hine drihten het" ("he had decided on one thing only, that he should do as the Lord had ordered him," 2893b–4); "Swa him bebead metod" ("as the Measurer had commanded him," 2872b); "swa hine drihten het" ("as the Lord had ordered him," 2894b); "swa him se eca bebead" ("as the Eternal One commanded him," 2898b).[121] So the end of the poem returns us to the beginning – "Us is riht micel ðæt we rodera weard,/wereda wuldorcining, wordum herigen/modum lufien" (1–3a) – and as McKill suggests, the episode "provides a fit conclusion to a poem revealing in concrete terms both sure punishment for the *wærlogan* 'pledge-betrayers' and rewards for the *wærfæst* 'pledge-firm' dear to God."[122] That last adjective is

---

118 But see, e.g., Estes, "Raising Cain."
119 Wright, "*Genesis A ad Litteram*," 153; for the earlier suggestion of figural meaning, see further Creed, "The Art of the Singer," 69–82.
120 See further, Greenfield and Calder, *A New Critical History*, 209.
121 Larry McKill, "The Offering of Isaac," 1–12, at 8.
122 Ibid., 4.

a phrase that describes the Lord is this passage (*wærfæst metod*, 2901), and we may add the fallen angels of *Genesis A* and Adam and Eve in *Genesis B* to the hosts of treaty breakers in the poem.

Conclusions

A.N. Doane succinctly captures the achievement of the *Genesis A*-poet when he says, "no one but an expert could have chosen verses so consistently, which to render, which to omit, which to alter, which to conflate, and have treated them so harmoniously, according to the various conflicting demands which his task imposed upon him."[123] The final product is a "close" rendition of the Bible, and it is remarkable how many of the basic practices in *Genesis A* reflect the versifying *modus operandi* of Juvencus and Cyprianus, however much distance stands between them. *Genesis B* is certainly a much freer response to the Bible and a completely different poem in many ways, but that poet is no less careful or deliberate. The entire sequence of the Temptation and Fall is thoughtfully orchestrated, as it is in Avitus, and the English (or Saxon) poet's use of repetition is key to interpreting the poem. Both *Genesis A* and *B* furthermore promote the need to praise God as a validation of faith, and both highlight the Fall of angels and man as a failure in that respect. Moreover, both *Genesis A* and *B* provide entrances into biblical exegesis, though the author of *Genesis B* appeals to the reader more often as a homilist, exhorting his audience to right action. The author of *Genesis A* is more like Juvencus or Cyprianus, who are subtle about the underlying symbolism of a given scene; but there is no doubt that the Old English poet invites his reader to explore it at times, especially in passages like the Flood. Finally, like the biblical poets of late Antiquity, the versifiers of *Genesis A* and *B* are obviously well-versed in the Latin Bible and the language of traditional poetry, and their fusion of the two has more in common with the late antique genre than not, allowing for the differences of language and secular sources of poetic inspiration. Our search for sources is not as important as our understanding and appreciation that all of this literature belongs to the same evolving body of Christian verse.

---

123 Doane, *Genesis A*, 92.

Exodus (8th or 9th Century)

The Old English *Exodus* dates roughly to the eighth century (before c. 825) and deals mainly with the incidents at the Red Sea (Ex. 13.20–14.31), culminating in the crossing and leaving the better part of forty biblical chapters unsung.[124] Nothing for certain is known about the author, but the language and style of the poem suggest a monk or priest who is familiar with the Vulgate and the Christological links between the Old and New Testaments.[125] Like Avitus, who "handles his source very freely" in *De transitu maris rubri* (*On the Crossing of the Red Sea*), the Old English poet ranges far from his scriptural source – this is no *paene ad uerbum* translation of the Bible.[126] Both writers also share a fondness for vivid language and turbulent action, and both elevate the story to "epic" proportions.[127] But while Avitus is explicit about the underlying message of the crossing – that it prefigures man's redemption through Christ and Baptism – the *Exodus* poet is quiet by comparison. Like Cyprianus in the *Heptateuch*, he

---

124 For the date of *Exodus*, see further Fulk, *History of Old English Meter*, 391, and the introductory discussion of *Genesis A* and *B* above, which summarizes his criteria for dating. Fulk, 391, does not hazard a *terminus a quo* for *Exodus*; but see Lucas, *Exodus*, 71, who suggests a date between the lifetimes of Bede (673–735) and Alcuin (735–804), that is, after *Caedmon's Hymn* (c. 657–80), and he allows that a date after 800 is also possible. On the basis of linguistic evidence, Irving, *Exodus*, 28, puts the date earlier, to the beginning of the eighth century. Krapp does not venture a date in *The Junius Manuscript*, xxvi, citing several conflicting arguments of his time. In the following discussion, I have used the edition of Lucas, *Exodus*, though I have consulted Krapp's edition in *The Junius Manuscript*, 91–107, that of Irving, *The Old English Exodus*, and that of Tolkien and Turville-Petre, eds., *The Old English Exodus*. Translations are my own, but I have also consulted Thorpe's literal rendering in *Caedmon's Metrical Paraphrase*, 177–216, and Anlezark, *Old Testament Narratives*, 206–45.

125 For evidence of the monastic origins of *Exodus*, see further Irving, *Exodus* 34; Lucas, *Exodus*, 72. The question of authorship is more difficult. See Krapp, *Junius Manuscript*, xxvii and xxxi. Irving, 23, on the basis of linguistic evidence, favours an Anglian origin, but he does not dismiss Northumbrian authorship, given that writers like Caedmon were producing biblical poetry in Northumbria much earlier, in the closing years of the seventh century; Lucas, 72, also on the basis of linguistic evidence, suggests "that *Exodus* may have been composed in a Northumbrian dialect and transmitted to Malmesbury via a West Mercian centre such as Worcester or Lichfield"; more recently, Remley has proposed Aldhelm of Malmesbury as a possible author; see "Aldhelm as Old English Poet," in 90–108).

126 The quote is from Roberts, *Biblical Epic*, 124.

127 *Exodus* has often been compared to *Beowulf* for its inventive poetic language and other similarities of style. See further Fulk and Cain, *History of Old English*, 115.

appears to favour the historical incidents of the Bible over the figural, but then at other times he invites the kind of extra-literal interpretation we might expect to find in a Latin poem on Exodus. The problem in our reading of the text is the author's silent movement between these two modes, the literal and figurative, and often the want of any clear indication of how we are meant to approach a given word, phrase, or scene. None of the Latin versifications of the Bible is so consistently inscrutable as *Exodus*, which challenges its readers, with riddling ambiguity, to guess its meaning. If the central message of this poem is one of Christian redemption, the author leaves it up to the reader for the most part to find his own "spiritual keys" (*gastes cægon*, 525b), to unlock that meaning, which is more than most Latin biblical poets ask of their audience.

Germanic-Heroic Context

The heroic tenor of *Exodus* leaves the strongest impression, and "though there is never an actual battle, the poet provides a spectacular setting for one."[128] God is *soðfæst cyning* ("Righteous King," 9a) and *sigora waldend* ("Lord of Victories," 16b), and He gives Moses "the power of weapons against the terror of his enemies" ("gesealde wæpna geweald wið wraðra gryre," 20). The Israelites are his "army" (*fyrd*, 54a), and Moses, their "glorious hero" (*tirfæste hæleð*, 63b), like his counterpart in Avitus' poem ("*uirgam forte manu gestabat legifer heros*" ["As it happened, that law-bearing hero held a staff in his hand," 5.67]). Pharaoh, too, is "a battle-keeper of men," who dons the "masked-helm" of war against the Israelites ("guðweard gumena grimhelm gespeon," 174). Like Moses, he is a bold and resolute commander, who bids his troops to be brave and hold the line ("het his hereciste healdan georne / fæst fyrdgetrum," 177–8a). That image evokes scenes elsewhere in more squarely secular verse, notably in the *Battle of Maldon*, where the nobleman Byrhtnoth pits his troops (unsuccessfully) against the Vikings in 991 CE (17–19): "Ða þær Byrhtnoð ongan beornas trymian, / rad and rædde, rincum tæhte / hu hi sceoldon standan and þone stede healdan" ("Then Byrhtnoth began to array his men, rode and counselled them, showed his warriors how they should stand and

---

128 Irving, *Exodus*, 30.

hold their place").[129] Evoking similar imagery, allowing that *Maldon* is later, the *Exodus* poet aims to introduce a Germanic-heroic backdrop for his versification of the Bible, to entertain his readers. So the Egyptians are vividly described as "sword-wolves" (*heorawulfas*, 181a), who rush into the sea with reckless abandon. Likewise, in *Maldon*, the Vikings are "slaughter-wolves" (*wælwulfas*, 96), who charge into the waters of the Panta equally heedless of the danger (96–9): "Wodon þa wælwulfas (for wætere ne murnon),/wicinga werod, west ofer Pantan,/ofer scir wæter scyldas wegon,/lidmen to lande linde bæron" ("Then those slaughter-wolves waded in, paid no attention to the water, the Viking host went west over the Panta, shouldered their shields across the shining water, the sea-farers bore their shields to land").[130] So there is a stylistic kinship between the poetry of *Exodus* and *Maldon* originating in the tradition of Germanic-heroic verse, and this spirit pervades the atmosphere of *Exodus*. As E.B. Irving put it, "all the emotional associations which clustered around the Germanic concepts of the necessity of loyalty to one's lord, the emphasis on warfare and stern performance of duty, and the munificent reward for faith and obedience have been transferred, and on the whole convincingly transferred, to the religious ties which bind man to God."[131] This kind of appropriation can be seen in *Genesis A* and in all of the Latin biblical epics, which share with *Exodus* great enthusiasm for the earlier traditions. In fact, we might consider that the source of all of his martial-heroic fanfare originates as much with the tradition of Latin biblical epic as Germanic-heroic verse, a suggestion Miranda Wilcox has also made.[132]

Biblical Context

On the surface, the textual relationship between *Exodus* and the Bible appears easy to characterize. The central action of the poem covers a mere

---

129 See also *Ex.* (215–20): "Moses bebead/eorlas … habban heora hlencan, hycgan on ellen,/beran beorht searo" ("Moses commanded his men … to take hold of their shields, to think of glory, to carry out their bright battle-gear").

130 See further Robinson, "Names in Old English Literature," 25–6, who mentions Israel with reference to line 359 as *onriht Godes*, as an etymological pun based on the Latin *rectus domini*. He does the same with Egypt in line 194 (*eorp werod*, "the dark host") on 26. As Robinson says, this darkness may account for other references to the Egyptian host as dark elsewhere in the poem (27).

131 Irving, *Exodus*, 30.

132 See further Wilcox, *Vernacular Biblical Epics*, 212–15. In fact, Wilcox's discussion of *Exodus* provides a very thorough discussion of the poem with respect to its potential Latin sources, and I would direct the reader there.

portion of the scriptural source (Ex. 13.20–14.31), which the author handles freely, and yet allusions to other books of the Bible, to Genesis, Numbers, Kings, Chronicles, the Psalms, and Wisdom, deepen and complicate the poet's debt to the Old Testament.[133] There is also evidence that the author is familiar with the liturgy and biblical commentaries on Exodus, which introduce the potential for the kind of spiritual interpretation we so often find in Latin biblical epic.[134]

For example, the author seems to suggest at the opening of *Exodus* that the journey of the Israelites is a metaphor for the Christian journey through life (*bealuside*, "the deadly journey," 5a). If this is true, it is tempting to interpret other scenes, if not the whole poem, in symbolic terms.[135] The problem is the author himself does not guide his readers in the way Sedulius, Avitus, or Arator do so that our interpretive progress through the narrative is often precarious. Understanding *Exodus* is also complicated by the author's use of exotic, figurative language and *hapax legomena* (words that appear nowhere else in Old English), which enhance the emotional and psychological depth of the story, but add shades of meaning that can and do obscure the sense of many passages. The pillar of cloud and fire, for instance, is called *lifes latþeow* (104a), "a guide to life," because it shows the Israelites the road to freedom, literally, and it measures out a *lifweg* (104b), "a path to life," for the same reason. Alternatively, if we accept the figural potential of the "deadly journey" (*bealuside*, 5a) which the poet mentions in the preface, the pillar may also represent the Christian path towards salvation.[136] Because the author offers no guidance one way or the other, it is up to the reader to decide which of these paths, if not both, to take. The question, then, is not whether *Exodus* promotes spiritual meaning – it does – but how much and how consistently the

---

133 See further Lucas, *Exodus*, 51–61, for a detailed account of the sources. It is unclear whether the poet uses the Vulgate or *Vetus Latina* as the basis of his poetic rendition, but Lucas offers some evidence (p. 53) to suggest that he was familiar with the Old Latin Bible.

134 See esp. the early article of Bright, "The Relation of the Caedmonian Exodus to the Liturgy," 97–103; also, Cross and Tucker, "Allegorical Traditions and the Old English Exodus," 122–7.

135 See further Fulk and Cain, *History of Old English*, 114.

136 See further Tolkien, *Exodus*, 45, on *lifes latþeow*: "the expression 'guide to Life (Salvation)' is found also of God in *El* 520, 898. To fully understand it here it is necessary to remember that Exodus throughout treats the escape of Israel as at once a historical narrative and a symbol of the soul's journey to the promised land of Salvation."

audience should pursue it.[137] Given the general silence of the poet in this matter, there can be no conclusive answer to the question.

Opening of *Exodus* (1–7)

Still, it is clear from the outset of *Exodus* that the poet presents much of the action of the narrative literally and according to values of the Germanic-heroic code. The actual judgments of Moses are most important in the preface (*Moyses domas*, 2b), his words and deeds, and the fact that he is a good leader to his people, that he guides and protects them, and gives them land and laws to live by. These are kingly virtues in the Germanic-heroic world and they serve to validate the legendary status of "the hero." On the other hand, the poet does include language in these lines, to indicate a different context for interpreting the experience of the Israelites, and many of his words suggest an alternative path for the reader (1–7):

> Hwæt, we feor and neah   gefrigen habbað
> ofer middangeard   Moyses domas,
> wræclico wordriht,   wera cneorissum –
> in uprodor   eadigra gehwam
> æfter bealusiðe   bote lifes,   5
> lifigendra gehwam   langsumne ræd –
> hæleðum secgan.   Gehyre se ðe wille!

[So, we have heard far and near over middle-earth that Moses spoke judgments, wondrous laws for generations of men: for each of the blessed, a reward for life in heaven after a hellish journey; for each of the living, for heroes, long-enduring wisdom. Listen, if you will.]

The full meaning of these first seven lines unfolds slowly, and the syntax is intricate, almost Latinate.[138] Withholding the object of *gefrigen habbað* ("we have heard …," 1b) until the end of the second verse (*Moysas domas* ["that Moses (spoke) judgments," 2b]), the poet intensifies the traditional feel of the opening line to create a sense of "antiquity" for *Exodus. Beowulf*

---

137 Wright's discussion in "*Genesis A ad Litteram*" is instructive here, and Wright makes a similar point about the interpretation of that poem on p. 127.

138 The verb *secgan* in 6a completes the sense of *gefrigen habbað* (lit., "we have heard that Moses … spoke judgments …").

exemplifies this spirit, but there the poet begins more directly and identifies the Danes immediately (1–3): "Hwæt, we Gardena in geardagum, / þeodcyninga þrym gefrunon, / hu ða æþelingas ellen fremedon" ("So, we have heard of the Spear-Danes, the glory of those people's kings in days gone by, how their princes performed deeds of valour").[139] Rearranging some common formulas and momentarily delaying the religious focus of the poem, the Old English versifier therefore aims to draw his readers into an imagined world of Germanic heroism that will accommodate the heavenly king (*soðfæst cyning*, 9a) and his saintly hero.

Remember that Juvencus uses a similar strategy at the opening of *Euangeliorum libri*, where he calls on the epic theme of immortality to create a traditional atmosphere for his poem. In fact, at every turn in his translation of the Bible, Juvencus shows how best to make good and pious use of pagan literature, by adopting and adapting classical-poetic diction and subject matter. We know that Aldhelm, Bede, and Alcuin benefitted a great deal from their knowledge of such Latin literature – and not just of isolated words but ways of using them – and so it is reasonable to expect that an Old English poet of the same period and one as learned as the *Exodus* author would not fail to grasp the value of these poems, which offered stylistic templates for his own versification of the Bible. Writers of Old English biblical verse had to retake many of the steps Juvencus once took, but there were clear footprints there for them to follow.

There were also many different paths to take. One could follow Juvencus on a direct road through the text of the Bible, or one could join Avitus on a more scenic route with symbolic detours. The latter course has left its traces on *Exodus* with one important difference. Avitus states in no uncertain terms that, although the story of Exodus is great on its own, its figural significance is greater still ("Historiis quae magna satis maiorque figuris,"

---

139 The word *hwæt* appears at the beginning of several other poems in Old English, including *Beowulf, Andreas, Fates of the Apostles, Dream of the Rood, Juliana, Judgment Day II, Vainglory, Solomon and Saturn*, and the *Meters of Boethius* (2.1, 9.1, 14.1, 17.1, 31.1). More often it appears as the first element in speeches; see *Genesis A* ("Hwæt sceal ic winnan, cwæð he," 278), *Exodus* ("Hwæt, ge nu eagum to on lociað," 278), *Daniel* ("Metod alwihta, hwæt!" 283), *Christ and Satan* ("Hwæt, we for dryhtene iu dreamas hefdon," 44). Huppé suggests the poet uses this device "to mark a stage in the development of the poem" (*Doctrine and Poetry*, 149). See also Klaeber's *Beowulf*, 4th ed., 110 n. 1–3. The expression "Gefrægn ic," is a common formula in Old English; it appears throughout *Beowulf* and at the beginning of both *Daniel* (*Gefrægn ic*, 1a) and *Judith* (*Gefrægn ic*, 7a). See further Parks, "I Heard Formulas in Old English Poetry," 45–66; Stanley, "Hwaet," 525–56.

5.17). The Old English poet on the other hand says nothing so explicit about the potential symbolism of his poem, and yet there is undeniably a sense that the "deadly journey" of the Israelites (*bealuside*, 5) represents man's journey through life, especially in the context of the Christian reference to the rewards of heaven ("in uprodor ... bote lifes," 4–5), which does not appear in the biblical Exodus.[140] Peter Lucas, who has edited the poem most recently, takes for granted that "the stylistic device" (i.e., the allegory of the journey), "is used to indicate to the audience the kind of response required for the understanding of the poem as a whole," which is to say the narrative promotes knowledge and awareness of salvation history.[141]

Certainly, a number of other Old English poems approach the journey ("sið") in these terms, as a metaphor. In Cynewulf's *Fates of the Apostles*, the narrator opens with a lamentation about his own spiritual despondence (1–2): "Ic þysne sang siðgeomor fand / on seocum sefan" ("Travel-weary, I have composed this poem with a sick heart").[142] That word, *siðgeomor* (1b), is a *hapax legomenon*, but its meaning is clear enough, which refers to man's spiritual journey through life. Thus the narrator tells the life-stories (i.e., deaths) of the twelve apostles, in the hope that they may alleviate some of his own self-obsessive woe. It does not, and in the end he returns to his initial focus on the journey, still troubled, and morbidly pondering his future demise and departure from this world (98b–101a):

>   Ic sceall feor heonan,
> an elles forð,   eardes neosan,
> sið asettan,   nat ic sylfa hwær,   100
> of þisse worulde.

---

140 See further Lucas, *Exodus*, 75; and Irving, *Exodus*, 67, who writes, "The specifically Christian reference here to the future life is worth noticing; obviously there is no such reference to be found in the O.T. version of the laws of Moses." Wilson, *Christian Theology and Old English Poetry*, 116, also suggests "wræclico" is a pun meaning both "wondrous" and "wretched, miserable," and that it relates to the noun "wrecca" or "wræca" meaning "exile, wanderer, pilgrim." He argues that "the pun gives added meaning to the lines by suggesting that the theme of the poem will have to do not only with the Laws of Moses but also with man's exile, as that exile is related to the covenant between God and man."

141 Lucas, *Exodus*, 75.

142 The text of *Fates* can be found in Krapp, ed., *The Vercelli Book*; see also Brooks, ed., *Andreas and the Fates of the Apostles*. A discussion of the journey motif in Old English can be found in McBrine, "The Journey Motif in the Poems of the Vercelli Book," 298–317.

[I must go far from here, forward elsewhere on my own, to seek out a land, to set out on a journey; I know not where myself, but from this world.]

Presumably, heaven is the hoped-for destination, but the narrator is not so sure of his merit that he will hazard to predict it, especially in his current state of mind. Elsewhere in Old English poetry, in *The Seafarer*, the narrator begins with a similar emphasis on the figurative path: "Mæg ic be me sylfum soðgied wrecan, / siþas secgan" ("I can sing a true song about myself, about my journeys," 1a–2a).[143] In this case, the travels are of a more literal nature, but like *Exodus*, there is a sense that the poet means life experience as well. In fact, many poems of the surviving corpus and writings elsewhere in prose promote the notion that literal journeys represent figurative paths. So there are good reasons to suspect that the author of *Exodus* has such a metaphor in mind.[144] The trouble, however, is a want of certainty that we should read the whole poem allegorically on the basis of this preliminary metaphor. If this were the opening of Avitus' *De transitu maris rubri*, where the author declares in no uncertain terms that spiritual meaning is the point, I would agree with Lucas and say that the references to the "deadly journey" and the "rewards of heaven" are "used to indicate to the audience the kind of response required for the understanding of the poem as a whole." But in the absence of certainty and the persistence of obscurity, it is clear only that figural language is woven into the fabric of *Exodus* in many places, yet not so coherently or consistently that it would suggest a preference for symbolism over the literal words and deeds of the Bible.

Pillar of Cloud and Fire (63–74)

Following the preface, the author moves quickly through the early chapters of Exodus, covering only the tenth plague (8–29) and the killing of the first-born (34–5).[145] At line sixty-three, a new section begins in the manuscript

---

143 See further Greenfield and Calder, *New Critical History*, 214; and the extended simile at the end Cynewulf's *Christ II* (lines 850–66), which compares life to a sea-journey and Christ as "safe harbour."

144 See also Howe, *Migration and Mythmaking in Anglo-Saxon*, for a suggestion that the journey of the Israelites in *Exodus* may have resonated with Anglo-Saxon readers who knew about the fifth-century migration of the Germanic tribes (i.e., their ancestors); and see Zacher, *Rewriting the Old Testament in Anglo-Saxon Verse*, for the appropriation of the myth of "chosenness" in Old English literature.

145 See further Lucas, *Exodus*, 78–9.

(63–135) which expands dramatically upon the details of the Bible, from the third encampment at *Æthanes byrig* ("Etham" in Ex. 13:20–2) to the fourth camp by the Red Sea ("*feorðe wic … be þan Readan Sæ*" 133–4), which is mentioned in Ex. 14:1–2 ("contra Phiahiroth, quae est inter Magdolum et mare contra Beelsephon" ["against Phiahiroth which is between Magdal and the sea over against Beelsephon"]).[146] These events cover just five verses in the Bible (13:20–14:2), or about eighty words, and yet the poetic rendition contains almost 350, including a striking metaphor depicting the pillar of cloud and fire as a great sail in the sky leading the Israelites through a virtual sea. Given the length of this section, I offer only an excerpt here, but this passage reveals something of the author's approach to the Bible and his inclination towards extra-literal meaning. Again, though it is later, I have included the Old English prose translation of Exodus, to help bridge the linguistic gap somewhat between the Latin and Old English Bibles (88b–97):[147]

20 Profectique de Soccoth castrametati sunt in Etham in extremis finibus solitudinis. 21 Dominus autem praecedebat eos ad ostendendam uiam per diem in columna nubis et per noctem in columna ignis ut dux esset itineris utroque tempore. 22 Numquam defuit columna nubis per diem nec columna ignis per noctem coram populo.[148]

20 And hig foron fram Socho and wicodon æt Etham, on þam ytemestan ende þæs westenes. 21 And Drihten for beforan him and swutelode him þone weg on dæg þurh sweart tacn, on sweres gelicnesse, and on niht swilce an byrnende swer him for beforan. 22 and symle him gelæste þæt sweorte tacn on dæg and þæt fyrene on niht.

– Ex. 13:20–2

---

146 See further ibid., 86; Irving, *Exodus*, 72.

147 Note that the Old English prose at this point is not believed to be the work of Aelfric, but some other translator. See further *The Old Hexateuch*, 3–4, and Marsden, "Translation by Committee?" 41–2 in the same volume.

148 Ex. 13:20–2: "And marching from Soccoth, they encamped in Etham, in the utmost coasts of the wilderness. And the Lord went before them to show the way, by day in a pillar of a cloud, and by night in a pillar of fire; that he might be the guide of their journey at both times. There never failed the pillar of cloud by day, nor the pillar of fire by night, before the people."

Fyrd eall geseah

hu þær hlifedon   halige seglas,
lyftwundor leoht;   leode ongeton,   90
dugoð Israhela,   þæt þær Drihten cwom,
weroda Drihten,   wicsteal metan.
Him beforan foran   fyr and wolcen
in beorhtrodor,   beamas twegen,
þara æghwæðer   efngedælde   95
heahþegnunga   Haliges Gastes,
deormodra sið   dagum and nihtum.

[The army all saw how they towered there, those holy sails, a bright wonder
in the sky. The people, the band of Israelites, recognized that the Lord had
come there, the Lord of hosts, to mark out a camp. The two pillars, fire and
cloud, went before them in the brilliant sky, each of which shared high service
to the Holy Spirit, the journey of the brave, day and night].

There is not much here to announce the context of Exodus. The persistent description of the Israelites as an "army" (*fyrd*, 88b) obscures the source, but the reference to *dugoð Israhela* ("the band of Israelites," 91a) begins to give away the biblical lineage. The *hapax legomenon*, *lyftwundor* ("sky-wonder," 90a), is at best an allusive counterpart to the "column" in the Vulgate (*columna*), which line ninety-three reveals more plainly through *fyr and wolcen* ("fire and cloud"), which in turn reflect the Latin, *nubis* and *ignis*. The phrase *Him beforan foran* relates to the Latin prose *praecedebat eos* (13:21) as well as *coram populo* (13:22), and there is a kinship with the Old English prose as well, which reads *for beforan him*, which reflects the poetry except for the use of the singular *for* (from *faran*, "to go"). This apparent similarity may suggest that the use of rhyme by the *Exodus* poet in this case is incidental and represents only his effort to render the prose. Apart from these allusions, the use of *Drihten* in the poetry and prose indicates that this word may echo the biblical "dominus" in the Vulgate; finally, the references to the "day" and "night" (*dagum and nihtum*, 97b) add further context to suggest the source (*per diem … per noctem*), which is still distanced from the Bible by metaphorical language.
The source of the sail metaphor has long preoccupied critics, and the author of *Exodus* takes pains to develop the image, which has been explained as a response to other nautical imagery in the poem, including later references to the Israelites as "sailors" (*flotan*, 133a, 223a, 331b) and

"sea-Vikings" (*sæwicingas*, 333a). In symbolic terms, the nautical imagery has also been linked to metaphors in Christian literature that describe the Church as a great ship on the ocean.[149] One such image can be found in the poetry of Avitus, who says that, like the ark, "the true Church weathers many storms" ("Non aliter crebras Ecclesia uera procellas / Sustinet," 4.493–4). The earlier description of the pillar of cloud as a "tent" (*feldhus*, 85) has been taken as a possible reference to the Tabernacle, and Lucas cites a variant reading of Psalm 104 (105).39 as potential inspiration, "expandit nubem in tentorium," but he allows that Ex. 40:32 may equally inspire the author: "operuit nubes tabernaculum testimonii; et gloria Domini impleuit illud" ("The cloud covered the tabernacle of the testimony, and the glory of the Lord filled it"). More recently, Miranda Wilcox has suggested that "the framework of this conceit relies on recognizing implicit allusions to Arator's *Historia apostolica* and Bede's *Expositio actuum Apostolorum*."[150] If so, that connection makes a strong case for the author's knowledge of at least one Latin biblical epic. Wilcox is certainly on the right track by broadening the discussion to consider the New Testament poems of the Latin genre, and it is hard to imagine that the *Exodus* poet could have known Arator without knowing Avitus, whose work is so obviously akin to his own. Wilcox's argument is too complex to cover in full here, but her conclusion provides a sufficient outline:[151]

> The nautical domain draws on Peter and fishing in Matthew and the conceptual metaphor The Ship Of the Church; the tentage domain draws on Paul and tent-making in Acts and the conceptual metaphor A Christian Life Is a Journey; and the third domain focuses on the meteorological shading that God provides the Children of Israel in Exodus and the conceptual metaphor Protection Is Covering.

If all of this is true, the tent-metaphor in *Exodus* speaks not only to the erudition of its author but the potential sophistication of his audience. Arator's poem is heavy-laden with allusive language and layers of meaning. It is just the sort of thing a learned Anglo-Saxon like Bede would have loved – and we know that he did love Arator – but how many other

---

149   For a recent assessment of the Church as ship metaphor in *Exodus*, see further Zacher, *Rewriting the Old Testament*, 63–70.

150   See further Wilcox, "Creating the Cloud-Tent-Ship Conceit in *Exodus*," 103–50, at 148.

151   Ibid., 148.

English readers would have been able to decode the text of *Exodus* in this way? It is a fair question. Wilcox suggests, and reasonably so, that "the *Exodus*-poet targets Anglo-Saxon Christians,"[152] but that audience would have been a small one, if they possessed the kind of knowledge the author seems to have, and that may have been the case. But why write in Old English, if not to appeal to a more general audience? Again, the difficulty with *Exodus* is the author's silent movement between passages of direct and literal action, and imagery such as this, which might have been passed over by a general audience as a simple sail, or contemplated more deeply by readers with greater knowledge.

There is more to consider here. The reference to *Haliges Gastes* ("The Holy Ghost") in this passage certainly invites the audience to read the *deormodra sið* (97a) as "the journey of brave souls," even though the subject of the sentence is the "army" (*fyrd*), "people" (*leode*), or host (*dugoð*) of Israel. Therefore, there must be a spiritual subtext to the passage of the Israelites through the wilderness towards a place of safety or salvation. Moreover, editors have not missed the potential of the two *beamas*, "bright in heaven" (*in beorhtrodor*, 94a), to refer to the "beams" of the cross, and in fact similar synecdoche can be found in the most famous Old English poem on the Crucifixion, *The Dream of the Rood*. There, the cross is likewise called *beama beorhtost* ("the brightest of beams," 6a) and "a beacon" (*beacen*, 5b). Like the pillars that "tower" over the Israelites (*hlifedon*, 89a), the rood does the same thing in the sky (88b–9a): "Glorious, I now tower under heaven" ("Forþan ic þrimfæst nu / hlifige under heofenum"). Also, like the pillars in *Exodus*, which offer a *lifweg* to the Israelites, the cross opens up "a life-way" to salvation through Christ ("lifes weg … gerymde," 88b–9a). All this to say, in the context of the imagery in the *Dream of the Rood*, imagery that is both heroic (*þrimfæst*) and spiritual (*lifes weg*, 89b), it is hard to dismiss the potential Christian message of this particular passage in *Exodus*.

Interpolation: The Flood (362–76)

It goes without saying, the Flood and the Crossing of the Red Sea are often presented in Christian poetry as metaphors for Baptism. Here, however, the episode favours the historical action of the Bible. If this scene is meant to suggest Christian Redemption, it is one of the more subtle such suggestions

---

152 Ibid., 150.

in the genre, Latin or English. To be fair, there is language here to invite such an interpretation, but much of it could just as easily be taken literally. Again, Avitus is clear from the outset of *Historia spiritalis* that his poem is a "spiritual history" of the Old Testament, and both Sedulius and Arator provide explicit statements about the symbolic meaning of biblical events, but the situation is different in *Exodus*, where we lack so much information about the author's desire to promote symbolic meaning (362–76):

Niwe flodas   Noe oferlað,
þrymfæst þeoden,   mid his þrim sunum,
þone deopestan   drencefloda
þara ðe gewurde   on woruldrice.   365
Hæfde him on hreðre   halige treowa;
forþon he gelædde   ofer lagustreamas
maðmhorda mæst,   mine gefræge.
On feorhgebeorh   foldan hæfde
eallum eorðcynne   ece lafe,   370
frumcneow gehwæs,   fæder and moder
tuddorteondra,   geteled rime,
missenlicra   þonne men cunnon,
snottor sæleoda.   Eac þon sæda gehwilc
on bearm scipes   beornas feredon   375
þara þe under   heofonum hæleð bryttigað.

[Noah, glorious prince, crossed over new floods with his three sons, the deepest deluge the world has ever known. He had holy faith in his heart, and so he led the greatest of treasure-hoards across the ocean-streams, as I have heard tell. He held the eternal remnant of the earth for all creatures of the world in his safekeeping, and kept count, the wise seafarer, of the first generation of every heir-maker, father and mother – creatures more diverse than men can know. Those men also ferried every kind of seed within the bosom of that ship that heroes use under the heavens.]

Immediately, the phrase *niwe flodas* ("new floods," 362a) begs the question, what does the poet mean by "new"? Quoting Hall, and evoking baptismal imagery, Lucas says that "the masses of flowing water (*flodas*) are *niwe* not in the sense of being unprecedented (the world was similarly inundated at the time of Creation, Gen. 1.1–10) but in the sense of being a change from what immediately preceded and a renewal of what had gone before that."[153] I would add that similar language also appears in *Genesis A* at the end of the Flood sequence, where fitt 24 marks a new section in the manuscript and a new stage in Noah's life. (1555–6): "Ða Noe ongan niwan stefne / mid hleomagum ham staðelian ..." ("Then Noah began anew with his kindred to build a home ..."). This passage may help to shed some light on *Exodus*, and Doane's commentary on *niwan stefne* ("anew" or "a second time," 1555b) is worth repeating:

> The expression, *niwan stefne* (8x in poetry), marks the second stage of the dragon's attack in BW (2594) and seems to mark the second stage of Noe's career here. It also marks the Second Age of the World, which was commonly held to have begun with Noe after the Flood (Bede begins it precisely at the time of Noe's sacrifice [*In Gen.*, CCSL 118A: 127]): "Et egressa post diluuium animantia de arca ingrediantur in nouam terrae faciem, nouis uernantem floribus, ibique multiplicentur et crescant" ("And emerging after the Flood from the ark let the living beings enter into the new face of the land, springing with new blossoms, and there multiply and increase").

The *Exodus*-poet may therefore be thinking of *niwe flodas* in these terms, that the Deluge brings "a new face to the land" (*nouam terrae faciem*) in "a new time" (*niwan stefne*). The adjective may also intimate the renewal of man through Baptism, but that meaning must be brought to the page by the reader, because the poet says nothing about the mystical significance of the ark or its cargo.

The *Exodus*-poet does call the ark "the greatest of treasure-hoards" (*maðmhorda mæst*, 368a), but that kenning accords with similar descriptions of the ship in *Genesis A*, where the ark is described as "a great sea-chest" (*micle merecieste*, 1317a), "the greatest of sea-houses" (*geofonhusa mæst*, 1321a), and "the greatest of ocean-houses" (*holmærna mæst*, 1422b) without any clear indication that symbolism is intended. The *Genesis A*-poet also refers to the contents of the ark as a "hord" (*horde*, 1439b) without any overt sense that the vessel must represent Christian redemption. In other words, despite their innately figural nature, kennings need not be taken as spiritual metaphors, and so when Noah holds the future of the human race in "safe keeping" (*feorhgebeorh*, 369a), the *hapax legomenon*

---

153 Lucas, *Exodus*, 123; Hall, *NQ* ccxx (1975), 243–4.

may be taken simply to mean the "seeds" of life (*sæda gehwilc*, 374b) that are holed up in the ark.

On the other hand, the poet does seem to pun when he says that this was "the deepest deluge the world has ever known" ("þone deopestan drence-floda/þara ðe gewurde on woruldrice," 364–5). Twice elsewhere in the poem he uses the phrase *deop lean* ("deep reward") as a play on words, first with reference to a soldier in the tribe of Judah, whose determination to enter the sea will earn him a "deep" recompense (314b–15): "Swa him mihtig God/þæs dægweorces deop lean forgeald" ("So mighty God gave him a deep reward for that day's work").[154] Later, the phrase appears in ironic terms as the "deep reward" the Egyptians receive for opposing God (506b–7): "Egyptum wearð/þæs dægweorces deop lean gesceod" ("A deep reward was paid to the Egyptians for their day's work"). Finally, the message Moses delivers to his people after crossing is also called *deop ærende* ("deep tidings," 519a). Therefore, the poet's use of *deopestan drencefloda* (364) may suggest an awareness of the "profoundness" of the Deluge in terms of Baptism, and the phrase, *halige treowa* (366b), which must mean "holy faith," may also be taken aurally as a pun on *halig treow* ("holy tree") with reference to the cross. Also, just as the reference to the remnants of the Flood in *Genesis A* (*wraðra lafe*, "remnant of the rebellious," 1496b) and *wætra lafe* ("remnant of the waters," 1549b), may suggest man's redemption, the phrase, "the eternal remnant" (*ece lafe*, 370b) in the *Exodus* account of the Flood may call for a Christological interpretation. If so, the subtle invitation to pursue such meaning is more like the kind of understated exegesis we find in the poetry of Juvencus than in the works of Avitus or Arator, who tend to be more explicit.

Abraham and Isaac (397–416)

This section maintains the focus on the lineage of the Israelite tribes. The biblical story of the Offering of Isaac often promotes figural connections between Abraham and God, and Isaac and Christ in Latin biblical epic, where the threat of sacrifice is aligned to the actual Crucifixion. Again, however, this episode, like the Flood, offers a more literal rendition of the scriptural narrative, including a core of biblical language (397–414):

---

154   The translation of this passage follows Anlezark, *Old Testament Narratives*, 227.

Veneruntque ad locum quem ostenderat ei Deus in quo aedificauit altare et
desuper ligna conposuit cumque conligasset (conligatis manibus et pedibus)
Isaac filium suum posuit eum in altari super struem lignorum. 10 Extenditque
manum et arripuit gladium ut immolaret filium.[155]

Hig comon þa to þære stowe þe him geswutelode God, and he þær weofod
arærde on þa ealdan wisan, and þone wudu gelogode, swa swa he hyt wolde
habban to his suna bærnytte syþþan he ofslagen wurde. He geband þa hys
sunu. 10 and his swurd ateah, þæt he hyne geoffrode on þa ealdan wisan.[156]

– Gen 22:9–10

To þam meðelstede magan gelædde	
Abraham Isaac, adfyr onbran	
(fyrst ferhðbana no þy fægra wæs),	
wolde þone lastweard lige gesyllan,	400
in bælblyse beorna selost,	
his swæsne sunu to sigetibre,	
angan ofer eorðan yrfelafe,	
feores frofre, ða he swa forð gebad,	
leodum to lafe, langsumne hiht.	405
He þæt gecyðde, þa he þone cniht genam	
fæste mid folmum, folccuð geteag	
ealde lafe (ecg grymetode),	
þæt he him lifdagas leofran ne wisse	
þonne he hyrde heofoncyninge.	410
Abraham æðeling up aræmde,	
wolde se eorl eaferan sinne,	
unweaxenne, ecgum reodan,	
magan mid mece, gif hine metod lete.	

[Abraham led his son, Isaac, to that meeting place. He lit the pyre – the foremost soul-slayer was not the more doomed for that; he wanted to give his

---

155 Latin: "And they came to the place which God had shown him, where he built an altar,
    and laid the wood in order upon it; and when he had bound Isaac his son, he laid him
    on the altar upon the pile of wood. 10 And he put forth his hand, and took the sword,
    to sacrifice his son."

156 Old English: "They then came to that place which God had shown him, and where he
    built an altar in the old way, and laid the wood on it, so as he it would burn his son after
    he was slain. He bound his son, 10 and drew his sword, to offer him in the old way."

heir to the fire, the best of men to the burning blaze, his dear son as a victory-offering, his only successor on earth,[157] whom he had awaited for so long as a comfort for his life, a long-enduring hope, as a legacy to his people. He made it known, when he seized his son firmly with his hands – the renowned man drew his ancient heirloom (the edge growled) – that the life-days of his dear son were not more dear to him than heeding the king of heaven. Noble Abraham arose, that man planned to redden his young son with the edge, his kinsman with the sword, if the Lord let him.]

Several words in this passage point to the underlying influence of the biblical narrative (Gen. 22:9–10). The initial phrase, *to þam meðelstede* ("to that meeting-place," 397a), alludes to the Latin (*ad locum*), which is also echoed by the Old English prose (*to þære stowe*). The *Exodus*-poet imitates the grammar of the original as well. The reference to the pyre, *Adfyr onbran* ("he lit the pyre," 398b), closely follows the prose (*aedificauit altare*/*weofod arærde*), while Abraham's intention to kill his son, *wolde … gesyllan* (400a), compares to the construction of the Old English prose, *wolde … habban* (cf. also *se eorl wolde* in 412a). Isaac is called a "dear son" in line 402a (*his swæsne sunu*) and this language reflects the Bible (*filium suum*/*his suna*), not to mention other apposite phrases referring to the boy in similar terms. The words *fæste mid folmum* ("firmly with his hands, 407a) may be a loose allusion to *conligatis manibus et pedibus* in the Latin, but the Old English refers to Abraham and not Isaac. In all probability, the poet is responding to *Extenditque manum* in verse ten of the Bible. Finally, the image of Abraham as he draws the sword, "Geteag / ealde lafe (ecg grymetode)," is a poetic amplification of *arripuit gladium* in the prose; and compare *swurd ateah* ("he drew his sword") in the Old English prose translation, which uses the same verb (*geteon*). There is therefore enough language here to suggest that the *Exodus*-poet is working from his memory of specific biblical language, however free his rendition is.

Much of the extra-biblical language in this scene gives pause, however. For one, the sense of line 399 is unclear: "fyrst ferhðbana no þy fægra wæs" ("the first soul-slayer was not the more doomed for that" (?)). Is this a reference to Abraham? If so, the *hapax legomenon*, *ferhðbana* ("life-destroyer" or "murderer," 399a), is not flattering. There is also the problem that Abraham is not actually a "killer," since he does not sacrifice his

---

157 The phrase, "his only successor on earth," is taken from Anlezark's translation, *Old Testament Narratives*, 233.

son, ultimately.[158] E.B. Irving takes the adjective *fyrst* to mean "foremost," since Abraham cannot be the "first" killer, who is Cain; but "first" would work, if, like Hill, we understand *fyrst ferhðbana* to refer to Adam, whose crime of eating the fruit brought death into the world.[159] Again, however, the *Exodus*-poet offers no guidance to the reader, and Adam is not normally mentioned in Latin poetic treatments of this scene, which is not to exclude the possibility. It makes sense to me to take *ferhðbana* as a reference to Abraham, who is not to be doomed for killing his son because God has commanded it. Whatever is meant here, the poet's exuberant language is problematic and requires interpretation.

Clearer symbolism is contained in the *hapax legomenon, sigetibre* (402b), which means something like "victory-offering." If the word is taken literally, it may apply to God's deliverance of the Israelites into the promised land; otherwise, it may be a reference to man's salvation through Christ. It is noteworthy in this context that Isaac is called "an enduring hope" (*langsumne hiht*, 405b), which is how Sedulius refers to the boy in the *Carmen paschale* ("spem gentis opimae "hope of a fertile race," 1.112), and Sedulius links the offering of Isaac explicitly to Christ's sacrifice (118–20): typicique cruoris/Auxilio uentura docet, quod sanguine Christi/Humana pro gente pius occumberet agnus." ("And with the help of figural bloodshed [Abraham] shows what is to come, that a pious lamb would die for the human race by the blood of Christ"). The *Exodus*-poet also says that the life of Abraham's son is not dearer to him than his obedience to God ("þæt he him lifdagas leofran ne wisse þonne he hyrde heofoncyninge," 409–10). These words are reminiscent of those of Sedulius in the same scene of the *Carmen paschale* (116–18): "pietate remota/Plus pietatis habens contempsit uulnera nati/ Amplexus praecepta Dei" ("Putting pity aside, having more piety, he turned away from the [potential] wounds to his child, embracing God's commands"). To anyone familiar with the *Carmen paschale* or other such depictions of the Offering of Isaac in Latin poetry, the symbolism of the scene is self-evident. But if such meaning is intended by the *Exodus* poet, it is subtle and latent rather than explicit and patent.

Crossing of the Red Sea (447–63)

The description of the converging waves and the destruction of the Egyptian army is the showpiece of *Exodus*. The entire sequence runs for

---

158 Lucas, *Exodus*, 126.
159 See further Hill, 204–5; and Lucas, ibid.

almost seventy lines (447–515), though it is based on just two verses of the Bible (Ex. 14.27–8).[160] While the epic tenor of the poetry coincides broadly with that of Avitus in *Historia spiritalis*, there is little sense of any baptismal imagery. In fact, it is the raw action of the passage that takes centre stage (447–63):[161]

> Cumque extendisset Moyses manum contra mare, reuersum est primo diluculo ad priorem locum: fugientibusque Aegyptiis occurrerunt aquae, et inuoluit eos Dominus in mediis fluctibus. 28 Reuersaeque sunt aquae, et operuerunt currus et equites cuncti exercitus Pharaonis, qui sequentes ingressi fuerant mare: nec unus quidem superfuit ex eis.[162]
>
> – Ex. 14.27–8

Folc wæs afæred; flodegsa becwom	
gastas geomre, geofon deaðe hweop.	
Wæron beorhhliðu blode bestemed,	
holm heolfre spaw, hream wæs on yðum,	450
wæter wæpna ful, wælmist astah.	
Wæron Egypte eft oncyrde,	
flugon forhtigende, fær ongeton,	
woldon herebleaðe hamas findan –	
gylp wearð gnornra. Him ongen genap	455
atol yða gewealc, ne ðær ænig becwom	
herges to hame, ac behindan beleac	
wyrd mid wæge. Ðær ær wegas lagon	
mere modgode (mægen wæs adrenced),	
streamas stodon. Storm up gewat	460
heah to heofonum, herewopa mæst;	
laðe cyrmdon (lyft up geswearc)	
fægum stæfnum. Flod blod gewod.	

---

160 See Lucas, *Exodus*, 132.

161 See also Zacher, *Rewriting the Old Testament in Anglo-Saxon Verse*, 49–53, for a spirited reading of several lines here and her comment that "the most striking change [to the original] is the poet's addition of martial imagery that pervades the entire poem."

162 Ex. 14.27–8: "And when Moses had stretched forth his hand towards the sea, it returned at the first break of day to the former place, and as the Egyptians were fleeing away, the waters came upon them, and the Lord shut them up in the middle of the waves. 28 And the waters returned, and covered the chariots and the horsemen of all the army of Pharaoh, who had come into the sea after them, neither did there so much as one of them remain."

[The people were terrified, fear of the Flood overcame the wretched souls, the ocean threatened death. The mountainous slopes were drenched with blood, the sea spewed gore, screaming surfaced on the waves, the water was full of weapons, a slaughterous mist arose. The Egyptians were turned back; terrified, they fled, and felt fear; cowards, they wanted to find their homes, their gloating grew sadder. A dreadful rolling of the waves darkened their path, so that none of that troop found their homes again, but fate sealed off their retreat with a wave. Where paths lay open before, the sea now raged, streams stood, the army was drowned. The storm rose up high to the heavens, great wailing from the troop. The hateful men cried out, the air darkened with their doomed voices. Blood filled the Flood.]

As Lucas puts it, this is a "a *tour de force* of dramatic description."[163] The lines are short. The action, swift, and only a few conjunctions link successive clauses. Thoughts collide. Commotion abounds, and in the space of two lines, the poet moves from references to "gore" (*heolfre*, 450) and "screaming" (*hream*, 450) to "weapons" (*wæpna*, 451) and "blood-mist" (*wælmist*, 451). The language is lurid and gory, and the chaos recalls the destruction of Pharaoh in *Historia spiritalis* (5.683–97). In both poems, a "mountain" of water rises up against the Egyptians (*lympharum monte leuata*, 684/ *Wæron beorhhliðu*, 449)[164] and blood mingles with the waters of the sea ("concolor et rubro miscetur sanguine pontus," 694/"blode bestemed," 449).[165] But the *Exodus* poet is less personal in his characterization of Pharaoh, who stands generally for sinfulness. He is less of an individual here.

As a further point of style, the *Exodus*-poet interrupts his train of thought with two parenthetical statements (459, 463). He says, for example, "where paths lay before, the sea now raged (the force was drowned), streams stood" ("Ðær ær wegas lagon/ mere modgode (mægen wæs adrenced),/ streamas stodon," 458b–60). The intervening statement, that the army has drowned, clips the logical sequence of thought, creating a sense

---

163 Lucas, *Exodus*, 132.

164 There are only seven occurrences of *beorhhlið* in Old English, all of them in poetry – *Elene* (2), *Exodus* (2), *Riddles* (2), *Genesis A* (1). In his edition of *Exodus*, Irving writes (p. 92) that "these must be the hills along the shore, but they have been understood as the waves themselves." But see Juvencus and the storm on the sea of Galilea in which the storm raises up furious mountains to the sky, which appear to be water ("ad caelum rabidos sustollere montes," 1.29). Also, see n. 53 on that page for the source of Juvencus (*Aen.* 1.105, *praeruptus aquae mons*).

165 Lucas, *Exodus*, 132, suggests a pun on bloody water and points to lines 463b and 478.

of disorder and alarm, as if the poetry were caught up in the chaos. A similar stylistic device is used by Juvencus in *Euangeliorum libri*, where the
violence of the tempest on the Sea of Galilee tears words apart at the caesura of the line (1.32): "Fluctus disiectoque aperitur terra profundo"
("And the earth is opened to the sundered deep"). Thus the style of *Exodus*
reflects the tumult of the storm. The violence comes to rest with a single,
striking instance of rhyme: Flōd blōd gewōd ("Blood filled the Flood,"
463), which abruptly slows the pace, allowing a moment's reprieve and
mingling all the disparate images of chaos into a single, bloody image. The
entire passage is carefully crafted to capture the physical violence of the
scene and the terror of the Egyptians.

Echoes of the biblical passage are scattered throughout the sequence
from lines 447–515, but an obvious example appears here with reference to
the biblical phrase "nec unus quidem superfuit ex eis" ("neither did there
so much as one of them remain," 14:28), which is covered by verses 456b–
7a ("ne ðær ænig becwom / herges to hame" [" ... that none of that troop
found their homes again"]).[166] That thought is repeated at the end of the
scene, which then forms an envelope pattern, bringing the episode to a
close (506b–9):

           Egyptum wearð
þæs dægweorces   deop lean gesceod,
forðam þæs heriges   ham eft ne com
ealles ungrundes   ænig to lafe ...

[Egypt earned a deep reward for that day's work, since no remnant of that
troop, that huge army, came home again ...]

The utter destruction of the Egyptian army, which leaves "no remnant"
("ne ... ænig to lafe," 508–9), can be contrasted with the survival of Noah
and his kin after the Flood, who return to dry land "as the eternal remnant
of the whole human race" ("eallum eorðcynne ece lafe," 370), or on a
smaller scale with the sparing of Isaac, who survives "as the remnant of his
people" (*leodum to lafe*, 405a) and Abraham's "heir" (*yrfelafe*, 403b).
Those two moments testify to the mercy of God towards the faithful, but
the Egyptians earn only wrath, whose annihilation serves as a warning to

---

166 See note by Lucas, *Exodus*, 132, who connects the language to the heroic ethos: "Acts
    of cowardice, even in the face of certain defeat, were considered ignominious in Ger-
    manic heroic society." Lucas also cites a parallel from *Beowulf* (*hames niosan*, 2365–6).

the reader, one that recalls the narrator's cautionary tale of Lucifer's fall in *Genesis B* (292–9):

> Ða hit se allwalda   eall gehyrde,
> þæt his engyl ongan   ofermede micel
> ahebban wið his hearran   and spræc healic word
> dollice wið drihten sinne,   sceolde he þa dæd ongyldan,   295
> worc þæs gewinnes gedælan,   and sceolde his wite habban,
> ealra morðra mæst.   Swa deð monna gehwilc
> þe wið his waldend   winnan ongynneð
> mid mane wið þone mæran drihten.

[When the Almighty heard all that, that his angel began to uplift great pride against his Lord and speak haughty words rashly against his ruler, he had to repay the deed, share the work of war, and have for his punishment the worst of all miseries. So does each man who sets out to contend against the renowned Lord.]

Such is the fate of Pharaoh and his army for their disobedience and pride and for doing what Lucifer and the rebel angels did: "they contended with God!" ("Hie wið god wunnon!" 515b). Those are also the final words in this sequence, and they testify less to the importance of symbolism than the need for obedience. Pharaoh's fall is therefore less symbolic in meaning and more of a homiletic exhortation to mend one's ways while there is time. That is something Avitus urges as well in his *Historia spiritalis*.

The Closing of *Exodus* (516–30)

In all, the Old English *Exodus* appeals to its audience on several levels. On the one hand, the action is, as Avitus would say, entertaining enough on its own. To that end, "the poet does not pause in his story to moralize (as does Cynewulf, for example, in *Christ II*) or to point out the explicit *significatio* of individual objects or events in the manner of exegetical commentators."[167] As Irving says, *Exodus* "offers its message of human

---

167 Irving, "*Exodus* Retraced," 203–23 at 212. Irving does not, however, deny "that the Christian typological pattern is also there, the same majestic series of great names one can find in the thirteenth chapter of Hebrews or in the liturgy" (p. 216). See also Sheppard, "Scriptural Poetry," 31: "the poet emphasizes the importance of spiritual meaning without elucidating it."

salvation largely in heroic terms."[168] That is true, but the poet, who is obviously very learned, also feels a degree of pressure to account for the symbolism that is so often linked to interpretations of Exodus. That pressure leads him to include language in his narrative that intimates deeper spiritual meaning, including many individual words and phrases but also the following statement at the end of the poem (516–30a):

> Ðanon Israhelum   ece rædas
> on merehwearfe   Moyses sægde,
> heahþungen wer,   halige spræce,
> deop ærende.   Dægweorc nemnað
> swa gyt werðeode,   on gewritum findað   520
> doma gehwilcne,   þara ðe him drihten bebead
> on þam siðfate   soðum wordum.
> Gif onlucan wile   lifes wealhstod,
> beorht in breostum,   banhuses weard,
> ginfæsten god   Gastes cægon,   525
> run bið gerecenod,   ræd forð gæð;
> hafað wislicu   word on fæðme,
> wile meagollice   modum tæcan
> þæt we gesne ne syn   Godes þeodscipes,
> metodes miltsa.   530

[Then through holy speech that noble man, Moses, spoke everlasting laws, a deep message, to the Israelites on the seashore. People still speak about the works in those days, and in the Scriptures one can find each of the judgments that the Lord enjoined to him in true words on that journey, if the interpreter of life, the keeper of the body, bright within its breast, will unlock those ample goods with the keys of the spirit. The mystery will be explained and wisdom will issue forth; [it] has wise words in its breast and earnestly wants to teach our hearts, so that we may not be without God's fellowship and mercy.]

This passage is about the power of the soul as *lifes wealhstod* ("interpreter of life," 523b) to unlock the meaning of the Old Testament. The allusions to "keys of the spirit" (*Gastes cægon*, 525), "mystery" (*run*, 526a), and "teaching" (*tæcan*, 528b) suggest the kind of "didaktische Intention" ("didactic intention") we have come to expect from Latin biblical epic, in which Sedulius, Avitus, and Arator make overt statements

---

168 Ibid.

about the mystical sense of the scriptures and their power to teach.[169] Unlike them, however, the *Exodus*-poet leaves it up to the soul to teach the individual how best to interpret these events. The author himself does not step in. What guidance, then, can the soul receive? Life experience can afford some understanding of the deeper meaning of such events, of "the deadly journey," but it is more likely that the poet reserves the keys of the spirit for those who are literate and familiar with the coded language of the Bible than those who are not.[170] If so, he means the kind of readers Wilcox suggests in her interpretation of the cloud-tent metaphor, learned and Latinate ones alongside general audiences, for whom this would have been primarily a poem of action.

It may also be that the Latin biblical epics themselves can explain the *Exodus* poet's unpredictable movement between the literal and figurative modes. For the English author, as for every writer of the Anglo-Saxon period, the genre of Latin biblical epic came not, as it did for their continental neighbours, as a series of individual poems appearing over a span of two centuries. The Anglo-Saxons inherited this literature as a collection of verse that had already run its course. While Juvencus initiated the Latin genre presumably without any other such poems at his disposal, the writers of the Old English period, if they were familiar with this literature, had several approaches to choose from. If the author of *Exodus* studied the Latin biblical epics in school, as so many of his contemporaries did, he would have been familiar with the literal method of Juvencus and Cyprianus as well as the progressively freer practices of Sedulius, Avitus, and Arator, who blend passages of literal description with spiritual interpretations. Without any of that later poetry or knowledge of extra-biblical literature, it may be the *Exodus* poet would have written a more literal rendition of the Bible in the style of the *Heptateuch* of Cyprianus, who probably wrote his own versification under such conditions. But under the influence of poets like Arator and Avitus, the Old English writer would have been more susceptible to the kind of spiritual interpretation we find so often in those texts, especially because he is inclined towards

---

169 See further Siegmar Döpp, *Eva und die Schlange*, 19–22, who surveys the purpose of biblical epic.

170 See also Zacher, *Rewriting the Old Testament*, esp. 72–5, who discusses the enigmatic nature of this passage and cites Augustine's *De ciuitate dei* (13.24.2), where the interaction of the rational and divine soul, working in unison, may be the "interpreter of life" (*lifes wealhstod*, 523b): "Like Augustine's 'inner man,' the function of the *wealhstod* is to 'translate' or 'interpret' precepts imported from external sources, such as books, teachers, and experiential sense perceptions."

florid, metaphorical language. Moreover, we should also not exclude the many other extra-biblical materials the poet may have known.

The problem is, while Arator can afford to pursue "whatever mystical sense is given to [his] heart" ("Et res si qua mihi mystica corde datur," *Epist. Vigil.* 22), since Avitus, Sedulius, Cyprianus, Juvencus, and others had already paved the way with all kinds of biblical verse, the English author standing at the beginning of the vernacular genre would have faced the problem of how best to proceed. He seems to know that a literal rendition would probably best serve his contemporary audiences, as they would not be familiar with much biblical poetry, Latin or English, and they would have been likely to respond more favourably to a literal rendition of Moses' heroic deeds. On the other hand, the author of *Exodus* also seems unable to ignore the kind of persistent commentary we get from Avitus, who says that the more beautiful image of salvation outshines the beauty of the story itself ("pulchramque relatu / Pulchrior exuperat praemissae forma salutis," 5.15–16). In other words, the symbolism is more important than the events. With words like that in mind, the Old English poet resolves that the message of salvation is too important to ignore and must be stated in some measure, even if it means diverting the primary focus on the praise-worthy deeds of Moses and the Israelites.

Chapter Nine

Conclusion

Accedat igitur paruulus ad huius libri lectionem quia in eo invenitur lac paruulo-
rum, accedat et perfectus quia in eo inueniet solidum cibum ... Accedat similiter
ingeniosus uel studiosus, quia reperiet unde possit et debeat exercere ingenium
suum.[1]

[So let the young come to the reading of this book, since there is milk in it for the
young; and if they are done with that, let them come still, for there is solid food in
it as well ... Likewise, let the bright and eager come, for here is a place to exercise
one's intellect.]

The above words appear in the "Teacher's Preface" to the *Aurora* of Peter
Riga, canon of Rheims, who died around 1209 CE. The *Aurora* is a 15,000-
line versification of all the major books of the Bible, or more properly a
verse commentary upon them, and it was written at the end of the twelfth
century (c. 1170–1200 CE). The existence of this work and others like it
shows that the genre of biblical versification persists into the later Middle
Ages and continues to evolve.[2] More to the point, the general purpose of
the *Aurora* aligns with that of the Latin and Old English biblical versifications, showing that the genre remained popular throughout the first

---

1 The quotation is from the preface in Beichner's edition, *Aurora Petri Rigae Biblia Versificata*.

2 See further Morris, ed. *Cursor mundi [The cursor of the world]: A Northumbrian poem
of the XIVth century*. Early English Text Society. Original series 57, 59, 62, 66, 68, 99,
101; and Agneta, ed., *Petris Comestoris Scolastica Historia: Liber Genesis* (Turnhout,
2004); also Morey, "Peter Comestor, Biblical Paraphrase, and the Medieval Popular
Bible," *Speculum* 68 (1993), 6–35.

millennium of Christianity.[3] Paul Beichner, who edited the *Aurora*, effectively captures the value of this literature: "For those who could read Latin, it supplied Scriptural lore in a popular form and it also served as a book of popular theology, devotional reading, moral instruction, and entertainment."[4] Allowing for the intervention of vernacular audiences in Old and Middle English, this is also the general purpose of late antique biblical epic and Anglo-Saxon biblical verse.

Sedulius would have appreciated the symbolic links in the Teacher's Preface between food and literature, that the *Aurora* offers "milk" for the young (*lac*) and more "solid food" (*solidum cibum*) for those with teeth, "the bright and eager" (*ingeniosus uel studiosus*). Such imagery accords well with the banquet-themed preface of his *Carmen paschale*, in which he promotes the humble but wholesome fare of the Gospels over the "waxen honey" of classical poetry ("Cerea gemmatis flauescunt mella canistris," *Cp. praef.* 13). The healthier diet, as Prudentius agrees, is made of "the leaves of greens" and "the pod that swells with varied beans," by which he means the Bible and Christian literature. This, he says, "will nourish us with an innocent banquet" ("Nos holeris coma, nos siliqua / Feta legumine multimodo / Pauerit innocuis epulis," *Cath.* 3.63–5). In fact, that is the greater purpose of the Christian genre according to its authors, that is, to provide a healthier alternative to classical poetry. That being said, the rich and complex intertexuality that characterizes biblical versification, which aims to blend the honeyed eloquence of the *Aeneid* with the vegetarianism of the Bible, ends up being a much fancier banquet that its authors would care to admit. Avitus may say, "I do not sing, so that my praise of so great a story may capture the eloquence it deserves" (non ut dignum tanti praeconia facti / Eloquium captent," *Hist. Spir.* 5.6–7), but the style of *Historia Spiritalis* suggests otherwise, and while Sedulius is ardent in his effort to be faithful to the Bible, he is also eager to make a name for himself and for Christian poetry.

Juvencus is the first to show that it is possible to combine the two traditions, that the message of the Bible can be heard through the tumult of epic, and that both benefit in the process: the one being allowed to live on; the other finding new life. With few (if any) models before him, Juvencus

---

3 Rigg, *History of Anglo-Latin Literature: 1066–1422*. See also Raby, *A History of Christian Latin Poetry*, 303–4. The author of the "Teacher's Preface" may be Albert of Reims, whose name is attached to the preface in at least two manuscripts.

4 Beichner, *Aurora*, xi.

adapts his classical sources to celebrate the Gospels and "the life-giving deeds of Christ" (*Christi uitalia gesta, praef.* 19), and the success of his enterprise cannot be overstated. The fact that *Euangeliorum libri* took precedence over Vergil on the Anglo-Saxon school curriculum is reason enough to acknowledge the work, but we also know that late antique and medieval readers admired the poem a great deal, and that, too, is cause to ask why this text was so influential.

For one, Juvencus was writing at a time when the Latin text of the Bible was itself still taking shape, and so an elegant rendition of the Gospels in the style of classical epic would have appealed to the literary elite, who regarded that literature highly. In fact, we know that *Euangeliorum libri* did receive the approbation of its intended audience, if the endorsement of Jerome is any indication, or the myriad allusions to the poem over the course of the next seven hundred years. In fact, as centuries passed, *Euangeliorum libri* settled into a place of distinction, which led to its adoption into the Anglo-Saxon curriculum. There, it became a model exemplum for the composition of Christian poetry in the "classical" style, which is to say, poetry in the style of late antique literature. Like their continental counterparts, Anglo-Saxon audiences admired this poem a great deal and adapted it for their own purposes. So there are good reasons for students and scholars of the Anglo-Saxon period to reconsider *Euangeliorum libri* again, given that we do not yet have a clear picture of its path through late Antiquity and the Middle Ages. Immediately, there is need for an English translation of the poem, which will help make the text more accessible to general audiences; moreover, there has also not been an edition of the text since 1891. Further analyses of the text will also help secure its status in the early years of Christian literature, and particular attention should be given to the work as a whole and how individual scenes contribute to the larger unity of the text. Finally, there is still much to be said about the reception of *Euangeliorum libri* in Anglo-Saxon England. This book has scratched the surface, but it is clear that Juvencus was an important source of inspiration for many English writers.

There is also probably a better case to be made for the *Exodus* poet's knowledge of Cyprianus and the *Heptateuch*. I have provided a sense of the author's work and his general approach to biblical versification, but there is more to be said about the shared emphasis on heroic dramatization in these two texts. If *Exodus* does indeed originate in eighth-century Northumbria, it is likely that its author was familiar with the *Heptateuch*, especially since Bede cites it in his eighth-century treatise, *De arte metrica*. That alone suggests the poem was being read more widely by the sorts of people who were most likely to have written a work like *Exodus*. What is more, the greatest virtues of the *Heptateuch* are its accessibility and economy of style, and these offer an easy entrance into the Latin genre and a poem that affords the kind of martial-heroic vigour we have thus far attributed to Avitus and others. Given knowledge of the *Heptateuch* among Aldhelm, Bede, and others, we should therefore consider the work of Cyprianus as a potential source for Anglo-Saxon poetry and for *Exodus* in particular.

A stronger case should also be made for knowledge of Sedulius and the *Carmen paschale* among any number of Old and New Testament works in Anglo-Latin and Old English. In fact, all of the New Testament versifications of the Bible in Latin should be regarded as potential sources for vernacular poetry, even if the given Anglo-Saxon text covers the Old Testament primarily. There are plenty of Old Testament scenes in New Testament versifications of the Bible, including those in the works of Sedulius and Arator, and Miranda Wilcox has shown, in "Creating the Cloud-Tent-Ship Conceit in *Exodus*," that this literature is important to our reading of Old English biblical poetry. In fact, we know from the large number of verbal echoes in Anglo-Latin verse, especially of the first books of *Euangeliorum libri*, the *Carmen paschale*, and the *Historia apostolica*, and from glossing in Old English on these texts, that the Anglo-Saxons were reading these works carefully. They could not, therefore, have missed the sensitive use of language by Juvencus or the allegorical style of Sedulius and Arator, which so often links the incidents of the Old Testament to the New. Broader consideration, then, should be given to the ways in which the Latin genre as a whole inspires the production of imitative works in Anglo-Latin and Old English literature.

There is no need to repeat the same argument for Avitus' *Historia spiritalis* and Arator's *Historia apostolica*. Both poems were known and studied throughout the Anglo-Saxon period and both make contributions to the evolution of Anglo-Latin poetry and no doubt to features of Old English verse as well. The extent to which this is true remains to be shown, but there is already sufficient evidence to warrant further enquiry. Above all, we should consider that viable connections between the two traditions may be made, if we move beyond our prior quest for verbatim evidence and begin to consider broader affinities of form and content. Even if we fail to make sources of those Latin texts for any given work in Anglo-Latin or Old English poetry, they remain important analogues, and there can be no question that knowledge of the earlier tradition informs and deepens our reading of Anglo-Saxon literature, which flows from the literary achievements of late Antiquity as much as from the Germanic past.

Finally, I am aware that, for some, a potential shortcoming of this study will be that it does not seek out and provide irrefutable evidence that, for example, the author of *Exodus* knew and imitated the work of Avitus or Cyprianus. I believe that he did, but my primary goal has been to advance knowledge of the late antique biblical epics themselves, since general knowledge of this literature has been lacking from discussions of sources. I have shown, I think, that Juvencus, Sedulius, and Arator are crucial to our understanding of Anglo-Latin poetry and that they are important sources of inspiration for Aldhelm, Bede, and Alcuin. All of this is Anglo-Saxon literature, and so we should not hesitate now to take the next step and look again at the potential connections between the Latin and Old English genres of biblical versification. If we do so with an open mind and a view towards the broader affinities of style, theme, and symbol, we shall appreciate that these traditions have more in common than we have hitherto supposed.

Outline of the *Carmen Paschale*

3.70–85   Miracle 8: exorcism of the Gadarene swine
3.86–102   Miracle 9: healing of a paralytic
3.103–42   Miracles 10/11: resurrection of the "sleeper" & the healing cloak
3.143–51   Miracle 12: healing of two blind men
3.152–7   Miracle 13: healing of a deaf and mute man
3.158–81   Jesus sends the apostles out to heal and convert
3.182–8   Miracle 14: healing of a withered hand
3.189–98   Miracle 15: healing of a deaf and mute demoniac
3.199–205   Miracle 16: healing of a crippled woman
3.206–18   Miracle 17: feeding five thousand
3.219–36   Miracle 18: Jesus walks on water
3.237–41   Miracle 19: healing at the touch of Jesus' cloak
3.242–50   Miracle 20: healing/exorcism of Canaanite woman's daughter
3.251–6   Miracle 21: healing the multitudes of various ailments
3.257–72   Miracle 22: feeding four thousand
3.273–95   Miracle 23: Transfiguration of Jesus
3.296–312   Miracle 24: exorcism/healing of an epileptic child
3.313–19   Miracle 25: coin from the mouth of a fish
3.320–39   Apostles ask Jesus what man will be considered greatest in heaven

4.1–8   Reiteration of God's omnipotence over nature
4.9–30   Vanity of earthly wealth vs. heavenly riches
4.31–9   Miracle 26: healing of two blind men
4.40–4   Miracle 27: healing in the temple
4.45–56   Miracle 28: withering of the fig tree
4.57–63   Miracle 29: healing of a mute
4.64–81   Miracle 30: woman washes the feet of Jesus with her hair
4.82–9   Miracle 31: healing of a mute demoniac, forbidding demons to speak
4.90–8   Satan and his demons are dismayed by the incarnation of Christ
4.99–105   Miracle 32: healing of a blind mute
4.106–8   Miracle 33: healing blindness
4.109–24   Miracle 34: abundance of fish caught by the apostles
4.125–41   Miracle 35: resurrection of a dead boy
4.142–9   Miracle 36: healing/exorcism of Mary Magdalene
4.150–71   Instruction of the twelve apostles
4.172–88   Miracle 37: healing of a man with edema
4.189–209   Miracle 38: healing of ten lepers
4.210–21   Miracle 39: healing of Bartimaeus, son of Timaeus
4.222–32   The Samaritan woman at the well (salvation)
4.233–50   Jesus forgives the adulterous woman

<table>
<tr><td>4.251–70</td><td>Miracle 40: healing of a man born blind</td></tr>
<tr><td>4.271–90</td><td>Miracle 41: resurrection of Lazarus</td></tr>
<tr><td>4.291–309</td><td>Jesus enters Jerusalem on a donkey</td></tr>
<tr><td></td><td></td></tr>
<tr><td>5.1–19</td><td>Introduction to crucifixion and resurrection</td></tr>
<tr><td>5.20–8</td><td>Jesus washes the feet of the apostles</td></tr>
<tr><td>5.29–68</td><td>Judas betrays Jesus, lengthy digression on Judas</td></tr>
<tr><td>5.69–112</td><td>Arrest of Jesus, Peter denies him three times</td></tr>
<tr><td>5.113–38</td><td>Judas refuses his reward and hangs himself</td></tr>
<tr><td>5.139–55</td><td>Jesus endures accusations at the trial</td></tr>
<tr><td>5.156–63</td><td>The narrator condemns Pilate</td></tr>
<tr><td>5.164–81</td><td>Jesus surrenders to torture</td></tr>
<tr><td>5.182–201</td><td>The Crucifixion</td></tr>
<tr><td>5.202–31</td><td>Two thieves crucified with Jesus</td></tr>
<tr><td>5.232–49</td><td>Jesus dies, darkness falls</td></tr>
<tr><td>5.250–60</td><td>Jews compared to vinegar on the sponge</td></tr>
<tr><td>5.261–75</td><td>Jesus descends into Hell</td></tr>
<tr><td>5.276–94</td><td>Climax. Apostrophe to personified Death.</td></tr>
<tr><td>5.295–314</td><td>Guards demand the tomb be well-protected from robbers</td></tr>
<tr><td>5.315–50</td><td>Tomb is empty and the narrator criticizes the guards</td></tr>
<tr><td>5.351–64</td><td>The narrator rebukes the Jews</td></tr>
<tr><td>5.365–91</td><td>Resurrected, Jesus reveals himself to the apostles (Thomas)</td></tr>
<tr><td>5.392–404</td><td>Miracle 42: fish from the right side of the boat (metaphor)</td></tr>
<tr><td>5.405–21</td><td>Jesus eats with the apostles, tests Peter, grants peace</td></tr>
<tr><td>5.422–38</td><td>Miracle 43: ascension of Jesus into heaven</td></tr>
</table>

Miracles in Book One of the *Carmen Paschale*

Miracle	Biblical book	Location	Total lines
1. The story of Enoch	Gen 5:18–24	103–6	4
2. Sara, Abraham and Isaac	Gen 17:16–21; 21:1–8; 22:1–13	107–20	14
3. Lot's wife turned to a pillar of salt	Gen 19:24–6	121–6	6
4. The burning bush	Ex 3:2	127–31	5
5. Moses' staff becomes a serpent	Ex 4:3; 7:10–12	132–5	4
6. The parting of the Red Sea	Ex 14:21–25	136–47	12
7. Manna from heaven	Ex 16:13–16	148–51	4
8. Water from the rock	Ex 17:1–7	152–9	8
9. The talking ass	Nu 22:22–30	160–2	3
10. The sun and moon stand still	Jos 10:12–13	163–9	7
11. Elijah, ravens, and chariot of fire	1 Kings 17:1–6	170–87	18
12. Hezekiah given an extra 15 years	2 Kings 20:1–6	188–91	4
13. Jonah and the whale	Jon 1:17–2.10	192–6	5
14. The three youths in the furnace	Dan 3:13–30	197–211	15
15. Daniel and the lions	Dan 6:16–24	212–19	8

Bibliography

Alberi, Mary. "'The Better Paths of Wisdom': Alcuin's Monastic 'True Philosophy' and the Worldly Court." *Speculum* 76.4 (2001): 896–910.

Anlezark, Daniel. *Old Testament Narratives*. DOML 7. Cambridge: Harvard University Press, 2011.

Arevalo, P., ed. *Vetti Aquilini Iuvenci Hispani Presbyteri Evangelicae Historiae libri IV*. PL 19 (1846): 9–346.

Arweiler, Alexander. *Die Imitation antiker und spätantiker Literatur in der Dichtung "De spiritalis historiae gestis" des Alcimus Avitus*. Berlin: De Gruyter, 1999.

Bailey, Cyril, ed. *De rerum natura*. 2nd ed. Oxford: Clarendon Press, 1963.

Baker, P.S., and M. Lapidge, eds. *Byrhtferth's Enchiridion*. EETS ss 15. New York: Oxford University Press, 1995.

Barnhouse, Rebecca, and Benjamin C. Withers, eds. *The Old English Hexateuch: Aspects and Approaches*. Michigan: Medieval Institute Publications, 2000.

Becker, Carl. *De Metris in Heptateuchum*. Diss. Bonn, 1889.

Behaghel, Otto ed. *Heliand und Genesis*. 10th ed. Tübingen: M. Niemeyer, 1996.

Beichner, Paul E., ed. *Aurora Petri Rigae Biblia Versificata*: A Verse Commentary on the Bible. 2 vols. Publications in Mediaeval Studies, University of Notre Dame, 19. Notre Dame: University of Notre Dame Press, 1965.

Belanoff, Pat. "The Fall (?) of the Old English Female Poetic Image." *PMLA* 104.5 (1989): 822–31.

Berlin, Gail Ivy. "Bede's Miracle Stories: Notions of Evidence and Authority in Old English History." *Neophilologus* 74 (1990): 434–43.

Best, Hermann. *De Cypriani quae feruntur Metris in Heptateuchum*. Diss. Marburg, 1891.

Biggs, Fred. "'Englum gelice': *Elene* line 1320 and *Genesis A* line 185." *NM* 86 (1985): 447–52.

Blackburn, F.A. *Exodus* and *Daniel*. Boston: D.C. Heath, 1907.

Bolton, W.F. *A History of Anglo-Latin Literature, Volume I: 597–1066.* Princeton: Princeton University Press, 1967.

Bonner, G., ed. *Famulus Christi: Essays in Commemoration of the Thirteenth Centenary of the Birth of the Venerable Bede.* London: S.P.C.K., 1976.

– "Saint Cuthbert: Soul Friend." *Church and Faith in the Patristic Tradition: Augustine, Pelagianism and early Christian Northumbria.* London: Variorum (1996): 24–41.

Bonner, G., David Rollason, and Clare Stancliffe, eds. *St. Cuthbert, His Cult and Community to AD 1200.* Woodbridge: Boydell, 1989.

Boren, James L. "Form and Meaning in Cynewulf's *Fates of the Apostles.*" In *The Cynewulf Reader (Basic Readings in Anglo-Saxon England)*, edited by Robert E. Bjork, 57–65. New York: Routledge, 2001.

Borrell, E. *Las palabras de Virgilio en Juvenco.* Barcelona: Publications UB, 1991.

Bright, J.W. "The Relation of the Caedmonian Exodus to the Liturgy." *MLN* 27 (1912): 97–103.

Brockman, B.A. "'Heroic' and 'Christian' in *Genesis A.*" *MLQ* 35 (1974): 115–28.

Brooks, Kenneth R., ed. *Andreas and the Fates of the Apostles.* Oxford: Clarendon Press, 1961.

Brooks, N. *Latin and the Vernacular Languages in Early Medieval Britain.* Studies in the Early History of Britain. Leicester: Leicester University Press, 1982.

Brown, George Hardin. *A Companion to Bede.* Woodbridge: Boydell, 2009.

– *Bede the Venerable.* Boston: Twayne Publishers, 1987.

Bullough, Donald A. *Alcuin: Achievement and Reputation.* Leiden and Boston: Brill, 2004.

– "Alcuin's Cultural Influence: The Evidence of the Manuscripts." In *Alcuin of York*, edited by L.A.J.R. Houwen and A.A. MacDonald, 1–26. Groningen: Egbert Forsten, 1998.

Canali, L., ed. *Aquilino Giovenco: Il poema dei Vangeli.* Milan: Bompiani, 2011.

Carrubba, R.W. "The Preface to Juvencus' Biblical Epic: A Structural Study." *American Journal of Philology* 114 (1993): 303–12.

Charlet, Jean-Louis. "L'inspiration et la forme bibliques dans la poésie latine chrétienne du IIIe au VIe siècle." In *Le monde latin antique et la Bible*, edited by J. Fontaine and C. Pietri, 613–43. Paris: Beauchesne, 1985.

Chase, Colin, ed. *The Dating of Beowulf.* Toronto: University of Toronto Press, 1981.

Clemoes, P., M. Lapidge, and H. Gneuss. *Learning and Literature in Anglo-Saxon England: Studies Presented to Peter Clemoes on the Occasion of His Sixty-Fifth Birthday.* Cambridge: Cambridge University Press, 1985.

Clubb, M.D., ed. *Christ and Satan: An Old English Poem.* Hamden: Archon Books, 1972.

Colgrave, B., and R.A.B Mynors, eds. *Bede's Ecclesiastical History of the English People.* Oxford Medieval Texts. Oxford: Oxford University Press, 1969.

Colombi, E. "*Paene ad verbum*: gli *Evangeliorum libri* di Giovenco tra parafrasi e commento." *Cassiodorus* 3 (1997): 9–36.

Costanza, Salvatore. *Avitiana I: I Modelli Epici Del "De Spiritalis Historiae Gestis."* Messina: Editrice Universitaria, 1968.

– "Da Giovenco a Sedulio: I proemi dagli *Evangeliorum Libri* e del *Carmen paschale*." *Civiltá classica e cristiana* 6 (1985): 253–86.

Constantinescu, R. "Alcuin et les 'Libelli Precum' de l'époque Caroligienne." *Revue de l'histoire de la spiritualité* 50 (1974): 17–56.

Crandall Amos, Ashley. *Linguistic Means of Determining the Dates of Old English Literary Texts.* Cambridge, MA: Medieval Academy of America, 1980.

Crawford, S.J., ed. *The Old English Version of the Heptateuch.* EETS os 160. London: Oxford University Press, 1922.

Creed, Robert P. "The Art of the Singer: Three Old English Tellings of the Offering of Isaac." In *Old English Poetry: Fifteen Essays*, edited by Robert P. Creed, 69–92. Providence: Brown University Press, 1967.

Cross, J.E., and S.I. Tucker. "Allegorical Traditions and the Old English *Exodus*." *Neophilologus* 44 (1960): 122–7.

Cunningham, M.P., ed. *Aurelii Prudentii Clementis Carmina.* CCSL 126. Turnhout: Brepols, 1966.

Curtius, E.R. *Europäische Literatur und lateinisches Mittelalter.* Bern: A. Francke, 1948.

– *European Literature and the Latin Middle Ages.* Translated by Willard R. Trask. New York: Pantheon Press, 1953.

Danielou, Jean. *From Shadows to Reality: Studies in the Biblical Typology of the Fathers.* London: Burns & Oates, 1960.

– *Sacramentum Futuri: Études sur les origines de la typologie biblique.* Paris: Beauchesne et fils, 1950.

– *The Bible and the Liturgy.* London: Longman & Todd, 1964.

Deerberg, D. *Der Sturz des Judas. Kommentar (5,1–163) und Studien zur poetischen Erbauung bei Sedulius.* Orbis Antiquus 43. Münster: Aschendorff, 2011.

De Lubac, Jean. *Exégèse médiéval: Les quatre sens de l'Écriture.* 2 vols. Paris: Aubier, 1959–64.

De Nie, Giselle. *Poetics of Wonder: Testimonies of the New Christian Miracles in the Late Antique Latin World.* Studies in the Early Middle Ages 31. Turnhout: Brepols, 2011.

– "'Whatever Mystery May be Given to My Heart': A Latent Image in Arator's History of the Apostles." In *Rome and Religion in the Medieval World: Studies Thomas F.X. Noble*, edited by Valerie L. Garver and Owen M. Phelan, 1–20. Farnham: Ashgate, 2014.

Deproost, Paul-Augustin. "*Ficta et Facta*: La Condamnation du 'mensonge des poètes' dans la poésie latine chrétienne." *REA* 44 (1998): 101–21.

– "La mise en scène d'un drame intérieur dans le poème sure le péché originel d'Avit de Vienne." *Traditio* 51 (1996): 43–72.

– *L'Apôtre Pierre dans une épopée du VIᵉ siecle: L'Historia apostolica d'Arator.* Paris: Institut d'études augustiniennes, 1990.

– "L'épopée biblique en langue latine: Essai de définition d'un genre litéraire." *Latomus* 56 (1997): 14–39.

– "Mise en oeuvre du merveilleux épique dans le poème *De deluvio mundi* d'Avit de Vienne." *JAC* 34 (1991): 88–103.

Dermott–Small, C. "Rhetoric and Exegesis in Sedulius' *Carmen Paschale*." *Classica et Mediaevalia* 7 (1986): 223–44.

Derolez, R. "*Genesis*: Old Saxon and Old English." *ES* 76 (1995): 409–23.

Di Berardino, Angelo. "Christian Poetry." In *Patrology*, vol. 4, edited by Johannes Quasten, 254–341. Allen, TX: Christian Classics,1999.

Doane, A.N., ed. *Genesis A: A New Edition*. Madison: University of Wisconsin Press, 1978.

– *Genesis A: A New Edition, Revised.* Tempe, Arizona: ACMRS, 2013.

– *The Saxon Genesis: An Edition of the West Saxon Genesis B and the Old Saxon Vatican Genesis.* Madison: University of Wisconsin Press, 1991.

Dobbie, E.V.K., and G.P. Krapp, eds. *The Exeter Book*. ASPR 3. New York: Columbia University Press, 1936.

Dobbie, E.V.K. *Beowulf and Judith*. ASPR 4. New York: Columbia University Press, 1953.

– ed. *The Anglo-Saxon Minor Poems*. ASPR 6. New York: Columbia University Press, 1942.

Dodwell, C.R., and P. Clemoes. *The Old English Illustrated Hexateuch: British Museum Cotton Claudius B. IV.* Early English Manuscripts in Facsimile. Copenhagen: Rosenkilde og Bagger, 1974.

Döpp, Siegmar. Eva und die Schlange: die Sündenfallschilderung des Epikers Avitus im Rahmen der bibelexegetischen Tradition. Speyer: Kartoffeldruck Verlag, 2009.

Duckworth, George E. *Vergil and Classical Hexameter Poetry: A Study in Metrical Variety*. Ann Arbor: University of Michigan Press, 1969.

Dümmler, E., ed. *Poetae Latini Aevi Carolini* 1. MGH. Berlin, 1881.

Dykes, Anthony. *Reading Sin in the World*. Cambridge: Cambridge University Press, 2011.

Earl, James W. "The Christian Tradition in the Old English Exodus." In *The Poems of MS Junius 11*, edited by Roy Liuzza, 137–72. New York: Routledge, 2002.

Eby, John C. "Bringing the Vita to Life: Bede's Symbolic Structure of the Life of St. Cuthbert." *American Benedictine Review* 48.3 (1997): 316–38.

Ehwald, R., ed. *Aldhelmi Opera*. MGH, Auct., Antiq. 15. Berlin, 1919.

Estes, Heide. "Raising Cain in *Genesis* and *Beowulf*: Challenges to Generic Boundaries in Anglo-Saxon Biblical Literature." *The Heroic Age* 13 (2010). Accessed 1 December 2014.

Evans, J. Martin. *Paradise Lost and the Genesis Tradition*. Oxford: Clarendon Press, 1968.

Evenepoel, W. "Prudentius' *Hymnus Ante Cibum* (*Cath.* 3)." *MAIA* 35 (1983): 125–37.

– "The Place of Poetry in Latin Christianity." In *Early Christian Poetry: A Collection of Essays*, edited by J. Den Boeft and A. Hilhorst, 35–60. New York: Brill, 1993.

Everson, David L. "The *Vetus Latina* and the Vulgate of the Book of Genesis." In *The Book of Genesis: Composition, Reception, and Interpretation*, edited by Craig A. Evans, Joel N. Lohr, David L. Petersen, 519–36. Boston: Brill, 2012.

Fagles, Robert, trans. *The Aeneid*. New York: Penguin, 2006.

Farrell, R.T. *Daniel and Azarias*. London: Methuen, 1974.

Fichtner, R. *Taufe und Versuchung Jesu in den Evangeliorum libri quattuor des Bibeldichters Juvencus (1, 346–408)*. Beiträge Zur Altertumskunde, Bd. 50. Stuttgart: Teubner, 1994.

Finnegan, R.E., ed. *Christ and Satan: A Critical Edition*. Waterloo, ON: Wilfrid Laurier University Press, 1977.

Fischer, Bonifatius. *Vetus Latina: Die Reste der altlateinischen Bibel*, Bd. 2: *Genesis*. Freiburg: Herder, 1951–4.

Flieger, Manfred. "Interpretationen zum Bibeldichter Iuvencus: Gethsemane, Festnahme Jesu und Kaiphasprozess (4, 478–565)." Stuttgart: Teubner, 1993.

Fontaine, J. *Naissance de la poésie dans l'occident chrétien*. Paris: Études Augustiniennes, 1981.

Fontaine, J., and C. Pietri, eds. *Le monde latin antique et la Bible*. Paris: Beauchesne, 1985.

Fox, Michael, and Manish Sharma, eds. *Old English Literature and the Old Testament*. Toronto: University of Toronto Press, 2012.

Fowler, David C. *The Bible in Early English Literature*. London: Sheldon Press, 1977.

Fraipont, J., ed. *Bedae Venerabilis Opera*. CCSL 122. Turnhout: Brepols, 1955.

Fraïsse, Anne, and Jean-Noël Michaud. "Pendant ce temps, à la poupe, Jésus goûtait au sommeil: La tempête apaisée (Juvencus E. L., II. 9–12, 25–42)." *EC* 74 (2006): 193–218.

Frank, Roberta. "Some Uses of Paronomasia in Old English Scriptural Verse." *Speculum* 47 (1972): 207–26.

Frey, Leonard H. "The Rhetoric of Latin Christian Epic Poetry." In *Annuale Mediaevale, Vol. II*, edited by John F. Mahoney, 15–30. Pittsburgh: Duquesne University Press, 1960.

Fritz, Donald. "Caedmon: A Traditional Christian Poet." *Medieval Studies* 31 (1969): 334–7.

Fulk, R.D. *A History of Old English Meter*. Philadelphia: University of Pennsylvania Press, 1992.

Fulk, R.D., and Christopher M. Cain, eds. *A History of Old English Literature*. Malden, MA: Blackwell, 2003.

Fulk, R.D., Robert E. Bjork, and John D. Niles, eds. *Klaeber's Beowulf, Fourth Edition*. Toronto: University of Toronto Press, 2008.

Gao, Feng-Feng. *Vergil and Biblical Exegesis in Early Christian Latin Epic*. Diss. Berkeley, 2002.

Gardner, John. *The Construction of Christian Poetry in Old English*. Carbondale: Southern Illinois University Press, 1975.

Gärtner, Thomas. "Die Musen im Dienste Christi: Strategien der Rechtfertigung christlicher Dichtung in der lateinischen Spätantike." *VC* 58.4 (2004): 424–46.

Giles, J.A. "Anecdota Bedae, Lanfranci et aliorum." *Publications of the Caxton Society* 12, London, 1851.

Gneuss, H. *Handlist of Anglo-Saxon Manuscripts: A List of Manuscripts and Manuscript Fragments Written or Owned in England up to 1100*. Tempe: Arizona Center for Medieval and Renaissance Studies, 2001.

Gneuss, H., and M. Lapidge, eds. *Anglo-Saxon Manuscripts: A Bibliographical Handlist of Manuscripts and Manuscript Fragments Written or Owned in England up to 1100*. Toronto: University of Toronto Press, 2014.

Godden, M., and M. Lapidge, eds. *The Cambridge Companion to Old English Literature*. Cambridge: Cambridge University Press, 1991.

Godman, P. "The Anglo-Latin *Opus Geminatum* from Aldhelm to Alcuin." *MÆ* 50 (1981): 215–29.

– *The Bishops, Kings, and Saints of York*. Oxford Medieval Texts. Oxford: Clarendon Press, 1982.

Goelzer, Henri. *Le Latin de Saint Avit*. Paris: Alcan, 1909.

– "Ovid et saint Avit." In *Mélanges offerts à M. Emile Chatelain par ses élèves et ses amis*, 275–80. Paris: Champion, 1910.

Gollancz, Israel. *Caedmon Manuscript of Anglo-Saxon Biblical Poetry, Junius XI in the Bodleian Library*. London: British Academy, 1927.

Green, R.P.H. "Approaching Christian Epic: The Preface of Juvencus." In *Latin Epic and Didactic Poetry: Genre, Tradition, and Individuality*, edited by Monica Gale, 203–22. Swansea: Classical Press of Wales, 2004.

– "Birth and Transfiguration: Some Gospel Episodes in Juvencus and Sedulius."
In *Texts and Culture in Late Antiquity: Inheritance, Authority, and Change*,
edited by J.H.D. Scourfield, 135–71. Swansea: Classical Press of Wales, 2007.

– *Latin Epics of the New Testament: Juvencus, Sedulius, Arator*. Oxford: Oxford
University Press, 2006.

– Review: *Christus, Nikodemus und die Samaritanerin bei Juvencus*. *Classical
Review* 55.1 (2005), 163–4.

– "The *Evangeliorum Libri* of Juvencus: Exegesis by Stealth?" In *Poetry and
Exegesis in Premodern Latin Christianity*, 65–80. Supplements to Vigiliae
Christianae 87. Ed. Willemien Otten and Karla Pollmann. Boston: Brill, 2007.

– *The Works of Ausonius: Edited with Introduction and Commentary*. Oxford:
Clarendon Press, 1991.

Greenfield, S.B., and D.G. Calder. *A New Critical History of Old English
Literature*. New York: New York University Press, 1986.

Gribomont, Jean. "Les plus anciennes traductions latines." In *Le monde latin antique et la Bible*, edited by Fontaine and Pietri, 43–65. Paris: Beauchesne, 1985.

Griffith, Mark. "The Register of Divine Speech in *Genesis A*." *ASE* 41 (2012): 63–78.

Groth, Ernst J. *Composition und Alter der altenglischen Exodus*. Göttingen:
Franz Ebhardt, 1883.

Gurteen, S. Humphreys. *The Epic Fall of Man: A Comparative Study of
Caedmon, Dante and Milton*. New York: Putnam, 1896.

Hall, J.B., A.L. Ritchie, and M.J. Edwards, eds. *P. Papinius Statius. Thebaid and
Achilleid*. 3 vols. Newcastle: Cambridge Scholars Publishing, 2007.

Hall, J.R. "The Building of the Temple in Exodus: Design for Typology."
Neophilologus 59 (1975): 616–21.

– "The Old English Epic of Redemption: The Theological Unity of Ms Junius
11." *Traditio* 32 (1976): 185–208.

Hall, T.N., ed. *Via Crucis: Essays on Early Medieval Sources and Ideas in
Memory of J.E. Cross*. Medieval European Studies. Morgantown: West Virginia
University Press, 2002.

Hass, Willy. *Studien zum Heptateuchdichter Cyprian mit Beiträgen zu den
vorhieronymianischen Heptateuchchübersetzungen*. Diss. Berlin: Universitats-
Buchdruckerei von G. Schade, 1912.

Hatfield, J.T. *A Study of Juvencus*. Bonn: Georgi, 1890.

Hecquet-Noti, Nicole, ed. and trans. *Avit de Vienne: Histoire Spirituelle*. Tome I.
Sources Chrétiennes 444. Paris: Les Editions du Cerf, 1999.

– ed. and trans. *Avit de Vienne: Histoire Spirituelle*. Tome II. Sources
Chrétiennes 492. Paris: Les Editions du Cerf, 2005.

– "Ève et le serpent, une réécriture chrétienne de la rencontre entre Médée et
Jason. Approche intertextuelle du récit de la tentation dans l'Histoire spirituelle d'Avit de Vienne (2.204–31)." *Dictynna* 4 (2007): 2–17.

– "La description du déluge dans Avit carm. 4, 429–540: Usurpation et rénovation du poncif épique de la tempête." *Antiquité Tardive* 8 (2000): 229–35.

– "Le corbeau nécrophage, figure du juif, dans le *De diluuio mundi* d'Avit de Vienne: à propos de l'interprétation de Gn. 8, 6–7 dans *carm.* 4.544–584." *REA* 48 (2002): 297–320.

Heinsdorf, Cornel. *Christus, Nikodemus und die Sameritanerin bei Juvencus*. Untersuchungen zur antiken Literatur und Geschichte 67. Berlin: De Gruyter, 2003.

Helm, R., ed. *Eusebius' Werke 7: Die Chronik des Hieronymus*. GCS, vol. 47. Berlin: Akademie Verlag, 1984.

Herbison, Ivan. "The Idea of the "Christian Epic": Towards a History of an Old English Poetic Genre." In *Studies in English Literature*, edited by M.J. Toswell and E.M. Tyler, 342–69. London: Routledge, 1996.

Herzog, R. *Die Bibelepik der lateinischen Spätantike: Formgeschichte einer erbaulichen Gattung*. Theorie und Geschichte der Literatur und der schönen Künste: Texte und Abhandlungen 37. Munich: Fink, 1975.

– "Exegese – Erbauung – Delectatio. Beiträge zu einer christlichen Poetik der Spätantike." In *Formen und Funktionen der Allegorie*, edited by W. Haug, 52–69. Stuttgart: J.B. Metzlersche, 1979.

– "Juvencus." In *Handbuch der lateinischen Literatur der Antike 5. Restauration und Erneuerung 284–74 n. Chr*, edited by Reinhart Herzog and Peter Lebrecht Schmidt, 331–6. Munich: C.H. Beck, 1989.

Hieatt, Constance B. "*The Fates of the Apostles*: Imagery, Structure, and Meaning." In *The Cynewulf Reader*, edited by Robert Bjork, 67–77. New York: Routledge, 1974. Rpt. 2001.

Hilhorst, A. "The Cleansing of the Temple (John 2, 13–25) in Juvencus and Nonnus." In *Early Christian Poetry: A Collection of Essays*, edited by J. Den Boeft and A. Hilhorst, 61–76. New York: Brill, 1993.

Hill, Joyce. "Confronting *Germania Latina*: Changing Responses to Old English Biblical Verse." In *The Poems of MS Junius 11*, edited by Roy Liuzza, 1–19. New York: Routledge, 2002.

Hill, Thomas D. "The Fall of Angels and Man in the Old English *Genesis B*." In *Anglo-Saxon Poetry: Essays in Appreciation for John C. McGalliard*, edited by Lewis E. Nicholson and Dolores Warwick Frese, 279–329. Notre Dame: University of Notre Dame Press, 1975.

– "The *uirga* of Moses and the Old English *Exodus*." In *Old English Literature in Context: Ten Essays*, edited by John D. Niles, 57–65. Suffolk: D.S. Brewer, 1980.

Hillier, Richard. *Arator on the Acts of the Apostles: A Baptismal Commentary*. Oxford Early Christian Studies. Oxford: Clarendon Press, 1993.

– "Arator and Baptism in Sixth-Century Rome." In *Studia Patristica* 71, edited by J. Day and M. Vinzent, 111–34. Paris: Peeters, 2014.

Hofmann, Dietrich. "Untersuchungen zu der altenglischen Gedichten Genesis und Exodus," *Anglia* 75 (1957): 1–34.

Holthausen, F., ed. *Die ältere Genesis*. Heidelberg: C. Winter, 1914.

Homey, H.H. "Evas Schuld (Alcimus Avitus *De spiritalis historiae gestis* 2.145–82)." *Hermes* 137 (2009): 474–97.

Hovingh, P.F., ed. *Alethia*, 125–93. Turnhout: Brepols, 1960.

Howe, Nicholas. *Migration and Mythmaking in Anglo-Saxon England*. New Haven: Yale University Press, 1989.

Hudson-Williams, A. "Virgil and the Christian Latin Poets." *Papers of the Virgil Society* 6 (1966–7): 11–21.

Huemer, J., ed. *Gai. Vetti Aquilini Iuuenci Euangeliorum Libri Quattuor*. CSEL 24. Vienna: F. Tempsky, 1891.

– *Sedulii Opera Omnia*. CSEL 10. Vienna: apud C. Geroldi filium, 1885. Rev. 2007 by Victoria Panagl.

Hunter Blair, Peter. *The World of Bede*. London: Secker & Warburg, 1970.

Huppé, B. *Doctrine and Poetry: Augustine's Influence on Old English Poetry*. Albany: State University of New York, 1959.

Irving, E.B. "*Exodus* Retraced." In *Old English Studies in Honour of John C. Pope*, edited by Robert B. Burlin and Edward B. Irving, 203–23. Toronto: University of Toronto Press, 1974.

– "On the Dating of the Old English Poems *Genesis* and *Exodus*." *Anglia* 77 (1959): 1–11.

– *The Old English Exodus, Edited with Introd., Notes, and Glossary*. New Haven: Yale University Press, 1953.

Jager, Eric. "Tempter as Rhetoric Teacher: The Fall of Language in the Old English *Genesis B*." *The Poems of MS Junius 11: Basic Readings*. Ed. Roy M. Liuzza, 99–118. New York: Routlege, 2002.

Jaager, Werner, ed. *Bedas Metrische Vita sancti Cuthberti*. Leipzig: Mayer & Müller, 1935.

Jones, C.W., ed. *Opera Didascalica*. CCSL 123A. Turnhout: Brepols, 1975.

Joyce, Jane Wilson, ed. *Statius, Thebaid: A Song of Thebes*. Cornell: Cornell University Press, 2008.

Jülicher, A., ed. *Itala: Das Neue Testament in Altlateinischer Überlieferung*. 4 vols. Berlin: De Gruyter, 1938, 1940, 1954, 1963.

Juster, A.M. *Saint Aldhelm's Riddles*. Toronto: University of Toronto Press, 2015.

Karkov, Catherine. *Text and Picture in Anglo-Saxon England: Narrative Strategies in the Junius 11 Manuscript*. CSASE 31. Cambridge: Cambridge University Press, 2001.

Kartschoke, Dieter. *Bibeldichtung: Studien z. Geschichte d. epischen Bibelparaphrase von Juvencus bis Otfrid von Weissenburg.* Munich: Fink, 1975.

Kendall, C.B., ed. *De Arte Metrica,* 81–141. CCSL 123A. Turnhout: Brepols, 1975.

Ker, N.R. *Catalogue of Manuscripts Containing Anglo-Saxon.* Oxford: Clarendon Press, 1957.

Kiernan, Kevin. *Beowulf and the Beowulf-Manuscript.* New Brunswick, NJ: Rutgers, 1981. Rev. ed., Ann Arbor: University of Michigan Press, 1996.

– "Reading Caedmon's 'Hymn' with Someone Else's Glosses." *Representations* 32 (1990): 157–74.

Kievits, H.H., ed. *Ad Iuvenci Evangeliorum Librum Primum Commentarius Exegeticus.* Groningen: M. De Waal, 1940.

Kirsch, Wolfgang. *Die lateinische Versepik* des 4 Jahrhunderts. Berlin: Akademie Verlag, 1989.

Klaeber, F. "Die christlichen Elemente im *Beowulf.*" *Anglia* 35 (1911): 111–36.

– *The Later Genesis.* Heidelberg: C. Winter, 1913.

Klinck, Anne. "Female Characterization in Old English Poetry and the Growth of Psychological Realism: *Genesis B* and *Christ I.*" *Neophilologus* 63 (1979), 597–610.

Kline, A.S. "Propertius, *Elegy* 1.16." Accessed 16 December 2015. http://www.yorku.ca/pswarney/3110/Propertius.htm#_Toc498857579.

Knappe, Gabriele. *Traditionen der Klassischen Rhetorik im angelsächsischen England.* Anglistische Forschungen 236. Heidelberg: C. Winter, 1996.

– "Classical Rhetoric in Anglo-Saxon England." *ASE* 27 (1998): 5–29.

Krapp, G.P., ed. *The Junius Manuscript.* ASPR 1. New York: Columbia University Press, 1931.

– *The Paris Psalter and the Meters of Boethius.* ASPR 5. New York: Columbia University Press, 1932.

– *The Vercelli Book.* ASPR 2. New York: Columbia University Press, 1932.

Kreuz, Gottfried, ed. *Metrum in Genesin, Carmen de Evangelio: Einleitung, Text und Kommentar.* Vienna: Österreichischen Akademie der Wissenschaften, 2006.

Kriel, D.M. "*Sodoma* in Fifth Century Biblical Epic." *Acta Classica* 34 (1991): 7–20.

Laistner, M.L.W., ed. *Expositio Actuum Apostolorum et Retractatio.* Cambridge, MA: The Medieval Academy of America, 1939.

– "The Library of the Venerable Bede." *Bede, His Life, Times, and Writings,* edited by A. Hamilton Thompson, 237–66. 1935. Oxford: Clarendon Press, 1969.

Lapidge, Michael. "An aspect of Old English poetic diction: the postpositioning of prepositions." In *Inside Old English: Essays in Honour of Bruce Mitchell,* edited by John Walmsley, 153–80. Oxford: Blackwell, 2006.

– *Anglo-Latin Literature, 900–1066*. London: Hambledon Press, 1993.
– *Anglo-Latin Literature, 600–899*. London: Hambledon Press, 1996.
– ed. *Beda Storia Degli Inglesi* (*Historia ecclesiastica gentis Anglorum*). 2 vols. Translated by Paolo Chiesa. Rome: Fondazione Lorenzo Valla, 2008 and 2010.
– "Hypallage in the Old English *Exodus*." *LSE* 37 (2006): 31–9.
– "Old English Poetic Compounds: A Latin Perspective." In *Intertexts: Studies in Anglo-Saxon Culture Presented to Paul E. Szarmach*, edited by Virginia Blanton and Helene Scheck, 17–32. Tempe: ACMRS, 2008.
– "Some Old English Sedulius Glosses from Bn Lat. 8092." *Anglia* 100 (1982): 1–17.
– "Surviving Booklists from Anglo-Saxon England." In *Learning and Literature in Anglo-Saxon England: Studies Presented to Peter Clemoes*, edited by Michael Lapidge and Helmut Gneuss, 33–90. Cambridge: Cambridge University Press, 1985.
– *The Anglo-Saxon Library*. Oxford: Oxford University Press, 2006.
– *The Cult of St Swithun*. Oxford: Clarendon Press, 2003.
– "The Study of Latin Texts in Late Anglo-Saxon England: The Evidence of Latin Glosses." In *Latin and Vernacular Languages in Early Medieval Britain*, edited by Nicholas Brooks, 99–165. Leicester: Leicester University Press, 1982.
– "Versifying the Bible in the Middle Ages." In *The Text in the Community: Essays on Medieval Works, Manuscripts, Authors, and Readers*, edited by Jill Mann and Maura Nolan, 11–40. Notre Dame: University of Notre Dame Press, 2006.
Lapidge, M., and M. Herren, trans. *Aldhelm: The Prose Works*. Cambridge: D.S. Brewer, 1979.
Lapidge, M., and J.L. Rosier, trans. *Aldhelm: The Poetic Works*. Cambridge: D.S. Brewer, 1985.
Lawton, David. "Englishing the Bible." In *The Cambridge History of Medieval English Literature*, edited by David Wallace, 454–82. Cambridge: Cambridge University Press, 1999.
Lendinara, Patrizia. "Was the Glossator a Teacher?" *Quaestio* 3 (2002): 1–27.
Liuzza, R.M. *The Poems of MS Junius 11*. New York: Routledge, 2002.
Lockett, Leslie. "An Integrated Re-Examination of the Dating of Oxford, Bodleian Library, Junius 11." *ASE* 31 (2002): 141–74.
Lombardo, Stanley, trans. *Metamorphoses*. Indianapolis: Hackett Publishing Company, 2010.
Longpré, André. "Aspects de métrique et de prosodie chez Juvencus." *Phoenix* 29 (1975): 128–38.
– "Structure de l'Hexamètre de Cyprianus Gallus." *Cahiers des Études Anciennes* 1 (1972): 75–100.

– "Traitement de l'élision chez le poète Cyprianus Gallus." *Phoenix* 26 (1972): 63–77.

Lucas, Peter, ed. *Exodus*. Exeter Medieval Texts and Studies. Exeter: Methuen, 1977. Rev. 1994.

– "Exodus." In *The Blackwell Encyclopaedia of Anglo-Saxon England*, edited by Michael Lapidge, John Blair, Simon Keynes, and Donald Scragg, 179. Oxford: Blackwell, 1999.

Magoun, F.P. "The Oral-Formulaic Character of Anglo-Saxon Narrative Poetry." *Speculum* 28 (1953): 446–67.

Malsbary, Gerald. "Epic Exegesis and the Use of Vergil in the Early Biblical Epics." *Florilegium* 7 (1985): 55–81.

Manitius, M. *Geschichte der Christlich-lateinischen Poesie: bis zur Mitte des 8. Jahrhunderts*. Stuttgart: J.G. Cotta, 1891.

– *Geschichte der lateinischen Literatur des Mittelalters*. 3 vols. Munich: Beck, 1923–59.

– *Zu Aldhelm und Baeda*. Vienna: Carl Gerold, 1886.

Marsden, Richard. "Aelfric as Translator: The Old English Prose Genesis." *Anglia* 109 (1991): 319–58.

– *The Old English Heptateuch and Aelfric's Libellus de Veteri Testamento et Novo*. EETS 330. Oxford: Oxford University Press, 2008.

– *The Text of the Old Testament in Anglo-Saxon England*. CSASE 15. Cambridge: Cambridge University Press, 1995.

Martin, Lawrence T. "The Influence of Arator in Anglo–Saxon England." In *Proceedings of the PMR Conference: Annual Publication of the International Patristic, Medieval and Renaissance Conference* 7, 1982, 75–81.

Mathisen, Ralph. "Epistolography, Literary Circles and Family Ties in Late Roman Gaul." *TAPA* 111 (1981): 95–109.

Maurer, Heinrich. *De exemplis quae Claudius Marius Victorius*. Diss. Bonn, 1972.

Mayor, John E.B. *The Latin Heptateuch Published Piecemeal by the French Printer William Morel 1560 and the French Benedictines 1733*. London: C.J. Clay & Sons, 1899.

Mayr, T. *Studien zu dem Paschale carmen des christlichen Dichters Sedulius*. Diss. Augsburg, 1916.

Mayr-Harting, Henry. "Alcuin, Charlemagne and the Problem of Sanctions." In *Early Medieval Studies in Memory of Patrick Wormald*, edited by Stephen Baxter et al., 207–18. Burlington, VT: Ashgate, 2009.

Mazzega, M., ed. *Sedulius, Carmen Paschale, Buch III*. Chraesis 5. Basel: Schwabe, 1996.

McBrine, Patrick. "The English Inheritance of Biblical Verse." Diss. University of Toronto, 2008.

– "The Journey Motif in the Poems of the Vercelli Book." In *New Readings in the Vercelli Book*, edited by Andy Orchard and Samantha Zacher, 298–317. Toronto: University of Toronto Press, 2009.

McClure, J. "The Biblical Epic and Its Audience in Late Antiquity." In *Papers of the Liverpool Latin Seminar* 3, 1981, 305–21.

McKill, L.N. "Patterns of the Fall: Adam and Eve in the Old English *Genesis A*." *Florilegium* 14 (1995–6): 25–41.

– "The Offering of Isaac and the Artistry of Old English *Genesis A*." In *The Practical Vision: Essays in English Literature in Honour of Flora Roy*, edited by Jane Campbell and James Doyle, 1–12. Waterloo, ON: Wilfrid Laurier University Press, 1978.

McKinlay, Arthur Patch, ed. *Aratoris Subdiaconi De Actibus Apostolorum*. CSEL 72. Vienna: Hoelder-Pichler-Tempski, 1951.

Menner, Robert J. "The Date and Dialect of *Genesis A*." *Anglia* 70 (1951): 285–94.

Meritt, H.D. *Old English Glosses (a Collection)*. London: Oxford University Press, 1945.

– "Old English Sedulius Glosses." *AJP* 57.2 (1936): 140–50.

Michel, L. "*Genesis A* and the *Praefatio*." *MLN* 62 (1947): 545–50.

Minkoff, Harvey. "Some Stylistic Consequences of Aelfric's Theory of Translation." *SP* 73 (1976): 29–41.

Monro, David, and Thomas Allen, eds. *Homeri Opera*. Oxford: Clarendon Press, 1920.

Moore, Samuel. "On the Sources of the Old-English Exodus." *Modern Philology* 9 (1911): 83–108.

Mora-Lebrun, Francine. *L'Enéide médiévale et la chanson de geste*. Paris: Presses Universitaires France, 1994.

Moretti Pieri, G. "Sulle fonte evangeliche di Sedulio." Atti e memorie dell' academia toscana di scienze e lettere "La Columbaria" 39.20 (1969): 125–234.

Morhmann, Christine. *La langue et le style de la poésie Latine chrétienne. Études sur le latin des chrétiens*, 151–68. Tome 1. Storia e Letteratura 65. Rome, 1947.

Morrell, M.C. *A Manual of Old English Biblical Materials*. Knoxville: University of Tennessee Press, 1965.

Mürkens, Gerhard. *Untersuchungen über das altenglische Exoduslied*. Bonner Beitrage zur Anglistik 2. Bonn, 1899.

Mynors, R.A.B., ed. *P. Vergili Maronis Opera*. Oxford: Clarendon Press, 1969.

Napier, Arthur S. *Old English Glosses: Chiefly Unpublished*. Anecdota Oxoniensia 4. Medieval and Modern Series, Pt. 11. Oxford: Clarendon Press, 1900.

Nodes, Daniel J. "Avitus of Vienne's Spiritual History." *VC* 38 (1984): 185–95.

– *The Fall of Man: De Spiritalis Historiae Gestis, Libri I–III*. Toronto Medieval Latin Texts 16. Toronto: PIMS, 1985.

– *Doctrine and Exegesis in Biblical Latin Poetry*. Arca, Classical and Medieval Texts, Papers and Monographs 31. Leeds: F. Cairns, 1993.

Norberg, Dag Ludvig. *An Introduction to the Study of Medieval Latin Versification*. Washington: Catholic University of America Press, 2004.

Norton, M.A. "Prosopography of Juvencus." In *Leaders of Iberian Christianity 50–650 A.D.*, edited by Joseph Marique, 114–20. Boston: St Paul's, 1962.

O'Brien O'Keeffe, Katherine. *Visible Song: Transitional Literacy in Old English Verse*. CSASE 4. Cambridge: Cambridge University Press, 1990.

O'Daly, Gerard. *Days Linked by Song: Prudentius' Cathemerinon*. Oxford: Oxford University Press, 2012.

O'Donnell, D.P. *Cædmon's Hymn: A Multimedia Study, Archive and Edition*. Cambridge: D.S. Brewer in association with SEENET and the Medieval Academy, 2005.

Ogilvy, J.D.A. *Books Known to the English, 597–1066*. Cambridge, MA: CEMERS, SUNY-Binghamton, 1967.

O'Neill, P.P. *The Old English Prose Psalms of the Paris Psalter*. Diss. Philadelphia, 1980.

Orbán, A.P., ed. *Aratoris Subdiaconi Historia Apostolica*. 2 vols. CCSL 130. Turnhout: Brepols, 2006.

Orchard, Andy. *A Critical Companion to Beowulf*. Rochester, NY: D.S. Brewer, 2003.

– "After Aldhelm: The Teaching and Transmission of the Anglo-Latin Hexameter." *Journal of Medieval Latin* 2 (1992): 96–133.

– "Intoxication, Fornication, and Multiplication: The Burgeoning Text of *Genesis A*." In *Text, Image, Interpretation: Studies in Anglo-Saxon Literature and its Insular Context in Honour of Éamonn Ó Carragáin*, edited by Alastair Minnis and Jane Roberts, 333–54. Turnhout: Brepols, 2007.

– *The Poetic Art of Aldhelm*. CSASE 8. Cambridge: Cambridge University Press, 1994.

– "Poetic Inspiration and Prosaic Translation: The Making of *Cædmon's Hymn*." In *Studies in English Language and Literature: Doubt Wisely: Papers in Honour of E.G. Stanley*, edited by Jane Toswell and Elizabeth Tyler, 402–22. London: Routledge, 1996.

– "Re-Reading *the Wanderer*: The Value of Cross-References." In *Via Crucis: Essays on Early Medieval Sources and Ideas in Memory of J.E. Cross*, edited by T.N. Hall, 1–26. Medieval European Studies. Morgantown: West Virginia University Press, 2002.

Overing, Gillian R. "On Reading Eve: *Genesis B* and the Readers' Desire." In *Speaking Two Languages: Traditional Disciplines and Contemporary Theory in*

Medieval Studies, edited by Allen J. Frantzen, 35–64. Albany: State University of New York Press, 1991.

Page, R.I. "Anglo-Saxon Scratched Glosses in a Corpus Christi College, Cambridge, Manuscript." In *Otium Et Negotium: Studies in Onomatology and Library Science Presented to Olof Von Feilitzen*, edited by Folke Sandgren, 209–15. Stockholm: P.A. Norstedt and Soner, 1973.

– "More Old English Scratched Glosses." *Anglia* 97 (1979): 27–45.

– "On the Feasibility of a Corpus of Anglo-Saxon Glosses: The View from the Library." In *Anglo-Saxon Glossography: Papers Read at the International Conference Held in the Koninklijke Academie voor Wetenschappen Letteren en Schone Kunsten van Belgie*, 77–95. Edited by R. Derolez. Brussels: Paleis der Academiën, 1992.

Peiper, R., ed. *Alcimi Ecdicii Aviti Viennensis Episcopi Opera*. MGH Auct. Ant. 6.1. Berlin, 1883.

– *Cypriani Galli Poetae Heptateuchos*. CSEL 23. Vienna: F. Tempsky, 1891.

Perkins, Larry J., trans. "Exodus." *The New English Translation of the Septuagint*, edited by Albert Pietersma and Benjamin B. Wright, 52–81. Oxford: Oxford University Press, 2009.

Poinsotte, Jean-Michel. *Juvencus et Israel: la représentation des Juifs dans le premier poème latin chrétien*. Publications de l'Université de Rouen 57. Paris: Presses universitaires de France, 1979.

Pollmann, Karla, ed. *Das Carmen adversus Marcionitas: Einleitung, Text, Übersetzung und Kommentar*. Göttingen: Vandenhoeck & Ruprecht, 1991.

– "Der Sogennante Heptateuchdichter und die *Alethia* des Claudius Marius Victorius: Anmerkungen zur Datierungsfrage und zur Imitationsforschung." *Hermes* 120.4 (1992): 490–501.

Porter, David. "The Latin Syllabus in Anglo-Saxon Monastic Schools." *Neophilologus* 78 (1994): 463–82.

Quadlbauer, F. "Zur "invocatio" des Iuvencus." Gräzer Beitrage, 2 (1974): 189–212.

Raby, F.J.E. *A History of Christian Latin Poetry from the Beginnings to the Close of the Middle Ages*. 2nd ed. Oxford: Clarendon Press, 1966.

Rambridge, Kate. "Alcuin, Willibrord and the Cultivation of Faith." *Haskins Society Journal* 14 (2005): 15–32.

Ratkowitsch, C. "Vergils Seesturm bei Iuvencus und Sedulius." *Jahrbuch für Antike und Christentum* 29 (1986): 40–58.

Reischmann, Hans-Joachim. *Willibrord: Apostel der Friesen. Seine Vita nach Alkuin und Thiofrid*. Sigmaringendorf: Glock und Lutz, 1989.

Remley, Paul. "Aldhelm as Old English Poet: *Exodus*, Asser, and the *Dicta Ælfredi*." In *Latin Learning and English Lore: Studies in Anglo-Saxon*

Literature for Michael Lapidge, vol. 1, edited by Katherine O'Brien O'Keefe
and Andy Orchard, 90–108. Toronto: University of Toronto Press, 2005.

– "Biblical Translation: Poems." In *The Blackwell Encyclopaedia of Anglo-Saxon
England*, edited by Michael Lapidge, John Blair, Simon Keynes, and Donald
Scragg, 66–7. Oxford: Blackwell, 1999.

– *Old English Biblical Verse: Studies in Genesis, Exodus and Daniel.* CSASE 16.
Cambridge: Cambridge University Press, 1996.

– "The Latin Textual Basis of *Genesis A.*" *ASE* 17 (1988): 163–90.

Renoir, Alain. "Eve's I.Q. Rating: Two Sexist Views of *Genesis B.*" In *New
Readings on Women in Old English Literature*, edited by Helen Damico and
Alexandra Hennessey Olsen, 262–72. Bloomington: Indiana University Press,
1990.

– "The Self-Deception of Temptation: Boethian Psychology in *Genesis B.*"
In *Old English Poetry: Fifteen Essays*, edited by Robert P. Creed, 47–67.
Providence: Brown University Press, 1967.

Richardson, E.C., ed. *Liber de Viris Illustribus.* In *Texte und Untersuchungen zur
Gescichte der altchristlichen Literatur* 14.1 (1896): 57–97.

Riché, Pierre. "La vie quotidienne dans les écoles monastiques d'après les colloques scolaires." In *Sous la règle de Saint Benoît: structures monastiques et
sociétés en France du Moyen Age à l'époque moderne*, 417–26. Hautes Études
Médiévales et Modernes 47. Geneva: Droz, 1982.

Rigg, A.G. *History of Anglo-Latin Literature: 1066–1422.* Cambridge: Cambrige
University Press, 1992.

Rigg, A.G., and G.R. Wieland. "A Canterbury Classbook of the Mid-Eleventh
Century (The "Cambridge Songs" Manuscript)." *Anglo-Saxon England* 4
(1975): 113–30.

Robert, Ulysse. *Pentateuchi Versio Latina Antiquissima e Codice Lugdunensi.*
Paris: Firmin-Didot, 1881.

Roberts, Michael. *Biblical Epic and Rhetorical Paraphrase in Late Antiquity.*
Arca, Classical and Medieval Texts, Papers, and Monographs 16. Liverpool:
Cairns, 1985.

– "Rhetoric and Poetic Imitation in Avitus' Account of the Crossing of the Red
Sea (*De Spiritalis Historiae Gestis* 5.371–702)." *Traditio* 39 (1983): 29–80.

– *The Jeweled Style: Poetry and Poetics in Late Antiquity.* Ithaca: Cornell
University Press, 1989.

– "The Last Epic of Antiquity: Generic Continuity and Innovation in the *Vita
Sancti Martini* of Venantius Fortunatus." *TAPA* 131 (2001): 257–85.

– "The Latin Literature of Late Antiquity." In *Medieval Latin: An Introduction
and Bibliographical Guide*, edited by Frank A. Mantello and A.G. Rigg.
Washington: Catholic University of America Press (1996): 537–46.

– "The Prologue to Avitus' *De Spiritalis Historiae Gestis*: Christian Poetry and Poetic Licence." *Traditio* 36 (1980): 399–407.

– "Venantius Fortunatus's Life of St. Martin." *Traditio* 57 (2002): 129–87.

– "Vergil and the Gospels: The *Evangeliorum Libri IV of Juvencus*." In *Romane Memento*: *Vergil in the Fourth Century*, edited by Roger Rees, 47–61. London: Duckworth, 2004.

Robinson, Fred C. *Beowulf and the Appositive Style*. Knoxville: University of Tennessee Press, 1985.

– "Some Uses of Name-Meanings in Old English Poetry." *NM* 69 (1968): 161–71.

– "Syntactical Glosses in Latin Manuscripts of Anglo-Saxon Provenance." *Speculum* 43.3 (1973): 443–75.

– "The Significance of Names in Old English Literature." *Anglia* 86 (1968): 14–58.

– "Two Aspects of Variation in Old English Verse." In *Old English poetry: Essays on Style*, edited by Daniel G. Calder, 125–45. Berkeley: University of California Press, 1979.

Röttger, Wilfrid. *Studien zur Lichtmotivik bei Iuvencus*. Jahrbuch für Antike und Christentum, Ergänzungsband 24. Munster: Aschendorffsche Verlagsbuchhandlung, 1996.

Sandnes, Karl Olav. *Gospel According to Homer and Vergil: Cento and Canon*. Supplements to Novum Testamentum 138. Boston: Brill, 2011.

Schäferdiek, Knut. "Willibrord." In *Theologische Realenzyklopädie* 36, 107–9. Berlin: De Gruyter, 2004.

Schenkl, Carl, ed. *Claudii Marii Victoris oratoris Massiliensis Alethia*. CSEL 16. Vienna, 1888.

Schrader, R.J. "Arator: Reevaluation." *Classical Folia* 31 (1977): 64–77.

– *Arator's On the Acts of the Apostles (De Actibus Apostolorum)*. Classics in Religious Studies 6. Atlanta, GA: Scholars Press, 1987.

Schwind, J. *Arator-Studien*. Gottingen: Vandenhoeck and Ruprecht, 1990.

Scragg, Donald. "The Nature of Old English Verse." In *The Cambridge Companion to Old English Literature*, edited by M. Godden and M. Lapidge, 50–65. 2nd ed. Cambridge: Cambridge University Press, 2013.

Shanzer, Danuta, and Ian Wood, trans. *Avitus of Vienne: Selected Letters and Prose*. Translated Texts for Historians 38. Liverpool: Liverpool University Press, 2002.

Shea, George W., trans. *The Poems of Alcimus Ecdicius Avitus*. Medieval and Renaissance Texts and Studies 172. Tempe, 1997.

Shepherd, Geoffrey. "Scriptural Poetry." In *Continuations and Beginnings*, edited by E.G. Stanley, 1–36. London: Nelson, 1966.

Shipley Duckett, Eleanor. *Latin Writers of the Fifth Century*. New York: H. Holt, 1930.

Sievers, E. "Caedmon und Genesis." In *Britannica: Max Forster zum 60. Geburtstage*, 57–84. Leipzig, 1929.

– ed. *Der Heliand und die Angelsächsische Genesis*. Halle: M. Niemeyer 1875.

– *Heliand*. Germanistische Handbibliothek 4. Halle: Buchhandlung des Waisenhauses, 1878.

Sigerson, G., trans. *The Easter Song: Being the First Epic of Christendom*. Dublin: Talbot Press, 1922.

Simonetti Abbolito, G. "Avito e Virgilio." *Orpheus* 3 (1982): 49–72.

Sisam, Kenneth. *Studies in the History of Old English Literature*. Oxford: Clarendon Press, 1953.

Springer, C.P.E. *Sedulius: The Paschal Song and Hymns*. Atlanta: Society of Biblical Literature, 2013.

– "The Biblical Epic in Late Antiquity and the Early Modern Period: The Poetics of Tradition." In *Antiquity Renewed: Late Classical and Early Modern Themes*, edited by Z. von Martels and V. M. Schmidt, 103–26. Leuven: Peeters, 2003.

– *The Gospel as Epic in Late Antiquity: The Paschale Carmen of Sedulius*. Supplements to Vigiliae Christianae 2. New York: Brill, 1988.

– *The Manuscripts of Sedulius: A Provisional Handlist*. TAPS 85.5. Philadelphia: American Philosophical Society, 1995.

Stancliffe, Clare. "Disputed Episcopacy: Bede, Acca, and the Relationship between Stephen's Life of St. Wilfrid and the Early Prose Lives of St Cuthbert." *ASE* 41 (2013): 7–39.

Stanley, E.G. "Hwaet." In *Essays on Anglo-Saxon and Related Themes in Memory of Lynne Grundy*, edited by Jane Roberts and Janet Nelson, 525–56. Exeter: King's College London Medieval Studies, 2000.

Steen, Janie. *Verse and Virtuosity: The Adaptation of Latin Rhetoric in Old English Poetry*. Toronto Old English Series. Toronto: University of Toronto Press, 2008.

Stella, Francesco. "Alkuins Dichtung." In *Alkuin von York und die geistige Grundlegung Europas*, edited by E. Tremp and K. Schmuki, 107–28. St Gallen: Verlag am Klosterhof, 2010.

Stenton, F.M. *Anglo-Saxon England*. 3rd ed. Oxford: Clarendon Press, 1971.

Story, Joanna. *Carolingian Connections: Anglo-Saxon England and Carolingian Francia 750–870*. Aldershot and Burlington: Ashgate 2003.

Stranks, C.J. *The Life and Death of St. Cuthbert*. London: S.P.C.K., 1964.

Talbot, C.H., trans. "The Life of St. Willibrord." In *Soldiers of Christ: Saints and Saints' Lives from Late Antiquity and the Early Middle Ages*, edited by

E.X. Noble and Thomas Head, 189–211. University Park: Pennsylvania State University Press, 1995.

Taub, Lisa. "Translating the *Phainomena* Across Genre Language and Culture." In *Writings of Early Scholars in the Ancient Near East, Egypt, Rome, and Greece*, edited by Annette Imhausen and Tanja Pommerening, 119–38. Berlin: De Gruyter, 2010.

Thornbury, Emily. *Becoming a Poet in Anglo-Saxon England*. Cambridge: Cambridge University Press, 2014.

Thraed, K. "Epos." *Reallexicon für Antique und Christentum* 5 (1962): 983–1042.

– "Iuvencus." *RAC* 19 (2001): 881–906.

– "Juvencus: Der Übergang zur Bergpredigt des Matthäusevangeliums." *Alavarium: Festschrift für Christian Gnilka. Jahrbuch für Antike und Christentum Ergänzugsband* 33 (2002): 377–84.

– "Nachträge zum Reallexikon für Antike und Christentum: Arator." *Jahrbuch für Antike und Christentum* 4 (1961): 187–96.

Tolkien, J.R.R., and J. Turville-Petre, eds. *The Old English Exodus*. Oxford: Clarendon Press, 1981.

Toswell, M.J. *The Anglo-Saxon Psalter*. Turnhout: Brepols, 2014.

Trask, R.M. "Doomsday Imagery in the Old English *Exodus*." Neophilologus 57 (1973): 295–7.

Tunberg, Terence O. "Prose Styles and Cursus." In *Medieval Latin: An Introduction and Bibliographical Guide*, edited by F.A.C. Mantello and A.G. Rigg, 111–21. Washington: Catholic University of America Press, 1996.

Utley, Francis Lee. "The Flood Narrative in the Junius Manuscript and in Baltic Literature." In *Studies in Honor of Arthur G. Brodeur*, edited by Stanley B. Greenfield, 207–26. Eugene: University of Oregon Press, 1963.

Van der Laan, P.W.A.T. "Imitation créative dans le *Carmen Paschale* de Sedulius." In *Early Christian Poetry: A Collection of Essays*, Supplements to Vigiliae Christianae 22, edited by J. den Boeft and A. Hilhorst, 135–66. Leiden, New York, and Cologne: Brill, 1993.

– *Sedulius, Carmen Paschale Boek 4, inleiding, vertaling, commentar*. Diss. Leiden, 1990.

Van der Nat, P.G. "Die Praefatio der Evangelienparaphrase des Iuvencus." In *Romanitas et Christianitas*, edited by W. den Boer, P.G. van der Nat, C.M.J. Sicking, and J.C.M. van Winden, 249–57. Amsterdam: North-Holland Publishing Company, 1973.

Vickery, John F. "*Micel Wundor* of *Genesis B*." *Speculum* 68 (1971): 245–54.

– "The Vision of Eve in *Genesis B*." *Speculum* 44 (1969): 86–102.

Vollmer, F., ed. *De Laudibus Dei*. MGH AA 14. Berlin, 1905.

Wacht, M. *Concordantia in Iuuenci Euangeliorum Libros*. Hildesheim: Olms-Weidmann, 1990.

– *Concordantia in Sedulium*. Hildesheim: Olms-Weidmann, 1992.

Walther, Hans. "Versifizierte *Pater Noster* und *Credo*." *Revue du Moyen Age Latin* 20 (1964): 45–64.

Wampach, Camillus. *Geschichte der Grundherrschaft Echternach im Frühmittelalter*. 2 vols. Luxembourg: Luxemburger Kunstdruckerei, 1929, 1930.

Ward, Benedicta. *The Venerable Bede*. Wilton, CT: Morehouse Publishing, 1990. Rept. Kalamazoo, MI: Cistercian Publications, 1998.

Wattenbach, W., and E. Dümmler. *Monumenta Alcuiniana*. Berlin, 1873.

Weber, R., ed. *Biblia Sacra Iuxta Vulgatam Versionem*. 4th ed. Stuttgart: Deutsche Bibelgesellschaft, 1994.

Whitelock, Dorothy. *The Audience of Beowulf*. Oxford: Clarendon Press, 1951.

Whiting, C.E. "The Life of the Venerable Bede." In *Bede: His Life, Times, and Writings*, edited by A. Hamilton Thompson, 1–38. Oxford: Clarendon Press, 1935. Rpt. 1969.

Wieland, G.R. "Alcuin's Ambiguous Attitude Towards the Classics." *JML* 2.2 (1992): 84–95.

– "British Library, Ms. Royal 15.A. V: One Manuscript or Three?" In *Beatus Vir: Studies in Early English and Norse Manuscripts in Memory of Philip Pulsiano*, edited by A.N. Doane and Kirsten Wolf, 1–25. Tempe: Arizona Centre for Medieval and Renaissance Studies, 2006.

– "*Geminus Stylus*: Studies in Anglo-Latin Hagiography." In *Insular Latin Studies: Papers on Latin Texts and Manuscripts of the British Isles*, edited by Michael Herren, 113–33. Toronto: PIMS, 1981.

– "Interpreting Interpretation: The Polysemy of the Latin Gloss." *JML* 8 (1998): 59–71.

– "The Glossed Manuscript: Classbook or Library Book?" *ASE* 14 (1985): 153–73.

– *The Latin Glosses on Arator and Prudentius in Cambridge University Library, Ms Gg. 5.35*. Toronto: PIMS, 1983.

Wilcox, Miranda. "Creating the Cloud-Tent-Ship Conceit in *Exodus*." *ASE* 40 (2011): 103–50.

– *Vernacular Biblical Epics and the Production of Anglo-Saxon Cultural Exegesis*. Diss. University of Notre Dame, 2006.

Wilson, James H. *Christian Theology and Old English Poetry*. The Hague: Mouton, 1974.

Witke, Charles. *Numen Litterarum: The Old and the New in Latin Poetry from Constantine to Gregory the Great*. Leiden and Köln: Brill, 1971.

Wood, Ian. "An Absence of Saints? The Evidence for the Christianization of Saxony." In *Am Vorabend der Kaiserkrönung: Das Epos "Karolus Magnus et Leo papa" und der Papstbesuch in Paderborn 799*, edited by Peter Godman, Jošrg Jarnut, and Peter Johanek, 335–52. Berlin: Akademie Verlag, 2002.

– "Avitus of Vienne: The Augustinian Poet." In *Society and Culture in Late Antique Gaul: Revisiting the Sources*, edited by Ralph Mathisen and Danuta Shanzer, 262–77. Aldershot: Ashgate, 2001.

Woolf, R. "Doctrinal Influences on *The Dream of the Rood*." *MÆ* 27 (1958): 137–53.

– "The Fall of Man in *Genesis B* and the Mystère d'Adam." In *Studies in Honor of Arthur G. Brodeur*, edited by Stanley B. Greenfield, 187–99. New York: Russell and Russell, 1963.

– "*The Wanderer, Seafarer*, and the Genre of *Planctus*." In *Anglo-Saxon Poetry: Essays in Appreciation for John C. Mcgalliard*, edited by Lewis E. Nicholson and Dolores Warwick Frese, 192–207. Notre Dame: University of Notre Dame Press, 1975.

Wright, Charles D. "*Genesis A ad Litteram*." In *Old English Literature and the Old Testament*, edited by Michael Fox and Manish Sharma, 121–71. Toronto: University of Toronto Press, 2012.

– "The Blood of Abel and the Branches of Sin: *Genesis A, Maxims I*, and Aldhelm's *Carmen de uirginitate*." *ASE* 25 (1996): 7–19.

Wright, N. "Arator's Use of Caelius Sedulius: A Re-Examination." *History and Literature in Late Antiquity and the Early Medieval West: Studies in Intertextuality*, 1 vol. (various paginations), 51–64. Aldershot: Variorum, 1995.

– "Imitation of the Poems of Paulinus of Nola in Early Anglo-Latin Verse." *Peritia* 4 (1985): 134–51.

– "The *Hisperica Famina* and Caelius Sedulius." *CMCS* 4 (1982): 61–76.

Würthwein, Ernst. *The Text of the Old Testament: An Introduction to the Biblia Hebraica 3rd Edition*. Trans. Erroll F. Rhodes. Grand Rapids: William B. Eerdmans, 2014.

Yaager, Verner, ed. *Bedas metrische Vita sancti Cuthberti*. Leipzig: Mayer and Müller, 1935.

Zacher, Samantha. *Rewriting the Old Testament in Anglo-Saxon Verse*. New York: Bloomsbury, 2013.

Ziolkowsky, Jan M. "Classical Influences on Medieval Latin Views of Poetic Inspiration." In *Latin Poetry and the Classical Tradition*, edited by Peter Godman and Oswyn Murray, 15–38. Oxford: Clarendon Press, 1990.

Index

speech, 293–9; temptation of Adam, 299–303; temptation of Eve, 303–5; theme, 280, 293–4; title, date, and authorship, 274–6
glosses, 213–14, 229
golden line, 70, 236

Heliand, 276
Hilary, *Metrum in Genesin*, 70, 140, 264
Hisperica famina, 236
Horace, 59, 133
Hrabanus Maurus, 66, 210, 260, 287n57

Jerome, 6, 22–3, 24, 26, 56, 62, 94, 277, 293
John the Baptist, 242–4
Judith, 273
Juno, 144–5, 145n47
Juvenal, 59, 126, 130, 186
Juvencus, 22–56; biography, 23; general influence, 59, 171, 258
– *Euangeliorum libri*: alliteration, 42, 48, 51; **book 1**: anonymous preface, 211–14, 250–2; — main preface, 27–33, 105, 129, 133, 134, 149, 155, 161, 179, 221, 253–4, 259, 261, 264, 271, 281; — general theme, 29–33; — Nativity and Magi, 36–9, 53, 88, 113, 144, 221; — sermon on the mount, 39–43; — Lord's Prayer, 43–5, 214–20; — centurion's servant, 45–9, 50; **book 2**: storm on the sea, 34–6, 80, 189–91; — healing of blind men, 49–51, 204; **book 4**, Crucifixion, 51–5; Christian sources (Bible, etc.), 26–7; classical sources, 24–5; economy of style,

26, 39, 48, 49, 53, 55; exegesis, 38–9, 56–7; metre, 25, 41, 52, 55, 217; theme of faith, 48–51, 118; title and date, 22, 24

Kontrastimitation, 9, 36, 41, 48n65, 90, 99, 101n25, 127n20, 138, 280

Lactantius, 211n2, 258
Lantfred: knowledge of Arator, 227–8; knowledge of Juvencus, 221; knowledge of Sedulius, 224
Leofric, bishop, 223, 226
Livy, 59
Lord's Prayer I, II, III, 274
Lucan, 24, 59, 96, 125, 134, 186, 195, 198
Lucifer. *See* Satan
Lucretius, 29n32, 64–5

Macedonius, 95, 96
Martial, 71, 103n34, 125, 126n8, 186
monastic schools, 210–11, 214, 222, 226, 229, 230, 258, 345

opus geminatum, 6, 93, 224, 230, 247, 262
Ovid: general influence, 24, 59, 70, 96, 186; *Heroides*, 77; *Metamorphoses*: **book 1**, 30n34, 80–2, 138, 155; **book 2**, 133; **book 3**, 53; **book 8**, 99n20; **book 11**, 71

paene ad uerbum: and Arator, 191, 192; and Avitus, 125; and Cyprianus, 62, 74, 77; and Juvencus, 9, 23, 26, 42, 43, 45, 56, 209; OE biblical verse, 277, 287, 322; and Sedulius, 94, 102

Toronto Anglo-Saxon Series

General Editor:
ANDY ORCHARD

Editorial Board
ROBERTA FRANK
THOMAS N. HALL
ANTONETTE DIPAOLO HEALEY
MICHAEL LAPIDGE
KATHERINE O'BRIEN O'KEEFFE